Dreamweaver MX 2004

SAVVY

Dreamweaver® MX 2004

CHRISTIAN CRUMLISH | LUCINDA DYKES

SAN FRANCISCO | LONDON

SYBEX®

Associate Publisher: Dan Brodnitz
Acquisitions Editor: Mariann Barsolo
Developmental Editors: Pete Gaughan, Willem Knibbe
Production Editor: Susan Berge
Technical Editor: Martin Reid
Copyeditor: Linda Stephenson
Compositor: Maureen Forys, Happenstance Type-O-Rama
Graphic Illustrator: Caryl Gorska, Gorska Design
CD Coordinator: Dan Mummert
CD Technician: Kevin Ly
Proofreaders: Laurie O'Connell, Amy J. Rasmussen, Nancy Riddiough
Indexer: Ted Laux
Cover Designer: Caryl Gorska, Gorska Design
Cover Photographer: Angelo Cavalli, The Image Bank

Dear Reader,

Thank you for choosing *Dreamweaver MX 2004 Savvy*. This book is part of a new wave of Sybex graphics books, all written by outstanding authors—artists and teachers who really know their stuff and have a clear vision of the audience they're writing for.

Founded in 1976, Sybex is the oldest independent computer book publisher. More than twenty-five years later, we're committed to producing a full line of consistently exceptional graphics books. With each title, we're working hard to set a new standard for the industry. From the paper we print on, to the writers and photographers we work with, our goal is to bring you the best graphics books available.

I hope you see all that reflected in these pages. I'd be very interested to hear your comments and get your feedback on how we're doing. To let us know what you think about this or any other Sybex book, please visit us at www.sybex.com. Once there, go to the book's page, click on Submit Feedback, and fill out the questionnaire. Your input is greatly appreciated.

Please also visit www.sybex.com to learn more about the rest of our growing graphics line.

Best regards,

Dan Brodnitz
Associate Publisher—Graphics
Sybex Inc.

Acknowledgments

It has been a long journey writing a book this long and detailed, and many have helped in many different ways to make this possible.

First, I have to thank Wali for his love and support during a difficult and challenging writing schedule. Without his support, none of this would have been possible.

Next, I would like to thank Macromedia and the Macromedia developers for allowing me to be part of the Beta team and to be involved first-hand in the final phases of testing and development of a new version of this software.

This book would not have been possible without the contributions of the writers who stepped in at just the right moment to ensure that all the chapters could be completed within a very short timeline.

I'd also like to thank all those who so generously agreed to the use of screenshots and/or trial versions of their products—in particular, Nick Bradford of TopStyle Pro, the team at StoreFront E-commerce software, Dave Shea of CSS Zen Garden, Manny Cline at Santa Fe Healing Art, and Dr. Ken Stoller of Simply Hyperbarics.

People I don't know personally but whose work has inspired me include Jeffrey Zeldman, Jeffrey Veen, and Eric Meyer. I also want to thank all those web pioneers who generously offered their help and knowledge to those of us trying to figure out how to create websites in the early '90s.

At Sybex, I'd like to thank Associate Publisher Dan Brodnitz and Acquisitions Editor Mariann Barsolo for their vision and support. Willem Knibbe, developmental editor, was always there as a friend and advisor throughout the long process of this book's development, and offered insightful and useful suggestions for making this the best book possible. Susan Berge did an outstanding job as production editor, juggling a multitude of changing schedules and outlines. A lot of other people at Sybex helped with this massive project without interacting with me directly, and I'd like to acknowledge their contributions as well. Thank you all!

I'd like to thank my agent, Danielle Jatlow, of Waterside Productions, for her incredible level of support and for helping me through all the tricky phases of bringing a book of this size to completion.

And finally, I'd like to thank all the readers—the web designers and developers at all stages of their web careers who are interested in growing and developing their web skills, and who help keep the Web alive as an evolving medium.

About the Authors

Christian Crumish and Lucinda Dykes have joined together again for this edition of *Dreamweaver MX 2004 Savvy*. Both of them have used Dreamweaver since Version 2.0 and continue to use Dreamweaver on a daily basis as their web design and development tool of choice.

Since the early '90s, Christian has been writing about technology, music, popular culture, and the media. Christian has packaged books and e-books, consulted on matters of information architecture and content-management strategy with Fortune 500 companies, represented other authors as a literary agent, and written nearly 20 books on technology, the Internet, and web development. He maintains the website for this book at `http://dreamweaversavvy.com`.

Lucinda started her career in a high-tech area of medicine, but left medicine to pursue her interest in the Web. She has been writing code and developing websites since 1994, teaches web-related classes both online at `eclasses.org` and in the classroom, and maintains a Dreamweaver MX 2004 blog at `http://radio.weblogs.com/0132492/`. She is the coauthor of *XML Schemas* (Sybex, 2002) and *Mastering XHTML* (Sybex, 2002) and a contributing author to *XML for Dummies*. In those rare moments when she's not online, other interests include cryptography, holographic technology, and science fiction.

In addition to Christian and Lucinda, other writers and designers contributed their specialized expertise to make this book as useful as possible for today's web designer and developer.

Contributors

Our contributing authors have a great deal of hands-on experience with Dreamweaver and the Web, and our contributing designer created beautiful designs for the tutorial files.

Eric Butow Eric Butow contributed Chapters 5, 9, 18, and 30. He is CEO of Butow Communications Group (BCG), a technical documentation and web design firm in Roseville, California, where he uses Dreamweaver as his primary web design tool. Eric has contributed to several books including *Creating Web Pages Bible* and has also authored two books including *FrontPage 2002 Weekend Crash Course.* Visit BCG and learn more about Eric at www.butow.net.

Michele Davis Michele Davis contributed Chapters 19, 20, 26, 31, and 32. She is a technical consultant for companies implementing new documentation for PDF manuals, websites, marketing brochures, instructional design, training, and online help. She is savvy in numerous applications and has written or coauthored several trade publications and works of fiction. She can be found on the Web at www.krautgrrl.com.

Jennifer Ryan Wilde Jennifer Ryan Wilde of chaotech design + development created the designs for the e-commerce, information, and intranet site examples used in the chapter tutorials. To see more examples of Jennifer's designs, visit www.chaotech.com.

CONTENTS AT A GLANCE

Contents

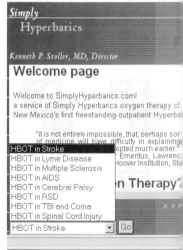

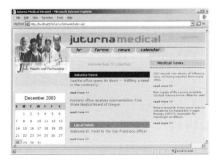

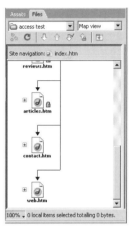

Introduction

Thankfully, we've come a long way since the early days of the Web when most pages had grey backgrounds and were filled with paragraphs of text punctuated by an occasional small graphic. Dreamweaver MX 2004 allows professionals at any level of web development to use its features to develop websites and web applications as easily and rapidly as possible. This book is designed for readers at all levels of experience with the Web and with Dreamweaver. If you are a beginner, you may choose to work your way through this book from Chapter 1 to Chapter 33, or if you are already experienced with web development, you might find it more productive to jump right in to your particular areas of interest.

For those of you who are familiar with the first edition of this book, eight new chapters have been added and every chapter has undergone major revision and additions to incorporate the new features of Dreamweaver MX 2004.

Who Needs This Book

The line between designer and developer has become less clearly delineated as the Web has evolved over time, and most people producing websites today need to use a combination of design and development skills. Dreamweaver is an ideal tool for providing features that are easy to use and learn for designers, developers, and the new breed of designer/developer.

This book provides information on planning, designing, and developing a website and a web application. For readers who are new to web design, we have provided detailed information on web graphics, including a bonus graphics chapter (included on the CD) on slicing and optimizing graphics in Fireworks, Photoshop, and Illustrator. For readers who are new to web development, we have provided comprehensive instructions on setting up a web server, connecting to a database, and using any of Dreamweaver's five supported server technologies to create web applications. For readers who are already familiar with web development, this book also includes specifics on using Dreamweaver for web application development, as well as myriad web development tips and techniques.

Conventions Used in This Book

To help you find your way through this book as effectively as possible and find the information you need, we've incorporated a number of design elements to call out material that might be of interest to you.

 New features in Dreamweaver MX 2004 are marked with this margin icon. For a detailed list of new features, see Appendix C.

Many procedures are broken down into numbered steps, and many chapters include tutorials that enable you to try out what you've learned with a specific project. All the files you need to complete the tutorials are included in the Chapter files on the CD.

> Tips, comments, and warnings are called out as Notes.

> **SIDEBARS**
>
> Interesting bits of information and additional details that might not be essential to your understanding of Dreamweaver MX 2004 are boxed as stand-alone sidebars, like so. These are usually much longer and more detailed than notes.

Because there are many different ways of working with Dreamweaver and you might not need to make use of every possible feature of Dreamweaver MX 2004, you should feel free to skip around from chapter to chapter as necessary. To minimize redundancy and pack as much fresh information as possible into this book, we've liberally included cross-references throughout to suggest when you might benefit from looking at another chapter.

How This Book Is Organized

This book has five parts and comprises 33 chapters and three appendices. Here's a quick rundown of what you'll find inside:

PART I ■ Planning Your Project and Setting Up Dreamweaver

This part is all about getting your project started and your site set up to optimize the development process. Chapter 1 covers the essentials of website planning and preparation.

Chapter 2 breaks down web pages into their component parts, based on how Dreamweaver works with HTML files and other web documents. Chapter 3 shows you how to get the new Dreamweaver MX workspace set up for efficiency and comfort, and how to set up a website for the first time. Chapter 4 explains how to use sitewide components—templates, assets, and library items—to save time and effort and maintain consistency.

PART II ■ Building a Web Page

This part is the heart of the matter: how to assemble the essential elements needed to construct a web page. Chapter 5 covers layout with tables or layers. Chapter 6 is all about working with text, including importing Word or Excel files. Chapter 7 explains how to set up framesets and frames. Chapter 8 explains how to insert local and external hyperlinks in your pages. Chapter 9 discusses all the new CSS features of Dreamweaver MX 2004 and shows you how to use these features to develop cutting-edge standards-compliant designs. Chapter 10 shows you how to add graphics and multimedia to your Dreamweaver pages. Chapter 11 explores the Flash features incorporated in Dreamweaver as well as the specifics on inserting Flash files in your Dreamweaver pages.

PART III ■ Adding Interactivity within Dreamweaver

This part takes you a step beyond flat, static web pages and shows you how to add movement and interactivity to your pages. Chapter 12 introduces Dreamweaver behaviors—pre-made JavaScript routines you can add to your pages without learning how to code JavaScript. Chapter 13 shows you how to incorporate navigation objects, including rollovers, navigation bars, and jump menus. Chapter 14 explains everything you need to know to use forms, including information on forms processing. Chapter 15 covers community-building interactive features, including guest books, discussion boards, and blogs.

PART IV ■ Developing Web Applications

This part takes you into the world of dynamic, data-driven websites and rapid web application development. Chapter 16 gets you started with setting up Dreamweaver for application development. Chapter 17 walks you through developing an e-commerce site. Chapter 18 helps you customize your coding environment for handcrafting your code. Chapter 19 is a crash course in database development for the Web. Chapter 20 shows you how to use Dreamweaver with ColdFusion. Chapters 21, 22, and 23 feature the specifics of using

Dreamweaver with ASP, PHP, and JSP. Chapter 24 details the use of XML and XHTML in Dreamweaver. Chapter 25 covers web services, ASP.NET, and Rich Internet Applications (RIA).

PART V ■ Site Administration from Start to Finish

This part is about wrapping up your development project and handing over the site. Chapter 26 explains how to control access with user registration and login. Chapter 27 introduces content management with Macromedia Contribute. Chapter 28 features dynamic content management using ASP and a database. Chapter 29 shows how to use Dreamweaver to test browser compatibility features. Chapter 30 discusses the issues involved with launching a site or turning it over to a client. Chapter 31 covers the details of using Dreamweaver for maintaining a site. Chapter 32 explains how to customize and extend Dreamweaver to get the maximum use out of it as your primary web development tool. Chapter 33 shows you how to use Dreamweaver's accessibility features.

Appendices

We've included three appendices this time. Appendix A includes useful Dreamweaver resources that are available online. Appendix B lists keyboard shortcuts in Dreamweaver. Appendix C details the new features of Dreamweaver MX 2004.

Note to Macintosh (and PC) Users

The authors of this book use both Macs and PCs for web design and development, and have used Dreamweaver MX 2004 on both platforms. The majority of readers of this book will be Windows users, so most (but not all) of the illustrations in this book show Windows XP screens.

Rest assured, though, that this book is perfectly designed for use with a Mac. We have tested every command on a G4 PowerBook running OS X, and where necessary we've included separate instructions or screen shots to illustrate when the Mac version of Dreamweaver looks or functions in some way different from the PC version.

About the CD

The accompanying CD includes demos, browsers, extensions, example files, and tutorial files.

Demos We've included trial versions of Dreamweaver MX 2004, Fireworks MX 2004, Flash Basic MX 2004, Flash Pro MX 2004, Flash Player 7, Contribute 2.0, Director MX, JRun 4, and Top Style Pro 3.1.

Browsers Internet Explorer 6, Netscape 7.1, Opera 7.0, and Mozilla Firebird are included on the CD.

Extensions We've included extensions that we refer to in the book, as well as an additional assortment of our favorite Dreamweaver extensions. Many more can be found at `www.macromedia.com`.

Visit Our Website

This book has a website that can be accessed at `http://dreamweaversavvy.com`. The site includes copies of the tutorial and example files; news about Dreamweaver, web design, and development; updates for the book; and a way to suggest improvements for the next edition.

Join the Discussion

There's a Yahoo!Groups discussion for this book, and any reader of the book is welcome to join in on the discussion. To visit the group's web page, go to `http://groups.yahoo.com/dreamweaversavvy/`. (To join the list, go directly to `http://groups.yahoo.com/group/dramweaversavvy/join/`—you'll need to set up a Yahoo ID to participate.)

Contact the Authors

To contact the authors by e-mail, you can send e-mail to `support@sybex.com`.

## PART I

Planning Your Project and Setting Up Dreamweaver

Although *it might be more exhilarating to start designing web pages on the first day of your project, experience has taught us that a successful web development project starts with some strategy. First you want to take a step back and look at the big picture. What is your site or application going to do? Who's going to use it? How does it have to work? How should it be organized?*

Next, to make the most of Dreamweaver, take a little time to understand how the software creates, interprets, and displays web pages. Get the software set up in a way that suits your workflow, and then finally start developing your site.

Even then, before you get into the process of building actual pages, you're going to need to spend some time setting up your site in Dreamweaver, and creating the shared templates, library items, and other assets that will enable a rapid, efficient development process.

## CHAPTER 1

Planning and Preparing for a Dreamweaver Project

Dreamweaver can help your project run more smoothly whether you are building a website from scratch all by yourself for yourself, collaborating with a multidisciplinary team to deliver a web application for a client, or anything in between. Regardless of the scope of your project, take some time in advance to think through the *architecture* of your site (fundamentally, the layout structure of the pages as a whole, and the options for navigating the site), develop a look-and-feel (graphic design and interface), and gather the *content* (the information you want to include on the site pages). When this preliminary work is done, you can plunge into the development, staging, launching, and maintenance of the site.

This chapter assists you in sorting through the elements of your preferred methodology before you get down to brass tacks with Dreamweaver. Topics addressed in this chapter include the following:

- **When to use Dreamweaver**

- **Nailing down your process**

- **Gathering requirements for your web project**

- **Designing the project's information architecture**

When to Use Dreamweaver

As the Web has grown and developed, so has Dreamweaver. Dreamweaver has evolved from an HTML editor to a full-featured web production and application development tool. Each version introduces new features that make the web development process easier and faster whether you are involved in the front end (design and page production) or the back end (scripting and application development).

Dreamweaver goes beyond enabling you to design and create web pages—it helps you manage your entire site from the top down. Best of all, it enables a team of people to work together on the same project. If you are working with collaborators, chances are not everyone is working in Dreamweaver. That's fine. Dreamweaver produces clean code that even the most hardcore code jockey can't complain about.

With Dreamweaver, though, you can keep your part of the project all in one place, and you can do all of your work inside the application (at least after you're done doodling on cocktail napkins).

Using Dreamweaver with Other Applications

Dreamweaver MX 2004 is an incredibly powerful web development tool, but of course it can't do every single thing a designer or developer would like to do. Macromedia wisely provides tight integration with its other popular web applications: Fireworks, Flash, HomeSite+, and ColdFusion. You can also use files from Macromedia Director, Microsoft Word and Excel, and other graphics programs in your Dreamweaver pages.

Fireworks and Other Graphics Software

Fireworks is a unique tool expressly designed for the development and optimization of web graphics. Fireworks is where you can develop and refine the graphical look-and-feel for the site—the site's logo, the graphics, the navigational elements, and so on. The entire site won't live inside Fireworks the way it will in Dreamweaver, but because they're both Macromedia products designed to work together, any graphics you develop or import into Fireworks will flow easily into your site templates and pages over on the Dreamweaver side.

> For more information on using Fireworks and other graphics programs, see the CD Bonus Chapter, "Slicing, Optimizing, and Exporting Images," and Chapter 13, "Designing Navigation Objects."

You don't have to use Fireworks to create and develop your site graphics, however. Dreamweaver accepts web graphic files (GIFs, JPEGs, and PNGs) from any graphics software program including Adobe Photoshop, Adobe Illustrator, and Jasc Paint Shop Pro.

In Dreamweaver preferences (Edit → Preferences / Dreamweaver → Preferences) you can select external editors for specific file types. For example, you can choose to have Dreamweaver open Photoshop when you want to edit a JPEG image. To open the external editor, select the image and click on the Edit icon in the Property inspector. For more details on using the Property inspector, see Chapter 3, "Setting Up Your Workspace and Your Site."

However, there are two major advantages to using Fireworks with Dreamweaver:

- Fireworks is specifically designed for creating web graphics and includes a multitude of special features for doing so.
- Fireworks is integrated with Dreamweaver and can export both HTML code and graphic files directly to Dreamweaver.

Flash

Flash is the web designer's favorite tool for developing interactive movies, animations, and every other kind of beast that slithers, crawls, runs, or flies across your screen. Flash movies are optimized for streaming over the Web, and widely accepted as a format. The newest version of Flash includes a professional version that features extensive video support as well as Flash application development. Flash is the first choice when you want your users to be able to, say, play a video game at your website. Artists love Flash too (see www.snarg.net/ for a hypnotic example of what we're talking about).

You can create Flash text and Flash buttons in Dreamweaver (whether or not you have Flash installed on your computer). Dreamweaver MX 2004 also includes support for *Flash elements*—prebuilt Flash components that can be downloaded and added to your pages.

Flash is integrated with Dreamweaver. You can export Flash files to your Dreamweaver site, insert Flash movies in your web pages, and use Dreamweaver to set playback and display options. If you have Flash installed on your computer, you can also use Dreamweaver to update the links in Flash movies or launch and edit Flash files from Dreamweaver.

For more details on working with Flash, see Chapter 11, "Getting into Flash."

Director

Director is a multimedia authoring tool used to create interactive multimedia files, including web content (Shockwave files), multimedia CDs and DVDs, games, movies, and cartoons. Files created in Director can include photo-quality images, digital video, audio, 2D and 3D animation, and even Flash content. Director files can be deployed to multiple environments, including the Web, kiosks, CDs, and DVDs. Chances are, last time you stuck a

CD in your drive and watched a little promo or clicked on a bulbous shiny set of interface buttons, they were developed in Director—this book's CD features a Director interface.

Macromedia statistics (`www.macromedia.com/software/player_census/shockwaveplayer/`) show that 375 million web users have the Shockwave Player. Although Director is not actually integrated with Dreamweaver, you can use Dreamweaver to insert Shockwave files in your pages, and set playback and display options.

For more information on Director, see Chapter 10, "Adding Graphics and Multimedia."

Getting Your Process Squared Away

Before you fire up the software and start cranking out web pages, take a step back to sort out your process (methodology). Nowadays, most web design and development projects are collaborative and require a lot of coordination among team members. Yes, it's true that if you're running a one-person project or shop, you don't have to answer to anybody, you don't have to use anyone else's lingo, you don't have to adhere to anyone's deadlines, and no one is going to second-guess your work. But even then you're going to have to figure out what to do first, what part of the project depends on other parts being completed first (sometimes referred to, for short, as *dependencies*), and what your timeline and milestones are going to need to be.

In most situations, you've got a "someone" to answer to, whether it's your boss, your client, or simply your audience. That's right, web design and development requires you to anticipate and meet your audience's needs if you expect them to come to your site, use your interactive application, register with your enterprise, or come back again after the first visit. Furthermore, in most commercial projects, you're going to have to collaborate with somebody, or with a whole team of somebodies. There might be a branding expert, a writer (perhaps called a content developer), some developers (technical architects, front-end scripters, back-end coders, middleware specialists, and so on), and possibly a project manager. Oh, yes, and a visual designer or graphic designer.

You may be working with people who cut their teeth in the field of professional services, interactive or advertising agencies, publishing, and software development. You're going to discover that everyone has a different name for the same thing (is it a *storyboard* or a *wireframe*, a *site map* or *thumbnail series*, *use cases* or *process flows*?), and most people see the project revolving around their discipline. In any collaborative project, some time—at least an hour—should be spent up front hashing out the division of labor, the dependencies (such as, "I can't develop the content inventory until you finish the site map"), the points of handoff or turnover, and the milestones and deliverables expected by the client (even if the client is just your boss).

For more ideas and discussion about various web-development methodologies (and there are a number of equally valid approaches), check out the author-created website for this book, at `http://dreamweaversavvy.com/`.

Gathering Requirements

How are you going to know what to put into your site or application unless you spend some time and effort learning the needs of your website's or application's eventual users? (Consultants call this stage of a project *discovery*—not to be confused with lawyers pawing through your files.) This discovery phase should involve interviewing representatives of every audience type or anyone else with a stake in the usefulness and success of the site. This means not just your boss or client, your client's boss or team members, and other obvious stakeholders, but also, if at all possible, some potential users of the site—often customers, partners, or vendors. Find out what they want. Your role is to meet the needs of both the client and the users. Clients do not always know what their users want as well as those clients think they do. Also, it makes a killer argument when the client has gotten attached to some horrible idea to be able to say, "But your site's users don't want that. See, here in these interview notes, they say they'd never come back if you had *that* as part of your site." It's also worth taking the time to check out the competition—look at their sites to get an idea about the features they offer, and what works and what doesn't.

This leads to the first commandment of web design (perhaps the only commandment—we're not sure):

Know Thy Audience

What if they built a website and nobody came? They did. And nobody did. It was called the dotcom bubble. Just because you can sell your boss, or your client, or a venture capitalist (VC) on an idea doesn't mean that people are going to come and pay you to keep executing that idea. Understand your audience. Go meet them if possible. Interview them, but also watch them as they work. Study what they like and dislike. Learn as much as you can about usability. If your ultimate product isn't useable, guess what? People won't use it. If your site doesn't meet a need, then no one will need it.

So think long and hard about the needs and desires of your audience. What are they reaching out for? How can you satisfy those needs? Get that straight and the rest of the project will practically take care of itself.

Once your site is up and running online, be sure to follow site statistics and usage patterns. See what your traffic actually is, and which parts of your site get visited and which parts are ignored. Pay attention to the feedback you receive from visitors. Good websites change over time to address the current needs of their audience.

Getting the Information Architecture Right

Information architecture is a $10 word that means how your site's information is organized. What do people see first when they come in the front door? How many levels down is certain information buried? How many clicks does it take to get to crucial information? What is the structure of the navigation? Dreamweaver won't figure any of this out for you. Sure, once you've sorted it out, Dreamweaver is an awesome tool for maintaining the site map, navigation links, and so on. But you have to do the hard thinking first.

Fortunately, because Dreamweaver is so flexible and easy to use, you can make mistakes when you start and still correct them later on in the project. That's right, no matter how carefully you gather your requirements, know thy audience, or massage your client, guess what? New requirements will emerge at the 11th hour. Projects you've never heard of will suddenly demand to be integrated into your pristine site map. With a few points and clicks in Dreamweaver, subsections can be promoted to top-level categories, and entire site areas can be snipped out and placed in limbo. I'd like to see a "real" architect try to rearrange a real building once the contractors are in the house!

Still, just because things are inevitably going to change, that's no excuse for not trying to get it right at first. In fact, getting your architecture clarified at the beginning makes it that much easier to *track the changes* as they emerge. Think about it. It's a lot easier to see what's changed if you know what it changed from!

Also, remember those other people on the team. They need to know where you're planning on putting stuff. They may be writing scripts and have to know what directory (a.k.a. folder) a certain piece of content is going to live in. They may need to know how many levels down their application is going to be running. Sorting out the site's architecture is step one of designing any substantial web project.

ENSURING THAT YOUR SITE IS ACCESSIBLE

One of the most important changes to the specifications for HTML in Version 4 is the inclusion of requirements that your site be accessible to people with disabilities. This means that your work can be used and appreciated by the estimated 10 percent of the world's population with some sort of physical disability that makes it difficult to access most websites. The World Wide Web Consortium (W3C) has set up a special organization and website that provide helpful checklists, guidelines, and ideas in support of the Web Accessibility Initiative (WAI). Check out www.w3.org/WAI/ to find out how to insert accessibility into your website relatively painlessly. Another very useful site that serves as both an example of a well designed, accessible website and as a tutorial is the Web Accessibility In Mind (WebAIM) site (www.webaim.org/). For information about using Dreamweaver's accessibility features, see Chapter 33, "Using Dreamweaver to Make Your Site Accessible."

Developing a Site Map

A great way to get an overview of a website at a glance is to create and maintain a site map. Ultimately, Dreamweaver can generate or show you a site-map type view of your site, but that's after you've actually created all the pages. When you're just getting started, you can literally just draw it by hand or use any illustration software to put it together. A site map looks something like a family tree. Pages are represented as boxes and labeled. You can indicate the name of a page or—if you really want to get into it at this stage—what the page will contain. Navigational links are represented as lines between boxes. Then, like a family tree, child and sibling pages all stem from a parent page, and you can take this organization down as many levels as you like. Some people make the boxes smaller as they go down in levels. Often the third level of links is represented as a simple text list. The level of detail depends on your own needs or those of your client.

Figure 1.1 shows a sample site map for an e-commerce site.

When you are developing an interactive application (as opposed to a series of static, linked pages), the site map can also be referred to as a *process flow*, because it shows how the user might flow through the various pages or screens to accomplish some task. For example, let's say you developed a new search engine for a site. You could create a process-flow diagram showing how users can go from the basic search box to the advanced search page or to the search tips, and then ultimately to the search results.

You can create whatever codes or symbols you'd like to indicate different types of pages. Use dotted lines for dynamic pages (pages that are created from a database), or use rounded edges for new pages. Have fun with it. This is information design without that tedious "making it work" part.

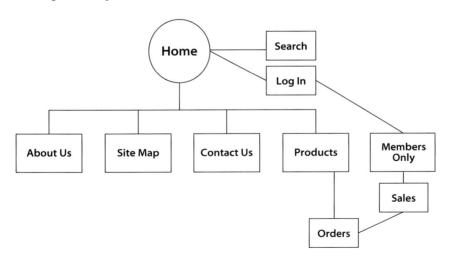

Figure 1.1

This e-commerce site has a main page with links for Search and Log In as well as links to four subsections reached from the main page. The Log In page links to another subsection for members only.

Creating Wireframes and Storyboards

If you are developing a large site with several subsections, you may want to create *wireframes* for the project. The name *wireframe* comes from the skeletal wires that underlie a piece of sculpture. A wireframe is a simple page of text that includes the purpose of one specific web page and all entry and exit points from the page—that's it! Wireframes do not include design or content elements.

Once you have created wireframes for every page in the site, and made final decisions about the overall site structure, you can then create *storyboards* for each page that show the content, layout, navigation elements, design elements and other graphics.

Figure 1.2 shows a mocked-up wireframe page for the home page in our imaginary e-commerce site.

For more information on using wireframes and storyboards for web projects, see www.grokdotcom.com/wireframing.htm.

Ready, Set, Rumble!

This chapter explained some of the planning and organizational work you'll need to do before you launch a serious web-development project. This includes determining when it's appropriate to use Dreamweaver, Fireworks, Flash, and other software; hashing out a process or methodology for developing your site or application; figuring out how to collaborate with other team members (if necessary); gathering requirements for your site; and developing an information architecture.

Figure 1.2

This simple wire-frame shows the purpose of the page as well as all links.

Home Page

Purpose: main entry page for e-commerce site

Links to: • Search
• Log In
• About Us
• Site Map
• Contact Us
• Products

This information is useful no matter what tools you use to assist you as a web designer and developer. Don't ignore these steps because they involve thought processes and decisions that your software applications can't do for you. Once you know how you're going to design your project, what you're going to do it with, how and when you are going to use your tools, who the product is for, and how the information at the site will be organized, you're ready to start cranking away in Dreamweaver. The next chapter will take you through the elements of a web page and a website and will even show you some actual Dreamweaver screens! Remember, have fun.

## CHAPTER 2

Web Pages Deconstructed

As you know, the basic unit of display on the Web is called a page. Like all metaphors in the electronic world, this one only partly conveys the idea. In a book, the pages are all the same length. On the Web, a page can be any length. In a book or magazine, the elements on each page are static (unchanging). On the Web, the elements of a page may be dynamic (changeable) and interactive. Generally, a book is read from start to finish in a linear fashion. Hypertext makes it possible for websites to be navigated in a nonlinear way by following hyperlinks to other pages on the same site or pages anywhere on the Web. In this chapter we discuss the components of a typical web page—content, design, and navigation—and explain how you can use Dreamweaver to manage these different types of web page elements.

- **Text, graphics, and other content objects**

- **Design, layout, and style sheets**

- **Navigation elements**

The Elements of a Web Page

From a human point of view, a web page consists of *content* (information in all its forms), *design* (how the content is displayed), and *navigation* (how users move around the site).

Of course, to server and browser software, web pages consist of text and code, which is made up of HTML tags and other coding representing embedded files and scripting elements. So *content* can be text, data, images, and other forms of information. *Text* is also called writing, copy, or just content. Other types of content appear on web pages in the form of embedded graphic files or multimedia objects such as Flash movies or audio files.

The *design* of a page is the way text formatting, graphic elements, and other style elements are used to produce the site's look-and-feel. *Navigation* is the system of interactive elements that lets the user move from page to page. Navigation can be in the form of text, though it is often handled with graphic elements and sometimes script objects that enable actions (as with a *rollover*, an animation activated by a script when the mouse moves over an object such as a graphic or a block of text).

From a Dreamweaver user's point of view, everything on a web page is either *text* or *objects*. Text and objects are integrated on the page by *code* (tags, mostly). Sure, you can view or touch code directly, but Dreamweaver's metaphor, at least in Design view, is of pages comprising text and objects. Text is written material, as always. Objects are everything else. Figure 2.1 shows how Dreamweaver displays text and objects held together by tags. Manipulating text and objects is web design in a nutshell.

Figure 2.1

Dreamweaver enables you to manipulate text and objects on a web page.

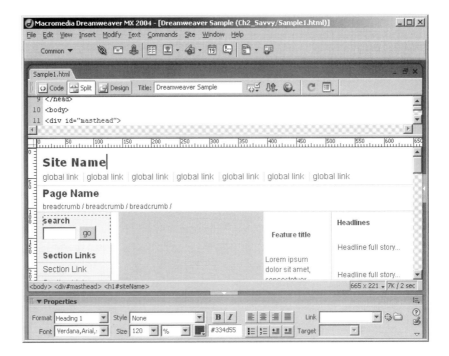

Working with Content

Before you can construct your web pages from the basic elements Dreamweaver recognizes (text and objects), you'll need to collect *assets*, meaning any prepared material or "ingredients" needed to build your pages. For example, you will insert the text on your web pages either by importing it from a word processing program or by typing it directly onto the page—either way, you need the text to be ready when the time comes to build the page. Assets for a Dreamweaver site can include images, color codes, URLs, movies (Flash, Shockwave, QuickTime, or MPEG), script files (JavaScript or VBScript), templates, and library items.

> For additional details on managing assets, templates, and library items, see Chapter 4, "Saving Labor with Templates and Libraries."

You'll need to have your artwork ready, and you may also need to collect scripts as well as Macromedia extensions (additional features you can add to Dreamweaver) to include any interactivity you wish to incorporate into the site.

Before you begin to work, you need to do one other thing: set up your directories or folders to receive the assets you collect. Chapter 3, "Setting Up Your Workspace and Your Site," discusses how to set up the structure of your site (folders and files) on your computer or on a local network, how to set up a site in Dreamweaver, and how to use Dreamweaver's site management tools.

Working with Text

You can type text content for your pages directly in the Document window in Dreamweaver or, if you have your text assets prepared (the text files, or *copy*), cutting and pasting them into Dreamweaver is a snap. Chapter 3 presents detailed information on setting up the Dreamweaver workspace and using the Document window. Formatting the text is a little more complicated, but we'll explore that in detail in Chapter 6, "Inserting and Formatting Text Content."

STAYING ON THE RIGHT SIDE OF COPYRIGHT LAW

Make sure you have the right to use any content (text, images, or multimedia) you intend to include at your site. The general rule of thumb about copying material from another person's website, by the way, is *don't do it* without proper permission. For more information, visit the Friends of Active Copyright Education (FACE) website (http://www.law.duke.edu/copyright/face/softint/index.htm).

There are many websites that discuss web design theory. One of the best is The Site Wizard at `www.thesitewizard.com`. These materials are practical and extremely easy to understand and implement. Another classic site for insight into web design theory and human interface design is Jakob Nielsen's `www.useit.com`. Joe Gillespie's Web Page Design for Designers at `www.wpdfd.com/` features articles on web design and typography and additional resources for designers. For a comprehensive list of web design sites and blogs, see `http://www.d.umn.edu/itss/support/Training/Online/webdesign/sites.html`.

Working with Graphics

How are web graphics different from any other electronic images (computer graphics)? They have to make it over your user's Internet connection, whether it is a "fat" broadband connection such as a T1, cable, or DSL link, or a connection with much less bandwidth, such as a dial-up modem. In every case, an optimized graphic (one that has been compressed in size as much as possible without sacrificing too much quality) is preferable. Although using a websafe color palette (216 colors of the standard 256) is the safest way to ensure that most users will see the same color, it is questionable whether this limitation is still necessary today. Browsers News (`www.upsdell.com/BrowserNews/stat_trends.htm`) statistics show that over 90 percent of current users have displays with 16-bit (65,536 colors) or 24-bit (16,77,216 colors) or greater color depth. Ultimately, it may be a personal decision, based on the needs of the site and/or client. In any event, testing your pages on a monitor set to 16-bit color display may be the best idea. This allows you to judge whether or not you have a color-shifting problem that needs to be addressed.

For a detailed discussion of the websafe color palette and web color issues, see "Death of the Websafe Color Palette?" at `http://hotwired.lycos.com/webmonkey/00/37/index2a.html?tw=design`.

For more information on color depth, see Chapter 10, "Adding Graphics and Multimedia."

The standard file formats for web graphics are JPEG (JPG), GIF, and PNG, which combines the best features of the other two formats. PNG is Fireworks' native format, but not all browsers currently handle PNG files, so you'll probably have to stick to JPEGs and GIFs for most projects.

Use the JPEG file format for images with smooth gradations of color, such as most photographs. Use the GIF file format for images that use large patterns of single colors. (You also use the GIF89a format for a type of animated graphic file.)

Designing for the Web

When you are designing for the Web, you must be cognizant not only of your local computer and software restraints, but your viewer's constraints as well (which, as you remember, you usually don't know). You can guess at what your viewers will be using to visit your website and base your designs on these suppositions. Your guess must address several factors.

You must design for the computer screen and not for the printed page. You usually don't know the size of the browser window on your visitor's computer or the quality of the color display, and you don't even have control over where on that screen the browser window is placed. For example, some people view web pages using a portable computer with a very small monitor that supports only 256 colors. In fact, monitors can get even more limited. Nowadays, portable digital assistants (PDAs), such as the Palm m130 and its competitors, are often used to view websites, and they have itty-bitty screens. Other people might view your pages using a 21-inch super VGA monitor that supports millions and millions of colors.

Not all monitors display colors the same way. One of the most important factors to control when you are designing web graphics is the quality of the images. Quality comes down to how color is managed by the software drivers used to control the monitors. Color calibration, color bit-depth, and resolution all affect how graphics are displayed. Your choices are best guided by knowledge of your audience as well as current trends in color depth and screen resolution.

People do not use the same tools to view the Web. The software used to view websites is called the browser. There are currently several browsers on the market, although this is rapidly changing. Netscape downsized in July 2003, and there will most likely be no new versions of Netscape (the latest release is 7.1). At the same time Microsoft announced that it is abandoning development of Internet Explorer for the Mac (the last version is 5.5).

Most viewers (currently more than 90 percent) use Microsoft Internet Explorer. There are alternative browsers available, such as Opera (www.opera.com), a popular European browser developed by a telecommunications company in Norway. Other popular alternative choices include Mozilla (www.mozilla.org) and Mozilla Firebird. Mac users may be using Apple's new browser, Safari, the Mac OS X default web browser (www.apple.com/safari/).

There are many different versions of each of these browsers still being used, each with its own support of a selection of the entire HTML standard as well as proprietary HTML tags not supported in other browsers. Each browser displays web pages differently. Also, the web medium is constantly "oozing" onto new devices, such as Web TV boxes, handheld organizers such as Palms, cell phones, and who knows what will be next? Usually these newer devices have severe limitations on what they can display. For example, the Wireless

Application Protocol (WAP) format, used for wireless devices like cell phones, displays only text and links—no graphics.

For more details on using Dreamweaver's browser compatibility features, see Chapter 29, "Checking Browser Compatibility."

Not everyone has a fat pipe. Your web graphics (and overall page sizes) must be made as small as possible so that users connecting to the Internet using dial-up modems can access your information quickly. According to Nielsen//NetRatings (`http://netratings.com`) statistics for May 2003, 51 percent of home users in the U.S. connect to the Internet at a speed of 56 Kbps, 9 percent at 28.8/33.3 Kbps, and 3 percent at 14.4.

To support users with slow connections, web images are compressed (using the three file formats we just discussed: GIF, JPEG, and PNG). Compression can mean degradation of the image, so you must design your graphics to work with this loss of detail.

Not everyone is using the same operating system. Designers often use Macs, but their users are more often running Windows on a PC. Some people use a flavor of Unix, such as Linux. Different operating platforms display graphics differently. For example, Macs and PCs use completely different color management methods to display images. In fact, even the same operating system running on different software/hardware configurations of video cards, audio cards, or drivers displays graphics differently. You must be aware of these differences and test your pages on as many platforms as you can to ensure their quality translates as well as possible across computer platforms.

You must consider users with disabilities. What about the user who uses a screen reader or other device to "view" your page? Visitors with visual, auditory, motor, or other disabilities may use a variety of software and hardware devices to access your web pages. Dreamweaver supports a variety of accessibility features, including screen reader support, keyboard navigation features, and operating system accessibility support. You can also choose to have Dreamweaver prompt you to add accessibility features to appropriate page items as you construct your pages. Dreamweaver offers sample pages designed for accessibility, and you can generate an accessibility report to test any of your pages against accessibility guidelines. Chapter 33, "Using Dreamweaver to Make Your Site Accessible," gives all the details about using Dreamweaver to make your site accessible, and we'll also point out relevant accessibility features as we go along.

Having considered some of the cross-platform and accessibility issues involved in planning a web project, you'll then also need to think about some of the specific design approaches available to you in the web medium, such as text-based design, use of style sheets, and methods of page layout.

Designing with Text

Text is the simplest element of a web page, but it is often the least controllable of your variables when you are laying out a page. Unless you can assume that your users have a specific font installed or a certain type of setup (as you sometimes can on, say, an intranet), stick to the most popular fonts, such as Times New Roman, Arial, MS Sans Serif, or Courier. If you specify a font that looks great to you, but your user doesn't have it installed on their computer, your page will be displayed with their default font. Table 2.1 shows the standard fonts in Dreamweaver by operating system. Additional fonts can be added to the standard font menu (Text → Font → Edit Font List).

PC	UNIX	MACINTOSH
Times New Roman	Times	Times
Arial		Arial
Courier New		Courier
Verdana		Verdana
	Helvetica	Helvetica
		Geneva
Georgia[1]		

Table 2.1

Standard Fonts in Dreamweaver

1 Georgia is installed by Internet Explorer 4+.

To overcome this constraint on available fonts, designers tend to rely on objects such as graphic files to display more sophisticated treatments of text. For instance, if they wish to use more typographically interesting fonts, they may create graphical text in a graphics program and import it into Dreamweaver as an object, or create Flash text in Dreamweaver itself (see Chapter 11, "Getting into Flash") for more information on creating Flash text and Flash buttons).

This practice is especially useful when you need complete control of the appearance of text. Any text that you wish to format with specific fonts, colors, graphics, and so forth (as you would with banners, logos, navigation buttons, and headlines), can be inserted as an object onto your page. In this case, the object is a graphic. The following are the main disadvantages to this approach:

- If the image file fails to download for any reason, the user may not be able to read the text contained in the graphic.

- Text presented in a graphic may not be available to users with visual disabilities who use screen readers or other devices to access web pages. For more information on using Dreamweaver to create accessible pages, see Chapter 33.

- Graphic files are the major contributor to overall page file size, so presenting blocks of text in graphics may greatly increase page download time.

A better approach is to use Cascading Style Sheets (described in the following section) to gain more control over the presentation of text in the body of your pages.

Cascading Style Sheets

As shown in Figure 2.2, there is another way to format—by using Cascading Style Sheets (CSS). *Style sheets* allow you to define how you want page elements, such as paragraphs, table cells, text boxes, and headings, to appear every time you use them. You just associate one or more formatting attributes with a style and give that style a name. All such style definitions can be stored in a single style sheet file. Once you associate that style sheet with a page, you can use any defined style by applying the name to the element. Best of all, if you revise your design specifications, you can make the change in one place (in the style sheet), instead of hunting through every page and making the change over and over and over.

Current versions of Microsoft Internet Explorer (5 and later), Netscape Navigator (6 and later), and Opera (5 and later) browsers offer very good style sheet support. However, many style sheet features do not work consistently or at all in earlier browser versions.

Dreamweaver MX 2004 includes many new CSS features. For more information about CSS in Dreamweaver, see Chapter 9, "Cascading Style Sheets."

Style sheets allow you to separate the presentation of a page from the content of the page, and make it possible to change the look of a page or a whole site quickly and easily. Both the HTML 4.01 and XHTML 1.0 specifications *deprecate* (make invalid and obsolete) formatting elements and attributes (such as the font element and the align attribute) in favor of style sheets.

Laying Out Pages with Tables or Layers

Because the web medium is less flexible than most print-design applications, laying out a web page usually requires a laborious process of manually situating objects in table cells that are nested within other table cells to give the illusion of columns, side-by-side graphics, or grids ("laborious" unless you use CSS, that is!).

We encourage you to use CSS for page layout rather than tables. Tables were originally created as a way to present tabular information, not as a page layout tool. Although tables have been used extensively for web page layout, this presents problems in older browsers, and can also make your page inaccessible to viewers with disabilities.

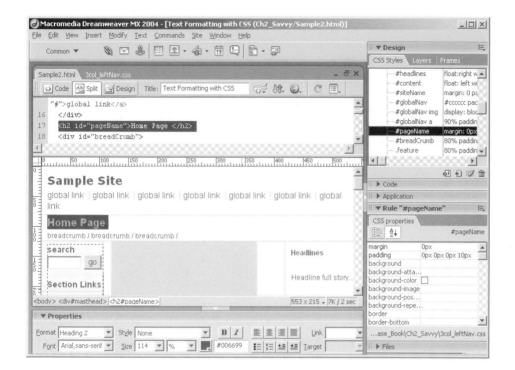

Figure 2.2

Text formatting can be managed using Cascading Style Sheets.

Layers are transparent areas on a page that can be hidden, overlapped, or displayed at will. Dreamweaver supports the use of layers in a way that makes web layout more natural and more like desktop publishing. In layout mode, you can design your page layout using Dreamweaver's layers, and then use Dreamweaver to convert the layers to tables and automatically generate the HTML code.

In Dreamweaver, the term *layer* refers to a layout option, not to Netscape's layer element. The layer and ilayer elements are proprietary Netscape elements that were only supported in Netscape 4.*x*. Dreamweaver recognizes these elements, but does not create layers by using them. Instead, Dreamweaver creates layers through the use of div and span as well as absolute and relative positioning.

Dreamweaver's layout mode enables you to lay out pages visually without having to manage the coding of the nested table cells. Figure 2.3 presents page layout and HTML code using layers. Figure 2.4 shows the same page layout and code after the layers are converted to tables. Tables and layers are discussed further in Chapter 5, "Page Layout."

You can also use HTML *frames* in order to display more than one HTML page at the same time, and create links so that other pages can open within these frames (see Chapter 7, "Interactivity with Framesets and Frames").

Figure 2.3

Dreamweaver supports the use of layers for page layout.

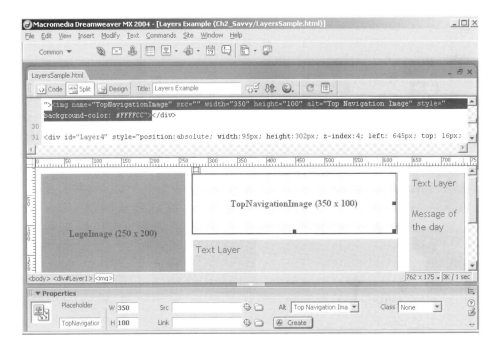

Figure 2.4

Dreamweaver can convert layers to tables.

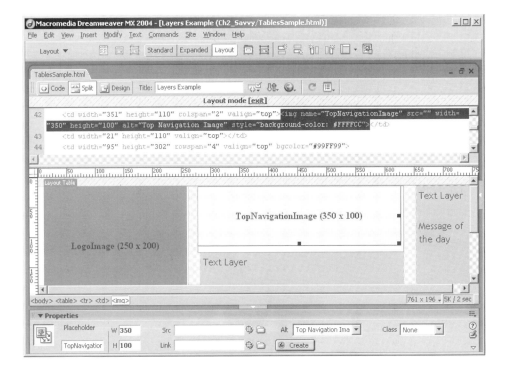

Along with Cascading Style Sheets, tables and layers help you control the placement of content and the look-and-feel of your site.

Setting Up a Navigation Scheme

One factor that distinguishes the Web from traditional print media is interactive, user-initiated navigation via hyerlinked text and graphics. Users experience this nonlinear navigation when they use various means to move from one page to another. In order to help your users understand their web experience and your website, you must provide them with an easy-to-grasp navigation scheme.

Organizing a Site

Sites are usually organized hierarchically, with a series of top-level pages that have sub-hierarchies. A good navigation scheme should make it clear what level the user is on and what related pages are available. (We'll explore navigation objects thoroughly in Chapter 13, "Designing Navigation Objects," and the chapters of Part IV.)

Designing Navigation with Hypertext

Before you can design an appropriate navigation scheme, you need to understand how hypertext works. Here is a little background for you.

The original purpose of the World Wide Web, as devised by Tim Berners-Lee, was to enable the visual linking of disparate types of information. This concept was revolution-ized with the development of the *Hypertext Transfer Protocol (HTTP)* and *Hypertext Markup Language (HTML)*. HTTP enabled browsers to request web pages, and web servers to respond to such requests. HTML provided the means to display pages on the Web and to link them to each other via hypertext. These hypertext links were set apart from the rest of the HTML page text by specific colors and underlining, and included a visual indicator to the user (usually a hand with a pointing finger) that their mouse was over a link.

Without hypertext there would be no Web. The more links you can build into your site, the more useful it becomes to your readers. The Web grows from these serendipitous interconnections that are built into each web page. Sometimes the most difficult part of designing a site is creating a useful and user-friendly navigation scheme. You should always think ahead about how you want to enable viewers to navigate through your site and what links you want to provide to other sites. At the same time, make requests for reciprocal links from related sites back to yours.

Links: Text, Graphics, and Hotspots

There are three ways to link information on web pages: by using text links, by using an entire graphic as a link, or by using a specific part of a graphic (*hotspot*) as a link.

Hypertext Links

The easiest way to create a connection between two pieces of information is by using a *hypertext link*. For example, if you wished to place a link to a page called `contactus.html` from a selection of text, your HTML code might look like this: `<a href="contactus.html"> Contact Us</a>`. By the way, Dreamweaver automatically generates this type of code when you select text or a graphic and type the target address into the Link text box or point to the target file from the Property inspector, but we'll get to that in Chapter 8, "Making and Maintaining Hyperlinks."

Graphic Links

Graphics can be used as links by simply enclosing the `img` tag within opening and closing a tags. A graphic link for the contactus page could be created with this code: `<a href= "contactus.html"><img src="contact.gif" width="100" height="50" alt="contact us"> </a>`. You could also include both a text link and a graphic link within the same set of a tags: `<a href="contactus.html"><img src="contact.gif" width="100" height="50" alt="contact us"><br>Contact Us</a>`.

Hotspots

Another very powerful way of linking areas of your page to related information elsewhere is by identifying an area of a graphic as a *hotspot* and then creating a link from this area. Hotspots are areas of an image on a web page that, when clicked, jump the viewer to another Uniform Resource Locator (URL). Hotspots can be created in Dreamweaver by first selecting an image and then using the Hotspot tools in the Property inspector to select one or more separate sections of the image and add links from those specific areas. (For more details on using the Property inspector and the Dreamweaver workspace, see Chapter 3.)

Hotspots and image maps can also be created in Fireworks and Flash. See Chapter 13 for more information.

Graphics with hotspots use *client-side image maps* to specify the areas of a graphic where links exist. Map code containing the link information is included in the web page that contains the code for the graphic image. This is called a "client-side" image map because the code is interpreted in the user's browser (the client-side). *Server-side image maps* are an older and more complex way of creating graphical links; they require special scripts that use a protocol called CGI (Common Gateway Interface) to transmit to the server the x,y coordinates of each click on the map graphic. Chapters 8 and 13 give more details on how to create linked graphics and how to build links in Dreamweaver.

Graphic Navigation Bars

Though pages can be hyperlinked with a perfectly adequate navigation scheme using only text links (we'll explain how to create and insert these links in Chapter 8), the most elegant navigation interfaces use graphic navigation bars. For these, you need to first use a graphics program to create the images to be used in the navigation bars (as described in Chapters 10 and 13).

> Graphic navigation bars may work using either hyperlinks or hotspots. If each of the navigation options is a separate image, then each one will be a hyperlink as well. If the entire navigation bar is a single image, then the options will all be hotspots.

Dreamweaver automates the process of using graphics to create a navigation bar through the use of *behaviors*. Behaviors are scripted actions that can be triggered by pointing to or clicking part of a graphic. They can be as simple as playing a sound or as complex as pulling in pictures for a slide show.

With behaviors, images may appear to change shape or appearance when you click them or roll over them with your mouse.

Jump Menus

There are several other specialized ways to navigate. Dreamweaver can assist you in building a jump menu containing linked items. This functions like the typical drop-down menus of choices that you see in dialog boxes in most common applications. Figure 2.5 shows a Dreamweaver jump menu with a Go button at the bottom of the page. The viewer selects one of these options and clicks the OK button to go to the chosen page.

Figure 2.5

**Dreamweaver
Jump Menu**

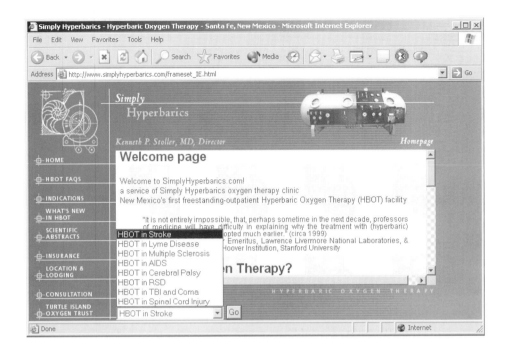

The Whole Enchilada

OK, now that you have an overview of the structure of a single page, we're going to zoom out a little, conceptually, and look at an entire site (or application, or project). Usually, a site consists of many pages, at least from the browser's point of view. To work with an entire site in Dreamweaver, you need to first set up the site's structure or "architecture." That's what we'll explore in the following chapter.

## CHAPTER 3

Setting Up Your Workspace and Your Site

So, you've worked out a site development plan and thought about what you're going to be putting on your pages. This must mean you're ready to actually work in Dreamweaver! In this chapter, we're going to start by giving you the cook's tour of the Dreamweaver workspace because you need to understand what assumptions the software makes about your development process. Most of the time the primary focus of your workspace will be a page, but tools for working at the site level, with files, links, styles, templates, assets, and so on, are never out of reach. When you're moderately comfortable with the interface, we'll show you how to set up a new site, telling Dreamweaver where to store the local files and where to publish the remote files.

Dreamweaver MX 2004 introduces many changes to the Dreamweaver interface and its design and coding environment. Many of the features initiated in Dreamweaver MX have been enhanced. New features have been added to make Dreamweaver more useable while incorporating a more sophisticated design model and application development environment. In this chapter, we'll explore the Dreamweaver workspace, pointing out new and changed features as we go.

Here are the topics that will be addressed:

- **Choosing a workspace style**

- **Understanding the Dreamweaver workspace**

- **Customizing your workspace**

- **Setting up a new site**

- **Importing an existing site**

- **Planning ahead for accessibility**

The Integrated Workspace versus the Floating Layout

Dreamweaver MX 2004 makes a clear distinction between the Windows workspace and the Macintosh workspace. Windows users have a choice between two versions of the integrated workspace, Designer or HomeSite/Coder-Style. Mac users have only the floating-panel workspace style, which is no longer available to Windows users.

The issue is always how to organize all the panels used to provide shortcuts and efficient workflow. With either integrated or floating style, Dreamweaver offers a Hide Panels command (Window → Hide Panels or View → Hide Panels) that instantly removes most of the clutter from the workspace.

For Windows users, the first time you run Dreamweaver, you will be asked to choose a default workspace style (see Figure 3.1). If you are not the first person to run this installation of Dreamweaver, then the decision already will have been made, but you can change the workspace style at any time (Edit → Preferences → General → Change Workspace).

The workspace is designed to ease clutter while retaining the availability of numerous shortcuts. The integrated workspace displays all the windows and panels within one larger window. Designer style displays the panel groups docked on the right side of the main window, and the Document window appears in Design view by default (see Figure 3.2). Coder style displays panel groups on the left side, and the Document window appears in Code view by default (see Figure 3.3).

The floating layout is the only choice of workspace for Macintosh users (see Figure 3.4). In the floating layout, each document is in its own window, but there is no multiple-document window (as in the Windows version). When windows are dragged or resized, they automatically align with each other, the edge of the screen, or the Document window. Panels are docked with each other by default, but they can be easily undocked into their own windows.

Figure 3.1

Choosing a Workspace in Windows

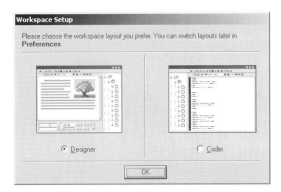

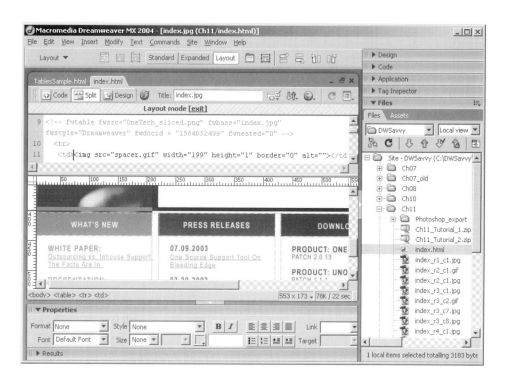

Figure 3.2

Designer style integrated workspace

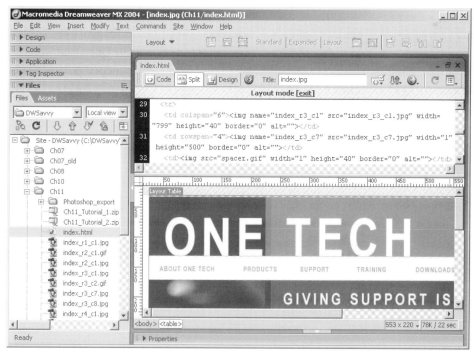

Figure 3.3

Coder style integrated workspace

Figure 3.4

The floating look, available for Macintosh users

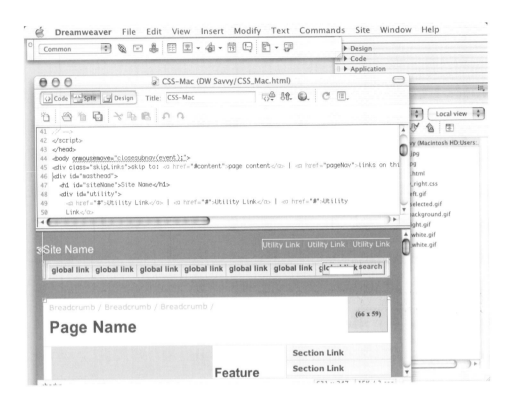

Getting Oriented

Dreamweaver offers numerous tabbed panels, a toolbar for switching among three working modes, and much information about the contents of whatever web page you've got open, as shown in Figure 3.5.

Let's first sort out what is important on the Dreamweaver desktop.

The Start Page

When you open Dreamweaver, the Start page appears in the workspace (see Figure 3.6). It also displays any time you don't have a document open. The Start page includes options to open a recent document, create a new document, and create a new document from sample files. In addition, there are links to a quick tour of Dreamweaver features, a Dreamweaver tutorial, the Dreamweaver Exchange, and the Dreamweaver section of the Macromedia site.

The Start page displays by default, but you can hide it by checking the "Don't Show Again" box at the bottom-left of the Start page. To display it again, select Edit → Preferences → General → Show Start Page.

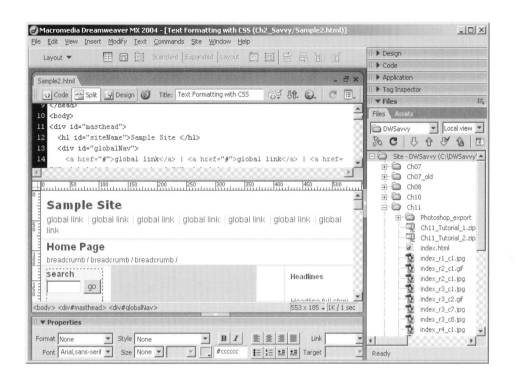

Figure 3.5

The Dreamweaver desktop

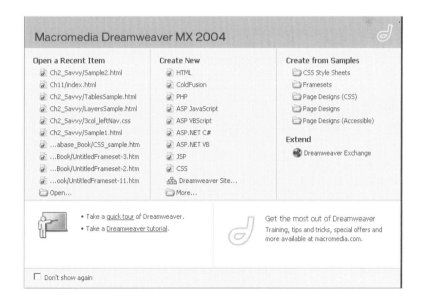

Figure 3.6

The Start page

The Document Window

The main focus of your attention in Dreamweaver will almost always be the Document window.

Among the many useful changes to the Dreamweaver interface in MX 2004 are the changes to the Document window. These changes are greatest for the Windows workspace. In Windows only, the Document window becomes tabbed when it's maximized (see Figure 3.7). The filenames of all open windows are displayed in the workspace; to bring a window into focus, just click on its tab.

The Document window has three parts:

1. The Document toolbar (modified in MX 2004 and discussed further in the following section)

2. An area for viewing the contents of the document in the middle

3. A status bar at the bottom

In both Windows and Mac, you can choose which toolbars (Insert, Document, Standard) are displayed by selecting View → Toolbars.

Figure 3.7

Document window changes to tabbed window when maximized (Windows workspace only)

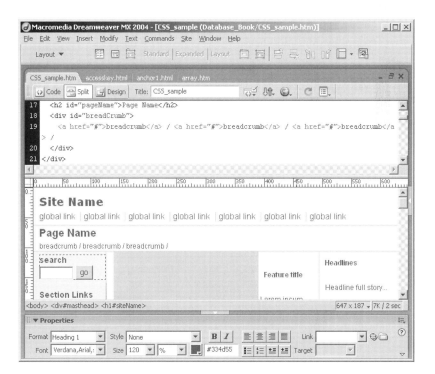

By default, the Property inspector displays below the document window. If it's not visible, select Window → Properties. The rest of the interface consists of panels that all have the ability to affect the contents of the Document window.

The Document Toolbar

The new Document toolbar includes more options and makes it easy to use features that were previously in separate locations in the Dreamweaver workspace. The Document toolbar provides quick and easy access to most of Dreamweaver's essential tools—tools that let you switch between viewing modes (Code, Split, Design), change the document title, manage files, check browser support, preview your site in a browser of your choice, refresh the page, and change view options. Consider the Document toolbar your chief navigational aid because its buttons and pop-up menus provide access to just about every area of the program. Figure 3.7 shows the new Document toolbar in Windows with the Document window maximized, Figure 3.8 shows the Windows workspace when the Document window is not maximized, and Figure 3.9 shows the new Document toolbar in Mac.

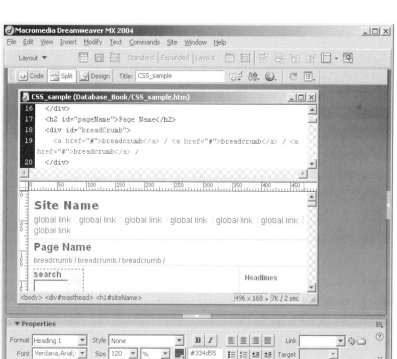

Figure 3.8

Document window not maximized (Windows workspace)

Figure 3.9

**Document window
(Mac workspace)**

Three Views: Code, Design, or Both

Dreamweaver offers three different ways of viewing your work, which you can access through the Document toolbar or the View menu in the Dreamweaver application window:

Design view This is the standard view used for doing layout. It lets you place objects visually with the Insert bar. Design view itself has two modes: *Layout mode* and *Expanded Tables mode*. Layout mode allows you to draw table cells and new tables, including nested tables. Expanded Tables mode is used to temporarily add cell padding and spacing to make table editing easier by making it simpler to select items and insertion points.

Code view This view shows the code on the page, including HTML and any associated scripts. The code will change automatically as you make changes in Design view, or you can edit the code directly in Code view.

Code and Design view This view uses a split screen, enabling you to work in Design view mode and check the resulting code in Code view at the same time. You can select an item in Design view, and the corresponding area in Code View will also be selected, and vice versa. The split screen can also be useful for controlling the placement of imported code, such as JavaScript scripts or Flash movies.

By the way, you might prefer to see the code peeking out at the bottom of the Design view instead of at the top. You can switch them easily—just click the View Options button at the right side of the toolbar and select Design View On Top. To see more design than code, drag the divider toward the bottom of the Document window.

Additional Document Toolbar Features

In addition to choosing a page view mode, the Document toolbar offers many other options:

Live Data view You can preview and edit dynamic content while in Design mode with Live Data view. Dreamweaver must first be configured to use live data because Dreamweaver runs the page on your specified application server before displaying it in Live Data view. See Part IV of this book for more information on web application development and setting up sites to use live data.

Title field The Title field shows your document's current title (by default, it will be something like "untitled3" or "Untitled Document"). You can alter the way the name of your page will be displayed in a browser's Title bar by typing it in the Title field. All you need to do to change the name is highlight the text, type a new name, and hit Enter. The Title bar immediately changes to show the new name. Note that giving the page a title does not automatically save the document to a file! You must also use the Save command (File → Save) to name the file. (Experienced HTML users will realize that this Title field is merely supplying the contents of the `<title>` tag in the `<head>` section of the document.) A document should always have a title—it helps the viewer to navigate your site (since it identifies which page they're on) and if they bookmark the page, it will be identified in their Bookmarks or Favorites list by the title.

Check Browser Support Check Browser Support enables you to specify browsers and browser versions and test your page for errors based on level of browser support for the features included in your page. Dreamweaver automatically tests to make sure you are not using tags or CSS features that the target browsers do not support. You can specify target browsers by selecting Settings from the pop-up menu. You can also choose Auto-Check On Open if you want Dreamweaver to automatically check target browser support when a document is opened.

File Management You can use the File Management pop-up menu to upload and download files. You can perform updates by quickly swapping files between the remote and local sites using the Get and Put or Check In and Check Out commands.

We'll explain more about your local site versus your remote site soon. The basic idea is that the real site that the public sees (or the production or staging version of the site) is "out there" on a remote server, but you keep a copy of the entire site on your own computer or on a local file server as well. Dreamweaver allows you to work with either the local file or with the remote file. For more details on working "live" with remote files, see Chapter 30, "Going Live or Delivering the Site."

Check In and Check Out are used to facilitate collaboration and prevent people from accidentally overwriting their colleagues' work. When you check a file out, Dreamweaver marks the remote file (so that no one else can change it) and copies it to your local site. When you check a file in, Dreamweaver replaces the file on the remote site and unmarks it (so others are free to alter it again).

Checking in or out will ensure that no other collaborator will be able to get the file while you are making your changes. This feature also records such changes so that you can trace who is working on which file either remotely or locally.

Check In and Check Out work only if everyone working on the site files is accessing them via Dreamweaver. Otherwise, all the files are available through FTP, and can be overwritten despite having Check In and Check Out enabled.

If you are working alone (without collaborators), you don't need to worry about checking pages in and out. Just use the Get (download) and Put (upload) commands. But be careful not to overwrite your own files unintentionally—save a copy of the current version of a file before you make changes.

The File Management pop-up menu also lets you open the Design Notes dialog box (where you can document changes you make to files as you work) and quickly locate the current page in the Files panel (explained later in this chapter) with the Locate In Site command (also available in the Main Menu bar—Site → Locate In Site).

Preview/Debug in Browser   When Tim Berners-Lee invented the Hypertext Transfer Protocol (HTTP) and its attendant Hypertext Markup Language (HTML) as the underpinnings of the World Wide Web, he intended that any browser should be able to display web pages identically as long as they follow HTML standards. Sadly, over the years, browser support for standard HTML has varied greatly. Both Microsoft and Netscape have often invented their own tags to "enhance" HTML, thus introducing different approaches to everything from how to indicate paragraph breaks to how to implement Cascading Style Sheets. As a result, today, individual browsers might not display your pages in exactly the same way.

In addition, Macintosh computers use a different default monitor resolution (72 dots per inch) than Windows machines (96 dots per inch); this results in drastic differences in the size of text displayed on the two machines. In addition, color support varies between the two platforms. Add in the fact that many people use Unix-based platforms, such as Sun Solaris or Linux, to view the Web and you have a virtual Tower of Babel when it comes to displaying pages.

One more variable is the age of the browser used to view the Web. For example, schools may use older browsers, as do many individuals who can't be bothered with constantly upgrading to the latest version of their software. These older browsers generally cannot display newer tags, such as those adopted in version 4 of HTML (and supported by Dreamweaver).

Using the Preview/Debug pop-up menu, you can test your site's appearance and performance. When you are designing a website, you must test it in as many browsers as you possibly can (depending, of course, on how much you know about the browsers your audience will or might be using), and on as many different computer platforms as possible to ensure that it displays correctly. Dreamweaver helps you with this process by providing access to any number of browsers on your computer via this portion of the Document toolbar menu.

> For more information on browser issues, see Chapter 29, "Checking Browser Compatibility."

Refresh Design View If you are working in Code view or Split view (Code and Design), you can edit your HTML directly. If you do so, however, changes will *not* be automatically reflected in the Design view until you refresh it. To do so, you can simply click anywhere in the Design view window, click the Refresh Design View button on the Document toolbar, select View → Refresh Design View, or press F5.

> A refresh button still appears in the Property inspector window after you make changes to the code, and the Refresh Design View button on the toolbar also becomes available for use (the button changes from grey to blue to indicate this).

View Options You can use the View Options pop-up menu to turn off and on hidden tags and other visual aids. This menu is contextual—meaning that what is shown on the menu depends on which view you are using (Design, Code, or Code and Design). In Design view, the options are Hide All Visual Aids, Visual Aids (with a submenu of individual visual aids to select or deselect), Head, Rulers, and Grid. In Code view, the options include Word Wrap, Line Numbers, Highlight Invalid HTML, Syntax Coloring, and Auto Indent. In Split view, all of the above options are included, plus the option Design View On Top, which moves the Design view to the top pane and Code view to the bottom pane.

> If you have used Dreamweaver MX, you may notice that the Reference panel button and the Code Navigator button are no longer available on the Document toolbar. The Reference panel is still accessible as part of the Code Panel Group, but the Code Navigator is no longer an available feature.

The Document's Title Bar

The document's own title bar (as opposed to the Title bar of the Dreamweaver application, although both appear together in Windows when the document is maximized) displays three pieces of information: the page title as it will appear in a browser's title bar, the file path that includes the filename of the document, and the saved file status (an asterisk means you've made changes since last saving). Dreamweaver will also indicate if the file is in XHTML format instead of HTML (see Chapter 24, "Working with XML and XHTML," for more on XHTML and XML).

The View Area

The main area of the Document window shows you the contents of the current document. For web pages, you can choose to see just the Design view (a visual representation of how the page will be rendered in a browser with click-and-drag shortcuts for manipulating the design), Code view (the literal HTML and script code that makes up the web page), or Code and Design view (a split view showing both views in two different panes). For some other file formats, such as script and style sheet files, you can only use Code view. You can change the view in the Document toolbar or by choosing View → Switch Views.

Most of what you'll do in the Document window is insert, paste, and enter text and objects, and then manipulate them by using the panels and other shortcuts.

The Status Bar

The status bar at the bottom of the Document window features a tag selector, a Window Size pop-up menu, and estimated document size and estimated download time.

Wherever the insertion point is in a document, the status bar will show any of the tags that currently have a bearing on that spot in the document (in HTML files, the <body> tag is in effect in much of the document). The tag selector displays the hierarchy of the tags surrounding a selection. Clicking a tag selects the tag. You can edit it by right-clicking on the tag (Ctrl-click on Mac) to open the context menu for the Quick Tag Editor, then selecting Edit

Tag. (See Chapter 6, "Inserting and Formatting Text Content," and Chapter 18, "Handcrafting Your Code," for more on using the tag selector, and tags and code in general.)

The Window Size pop-up menu is visible only in Design view. The window's current dimensions in pixels are displayed. You can adjust this size by using the pop-up menu to choose any of the preset sizes, or create a new size.

The estimated document size is based on the entire page content, including linked objects such as images and multimedia files. The estimated download time is based on the connection speed entered in the Status Bar preferences (Edit → Preferences → Status Bar).

Experienced users may wonder about the Launcher, a set of icons at the bottom of the Document window that open specific panels. The Launcher no longer exists—it has been replaced by all the new features of the user interface in Dreamweaver MX 2004.

See Figure 3.7 for a view of a maximized Document window, with the Document toolbar at the top and status bar at the bottom.

The Insert Bar

The most important panel in your Dreamweaver arsenal is the Insert bar, introduced in Dreamweaver MX and streamlined and improved in Dreamweaver MX 2004. The Insert bar contains almost every tool you need to insert, edit, and manage text and objects on your web page. The Dreamweaver MX 2004 Insert bar takes up much less room in the workspace than the MX version, and includes many of the Dreamweaver MX Insert bars as pop-up menus within other Insert bars. You'll have at least eight different choices in the Insert bar drop-down menu, including the following: Common (see Figure 3.10), Layout, Forms, Text, HTML, Application, Flash elements, and Favorites. Dreamweaver will automatically populate an Insert bar with the appropriate objects depending on the file format and server model you're using for your site; for example, if you're working on an ASP file, an ASP Insert bar will become available.

Figure 3.10

The Insert bar with Common objects option

> The Insert bar replaces the Objects palette or Objects panel used in Dreamweaver 4 and earlier.

If you prefer working with a tabbed view of the Insert bar, you can choose that option by clicking on the Insert bar pop-up menu and selecting "Show as Tabs." To return to the menu view, right-click on any of the tabs and choose "Show as Menu."

The Flash Elements Insert bar, new in Dreamweaver MX 2004, can be used to insert Flash elements. For more information on using Flash elements, see Chapter 11, "Getting into Flash."

The Favorites Insert bar, also new in Dreamweaver MX 2004, can be used to include those objects you use most frequently. Objects can be easily added to the Favorites Insert bar by right-clicking on any object in an Insert bar and selecting Customize Favorites. This opens the Customize Favorite Objects window, where you can copy objects from any Insert bar and add them to your Favorites Insert bar.

If the Insert bar is not visible when you start up Dreamweaver, choose Window → Insert or press the keyboard combination Ctrl-F2 (no keyboard shortcut available for Mac). This command toggles the Insert bar on or off.

Table 3.1 describes the contents of most of the selections on the Insert bar. (Remember that some selections will appear only when needed.)

Table 3.1

The Insert Bar

SELECTION NAME	CONTENTS	DESCRIPTION
Common	Insert Hyperlink, Insert Email Link, Insert Named Anchor, Insert Table, Insert Image Pop-up Menu, Insert Media Pop-up Menu, Date, Comment, Templates, Tag Chooser	These are the most common objects you will use in Dreamweaver. These objects are described as they are encountered throughout the book.
Layout	Insert Table, Layout Table, Draw Layout Cell, Insert Row Above, Insert Row Below, Insert Column To The Left, Insert Column To The Right, Insert Div Tag, Draw Layer, Frames Pop-up Menu, Tabular Data	All the commands you need to rough out layouts and designs using tables or layers.
Forms	Form, Text Field, Hidden Field, Textarea, Checkbox, Radio Button, Radio Group, List/Menu, Jump Menu, Image Field, File Field, Button, Label, Fieldset	Forms are specialized areas of your Document window that are linked to a server-side script. This tab lets you rapidly insert Form object types and their variables. See Chapter 14 for more about Forms.
Text	Font Tag Editor, Bold, Italics, Strong, Emphasis, Paragraph, Block Quote, Preformatted Text, Heading 1, Heading 2, Heading 3, Unordered List, Ordered List, List Item, Definition List	These are the standard HTML formatting options. They all correspond to well-accepted HTML tags. For tags with further attributes to select, a dialog box pops up to collect that information from you.
HTML	Horizontal Rule, Head Pop-up Menu, Text Pop-up Menu, Character Pop-up Menu, Tables Pop-up Menu, Frames Pop-up Menu, Script Pop-up Menu	These are the standard HTML formatting options. They all correspond to well-accepted HTML tags. For tags with further attributes to select, a dialog box pops up to collect that information from you.

SELECTION NAME	CONTENTS	DESCRIPTION
Application	Recordset, Stored Procedure, Dynamic Data Pop-up Menu, Repeated Region, Show Region Pop-up Menu, Recordset Paging Pop-up Menu, Go To Detail Page Pop-up Menu, Recordset Navigation Status, Display Record Count Pop-up Menu, Master Detail Page Set, Insert Record Pop-up Menu, Update Record Pop-up Menu, Delete Record, User Authentication Pop-up Menu	You'll only need these if you're developing a database backed site.
Flash Elements	Contains available Flash elements	These are pre-built Flash components. Image Viewer is installed with Dreamweaver MX 2004; other Flash elements can be downloaded from the Macromedia Exchange.

In addition to these selections, other Insert Bar choices become available when you open certain file types. These include Insert Bars for CFML Basic, ASP, ASP.NET, JSP, and PHP. For more information on web application development and scripting languages, see Part IV of this book.

The Insert Bar selections reflect folders in the Objects folder, and you can actually customize the Insert Bar further by modifying the contents of these folders, as discussed in Chapter 32, "Customizing and Extending Dreamweaver."

The Property Inspector

Every object in Dreamweaver can be modified by adjusting its attributes (such as foreground color, background color, width, and so forth). The place where you can make these adjustments without resorting to menu commands is called the *Property inspector* (see Figure 3.11).

The Property inspector is context-sensitive, meaning that its contents change based upon which object you select in the Document window. In addition, the Property inspector expands to include more options, such as creating hotspots for an image map. Tables can be extensively edited using the expanded Property inspector. Toggle the arrow at the bottom-right of the Property inspector to open or close this expanded view.

Figure 3.11

The Property inspector

The Property inspector lets you change attributes by either typing new information into text boxes (such as the size of a font) or by using pop-up menus that open related panels. One of the most powerful uses of the Property inspector is to create links from an object to a file simply by dragging the pointer on the Property inspector to the target file in the Files panel. The full path of the link is entered into the Link text box.

New additions to the Property inspector in Dreamweaver MX 2004 include a Class text box to apply CSS classes to selected objects, a Styles text box to apply CSS styles to selected text, and additional Image editing buttons, including Edit In Fireworks, Optimize In Fireworks, Crop, Brightness And Contrast, and Sharpen. The Image editing features are new to Dreamweaver MX 2004 and will be covered in more detail in Chapter 10, "Adding Graphics and Multimedia."

> We'll be referring to the Property inspector throughout the book, offering tips and tricks to enhance your efficiency with Dreamweaver through its use.

The Panels

The Insert Bar and the Property inspector are both, technically, panels, but they tend to dock at the top and bottom of the screen respectively, while the rest of the panels hang out at the side of the screen. All panels have an expander arrow at their left edge for opening or closing the view of the panel or the panel group. When a panel group is opened, each panel appears as a tab. Each panel in a group can be separated and joined to a different group or display on its own. When a panel is opened, the Options menu in the upper-right corner becomes visible. Click on this icon to view the available options for that panel, including options for panel display. They also all have a textured "gripper" area to the left of the expander arrow for dragging the panel around the screen or for docking it with the rest of the panels. When panels are closed, they take up very little space. If you open just one panel, it will get all the space available. If you open more, they have to share the space.

Let's take a quick walk through the available panels.

The Design Panel Group This panel features two panels and is geared toward page layout and composition:

> **CSS Styles** For designing with Cascading Style Sheets (see Chapter 9)
>
> **Frames** For designing with frames (see Chapter 7)

The Code Panel Group This panel features two panels and is geared toward working directly with code (see Chapter 18):

> **Snippets** Used to store useful bits of code, and it comes with a pretty cool starter set
>
> **Reference** Contains hyperlinked versions of references for various markup and scripting languages

The Application Panel Group This panel features four panels, all geared toward web application development (see Part IV):

> **Databases** Used to connect to your data source
>
> **Bindings** Helps make data available
>
> **Server Behaviors** Takes advantage of server-side features for working with dynamic data
>
> **Components** Used for introspection into the properties and methods of a component such as a JavaBeans. Now, aren't you glad you asked?

The Tag Inspector Panel Group This panels features three panels, allowing you to view and edit attributes, behaviors, and relevant CSS styles for selected tags:

> **Attributes** Shows available attributes for the selected tag, as well as current values for those attributes already included in the selected tag. Attributes can be seen in Category view or in List view.
>
> **Behaviors** Shows built-in JavaScript actions that can be automatically added to user and browser events (see Chapter 12).
>
> **Relevant CSS** Shows CSS rules for the selected tag, available CSS properties for this tag, and current values for those properties. CSS properties can be seen in Category view or List view.

The Files Panel Group This panel features two panels. It gives you easy access to the files (both documents and assets) used in your site:

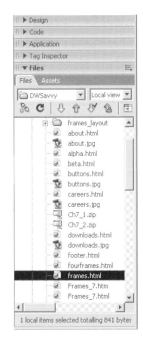

> **Files** Offers direct access to your local computer's or network's files through an explorer-type icon in the list view. The Files panel can be expanded to a full-size window that displays remote files on the left and local files on the right.
>
> **Assets** Functions as a repository where you keep all your objects handy. More on this in Chapter 4.

The Results Panel Group This panel group is not shown by default, but like all panels, you can bring it up by choosing it from the Windows menu. When you display this panel, it appears like the Property inspector, docked to the bottom of the screen. Here are its panels:

> **Search** Shows search results
>
> **Validation** Checks your code for syntax errors and for compliance with W3C specifications (see Chapter 18)
>
> **Target Browser Check** Checks for browser compatibility (see Chapter 29)
>
> **Link Checker** Check links sitewide (see Chapter 8)
>
> **Site Reports** Generate statistics about your site
>
> **FTP Log** Tracks FTP downloads (Gets) and uploads (Puts)
>
> **Server Debug** Debug scripts code

Other Panels As in all systems, there are a few miscellaneous panels:

> **Code Inspector** Shows code view in a floating-panel layout
>
> **History** Shows the undoable history of commands you have used
>
> **Layers** Shows name and z-index value for any layers in the current document

Several panels are no longer available, including the Answers panel, HTML Styles panel, Sitespring panel, and the Timelines panel. The Site panel has been replaced with the Files panel. For more information on using Dreamweaver with and without site management, see the section "Setting Up Your Site" later in this chapter.

Customizing Your Workspace

As you begin working with Dreamweaver, you'll find your own preferred style of working with the interface. You may find some layouts easier to work with in specific circumstances, and you may therefore find yourself jumping back and forth or changing things around as you go. Dreamweaver makes it pretty easy to set up the workspace the way you want it.

Changing Your Workspace Style (Windows Users Only)

As mentioned earlier in this chapter, Windows users are asked to choose a workspace layout when they first start running the program—Mac users don't have any such choice. Windows users can also change the preferred workspace at any point from the Preferences dialog box (Edit → Preferences, or Ctrl-U). In the General category, click the Change Workspace button. This brings up the Workspace Setup dialog box shown earlier in Figure 3.1. Choose a new workspace (Designer or HomeSite/Coder-Style) and click OK to switch. Dreamweaver will inform you that the change will take place the next time you start the program.

Hide Panels

One quick way to maximize the screen space available for your Document window is to instantly hide all the panels with the Hide Panel command (F4, or View → Hide Panels); the result of this action is shown in Figure 3.12 for the integrated workspace (Windows).

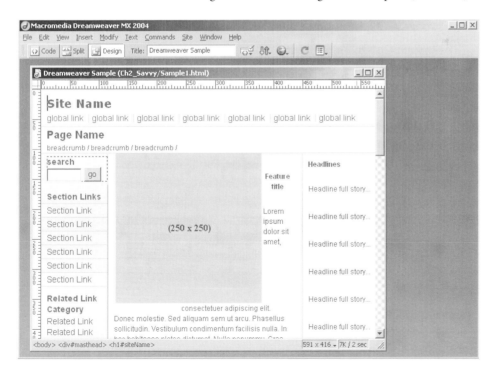

Figure 3.12

The Hide Panels command (integrated workspace) has been used to maximize the workspace for your document.

Figure 3.13 shows the result of hiding panels in the Floating layout workspace (Mac). Because the Site panel is not functioning as a panel in this layout, it remains visible (if open) after panels have been hidden.

In the integrated workspace, you can also click and drag the little handle in the middle of the left (inner) edge of the panels docked on the right side. (These directions are reversed, of course, in the Coder style layout.) Double-clicking the handle hides those panels all at once. Click it once to restore the panels docked along the right side.

Docking and Undocking Panels

To undock a panel, drag it from where it's docked until it floats free.

To dock a panel, drag it by its gripper (the textured area to the left of the panel's name) into the panel area. A black outline will appear to show where the panel will be docked when you release the mouse button.

A floating undocked panel will have a Close button on it like any other window (this is true in both Windows and Mac operating systems). You can hide the panel by clicking the Close button. To bring it back (docked or undocked), select any of the panel's tabs by name from the Windows menu.

Setting Up Your Site

OK, enough of the grand tour. Let's get down to business! As you probably know, a website is a conglomeration of web pages grouped together via associated hypertext links. Dreamweaver allows you to work with entire websites, not just individual pages, by designating a group of folders on your computer or local network as a "site."

As soon as you designate a group of folders as a site in Dreamweaver, you can start to take advantage of Dreamweaver's site management tools. Dreamweaver keeps track of every link on every web page within a site, inserting the source and link information for each page into that page's properties; it also ties the same information into the site's folders. This tracking capability enables you to move around files within the site while maintaining their links. You can also rename files and folders without disturbing these links.

Remember, the links essentially *are* the website. Do not move any folder or rename a file manually (outside of Dreamweaver). That way you won't accidentally disturb the integrity of your website.

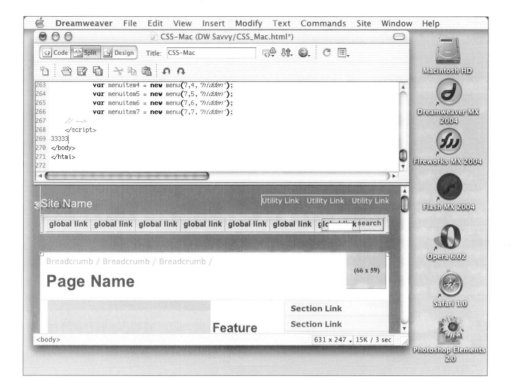

Figure 3.13

Hiding panels in the Floating layout workspace

For those users who want FTP access without using Dreamweaver's site management tools, Dreamweaver now offers the option of connecting to an FTP or RDS (Remote Development Services) server to upload and download files without formally setting up a Dreamweaver site.

To access files on a server that is not in a defined Dreamweaver site:

1. Open the Files panel.
2. Select Desktop from the drop-down menu on the left.
3. Right-click (Windows) or Control-click (Mac) on FTP And RDS Servers.
4. Select "Add FTP Server" or "Add RDS Server."
5. Complete the dialog in the Configure Server dialog box that then displays. (You will need the FTP hostname, username, and password.)

The Files panel displays the contents of the folder you connected to on the remote server, and the server name appears in the drop-down menu. To access the files again, just select the server name from the drop-down menu.

RDS (Remote Development Services) access is only available on computers running Cold Fusion. For more information on Cold Fusion, see Chapter 20.

Setting Up Local Site Folders

Setting up your website in Dreamweaver is a two-part process:

1. First, you create your folders on your hard drive or local network.

2. Then you designate those folders as a site in Dreamweaver.

One of the most important issues in developing a site is project file management. Before you start, you need to develop a system for managing all the files associated with the site. When you're working on a large site, you are usually dealing with a large number of files of different formats, possibly spread over many drives and being worked on by a number of people. If you plan how you're going to handle your HTML pages, image files, and related documents (such as text files used as source material, Fireworks source files, etc.), you'll make your life a lot easier.

The front page or first page of your site should always be stored at the site's root level and is nearly always named index.html.

Unless the site consists of only a few pages and no images, avoid putting everything into just one folder (directory). At the very least, you'll want to keep the files you need to upload to a web server separate from your working files. Set up your own structure and ensure everything gets saved into the correct folder. See Figure 3.14, which shows the folder structure for the sample One Tech site files. The source files are separate from the finished website files that are posted on the web server.

Here are some general guidelines for naming your folders.

Create a master location. Create a master location on your hard disk or file server to hold all your websites. Then store all of your sites in this folder.

Create a folder for the specific site. Create a folder for the specific site you are setting up and give it a descriptive name without any spaces or special characters. This will become the name of the site in Dreamweaver. (For example, the site for One Tech [introduced in Chapter 1] was stored in a folder called OneTech.) This folder is also called the *root* level of your site.

Keep subfolder names simple. Keep the names of your subfolders simple so that they are easy to navigate in the Property inspector and Files panel. For example, a good name for your graphics folder is "images" or "graphics." The simpler the name, the shorter the

pathname you have to remember (at some point, you may be required to edit the pathname by hand or you may have to type it into the Property inspector). You can specify a
default images folder in the Advanced tab of the Site Definition
window. Dreamweaver will place any images you add to your
site in this folder, and this folder will open whenever you insert
an image. If you drag an image from the desktop to an active
document in your site, Dreamweaver will automatically place
it in the Default images folder.

Figure 3.14

**Folder structure for
One Tech site files**

For more information on the Site Definition window, see the
section "Advanced Site Setup" later in this chapter.

Don't use spaces or special characters. Make sure that your folder (and file) names do not
contain spaces or special characters. It is also a good idea to use only lowercase letters
without any spaces because some server software, such as the ubiquitous Apache Server, is
based on Unix, and thus requires case-sensitive naming. Any spaces in a file or folder
name will display as %20. For example, if you name a page my page.html, it will display in
the browser address bar as my%20page.html.

In addition to the above advice, you should get into the habit of naming your files in a
way that makes them easy to find:

- Use meaningful filenames.
- Include the file extension (.html, .gif, etc.).

Planning your file and folder management is an important part of efficient project
planning and development and will make your life much easier! Once you have created
the folders that will contain your site, you are ready to designate these folders in
Dreamweaver as your local site.

Using the Site Setup Wizard

To define a new site, select Site → Manage Sites to bring up the Manage Sites dialog box,
then select New... → Site. The Site Definition dialog then displays. To make site setup easier, Dreamweaver provides a Site Setup wizard as the basic option in this dialog box (see
Figure 3.15). Experienced users will probably prefer the Advanced options (discussed in
the next section), and can skip the Wizard by choosing the Advanced tab (selected by
default) at the top of the Site Definition dialog box.

> You can also set up FTP access without defining a site, as described in the previous section,
> by selecting Site → Manage Sites → New... → FTP And RDS Server. The Configure Server dialog
> box then displays.

Then follow these steps:

1. Type a name for your site and click the Next button.

2. For now, leave "No, I do not want to use a server technology" selected (unless you know for a fact that you do, in which case, see Chapter 16 for further details), and click Next.

3. If you plan to edit your local site on your own computer, leave the first option selected. If your local files are on a network, choose "Edit directly on server using local network."

   - If you choose to work with local copies, type or browse to a root folder where the site will be stored on your computer.

   - If you choose to work on files over a network, type or browse to the network folder you'll be using as your root.

   Either way, after indicating your local root folder, click the Next button (see Figure 3.16).

Figure 3.15
The wizard starts simple by asking you to name your new site.

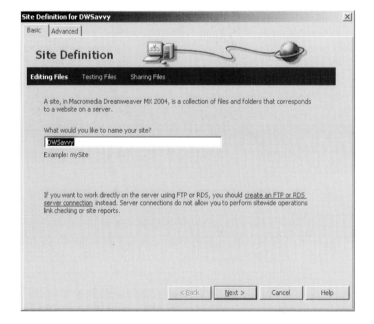

Unless you chose a server technology in step 2 (in which case you've moved on to Chapter 16, right?), the wizard won't ask you anything about where your testing server can be found. Instead, you'll be asked about the remote site—the public site or staging area where the site is actually being built, as opposed to the local site where your working files are kept conveniently available for you at all times without any risk of compromising the integrity of the public site… phew). The most common choice here is FTP, but Dreamweaver also supports other ways of connecting to remote sites, such as via a standard network connection with Remote Development Services (RDS), or by using code-integrity database/authentication tools such as SourceSafe or Web-based Distributed Authoring and Versioning (WebDAV), which is an extension to the HTTP protocol.

To set up your remote connection, follow these steps:

1. Choose a connection method, and then either add your FTP remote hostname, folder, and login info (see Figure 3.17), browse to the remote network location, or for any of the other options, click the Settings button and enter the connection information. Then click Next.

If you're not sure about your FTP information yet, you can choose None from the drop-down list at this step and add the information when you have it available.

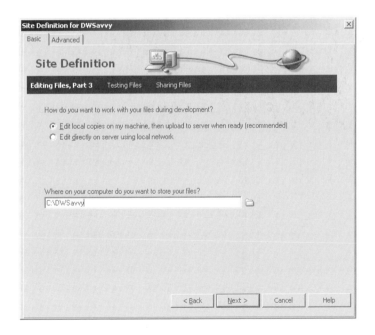

Figure 3.16

Dreamweaver is flexible about where you store and how you access both local and remote files.

Figure 3.17

Dreamweaver offers a Test Connection button that helps ensure your FTP (or other access method) information is correct before you move on.

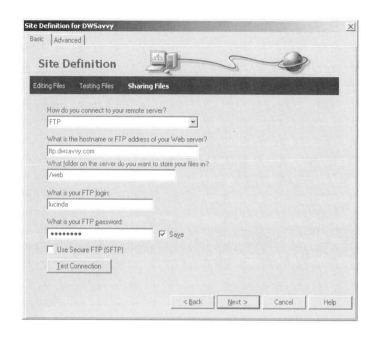

2. If you chose any of the secure connection methods, then file Check In/Check Out is enabled by default. For FTP or network connections, you can choose whether or not to turn on Check In/Check Out. (A good rule of thumb is that you do want it on unless you are working alone.) To turn it on, leave "Yes, enable check in and check out" selected. (To decline to use Check In/Check Out, select "No, do not enable check in and check out," then click the Next button, and then skip to step 6.)

3. Leave "Dreamweaver should check it out" selected as the answer to the next question, unless you want to shadow the project by viewing read-only files and preventing any opportunity for accidentally overwriting files.

4. Type your name or a unique, recognizable moniker in the next box.

5. Type your e-mail address in the last box so that other collaborators can send you e-mail based on your check-out name, and then click the Next button.

6. Review the information you have entered and then click the Done button.

Whenever a file is checked out, Dreamweaver places a small text file with a .1ck (lock) extension on both the server and remote site. The LCK file stores the Check Out name of the person who has the file as well as their e-mail address. Do not delete this LCK file from the server or the status of the checked-out file will be lost.

SETTING UP FOR COLLABORATION

In today's world, few commercial sites are built by a single person anymore. (Did I ever tell you about the old days…?) The more common practice is to assemble a team with different specialties and divvy out responsibilities for different portions of the site. In order to manage this potentially chaotic situation, Dreamweaver supports collaborative web design via the secure connection methods mentioned in this section, as well as by Check In/Check Out management, which is available even over an ordinary FTP connection.

You can manage who checks files in or out of the server during the design process by using Dreamweaver's Check In and Check Out commands (instead of just Put and Get). This prevents collaborators from accidentally overwriting someone else's work, because only one person can have access to a file at any one time—if all the collaborators are using Dreamweaver with Check In and Check Out enabled. Ever had someone upload an old version of a file over one you've just spent hours fine-tuning? It's not pretty.

See Chapter 27, "Static Content Management with Contribute," for information on an alternative method of collaboration, website management, and updating sites.

Advanced Site Setup

If you don't need or want to use Dreamweaver's Site Setup Wizard, click the Advanced tab at the top of the Site Definition dialog box and then just work your way through the categories (Local Info, Remote Info, Testing Server, Cloaking—which means hiding files so they don't get uploaded to the site—Design Notes, Site Map Layout, File View Columns, and Contribute). Most of the information covered is the same as in the Basic approach, but the presentation is more like a series of forms and less like a conversation (see Figure 3.18).

Here are some of the issues to consider:

- The Local Root folder identifies where you do your work locally, as opposed to the server where your site will ultimately be stored for serving over the Internet.

- The Default images folder identifies the folder where the site graphics are stored.

- If you know the URL (the domain name) of the server where your site will ultimately reside, type its address in the HTTP Address text box.

- Leave Enable Cache checked as long as you want Dreamweaver to track all the links at your site and update them automatically when you rearrange the furniture.

Figure 3.18

Advanced Setup doesn't hold your hand, but it can be faster for experienced users.

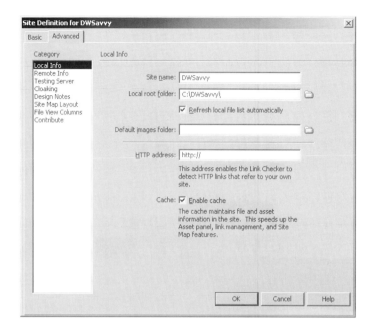

Setting Up Your Remote Site Server

In the Remote Info category, enter your access method and authentication information. For FTP or network-type connections, also indicate the path of the root folder on the remote server.

To set up a testing server for web applications, choose the Testing Server category and enter the connection information required there. (See Chapter 16 for more on setting up web applications).

The Cloaking category enables you to shield files with specific extensions from upload or download. Dreamweaver suggests, for example, that you cloak .png files, which are Fireworks working files, because they cannot be displayed by all browsers—they are generally used as source files for .jpg or .gif files.

The Design Notes category enables you to turn on a collaborative feature for sharing comments about specific pages among the members of the design team.

The Site Map Layout category offers options for customizing the appearance of your site map. Details are covered in the following section, "Initializing a Site Map."

The File View Columns category enables you to change the order of the columns in the Files panel, and to add or delete columns.

The Contribute category, new in Dreamweaver MX 2004, enables you to work with Contribute users. For more details on Contribute, see Chapter 27.

Initializing a Site Map

Dreamweaver uses the Map View option in the Files panel to display file associations for your site. To set up your site map, you need to designate a file as the home page. If the page does not yet exist, Dreamweaver will create it as a blank document. This home page is generally the first page a reader will see when surfing to your site. (You can call this file anything, but `index.html` is the standard name on most web servers. Microsoft server software uses `default.htm`—or `default.asp` for dynamic pages, but that's another story.)

To initialize your site map, follow these steps:

1. Choose the Site Map Layout category from the Advanced tab of the Site Definition dialog box.

2. Type the filename of the home page or browse to it in the file hierarchy if it already exists.

3. Click OK.

Dreamweaver will then collect the folders, any contents such as graphics and so forth, and build its cache, effectively indexing the website such as it is so far.

> In the Files panel, choose Map View from the drop-down menu on the right, then click on the Expand/Collapse button to the right for an expanded view of both the site map and the site files, side by side.

Importing an Existing Site

You will not always be fortunate enough to be there at the start of a new site or project. Often, you will be inheriting someone else's partially completed site, working on a site upgrade or revision, or even converting a site to Dreamweaver that you started with some other software or method.

To import a site, follow these steps.

1. First use the Site Definition Wizard or Advanced mode to set up your remote site and your local site (this was described in the previous sections).

2. Then, with the Files panel open, connect to the remote site by clicking the Connect button.

3. Then, click on the Options menu on the right of the Files panel group, and select Site → Synchronize (Figure 3.19).

Figure 3.19

You can find the Synchronize command in the Options menu, Files panel group.

4. From the resulting Synchronize Files dialog box (see Figure 3.20), choose Entire *'Name Of Your Site'* Site in the first drop-down list menu and Get Newer Files From Remote in the second one.

Figure 3.20

Synchronize Files dialog box

5. Then click the Preview button. Dreamweaver will review the selected files, and it will show you which ones it plans to download in the Synchronize Preview dialog box that pops up (see Figure 3.21).

Figure 3.21

You can uncheck any files you, on reflection, decide not to synchronize, but if you want to download the entire remote site, just click OK.

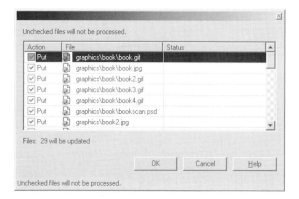

6. Click OK to begin the synchronization process. When you're done, you should have an entire mirror of the remote site at your local location.

Turning On Accessibility Reminders

One last thing you should consider doing before plunging with both feet into your web development schedule is to turn on reminders that help you develop a more accessible website (one that can be read by people with different abilities using special browsers, for example). Accessibility is a worthy topic unto itself, and in fact, in Chapter 33, "Using Dreamweaver to Make Your Site Accessible," we'll show you how to fully implement accessibility features in your site, but for now let us show you how to turn on the reminders, and then you can decide on your own design criteria.

To turn on accessibility reminders, go the Preferences dialog box (Edit → Preferences) and choose the Accessibility category (see Figure 3.22).

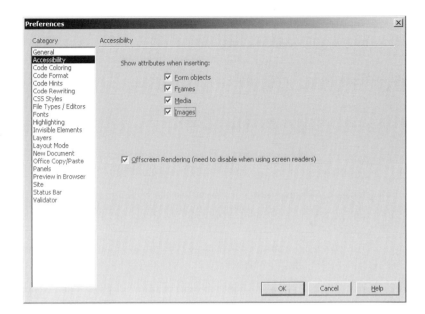

Figure 3.22
Tell Dreamweaver here that you want to be reminded about accessibility practices when inserting objects.

Check the first four check boxes (Form Objects, Frames, Media, Images) to turn on the reminders. These reminders will take the form of a prompt—for example, one that prompts you to supply alternative text for images when inserting them.

When you insert a new table, accessibility attribute options automatically appear in the Insert Table dialog box. The last check box enables screen readers for those who cannot read from the screen directly. Click OK.

See Chapter 33 for detailed information about using Dreamweaver's accessibility features.

Look-and-Feel Standards

Admittedly, this chapter is somewhat dry. It's that necessary housekeeping you have to do, at least once, so that Dreamweaver can count the beans for you and perform all of its automated tasks neatly, without error or complaint. In the next chapter, you get to work on the more interesting part of setting up a site: establishing design templates, and using other tools to impose a consistent look-and-feel sitewide, with efficient use of repeating elements.

## CHAPTER 4

Saving Labor with Templates and Libraries

With a team in place, a plan on the easel, and your site folders assigned, one last aspect of sitewide setup remains: establishing a consistent look-and-feel for your site using Dreamweaver's powerful template feature. When you update a template, every page using that template is updated automatically. Beyond templates, you can also build up a collection of reuseable objects and store them in something called the Library to make them available for any page. You'll access your templates, library items, and other reuseable page elements through the Assets panel. If you take the time to arrange your toolkit of resources before building pages, you can save a lot of time and effort during the development process, especially when changes are required or the work is shared among members of a collaborative team.

This chapter discusses the following items:

- **Creating templates from example pages and from scratch**

- **Nesting templates within other templates**

- **Developing pages with a template**

- **Editing a template's contents**

- **The Assets panel and the Library**

- **Server-side includes (SSIs)**

What Is a Template?

The concept of a template comes to us from crafts and manufacturing: a *template* is a model used to replicate a design, as with a sewing pattern used to make clothing or a stencil used to guide a design in woodworking. Today, most applications that produce documents offer some sort of template that helps enforce a master design. In word-processing applications, templates are collections of content, styles, and page-formatting selections that can be used to create new documents with consistent design elements.

Dreamweaver's templates enable you to lock down some layout elements while allowing other content to be customized; this enables you to enforce consistency across a website. When you create a new page from a template, the page is linked to the template, so changes to the template update the linked page.

Although Dreamweaver MX 2004 gives you the option to upload and download files without defining a site, as described in Chapter 3, "Setting Up Your Workspace and Your Site," you must create a Dreamweaver site if you want to use site management tools, such as templates.

Templates can have four different types of regions:

- Locked (noneditable regions)
- Editable regions
- Repeating regions
- Optional regions

Figure 4.1 shows editable and repeating regions in a Dreamweaver template.

By default, all regions of a new template are locked. You must make specific regions editable (or repeating or optional). Templates can also make tag attributes editable, which means that the tag will be required, but some of its attributes may be up to the individual page designer.

Templates can help speed up the development of pages for a site. Without such a method for enforcing consistency, a team of collaborators will inevitably produce slightly inconsistent pages, requiring a reconciliation phase or, if that phase is skipped, resulting in an unprofessional-looking result. With templates, a large team can confidently build numerous pages rapidly, and as a result, updating a site becomes easier. This is a real plus in today's extremely competitive web environment where the more quickly new information is uploaded, the more visitors will gravitate to your site.

Figure 4.1

Editable and repeating regions in a template

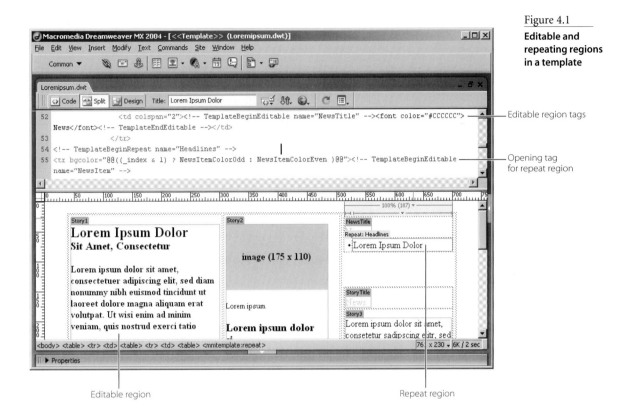

Editable region tags

Opening tag for repeat region

Editable region Repeat region

Macromedia Contribute is a program designed to integrate with Dreamweaver and assist collaboration and teamwork in site updates and maintenance. Contribute was created to make it possible to update and publish to established sites without the need for technical web skills. At the same time, it allows the site administrator to maintain control over the site style and code standards. Contribute users can also use templates, both inside and outside of Dreamweaver. For more details on Contribute, see Chapter 27, "Static Content Management with Contribute."

Templates are wonderful prototyping tools because any changes you make to a template will be replicated on all of its attached pages. You can build and edit a prototype page until all the elements are finalized, and then you can make the page a template and apply it to existing pages, automatically updating them to the new design.

ECONOMIES OF SCALE IN WEB DEVELOPMENT

Many of the tools that have evolved to help web developers function in one way or another—by abstracting content and layout information from the individual page level and by sharing this information among multiple pages—speed development and make updating easier. Templates offer a Dreamweaver-specific method of doing this. Server-side includes (SSIs), discussed at the end of this chapter, represent another way to share page elements, and Cascading Style Sheets (CSS), discussed in Chapter 9, "Cascading Style Sheets," offer a web standards–compliant way of abstracting and sharing design information.

Templates can contain not only text and HTML tags but also CSS (Cascading Style Sheet) styles and pre-programmed JavaScript code that can do such things as these:

- Display current date and time.
- Compare browsers for compatibility.
- Download snippets of HTML (called *server-side includes*) from databases or outside files (discussed at the end of this chapter).

For more information on CSS, see Chapter 9, "Cascading Style Sheets." For details on using JavaScript behaviors, see Chapter 12, "Incorporating JavaScript Behaviors." Code snippets and other details of the Dreamweaver coding environment are covered in Chapter 18, "Handcrafting Your Code."

Templates can also include any objects in your Library items directory (accessible via the Assets panel, both discussed later in this chapter). The more detail you include in your template, the quicker your team can turn around a project.

Fitting Templates into Your Development Process

Templates and pages represent a bit of a chicken-and-egg paradox. An efficient development process requires templates to make page production quick and accurate, but templates have to come from somewhere. Whether you create a template from scratch or convert an existing page into a template (we'll explain both methods soon), you must know a thing or two about page development to do so. The truth, therefore, is that the process is usually a loop, from templates to pages to templates, and so on—something like this:

1. Plan templates based on page content, navigation, site information architecture, and overall design theme(s).

2. Develop sample pages for various parts of the site, including a sample home page, subordinate pages, and navigation dummies (pages with navigation but no content).

3. Turn reviewed and finalized samples into templates.

4. Develop actual site pages from templates.

5. Launch site and hand over templates to whoever will be administering and maintaining the site.

Because making templates is a key part of setting up a site for development, we have chosen to include this chapter here in the first part of the book. But as we just alluded to, making templates depends on some skills related to page development, so you will probably have to read this chapter for informational purposes and then work on Parts II and III of this book to learn how to construct web pages. Eventually, you might want to come back to this chapter to turn those pages into templates.

Making Templates

There are two ways to prepare a template: by creating a blank template and then adding the design elements, or by opening an existing page and saving it as a template. Both approaches are appropriate in different situations. When you have detailed formatting information at hand before creating any pages, you can create a blank template, implement the design on the template, and then make new pages based on that template. If you decide to use the design of an existing page as a template for other pages, then use the latter approach (open the model page and save it as a template).

Figure 4.2

Creating a blank template in the New Document window

Making a Template Page from Scratch

Creating a blank template page is a simple process. Just follow these steps:

1. Select File → New from the Dreamweaver application menu bar.

2. From the General tab in the New Document window (Figure 4.2), select Template Page from the Category list on the left, and HTML template from the Template page list on the right.

You can also create a blank template using the New Template button in the Templates area of the Assets panel, in the Files panel group (see Figure 4.3). The Assets panel is a

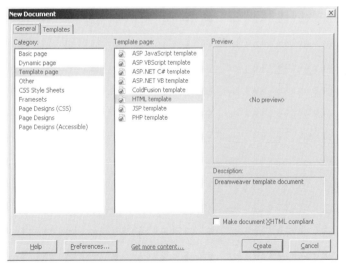

tool that collects all of your site objects together in one handy panel from which you can drag and drop objects onto pages. For more information on the Assets panel, see the section "Managing Your Assets" later in this chapter.

To create a blank template from the Assets panel:

1. Open the Assets panel (Window → Assets, or F11).

2. Click on the Templates icon on the left side of the Assets panel (Figure 4.3).

3. Click the New icon (looks like a piece of paper with a plus sign) at the bottom of the Assets panel.

> On the bottom of every panel in Dreamweaver you will see a series of small icons. These buttons let you quickly perform four functions: refresh, create a new item, edit an item, or delete an item.

4. Type a name for the template in the outlined area in the Template list.

5. Click the Edit icon at the bottom of the Assets panel to display the new template.

Whether you create a template from the File menu or from the Assets panel, the next step is to define template regions (editable, optional, repeating). See the section "Configuring a Template" later in this chapter, for all the details.

Making a Template from an Existing Page

There are times when you will have a page already designed and you'll realize you want to turn it into a template (or, more properly, create a new template based on the existing page). For example, if there is a section of your site with many pages that have the same overall design, but different graphics and/or different text, you may be able to create new pages for this section much faster if you use a template. Or if you have a page—for example, a "What's New" page—that is frequently updated with new graphics or new text, but the formatting stays the same, a template could be useful for streamlining the page updates.

> If your site includes a "What's New" page, be sure to update it frequently so the information actually is new. You can use the Dreamweaver's Date object (Insert → Date) to create a "Last modified on xxx" feature that automatically updates the date information when the file is saved. That way, viewers know how new the information is.

To make a template from an existing page, open the page, then choose File → Save as Template (or click the Make Template button on the Templates drop-down menu of the Common Insert bar). Dreamweaver displays the Save As Template dialog box (see Figure 4.4). Indicate which site the template is for with the Site drop-down menu, and give the template a descriptive name.

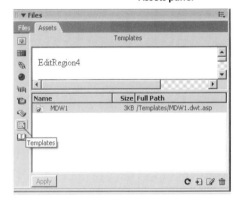

Figure 4.3

Creating a blank template in the Assets panel

Tips for Creating Templates

You will make it easier on yourself and your collaborators if you follow these "best practices":

- Document your design.
- Finalize as much material on the page as possible.
- Set up underlying parameters.
- Include `<meta>` tag information.
- Add your Dreamweaver extensions and their behaviors to the template.

Documenting Your Design

Document your design so that your collaborators understand the types of materials they will need to add to each editable region. The easiest way to communicate your wishes is to add dummy text or graphics to the editable areas of your template that indicate the types of information that should be inserted. For example, if your page is a "contact us" page, add a dummy e-mail address table in the space provided. Your coworkers then simply have to replace the dummy with the real thing. Another trick is to make the dummy content a Library item. In this way, your collaborators simply have to edit the object and Dreamweaver automatically updates any page using that element via the template. See the "Building a Library" section below for further discussion on how to update Library items.

Figure 4.4

Using the Save as Template dialog box to create a template from an existing page

Finalizing Content

The more structure you provide to the page, the faster it is completed. For this reason, you should finalize as much material on the page as possible, without compromising the ability of your team to diversify pages as required. For example, if you have a masthead, advertising banner, navigation bar with links or rollover buttons, copyright blurb, and web ring links on every page, add these objects to the template. Also add a table or layer to indicate any block where new content is to be placed.

Setting Up Parameters

Set up underlying parameters for areas where a graphic or multimedia object is to be placed, such as borders, cell height and width, background color, and so forth, so that any new object inserted will inherit and thereby comply with the layout requirements of the page. Use the Property Inspector to preset parameters.

Including <*meta*> Tag Information

Some search engines find sites through the keywords coded into the <meta> tag area of the <head> tag. It is a good idea to precode these keywords, or any other type of information you wish to document to browsers in the template, so that they appear on every page of your site. Choose Insert → HTML → Head Tags → Meta (or select Meta from the Head pop-up menu in the HTML Insert bar) to display the Meta dialog box as shown in Figure 4.5. In the resulting dialog box, type "keywords" in the Value text box. Enter your keywords separated by spaces (and bound with quotation marks for multiword phrases) in the Contents text box. See Chapter 30, "Going Live or Delivering the Site," for further discussion of advertising your site and the use of <meta> tag data.

> If your site includes distinct sections, consider using section-specific templates that include a separate list of keywords related to that section.

Adding Extensions and Behaviors

Figure 4.5

Use this dialog box to add keywords to aid successful retrieval of your site by search engines.

Add all your Dreamweaver extensions into the template. Also attach Cascading Style Sheets (CSS) to the template and prebuild all of the styles you wish to use. One problem with using a template is that the <head> area (where most JavaScript behavior code is stored) is automatically locked and cannot be defined as an editable region in a template. Therefore, all information, including JavaScript code, that is included in the <head> area must be in place prior to saving a page as a template. Don't get scared yet; we'll walk you through how to use CSS and behaviors in later chapters in the book. Just be aware that templates should contain this information because it cannot be later hard-coded into separate pages.

When you create a template page, Dreamweaver saves the file with a special extension, .dwt, in the Templates folder that is automatically created for each defined site. Dreamweaver adds the word <<Template>> to the file title whenever you save a page as a template, to indicate its special purpose. All of the contents of the Templates folder are reflected in the Templates category of the Assets panel.

Configuring a Template

At this point, you have a template, but it is not useable by anyone because, by default, all of its elements are locked and cannot be changed.

To unlock areas for editing, you need to define editable regions. There are two ways to do this:

- You can assign an existing layout element as editable.
- You can add new editable areas.

Give each editable area a unique descriptive name. Anybody building a page for your site from the template can press the Tab key to jump through the editable areas, skipping the locked areas.

Assigning an Editable Area

To choose a layout element (for example, a table cell or an image) and make it editable, do the following:

1. Select the element with your mouse or, in the tag selector in the Document window's status bar, select the `<td>` (table cell) tag for tables or the `<img>` (image) tag for images.

2. Click the Editable Region button on the Templates pop-up menu of the Common Insert bar (or choose Insert → Template Objects → Editable Region). You can also use the keyboard combination Ctrl-Alt-V (Cmd-Option-V on the Mac) to do the same thing.

3. In the New Editable Region dialog box, type a name for the editable area (see Figure 4.6) and click OK.

Figure 4.6

Give the new editable region a name identifying its purpose.

Template filenames can contain spaces (although it is not recommended to include spaces in any filenames). When naming your template, do not use the following characters: ampersand (&), double quotation mark ("), single quotation mark ('), or the left or right angle brackets (</>). This rule is a general naming convention for all filenames within Dreamweaver.

4. Dreamweaver puts a blue outline around the editable region and displays its name.

You can also create editable tag attributes in a Dreamweaver template. This allows you to specify any attributes that can be edited by the template user. To enable this feature, select an item and then choose Modify → Templates → Make Attribute Editable (see Figure 4.7).

Figure 4.7

Making a template attribute editable in the Editable Tag Attributes dialog box

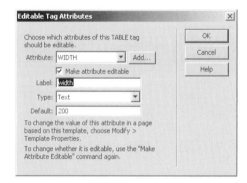

The original attribute value will be used when a new page is created from the template, but you can modify the value by selecting Modify → Template Properties and changing the attribute value in the Template Properties dialog box, shown in Figure 4.8.

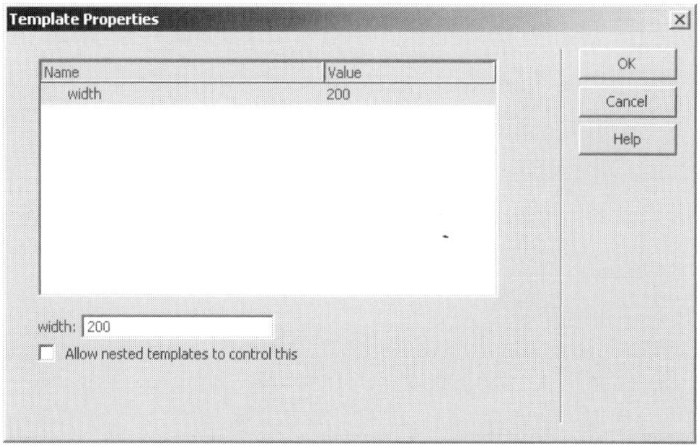

Figure 4.8

Changing an attribute value in the Template Properties dialog box

Creating a New Editable Region

You can also insert blank editable regions anywhere with the Editable Region command. To do so, click your mouse where you wish to add the region and Insert → Template Objects → Editable Region (or click the Editable Region button on the Templates pop-up menu of the Common Insert bar). Give the region a name that identifies the type of content to be entered into the space.

> You can edit the region label by selecting the label in Design view and changing the name in the Name textbox in the Property Inspector, or you can select the name value in Code view and type a new label.

Repeating Regions and Optional Regions

You insert the other types of regions the same way you do editable regions. Actually, the terminology can be a little confusing. For example, repeating regions are themselves editable. Optional regions can be editable or not. Also, there are really two types of repeating regions: one type is called simply *repeating regions,* and the other is called *repeating tables.* Repeating tables are still repeating regions, but they include table tags automatically, since tables are the most common type of repeating page element.

The Common Insert bar is the most useful tool for inserting the other types of regions. Just select the area you want to designate and click the Templates pop-up menu and choose Optional Region, Repeating Region, Editable Optional Region, or Repeating Table (or Insert → Template Objects). If you insert an optional region, you'll be prompted to specify the conditions (such as variables that can be set and checked) that will determine whether the optional region should appear. You can also leave the conditions unspecified to allow individual page designers discretion about whether to include or exclude the optional template region in their page.

Relocking Regions

To lock a region so that it is no longer editable, chose Modify → Templates → Remove Template Markup. Dreamweaver unmarks the area, relocking it from use. When you save the template, Dreamweaver updates all of its associated pages.

> Dreamweaver removes the editable area, but leaves the name of the area in place as freestanding text; you'll need to remove this name from any pages based on the template.

Adding Links to a Template

You must be careful when you add links to a template because making those links work correctly on attached pages is a tricky business. If you wish to anticipate links in the template to pages that have not yet been created, their (prospective) filenames must be typed by hand.

For example, in our sample template, we have a link to a file called `employment.html`. Because the page does not yet exist, Dreamweaver places a blank placeholder page in the Templates folder called `employment.html` (with a pathname of `.../Templates/employment.html`).

TIPS AND TRICKS FOR EDITABLE REGIONS

Here are some important tips to remember when assigning editable regions.

Always select a complete tag pair (for example, a table begins with the `<table>` tag and concludes with the `</table>` tag). Note that HTML uses pairs of tags to indicate the beginning of a formatting selection and its ending. Everything between the opening tag and the closing tag uses the specified formatting. This has very important ramifications for tables because it allows you to select an entire table or any area within the table that is enclosed within opening and closing tag pairs. For example, you can select an entire row (`<tr>...</tr>`, adjacent rows (`<tr>...</tr><tr>...</tr>`), a single cell (`<td>...</td>`), or adjacent single cells (`<td>...</td><td>...</td>`). You can see that although you can select multiple rows, you can't select multiple columns in different rows. One easy way to ensure that you have selected an entire tag pair is to choose the tag label from the status bar. Dreamweaver will indicate on the Document window the extent of your selection.

Be sure to include the `<p>` tag in your editable region if you want to use paragraph returns within an edited area. If you don't include the `<p>`/`</p>` tag pair, you will be limited to the use of the less powerful soft-return `<br>` option between paragraphs, and subsequently you will have formatting issues to deal with because the `<br>` tag does not complete a formatting instruction in the same way that the `<p>` tag does. To ensure that you include a least one hard return within a selection, choose the `<p>` tag in the Tag Selector in the status bar.

Be sure to apply all text formatting. You should apply all text formatting, including any CSS styles, before you define an editable region because you will want to carry your formats across pages via the template's editable regions.

Open the Code and Design view. A good technique when creating editable regions is to open the Code and Design view (Split view) so that you can watch the code as you define editable areas. This way you can ensure that you pick up the entire tag pair.

The potential problem is that if you make any typing mistakes, the link is nonfunctional, and will be nonfunctional in all the pages created from the template.

The best solution is to pre-create all pages that will exist in the site (at least set up files with formal filenames in the proper folder) prior to creating the template. Then, use the point-to-file icon or folder icon next to the Link text box in the Property inspector and let Dreamweaver manage filenames and locations.

> Templates must be saved in the Templates folder on the root level of the site. Do not move the Templates folder or its contents or you will detach the template from the site, and it will be inaccessible (although it will still show up in the Templates category).

Closing and Reopening Templates

To close a template you're working on, just close its window, as you would with any other kind of document. After closing a template, you can open it again in several ways. The easiest way is to select its name from the Template category of the Assets panel and click the Edit button on the bottom of the Assets panel.

You can also double-click the template name in the Template category or choose File → Open (keyboard combination Ctrl-O, or Cmd-O on the Mac) and choose the template straight from the Templates folder inside your site folder. One further way to open the template is to locate it in the Files panel and double-click it.

Nested Templates

You can also base a new template on an existing template. Such templates are referred to as *nested templates*. The nested template inherits the design and editable regions from the parent template, but you can define further locked and editable regions in the nested template.

Why would you want to do this? Well, let's say that all the pages at your site are going to have the same banner and universal navigation at the top, but that different site sections will have different subnavigation, say, down the left side of each page below the banner. Well, then, an easy way to control this standard and its variations would be to create a master template that defines the top area of the page. Then templates for each subsection of the site could be based on (nested from) the master template, with different subnavigation defined for each. Changes to the master template would trickle down to all pages based on these subtemplates, but changes to the side navigation on a nested template would change only the pages in that section (that is, those based on the nested template).

To make a nested template, first make a new document based on the master template (as explained in the next section), and then select the Make Nested Template option in the Templates pop-up menu of the Common Insert bar (or select File → Save As Template), and save the new document as a template.

You can nest as many templates as you like, although if you get too creative it can get pretty confusing! To simplify your site management, it's best to stick with one level of nested templates. You can always create more than one nested template from the original template.

Applying a Template

There are several ways to apply your template to pages in the site. The typical way is to create a new page from the template and then work on it. The benefit of this method is that you do not have to deal with existing information on the page; instead, you can start fresh using the template as a layout guide. Most of the time, this is the tactic you'll take in collaboration scenarios.

An alternative way of using the template is to apply the template to an existing page. This method is best implemented when you wish to update existing pages and use a new template. This happens when sites are radically altered.

Let's look at these two options more closely.

Creating a New Page from a Template

The cleanest and easiest way to use a template is to create a new page from it. There are two ways to do this:

- Right-click (Ctrl-click on the Mac) the template name in the Assets panel and choose New From Template.

- Click File → New, and choose the Templates tab, choose your site in the Templates For list, and then choose the template you want to base your new page on from the Site template list (see Figure 4.9).

Figure 4.9

You can use a template from any site by using the New From Template command.

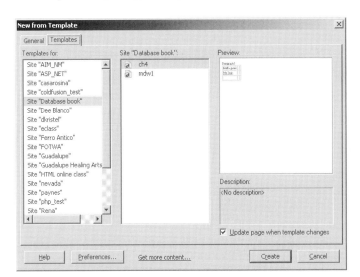

Applying the Template to an Existing Page

Templates are easily applied to existing pages, but the resulting confusion between new information and existing information can be difficult to manage.

To associate a template with an existing page, open the page in question from either the Files panel or by using the File → Open command. Then, drag the template from the Assets panel onto the open page window. You can also choose Modify → Templates → Apply Template To Page and choose the template that you wish to attach to the page from the resulting dialog box. In both cases, if there's any existing content on the page, you have to assign it a region of the template, using the Inconsistent Region Names dialog box (see Figure 4.10).

Remember that templates contain locked and editable areas. Dreamweaver's template assumes that all areas of the page that are to be attached are locked until you associate them with existing editable areas. The only option Dreamweaver offers is to dump the entire contents of the existing page into one of the editable regions of the templated page. Yech. The best option is to delete everything on the existing page by selecting the Nowhere option from the dialog box. If you wish to keep information from the original page, choose an editable region and dump the material in it. You then must manually delete those pieces that you do not wish to retain.

One of the most frustrating things about creating template-based web pages is the fact that when you are building the template, you must take into account the largest size block required by every page so that you can make allowances should you wish to add a repeating object, such as a copyright notice, beneath the block. If you don't calculate the height and width of a table in advance, then you run the risk of overlapping the locked item lying below the editable region with the contents of the editable region, and you have no way to fix the problem without detaching the template from the page with the error. To avoid this problem, specify the maximum size of an editable region and size your content accordingly.

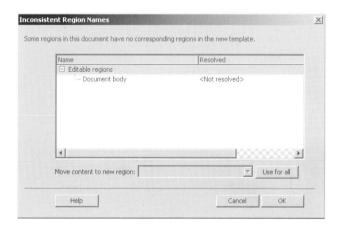

Figure 4.10

When you attach a template to an existing page, you must select where you wish existing content to be placed.

Modifying Template-Based Pages

When you attach a template to a page, you carry across every item that exists on the template to the attached page. This is both good and bad. The good part is that you don't have to reproduce difficult JavaScript code or replace graphics because they already will be available from the template. *The bad part is that you cannot add JavaScript behaviors to the <head> tag section of individual pages that use templates because the <head> tag section is always locked.* There are four possible solutions to this problem:

• Add the template, detach it from the page (by doing this you'll get the formatting and layout but you'll be unlocking every element, thus losing one of the more useful features of a template), and then add the behavior to the page.

• Add the behavior to the template, or add a special code in the <head> area to hold the place where you can later add code as required. (See "Adding Behaviors to a Template," at the end of this section for additional information.)

• Add the JavaScript behavior in the <body> section of the page. Be sure the JavaScript code appears before the behavior is called into action by the page code.

Detaching a Template

To detach an attached template from a page, choose Modify → Templates → Detach From Template. Don't reapply the template again later once you've changed the page, though, because if you do, any changes you have made to the detached page will be lost.

Editing a Template from an Associated Page

If you have permission to work on the template, you can edit the template from an associated page. From the linked page, choose Modify → Templates → Open Attached Template. Make the changes to the template and update only the page you are working on by choosing Modify → Templates → Update Current Page.

ADDING BEHAVIORS TO A TEMPLATE

The Dreamweaver support section of Macromedia's site includes two tech notes that feature workarounds for adding behaviors to the locked <head> section of templates. There is no one method that works in all cases, but several workarounds depending on the specific behavior you want to add.

For more information, visit www.macromedia.com/support/dreamweaver/ and search for Tech Note 14797, "Adding behaviors to templates and documents created from templates," and Tech Note 14852, "Using Library items to add behaviors to documents created from templates."

Updating Pages Linked to Templates

Whenever you make or edit a template, you have to save it before Dreamweaver will update any pages linked to it. To save the template, choose File → Save (or press the keyboard combination Ctrl-S or Command-S on the Mac). The Update Template Files dialog box (Figure 4.11) displays, and you can choose to apply the changes to files associated with the template—or not. However, your only choice is to update *all* the associated files or *none* of the associated files.

To update only an individual file, modify the template from that page (as described in the previous section) and choose Modify → Templates → Update Current Page. When you save the template page, the Update Template Files dialog box will display as usual, but if you select Don't Update, changes will not be applied to any additional files.

> If you are working with a Dreamweaver template in Dreamweaver MX 2004 (or Dreamweaver MX) and you insert a new region into the document, the syntax of the tags used to create the new region will be the newer MX and MX 2004 style, and this will make the template unreadable in older versions of Dreamweaver.

Managing Your Assets

The Assets panel is the collection point for all of the objects and elements you use in your site. As you build the site, the Assets panel grows. All colors, external and internal links, images, Flash files, templates, scripts, Library items, and HTML files are available via the Assets panel for dragging and dropping into a page. In this way, you have at your fingertips all of the things you need to efficiently build a consistent site.

As mentioned earlier, the Assets panel is part of the Files panel group (see Figure 4.3), and you can open it by choosing Window → Assets if it's not already visible.

The Assets panel consists of nine category buttons, a file list section, and a display section along with the ubiquitous drop-down menu and bottom icons. Table 4.1 lists the contents of each category and how it is used.

One of the shortcomings of the Assets panel is the way it lists files: alphabetically and without their containing folders. This makes it especially difficult to locate specific files, especially if you have grouped collections of files in different folders. Take for example the Images category. As you will see later on in this book, rollovers often have arcane names based on the location of the image on the page and their rollover type (see Chapter 13, "Designing Navigation Objects," for more on rollovers). These multiple images are included in the list, as is every version of a graphic ever saved in your local site.

Figure 4.11

Update template files in the Update Template Files dialog box.

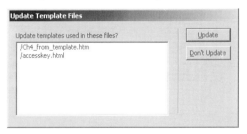

All of these files are listed without folders in a linear fashion. The only saving grace of this system is that, when you select a file, its contents are displayed in the Contents window above the file list. But you definitely cannot browse quickly through the list depending upon filenames alone to find your way.

Dreamweaver does include a Favorites view for each category (except Templates and Library) in which you can save favorite objects for quick access. The Favorites view is accessed at the top of the tab view for each group of assets. Files can be added to your Favorites list by selecting them in the Files panel and then clicking on the Add to Favorites icon at the bottom of the panel. In Favorites view, you can give your files names that help organize them alphabetically, preceding common elements with the same prefix (such as movie-, flash-, graphic-, and so on). You can also add a Favorites folder within the Favorites list by clicking on the New Favorites Folder icon at the bottom of the Assets panel. For more details, see the section "Using the Favorites Tab" later in this chapter.

To jump to a file (if you know its name) type the first letter of its name.

Table 4.1

The Assets Panel Categories

CATEGORY	CONTENTS
Images	All of the graphics contained in every page along with any other graphics saved in the Site folder.
Colors	All of the actual colors used in the site. In addition, any colors extracted from a graphic with the Eyedropper tool are also included. Drag colors from the palette to color layers, table cells, and so forth.
URLs	The Uniform Resource Locator (URL) addresses, both external and internal to the site, are listed. All hypertext links to e-mail addresses, external graphics, scripts, server-side includes, or web pages are listed. Drag an address onto an object to create a new link.
Flash	The Shockwave Flash files (identified by the .swf extension) that you use in the site are saved here. See Chapter 11, "Getting into Flash," for a discussion of these.
Shockwave	Macromedia Shockwave files are listed in this category. See Chapter 10, "Adding Graphics and Multimedia," for a discussion of multimedia plug-ins.
Movies	QuickTime movies and MPEG video files are listed in this category. See Chapter 10 for a discussion of multimedia plug-ins.
Scripts	This category lists script files that are called by the site files. These include JavaScript, VBScript, SSI, and applet files used by the site. See Chapter 12, "Incorporating JavaScript Behaviors," for information about applying behaviors to the site.
Templates	Templates used by the site are listed here. But you know all about these already, right?
Library	This is a special category that holds objects used on multiple pages. When you change a Library item, it is updated throughout the site. These objects can be scraps of text, graphics, tables, and more. You can pre-create Library items and repeat their use throughout the site. See the discussion in "Building a Library" later in this chapter for a description of how this works.

Working with the Assets Panel

To use an asset from the Assets panel, click a category button and then select a filename from the resulting list. (You may need to click the Refresh button at the bottom of the panel in order for the filenames to display.) To use the element, drag it on to the page. The Assets panel has several other interesting features that you can access through the following tabs: Favorites, Renaming, Editing, and Updating.

Using the Favorites Tab

When you start to use Dreamweaver and its Assets panel, you will quickly notice how fast objects build up in its categories. It becomes very time-consuming to browse down the file list trying to locate the one file you need to complete a page. The solution is to switch from the Site view to the Favorites view within the Assets panel. Click the Favorites radio button to switch views. The Favorites view provides seven categories (Templates and Library are not included), but you get to select what is included in the file list in each category.

To add an item to its Favorites view, select the filename and click the Add To Favorites icon (it looks like a little purple ribbon with a plus sign) on the bottom of the Assets panel. You can also use the Shortcuts menu by right-clicking and choosing Add To Favorites (you Mac users will need to press Ctrl-click and open the pop-up menu and then do the same thing).

ADDING COLORS TO THE FAVORITES VIEW

One of the best uses for the Favorites view is to copy colors from any source. When you collect colors on the Favorites view, you can quickly add them to other objects by dragging and dropping them from the Assets' Color category onto an object. To copy a color, do the following.

1. Click the Favorites radio button to switch to Favorites view.

2. Click the Color category button.

3. Click the New Color button on the bottom of the Assets panel (it looks like a piece of paper with a plus sign).

4. In the resulting color palette, use the Eyedropper to either choose a color from the palette or click anywhere on the Document window to pick up that color.

5. The color is added to the Favorites file list along with its hexadecimal value. As you see, the color's name reflects this value. Because it is difficult to identify a color by its numerical value, give the color a nickname by right-clicking the color. In the resulting shortcut menu, choose Edit Nickname. Type a new name in the resulting text box. (Mac users, you should Ctrl-click to reveal the pop-up menu and do the same thing.)

The colors you add to the Favorites list won't appear on the Site view in the Assets panel until you use them on a page.

Add a URL to the Favorites view by selecting the URL category and clicking the Add To Favorites button on the bottom of the Assets panel. In the resulting dialog box, type the URL's address and a nickname by which to remember the link. The URL is added to the Favorites view. Use the URL in another page to add it to your Site view in the Assets panel.

Inserting an Asset on a Page

There are three ways to insert assets: you can drag and drop them, you can insert them using the Insert bar, or you can insert them using the Insert menu in the main Dreamweaver application window. Dragging and dropping an object is the easiest way of applying it to a page. To do this, simply select the object and drag it onto the Document window. Dragging and dropping works well for images, applets, multimedia files and such, but it does not work well for certain applications, such as colors or URLs. For these objects, you need to use the Insert button on the bottom of the Assets panel. (Note that depending on the object you are inserting, the command might say "Apply" rather than "Insert," but it means the same thing.) The Insert (Apply) command is only visible if a file is open in the workspace.

When you use the Insert button to change the color of text, the color will apply only to text you type from that point forward. To change the color of existing text, always select it first before you drag and drop the color or use the Insert button.

Building a Library

One of the most tedious and laborious things you have to do when you are maintaining a website is update every page when one tidbit of information changes. Dreamweaver has conquered this tedium by providing you with a way to edit a repeating item once and then have its appearance updated on every subsequent page where it is used. The magical device that performs this service is the Library.

Before the advent of the Library in Dreamweaver 4, the only way to include repeating information was through a piece of scripting called a server-side include (SSI). SSIs are bits of HTML (which lack the <head> tag pair) that can be inserted into documents by the server before the document is sent to the browser. SSIs are most useful when they are used for shared content, such as standard navigation elements. SSIs have their uses—such as when you wish to create a dynamically changing piece of content (a query report from a database or a real-time news report, for example). In fact, we'll show you how to insert SSIs in the next section of this chapter, but repeatedly calling in server-side objects is a very processing-intense, I/O-intense drain on the web server. For this reason, many ISPs and IP organizations do not allow the use of SSIs.

Fortunately, Dreamweaver eliminates the need for most SSIs with the Library, accessed from the Assets panel (it's the last category button).

> Library items are saved in the Library folder at the root level of your site directory and given the file extension .lbi. Do not move items from the Library folder or rename the folder; if you do, the links to and from the Library items will be lost.

Adding Content to the Library

You can create Library items before you begin building your website, or you can select existing items on a page and add them to the Library. There are, of course, a couple of methods available for building up the Library's contents.

- Use the New Library Item button in the Assets panel.

  To do this, select text, graphic, or other objects on the web page and click the New Library Item button on the bottom of the Assets panel in the Library category. As shown in Figure 4.12, your item is added to the file list, displayed in the Contents screen, and given the name "untitled." Give the item a name that you will remember. The selected object is also highlighted in yellow on the web page to indicate that it is a Library item.

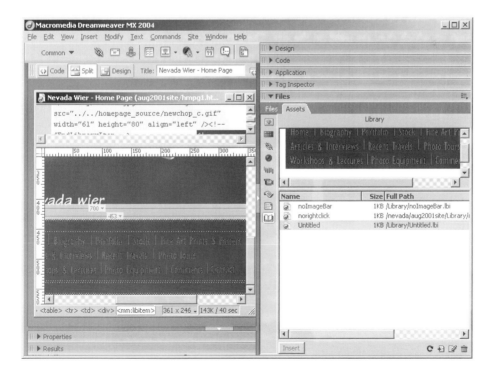

Figure 4.12

When you create a new Library item from an existing object, the object is highlighted on the page, indicating that it is now a reuseable element.

- Drag and drop the object into the Library category.

  To do this, select the item from your web page and drag it on to the File List section of the Library panel. The result is the same as what happens when you use the New Library Item command.

- Select Modify → Library → Add Object To Library.

> When you create a Library item from text that has been styled using a Cascading Style Sheet, be aware that the style sheet does not transfer with the Library item—thus, the formatting will not appear the same on a page that doesn't use a style sheet or uses a different style sheet than the one attached to the page that the element came from.

Inserting a Library Item on a Page

The easiest way to insert a Library item on a page is to drag it from the Assets panel Library category onto the page. You can also select the filename of the Library item and click the Insert button at the bottom of the panel. The element is placed where you clicked your cursor on the page.

Editing a Library Item

Library items are particularly useful because they can be edited once and updated on every page on which they are used on the site. The element can be edited either in the special Library Item window or via its originating program. To edit a Library item, select its filename and click the Edit button at the bottom of the Assets panel. Make your changes in the resulting Library Item window, which, for objects Dreamweaver can edit, is just like an ordinary document window.

Figure 4.13

The Library Item window enables you to open, re-create, or detach Library items from a page.

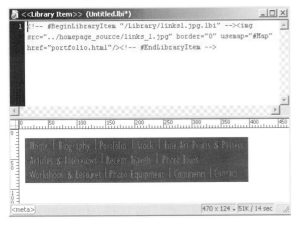

To edit Library items that originated in another Macromedia application (such as Fireworks), click the small arrow at the bottom right of the Property inspector to expand the panel and then click the Edit button.

You can also edit a Library item by selecting it directly on the page and then clicking the Open button on the Property inspector, which opens the Library Item window (see Figure 4.13).

You also have the option of editing a Library item for an individual page, i.e., editing it and applying the changes only to an individual page, not every page that uses that item. Select a Library item, then choose

Detach From Original in the Property inspector. The yellow highlighting disappears, and this item will no longer be updated when changes are made to the original Library item.

Updating the Website When Library Items Change

Whenever you make changes to a Library item or add a new one to a page, you must save the page and update the site so that Dreamweaver can propagate the change to pages that incorporate the Library item. To update the Library, choose Modify → Library → Update Pages. In the Update Pages dialog box that appears, choose Entire Site and then click the Start button (see Figure 4.14).

You can also update the current page (with Modify → Library → Update Current Page) to reflect changes and see how they work before applying the change or addition to every page that uses the element.

Figure 4.14

Updating a site after changing a Library item

Deleting a Library Item

If you no longer wish to use a Library item, you can delete it from the Assets panel. Actually deleting it from a page requires a second step in which you detach the Library item from the page, thus breaking the link. The element is now fully editable in the document.

To delete an element, select it from the file list in the Library category and click the Delete button on the bottom of the Assets panel (the little trash can). You can also delete an item by selecting it and choosing Delete from the shortcut menu (contextual menu for you Mac fans).

To detach the deleted Library item from the actual element on the page (and thus release it from bondage), select the element and click the Detach From Original button on the Property inspector.

Should you accidentally delete a Library item from the Library category, you can retrieve it if you still have a web page that uses the element. Open that web page and select the element. In the Property Inspector, click Recreate. Dreamweaver re-creates the Library item, thus restoring the element. Whew, no harm done. You will need to rename it, though; Dreamweaver re-creates it as an untitled library item.

Using Server-Side Includes (SSIs) as Repeating Elements

As discussed in the previous section, some site developers like to use server-side includes (SSIs) to store a piece of reusable content in a single file and let the web server include that content when pages containing an SSI referring to that file are served up to the requesting browser. Dreamweaver makes it very easy to insert SSIs and even shows you how the included content will appear in Design view.

> The use of SSIs is being superseded by content management systems and more sophisti-cated server-side scripting languages, such as PHP (which stands for PHP: Hypertext Pre-processor). See Chapters 27,"Static Content Management with Contribute," and 28,"Dynamic Content Management," for more information on content management. For more details about PHP, see Chapter 22,"Using PHP with Dreamweaver."

The following example shows an SSI for an Apache server. This SSI inserts the current date on the page when it is served to the browser.

```
<!--#echo var="DATE_LOCAL" -->
```

Note that this is not a very efficient use of server resources, especially when you could easily display the current date with client-side JavaScript, for example, which doesn't require any additional server resources.

By the way, to use SSIs, you'll have to make sure that your web server has enabled server-side includes. If you don't know how to do this, talk to your host or your system administrator and let them know what you're planning to do.

> For more information on using server-side includes, see BigNoseBird.Com's Server-Side Include Page at www.bignosebird.com/ssi.shtml, and WDVL: Server-Side Includes at www.wdvl.com/Authoring/SSI/.

Inserting an SSI

To insert an SSI, select Insert → HTML → Script Objects → Server-Side Include. In the Select File dialog box that appears, browse to a local file, choose a data source, or indicate a URL (see Figure 4.15). For included scripts, you can select parameters as well.

Editing an SSI

Although Dreamweaver will display the contents of an included file in Design view, you can't edit the included file directly from the including page. You can, however, right-click (Ctrl-click for Mac users) the include and select Edit from the pop-up menu to edit the SSI. Dreamweaver will open the included file in a new window. After you edit and save the file, its display will be updated on the page in which it is included.

Taking a Jump Backward

In this chapter, we took a big jump forward to discuss the use of collaborative tools. Templates, assets, and Library items are used to maintain the consistency of your web pages throughout a site. Contribute adds even more collaborative capabilities, which we'll explore in Chapter 27.

Your problem is that you now know how to apply templates and their contents, but you still might not know how to build a page. In Part II, you'll learn to construct a web page in Dreamweaver using layout tools, text formatting, frames, hyperlinks, and Cascading Style Sheets. If you're already experienced with page construction in Dreamweaver and would prefer to start working with web graphics and multimedia at this point, skip ahead to Chapter 10, "Adding Graphics and Multimedia," or any of the chapters in Part III.

Figure 4.15

Use the Select File dialog box for SSIs to pick a local file, a data source, or a URL.

## PART II

Building a Web Page

Finally, *we get to the hands-on web-page-design-oriented features of Dreamweaver. With your site set up and your graphical assets gathered, you can start building the most important pages (such as landing pages for key sections of your site) and then move very quickly on to the supporting pages.*

In this part, we show you how to construct web pages out of their component parts. We start with page layout because you must have some structure in your page design before you can insert text and other elements onto the page. Then we cover the two most common page elements: text and graphics. We explore using frames and framesets next, and then we get to the page element that makes the Web the Web: hyperlinks. We look at Cascading Style Sheets (CSS), the web-standards way to separate style from content, and introduce Dreamweaver MX 2004's new CSS features. Finally, we show how to incorporate graphics and multimedia objects into your pages, and then take a look at how Flash can aid your design goals.

## CHAPTER 5

Page Layout

Professionals who design printed material, such as brochures and booklets, expect to be able to position objects anywhere on a page and control spacing precisely. When the Web first appeared without offering that kind of control over the look of a "page," designers couldn't believe it. Then, when popular browsers introduced support for HTML tables, designers regained some degree of precision in placement, but ran into browser problems (especially in Netscape 4.*x*) and accessibility issues as they designed more and more complex table layouts. HTML tables were not created as a page layout tool, although they have been used (and abused) for that purpose. This chapter examines the ways you can use tables and layers as page layout tools in Dreamweaver, but we encourage you to use CSS for page layout rather than tables. For more details on using CSS in Dreamweaver, see Chapter 9, "Cascading Style Sheets."

This chapter includes the following:

- ▪ **Choosing a layout method**

- ▪ **Using predesigned layouts**

- ▪ **Creating tables in Standard mode**

- ▪ **Using Expanded Tables mode to edit tables**

- ▪ **Using Layout mode to draw tables and cells**

- ▪ **Editing tables**

- ▪ **Importing and exporting tabular data**

- ▪ **Controlling layout with layers**

- ▪ **Creating complex layouts by combining tables and layers**

Layout Methods

You have several options when you want to create a layout in Dreamweaver. The tried-and-true way is to use the traditional HTML table, where you create a grid of rows and columns and place information into the table's individual cells in an HTML page. Dreamweaver enables you to create tables easily in Standard mode by inserting a table or inserting Dreamweaver layers and then converting the layers to a table. Layout mode allows you to draw tables and table cells, and arrange them however you choose. Layout mode automatically creates HTML table code from your visual layout.

Dreamweaver MX 2004 adds Expanded Tables mode to your layout options. Expanded Tables mode makes table editing faster by adding temporary padding and spacing to table cells and increases table borders so it's easier to set an insertion point or select items within tables. The added padding, spacing, and borders disappear when you return to Standard mode.

No matter what type of table design you decide to use, tables display in their standard grid format. However, Dreamweaver gives you the flexibility to set the size of the table to your needs. After setting a fixed size for your table, you can then make the table "float" on your page with the text wrapped around it. You can also set your table to a specific percentage of the window size so the table will always be visible inside your visitor's browser window.

Using Cascading Style Sheets for Layout

Using Cascading Style Sheets, better known as CSS, is becoming a popular way to design pages and tables. CSS lets you define styles for designing web pages in much the same way as a word processor lets you define styles for your documents. You can embed CSS styles within your HTML page or you can create a separate CSS page that defines all the styles you use for all the pages contained within a site. Dreamweaver lets you create new styles within Dreamweaver or use an external style sheet and the CSS editor of your choice.

Creating new styles in Dreamweaver MX 2004 is easier than ever. Now you can use the text Property inspector to automatically create style classes for formatting text, and use the Style drop-down menu to preview style properties or apply styles to selections of text.

Some designers like to use CSS and traditional HTML tables together. For example, you can design a traditional table but have the text within it follow the styles set in your CSS document. Such "hybrid" table design is called transitional design.

You can also use CSS to position your table on a page in a certain way. For example, you may want to have a CSS page define the size of a table and its placement on a page.

See Chapter 9 for more information on CSS and Dreamweaver's new CSS features.

FLASH FOR PAGE LAYOUT?

Macromedia Flash is the leading vector animation design program for multimedia developers. Developers use Flash to design website components or entire sites. Macromedia closely ties Dreamweaver and Flash in both functionality and marketing.

You can use Flash by itself to create websites, but should you? It depends on the functionality and look you want your site to have. If you want graphic animations constructed with multiple layers with, for example, numerous graphic images in your navigation menu that animate when you mouse over them, then creating your site in Flash is something to consider. However, keep in mind that Flash animations increase file size, and that means slower loading times—something to consider, especially for web surfers using dial-up access.

Dreamweaver itself includes behaviors for creating modest animations for such things as text or buttons that change when you mouse over them. You can also create Flash buttons and Flash text with rollover effects in Dreamweaver. Behaviors, Flash buttons, and Flash text add little to your overall file size. (See Chapter 11 for more details on Flash buttons and Flash text, and Chapter 12 for additional information on behaviors.)

The bottom line? As with any website you design, consider your audience before you decide on your design tool.

Selecting a Predesigned Layout

If you're working with tables for the first time, you can save yourself some design time by starting with a template that already contains them. Templates give you the opportunity to build on someone else's experience. If you use a template as a starting point, you can then fine-tune the layout using the techniques described later in this chapter. (See Chapter 4, "Saving Labor with Templates and Libraries," for an introduction to templates.)

Starting with a Template

In Chapter 4, you learned how to create and apply templates to add consistency to a website. If you create a template that uses tables, you can carry out that table design throughout your website.

You can also use a different kind of template—a web page that someone else has designed and that you can use as a starting point for your own site. You just copy the page (or pages; some templates consist of sets of interlinked web pages) to your computer and alter the content to fit your needs.

Dreamweaver MX 2004 includes several pre-built Sample design files, including CSS Style Sheets, Page Designs (Table Based Layouts), CSS Page Designs, and Accessible Page Designs. These are not Dreamweaver templates—Dreamweaver automatically creates a copy if you make a page based on a design file.

Where do you find templates? The first and most obvious place to look is Macromedia. Go to www.macromedia.com/software/dreamweaver/download/templates. You can also purchase templates that talented web page designers have created and made available. Try Project Seven Development (www.projectseven.com) or the other sites listed in Appendix A.

SETTING THE TABLE FOR WEB PAGE LAYOUT

Before you can start using tables as web page layout tools, you need to know the basics about HTML tables and how they're structured.

Tables were originally added to Hypertext Markup Language (HTML) as a way of arranging tabular data in an orderly way. Tables consist of horizontal divisions into rows and vertical divisions into columns. Each row and column contains one or more subdivisions called cells. Each cell has its own border, as does the table itself. Conventional tables display information in a grid, much like a spreadsheet.

The table shown here, for instance, has two rows and two columns. The borders around each cell are visible, as is the border around the outer edge of the table itself.

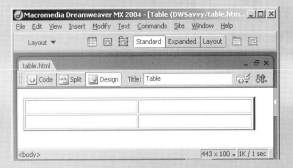

The savvy web designer can turn off the table's border display by setting the border value to 0 so that the viewer sees only the contents, not the borders. By filling the table cells with text and images rather than simple figures, the table becomes a layout tool for designing a whole web page. Dreamweaver gives you plenty of options for creating such tables, as described throughout this chapter.

It isn't difficult to locate templates that use tables for page layout because they are a very popular starting point for many web page designs. Follow these steps to locate a template and start working with it:

1. Start your browser and go to Macromedia's Dreamweaver templates page:

   www.macromedia.com/software/dreamweaver/download/templates

2. Scroll down and look for a page that's been divided into columns or that has a design similar to one you want to use. Chances are that a columnar layout uses tables.

> You can verify whether or not a web page uses tables by viewing the source code for the page. In Internet Explorer, choose View → Source; in Netscape Navigator, choose View → Page Source. Scan the HTML for tags such as <table> </table>, which enclose a table; <tr> </tr>, which define a row within a table; or <td> </td>, which define a cell.

3. Click Preview to view a closeup of the template in your browser window. The template called Department of History, for instance (see Figure 5.1), uses a common three-column design. The column on the left can be altered to contain a set of links to other parts of your site. The column on the right can contain a list of personnel or other facts about your organization; in the center is a spacing or placeholder column.

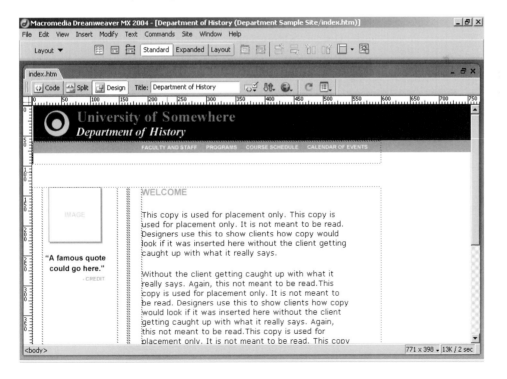

Figure 5.1

Dreamweaver makes it easy to edit tables because borders are always visible in the Document window. You can select images and text within cells and edit them just like regular web page content.

4. To copy the template, return to the Templates page and click either PC or Mac next to Download. Your system will now begin to download a Zip archive containing the template pages to your computer.

5. Extract the archive to a directory on your computer using WinZip or a similar application.

6. Start Dreamweaver, choose File → Open, and open the `index.htm` file.

After you have the template open in Dreamweaver, you can begin editing the content. The tables that contain the content appear in the Dreamweaver window (see Figure 5.1).

Using a Preset Table Format

Dreamweaver provides you with preformatted tables that give you another sort of design jump-start. They're a great source for innovative ideas of how to present the information within a table—particularly a borderless table. The preset table designs enable you to choose and preview tables that have different background colors assigned to individual rows, and type fonts that are chosen to convey a particular feeling (simple, businesslike, high-tech, and so on).

To view the preset designs, create a table on your page (Insert → Table), then choose Commands → Format Table. The Format Table dialog box opens (see Figure 5.2). Select an option from the list in the upper-left corner of the dialog box to see a preview on the right.

Figure 5.2

Each row or column within a table can be assigned a color to provide additional graphic interest.

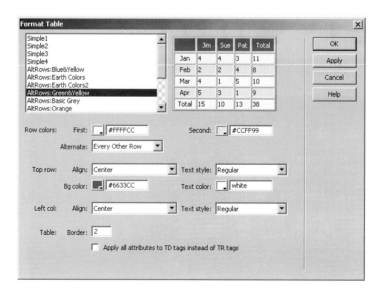

You can use Dreamweaver's preset table designs at any time, not just when you're first creating a table. To format an existing table, select the table by choosing Modify → Table → Select Table. Then choose Commands → Format Table to open the Format Table dialog box. The design elements you choose are applied to the currently selected table.

Use the controls at the bottom of the dialog box to adjust the attributes of the table. One benefit of doing this is that, when you make a choice, you instantly see the choice reflected in the preview at the top of the dialog box.

Creating a New Table

Using tables as design tools can help designers gain some control over a page's appearance. The three modes for creating and editing tables—Standard mode, Expanded Tables mode, and Layout mode—are described below.

PERCENTAGES VS. ABSOLUTE MEASUREMENTS

You can define the width of a table and/or the widths of the rows, columns, and cells within it in one of two ways:

- As a fixed measurement
- As a percentage of the width of the page or table itself

Setting a fixed, or static, table width can be advantageous in certain situations. For example, you may want to have a smaller column at the left for such things as graphics, and a larger column to the right for text. However, static tables have their drawbacks. Users of 800×600-pixel resolution (or Super VGA) monitors display web pages in browsers that cannot display the full 800-pixel width or 600-pixel height of a web page because the edges of the window (e.g., scroll bars) take up some of that space. If you have a table that is fixed at 800×600 pixels exactly, some visitors to your site will not be able to see the table in its entirety on the screen—they will have to scroll around to see everything.

In most cases, it's better to set the table as a percentage of the width of the page. This "liquid" table design sets the table size to the exact size of the window if the percentages for width and height are both 100%. This approach ensures your visitors will see the table in its entirety.

If you have columns or rows in your liquid table, you can establish fixed widths and/or heights for some columns and rows and assign other columns percentage values. For example, you may want to have a table with two columns that takes up 100 percent of the browser window height and width. You may also want the left column width to be an exact size that matches the width of your 150-pixel wide company logo. HTML is flexible enough to allow you to set the size of the left column to 150 pixels and the right column to 100%. The left column will remain at 150 pixels and the right column will always be visible in the browser window.

Using Standard Mode

Standard mode gives you a way of creating a table through parts of the Dreamweaver interface that you're already familiar with, such as menus and dialog boxes. Use it if you're not artistically inclined, you don't like to draw, or if you want the control over table attributes that the Insert Table dialog box provides.

Before you start creating a table from scratch, it's a good idea to sketch out on paper how you want your finished web page to look. That way, you'll know exactly how many rows and columns you'll need before you start filling in the table specifications in the Insert Table dialog box.

It's easy to begin creating tables in Standard mode. Just open the page you want to work on in Dreamweaver, and then position the cursor where you want the table to appear. Then, you create the table in one of three ways:

- Click the Table icon in the Common Insert bar or the Layout Insert bar, or drag the icon into the Document window
- Choose Insert → Table
- Press Ctrl-Alt-T

No matter which way you chose, the Insert Table dialog box should now appear (see Figure 5.3).

Enter the following specifications for your table:

Rows Enter the number of rows the table should have.

Columns Enter the number of columns the table should have.

Figure 5.3

The Insert Table dialog box lets you choose the attributes for your table.

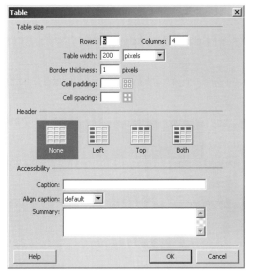

Width The width of a table can be expressed either as a percentage of the width of the page, as displayed in the browser window, or as a fixed number of pixels. Choose Percent or Pixels from the drop-down list to switch between the two types of measurement.

Border Set the border to 0 if you want it to be invisible. (The width shown is in pixels; set the value to 3 if you want a three-pixel-wide border.)

Cell Padding This is optional; it controls the space (in pixels) between the contents of the cell and the cell border.

Cell Spacing This is optional; it refers to the space between cells, in pixels.

Caption This is an optional accessibility feature; you can add a caption in a row above your table by default.

Align Caption If you have a table caption, select the location where the table caption will appear. The default value is above the table.

Summary This is an optional accessibility feature; you can enter additional information describing the table content and purpose.

You can always make revisions to the table specifications by selecting the table (choose Modify → Table → Select Table) and then making changes in the Property inspector.

To create a table for page layout, you should not only set borders to zero, but you may want to create columns or rows that are empty except for a non-breaking space ( ). This creates space between columns that do contain content.

Once you're finished entering values in the Insert Table dialog box, click OK. The table appears in your page (see Figure 5.4).

After the table's outline appears, you need to fill in its cells with content. You do this by clicking within each cell to position the cursor there. You can then begin typing or pasting text or images that you have already copied. You can also choose Insert → Image to insert an image.

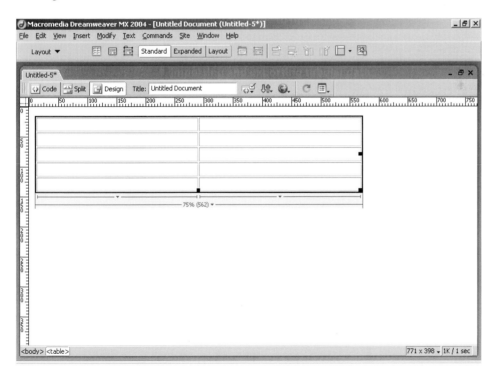

Figure 5.4

This table has two columns and five rows.

Using Expanded Tables Mode

Dreamweaver MX 2004 introduces a new layout option called Expanded Tables mode. Expanded Tables mode is mainly designed for easier table editing, but you can also create a table in this mode:

1. Open an HTML page in Dreamweaver, or create a new page from the Start page (or File → New).

2. From the Layout Insert bar, choose Expanded Tables Mode.

3. Insert a table on the page from the Common Insert bar, Layout Insert bar, or by selecting Insert → Table.

The real utility of Expanded Tables mode, however, is to make table editing easier. Increased cell spacing, cell padding, and border width is temporarily added in Design view so that you can position an insertion point more easily and precisely or, for example, select part of a cell's content without selecting the cell itself.

Once you have positioned the insertion point or made a precise selection, you can return to Standard mode to make the actual edits. All the options of Standard mode are also available in Expanded Tables mode, but some operations, such as visual resizing, might give unexpected results if performed in Expanded Tables mode. Figure 5.5 shows the same table in all three modes.

Figure 5.5

Three different layout modes for the same HTML table: top, Standard; middle, Expanded Tables; and bottom, Layout.

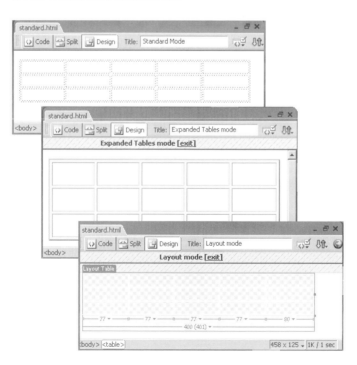

Using Layout Mode

Layout mode lets you arrange a page's contents visually. One advantage of using Layout mode is that tables and cells drawn in Layout mode have a border width set to zero automatically. Another is that you see the table being created as you draw it. To work in Layout mode, do one of two things:

- Choose View → Table Mode → Layout Mode.
- Click the Layout button on the Layout Insert bar (see Figure 5.6).

Figure 5.6

The three buttons in the Layout Insert bar let you switch between Standard, Expanded Tables, and Layout mode.

When you click Layout mode and then click either Layout Cell or Layout Table, the cursor turns into crosshairs when you pass it over the Document window.

Draw Layout Cell Click this icon, and then draw an individual cell within a table in Design view.

Layout Table Click this icon, and then draw a table in Design view.

Let's say you want to draw a table with two columns and only one row—essentially, you can use this table to design the entire page layout. Follow these steps:

1. Click the Layout button in the Layout Insert bar.
2. Click the Layout Table icon in the Layout Insert bar.
3. Click in the Document window, hold down the mouse button, and drag down and to the right. Release the mouse button, and the table is created.

> The mouse arrow turns into crosshairs when you click Layout Table or Draw Layout Cell. If you click Draw Layout Cell before you create a table, Dreamweaver automatically creates a table to contain the cell that you draw.

4. Resize the table, if needed, by clicking one of the handles around it.
5. Click Draw Layout Cell.
6. Click in the upper-left corner of the table and drag down and to the right to draw a cell.
7. If you need to resize the cell, click it and click and drag one of its handles.
8. Repeat steps 6 and 7 until you have drawn all of the cells you need.

> Each time you draw a cell, you need to click Draw Layout Cell first—unless you hold down the Ctrl key as you draw.

You can cut, copy, or paste individual cells within a table just like any other web page contents. If you select a cell within a table, you can view that cell's properties in the Property inspector so that you can adjust them if you need to. But whatever mode you're working in, Dreamweaver lets you adjust a table or cell by clicking and dragging: In Layout mode, you click and drag handles; in Standard or Expanded Tables mode, you click and drag the borders.

Finessing Table Properties

When laying out a page on-the-fly, your initial specifications don't have to be your final ones. As you work with your web page, you'll probably adjust spacing so its contents are readable. When your table covers most of your web page and controls the design for most or all of the page, you'll almost certainly need to adjust the spacing between columns so the columns of your page are far enough apart. (Of course, if you are simply building out a page from a pre-existing template, then you probably won't need to change any of the table settings.)

Maintaining some empty space on a page helps a viewer read the contents more easily and directs the viewer's eye toward the most important contents. This section examines Dreamweaver's tools for fine-tuning the dimensions of a table and its components, including the Property inspector and the Table submenu of the Modify menu.

> Dreamweaver displays tables with dashed lines around the borders. You can view the table without visible borders either by previewing the page in a browser window (choose File → Preview In Browser) or by choosing View → Visual Aids → Table Borders to toggle between turning border display on or off.

Selecting Parts of a Table

Before you can work with a table or individual cells, you should practice selecting them. It's not always easy to select an entire table, row, or column simply by clicking it; you need to know exactly where to click, and what menu options to choose if you don't select exactly what you want the first time.

Selecting in Standard or Expanded Tables Mode

The easiest way to select an entire table in Standard or Expanded Tables mode is to choose Modify → Table → Select Table.

You can select a table, or rows or columns within it, by clicking. Sometimes, clicking parts of a table to select them requires you to place the mouse cursor in exactly the right place. Here are some suggestions:

- Position the cursor just above or below the table to get this four-headed arrow ✛ . When you click, you select the entire table.

- If you can position the mouse cursor atop a table border, you get this arrow ⊥ . When you click, you select the adjacent row or column. (If the arrow points down, you select a column. If the arrow points to the left, you select a row.)

- If you click a cell border while this double-arrow ╪ appears, you select the entire table—not the cell. (To select a cell, click and drag across it.)

Selecting in Layout View

It's easier to select individual cells within a table by working in Layout view. You can click anywhere within the cell to display the handles around it, which means it's been selected.

However, when it comes to selecting rows that consist of multiple cells, you run into a limitation: you can't select multiple cells by pressing Shift-click (Ctrl-click on the Mac). You can, however, easily select the entire table by clicking the Layout Table label just above its upper-left corner.

Adding a Spacer

One of the advantages of using a table to design an entire web page is that you can easily add space between rows or columns by adding a new row or column that contains only blank space.

In the template table layout shown in Figure 5.7, some "spacer" empty columns have been added to provide extra separation between the column on the left and the middle column, and between the middle and right columns. If you want to add a few points of space, you can adjust cell spacing or cell padding. But to add large amounts of space, such as a quarter or a half of an inch, consider adding an extra column or row to the table to function as a spacer.

You can easily add a spacer to a table in Layout mode. In this case, though, the spacer is a graphic image rather than a row or column. In Layout mode, click the Down arrow next to the number indicating the size of the column in pixels. Choose Add a Spacer Image from the pop-up menu that appears. If you have not yet used a spacer image in your website, a dialog box appears asking you to choose such an image. Click one of the two options—Create a New Spacer Image or Choose an Existing Spacer Image File. If you choose to create a new spacer image, Dreamweaver asks you to name the file and choose where you want to save it, and then it creates the image for you.

Autostretching a Column

When you're working in Standard or Expanded Tables mode, you can adjust the width of an entire table using the Property inspector. Select the table, display the Property inspector, and choose Percent from drop-down menus next to the W (width) or H (height) boxes to change the table to variable width.

Figure 5.7

You can add table cells to increase space between columns.

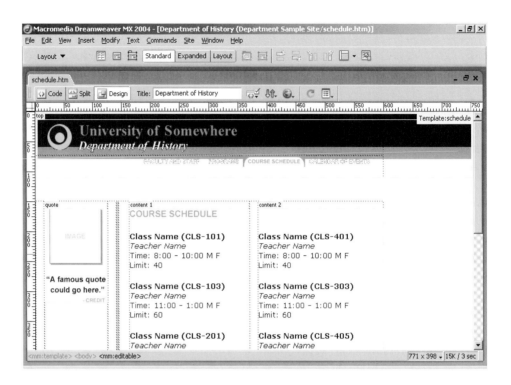

If you're working in Layout mode, in order to change a table from fixed to variable width, you need to use a Dreamweaver feature called *autostretch.* Autostretch enables you to insert a spacer image in a column of the table. The autostretch column width is set to 100 percent so that it can expand or contract to fill as much of the browser window as possible.

If you use autostretch, the table width is always 100 percent. You can specify a fixed width for other columns in the same table, but the overall table width is always 100 percent if you use autostretch in any column.

In Layout mode, you can make one column a variable width in one of two ways:

- Go to the column you want to make variable and click the down arrow next to the numbers that denote its size. Choose Make Column Autostretch from the pop-up menu.
- In the Property inspector, select the column you want to make a variable width, and then click the Autostretch button.

When you make a column autostretched, Dreamweaver inserts a spacer image in that column. In Layout mode, a wavy line displays at the top or bottom of the autostretch column. The image, which is transparent and not visible to a viewer, changes in width along with the browser window so that the other columns in the table can stay the same width.

> Though it's most common to set the rightmost column in a table to autostretch, you can choose autostretch for any column. But only one column in the table can be set to autostretch.

Adding or Removing Rows and Columns

Use the Modify menu when you need to add or remove rows or columns or make other changes that affect all of the table's rows or columns at the same time. Position the text cursor within the table, then choose Modify → Table. The Table submenu appears.

To add an element, select Insert Row or Insert Column. To add both rows and columns at the same time, choose Insert Rows Or Columns, then specify what you want to add in the Insert Rows Or Columns dialog box. To delete elements, choose Delete Row or Delete Column.

The options in the bottom section of the Table submenu (and in the expanded view of the Table Property inspector) let you fine-tune cell spacing:

Clear Cell Heights/Widths Sometimes, you add content to a cell that doesn't fill out the cell. To eliminate unnecessary space at the top or side of the cell, you can do any of the following:

- Drag the cell border to resize the cell.
- Choose Modify → Table → Clear Cell Heights, or Modify → Table → Clear Cell Widths.
- In the Table Property inspector in Standard or Expanded Tables mode, click the Clear Column Widths or Clear Row Heights icons.
- In the Table Property inspector in Layout mode, click the Clear Row Heights icon.
- In Layout mode, click the Table Header menu and choose Clear All Heights.

Convert Widths to Pixels/Percent This option lets you switch the width of the selected cell(s) from a fixed value to a percentage of the table, and vice versa.

Convert Heights to Pixels/Percent This option lets you switch the height of the selected row(s) from a fixed value to a percentage of the table, and vice versa.

Using the Table Property Inspector

As stated earlier in "Selecting Parts of a Table," you can resize an individual cell by dragging either its border (in Standard or Expanded Tables mode) or its selection handles (in Layout mode). When you resize a cell by dragging, it automatically snaps to align with the borders of adjacent cells so that they don't overlap.

You can also adjust properties that apply to all cells at once by using the Table Property inspector, which appears when you position the cursor within a table. It contains a variety of tools for fine-tuning spacing, alignment, and other attributes (see Figure 5.8).

The Merge Cells option is only active when more than one cell within a row or column is selected. Click this option to combine the selected cells into a single cell. Split Cells is only active when one cell is selected. Click it to split the cell into two cells.

Figure 5.8

The Table Property Inspector gives you control over row, column, and cell spacing.

Adding Colors

Each individual cell in a table can have its own background color. This enables you to create areas of spot color on the page—areas that call attention to a heading or a section because they have an accent color. On the other hand, for a simpler look you can assign a single background color to the table as a whole.

To add color to a cell, select it and then click the Background (Bg) button in the Property inspector. Select a color from the color selection box that appears (see Figure 5.9). The color immediately appears behind the cell's contents. To assign a background color to a table, the process is virtually the same—select the table, then click the Bg color button and select the color.

You can also assign a color to the outer border of the table—select the table, click Brdr Color in the Property inspector, and select a color. But this requires that the table border

Figure 5.9

Dreamweaver's color picker helps you assign a background color to a table or to an individual cell.

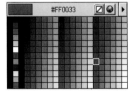

be visible to the viewer, with a value greater than zero pixels. Each cell within a table can have a border color. However, you need to be in Standard or Expanded Tables mode to see the Brdr Color box displayed in the Property inspector; it isn't available when you select a cell in Layout View.

Individual cell borders are often difficult to see on the finished web page unless the border is several pixels wide. The same rules that apply to backgrounds and other web page colors apply to table colors: they should not clash with other colors on the page, and they should make the text readable, not obscure or overshadow it.

Controlling Alignment

If you use a table for page layout, you may want the table to cover the entire width of the page at all times, in which case you should specify its width at 100 percent.

However, if you have a table that is less than the width of the page (such as a nested table, as described in the following section), you can align the table easily by selecting it, then selecting one of the alignment options (Default, Left, Center, Right) from the drop-down menu.

To align the contents of a row, cell, or column, select it and then click one of the alignment buttons (Align Left, Align Center, Align Right) in the Property inspector.

Nesting Tables

Just as you can put a cell within a table, you can place, or *nest*, an entire table inside a larger one. Nested tables can be useful when you need to arrange two or more objects at a fixed distance from one another on a page. Nesting allows you to keep the contents of both tables the same distance from one another regardless of the size of the browser window.

We recommend Cascading Style Sheets for page layout rather than nested tables. Complex tables can be rendered incorrectly in browsers, will increase page loading time as the browser interprets the complex layout code, and might create accessibility problems for visitors with disabilities.

Nesting can be a good strategy for handling photos that need to have lists next to them at all times. Nesting is also a good way to gain more flexibility over your text in certain cells of the parent table. In a table, you cannot set the cell padding and spacing in a single cell of the table; cell padding and spacing are the same for all cells, and that can be a problem if you want one cell to have different padding and spacing settings than the rest of your table cells.

To get around this conundrum, you can place a nested table within the cell that you want to have different cell padding and/or spacing. Then you can set the nested table cell padding and/or spacing settings as desired. When you type text into your nested table, the text will appear with the correct spacing.

Layout mode makes it easy to nest tables. Follow these steps:

1. Display the page that contains the table within which you want to nest another table.

2. From the Layout Insert bar, click the Layout button.

3. Click the Layout Table icon.

4. Position the cursor near the upper-left corner of one of the table cells. The cursor turns into a plus (+) sign when you're in the right spot.

5. Click and drag the cursor down and to the right to draw the nested table within the cell (see Figure 5.10).

6. Draw individual cells within the nested table.

7. Add content to the cells, save the changes, and preview the page to check it.

The limitation with a nested table is that the width of the table is limited by the width of the cell that contains it. However, the nested table can also use small cells of varying size that function as spacers; these spacers enable you to offset cells that do contain contents.

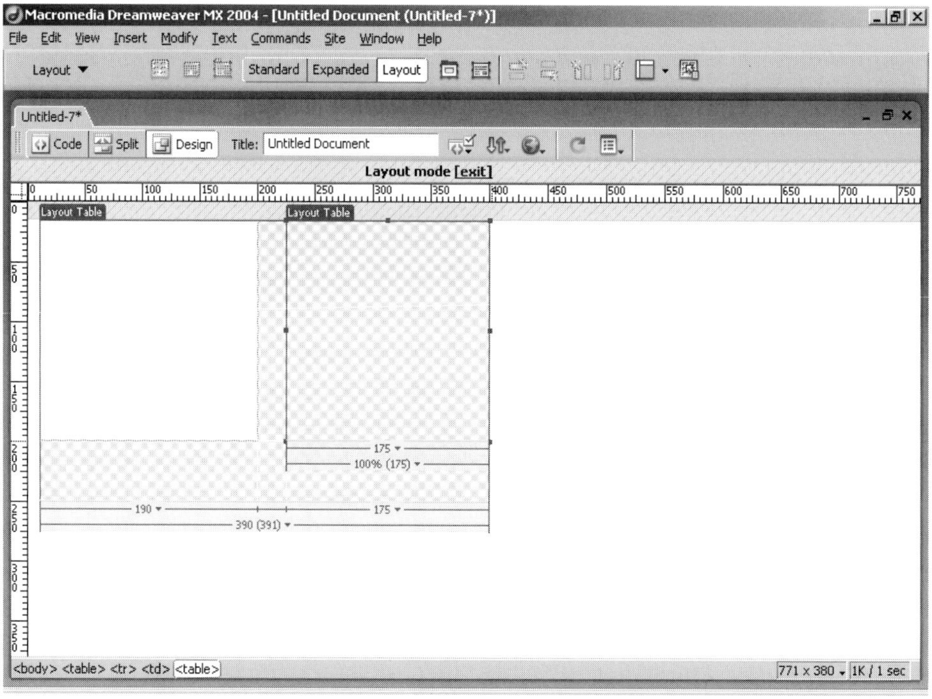

Figure 5.10

Nesting a table within a larger table gives you a great deal of control over positioning of text and images.

Using Tabular Data

You can import tabular data from another application that has been saved in a delimited text format (items separated by tabs, commas, semicolons, colons, or other delimiters). Choose Insert → Table Objects → Import Tabular Data (or File → Import → Tabular Data) to display the Insert Tabular Data dialog box. Click Browse to locate the tabular data file you want to add to the current web page.

You can also export a table from Dreamweaver into a delimited text file. Choose File → Export → Table, and choose a Delimiter, Line Break type (Windows, Mac, or Unix). Click OK and then enter a name for the file.

> You can also import Word or Excel documents directly. See Chapter 6, "Inserting and Formatting Text Content," for more details.

Designing with Layers

Tables give you a way to design a web page by containing contents within rows, columns, and cells. But the contents of a table's components can't overlap one another, and they can't bleed over the edge of a table border. Designers who want to break through the limitations of the table grid and add sophistication to their web pages can use layers.

A *layer*, like a table, is a container that can hold text, images, colors, and other web page contents. Dreamweaver MX 2004 supports the use of layers as an additional page layout option. Dreamweaver creates layers through the use of div and span as well as relative and absolute positioning, not through layer and ilayer elements. You can save your page layout in layers, or you can convert the layers to tables.

> Previous versions of Dreamweaver included a Timeline feature for creating simple animations with layers. This feature is superseded by Flash animation, and is no longer supported in Dreamweaver MX 2004.

Draw a Layer

As usual, Dreamweaver gives you multiple options for creating a layer without having to write the code. If you're an artist, you'll probably want to draw a layer. Just follow these steps:

1. Click the Draw Layer icon 🔲 in the Layout Insert bar.

> When you are in Layout mode you cannot add Layer objects to a page. Make sure you are in Standard or Expanded Tables mode before you start creating layers.

2. Position the cursor inside the Document window (the cursor turns into a plus (+) sign), and click and drag down and to the right. Release the mouse button when the layer is the size you want.

Grids make creating layouts or tables a snap—literally. Choose View → Grid → Show Grid to turn on the Grid to draw layers more accurately. If you choose View → Grid → Snap To Grid, the table cells or layers you draw will "snap" (in other words, jump to) the nearest grid line, which can help you achieve precise alignment.

You don't have to worry about drawing the layer perfectly the first time. You can resize it by clicking and dragging one of its resizing handles. These handles appear when you select the layer by clicking its selection handle. You can also move the layer freely around the document window by clicking and dragging its selection handle (see Figure 5.11). Although the border is visible in the Document window, it's invisible when you view the page in a web browser.

If you plan to draw more than one layer at a time, you need to click the Draw Layer button each time—unless you hold down Ctrl (Windows) or Cmd (Macintosh) while you draw each layer in succession.

Figure 5.11

You can reposition a layer by clicking and dragging either its selection handle or the handles around its border.

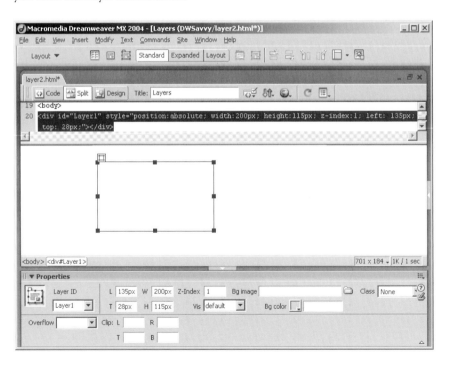

Insert a Layer

You can also use Dreamweaver's menus to create a layer. Just position the cursor at the spot on the page where you want the layer to appear. Then choose Insert → Layout Objects → Layer while you're in Standard or Expanded Tables mode. A layer instantly appears.

The size of a layer when you first insert it is predetermined by Dreamweaver's layer preferences. You can change the preferences if you want: choose Edit → Preferences, click Layers in the Preferences dialog box, and then change the values in the Width and Height boxes.

Use a Tracing Image

Some conventional page layouts are so complex, using overlapping layers of content, that they can only be replicated in Dreamweaver using layers. Dreamweaver lets you use a tracing image as a shortcut that can save you time as well as produce more faithful layouts.

A *tracing image* is a GIF, PNG, or JPEG file that you open in Dreamweaver in the background of the page being displayed in the Document window. The tracing image doesn't show up in the web page, even when it is previewed in a browser. It's only used as a model that you follow when you are assembling the page's contents. You create layers and fill those layers with images and other content that you then drag over the same images and content in the tracing image. When you're done, your web page displays a reasonably close approximation of the original design.

Suppose you scan a printed page that you have saved in GIF, JPEG, or PNG format and that you want to duplicate in a web page layout. Follow these steps to duplicate the image in Dreamweaver:

1. Select View → Tracing Image → Load.

2. In the Select Image Source dialog box, locate the image you want to trace, and then click Open. The Page Properties dialog box appears.

3. Adjust the Image Transparency slider to indicate how transparent you want the tracing image to be, then click OK. The image appears in the background of the web page.

4. Assemble the page, drawing layers over successive parts of the design.

5. Check your design while hiding the tracing image by deselecting View → Tracing Image → Show.

You can try out a more detailed version of this process in the tutorial at the end of this chapter.

You can align your tracing image with an image or paragraph in the Document window. Choose View → Tracing Image → Align With Selection. The upper-left corner of the element you've selected is aligned with the upper-left corner of the tracing image.

Finessing Layer Variables

You can fine-tune a layer's positioning, size, and properties just as you would with tables. You have two options: first, if you want to do hands-on adjustment, do it by clicking and dragging the layer. Sometimes, though, you want to really make some precise measurement adjustments, and in that case, you need to use the Layers panel and the Layer Property inspector.

Using the Layers Panel

When you are working on a web page that contains multiple layers, you can control their visibility and other properties by selecting Window → Layers to display the Layers panel.

The Layers panel displays layers in their stacking order, whether they're actually stacked atop one another or not. The layer at the top of the list is considered to be on top of the stack, and the others follow in order beneath it. You can change the stacking order by doing one of two things:

Figure 5.12

The Layers panel lists all the layers in the current web page.

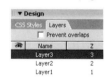

- Click a layer in the list in the Layers panel and drag it to another position in the list.

- Click the layer's number in the Z column of the Layers panel (see Figure 5.12) and type a higher or lower number to move the layer higher or lower in the stacking order.

You can change the visibility of all layers at once by clicking the eye icon at the top of the panel. You can also click an individual layer's eye icon to toggle between hiding or displaying it. An open eye means the layer is visible; a closed eye means it is hidden.

Using the Layer Property Inspector

Once you've created one or more layers, the Property inspector gives you a place to manage and adjust them. Some of the items in the Property inspector are obvious, but others are unique to layers:

Layer ID A default id value appears in this box, but you can change it to make it easier to keep track of objects in the Layers panel or if you're writing scripts for the page.

L/T This stands for left and top, and it describes the layer's placement relative to the top-left corner of the page.

W/H This stands for width and height, and it describes the size of the layer.

Z-Index This refers to the order of the layer in stacking, and it is used in case the currently selected layer is part of a stack of multiple layers.

Vis This describes whether the current layer is initially visible or invisible. Default is usually interpreted by web browsers to mean visible; inherit means the layer uses the same visibility as its parent, if there is one; visible means the layer will be displayed regardless of the parent's visibility; and hidden means the layer will be hidden.

Overflow This tells a browser what to do if the contents of the current layer exceed its borders.

Clip If you need to trim some of the edges of a layer's contents to fit within the layer borders, enter a value here.

You can set properties for more than one layer. To do so, select the layers you want to format one at a time, and then enter specifications in the Property inspector.

> The last two items—Clip and Overflow—are only visible when you click the expander arrow to display the bottom half of the Property inspector.

Changing Units of Measurement

By default, layer measurements are expressed in pixels, but you can change this if you're used to working with inches or centimeters. The ability to adjust units of measurement is especially handy if you're using a tracing image that was designed in a common measurement used in printing, such as points or picas. Table 5.1 describes the different layer measurements you can use in the Property inspector.

UNIT	ABBREVIATION	DESCRIPTION
Pixels	Px	Used in computer graphics; approximately 72 pixels equal one inch.
Points	Pt	Twelve points equal one pica; 72 points equal one inch.
Picas	Pc	Approximately 6 picas equal one inch.
Inches	In	Unit of measurement commonly used in the United States.
Centimeters	Cm	2.54 centimeters equal one inch.
Millimeters	Mm	10 millimeters equal one centimeter.
Percentages	%	Expresses size in relation to the size of the parent layer, if the current layer is nested.

Table 5.1

Units of Measurement

> You don't need to capitalize measurements when you enter them, but they do need to follow a numeric value without a space (for instance, 3px or 12pi).

Working with Complex Page Layouts

Tables and layers share a lot of common characteristics: they can contain images and text; they can be assigned background colors; they can be resized; and they can be used to design all or part of a web page.

The differences between tables and layers mean that, for many complex web designs, it's a good idea to combine the two types of objects. Layers, unlike tables, can overlap other objects. On the other hand, layers don't have visible borders that can be assigned a color and given different widths like tables. Tables give you great control over cell padding and cell spacing, and they're visible to virtually all browsers.

Dreamweaver gives you the best of both worlds by enabling you to use both layers and tables in the same layout, and by letting you convert tables to layers and vice versa as needed.

Combining Tables and Layers

The flexibility with which Dreamweaver lets you use both tables and layers in the same page layout is one of its most powerful features. You can, for instance, draw a layer, position the text cursor within the layer, and then choose Insert → Table to place a table within that layer.

Why would you want to place a table inside a layer? Just click and drag the layer's selection handle to find out: When a table is inside a layer, you can move the table freely anywhere on the web page you're designing. You can even overlap tables, if you want, by containing them within layers.

Similarly, if you divide a web page into two or more columns using a table that contains all of the page's content, you can insert two or more overlapping layers into a single column. This not only breaks up a long column of text, but it also adds graphic interest to the page.

Switching between Tables and Layers

Another powerful layout feature is Dreamweaver's ability to convert tables to layers and layers to tables. Converting tables to layers and layers to tables allows you to adjust and optimize your page layout. Converting tables to layers enables you to position the contents within tables in precise, innovative ways.

TABLES VERSUS LAYERS: PROS AND CONS

When is it best to use a table, and when is it best to use a layer? Dreamweaver's flexibility means that this isn't an either/or decision. You can mix tables and layers in the same page. You can also begin working in layers and then convert the layers to tables, and vice versa.

One factor is your own working style. You might be attracted by the flexibility that layers give you in overlapping and stacking content. If so, you can design the page's content using layers. Use them when you need to bleed content over a page or overlap content.

You can then convert the layers to tables if you choose. Be aware, though, that you can't convert a single layer or table; you have to convert all the layers or tables on the page. You will also be unable to overlap or stack content if you switch from layers to tables.

To convert layers to a single table, choose Modify → Convert → Layers to Table. The Convert Layers To Table dialog box appears (see Figure 5.13).

When you're switching from a "layered" layout to one that uses tables, you are likely to end up with lots of tables of all shapes and sizes and a very complex layout. But you can control the conversion with one of the following options.

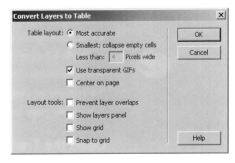

Most Accurate Choose this if you don't care how many table cells will be created—a cell will be created not only for each layer but also for the spaces between layers.

Smallest: Collapse Empty Cells This means fewer cells will be created, but your original "layered" layout might not be matched exactly.

Figure 5.13

If you convert layers to a table, you can choose options that control how accurately your original layout is duplicated.

Use Transparent GIFs If you choose this, a series of transparent GIF images is inserted in the bottom row of the table in order to keep the other rows the same size as in your original layout.

> If your layout contains overlapping layers, they won't be converted to a table. You'll have to separate the layers in order to convert them.

Converting a table to layers is similar: choose Modify → Convert → Tables to Layers. The table cells that contain content will be converted to layers, and the Document window will display the grid so that you can reposition the layers if needed. In addition, the Layers panel will open with a list of the layers that have been created.

WHAT HTML CAN AND CANNOT DO

Dreamweaver can enable you to achieve many complex design effects on a web page by combining tables and layers, but it can't do everything. It is limited by the limitations of HTML. Because HTML isn't a sophisticated layout language like PostScript (which is used by page layout programs like Adobe PageMaker) it can't handle these tasks:

- Run text around in a circle or abstract design
- Create gradations of color or grayscale
- Allow you to draw circles, polygons, or other complex shapes

  However, you *can* get some of these effects by creating an image in a graphics program. Just create a file that contains the effects you want in a page layout or graphics program, then save the image in GIF, JPEG, or PNG format, and insert it on your web page. (See the bonus graphics chapter on the CD for more about understanding web graphic formats and optimizing images for the Web.)

Hands On: Design a Page with Tables and Layers

Now you can try out some of the ways you can use layers and tables to design a web page. You'll open a tracing image, create a table, add layers, and nest a table inside another table. All of these techniques will help you duplicate an existing printed page design.

In the Chapter 5 folder on the accompanying CD, copy the folder complex_layout to your computer. Start Dreamweaver, and open a new blank page. If you want a preview of the completed page, you can open complex.htm, which is also in the Chapter 5 folder. The completed page is shown in Figure 5.14.

Open the Tracing Image

Begin by loading a tracing image that you can try to duplicate using layers and tables. Follow these steps:

1. Choose View → Tracing Image → Load.

2. Locate the file tracing.jpg in the Chapter 5 folder on the CD, and click Open.

3. In the Page Properties dialog box, adjust the Image Transparency slider to 50%.

4. Click OK.

Figure 5.14

This web page combines tables and layers for complex layout effects.

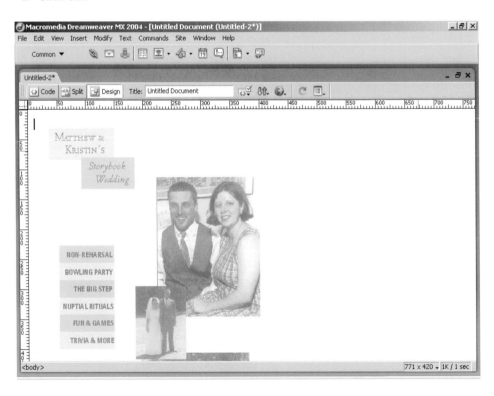

Add a Table

Next, you'll create a table to contain the page's contents. The primary purpose of the table is to provide a three-column layout. You could trace the layout using only layers, but the table will allow you to create the middle column. The middle column is needed in order to anchor both graphics and photos.

1. Switch to Layout mode and click Draw Layout Cell.

2. Draw the first table cell so that it aligns with the right edge of the yellow box. Drag the bottom of the cell all the way to the bottom of the tracer image.

3. Draw the other two table cells as shown in Figure 5.15.

Add Layers

The easiest way to duplicate the graphics and photos in the tracing image is to draw layers over each of them. The layers can overlap, just like the elements in the tracing image.

1. Click the Standard button in the Layout Insert bar.

2. Click the Draw Layer icon, also in the Layout Insert bar.

3. Draw a layer over the yellow box.

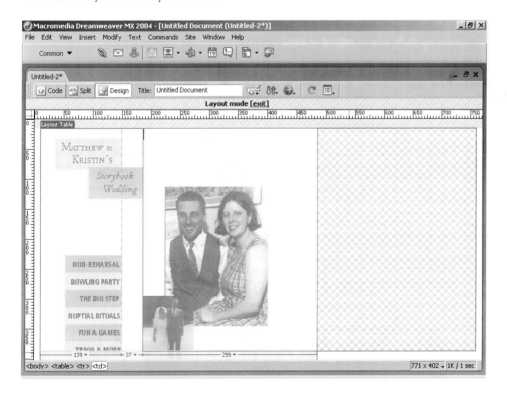

Figure 5.15

Drawing a table to enclose the web page contents and establish a three-column layout

4. Draw a layer over the light red box, overlapping the first and second columns of the table you drew earlier.

5. Draw layers over each of the photos.

Wherever photos overlap in the tracing image, you should first trace the photos in the back—the photos that are partially hidden. Trace each photo completely, even if part of it is behind another photo. Then trace the photos that are in front. That way, the layers you draw will overlap just like the photos in the tracing image.

6. Make sure the layers overlap the tracing image graphics and photos as closely as possible. Select each layer's selection handle and move it by adjusting the border if needed.

Insert Graphics

Next, you add graphics to each of the layers you created.

1. Position the cursor in the topmost layer and choose Insert → Image.

2. In the Select Image Source dialog box, choose `Logo1.gif` and click Select.

3. Resize the image to fit in the layer by clicking the handle in the lower-right corner, pressing Shift, and dragging inward.

4. Repeat steps 1 through 3 for each of the following images, from top to bottom: `logo2.gif`, `photo1.jpg`, `photo2.jpg`, and `photo3.jpg`.

Create a Navigation Bar

Next, you create a navigation bar in the left column of the table.

1. Draw a layer over the set of links on the left side of the tracing image.

2. Position the text cursor in the layer.

3. Choose Insert → Image, and insert the file `links1.gif`.

4. Resize the image so that it fits within the table.

5. Repeat steps 3 and 4 for `links2.gif` through `links6.gif`.

6. Associate each of the image files with a link.

7. Save your changes, and check your work.

Hopefully this tutorial has acquainted you with some of the ways you can use layers and tables to design a web page. You learned why tables are good for giving structure to a web page, and why layers are good when you need more flexibility and need to overlap objects.

Filling the News Hole

In the magazine business, the space between the ads and design elements on a printed page is sometimes referred to as the "news hole"—the place where you provide real content, in the form of words. The next chapter talks about managing the words on web pages.

## CHAPTER 6

Inserting and Formatting Text Content

In the beginning, there was the word, but now we've got pulsating 3D graphics, animated screechfests, and shiny, beveled, squirmy navigation. But guess what, most—nearly all—of the information on the Web is in the form of plain old text. Yes, it helps if the design of the page is clean and the copy is well groomed. We'll get to that. But in the excitement of interactive networked multimedia, don't overlook the most powerful medium of them all: the written word.

In this chapter, you'll learn about the following topics:

- Getting words onto pages

- Importing copy from Word and Excel documents

- Editing and proofreading copy

- Designing with text (format and style), design, and style

- Cleaning up HTML directly

- Creating complex layouts by combining tables and layers

Getting Copy onto the Page

Before you start inserting text willy-nilly, it helps to gather all your content assets together. As discussed in Chapter 2, "Web Pages Deconstructed," you must try to gather together all of your text content (also known as *copy*) in advance of building your site. At the very least, put together a strict submission, edit, and review schedule with some padding so that you don't hold up a launch because the copy isn't ready.

Chances are, you will have to manage copy coming from multiple sources. When this is the case, it can help if you establish what format you'd prefer to receive the copy in (such as Word documents, plain text, HTML files, and so on). Generally, it's preferable to keep the source copy as plain as possible (although fairly standard ways of indicating emphasis, such as Italics and boldface, can usually survive the importing process) so you minimize the amount of inappropriate formatting or badly formed HTML tags you have to strip away when you go to clean up the copy.

There are three main ways to get text content onto web pages in Dreamweaver:

- Copy the text from the source document and paste it into the page in Dreamweaver.
- Import the text from Microsoft Word.
- Type the text directly.

They're all pretty easy. In fact, if you're at all used to working with word processing programs, then you should find that most of the text-handling you'll have to do feels very familiar.

Inserting Text with Copy and Paste

Copy and paste is not the most powerful method for getting text onto a page, but it's extremely convenient, especially when the source text is not yet formatted (because Dreamweaver will only paste the plain text). The method should be utterly familiar to you already:

1. Select the text you want to copy in the source document.
2. Choose Edit → Copy (or Ctrl-C/Command-C).
3. Switch to Dreamweaver by your preferred method of switching programs.
4. Position the insertion point where you want the pasted text to appear in the web page.
5. Choose Edit → Paste Text.

Figure 6.1 shows some pasted plain text.

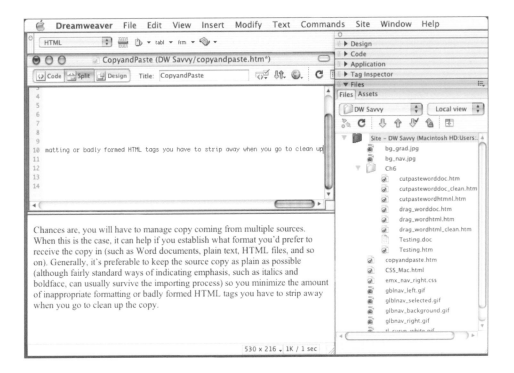

Figure 6.1

Whether the source of the copied text is a Word document, a web page, or an e-mail message, it gets pasted in without any formatting.

Copy and Paste from Word

Dreamweaver MX 2004 allows you to copy and paste directly from a Word document without saving it as HTML in Word. To preserve Word formatting, use Edit → Paste Formatted. If you don't want to preserve Word formatting, use Edit → Paste Text.

Would anyone ever need to keep Word's flavor of HTML in a document? Sure! For example, intranet users who have standardized on Microsoft Office and use Internet Explorer, Word, PowerPoint, and so on, seamlessly together might be perfectly comfortable with Word's non-compliant coding. It's also useful if you want to, for example, display a page sample from a Word document on a web page, and preserve Word styles and formatting. Remember—the only way to preserve Word formatting is to use the new Paste Formatted command.

You can also drag a Word document into a Dreamweaver page in Design view. The Insert Microsoft Word Or Excel Document dialog box appears (see Figure 6.2). Choose either Insert The Contents (if you want to paste the document to the current page) or

Create A Link (to link to the Word file). Any Word formatting will not be preserved in the pasted document. If you drag a Word HTML file into a Dreamweaver page, it will automatically create a link to the HTML file.

Microsoft has added Information Rights Management (IRM) to Word 2003 to allow document creators to restrict access to documents. An Internet Explorer (IE) feature is also available that allows visitors to view protected Word 2003 documents in IE if they have the appropriate permission. For more information, see `www.microsoft.com/office/editions/prodinfo/technologies/irm.mspx#XSLTsection128121120120`.

Importing Text and Tables

You can open a variety of document types in Dreamweaver, even if the files were originally created in another application. You can open HTML files as well as text files such as style sheets, JavaScript, XML, or plain text. Dreamweaver also includes special commands for use with Microsoft Word and Excel documents.

In addition to text documents and HTML files, Dreamweaver can also import *tabular* data, literally meaning information in tabular form (a table of rows and columns). That mainly means spreadsheet and database tables, which must be exported from their source applications using a standard text-with-delimiters format. But first, let's talk about Word documents.

Importing a Word Document

The Windows version of Dreamweaver MX 2004 enables you to import Word documents directly without first saving them as HTML documents in Word. First, open a new file from the Start page (or File → New), and then select File → Import → Word Document. The Word document will be pasted into your Dreamweaver file as plain text.

The Mac version of Dreamweaver MX 2004 does not include the Import Word Document or the Import Excel Document commands.

Figure 6.2

The Insert Microsoft Word Or Excel Document dialog box

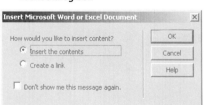

To open a Word file without importing it, the Word file should be saved in Word as an HTML file. (If you open a DOC file in Dreamweaver, the file displays with added garbage characters that you have to manually remove.) Word has a normal Save As command with which you can specify HTML format—the option is listed as Web Page (*.htm, *.html) in the Save As dialog box—and it also has a dedicated Save As Web Page format on the File menu. Similarly, you can open a Word HTML file in Dreamweaver the same way you open any document (use File → Open, or Ctrl-O/Command-O).

Clean Up Word HTML

Word HTML is messy and includes many tags that do not comply with standards. Open the Clean Up Word HTML dialog box (Command → Clean Up Word HTML) to remove extra HTML code generated by Word (see Figure 6.3).

> Importing from Word in HTML format and then cleaning up the HTML might render the file illegible to Word, so make sure you have saved a copy of the original document before you clean up the HTML version. If you're using Word 2003, however, you can still open the file in Word after a cleanup of the HTML in Dreamweaver.

The options on this dialog box are on two tabs (Basic and Detailed); you might as well look at them all at least once. After the first time you clean up some Word HTML, the dialog box uses your previous selections as the default. Be sure to select the version of Word the imported document was created in with the Clean Up HTML From drop-down list (the command is available for Word 97 or later Word documents).

The basic choices clean up the majority of Word's most egregious HTML output:

Remove all Word-specific markup This option is self-explanatory. If it's only in there to help Word display the document and it's not real HTML, chuck it.

Clean up CSS Takes out any redundant, unused, or nonstandard style declarations (more about Cascading Style Sheets [CSS] in Chapter 9).

Clean up <font> tags Fixes Word's habit of wrapping <font> tags around other tags.

Fix invalidly nested tags Corrects tag entanglements that can render a design incorrectly in a strict browser.

Set background color Reminds you that Word HTML documents will get a default gray background unless you set the background to White (#FFFFFF) or some other color.

Apply source formatting Permits Dreamweaver to apply your specified Code Format preferences (Edit → Preferences → Code Format).

Show log on completion Gives you a detailed "receipt" of all the changes made, which are especially useful in case anything goes wrong with the cleanup.

The choices on the Detailed tab differ depending on the version of Word from which you are importing. If the document was created in Word 97 (for Windows) or

Figure 6.3

We generally use all of the available options unless we have a specific reason to preserve some Word-style HTML.

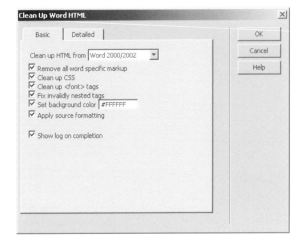

Word 98 (for the Mac), then the Detailed tab offers more choices about Word-specific markup and cleaning up `<font>` tags:

- If you checked Remove All Word Specific Markup on the Basic tab, then the Remove Word Specific Markup check box and the Word Meta And Link Tags From `<head>` check box will both be checked on this tab. (If not, not.) The only variation besides having them both checked or both not is having the first checked and the second (relating to the `<head>` portion of the web page) not.

- If you checked Clean Up `<font>` Tags on the Basic tab, then the same option will be checked on the Detailed tab, along with a set of mapping suggestions for Word's use of font sizes 1 through 7. (Dreamweaver suggests turning size 7 into a first-level header, size 6 into a second-level header, and so on, but you can assign any size to any standard HTML formatting tag. (More about HTML tags later in this chapter.)

If the document was created in Word 2000/2002, then the Detailed tab offers different choices for Word-specific markup and some detailed choices about cleaning up CSS:

- If you checked Remove All Word Specific Markup on the Basic tab, then Remove Word Specific Markup will appear checked here with five suboptions—XML From `<html>` Tag: Word Meta And Link Tags From `<head>`, As With Word 97/98; Word XML Markup; Word-Style Conditional Tags (of no use outside of Word); and Remove Empty Paragraphs And Margins From Styles. Unless you specifically know what you're doing with one of these choices, leave them all checked!

- If you checked Clean Up CSS on the Basic tab, then the same option will be checked here with five suboptions—Remove Inline CSS Styles When Possible; Remove Any Style Attribute That Starts With "mso"; Remove Any Non-CSS Style Declaration; Remove All CSS Styles From Table Rows And Cells, And Remove All Unused Style Definitions. Again, unless you're a CSS maven, leave these checked.

Dreamweaver does not yet include a Word 2003 option for Clean Up Word HTML.

When you're ready to clean up the imported page, click OK. Dreamweaver may take a while to crunch through the file if it's complicated. When finished, Dreamweaver displays the changes.

You can undo or redo a Clean Up Word HTML command, as needed.

Using Excel Documents in Dreamweaver

Dreamweaver MX 2004 allows you to copy and paste directly from an Excel document. To best preserve Excel formatting, use Edit → Paste Formatted. If you don't want to preserve Excel formatting, use Edit → Paste Text to paste unformatted plain text. For an intermediate choice, choose Edit → Paste; this creates an HTML table, but the formatting is not as close to the original as in the Paste Formatted command. See Figure 6.4 for a comparison between the Paste and Paste Formatted options for Excel.

You can also drag an Excel document into a Dreamweaver page in Design view. The Insert Microsoft Word or Excel Document dialog box appears (see Figure 6.2). Choose either Insert The Contents (if you want to paste the document to the current page) or Create A Link (to link to the Excel file). The inserted contents display the same as in the Edit → Paste option discussed in the previous paragraph. Dreamweaver MX 2004 enables you to import Excel documents directly, in .xls format, and converts this to HTML output. Select File → Import → Excel Document. The HTML representation of the Excel document is the same as that for the Edit → Paste option.

Importing Tabular Data

If you need to import a portion of a non-Excel spreadsheet or a database table, you must first export or save the source data as a tab-delimited text file. *Delimiter* is a computer-science word meaning something that indicates the limit of a field entry—the database equivalent of punctuation. A tab-delimited file separates each field in a record (or cell in a row) from the other fields (cells) using the tab character (or ASCII character 9, for obscurantists). Dreamweaver will actually support any delimiter character you want, but tab is often the only choice that Dreamweaver supports correctly.

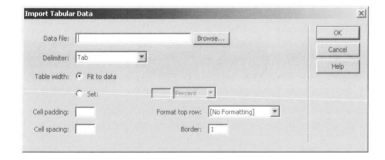

You can also use this option for Excel files if you export them from Excel as tab-delimited text files. Figure 6.5 shows the Excel file from Figure 6.4 after import to Dreamweaver as a tab-delimited text file.

In most spreadsheet and database programs, you do this by selecting File → Save As, and then choosing an option along the lines of "Text (Tab Delimited File)." Pick a filename, save it, and as always, note where you are saving the file.

Figure 6.4

Dreamweaver's new Paste Formatted option preserves the Excel format. The Paste option creates an HTML table, but most of the original formatting is not preserved.

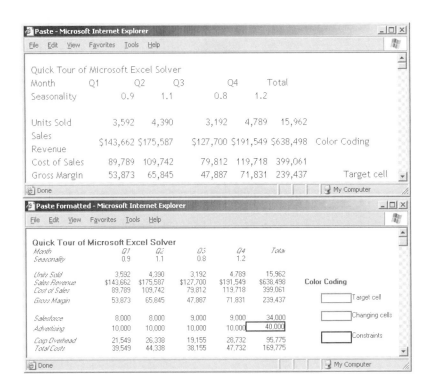

Back in Dreamweaver, select File → Import → Import Tabular Data (or choose the Tabular Data button on the Layout Insert bar to bring up this dialog box.)

Click the Browse button and find the text document you just saved. Make sure the delimiter shows Tab selected. If you want to control the width of the table in advance, click Set and enter a width in pixels or as a percentage of the browser window. A few more table formatting options are available (but remember, you can format this table all you want once you get the dang thing imported): Cell padding, Cell spacing, Border (set to 1 pixel by default), and Format top row, which has space options of Bold, Italic, and… wait for it, Bold Italic. When you become overjoyed with your choices (or before), click OK.

Entering Text Directly

The third, most humble way of getting text into Dreamweaver is by typing it yourself! Now, for any extended length of copy, this is probably not a good idea. Unless you are also the word-processing expert on the team (even then, I'd expect you'd prefer your own favorite word processor for the task), it's probably not the best use of your time. But for small segments of copy, headlines, and minor changes, Dreamweaver is perfectly serviceable. For the purposes of entering text, Dreamweaver more or less functions like a word processor.

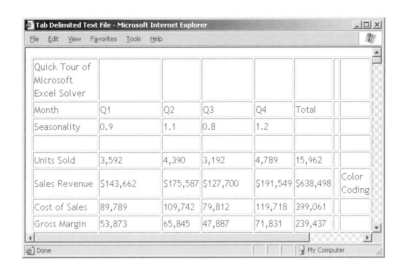

Figure 6.5

Importing an Excel document as a tab-delimited text file

So just position the insertion point and type. To insert line breaks (single) instead of paragraph breaks (double), use Shift-Enter (or choose the Characters category from the HTML Insert bar and click the Line Break option).

You can also format on the fly if you like. To do so, just boldface a selection or text you're about to type by first pressing Ctrl-B/Command-B or by clicking the Bold button on the Property inspector, as we'll get to soon.

Inserting Special Characters

HTML supports a number of other symbols (mostly commerce and typographical), a few of the most useful of which are on the Characters category of the Text Insert bar (see Table 6.1).

ENTITY	APPEARANCE	USE
non-breaking space		When multiple spaces are needed or a pair of words needs to be kept together around line breaks
copyright	©	Used to assert copyright
registered	®	Used to indicate a registered trademark or service mark
trademark	™	Used to indicate a trademark
Pound	£	British currency
Yen	¥	Japanese currency
Euro	€	European currency
left quotation mark	"	Curly, smart quote marks look better in print than the old inch mark (")
right quotation mark	"	Same as above. They do, really.
em-dash	—	Used for punctuation (not supported by all browsers)

Table 6.1

Special Characters

Can't find the Characters category? Click on the down-pointing arrow on the BR icon in the Text Insert bar to display the full Characters menu.

There's also the very useful Other option on the Characters category (the last choice). It brings up a larger selection of special characters in a big dialog box (see Figure 6.6).

Choose the character you want to insert and click OK.

Inserting Dates

You can insert the current date and time into a document at any time by clicking the Date button on the Common Insert bar (or by choosing Insert → Date). Choose a date and time format in the Insert Date dialog box that appears.

You can leave off the day of the week or the time if you like. The cool part is the Update Automatically On Save check box at the bottom. If you choose that, then the date always shows the day (or even time) of the last change to the document, which can be useful for your readers in a "This page was last updated…" kind of way when you post your pages live.

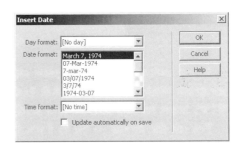

Figure 6.6
For each of these choices, Dreamweaver shows you if it's going to use an entity code (® for ®, for example) or a numerical code (— for —, for example), but this is only useful information if you discover that something is not displaying right.

The Text in Persistent Page Elements

There are a few other ways that text might appear on one of your pages. Any text in the template used to create your page, for example, will end up on the new page, either editable or not. (See Chapter 4, "Saving Labor with Templates and Libraries," for the skinny on templates and their editable areas.)

You can also use a Server-side include (SSI) to add any content to your pages (Chapter 4 also explains how to work with SSIs). If you do this, then that content won't appear on the page in Dreamweaver or in a preview. To view the complete page, you'll need to view it in a browser directly from the server that is handling the include statements. You can edit the included file, of course, but you have to open it separately to do so.

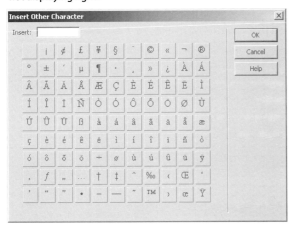

Editing Text

As with text entry, text editing in Dreamweaver is very similar to text editing in any standard word processing program. You select text by clicking and dragging. You delete a selection by pressing Delete. You can cut (Ctrl-X/Command-X), copy (Ctrl-C/Command-C), or paste (Ctrl-V/Command-V) a selection. And you can drag and drop a selection. As with other word-processing tasks, it doesn't make sense to do too much text editing in Dreamweaver, but for spot corrections here and there it's a breeze.

Spell Checking

To check the spelling of a document (or a selection), select Text → Check Spelling (or press Shift-F7). If Dreamweaver finds any questionable spellings, it will bring up the Check Spelling dialog box (if not, it will pop up a "Spelling Check Completed" message, and you'll have to click OK to continue).

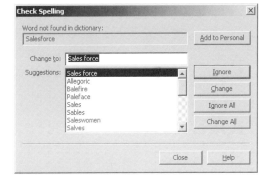

The dialog box indicates the suspect word (anything not listed in Dreamweaver's dictionary nor added by you in the past). As with spellcheckers in word processors, the dialog box will suggest alternative spellings when possible. Your choices are as follows:

- Accept the top suggestion (listed in the Change To box), select another suggestion, or type your own corrected spelling in the Change To box and then click the Change button (to correct the misspelled word this one time), or the Change All button (to correct it throughout the page).

- Click the Add To Personal button to add the suspect word to your personal dictionary (as when the word is a proper name or other jargon you expect to encounter repeatedly).

- Click the Ignore button to skip the word this one time.

- Click the Ignore All button to skip this word throughout the page.

After you make your decision, Dreamweaver will repeat the process until it reaches the end of the page, at which point it will tell you that it has completed the spelling check and you'll need to click OK to finish.

Editing with Find and Replace

Let's say that you're almost done building a company's site when you learn that the company is changing its name from, say, Dynergix to EnerGlobe, and this means you've got to change any references to the old name throughout the site. Dreamweaver can help.

To find all the instances of a specific word, phrase, or string of characters, use Dreamweaver's find and replace feature, which is—again—analogous to that in word processing programs but is more powerful: you can use it to make changes across multiple files, or even to your entire site.

To start searching, choose Edit → Find And Replace (Ctrl-F/Command-F).

Find Options

In the dialog box that appears, first decide the scope of your search. Dreamweaver MX 2004 has added additional options to the Find In drop-down menu. Your choices are:

Current Document searches the currently active document.

Open Documents searches all currently open documents.

Entire Current Local Site searches all files in the current site, including library items and text documents.

Selected Files in Site searches files and folders selected in the Files panel.

Folder searches a specific folder.

Selected Text searches the text that's currently selected in the active document.

Most of the time, you'll want to leave the Search drop-down menu on Text, although for a company name change, you'd want to make sure that the change is made throughout the HTML code as well, especially in the title section of any page! (See "Working with Raw HTML" later in this chapter, for more on the tag-related choices in this list.) Naturally, you'll need to type or insert the text you're searching for in the Find box (see Figure 6.7).

Use Ctrl-Enter/Command-Return if you need to insert a line break. (Use copy and paste if you need to insert a new paragraph break.)

Figure 6.7

The Find And Replace dialog box

Then in the Replace box, type or paste the new text with which you're replacing the old text.

- Use the Match Case check box to choose text that matches the case of the selection.

- Use Match Whole Word to search only for complete words.

- Leave Ignore Whitespace checked unless you have a good reason for caring about things like line breaks in the HTML code.

- Use Regular Expression if you are familiar with Unix-type search syntax. Regular expressions are patterns of character combinations, and make an extremely powerful search tool. If you are doing an advanced search—for example, all attribute values that contain an uppercase *A*, regular expressions are an extremely useful tool.

> Basic regular expression syntax is not difficult to learn. Check the Dreamweaver manual and help pages—they are the same—for a table of regular expressions with some explanation, or books such as *Perl, CGI, and JavaScript Complete, Second Edition* (Sybex, 2003), or *Mastering PHP 4.1*, by Jeremy Allen and Charles Hornberger (Sybex, 2002). Perl is the language best known for its use of regular expressions.

If you expect that you'll need to do this same search again repeatedly, you can save the search by clicking the Save Query button (the now old-fashioned-looking disk icon). Dreamweaver saves the query with a `.dwr` file extension. If you open this file, you'll see that it's an XML file.

> For additional information about XML, see Chapter 24, "Working with XML and XHTML."

To reuse a saved search, click the Load Query icon and browse to the saved query file. Saved queries from older versions of Dreamweaver may have a `.dwq` file extension.

> If you save or reuse a search, you'll notice that Dreamweaver calls this saving or loading a *query*, not saving a search—it amounts to the same thing. Query is just computer-science jargon for the request being put to the search function.

Executing the Search

To search for one instance of the text at a time, click the Find Next button. If Dreamweaver finds the text, it will highlight the selection for you, opening the page first if necessary.

To find all the instances of the text at once, click the Find All button. If the Results panel isn't currently open, Dreamweaver will open it to show you its progress:

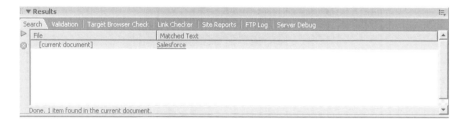

If you are hunting for your items one at a time, you can decide whether to replace each one individually.

- To make the change, click the Replace button. Dreamweaver will execute the replacement.
- To continue the search without replacing the current instance, click the Find Next button.

Either way, Dreamweaver will then automatically look for the next instance of your item. If it doesn't find any more items, it will tell you the search is done.

If you're comfortable making all the changes at once, click the Replace All button (you can do this even if you've already been using the more conservative one-at-a-time Find Next button).

Be careful not to globally replace something with nothing across your search domain by clicking Replace All when the Replace box is empty (that is, unless you do want to snip some text out everywhere).

When you're done with your replace operation, click the Close button. If you were using the box just to find stuff and not replace it, you can find that same stuff again at any time (until you go and find something else) without opening the Find and Replace dialog box by pressing F3/Command-G.

You can use the Search panel, part of the Results panel group, to work with a search result in context. After performing a Find All search, double-click a line in the Search panel. If the search involves only the current file, the search result is highlighted in Design and Code view in the Document window. If the search involves a group of files, the file containing the search result opens, and the search result is also highlighted in Design and Code view.

Formatting Text

There are several ways to format text, each with its own pros and cons:

- Apply standard HTML formatting with the Property inspector (we'll get to this in the next section).

- Use Cascading Style Sheets (CSS) either within a page or linked from a central location.

- For precise control over typeface and appearance, create graphical text.

We recommend using CSS (see Chapter 9, "Cascading Style Sheets," for more details), but we'll touch on each of these three options in this section. First, it helps to know a little about the basic formatting that is supported by the HTML standard and thus by most or all browsers.

Widely Supported Text Formatting

One of the longstanding ideals of the Web is that form should follow function, and that the formatting, layout, and style (usually called the *design* or *presentation*) of a document are not as important as the information (the *content*) displayed in it. Of course this is overly simplified—the presentation of information plays a large role in its comprehensibility and usefulness, and in the likelihood that it will get used.

Nonetheless, the goal of keeping the design separate from the information and its structure makes good sense. By structure, we mean information about the purpose of each text element (such as whether it's a heading, a caption, and so on), as opposed to the physical design of the copy, meaning its typeface, weight, color, size, and so on. Both cascading style sheets (see Chapter 9) and database-backed sites (see Chapter 19, "Database Connectivity") offer ways of separating content and presentation.

Having said all that, the fact remains that there are certain formatting tags long accepted in the HTML standard, and chances are you'll be using at least some of these in your work:

- Basic typographical enhancements, such as bold and Italic, that are interpreted essentially the same way in almost all contexts.

For web-standards compliance and improved accessibility, the `<strong>` and `<em>` tags are preferred over the `<b>` and `<i>` tags. You can choose this option in Preferences → General.

- Standard HTML that communicates structure, such as bulleted and numbered lists.

- Left, center, and right alignment methods that correctly comply with HTML by adding an `align=` attribute to the paragraph or heading tag, or by wrapping a `<div>` (divider) tag containing the correct `align=` attribute around the selection.

- Structural tags that have been unofficially associated with certain text effects. For example, there's the way Dreamweaver uses the `<blockquote>` tag to produce indentation effects—this does not comply with the spirit of HTML standards, although it may validate just fine because a validator can't tell semantically whether the text is actually a quotation or not.

- The `<font>` tag-based formatting that, for the time being, works correctly on most browsers. For example, providing a list of preferred typefaces in descending order or specifying a color for the text can be accomplished safely with `<font>`, whereas specifying the type *size* consistently across platforms and browsers is not always possible with that same tag.

Formatting Text with the Property Inspector

The Property inspector makes it really easy to apply most basic formatting options to a selection. To use it, first select the text you want to format. Then, choose the formatting options you want. Not all available text formatting options are on the Property inspector. The Text menu contains a few more—which we'll get to in a moment. Instead of just walking you around the panel, we'll cover the choices in conceptual groups:

- Phrase elements (also called character formatting or text styles)
- Fonts and font lists (typefaces)
- Size
- Color
- Paragraph formats
- Alignment
- Indentation
- Style

> If you need to apply the same formatting to a number of different items, do the first one and then, for the rest, just make the selection and then press Ctrl-Y/Command-Y (or choose Edit → Redo *Last Action*).

Phrase Elements

To boldface or italicize a selection, just click the Bold or Italic button. For other standard HTML character formatting, use the Text → Style submenu. Additional choices include the following:

Strikethrough Not universally supported.

Teletype Traditionally used for monospaced characters.

Emphasis Conceptual, often interpreted as Italic and preferred for accessibility reasons over the Italic format because it communicates the purpose of the formatting instead of its appearance.

Strong Conceptual, often interpreted as boldface and preferred for accessibility reasons over the bold format.

Code Used to display lines of code examples, including scripting languages and markup tags, mainly useful for technical writing, usually interpreted as a monospaced font.

Variable Used to display computer programming-code variables, useful mainly for technical writing, interpreted as Italic by most recent browsers.

Sample Used to display sample computer program or script output in technical writing; again, usually monospaced.

Keyboard Used in technical writing to indicate text, often code, that the reader should type, usually monospaced.

Citation Used for citations, usually interpreted as Italic.

Definition Used for the first or defining appearance of a word or phrase in a document.

> You can override a browser's default interpretation of any of these formats using a style sheet (see Chapter 9). You can also apply a longer list of formatting effects, including superscript and subscript.

Fonts and Font Lists

Although applying typefaces using the `font` tag is no longer the preferred method, it is widely supported by most browsers and is still the most common way of controlling typeface. Because you can't be sure what typefaces (fonts) your users have available, it's customary to specify a list of fonts in descending order of preference, such as "Arial, Helvetica, sans-serif." Using this example, if the system has Arial installed, then that font will be used. If not, it will check for Helvetica and use that if possible. Failing that, it will use whatever default sans-serif font is installed. (*Sans serif* is French for "without little thingies on the tips of the letters.")

   The Property inspector offers a few lists of commonly available fonts:

- Arial, Helvetica, sans-serif
- Times New Roman, Times, serif
- Courier New, Courier, mono

- Georgia, Times New Roman, Times, serif

- Verdana, Arial, Helvetica, sans-serif

- Geneva, Arial, Helvetica, sans-serif

To choose one, click the Font drop-down menu arrow.

If you want to make your own list of preferred fonts, choose Edit Font List from the Font drop-down menu to bring up this dialog box.

Choose an available font from among those installed on your system (or one of the HTML-defined generic font types, including Cursive, Fantasy, Monospace, Sans-serif, or Serif) from the Available Fonts list box or type the name of a font not present on your Dreamweaver list in the text box below and then click the button with the left-pointing

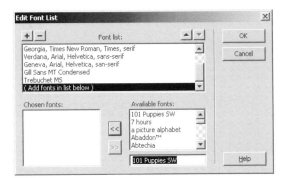

guillemet (<<) to add a font to the new sequence in your font list. Repeat to add a second choice (if you wish), a third, and so on. If you change your mind about a font, highlight it and click the right-pointing button (>>) to remove it from the choices.

To add another sequence to the list, click the button with the plus (+) sign. To remove a sequence, highlight it and click the button with the minus (–) sign. To rearrange the order of the list, click the up-arrow or down-arrow buttons. When you're done editing the font list, click OK.

Size

The Size menu options vary depending on the file that's active. If no styles are specified, you can choose a size number ranging from 1 to 7 (with 3 being the default), or you can choose a size *change*, either ranging from –7 to –1 or from +1 to +7. How the exact size or size change is rendered depends on the browser and varies from one platform to the next. The Size drop-down menu includes all of these options. Choose one to apply it to the selected text.

FULL UNICODE SUPPORT

Dreamweaver MX 2004 offers full Unicode support, so it supports all text encodings supported by Internet Explorer. In the New Document category of Dreamweaver preferences (Edit → Preferences), you can not only specify a default encoding type, but you can also choose a Unicode normalization form and a Unicode signature (byte order mark). For more information on Unicode, see the home page at www.unicode.org.

In a file that includes style information, the size menu displays a range of standard text sizes in pixels, points, or ems, depending on the current style options. The text measurement options (pixels, points, ems, %, etc.) can be changed in the drop-down menu next to the Size list.

> Relative units (such as ems and exs) are preferred over absolute units (such as points and picas) because they give the viewer more choice and make your page more accessible to users with visual disabilities. For example, if you use em to specify the text size, then the text will scale to the appropriate size when the user chooses to make the text larger or smaller in a browser. For more information on type sizing and relative and absolute units, see "Typography Measurements" at http://webdesign.about.com/cs/typemeasurements/.

Color

As with the other `<font>` tag-based formatting options, setting text color this way is now considered less desirable than using Cascading Style Sheets (Chapter 9), but if you want to add spot color to a selection on the fly, it's awfully convenient. To color a selection, click the color selector on the Property inspector (hey, that rhymes).

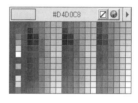

Dreamweaver will only offer web-safe colors unless you override the default (by unchecking Snap To Web Safe on the drop-down menu you get to by clicking the right-pointing arrow in the upper-right corner of the color picker—do this only when you are sure that the systems that will be used to view the site can handle a wider range of colors).

> See the bonus chapter on the CD for in-depth information about web graphic file formats as well as the web-safe color palette, and Chapter 9 for details on setting page colors with style sheets.

Paragraph Formats

Most stretches of text in web pages are treated as paragraphs, except for headings, lists, or what's called "preformatted" text, which basically means plain text rendered exactly as is from the original source. To change a selection to (or back to) the paragraph type, to a type of heading, or to preformatted text, click the Format drop-down menu and choose Paragraph, Heading 1 through Heading 6, or Preformatted. Headings are generally rendered in descending sizes, with boldface, although heading formatting can be customized with style sheets, which by now you should know will be discussed in Chapter 9!

There's an old HTML tag called <address> that is used to indicate, well, an address, and is usually rendered as Italic. Dreamweaver doesn't directly support it, but it knows about it (Dreamweaver also displays it as Italic if you insert it). The only way to apply this tag is to enter it directly in Code view. I'll explain about how to do that kind of thing in the last section of this chapter, "Working with Raw HTML."

Various Types of Lists

Similar to paragraph formats are list formats—in that they apply to sections of text and not to specific individual characters. There are several types of lists, each of which has different kinds of items in it, but the first two types of list are by far the most common. The list types are as follows:

- Unordered list (bullets)
- Ordered list (numbers)
- Definition list
- Directory list
- Menu list

To format a selection as an unordered list, click the Bulleted List button in the Property inspector. To make a selection into an ordered list, click the Numbered List button.

Definition lists have two types of items, terms and definitions. To make a definition list, select Text → List → Definition List. Dreamweaver automatically treats the first item in the list as a term, the second as a definition, and so on, alternating.

To make a Directory or Menu list, first create an unordered list and then choose Text → List → Properties to bring up the List Properties dialog box. Then choose the type of list you want from the List Type drop-down menu.

You can also use this dialog box to customize your bullets or numbering system. To customize the entire list, select a bullet or numbering type in the Style pop-up menu. Dreamweaver supports round (Hollow Bullet) and square (Square) bullets—although the HTML spec provides for a third kind (Disc—Solid Bullet)—and five numbering schemes:

- Number (1, 2, 3…)
- Roman Small (i, ii, iii…)
- Roman Large (I, II, III…)
- Alphabet Small (a, b, c…)
- Alphabet Large (A, B, C…)

You know—the familiar choices from outline numbering—imagine that you're back in some college-level class, copying copious amounts of information from a blackboard that's about to be erased.

You can also start the numbering somewhere besides at *1*. (Use a numeral in the Start count textbox, even if the list type is Roman or Alphabet. For example, if you want the list to start numbering at c, enter 3 in the Start count textbox in the List Properties dialog box.)

The List Item part of the dialog box enables you to override the list style for a specific item or restart the numbering of the list with that item.

> HTML and Dreamweaver also support lists within lists. For example, to create a bulleted list within another bulleted list, first apply the bulleted list formatting to the entire list. Then select the items for the sublist and click the text indent button. Dreamweaver will indent the sublist and—for bullets—change the graphical element to indicate another layer down (such as using hollow bullets instead of solid ones for these items).

Alignment

Dreamweaver handles alignment in a way that's smart and compliant with HTML standards. If the selection is a paragraph, Dreamweaver adds the alignment information to the paragraph tag. If the selection is an item that doesn't permit alignment attributes, then Dreamweaver wraps a `<div>` tag around the selection and includes the alignment attribute there.

To align a stretch of text, select it, and then click the Align Left, Align Center, Align Right, or Justify buttons.

Indentation

Dreamweaver offers a serviceable, if not perfectly compliant, approach to indentation using a tag for block quotations. It's preferable to use style sheets (Chapter 9) for indentation, but if you must, indent a selection by clicking the Text Indent button or outdent it by clicking the Text Outdent button.

> If the selection is already flush left, the Text Outdent button won't do anything.

Style

The Style drop-down menu enables you to format selected text on your page. This menu displays the names of currently defined text styles for the page, and displays them graphically with the font family, font size, font weight, text color, and background color that are specified in the selected text style definition.

The Style menu also includes options for Rename and Manage Styles (opens the Edit Style Sheet window).

Graphical Text

If you want total control over the appearance of text (as you sometimes might when you are creating headlines, advertisements, and so on), then you're better off creating graphical or Flash text instead of relying on the vagaries of HTML. There are pros and cons to this approach:

It's not really text. One problem with graphical text is that it's actually graphics and not text. It may read just fine to the human eye, but from the computer's point of view, there's no text there. Be sure to include alternative text with any graphical text so that the information will still be available to those who cannot or do not want to view graphics. And don't forget that any additional graphics increase the download time for your page.

But it looks exactly right! The argument for graphical text is that it brings back the level of control over typography that designers have been accustomed to for years in print and other media. Of course, it may only look *exactly* right on your own screen. It's a funny thing about the Web, but you can never be sure exactly how things are going to look for others.

For more information on creating graphical text, see Chapter 10, "Adding Graphics and Multimedia." Creating Flash Text in Dreamweaver is covered in Chapter 11.

Working with Raw HTML

Hey, look, we're six chapters into this book and we've managed to pussyfoot around HTML this whole time! If you're determined to stay away from the code as much as possible, go ahead and skip this last section, but remember that all Dreamweaver really is—for the most part—is an HTML-generating program, a bunch of very clever labor-saving shortcuts for generating clean HTML code. And for that matter, there's no way that Dreamweaver can provide a widget for every conceivable HTML effect. The time may come when you need to edit the code yourself to accomplish the results you seek. When that time comes, this section will help you to have a clue about how HTML works and how Dreamweaver gives you direct access to it.

THERE'S NO ESCAPING HTML

Experienced hand-coders like the authors of this book tend to be somewhat biased. We think it helps to understand the HTML tags, CSS, and other standards used to build the Web. While we're sympathetic to those who'd rather keep things on a visual level, we feel that there are times when there's no substitute for rummaging through the code yourself and rooting out some entangled problem. If you come to agree with us, you may find yourself looking for more detailed sources of HTML information. Of course the best place to start is the World Wide Web Consortium site where the standards are maintained and promulgated (www.w3c.org), but you may want to refer to a book, such *Mastering HTML and XHTML* by Deborah and Erik Ray. (Sybex, 2002).

   Macromedia also thoughtfully provides an HTML reference in a help/reference-style panel (Window → Reference or Shift-F1). It's a customized interactive version of some other reference books.

Editing HTML in Code View or with the Code Inspector

As you already know if you read Chapter 2 of this book, Dreamweaver can display pages in Design view (what you see is what you get), Code view ("Just the HTML, ma'am"), or in a combined view.

When viewing both the design and code, don't lose track of which panel is active, or you may end up typing code into the Design view. You can switch between views with View → Switch Views.

To resize the Code view window, click the divider and drag it up or down.

Using the Quick Tag Editor

If you prefer to work in Design view, you can still edit tags directly using the Quick Tag Editor, which has three modes:

- Insert HTML mode (for inserting new HTML tags into a page)
- Edit Tag mode (for changing an existing tag)
- Wrap Tag mode (for wrapping an opening and closing tag pair around a selection).

The mode is selected depending on what you do before you invoke the Quick Tag Editor:

- To insert new HTML, just place the insertion point where you want the new code to go.

- To edit an existing tag, first click in Design view or select the object in Design view to which the tag applies and then click the tag you want in the tag selector at the bottom of the page window.

- To wrap a new tag around a selection, first select the text you want to wrap the tag around (it must currently be unformatted).

Then press Ctrl-T/Command-T or click the Quick Tag Editor icon on the right side of the Property inspector.

The Insert HTML (or Edit Tag or Wrap) dialog pops up showing either the opening and closing angle brackets of an HTML tag (</>) or—for the Edit Tag—the current tag itself. You can cycle through the three modes of the Quick Tag Editor by pressing Ctrl-T/Command-T.

```
Edit tag: <span
          style='color:red'>
```

Now type or edit the HTML code to your liking. Now here's the cool part. If you pause while editing the tag, Dreamweaver will offer you a pop-up list of valid attributes you can apply. If you're editing multiple tags in the Quick Tag Editor, use the Tab key to jump between them.

When you are done, press Enter and then press Esc to leave the Quick Tag Editor.

> For more details on editing code and using the Tag Inspector to edit or add attributes, see Chapter 18, "Handcrafting Your Code."

Finding and Replacing HTML Tags

Earlier in this chapter, when we discussed editing with Find And Replace, we mentioned that it's possible to use the same tool to make changes in source code. There are three different modes for doing this:

Source Code Works just like regular Find And Replace but sifts through the text in Code view instead of the text shown in Design view.

Specific Tag Works like an ordinary Find And Replace, but looks for a single tag in the code instead of a word in the ordinary text. You can also choose these additional options to further refine your search:

- *With Attribute:* searches for tags containing a specific attribute name (and optionally, a specific attribute value)

- *Without Attribute:* searches for tags that do not contain the specified attribute

- *Containing:* searches for tags that contain the specified text or another particular tag

- *Not Containing:* searches for tags that do not contain the specified text or another particular tag
- *Inside Tag:* searches for tags that are contained within a specified tag
- *Not Inside Tag:* searches for tags that are not contained within a specified tag

You can also further limit the search by clicking on the + (Plus) button to add additional combinations of the above constraints to the search.

Text (Advanced) Enables you to hunt for ordinary text based on the tags that are or are not surrounding it (see Figure 6.8). Choose Inside Tag or Not Inside Tag. You can also click the + (Plus) button to further refine your search with the options as listed for the Specific Tag search (With Attribute, Without Attribute, Containing, and Not Containing).

Layout, Words, Frames!

OK, so far in this part we've covered laying out web pages with tables and layers, and inserting and formatting text. In the next chapter, you'll learn how to display multiple HTML pages simultaneously, using frames (and when not to use frames at all).

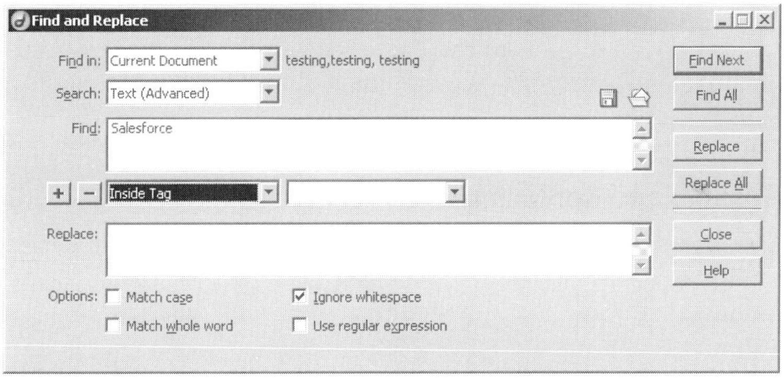

Figure 6.8

Choose Inside Tag or Not Inside Tag, select a tag, and then use the Plus (+) button to add further parameters, requiring or excluding attributes of certain values or ranges.

## CHAPTER 7

Interactivity with Frasemets and Frames

The first few chapters in this part showed you how to work with layouts and how to add and format text. Before we proceed to more objects you can add to a web page, such as hyperlinks, and how to format a page using Cascading Style Sheets, we'd first like to show you some further layout options in this chapter—frames and framesets.

Using frames and framesets enables you to display two or more web pages at the same time in a single browser window. A *frameset* page specifies the layout of the individual pages, or *frames*, that make up the page. A web page can be divided into two or more frames; each contains an individual web page with its own URL, content, and hyperlinks.

This chapter examines the ways you can use frames to your benefit and add interactivity to your site; luckily, Dreamweaver makes it a matter of point-and-click. The following topics highlight the uses of frames:

- Whether or not you should use frames

- Creating an interactive frameset

- Using Dreamweaver's predefined frames objects

- Adding navigation bars, targeted frames, and other linking options

- Fine-tuning borders, scrollbars, and other frame properties

- Creating NoFrames content to reach the widest possible audience

To Frame or Not to Frame?

After frames were introduced in HTML 4.0, they quickly became very popular and were overused. Worse yet, they interfered with ordinary bookmarking of websites, hiding the content and page source away from the base URL of a page's master frameset.

When you're planning your page layout, take a moment to consider accessibility, useability, and design issues and decide whether frames are really necessary for the purpose you want to achieve. Many designers and web users alike are opposed to frames because they are so frequently misused. (In fact, there's a whole website devoted to banning the use of frames—see www.noframes.org).

Here are some of the main disadvantages of using frames:

- Frames make it difficult for the viewer to bookmark a particular page on a site. Unless a new frameset is opened, the URL in the browser location bar stays the same, even when new pages are loaded into the frames.

- It is not as easy to view the source on a page created with frames. If you click on "View Source" in the browser, what is displayed is the frameset source code, not the code of the individual pages that are being displayed in separate frames.

- Frames can complicate layouts and increase download time. The chances of an error in display are also much higher with complicated nested framesets.

- Frames are often particularly inaccessible for users with visual impairments, including the following:
  - Visually impaired visitors who use screen readers or screen magnification software
  - Visitors who increase the text size; text may be cut off if the frame is not scrollable
  - Users who become visually disoriented when a frame opens in a new window

For more information on frames and accessibility, see "Frames: accessibility techniques and issues," by Jim Byrne, at http://www.mcu.org.uk/articles/noframes.html.

In the following quote he presents a very compelling reason for not using frames:

"Using frames means the pages will not conform with the way the rest of the Web works—i.e., on the majority of pages, each page is a single unit, with a single address, and the back button takes the user back to the page previously visited. Straying from this model means that skills learned on a frames based site can't be generalised to the rest of the Web."

—*JIM BYRNE, WWW.MCU.ORG.UK/*

The most common reason to use frames is to keep one sort of content static and always on screen while the content of other frames changes. The static content is usually a logo, an advertisement, or a navigation bar. As an alternative to using frames, you can choose from these techniques:

- Divide web page content into multiple sections using tables or layers (see Chapter 5, "Page Layout")
- Use Cascading Style Sheets for page layout (see Chapter 9, "Cascading Style Sheets.")
- Add a navigation bar without placing it in a frame (see Chapter 13, "Designing Navigation Objects")

Frames or CSS?

One of the dreams of the designers of the Web is to be able to separate content from presentation (also called formatting or style). The CSS (Cascading Style Sheets) standard offers a forward-thinking approach to this goal. CSS and XHTML are the future of web design. So, if you would like to explore alternatives to frames, feel free to move on to Cascading Style Sheets in Chapter 9.

If you've inherited some websites done in frames and haven't switched them over to a CSS design yet (or, more commonly, haven't quite convinced the client of the utility of switching to a CSS-based site), you will be interested to see that the rest of this chapter explores the use of frames in Dreamweaver.

For a W3C alternative to frames that uses the `object` element and CSS, see `http://www` `.w3.org/TR/WCAG10-HTML-TECHS/#alt-frames`.

The use of frames to divide pages or to handle persistent navigation might be considered out-of-date. However, although frames are not included in the current version of XHTML (XHTML 2.0), they have not disappeared. As an indicator of web designers' continuing fascination with frames, XFrames was released as a W3C Working Draft in 2002. XFrames is an XML application and not technically part of HTML or XHTML. However, XFrames is a module designed to replace HTML (and XHTML) frames, and to address many of the problems with using frames. So, stay tuned—frames continue to be part of the ongoing growth and development of the Web, and the final word on frames is not in yet!

Creating a New Frameset

Now that you have a realistic idea of the limitations of frames layouts, it's about time you created your own frameset so that you can start using frames-based web pages.

As usual, Dreamweaver gives you a variety of options for performing the task at hand. But before you can begin to create a frameset, you need to know something about such a page's component parts. When you divide a web page into frames, you create a set of frames called a *frameset*. The term comes from the HTML tags used to contain the frames instructions, `<frameset> </frameset>`. Framesets can be set up as groups of columns, groups of rows, or a mix of both. (See "Rows and Columns" later in this chapter.) Figure 7.1 shows the HTML for a simple frames page displayed in Code view.

The HTML shown in Figure 7.1 describes a web page that has been divided into three frames, as shown in Figure 7.2.

> The Code view in Figure 7.1 shows elements and attributes in lowercase. You can set your preferences for Code view in Edit → Preferences → Code Format. We've chosen lowercase to comply with web standards for XHTML and because we find lowercase more readable. For more details on working with code, see Chapter 18, "Handcrafting Your Code." For more information on XHTML, see Chapter 24, "Working with XML and XHTML."

In a web page that consists of three frames, those three frames each contain their own web page. But there's also a fourth page—the frameset page—that contains the instructions that describe the frames layout, including the number of frames as well as their sizes and attributes.

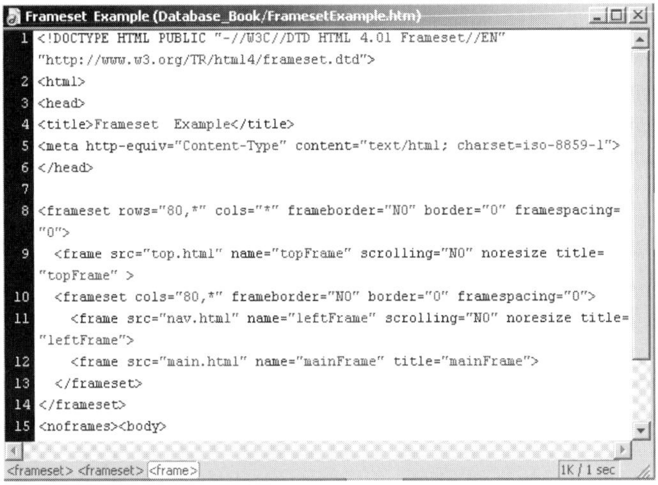

Figure 7.1

Frames commands are enclosed by `<frameset>` `</frameset>`.

```
Frameset Example (Database_Book/FramesetExample.htm)
 1  <!DOCTYPE HTML PUBLIC "-//W3C//DTD HTML 4.01 Frameset//EN"
    "http://www.w3.org/TR/html4/frameset.dtd">
 2  <html>
 3  <head>
 4  <title>Frameset  Example</title>
 5  <meta http-equiv="Content-Type" content="text/html; charset=iso-8859-1">
 6  </head>
 7
 8  <frameset rows="80,*" cols="*" frameborder="NO" border="0" framespacing=
    "0">
 9    <frame src="top.html" name="topFrame" scrolling="NO" noresize title=
    "topFrame" >
10    <frameset cols="80,*" frameborder="NO" border="0" framespacing="0">
11      <frame src="nav.html" name="leftFrame" scrolling="NO" noresize title=
    "leftFrame">
12      <frame src="main.html" name="mainFrame" title="mainFrame">
13    </frameset>
14  </frameset>
15  <noframes><body>
```
`<frameset> <frameset> <frame>`   `1K / 1 sec`

Designers considering whether or not to create frames on a page should keep in mind that Dreamweaver's options for creating frames aren't as visually oriented as with tables or layers. You can't draw frames, as you can with layers. You can't use Layout view to create or edit frames, as you can with tables. You can create a frameset instantly with the Start page (Create From Samples → Framesets), the File menu (File → New → General → Framesets), or the Frames pop-up menu in the Layout Insert Bar, as described later in the sections "Using a Predefined Frameset" and "Creating Frames from Scratch."

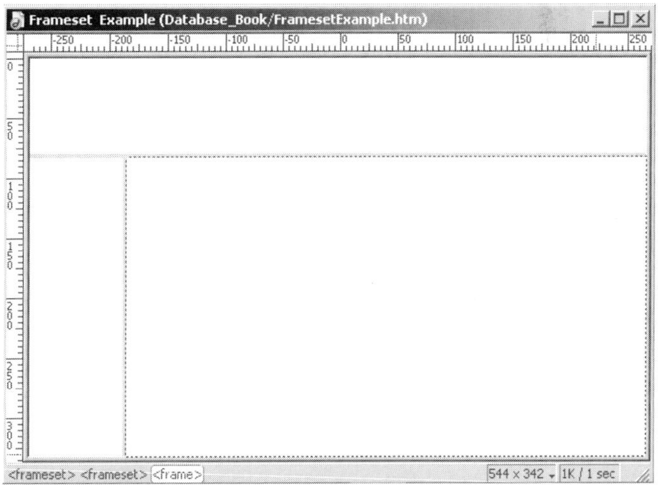

Figure 7.2

A web page with three frames that actually contains four separate documents—one for each frame and one for the frameset page.

Setting Accessibility Options for Frames

If you have enabled accessibility options for frames, the Frame Tag Accessibility Attributes dialog box (Figure 7.3) will display after the frameset is created.

To enable the accessibility dialog box for frames, choose Edit → Preferences → Accessibility. From the list labeled "Show attributes when inserting:" check the Frames box. This dialog box checks that a name is assigned to each frame.

For more details on making frames accessible, see the section "Putting the Viewer in Control" later in this chapter. See Chapter 35, "Using Dreamweaver to Make Your Site Accessible" for more information on using accessibility features in Dreamweaver.

Framing Your Layout

For many designers, the first step is to draw your frameset on paper before you start to use Dreamweaver. That way, you can decide whether to use one of Dreamweaver's predefined frame layouts or to create one from scratch. In order to make such a sketch, you need to know about the various components that make up a frameset as well as the tools for adjusting frames—the Property inspector and the Frames panel.

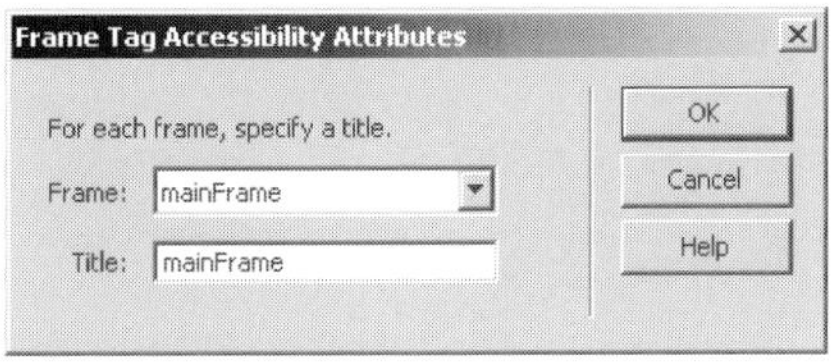

Figure 7.3

Frame Tag Accessibility Attributes dialog box

Framesets and Individual Frames

The frameset page and each frame page are distinct and separate pages, and need to be saved with different filenames. To save a frame, click to position the text cursor within it. Then choose File → Save Frame As. Be sure to save every individual frame you create with a separate filename.

> Instead of clicking in each frame separately and choosing File → Save Frame As, choose File → Save All. Dreamweaver prompts you to save each frame successively as well as the frameset page. Be sure to give the frameset web page a name that clearly describes the frameset as a whole so that you don't confuse it with an individual frame's web page.

Each frame, as a separate web page, has its own properties. You have to set them separately using the Property inspector (see "Modifying Frames and Framesets" later in this chapter).

Each frame also has a name that's separate from the filename of the web page it contains. For instance, a frame on the left side of a frames-based page might contain a web page named links.htm. But the frame itself might be named left or links. You can name a frame using the Property inspector. Dreamweaver automatically gives names to the individual frames when you use its collection of predefined frames layouts. You can easily change any frame name in the Property inspector; enter a new name in the text box labeled Frame Name in the upper-left corner.

> Framesets can be nested, but, just as with tables, be careful about nesting framesets further than one level in.

Frame names are crucial when you want to target links—you create a hyperlink in one frame and target another frame so that the linked content appears there. (See "Targeting Linked Content" later in this chapter for more on this.)

When you design a web page with a set of frames, which page within those frames contains the title that the viewer sees in the browser's Title Bar? The frameset itself has its own title, and that's what the user sees. When you want to edit the title, open the frameset page in Dreamweaver and enter a title that describes the whole frameset in the title box.

Frame Borders

Each frame within a frameset is enclosed by a border on all four sides, much like that of a table. You can click and drag the border that's within the Document window (as opposed to a frame border that's around one of the edges of the web page) to quickly resize a frame.

By default, the borders you see around the frames in Dreamweaver are only guides to help you design the page. When you preview the page in a browser window, the borders aren't actually visible because, by default, their width is set to zero.

You can change the border width—and even assign a color to borders—by following these steps:

1. Select the frameset by clicking on one of the internal frame borders in Design view. If frame borders aren't visible, choose View → Visual Aids → Frame Borders. You can also select the frameset (or an individual frame) in the Frames panel (part of the Design panel group). A dashed line appears around all borders in the frameset to show that the entire frameset has been selected. The tag `<frameset>` also appears in the tag selector at the bottom-left of the window to indicate that the frameset has been selected.

2. Choose Window → Properties (or press Ctrl-F3) to display the Property inspector if it's not already displayed (see Figure 7.4).

3. Enter a value other than 0 in the Border Width box to assign a width to the frameset's borders.

4. Choose Yes from the Borders drop-down list to display borders in the browser window.

If you select the entire frameset, you can only change the borders for all of the frames at once. But you can assign different colors to the borders of an individual frame. Begin by either Alt-clicking within the frame or by clicking that frame in the Frames panel. Then display the Property inspector for that frame and click the Border Color box to select a color.

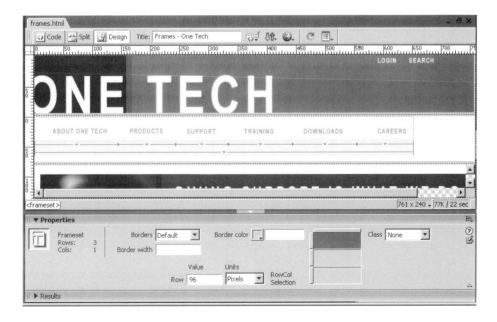

Figure 7.4

Click a border to select the frameset and adjust borders and other properties in the Frames Property inspector.

The Border drop-down list contains two other options. Choose No if you don't want borders to appear in the frameset. Choose Default if you want to leave it up to the user's browser settings to determine whether or not frame borders are displayed.

> Even if you don't want borders to show in your final frameset and frame pages, it can be useful to use them during the initial page design process as a way to keep track of where each individual frame is located. An alternate technique is to set a different background color for each frame.

The Frames Panel

The Frames panel, which appears when you choose Window → Frames or press Shift-F2, provides a miniature representation of the frames within a frameset. The Frames panel also gives you a clear, visual way to select either an individual frame or an entire frameset.

Figure 7.5

Selecting a frame in the Frames panel

When you click a frame in the Frames panel, the borders of that frame are highlighted to indicate that it's currently selected (see Figure 7.5). Once an individual frame is selected, you can adjust its properties in the Property inspector (Figure 7.6).

> To select a single frame, Alt-click (Option-Shift-Click for the Macintosh) anywhere within it.

Rows and Columns

Like tables, framesets are divided into rows and columns; when you divide a page into two vertical frames—one on the left and one on the right—you create a frameset with two columns. If you split one of those frames into two horizontal frames (by creating a nested frameset), you create two rows within that column of the frameset. Figure 7.2 shows a nested frameset, with two columns in the second row of the first frameset.

When you select a frameset and view the Property inspector, you see a RowCol Selection box (see Figure 7.4) that you can use to adjust width and height. (See "Specifying Row Height and Column Width" later in this chapter.)

Figure 7.6

The Property inspector displays attributes for a single frame.

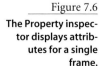

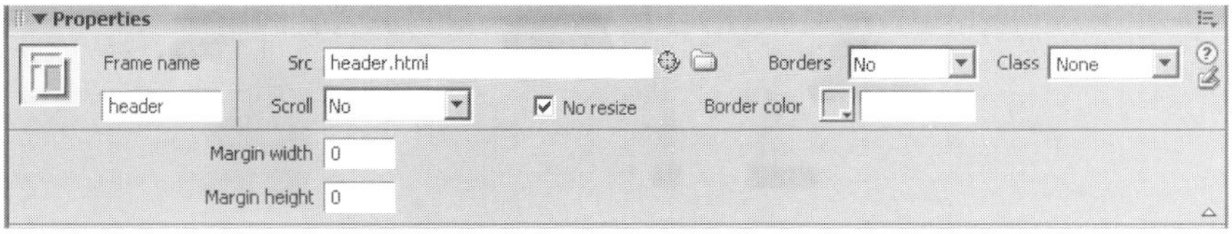

Using a Predefined Frameset

Now that you know how frames are organized, you can start creating your own framesets. Dreamweaver provides you with preformatted frames layouts that give you a design jump-start. If you haven't worked with frames before, or if you just want to save some time, look at the predefined frames layouts first.

To view the preset designs, choose Window → Insert to display the Insert Bar. Select the Layout Insert Bar from the Insert Bar pop-up menu, and then click the Frames pop-up menu button in the Insert Bar. A set of common frames designs appears (see Figure 7.7). Click an option to instantly create the frameset in the Document window.

You can use the Frames pop-up menu, the Start page (Create From Samples → Framesets), or the File menu (File → New → General → Framesets) to create one of the predefined frame designs. Select an option from the Frames submenu: Left, Right, Top, Bottom, Bottom Nested Left, Bottom Nested Right, Left Nested Bottom, Right Nested Bottom, Top And Bottom, Left Nested Top, Right Nested Top, Top Nested Left, or Top Nested Right. You can't preview the arrangement before you insert it, but if you don't like the layout you've chosen, just choose Edit → Undo and choose another one.

You can't create a template from a frameset page, although you can make templates for individual frames. When you use Dreamweaver's predefined framesets, only the frameset structure is provided. You'll still have to create the pages and content for the individual frames.

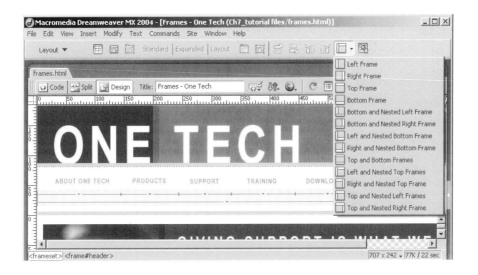

Figure 7.7

The Frames pop-up menu on the Layout Insert Bar presents you with a set of common frameset arrangements that you can quickly add to a web page.

Creating Frames from Scratch

You don't have to use the predefined frame layouts, of course. You can insert your own frames one at a time. Or you can start with one of the predefined arrangements and then modify it to suit your needs.

You can use the Modify menu to create a frameset or modify one you've already created. You can also split a web page or a frame within a page into two frames.

> Make sure you've configured Dreamweaver to display frame borders to make it easier to work on framesets. Choose View → Visual Aids → Frame Borders to see the borders displayed in the Document window while you are assembling your pages. When you want to preview your pages, you can turn the borders off by choosing View → Visual Aids → Frame Borders once again. That way, you'll be able to see the page as your viewers will see it. (You can, of course, choose File → Preview In Browser to preview the page, too.)

Inserting Frames

A single web page can be considered a frameset consisting of only a single frame. Thinking of a page this way comes in handy when you want to create a new frame. You do it by splitting the current single frame. Follow these steps:

1. Display the web page you want to divide into frames, or position the text cursor within a frame you want to divide.

2. Choose Modify → Frameset.

3. Choose one of the following options from the Frameset submenu:

    Split Frame Left Creates a frame to the left of the current one (or two vertical frames in a page without frames)

    Split Frame Right Creates a frame to the right of the current one (or two vertical frames in a page without frames)

    Split Frame Up Creates a frame above the current one (or two horizontal frames in a page without frames)

    Split Frame Down Creates a frame beneath the current one (or two horizontal frames in a page without frames)

The Frames submenu comes in handy when you want to create an unusual frames layout, such as three or four horizontal frames in succession, or when you want to adjust an existing frameset.

Dragging Frames

If you're a fan of clicking and dragging, Dreamweaver gives you the option of creating frames with your mouse. Remember that every web page, whether or not it has already been divided into frames, has a border around it. You can use this border to split the page into two frames by following these steps (make sure frame borders are visible by choosing View → Visual Aids → Frame Borders if necessary):

1. Click the left or top border of the currently displayed web page.

2. Drag the border into the Document window in one of the following ways:

   • Drag the top border (the mouse arrow becomes a two-headed arrow when it is positioned over the border) down to split the page into two horizontal frames.

   • Drag the left border to split the page into two vertical frames.

   • Drag the corner (the mouse arrow becomes a four-headed arrow) to split the page into four frames (see Figure 7.8).

You can also drag an inner frame border—one that's already a frame border and within the Document window rather than around the edge of the Document window. For an inner border, Alt-drag (Option-drag for the Macintosh) to split the frame into two frames.

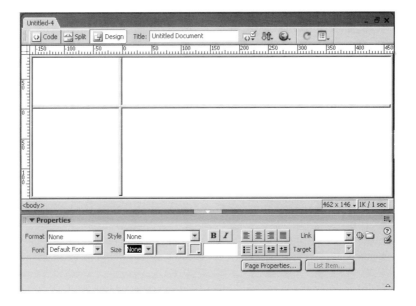

Figure 7.8

Click and drag a page to split the page into two or more frames.

Saving Framesets

Once you've created a frameset, you need to save it. This isn't as straightforward as choosing File → Save to save a stand-alone web page. You need to save both the frameset page and its component frames before you can preview the frames page in a browser.

When you use Dreamweaver to create a frame, a blank document is created within that frame and given a temporary filename. The first frame you create is given the temporary name Untitled-1, the second becomes Untitled-2, and so forth. The frameset page is called UntitledFrameset-1.

To save a frameset, you first need to select it by clicking any frame border. Then you can choose from the following options:

- Choose File → Save All to save the frameset and all frames in succession. Dreamweaver displays the Save As box and highlights the frame you're being prompted to save (though you might need to move the Save As box slightly to see which frame is being highlighted so that you can give it the name you want).

- Choose File → Save Frameset Page to save only the frameset page and not the individual frames.

- Choose File → Save Frameset As to save the current frameset with a different name.

When you click anywhere in an individual frame, a different set of frame-related File menu options appears:

- Choose File → Save Frame to save the currently selected frame.

- Choose File → Save Frame As to save the current frame with a different name.

- Choose File → Save Frame As Template to save the current frame as a template that you can use to create similar pages (see Chapter 4, "Saving Labor with Templates and Libraries").

Modifying Frames and Framesets

Simply creating frames with a few mouse clicks and menu choices is only part of the way Dreamweaver helps you "frame" web pages. Once your frames layout is in place, you add content to the frames as you would any other series of web pages. Then you can modify the attributes of each frame using the Property inspector.

The following sections describe how to turn scrollbar display on or off, keep a user from changing a frame's size, and make adjustments to a frame's appearance.

Changing a Frame's Appearance

Frames pages, like conventional web pages, need to complement rather than clash with their contents. But there's no reason why you need to limit yourself to a default white background for every frame. By giving your frames some visual interest, you can dramatically improve the overall appearance of your website.

At the same time, you can make the content being presented within the frames more readable by controlling alignment and other visual attributes. The ultimate goal is to get your message across in a compelling way so that the viewer will explore your site.

Adding Colors

Each individual frame in a frameset can have its own background color. By changing the background color of a single frame, you can call attention to a logo or section. On the other hand, for a simpler look, you can assign the same background color to the frames-based page by first assigning that color to all of the frames within it.

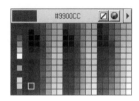

Figure 7.9

Dreamweaver's color picker helps you assign a background color to an individual frame page.

To add color to a frame's background, follow these steps:

1. Click anywhere in the frame you want to adjust.

2. Choose Modify → Page Properties to display the Page Properties dialog box.

3. Choose the Appearance category, click the color box next to Background color, and select a color from the color picker that appears (see Figure 7.9).

4. Click OK to close Page Properties and return to the Dreamweaver window, where the frame displays a page with the new background color.

> Remember that you're adjusting only the *currently* displayed page. If the contents of the frame change due to clicks on hyperlinks in other frames, you'll need to adjust the backgrounds of all the pages that might appear in that frame.

You can't select more than one frame at a time—after all, they're separate pages—but you can select the next or previous frame (or frameset) at the same hierarchical level by clicking Alt-Left-Arrow or Alt-Right-Arrow (Command-Left-Arrow or Command-Right-Arrow for Mac) to cycle through frames and framesets in code order (the order they're defined in the frameset page code).

> Alt-clicking within a frame displays the Property inspector, which enables you to assign a color to that frame's border but not to the background of the web page within the frame.

Adjusting Frame Margins

Another way to make a frame's contents more readable is to adjust the margins. The margin of a frame is the space between any one of the four borders and the text or images within them. By default, the margin space is about 8 pixels. By making the margin bigger, you can call attention to contents within the frame.

To adjust margins, follow these steps:

1. Alt-click to select the frame you want to adjust.

2. Choose Window → Properties to display the Property inspector if it isn't already displayed.

3. Enter **25** for Margin Width and **18** for the Margin Height boxes.

4. To see the changes on screen (see Figure 7.10), press Enter or click the miniature frames layout on the left side of the Property inspector.

> By setting margins to 0, you make the frame's contents "bleed" to the border. This enables you to align the images in one frame with images in another frame.

Specifying Row Height and Column Width

Dreamweaver makes it easy to change the size of frames: simply drag borders until each frame is the size you want. An alternative is to select one or more rows or columns and enter a value in the Property inspector. However, you need to begin by selecting the entire frameset. To do so, follow these steps:

1. Click directly on a frame border to select the frameset. If the borders are not visible, choose View → Visual Aids → Frame Borders.

Figure 7.10

Increasing frame margins can direct more attention to a frame's contents.

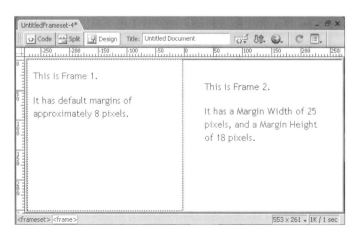

2. Click the expander arrow in the bottom-right corner of the Property inspector to display the expanded version if you need to.

3. Click a row or column in the RowCol Selection Box on the far right side of the Property inspector (see Figure 7.11). When you click a row, all the frames in that row are selected. When you click a column, all the frames in that column are selected.

Figure 7.11

Select a row or column in your frameset so that you can specify a different height or width, respectively.

You can express the size of a row or column within a frameset as a fixed number of pixels or as a relative value. Select the frameset, view the Property inspector, and select the row or column you want to adjust by clicking the RowCol Selection box on the right side of the Property inspector. Then choose one of three measurements from the Units drop-down list:

Pixels Assigns a specific pixel size to the frame. The frame size will remain constant no matter what the size of the browser window.

Percent Expresses the row or column size as a percentage of the frameset height (for a row) or width (for a column).

Relative Describes the size of the selected row or column in relation to other frames that have been given pixel or percentage measurements.

If you choose Pixels, enter a number of pixels in the Value box. If you choose Percent or Relative, enter a percentage in the Value box.

If you have trouble selecting a row or column in the RowCol Selection box, click one of the rectangles either above the top row or to the left of the first column.

If you are used to working with HTML, an alternative to dragging frame borders or using the RowCol Selection box is to edit the HTML code:

1. Alt-click to select the frame you want to edit.

2. Choose View → Code to open the frameset in Code view. The frameset code is highlighted.

3. Specify a precise width for columns or height for rows by changing the values that follow the `frameset` tag. For instance, the two-column layout shown in Figure 7.10 is described by the following HTML:

```
<frameset cols="350,*" frameborder="no" border="0" framespacing="0" rows="*">
```

The `"350,*"` value after the `cols` attribute means that the frameset contains two columns. The first column is 350 pixels wide. The width of the second one is not a fixed value; rather the width as symbolized by the asterisk (*) varies depending on the width of the browser window. You can change 350 to a different value or use an asterisk for the first column and give a fixed value to the second column, `"*, 350"`. You can also use percentages rather than fixed values or asterisks—the first column can be 40 percent of the browser window width and the second, 60 percent, for instance.

Another key concept regarding frames is this: you can't specify the exact size of the browser window on a user's computer using HTML, so you must give the browser some ability to control the relative size of the frames. You must either give the `cols` attribute percentage values, or else use absolute pixel numbers combined with at least one relative width (*). This allows flexibility in the display, and helps prevent unexpected results when your page is displayed.

Putting the Viewer in Control

Some frame attributes are ones that give the viewer the ability to resize frames or scroll to view their contents. Remember that frames can be difficult to view for those whose web browsers are older or who have only a limited amount of screen real estate to allocate to the web browser window. You can provide some enhancements to help visitors use your frames layout.

Controlling Scrollbar Display

By default, Dreamweaver displays scrollbars when a frame's contents can't be displayed in their entirety. For instance, when the text in a frame extends beyond the length of the Document window, a scrollbar appears on the right side of the frame so that you can scroll down and edit all of the frame's text. If images extend beyond the width of the frame, scrollbars appear at the bottom of the frame so that you can view them.

But you don't always need scrollbars. For instance, if a frame only contains a single logo or banner ad, it doesn't make sense to include scrollbars that interfere with the image (see Figure 7.12).

Figure 7.12

Some contents, like images, don't need scrollbars, so you should turn them off.

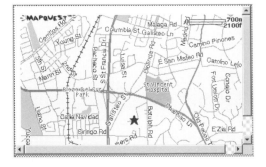

By selecting the frame and changing the Scroll drop-down list in the Property inspector, you can specify one of four settings:

Yes Means that the frame will always display scrollbars, even if they are not needed.

No Means that the frame will never display scrollbars.

Auto Means that the frame will display scrollbars only when needed.

Default Means that the viewer's browser can determine whether scrollbars should be shown. Most browsers use Auto as the default—they show scrollbars if the frame's contents aren't fully shown.

By choosing Auto or Default, you enable your visitors to control how the frames appear. Because you can't control the size of the browser window, it makes sense to give visitors control over scrollbars unless you're absolutely sure that the Yes or No options should be used. The four scrollbar options apply to both horizontal and vertical scrollbars.

> If you set scrolling to **no**, be sure that you have set a frame width or height that is large enough for the frame content. Otherwise, if the frame is not large enough, the viewer has no way to see all the content.

Allowing Frame Resizing

By default, when a frame is created, the viewer can resize that frame by dragging its borders. If you want to let visitors to your website resize a frame, Alt-click the frame, then make sure the No Resize box is unchecked in the Property inspector.

You might not always want to give viewers the ability to resize a frame, however. If one of your frames displays an ad that a customer has paid to display on your pages, you don't want to give visitors the chance to obscure part of it. In such a case, make sure the No Resize box is checked.

> To delete a frame, Alt-click to select it, then press Delete. Or, if you're a fan of clicking and dragging, click the frame, hold down the mouse button, and drag the frame off of the page. Release the mouse button, and the frame is gone.

Adding Navigation Elements to Frames

When you divide a page into frames, links get more complicated. A link in a frame should cause the viewer's browser to display some new content. The question is: where should that content appear? Should it appear in another frame in the frameset, the current frame, or a new web page altogether?

By *targeting* a link, you make sure that link produces the effect you want. Targeting a link means that you select a destination page—the target page—that displays the file that you have associated with the link.

This section describes one of the most useful features of frames: their ability to interact with one another through hyperlinks. By the way, Part III of this book discusses navigation elements and linking in greater detail.

Targeting Linked Content

It's important to select a target for the content that is associated with a link when the link occurs in a frames-based web page. Unless you identify a target where the linked content will appear, the content will appear in the same frame in which the link appeared before you clicked it.

For example, if one of your frames contains a set of links leading to the various important pages on a website, chances are you want those links to remain on screen while someone explores your site. If someone clicks one of the links and it is replaced by a new page, that person might have a hard time navigating your site.

To target a link in a frame, follow these steps:

1. Create the text, image, or other object you want to turn into a link.

2. Identify the file to link to in the Property inspector's Link field by doing one of the following:

   • Enter the URL for the file in the Link box.

   • Click the folder icon and select the file in the Select File dialog box.

   • Click the Point-to-File icon and drag it to a file, such as a web page that's displayed in another frame in the Document window.

3. Once you've created a link, the Target drop-down list in the Property inspector is enabled. Select the location where the linked content should appear by choosing an option from the Target drop-down menu in the Property inspector. This menu includes all the frames in the currently displayed frameset as well as four other options:

   _blank Causes the linked file to open in a new, blank browser window. The original window with the link remains open, but is displayed behind the new window. The browser back button in the new window is grayed out—this can be confusing for users who don't realize the original window is still open.

   _parent Opens the linked file in the parent frameset. This applies when you have nested one frameset inside another.

   _self Causes the linked file to open in the same frame that contained the link. (This is also the default condition when a target is not used.)

   _top Opens the linked content in the top level of all frames, replacing the frameset and all the frames with the new content. The browser back button is still available to the user. Except in rare cases, this option is preferable to _blank.

Most designers who use frames target linked content to open in an adjacent frame. In Figure 7.13, a row of links in a frame near the top of the page causes content to appear in a larger frame in the middle of the page.

Figure 7.13
A link in one frame is often targeted to an adjacent frame.

ASSIGNING BEHAVIORS TO FRAMES

You can also control how frames interact with one another and display linked content by assigning behaviors to them. To do so, you create the frameset and add content. Select an object in one of the frames, and then display the Behaviors panel. Click the plus (+) sign, then choose one of the following frames-related behaviors from the Actions pop-up menu:

Set Text → Set Text Of Frame Replaces the content and formatting of a frame with the content you specify. The content can include any valid HTML. Use this action to dynamically display information.

Go To URL Lets you specify one or more documents to open in targeted frames. You create a link, then identify multiple documents to open in different frames. Go To URL, in other words, lets you change the contents of multiple frames in response to a single mouse click.

You can also add these behaviors from the main Dreamweaver application window:

Insert Jump Menu (Insert → Form → Jump Menu) Lets you create a pop-up menu with a series of clickable list items. Each item can be targeted to a frame in your frameset. (This option can also be selected from the Forms Insert Bar.)

Insert Navigation Bar (Insert → Image Objects → Navigation Bar) Lets you create a row of clickable buttons that can be linked to individual frames.

For more information on using Behaviors, see Chapter 12, "Incorporating JavaScript Behaviors."

Creating NoFrames Content

Frames aren't going to be viewable by many users with disabilities as well as the growing number of wireless users who access the Web with handhelds, phones, pocket PCs, or other small devices. The handful of web surfers who still use old versions of web browsers won't be able to see frames, either. For such users, you need to set up NoFrames content.

> *NoFrames* pages are alternate versions of frames-based pages that use other design elements, such as tables, to present the same content. Browsers that can't view frames will instead display the NoFrames content, so the users can still get an idea of what's on the frames page.

> When a search engine searches and indexes a website for inclusion in its search listings, the contents of the <noframes> tags are added to the listings. If you have placed a string such as "Your browser doesn't support frames" there, then your search-engine listing will more than likely have "Your browser doesn't support frames" as the description of your website. To avoid this situation, put meaningful text in this location, including links to some of the other primary pages on your site.

The Edit NoFrames Content command lets you see what viewers who can't see frames see. After you create a frameset, edit the NoFrames content as follows:

1. Save your frameset. You may want to copy some content from one of your frames for use in the NoFrames page.
2. Choose Modify → Frameset → Edit NoFrames Content. A new blank page appears in the Document window, replacing your frames pages.
3. Enter the NoFrames text in the Document window or paste any text you have copied.
4. To return to your frames layout, choose Modify → Frameset → Edit NoFrames Content again.

For some designers, NoFrames content is as simple as a sentence saying, "This page is designed with frames, and your browser does not support them." Others attempt to duplicate the frames layout with tables. The important thing is to provide alternate content so that none of your viewers will see a blank browser window when they come to your frames-based page.

Prevent Others from Framing Your Pages

Some websites that contain links to other websites (for example, the Internet index site About.com) choose to "frame" the remote site's pages. When a visitor to About.com clicks a link to another website, the new site's content opens as a frame in a frameset. The originating site's content frames the new site. The purpose of such "framing" is so that the visitor always has a link to the original site that contained the link. However, many web designers are offended by the thought that their web pages would appear beneath another site's name, logo, and advertisements for other websites, and many users find it irritating to be trapped inside a frame without an obvious way out.

If your site already contains frames, it can be confusing for your frames-based pages to appear as a frame in someone else's frameset. You can, however, prevent other sites from framing your own pages. Add the following JavaScript code to the head section of any pages you want to block from being framed:

```
<script language=javascript type="text/javascript">
    <--! Hide script from old browsers
    if(top.location != self.location)
    { top.location =self.location }
    // end hide from older browsers -->
```

You can use the preceding script to prevent framing of conventional web pages as well as frames-based pages. The HTML Goodies website has an alternative script for preventing framing—check it out at www.htmlgoodies.com/tutors/yesnoframes.html.

See the Ask Jeeves search site at www.ask.com for an example of a user-friendly way to handle "framing." Although the site default is to "frame" the pages from the search result links, the URL of the new page is displayed as a link at the top of the page. If you click the URL link, the new page is "unframed" and displays in the browser window as a separate page. The Ask Jeeves page also includes a "Removes Frames" button at the top right of each search result page that "unframes" the page when clicked.

See this book's color insert for examples from a frames-based website.

Hands On: Design a Frames-Based Page

Now you can try out frames yourself by designing a web page. You'll divide a page into frames, add a navigation bar to a frame, and target links to open in another frame.

In the Chapter 7 folder on the accompanying CD, copy the folder frames_layout to your computer. Start Dreamweaver, and open a new blank page. If you want a preview of the completed page, you can open frames.html, which is in the frames_complete folder in the Chapter 7 folder on the CD. The completed page is shown in Figure 7.14.

Figure 7.14

**This web page
(frames.html) uses
frames to add inter-
activity and to pre-
sent multiple pages
simultaneously.**

Create the Frameset

To begin, create a frameset that you can work with. Follow these steps:

1. Start Dreamweaver.

2. In a new blank Document window, choose View → Visual Aids → Frame Borders.

3. Click and drag the top of the frame border into the center of the Document window, then release the mouse button.

   The web page is split into two horizontal frames.

4. While holding down the Alt key (or the Option key on a Mac), drag the middle frame border to create another horizontal frame. Repeat this to create an additional horizontal frame.

   The web page is now split into four horizontal frames.

5. Click and drag the frame borders until the frames resemble those in Figure 7.15.

6. Select the frameset by clicking on a frame border.

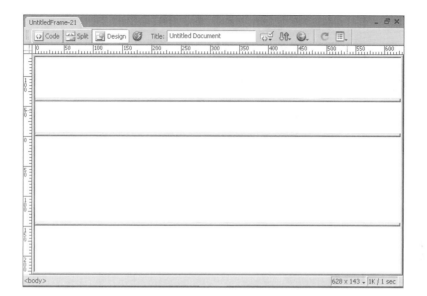

Figure 7.15

Divide a web page into four frames.

7. In the Property inspector, select each row in the RowCol selection. Set the row height for each one in the Row text box. Set the top frame to 96 pixels, the second frame to 40 pixels, the third frame to 247 pixels, and choose relative units and no value for the bottom frame.

8. Open the Frames panel. Select each frame and give it a name in the Property inspector in the text box below Frame Name. The top frame is named *header*, the second frame is named *navbar*, the third is named *main*, and the bottom frame is named *footer*.

Set Frame Properties

Next, you'll set frame properties for the four frames. The frame in the first row of the frameset is intended to hold an image, and the frame directly below this one will hold a navigation bar. These two frames are static: their contents don't change. The third, largest frame in the frameset is mobile—its contents change in response to links. The fourth frame has a relative size, and can scroll as needed.

1. Choose Site → Manage Sites → New and define a site where you can locate this frameset unless you have a site already open in Dreamweaver.

2. Open the Frames panel and select the top frame.

3. In the Property inspector, select No from the Scroll drop-down list to turn off scroll-bars. Select No in the borders pop-up menu, and check the No resize box. Set Margin width and Margin height to 0.

4. Select the second frame in the Frames panel. In the Property inspector, change the properties as in step 3. Select the third frame in the Frames panel, and repeat.

5. Select the bottom frame in the Frames panel. In the Property inspector, select Auto from the Scroll drop-down list so that scrollbars appear only when needed, depending on the size of the page content and the size of the browser window. Select No in the borders drop-down menu, and check the No resize box. Set Margin width and Margin height to 0.

Insert Web Pages into the Frames

You've got a number of options for adding content to your frames. In this case, you don't have to type content from scratch. You'll add a complete web page that's provided in the frames_layout folder to each of the three frames.

> We'll be creating the slices for the bottom frame in the Hands On tutorial in the bonus chapter, "Slicing, Optimizing, and Exporting Graphics, on the CD." For now, use footer.html in the frames_layout folder. We'll be creating the Navigation Bar and Rollovers in navbar.html in the Hands On tutorial in Chapter 13, "Designing Navigation Objects." For now, use the finished navbar.html file in the frames_layout folder.

1. Position the cursor in the top frame and choose File → Open In Frame.

2. Choose the file header.html in the frames_layout folder and click Select to insert it in the frame.

> As soon as you click Select, a window will display with the message, "To make a document-relative path, your document should be saved first …." Click OK to close the window. We'll save the documents in the following section.

3. Position the cursor in the second frame and choose File → Open In Frame.

4. Choose the file navbar.html in the frames_layout folder and click Select to insert it in the frame.

5. Repeat steps 3 and 4 in the third frame and insert main.html in this frame.

6. Position the cursor in the bottom frame and choose File → Open In Frame.

7. Choose the file footer.html in the frames_layout folder and click Select to insert it in the frame.

8. Click any frame border to select the frameset and enter a title in the Title box. This is the frameset title that the viewer will first see upon visiting your frames-based page.

Save the Frames

Now that you've created the frameset and added content to all frames, you'll save your frames and the frameset page itself.

1. Choose File → Save All.

2. In the File Name box of the Save As dialog box, enter a name for your frameset, such as `fourframes.html`, and then click Save.

3. Since you inserted web pages into the four frames, you don't have to save them. Otherwise, the Save As dialog box reappears so that you can save the individual frames one at a time. In that case, you would assign a filename to the frame and click Save.

4. Your page should look like the one shown in Figure 7.14.

> The targeted links are included in the Navigation Bar code. We will set the targets when we create the Navigation Bar in Chapter 13.

Target Links

Next, you need to target each of the links in the `header.html` page. You'll create an image map for the hyperlinks in Chapter 8, "Making and Maintaining Hyperlinks." Now you will target the links so that they will display in the main frame.

1. Open the `header.html` file from the `frames_layout` folder.

2. Select the first link (`LOGIN`) in `header.html`. In the Property inspector, choose Main from the Target drop-down list so that the link will open in the main frame.

3. Repeat this process for the SEARCH link.

4. Choose Save All Frames to save your changes. You can now preview your page in a browser window and test out your links. The additional linked pages (`search.html`, `login.html`, `products.html`, `support.html`, `training.html`, `downloads.html`, and `career.html`) are included in the `frames_layout` folder. Only `main.html` and `products.html` have any content so far, but each of the other pages has a different background color so that you can easily test your links and targets.

5. Create a NoFrames page to display in place of the One Tech home page, following the instructions given in the section "Creating NoFrames Content" earlier in this chapter. A NoFrames page does not necessarily have to include a lot of content—one effective technique is to add links in your NoFrames page to many of the individual frame pages themselves. The viewer then has an opportunity to see all of the page content—it's just not displayed within a frameset.

If you want frame borders to appear in the browser window, click a frame border and enter a value other than 0 in the Border Width box in the Property inspector.

One Holy Grail

So far in this Part, you've learned how to lay out pages and populate them with text and graphics. You've seen how to work with frames and framesets in this chapter. But there are also page elements that connect your web page to other pages or objects, or that make things happens. In Chapter 8, you'll learn how to weave pages together with hypertext links.

Making and Maintaining Hyperlinks

Hyperlinks (also known as *hypertext links* or just *links*) are the essence of the Web. Hypertext links make it possible to navigate the Web in a nonlinear way—going from page to page on the same website, or leaving one website for a different one altogether. This makes it possible for the user to choose a unique pathway through the massive collection of information that is the Web today.

To work with links, you need to understand a little about the folder (directory) structure of your site and how references are made from one page to another. Dreamweaver makes this as easy as possible for you, but we'll still start you off with some fundamentals (skippable if you're already an old hand) so that you know what you're doing.

In this chapter, you'll learn about the following topics:

- **Understanding links, anchors, and paths**
- **Making a link with the Property Inspector**
- **Inserting a link**
- **Creating links from the site map**
- **Making an image map**
- **Managing links with the cache**
- **Checking and fixing links**

Fundamental Link Concepts

One of the unique aspects of the Web as a medium is that the "page-turning" mechanisms are built into the content of the pages. Hidden in the HTML of your web pages, tags indicate *links*. These links allow the user to move to a different part of the same page, a different page on the same site, or another site.

> The word *link* is also used to refer to the link tag. The link tag indicates relationships between an HTML document and an associated file, such as a style sheet or script. The link element can only be used in the Head of a document. This should not be confused with hyperlinks. Hyperlinks are created with the a (anchor) element, and surround text or images to create physical links in the body of your document.

Links on the Web connect two points—one in the source document (that is, a link *from* a web document, usually activated by clicking), and one in the target document. Most of the time, only the source link requires a specific tag.

Where From?

To create a link, you insert an a tag (the HTML syntax is `<a href="`*address*`">`*linktext*`</a>`) that specifies an `href` (a hypertext reference) in the form of a URL or path and filename. You can avoid the hand-coding and let Dreamweaver fill in the address (path and filename) for you. It's generally much faster and more accurate to let Dreamweaver fill in the link address. Not only do you avoid broken links from typing errors, but you can save time and increase accuracy by browsing to the linked file rather than figuring out the code details for linking to specific levels of your folder hierarchy. "Inserting Links," later in this chapter, reviews the options Dreamweaver offers in place of typing every URL by hand. And, if you prefer, you can still choose to hand-code in Dreamweaver.

ANCHORS OR LINKS?

In this chapter, the term *anchor* is used only for *named anchors*, which create links to a specific part of a page. See the section "Creating a Named Anchor" later in this chapter for more details. Technically speaking, the a tag is an anchor tag, and anytime you use an a tag you're using an anchor. However, most people use the term *anchor* only to refer to named anchors. If you'd like more information on the technicalities of links and anchors, see "Links in HTML Documents" at www.w3.org/TR/html4/struct/links.html.

Where To?

Most of the time, the specification of the address or path in the link's href attribute suffi-ciently defines the destination—the top of the destination document. When it's necessary to reach a specific section of a target document (as in a page with a dynamic table of con-tents), you can insert *named anchors* at the specific point you want to link to in the target document. This is the same HTML a tag <a> with a different attribute (name="*anything*").

There are two parts to using a named anchor —the named anchor (in the target docu-ment) and the link to the named anchor (in the source document).

For example, if you open a target document and add a named anchor to a piece of text—in this case, *About Us*—the code looks like this:

```
<a name="about">About Us</a>
```

The link in the source document to that specific part of the target document (rather than the top of the document) includes the anchor name; for example:

```
<a href="info.html#about">About Us</a>
```

and goes directly to the part of the target page where the named anchor is located (you do have to open the target doc and insert the named anchor there if you haven't already done so).

What Will Happen?

Links from one HTML document to another tell the browser to load the target page in the current window or open it in a new window A link, however, can refer to any kind of file, not just an HTML document. If the user's browser knows what plug-in or helper applica-tion to invoke in order to display or play back the target file, then the user will experience the link as if he were directly opening the file. If not, the user will be given the opportunity to save the file.

Similarly, links can be made to run scripts. See Chapter 12, "Incorporating JavaScript Behaviors," for more on scripts and how to trigger them.

FILE MANAGEMENT

One of the most important issues in developing a site is project file management. Before you start creating links, you need to develop a system for managing all the files associated with the site. See the section, "Setting Up Your Site," in Chapter 3, "Setting Up Your Workspace and Your Site," for more information on file and directory (folder) management.

If you want a link to open a new mail message from the user to an address (such as a webmaster@ or info@ address), the HTML syntax is `<a href="mailto:youraddress">linktextorimage</a>`, but of course you don't really have to know this because Dreamweaver provides a specific shortcut for inserting a mailto link (the Email Link icon on the Common Insert Bar).

Paths Lead to Destinations

When specifying an `href`, you can use either an absolute path (a complete URL, such as `http://groups.yahoo.com/group/dreamweaversavvy/messages`) or a relative path. A relative path can be relative to the current document or to the root of the current site. To specify a path relative to the current document, do not precede the path with a forward slash. To

Figure 8.1

Adding files to the OneTech directories

specify a path relative to the root of the site, start the path with a forward slash. To indicate "up one level" in a path, you use the Unix format (`../`). And, of course, you can use Dreamweaver's link options to do this automatically!

Figure 8.1 shows the OneTech website files and folders after a few HTML and image files have been added to the site. A OneTech site has been created in Dreamweaver, and the `website` folder has been designated as the root folder.

A link from the contact page to the home page is specified as follows:

```
<a href="hmpg.html">home</a>
```

Or, if you add an image from the graphics folder to the about page, it's designated in this way:

```
<img src="../graphics/about.gif">
```

to indicate that the image file is in the graphics folder, one level up from the `about.html` file.

Root-relative paths specify the path from a site's root folder to a document. Root-relative links are useful if you frequently move files around from one directory to another. To use root-relative links, create a root directory in a Dreamweaver site to match the root directory on the remote server for the site. For more details on creating a site in Dreamweaver, see Chapter 3, "Setting Up Your Workspace and Your Site."

Understanding the Different Kinds of Links

Creating links using the a tag and the `href` attribute creates hypertext links, also known as hyperlinks. An a tag is not limited to text, though; it can contain either text or an image—or both.

The most common types of links, then, are the following:

Text links The basic link—highlighted text. You click it and something happens.

Image links Just like text links, but the thing you click is a picture instead of text (pictures can, of course, still include text, or you can include both an image and text in the same link).

Image maps These are images with variously shaped regions called hotspots, each of which links to an individual destination.

Navigation bars These are text or images (but usually images) that are used to create a consistent set of navigation links throughout a site or section of a site. These often include JavaScript behaviors that create rollover effects to display a different image when the user moves the cursor over the image link, or clicks on the image link. See Chapter 12 for the straight skinny on using JavaScript behaviors. For details on Dreamweaver's navigation objects, such as rollovers, navigation bars, and jump menus, see Chapter 13, "Designing Navigation Objects."

Link Color Schemes

One last conceptual topic deserves mention before we get into the nitty-gritty of inserting links into pages: link color schemes. When designing your pages, if you don't specify a color scheme for links (before, during, and after they're clicked) versus regular text, then your viewers will see whatever their browser shows by default (links are usually blue and underlined before they're clicked and purple afterward, in comparison to the rest of the text, which is black).

There are several approaches to standardizing your use of colors in a site, including basing pages on templates, using the Page Properties dialog box to set the colors for a specific page (or template), or through the use of CSS styles and style sheets.

Templates See Chapter 4 for a discussion of using templates to maintain consistency among such page elements as link coloring.

PageProperties dialog box Use Modify → Page Properties → Appearance (Ctrl/Cmd-J) to select colors for the text and background, and Modify → Page Properties → Links to select colors for links, visited links, and active links of a specific page or template.

Cascading Style Sheets (CSS) Use CSS (as discussed in Chapter 9, "Cascading Style Sheets,") to control color *and appearance* of links as compared to regular text, including how the link should look when the mouse pointer hovers over it.

Inserting Links

Naturally, there are about 17 different ways to insert links into a web document with Dreamweaver. Well, maybe not quite that many, but it seems that way. We'll run through the most useful techniques and you'll probably end up using just one method most of the time, but, as you'll see, some of the methods are more convenient in particular situations.

> Save your document before you insert links or you'll have to wade through various reminder dialog boxes and Dreamweaver will use absolute references to your local files until it knows how they relate to the current document (Dreamweaver can't know this until you've saved your document at least once).

Entering a Link with the Property Inspector

As is often the case with Dreamweaver, most of the time we find it easiest to make a link by just selecting the source file and entering the target information in the Property inspector. If you don't have the Property inspector visible, make it so with Window → Properties or Ctrl/Cmd-F3. Then follow these steps:

1. Select the text (or image) that will trigger the link.

2. Indicate the `href` target using any of these four techniques:

    - Type an absolute or relative pathname and filename in the Link box on the Property inspector (see Figure 8.2).

    - Click the drop-down menu next to the Link box to get a list of recently-linked-to addresses (Figure 8.3).

    - Click the Point-to-file icon (shown in Figure 8.4) and then point to a file in the Files panel. Make sure you have the folder open before you try to point to a file in the folder. You may have to do some window rearranging to get a clean sightline).

    - Click the Browse icon and choose a file from the Select File dialog box that results (see Figure 8.5). If it's not already within your site, Dreamweaver will offer to copy it there for you.

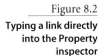

Figure 8.2

Typing a link directly into the Property inspector

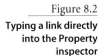

Figure 8.3

Choosing a recent link in the Property inspector

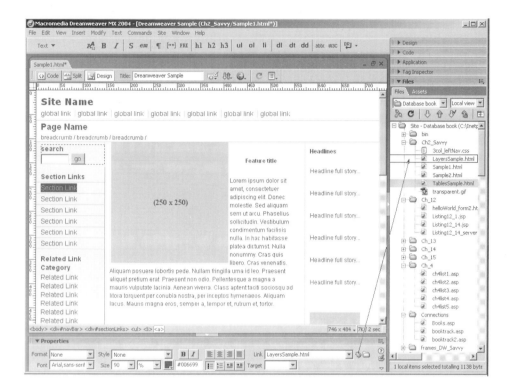

Figure 8.4

Using the Property inspector's Point-to-file icon to select a link from the Files panel

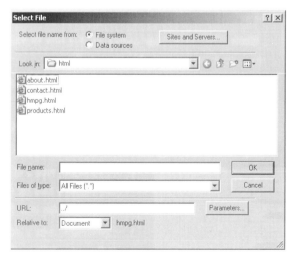

Figure 8.5

Browsing to your link anchor through the Select File dialog box

You can use Point to File even without going through the Property inspector—just select the source text for the link, hold down the Shift key, and then click-drag to the target document in your Files panel.

Using the Insert Hyperlink or Insert Email Link Commands

To insert a link entirely (as opposed to turning existing text into a link), click the Hyperlink button on the Common Insert Bar for links to documents, or click the Email Link button on the same panel for mailto links. (You can also choose Insert → Hyperlink or Insert → Email Link to get the same effects.)

Creating an Ordinary Hyperlink

When you insert a hyperlink, Dreamweaver brings up the Hyperlink dialog box (see Figure 8.6).

To insert a link, follow these steps:

1. Type the link text in the Text box.

2. Press the Tab key and then enter the link address, or choose it from the drop-down menu or by browsing (there's no Point to File option on this dialog box).

3. Optionally, most often if you are using frames, you can direct the link toward a target window or frame, using the Target drop-down menu. The Target menu will include frames defined in the frameset of your current page, if any, as well as these standard target names:

   _blank The linked page comes up in a new browser window; the original window stays open underneath the new window.

   _parent The linked page comes up in its parent window (if any) or the full window (removing all frames, if any).

   _self The linked page comes up in the same frame (if any) as the source link.

   _top The linked page comes up in the full window (removing all frames, if any).

4. Optionally, type a label for the link in the Title box. This will create a tool tip that appears if the user hovers the mouse pointer over the link.

5. Optionally, type a single keystroke in the Access Key box. If the user clicks Ctrl/Cmd-*AccessKey* while viewing this page, this will activate the link. (In Internet Explorer, you also need to press Enter to make Access Keys work.)

Figure 8.6

The Hyperlink dialog box enables the rapid assembly of a hypertext link.

The accesskey attribute is an accessibility feature introduced by the W3C to enable users who have difficulty controlling the mouse and selecting links to select the appropriate key and navigate to a specific link. For more details on using Access Keys, see "Unlocking Hidden Navigation: Access Keys" at www.alistapart.com/stories/accesskeys/.

6. Optionally, enter an ordinal number in the Tab Index box.

7. Click OK.

Creating an E-Mail Link

To insert an e-mail link, click on the Email icon in the Common Insert Bar, or choose Insert → Email Link. Dreamweaver brings up the (much simpler) Email Link dialog box (shown in Figure 8.7). When this figure appears, follow these steps:

1. Type the link text in the Text box.

2. Type the e-mail address in the Email box.

3. Click OK.

Creating a Named Anchor

When you need to link to a specific area in a document, you must first name it with an anchor tag. To do so, first select the target area and then click the Named Anchor button on the Common Insert Bar (or select Insert → Named Anchor). This brings up the Named Anchor dialog box shown in Figure 8.8.

All you need to do to create a named anchor is type a name in the Anchor name text box and click OK. An Anchor icon is placed in Design view to indicate the anchor.

Then, any time you are making a link targeted to this anchor, you will either use "*#thatname*" as the href or append *#thatname* to the end of the path and filename (URL).

A link that references a specific area in a page uses # plus a fragment identifier. For example, #thatname—thatname is the fragment identifier.

Figure 8.7

The Email Link dialog box

Figure 8.8

Named Anchor dialog box

Making a Link with the Make Link Command

If you select your source text, you can also create a link by selecting Modify → Make Link (Ctrl/Cmd-L). This brings up the Select File dialog box (refer back to Figure 8.5). Use it to browse to a destination file or to enter a URL.

Making Links from the Site Map

The same Point-to-file icon available on the Property inspector can also be used with Map view in the Files panel. First, choose Map view from the drop-down menu at the top-right in the Files panel. You must set a home page for your site before you can create a site map. Right-click on the home page file name, and then select Set As Home Page from the context menu. Then, click the Expand/Collapse button to maximize the Files panel if you're working in the Windows workspace. (If you are using the Mac floating layout, just choose Map view in the Files panel.) Figure 8.9 shows a set of links created directly from the site map.

Figure 8.9

When starting a project, you can insert the basic navigation links into the key pages for a site from Map view.

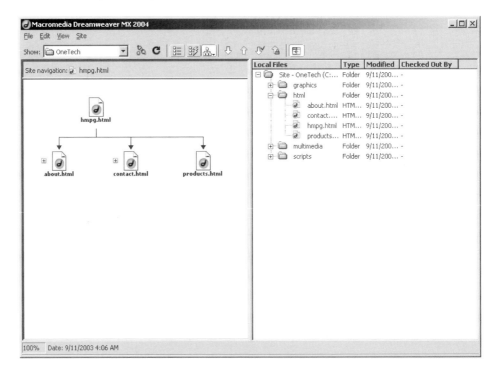

To create a link in this view, follow these steps:

1. Select the document *from which you want to link.*

2. Click the Point-to-file icon and hold down the mouse button.

3. Drag to the file you want to link *to* in Files view (see Figure 8.10).

4. Repeat as necessary.

To remove a link in this view, follow these steps:

1. Select the page you want to unlink.

2. Right-click (Command-click) on the Page icon.

3. From the context menu, select Remove Link

4. Repeat as necessary.

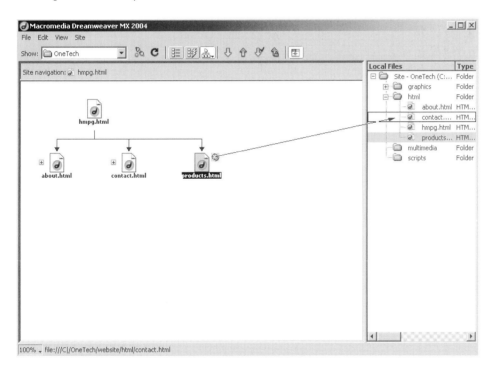

Figure 8.10

Use the Point-to-file icon to link up files quickly in Map view

Building Image Maps

An image map is a graphic with one or more designated hotspots that function as links. The first types of image maps to be supported on the Web were processed by web servers and hence called *server-side* image maps. These sent *x* and *y* coordinates from the selected point in the image, and the server would determine what link that particular (*x,y*) pair corresponded to.

These have now been largely supplanted by *client-side* image maps that are interpreted by the user's web browser. This means that all the shape and link information is stored in the page—in fact, the information is stored in the map code for the image. When the user hovers over a hotspot on a client-side image map, they can actually see the target of the link in the status bar (unless you've overridden this info, as discussed in Chapter 12) instead of a series of *x* and *y* coordinates. Dreamweaver only makes client-side image maps, but this should not be a problem!

The process for creating an image map is straightforward:

1. Insert an image or placeholder onto a page.

2. Select the image or make sure it's selected.

3. Expand the Property inspector to show all available options (see Figure 8.11).

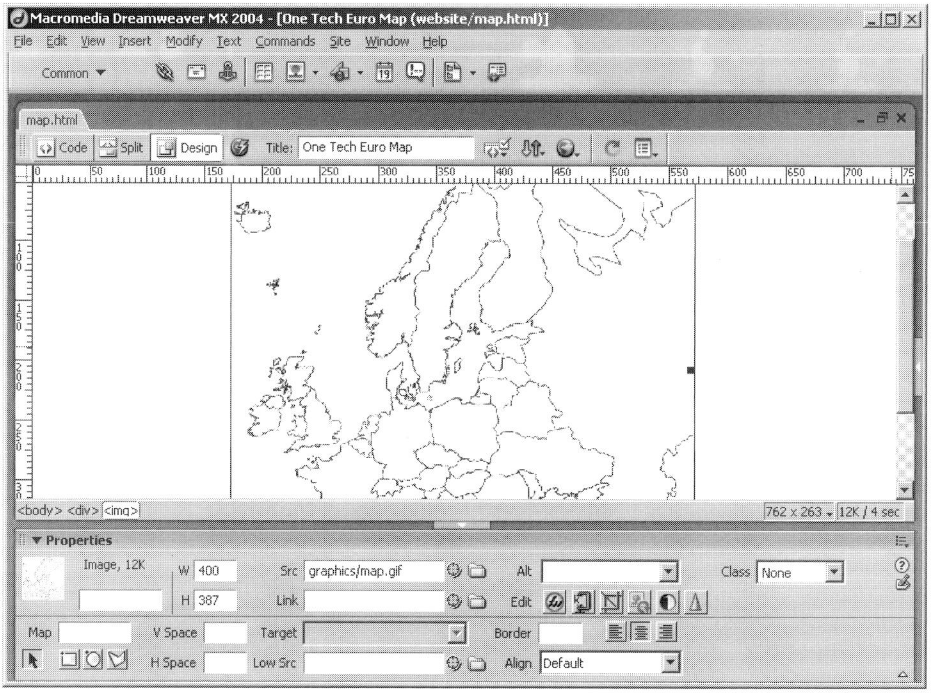

Figure 8.12

An image has been inserted and highlighted and the Property inspector has been expanded to show the image-map creation features.

4. Draw circles, rectangles, and/or irregular shapes on the image to indicate the hotspot areas (see Figure 8.12).

Rectangles and circles are drawn from upper-left to lower-right. For rectangles, this means that you should drag from the top-left corner to the bottom-right corner of the rectangle. For circles, this means that you should drag from an imaginary top-left corner of an invisible square containing the circle.

5. Select each hotspot and supply a destination address in the Link box that appears in the top half of the Property inspector (much as you would to select an ordinary link in the Property inspector, as discussed in the previous section). See Figure 8.13 to view the Property inspector options when a hotspot is selected.

6. Indicate a default link (for the rest of the image), if so desired, by clicking outside of all the hotspots and specifying a link destination for the image as a whole.

See the "Hands On" tutorial at the end of this chapter to create an image map and hotspots.

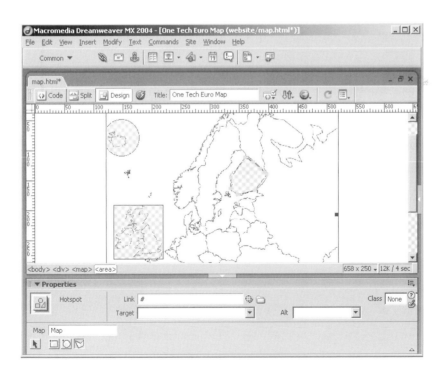

Figure 8.12

After indicating a rectangular hotspot and a round one, we're now specifying an irregular shape by clicking from corner to corner.

Figure 8.13

Expand the Property
inspector to see the
hotspot options
needed to build an
image map.

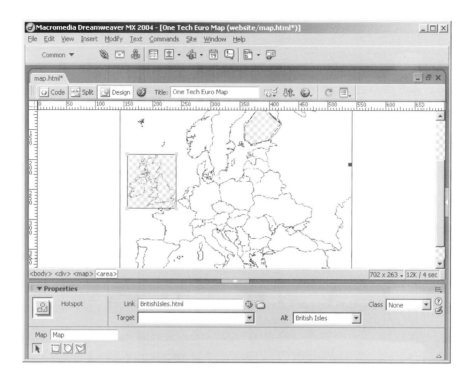

Figure 8.13

Expand the Property inspector to see the hotspot options needed to build an image map.

Avoiding or Fixing Broken Links

It's definitely a time-saver to be able to create links automatically using Dreamweaver's various shortcut features, and using these features also minimizes the risk of typos in path names when you can select a link by browsing, but perhaps the most valuable advantage to be gained from defining a site in Dreamweaver is the ability to use Dreamweaver's site management tools to track, manage, and correct links across an entire site. Without a site-management tool, one of the banes of web publishing is that hand-coded pages may contain broken links, especially after a site revision that involves renaming or moving pages or changing the site's directory structure. Without Dreamweaver (or a similar tool), hunting for all the broken links and fixing them by hand can be prohibitive.

Managing Links as You Go

To enable Dreamweaver so that it can help you maintain working links, you have to first turn on Link Management (if it's not already turned on) and create a cache for the site (if the site does not already have a cache created).

Turning On Link Management

To turn on Link Management, follow these steps:

1. Open the Preferences dialog box (Edit → Preferences/Dreamweaver → Preferences).

2. Select the General category (see Figure 8.14).

3. In the Document Options area, next to Update Links When Moving Files, select Always or Prompt. (If you select Always, Dreamweaver will automatically correct links to or from documents whenever you move them. If you select Prompt, Dreamweaver will always check with you first before correcting such links.)

4. Click OK.

If you did not create a cache when you first defined your site (see Chapter 3), you should do so now. To do this, select Site → Manage Sites, and choose the current site from the Manage Sites dialog box. Click on the Edit button to open the Site Definition dialog box. In the Advanced tab, select the Local Info category, click the Enable Cache check box, and then click OK. Remember that you can use Dreamweaver's site management tools only if you have defined the site in Dreamweaver.

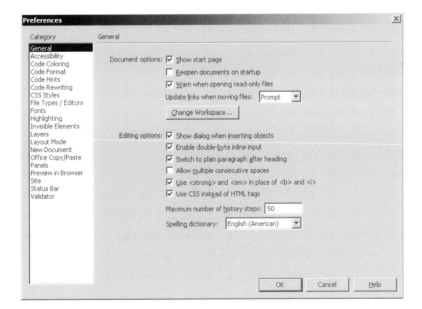

Figure 8.14

The General category of the Preferences dialog box

Allowing Dreamweaver to Update Links for You

Once Link Management is turned on, you can freely move documents around your site without worrying about tracking down all the affected links (including those links from other documents to the moving file and the links from that file to other documents) and correcting them by hand.

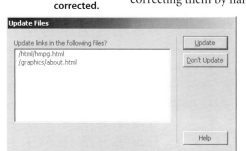

When you move a document, Dreamweaver will either fix affected links automatically without checking with you first for confirmation (if you selected Always in the previous section), or it will double-check with you first by displaying the Update Files dialog box, which lists all the links it intends to correct (see Figure 8.15).

Click the Update button to allow Dreamweaver to proceed. Dreamweaver will track its progress until the changes are completed.

Manually Changing a Link throughout Your Site

In addition to this automatic approach to changing links, you can also redirect all links to any specific destination with a single change (much like the Find/Replace feature). This is most useful when the link points outside your current site and can't be simply redirected by moving the destination file, or when you want to redirect all links to a file before deleting it. To do this, follow these steps:

1. Select a file in Local view in the Files panel.

2. Click on the arrow in the upper-right corner of the Files panel group, then select Site → Change Link Sitewide. This brings up the—wait for it…—Change Link Sitewide dialog box (see Figure 8.16).

3. Enter the old link address in the Change All Links To box.

4. Press the Tab key and enter the new link address in the Into Links To box below.

5. Click OK.

Figure 8.16

Make global link changes in the Change Link Sitewide dialog box

Editing Links from the Site Map

If you're rearranging some of the basic navigational or structural links in your site, you might want to consider doing this from Map view in the Files panel. To change a link from Map view, right-click/Ctrl-click the file representing the destination link and choose Change Link from the context menu that pops up. The Select HTML File dialog box displays. Browse to a new destination file or type a URL directly to indicate a destination outside the current site, then click OK. Dreamweaver will update the link for you.

Testing and Checking Links

In large, complicated sites, links can still end up broken—either from being typed incorrectly or from being changed without Link Management updating all affected files. In an ideal world, you wouldn't have to worry about this, but fortunately you can check individual links to make sure they go where they're supposed to, or you can check all links throughout your site, and you can have Dreamweaver fix any broken links it finds.

Testing a Single Link

You've probably noticed by now that hyperlinks shown in Dreamweaver are not "active" as they would be in a web browser; that is, you can't click a link and automatically browse to or open the destination of the link. However, for documents in your local site, you actually can browse through the links—just hold down Ctrl/Cmd and then double-click the link in Design view. If the destination is a local file, Dreamweaver will open it. If the destination is a web address, Dreamweaver will explain that it can't open "http, mailto, or other remote addresses."

Checking All the Links in a Site

You can actually check links for a single document, any subportion of a site, or across an entire site.

> For more on testing a site before it goes live, see Chapter 30, "Going Live or Delivering the Site."

To check links for one document or a subset of a site, the steps are as follows:

1. Open a document or select any number of files and folders in the Files panel.

2. Right-click (Ctrl-click on a Mac) on the file name in the Files panel. From the context menu, select Check Links → Selected Files/Folders.

3. Dreamweaver creates a report on broken and external links and displays it in the Results panel group in the Link Checker tab (see Figure 8.17).

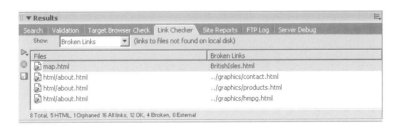

Figure 8.17

View a report of broken links in the Link Checker tab in the Results panel

4. To see broken links, choose Broken Links in the drop-down menu to the left of the Link Checker tab. To see links to external sites (which Dreamweaver can't check), choose External Sites. To see orphaned files (files in the local folders that are not linked from anywhere within the site), you must check the links in the entire site.

Or, alternatively, to check links for the entire site, follow these steps:

1. Click the arrow in the upper-right corner of the Files panel group. Select Site → Check Links Sitewide (or Shift - F8).

2. In the Link Checker tab of the Results panel, you can view broken and external links across the site as well as orphaned files.

Fixing Broken Links

Naturally, you can fix any broken links you find manually by using the techniques discussed earlier in this chapter, or you can do it directly from within the Results panel. To do so, follow these steps:

1. Select a broken link in the Broken Links column (not the Files column) on the right side of the Broken Links report.

2. Click the Folder icon that appears.

3. Browse to the correct destination file.

4. Select a new file to link to in the Select File dialog box that displays.

5. Press the Tab or Enter key.

6. Dreamweaver will select the next broken link to the same file you just selected. Repeat steps 2–4.

> Dreamweaver automatically uses the Check Out feature to hold any files that have changed so that they can be updated on the remote site if you have File Check In/Check Out turned on, as discussed in Chapter 3.

Updating Links—Publishing the Changes

Once you've corrected links in the local version of a site, if the site is already live on a remote server, you'll need to update the remote site with all the changes. The easiest way to do this is with the Synchronize command:

1. Click the arrow in the upper-right corner of the Files panel group, Select Site → Synchronize. This brings up the Synchronize Files dialog box, shown in Figure 8.18.

2. Select Entire *site name* Site and then select Put Newer Files To Remote.

3. Click the Preview button.

4. When Dreamweaver has compared the local and remote files and indicated the documents that need updating, uncheck any files you don't want updated and then click OK (Figure 8.19).

5. When the synchronization is complete, click the Save Log button if you wish to keep a record of the update.

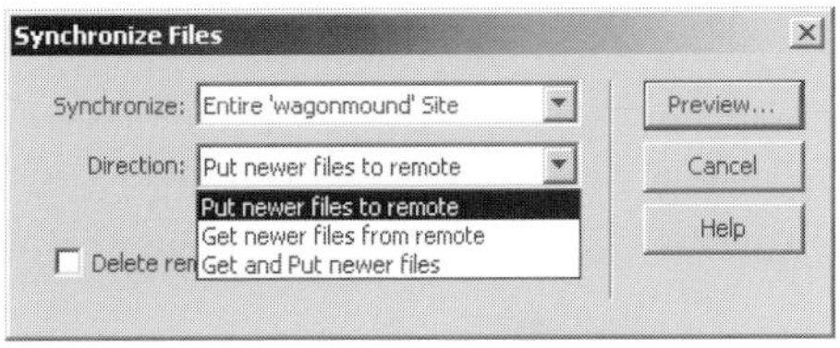

Hands On: Create an Image Map

Now you can try out an image map yourself and discover how easy this is to do in Dreamweaver! Hand-coding an image map involves using a graphics program to define areas and find coordinates and then writing a block of code to define the map. Dreamweaver enables you to do all that without leaving Dreamweaver itself, and it's easy and fast!

In the Chapter 8 folder on the accompanying CD, find the page named `header_nomap.html`. This page is used in the top frame in the One Tech site, and contains the header graphic.

Create Hotspots

You will create two hotspots for links to the LogIn page and the Search page:

1. Open Dreamweaver.

2. Open `header_nomap.html` from the CD.

3. Select the graphic (`header.jpg`).

4. Open the Property inspector if it's not already visible in the Dreamweaver window (Window → Properties).

5. Click on the downward-arrow in the bottom-right corner for the expanded view of the Property inspector.

6. Choose the rectangular selection map tool.

7. In the upper-right corner of the graphic, click and drag with the rectangular selection map tool to create a rectangular hotspot around the word *Login*.

8. Change the size of the rectangle, if needed, by using the Pointer Hotspot tool (the arrow on the left) on any of the four highlighted spots in the corners of the rectangle.

9. Repeat step 7 to create a rectangular hotspot around the word Search.

10. By default, Dreamweaver names the map and puts this name in the Map text box. To change it from the default Map, just select the text and replace with a name of your choice.

Figure 8.18

Update corrected links to your remote site with the Synchronize Files dialog box

Figure 8.19

The Synchronize command makes you preview the intended changes so you have a chance to verify the files to upload before proceeding.

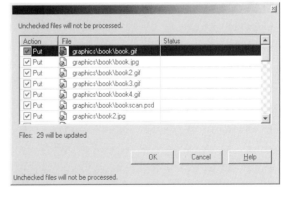

Link the Hotspots

Now the map is complete except for putting in the links:

1. Select the LogIn hotspot.

2. In the Property inspector, type in `login.html` in the Link text box. (Be sure to delete the # that appears there by default.).

3. Type LogIn page in the Alt text box.

4. Repeat for the Search hotspot. Link to search.html and type Search in the Alt text box.

It's that easy! And it doesn't matter if you're creating two hotspots or 20 hotspots, it's still easy.

To view the completed map page, open `header.html` from the Chapter 8 folder on the CD. To view the completed map page within the frameset, open `Map_8.htm`.

Separating Content from Presentation

Now you know how to create and manage the links that make your website an interconnected part of the Web and not a series of disconnected web pages. In the next chapter, we'll take an in-depth look at Cascading Style Sheets (CSS) and all the new features Dreamweaver MX 2004 has added for using CSS in Dreamweaver. Or, if you prefer to continue with links and navigation, skip ahead to Chapter 13, where we discuss jump menus and other navigation objects.

## CHAPTER 9

Cascading Style Sheets

In the ongoing effort to separate content from presentation on the Web, CSS (Cascading Style Sheets) is a powerful weapon. It's also, in some ways, a well-kept secret. Although CSS has been available since 1996, browser support in the past has been partial and inconsistent. With the advent of CSS 2.0 and the appearance of the Level 6 browsers (IE 6, Netscape 6+, Opera 6+), it has become more practical to use style sheets in recent years.

After explaining a little bit about how style sheets work and what they can do, we'll show you how Dreamweaver MX 2004 makes working with CSS easier than ever. Here are the topics we'll discuss:

- Using style sheets
- Internal and external style sheets
- Understanding the box model
- Working with the CSS Styles panel
- Making, attaching, editing, and viewing a style sheet
- Coding CSS on the fly
- Validating CSS code
- Using external CSS editors and importing external style sheets

What to Use Style Sheets For

Style sheets separate style (presentation) from content for anything from a single document to an entire site. Using them makes it easier to update, correct, or otherwise change the look-and-feel of a page or site without individually recoding all the formatting tags.

OK, so style sheets control "style," but what does that mean? For many people, previous experience with Microsoft Word provides one example of how styles can be defined and then applied to the contents of a document, but Word's styles are primarily focused on text formatting, which is only one of the applications of CSS. Style sheets can also define how links will appear in different circumstances, set background colors for an entire page or individual elements, control tiling of a background image, add borders, and set page layout—allowing you to control almost every aspect of the look of your page. And you can update the look of the site in one place—the style sheet—and it's immediately applied to every HTML page that's linked to that style sheet!

With CSS, you can apply style definitions to existing tags or create new subclasses of existing tags, each with their own style. You can also define freestanding styles that can be applied to any number of different tags.

Formatting with Styles

Text formatting options include font (typeface, size, color, weight, and so on), alignment, indentation, and paragraph spacing.

Link formatting options allow you to specify how links will look when unclicked, when hovered over, when being clicked, and after having been clicked.

OTHER APPROACHES

You can also separate style and content in other ways. For example, you can use a database to assemble documents on-the-fly using a single web boilerplate file that can be changed once to affect an entire dynamic site (see Chapter 19, "Database Connectivity," for more on developing database-driven sites). You can also use Dreamweaver templates to establish the look-and-feel for a site (as discussed in Chapter 4, "Saving Labor with Templates and Libraries").

We recommend using CSS for setting the look of your pages. (And, of course, you can add CSS to database-assembled pages and templates.) It's not only a web-standards-compliant method for page presentation, but you'll find that using CSS can save you enormous amounts of time and effort in designing, maintaining, and updating your pages. Dreamweaver MX 2004 makes it easier than ever to use CSS in your sites.

Layout with Styles (The CSS Box Model)

Page layout options are governed by something called the CSS *box model* (see Figure 9.1, which shows the CSS box model diagram from the W3C CSS specification at www.w3.org/TR/CSS2/box.html#box-dimensions). In CSS layout, a *box* is defined as a series of nested rectangular frames around a content rectangle. The outermost frame is the margin and is always transparent, next comes the border, then the padding (which gets the same background as the content area), and finally the content box. These areas can be styled the same on all four sides or with different styles for top, bottom, left, and right.

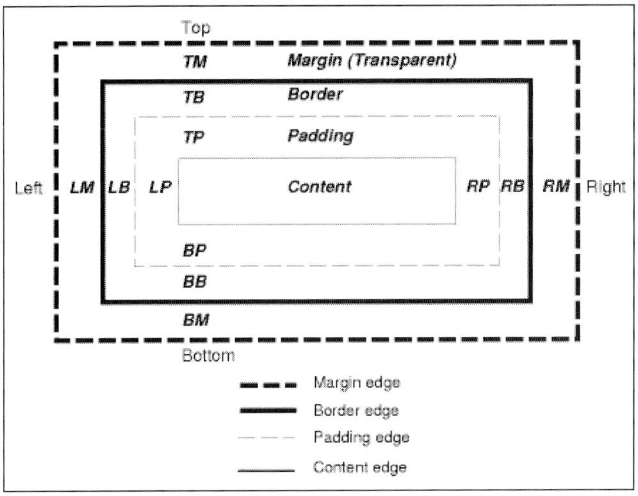

Positioning

Positioning, which is a CSS2 feature, lets you specify where you place certain elements, such as a graphic within a block of text. (If you've ever worked with a desktop publishing program for any length of time, the concept of positioning will be familiar.)

Dreamweaver MX 2004 gives you the ability to place a particular element in one of three ways. We'll take a look at how to apply these positioning features in the hands-on tutorial later in this chapter.

Figure 9.1

CSS box model diagram (from the W3C CSS specification at www.w3.org/TR/CSS2/box.html#box-dimensions**)**

Normal Flow

CSS2 has two different "flavors" of normal flow depending on how you want your text laid out on the page:

- Block formatting lays out boxes vertically, one after another, at the top of a containing box. You can set margins between each box using the margin property.

Every positioned element has a containing block, but exactly what constitutes a containing block depends on the type of positioning you're using. For relative positioning, the containing block is defined by the box the element would have occupied in the normal flow of the document. For absolute positioning, it's the closest ancestor element that has a defined position different from the default.

- Inline formatting lays out boxes horizontally, one after another, beginning at the top-left of the containing box. When horizontal inline boxes exceed the width of the containing box, the boxes perform something similar to word wrap in a word processor—the box that doesn't fit moves down vertically just below the first row of inline boxes.

You can also shift the position of your box relative to its default position. Relative positioning lets you move the box above, below, or to the right and left of its default position.

Floating and Clearing

Within a box, you can create another box and apply the float style that makes the second box appear as if it's "floating" on top of the containing box. Elements in the containing box either appear behind the floating box or wrap around the floating box. For example, you can have the floating box contain a picture and the original box contain text that appears to wrap around the picture.

If you don't want elements in the original box to appear on one or more sides of a floating box, you can apply the clear style to those elements. For example, if you want a block of text in the containing box to appear below the floating box, you apply the clear style to that block of text. It then displays below the floating box.

> For a tutorial on the basics of using floating elements, see `http://css.maxdesign.com.au/floatutorial/`.

Absolute Positioning

The third type of positioning is absolute. As the name implies, the box is placed in an absolute position outside of its containing box. This absolute box cannot overlap its containing box or any other box, and is completely separate from the normal flow.

How Styles Are Applied

Styles are applied by using style rules. Each rule specifies an individual CSS style, and can also specify the tags that can use this style. A group of style rules can be embedded in a single document or can be combined to create an external style sheet. An external style sheet can be applied to any document by adding a link to the style sheet from the HTML document.

Selectors and Classes

CSS styles are applied to content using selectors. If you've redefined a tag entirely, then the ordinary HTML tag functions as the CSS style selector. When you need to apply multiple styles to variants of the same tag (for example, when you are defining different types of paragraph tags for different design elements), and when you want to be able to apply a style to many different tags, then you define the style as a class or ID. (Classes can be specified for one specific tag or defined individually and applied to any tag or selection of text. IDs are unique, and should be used only once in the same document.)

CSS also provides for *pseudo-classes*, which are distinctions applied to text and links that the browser—what the W3C calls the user agent (UA)— determines when displaying the document. The most common application of pseudo-classes is for link formatting. They are called pseudo-classes because you don't actually apply the classes manually: you can't! There's no way to know when building a page whether the link will ultimately have been clicked or not. It doesn't make any sense to apply that determination in advance. This is something only the browser can do.

Similarly, the other common use of a pseudo-class is paragraph formatting applied to the first line of a paragraph. Until the page is rendered in a browser window, there's no way to know which words will end up on the first line, but the UA can make this determination on-the-fly and apply small caps (for example) to the first line when displaying the page.

Types of Style Sheets

There are essentially two different types of styles: external and internal. You apply external style sheets to documents by either *linking* to them or *importing* them. Dreamweaver supports both approaches. Internal styles, also called embedded styles, are defined directly within the document (in its <head> area). We recommend using external style sheets because the same style sheet can be applied to several documents, and several documents can be updated at one time just by updating the style sheet. That's the power of CSS.

CSS also permits styles to be defined and applied *inline* by using style as an attribute. This type of style only applies to the element where it's defined, and can't be reused without being defined again.

CSS Tools in Dreamweaver

You create and apply CSS styles in Dreamweaver using the CSS Styles panel, which is part of the Design panel group (see Figure 9.2). The buttons at the bottom of the panel allow you to attach an external style sheet to your HTML page, add a new style, edit an existing style, or delete the selected style in the list.

Whenever you create or edit a style in Dreamweaver itself you end up at the CSS Style Definition dialog box (see Figure 9.3). You can also use an external CSS editor with Dreamweaver—see "Using an External Editor" later in this chapter.

Figure 9.2

The CSS Styles panel has one mode for applying styles and another for editing them.

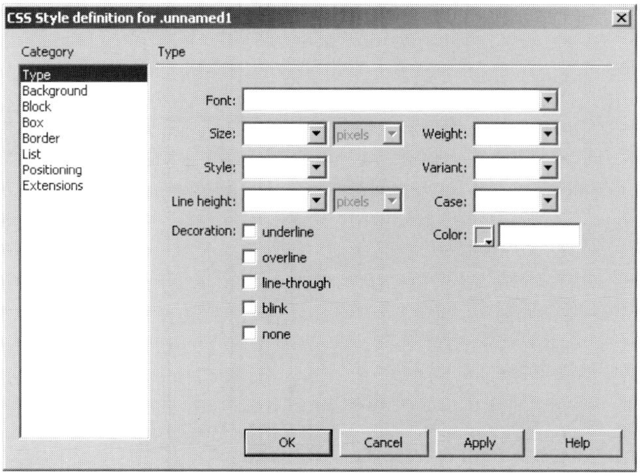

Figure 9.3

The CSS Style Definition dialog box compactly offers a wealth of CSS definition options organized into eight categories.

Working with Styles

Working with styles boils down to three things:

- Making new styles
- Applying existing styles
- Editing existing styles

   The hard part of all of this is not Dreamweaver. The program's interface enables you to develop CSS styles relatively quickly, but you still have to have some idea of how CSS works, because there's little visual feedback as you're working your way through multiple categories in dialog boxes.

Making a Style

To make a new style, start with these steps:

1. Open an existing HTML document in Dreamweaver, or create a new HTML document (File → New → Basic page → HTML).

2. Open the Property inspector or open the Design panel group to access the CSS Styles panel.

3. Choose New CSS Style in the Property inspector or click the New CSS Style button at the bottom of the CSS Styles panel (Figure 9.1).

If the new style you're making is largely similar to an existing style, then skip ahead to "Editing a Style" so that you can base the new style on a duplicate of the existing one and save some effort.

4. After you have done this, the New CSS Style dialog box will appear (see Figure 9.4).

Now choose one of the three Selector types from the New CSS Style dialog box: Class:

1. Click the Class radio button to make a style that can be applied to multiple tags.

2. In the Name field above the radio buttons, Dreamweaver will suggest a name such as .unnamed1 to remind you to start your class name with a dot. Give the selector any name that makes sense to you, but be sure to include a . before the name.

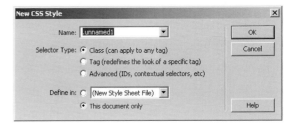

Figure 9.4

The New CSS Style dialog box

Tag:

1. Click the Tag radio button to make a style for a specific tag.

2. In the Tag field above the radio buttons, select an HTML tag from the drop-down menu.

Advanced:

1. Click the Advanced radio button to make a pseudo-class style, add an ID, or use contextual selectors.

2. In the Selector field above the radio buttons, you can choose a link pseudo-style (a:link, a:visited, a:hover, or a:active) from the drop-down menu or you can enter text for an ID or contextual selector.

To finish creating your new style:

1. Use the "Define in" radio buttons to indicate if this style should be saved to a new or existing external style sheet or applied only to the current document. If you choose to create a new style sheet at this point (as discussed later in this chapter), you won't be prompted to name and save the new style sheet until you click OK.

2. Click OK. The CSS Style Definition dialog box will appear (refer back to Figure 9.2).

See the hands-on tutorial at the end of this chapter to work with creating new styles.

Now you're ready to define your style in the CSS Style Definition dialog box. The settings you wish to apply may well be scattered over five or six of the categories, so we recommend checking each category to determine whether its options are applicable. Following is some context to understand the purpose of the options for each category.

You'll learn how to apply a style later in this chapter.

Type Options

When styling type, you can select a font or font list. Choose Edit Font List in the drop-down menu to create your own font lists, size, weight, style, variant (small caps or not), line height, case (capitalization), decoration (underline and its variations), and, perhaps most importantly, color.

Background Options

Choose the Background category to define the background color or pattern for this style element (see Figure 9.5).

If you use an image, you can have it repeat across (repeat-x) or down (repeat-y) or both (repeat). In the Attachment choice, you also can determine if the background will scroll with the page or stay fixed. Finally, you can position the image horizontally and vertically.

Block Options

Options in the Block category control spacing and alignment (see Figure 9.6).

The spacing and alignment choices are fairly self-explanatory. The Display option permits you to define whether the style is applied to inline text (without starting a new box or paragraph) or as a block. There are a number of other choices for specific layout situations, such as table headers and the like.

Box Options

The Box category controls most of the features of the box model we described earlier (see Figure 9.7).

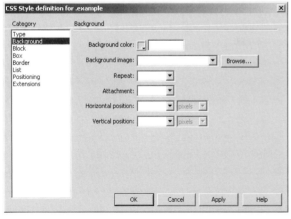

Figure 9.5

Choose a background color or image here.

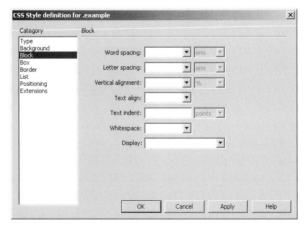

Figure 9.6

Choose text alignment, indentation, and display options here.

First define the box's height and width. (The most important thing to remember here is that padding is added to the size of the box and not subtracted from it!) Then decide if you want the box to float left or right.

Then define the padding and margins. If you want margins or padding that differ on each side, uncheck the Same For All check box.

Border Options

The Border category controls the other element of the box model—the optional border inside the margins and outside the padding (see Figure 9.8).

Here you should choose a style for the border (solid, dashed, groove, ridge, and so on), then define a width (use pixels if you need precise control), and then choose a color for the border. Remember that the background color for the style will fill the box and padding out to the border, and that the margins will be transparent.

List Options

List options are useful only for list elements, such as ordered (numbered) and unordered (bulleted) lists. You can use them to define the bullet symbol or image and to control positioning of list elements.

Positioning Options

Positioning options are useful for sophisticated page layout where you need to place boxes precisely on the page relative to other elements or relative to the page itself.

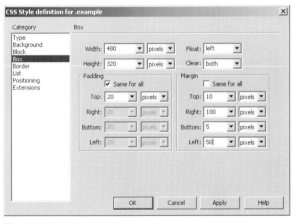

Figure 9.7

Define the box dimensions, padding, and margin here.

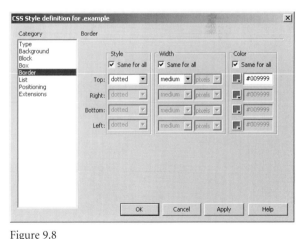

Figure 9.8

Get that dotted teal border you always wanted.

Extensions Options

Extensions options include the relatively mundane choice of calling for a page break before or after the styled element (useful when pages are printed), to funky cursor substitutes (such as a crosshairs symbol), to a number of filter effects that may or may not be supported by your target browsers.

Finishing Up

When you've finished defining your style, click OK. The new style will now appear in the style list on the CSS Styles panel. If it's a CSS class, it will also appear in the drop-down menu in the Property inspector.

Applying a Style

To apply a style, first select the text or other objects you want to apply it to and then select it with the Property inspector or right-click the name of the style in the CSS styles panel and then choose Apply from the context menu.

Editing a Style

To edit a style, follow these steps:

1. In the Document window, insert the cursor in the item you wish to edit. The current style rules display in the Relevant CSS panel (Tag panel group) and the CSS Styles panel (Design panel group).

2. Then do one of the following:

    -   Double-click the selected style in the CSS Styles panel and edit the selected style in Code view or directly in the Relevant CSS panel.

    -   Right-click the selected style in the CSS Styles panel and then select Edit to show the CSS Style definition dialog box for the selected style. Change the settings in the dialog box.

    -   Select the style in the CSS Styles panel. Click the Edit Style Sheet button in the Property inspector, then select the style name from the dialog box and click Edit to open the CSS Style definition dialog box. Change the settings in the dialog box.

    -   Click the Edit Style icon at the bottom of the CSS Styles panel. The CSS Style definition dialog box shows the current settings for the selected style. Change the settings in the dialog box.

The changes are immediately applied to the current document and can be previewed in the Document window.

If no style is currently selected when you click the Edit Style icon in the CSS Styles panel, this brings up the Edit Style Sheet dialog box (see Figure 9.9).

From here, you can choose one of two options:

- To edit an existing style, choose it and click the Edit button.

- To duplicate an existing style, click the Duplicate button, edit the name in the Duplicate CSS Style dialog box, and click OK. Then click the Edit button.

Either way, you arrive at the Style Definition dialog box. See "Making a Style" above for an explanation of the various categories and options there.

Figure 9.9

Edit or duplicate an existing style here.

Working with Style Sheets

Just as with individual styles, there are three main things you do with style sheets:

- Make them

- Attach them

- Edit them

We'll take them one at a time.

Making a Style Sheet

So far, you've seen how to create, apply, and edit a single style. A style sheet is a collection of styles. If you've been making your styles within the current document, you can export

Figure 9.10

Export your styles to an external style sheet all at once.

them to an external style sheet so that they'll be available to any document. You can also just choose to create a new style sheet when you first make a style and then add all subsequent styles to that sheet (as described in "Making a Style" above).

To export a set of styles as a style sheet, follow these steps:

1. Open a file that contains at least one CSS style.

2. Select File → Export → CSS Styles. This brings up the Export Styles As CSS File dialog box (see Figure 9.10).

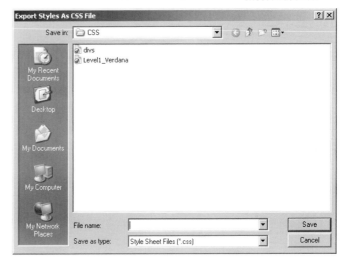

3. Choose a folder for the style. It often makes sense to put all your style sheet files in the same folder at a site.

4. Give the style sheet a name. Dreamweaver will take care of adding the .css extension.

5. Click Save.

Attaching a Style Sheet

To make the styles in a style sheet available to a new document, all you need to do is attach the style sheet to the document using either the link or the import method. In most cases, either method works fine. If you attach multiple style sheets to a single document (and there's no stopping you from doing this), then linked style sheets will be read first with imported style sheets read afterward, superseding any styles with the same names.

To attach a style sheet, click the Attach Style Sheet button in the CSS Styles panel.

The Link External Style Sheet dialog box appears. Once it does, follow these steps to complete the process of attaching a style sheet:

1. Browse to the CSS file you want to attach (or type a URL if you want to use a style sheet located elsewhere on the Web).

2. Choose the method for attaching the file: Link or Import.

> Usually, you'll want to choose the Link option to create a link to an external style sheet. However, if you want to created nested style sheets, use the Import option. For more information on the difference between these two options, see "Linking Style Sheets to HTML" at www.htmlhelp.com/reference/css/style-html.html.

3. Click OK. The styles in the style sheet are now available to the current document.

Generally, it won't matter what method you use for attaching the style sheet, but some designers use the import syntax to hide style sheets from older, noncompliant browsers, particularly Netscape 4.*x*.

> One easy way to make a style sheet available automatically to a given class of pages at your site is to link the style sheet to a template file and then attach the template to the documents in question (or build new documents based on the template). See Chapter 4 for more about working with templates.

Editing a Style Sheet

Editing a style sheet is merely a matter of editing the styles in the style sheet, as described above in the section "Editing a Style." However, if you are a hand-coder, you can edit your style sheets directly just by opening them in Dreamweaver. Use File → Open or double-click the style sheet file in the Files panel. Dreamweaver will open the CSS file as code only (see Figure 9.11). You can now hand-edit the code.

You can edit a style sheet with an external editor by selecting the style sheet in the CSS Styles panel, right-clicking it, and then choosing Use External Editor from the context menu.

Coding CSS on the Fly

The new features of Dreamweaver MX 2004 are numerous, but nowhere did Macromedia pay more attention to detail than with Dreamweaver's CSS tools. There are four new features for coding CSS that let you set CSS styles on the fly as you work on your site rather than having to open menus and windows. These new CSS features include the following:

- The CSS Properties tab, which lets you view and change CSS style rules
- The Style menu in the Property inspector
- CSS coding hints available as you hand-code your CSS style sheet
- The Relevant CSS panel so you can see what CSS style rules apply to your tags

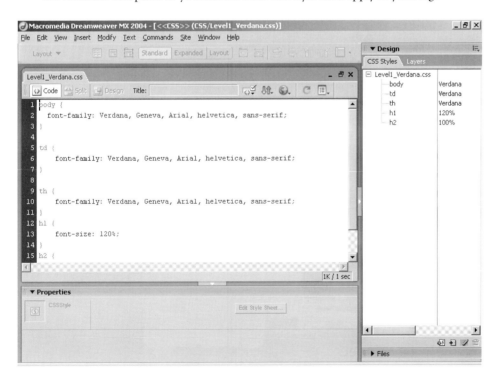

Figure 9.11

A style sheet file in Code view

The CSS Properties Tab

Previously we discussed setting CSS style rules using the New CSS Style dialog box. Dreamweaver MX 2004 makes it easier to establish style rules on-the-fly using the CSS Properties tab. The CSS Properties tab is part of the Tag Inspector, and appears when you select a CSS style in the CSS Styles panel, when you select a rule in Code view, or when you double-click a rule or property in the Relevant CSS panel (see Figure 9.12).

When you select a CSS style in the CSS Styles panel, the CSS Properties tab displays in the Tag Inspector and shows every single property associated with that style. The style property names appear on the left side of the list, and associated values appear to the right of each property name. From the CSS Properties tab, you can click on the property and change it. For example, if you want to change the text alignment of a style, you can click the value to the right of the text-align property, and select the new value from the list. If the style requires a text or numeric value, you can enter that new value directly in place of the old one.

Figure 9.12

The CSS Properties tab

Text Style Properties

Now Dreamweaver MX 2004 lets you select and change text styles on-the-fly in the Style drop-down menu, located within the Property inspector (see Figure 9.13).

When you click the style menu, a list appears with all the CSS text styles you have defined. Dreamweaver represents the styles by how they will appear on your page, not the code itself. You can scroll through the Style list to pick the text style you want to use for the selected text on your HTML page.

If you don't like any of the CSS text styles, you can add a new one by scrolling down to the bottom of the list and clicking Manage Styles. After you click Manage Styles, the Edit Style Sheet dialog box appears so you can add new styles or edit existing ones, just as you would by clicking the Edit Style button in the CSS Styles panel.

Figure 9.13

The Style drop-down menu

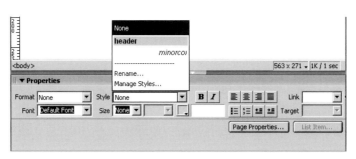

You can also rename your CSS text style directly from the Style list. Just scroll down to the bottom of the style list and click Rename. Then you can enter the new name in the Rename Style dialog box.

> Dreamweaver MX 2004 automatically creates embedded styles in your HTML page when you apply font face, color, or size properties to text. You can access these styles via the Property inspector or the CSS Styles panel and apply them to other selections on the same page. Dreamweaver also automatically creates styles for page properties such as background color and margins.

CSS Code Hints

When you hand-code your CSS style sheets, have you always wanted to find out what your options are for a certain piece of code without having to pick up a book or look through the online help? Dreamweaver MX 2004 now has code hints available at a keystroke. Actually, you press a keystroke combination—Ctrl-Space in Windows, or Command-Space on the Macintosh—when the cursor is located on a particular line in your CSS code. After you summon the code hints, a pop-up list of possible values appears (see Figure 9.14).

You can select from one of the code values, and once you click on the code value, Dreamweaver automatically places that information in your code. For example, if you don't know what text alignment options are available, you can enter text-align and then click Ctrl-Space or Command-Space. The list of possible values displays so you can choose the value you're looking for.

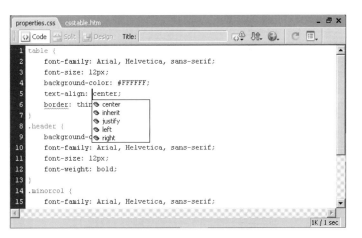

Figure 9.14

The list of CSS code hints

Relevant CSS Inspector

The Relevant CSS panel is part of the Tag Inspector panel group. When you click the Relevant CSS tab, the tab not only displays a list of HTML tags and the CSS rules that apply to those tags in your document, but also a list of all the CSS styles that apply to your HTML page (see Figure 9.15).

Figure 9.15

The Relevant CSS Panel

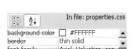

As with the CSS Properties tab, the names of the styles that apply to your page appear on the left side of the list, and their associated values appear to the right of each style name. You can click on the value to change it in a list or, if the style has a text or numeric value, enter that text directly in place of the old value. For example, if you want to change the page background, you can select a new color when you select the value to the right of the background style name.

Previewing Styled Pages

Dreamweaver does its darnedest to render CSS-styled pages accurately, following the CSS 2.0 specification, but it doesn't always get everything right (for instance, it doesn't always render borders). The fact is, your pages may very well look different in different browsers, so you will probably want to preview them.

Viewing a Style Sheet Layout

To preview a page in a browser, select File → Preview In Browser → *browser name*. You can add browsers with File → Preview In Browser → Edit Browser List. Any good web designer, developer, or information architect should have older versions of Internet Explorer and Netscape available as well as Opera and Mozilla (two relatively CSS-savvy browsers). So make sure you have these too, unless you know for sure that your users standardized on a specific browser, of course.

Design Time Style Sheets

One approach that some developers use to get around inconsistent style sheet interpretation by different browsers is to use scripting to serve up different style sheets depending on the user agent (browser) at any given time. If you need to do this, you will find that it becomes increasingly difficult to design pages without being able to see how the pages will render depending on which style sheets are being attached. Fortunately, Dreamweaver includes a feature called Design Time Style Sheets that allows you to select which style sheet(s) you want to use for displaying on-the-fly while you are designing.

To choose or hide style sheets, select Text → CSS Styles → Design-time, or right-click (or Ctrl-click) on the CSS Styles panel and choose Design-time. Either move brings up the (can you guess?) Design Time Style Sheets dialog box (see Figure 9.16).

Use the top portion of this dialog box to choose one or more style sheets to control display of the pages. Use the bottom portion to choose style sheets to hide (prevent from controlling the display of pages).

Checking for Browser Compatibility

As you write your CSS code, you need to be certain that visitors, no matter what browser they use, can read your code. Given that browsers can interpret CSS differently depending on the styles you use, it's always important to check your CSS code so you know any problems you encounter are not due to a faulty style sheet.

Figure 9.16

The Design Time Style Sheets window

You can check your CSS code the same way you verify that the rest of your page code works in your browsers of choice: by using the Target Browser Check. You will learn more about how to use the Target Browser Check from the Results panel in Chapter 29, but for the purposes of this chapter, you'll learn how to check your CSS Style Sheet using the Target Browser Check available in the Document toolbar.

Before you initiate the browser check, you must save your CSS file (and Dreamweaver will prompt you to do so if you haven't). Start the check by clicking the Target Browser Check button to the right of the Title text box in the Document toolbar (see Figure 9.17).

When you click the Target Browser Check button, a menu appears so you can check the CSS style by clicking the Check Browser Support option. If errors exist, the Target Browser Check button changes—instead of containing a check mark in the button, the button contains a warning sign (an exclamation point inside a yellow triangle). The Results panel also displays at the bottom of the screen and lists the error(s) on your page (see Figure 9.18). The errors contain not only a description, but also the browser that has a problem with the code causing the error. When you double-click the error on the page, Dreamweaver highlights the offending code block.

Figure 9.17

The Target Browser Check button

Figure 9.18

The Results panel

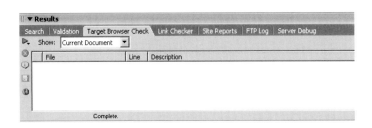

The Target Browser Check menu also lets you determine the target browsers and versions against which you want to check your CSS code. By default, Dreamweaver checks your code against Internet Explorer 5.0 and Netscape Navigator 4.0. You can change these versions to match your intended audience's browser(s). You can also check or uncheck up to six different browsers including Internet Explorer for the Macintosh, Mozilla, Opera, and Safari.

Note that testing your CSS file with Dreamweaver's Target Browser Check does not guarantee that you will have problem-free HTML pages when you let your website loose in the real World Wide Web. You can add an extra measure of CSS protection by downloading and running the World Wide Web Consortium CSS Validator to check your code a second time. You can download the CSS Validator at `http://jigsaw.w3.org/css-validator/`.

Using an External Editor

Editing your CSS in Dreamweaver is nice, but you may prefer to edit your CSS in an external editor. Fortunately, Dreamweaver doesn't make you choose between it and the CSS editing program you already know and love. Dreamweaver lets you attach style sheets from another program or a location on the Web, or edit your style sheets in an external program.

You can attach an external CSS style sheet by clicking the Attach Style Sheet button at the bottom of the CSS Styles panel. (When you have the CSS Styles panel selected, the button is the first of the four buttons.) When you click the button, the Attach External Style Sheet dialog box appears so you can link to the CSS style sheet or import it directly into Dreamweaver (see Figure 9.19).

Figure 9.19

The Attach External Style Sheet dialog box

Dreamweaver also lets you open documents with certain file extensions in external programs by associating an editor with the extension in the Preferences window (see Figure 9.20). To do this, choose Edit → Preferences and then click File Types/Editors in the Category list. Then remove the .css extension from the Open In Code View

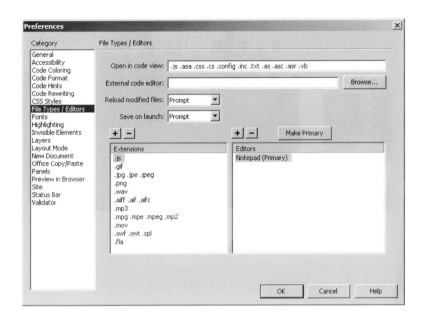

Figure 9.20

The Preferences window File Types/Editors area

text box, and add the .css extension to the Extensions list. Then you can add the external editor to the Editors list by clicking the plus (+) button above the Editors list and then select the external program from the Select External Editor window.

We've included the trial version of one of the top CSS editors available, in case you're inclined to try it. TopStyle Pro 3 from Bradbury Software is considered one of the best CSS design packages available for several reasons, including its easy-to-use GUI interface and excellent preview features. TopStyle Pro is a great production tool, and if you're not already familiar with CSS, it's a straightforward way to learn (see Figure 9.21).

If Bradbury Software sounds familiar, that's because Nick Bradbury, the creator of HomeSite, founded the company. HomeSite is the HTML editor that Bradbury developed in 1996 and is now owned by Macromedia. (It's a small world, indeed.)

For Further Reading on CSS

There is much more to say about CSS and its capabilities—at least an entire book's worth. If you want to learn more about CSS, start by visiting some of these sites:

- Access the original CSS specifications at www.w3.org/TR/REC-CSS1.
- Access the CSS2.1 working draft at www.w3.org/TR/CSS21/.
- Visit the CSS Zen Garden to see beautiful demonstrations of the visual power of CSS design at www.csszengarden.com/.

Figure 9.21

TopStyle Pro 3

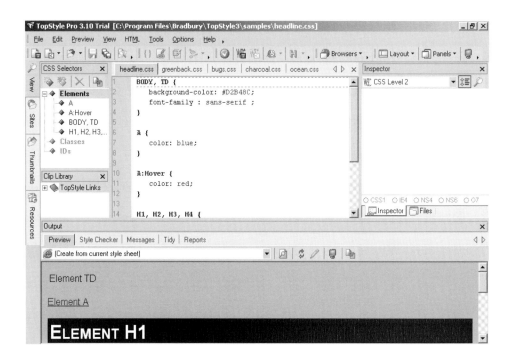

- Browse the New York Public Library's Online Style Guide (CSS: Steal These Style Sheets) at www.nypl.org/styleguide/css/opensource.html.
- Visit Eric Costello's site for CSS examples, techniques, resources, and tutorials at http://glish.com/css/.
- Look at Eric Meyer's site, which also has many CSS examples: www.meyerweb.com/eric/css/.

> In *Cascading Style Sheets: The Designer's Edge* (Sybex, 2002), author Molly E. Holzschlag explains CSS technology, then reveals how designers are using CSS to achieve advanced goals involving typography, color, layout, and more. The book includes a foreword by Eric Meyer.

- Try the Web Design Group's guide to style sheets at www.htmlhelp.com/reference/css/.
- Learn about using CSS layouts at www.bluerobot.com/web/layouts/.
- If you use a Mac, learn about CSS oddities and how to get around them at www.l-c-n.com/IE5tests/.

- Visit the css-discuss wiki to learn about writing good style sheets, get hacks and workarounds for CSS problems, and learn about code validation at `http://css-discuss.incutio.com/`.

- Take a look at Simon Willison's web log to learn how to use bookmarklets (bookmarks that embed JavaScript) with CSS at `http://simon.incutio.com/archive/2003/06/03/bookmarkletsAndCSS`.

Hands On: Design a CSS Table

Now it's time for you to put all this CSS knowledge to work. If you remember, in Chapter 5, "Page Layout," we talked about how you can use CSS to create tables. In this exercise, we're going to create a table and position the properties inside it using a CSS style sheet. The finished version of the HTML page, named `table.html`, is in the Chapter 9 folder on the CD and is shown in Figure 9.22.

Create the Table in HTML

The first step is to create the table. Follow these steps:

1. Open a new HTML document.

2. Choose Insert → Table.

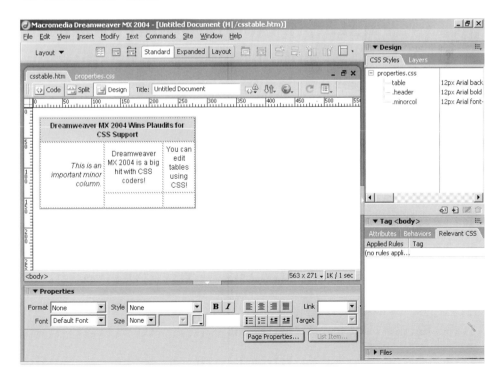

Figure 9.22

The CSS-created table when it's finished

3. In the Table dialog box, construct a table with the following parameters:

   - Three rows.
   - Three columns.
   - 50 percent table width.
   - 0-pixel border thickness.
   - 5-pixel cell padding.
   - No cell spacing.
   - No caption.
   - You can add a summary if you want.

4. Enter `Table1` in the Property inspector Table ID field.

5. Save the HTML file as `table.html`.

Create the CSS Table Properties

Now, with the HTML page still open, create a new CSS style and style sheet.

1. Click the New Style button in the CSS Styles panel.

2. Give the tag the name `table`, choose Tag from the Selector radio buttons, and define the file as a new style sheet file.

3. In the Save Style Sheet File As dialog box, browse to the location where you want to save your new style sheet and save the file with the name `properties.css`. Click OK. Click OK again if a message displays re: document-relative paths—this message indicates that you haven't yet saved the HTML file that you're linking to the style sheet.

4. In the CSS Style Definition dialog box, set the text properties as 12-point Arial, Helvetica, sans-serif.

5. Set the background color at #FFFFFF (white).

6. Set the block text alignment to center.

7. Give the block a thin, solid border.

8. Click OK, then click Done on the `properties.css` dialog box to save the file.

Customize Your Table

Next, customize your table to make it look like more than just a plain table. You do this by adding a class to your existing style.

1. In the `properties.css` file, click the New Style button in the CSS Styles panel.

2. Give the style the name `header`.

3. Keep the selector type as a class and the definition in `properties.css`.

4. Set the text properties as 12-point bold Arial, Helvetica, sans-serif.

5. Set the background to #CCCCCC (light gray).

6. Save the CSS file.

7. Switch to the HTML file.

8. Merge all three cells in the first row.

9. Place your cursor in the header row.

10. Apply the header style in the Property inspector. The header row turns light gray.

11. Enter text in the merged header row in your table. The bold text is centered in the merged header cell.

12. Enter text in the middle cell directly underneath the header cell.

13. Enter text in the right cell directly underneath the header cell.

14. Save the HTML file.

Create a Minor Column

Finally, tweak your table so you can create a minor column on the left side and position the text in that minor column so it appears at the bottom of the column.

1. Switch to the `properties.css` file.

2. Click the New Style button in the CSS Styles panel.

3. Give the style the name `minorcol`.

4. Keep the selector type as a class and the definition in `properties.css`.

5. Set the text properties as 12-point italic Arial, Helvetica, sans-serif.

6. Set the block text alignment to the right with a 2-point text indent.

7. Set the box width to 100 pixels.

8. Save the CSS file.

9. Switch to the HTML file.

10. Merge the middle and bottom cells in the left-hand column.

11. Place your cursor in the merged column.

12. Apply the header style in the Property inspector.

13. Enter text in the merged header row in your table. The italicized text appears right-aligned.

14. Save the HTML file.

We hope this tutorial has served to acquaint you with some CSS creation techniques using Dreamweaver's built-in CSS tools. You learned how to add new styles and classes in a CSS document and apply those to elements in an associated HTML file. You also learned how to add styles to change existing HTML elements.

Time for Jazz

So far in this part, you've learned how to lay out pages and populate them with text and graphics. You've seen how to work with framesets (if you must), and now you've been initiated into the mysteries of CSS. Now it's time to learn how you can place graphic and multimedia elements on your page. In Chapter 10, "Adding Graphics and Multimedia," you'll jazz up your site by learning how to insert graphics and multimedia files in your Dreamweaver pages.

Adding Graphics and Multimedia

The first web browsers were text-based only, with no graphic content. Web graphics first became a reality in 1993 when Marc Andreessen added the <img> (image) tag to his Mosaic browser. Andreessen and other developers created Netscape, first released in October 1994, which also included the <img> tag. Almost overnight, web pages changed from text-only pages with uniform gray backgrounds to pages that incorporate graphic content. The earliest web graphics were usually too large (by today's standards) and without transparent backgrounds. In other words, all the graphics had visible rectangular edges. It would be years later before other media could be added to web pages using <embed> and <object> tags.

As computer technology changed, web graphics evolved and multimedia elements emerged. Today, web pages can include graphics, interactive images, animated GIFs, Flash movies, Shockwave movies, Java applets, and sound and video files.

You must learn how to use graphics and multimedia elements wisely so they don't become a liability and deter visitors from visiting your site. This chapter reviews factors you should consider when you are making decisions about using multimedia content, and details how to use Dreamweaver to insert this content in your pages. Topics include the following:

- **Placing graphics on a page**

- **Fine-tuning the display of images**

- **Designing with placeholders**

- **Modifying a graphic for use on the Web**

- **Deciding to include multimedia**

- **Understanding web audio and video formats**

- **Using multimedia players**

- **Adding sound and movies**

- **Adding media elements**

- **Controlling media elements**

Inserting a Graphic

First, we'll look at how to insert graphics in your Dreamweaver pages. In the section, "Setting Image Options," later in this chapter we'll review the new image-editing features that make it easier than ever to use images in Dreamweaver.

Placing Your Image

Once you've decided upon a general layout scheme for your web page (as discussed in Part I), you're ready to start placing graphics where you want them.

The process is a fairly simple one:

1. In the Dreamweaver workspace, click the place in your design where you would like to place your graphic. You'll see a blinking cursor.

2. Without clicking anywhere else, move your mouse over to the Insert bar, make sure the Common tab (or the Common Insert bar if you haven't selected Tab view) is selected, and click the Images button to display the Images drop-down menu. You can also use Ctrl-Alt-I in Windows or Option-Cmd-I on Mac to insert an image. Figure 10.1 shows you the Insert bar and the location of the button.

Figure 10.1

Simply place a cursor on your page where you'd like a graphic and press the Images button on the Insert bar to place a graphic in your web page.

When you select Image from the Images drop-down menu, the Select Image Source dialog box appears (see Figure 10.2). You will now navigate to your computer's hard drive and locate the image you'd like to place into your web page. We'll assume that you've already decided what size your image should be based on your design.

Once you've found and selected your image, you'll notice a small drop-down menu in the Select Image Source dialog box labeled "Relative To:" (just below the URL or path to your image file).

If you are publishing HTML that will only appear on your computer (not on the Web) or on a CD or DVD, you should select the Document option because the path (in the code, the page has to refer the browser to the location of the file) will be relative to the HTML document you are working on.

On the other hand, if you are publishing this HTML page to the Web, you may opt to choose Site Root from this drop-down box. Choose this option only if you have already set up a definition for your site by going to Site → Manage Sites → New from the application menu at the top of the screen. (See Chapter 3, "Setting Up Your Workspace and Your Site," for more on setting up your site).

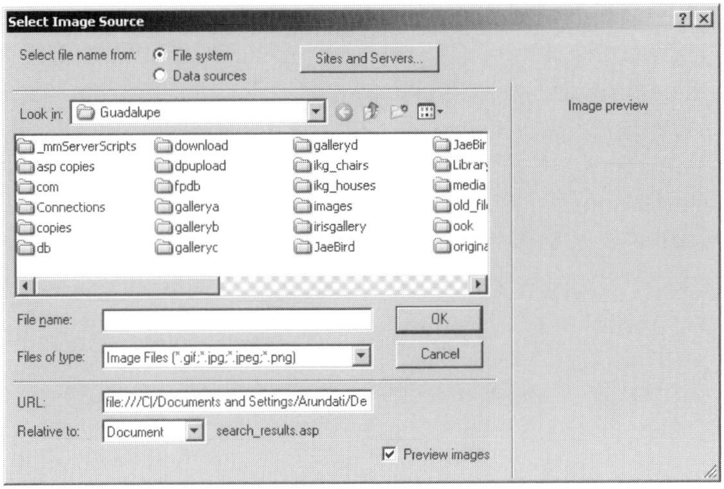

Figure 10.2

**The Select Image
Source dialog box**

If you work with a site with a "mirror" copy on both your drive and the web server, and you use the Relative To: Site Root image source, you will have a duplicate of your website/server file and folder hierarchy on your hard drive. This copy will help you keep your file locations organized, thus making it easier to locate files quickly and compare them to the copies on the live web server. The other thing that this process provides—and this is a big benefit—is an exact backup of your site.

Many programmers like to work on their live sites directly on the web server—probably because they know how. That's all fine and good, but if your web server crashes or your service provider goes belly up ("That'll never happen!" Quote circa 1999), you are out of luck. Of course, if you work on your site offline and this happens, you simply upload the latest version of your site files because they live right on your computer.

Because the Select Image Source's Relative To setting is an important one, I'd like to wrap it up with this bit of information—the local root folder in the Site Definition dialog box will act as your `/public_html/` directory, which is the typical directory for web hosting providers. The forward slash (/) that Dreamweaver will place in front of the path to your image (for example, `"<img src="/images/file.gif">"`) will be relative to the directory your service provider gave you as your account's public directory.

Make your selection and press Open to insert the image into your page. There it is! Looks good. If the image source is located outside the current Dreamweaver site, you'll be prompted to see if you want to copy the image to the current site files. Now you're done, right? Not quite. You still have to decide on a few image settings so that a web browser knows exactly how you want your image displayed.

CONTROLLING YOUR IMAGE SIZES

One more thing to note when you are creating a layout for your web page is that web pages are viewed on a computer monitor, not on paper. This means that your design and your graphics need to be optimized for this medium. Most novice web designers start creating graphics in an application using inches as their unit of measure for determining the size of their graphics. While that isn't technically wrong per se, you'd be wise to start thinking in pixels (the unit of measure for monitor screen resolution).

If you are using a graphics application such as Photoshop, you can change the unit of measure to pixels in Photoshop's preferences. This will get you thinking screen resolution instead of inches and it will help you tremendously when you go to size your images for a particular design. The more control you have over your design and its size, the cleaner your web pages will look to visitors.

Setting Image Options

If your design is simple or you are placing a graphic onto an empty page just to learn the process, most of the image settings will not apply to you. But if you are trying to make an exact design that needs to have images that fit where they are and work properly in relation to other elements (images, text, and so on) on the page, you will want to work with the Property inspector (see Figure 10.3). In order to make changes to your image in the Property inspector, you must select the image (but it will automatically be selected immediately after you place it into your page) by single-clicking it.

You'll quickly see that there is a lot to digest when reviewing the properties of an image. Some properties are more complicated than others, so we'll briefly run through each setting so that you can decide which one applies to your particular situation and/or situations to come.

For more details on changing graphics to make them "web-ready," see the Hands On tutorial, "Modifying a Graphic for Use on the Web," at the end of this chapter.

Figure 10.3

Use the Property inspector to modify how a browser will display your image.

IMAGE OPTIMIZATION

So what do we mean when we say an image has been optimized? We mean that we have chosen the optimal image size and format for display on a web page, and that we have selected the best balance between image quality and image compression.

When calculating file size of a page, you must add the file size of all the files—the HTML file, any associated script or CSS files, and all the graphics and multimedia elements. Graphics (and multimedia files) generally determine the overall file size of a web page.

Although the perfect file size varies, the general rule is to keep the total file size of a page at or under 48K. If your audience is all on a corporate intranet or broadband connections, a larger file size may be appropriate.

One of the most useful image-related features of Dreamweaver is its automatic placement of the image size in the HTML code. This may seem trivial to some, but it's a huge reason why some sites—even with graphics optimized for the Web—load slowly. If a site has image sizes set properly in the HTML code, the site visitor's browser doesn't have to guess where to place everything. It sees the graphic size and says, "Oh, okay. I know how to lay this page out." It does this without having loaded the image completely. Without those simple little numbers, the browser has to wait until the images are almost totally loaded in order to "know" where to place everything in order to display the page the way the page designer put it together.

Here are more features to get familiar with when working with images. (You can expand the Property inspector to show all image-related options by clicking the little arrow in its bottom-right corner.) Naturally, you'll have situations arise when you will need to handle images differently than the norm (for example, large images where you need to have multiple "hotspots," small spacer images where you'll change their size from the original file, and so on).

Image Map Creating an image map allows you to select portions of a single image and make them *hotspots*—clickable areas that send visitors to different URLs using *x* and *y* coordinates. This option is typically used with larger images for navigation. You can access the map options in the lower-left corner of the expanded Property inspector. See Chapter 8, "Making and Maintaining Hyperlinks," for more details on creating image maps in Dreamweaver.

Image Size You'll see the exact pixel size (see, you need to understand pixels!) of your image displayed automatically in the W (width) and H (height) text boxes. You can set this size manually, but be aware of how doing so alters your image when it is displayed in the browser. First, when you make the file size larger, you will probably see the visual quality of your image degrade. Secondly, if you make the size smaller, it may look okay, but the actual file size that a site visitor has to download is larger than it needs to be. Use this feature to visually place a graphic and find the right size, but go back to your graphics editing application and make sure the final image is the exact size you want it.

Image Source (src) As you can see in Figure 10.3, this is the URL (path) to your image.

In Figure 10.3, the path name and the filename are exactly the same (about.jpg), but that's not always the case. For instance, if the file is in a folder named Graphics, the path name is Graphics/about.jpg.

Image Link This is where you would place a URL (or web address) that you would like to point visitors to if they click your image. You may link to a file in your file structure or to another website altogether. Be aware that if you link to an outside website (outside your domain), you must provide a full path to the URL, such as http://www.example.com/somewhere/something.html. (See Chapter 8 for more about hypertext links.)

Image Align This setting can be important depending on how you intend to place your image on your page and how you want it to interact with other elements around it. The default setting is Browser Default. This aligns your image to the left of whatever placeholder it's in, such as a table cell or the entire web browser page. Play with each of these to see what it does for you.

We will explain the Left and Right options here. If you want an image to be displayed within a block or paragraph of text, you can place the image at the beginning of a line of text and choose the Left or Right Align option. This will align the image and allow the text to "flow" around it on whichever side is away from the alignment setting.

Image Alternate The alt tag is rarely used correctly. Alt is an alternate description of your image displayed in text. Originally, it was used for non-graphical browsers (yes, they existed…and still do) so that they could "see" what the image was or what it said. Nowadays, it's used as a descriptor (place your cursor over an image on the Web and see the little text box pop-up) or more importantly it's used to assist visitors with disabilities and those who have turned images off for faster page downloads. The alt tag should describe the image, and if the image is associated with a function, describe the function. It's also useful as a way to optimize your page for certain search engines. You can use alt tags as a way to increase the frequency of keyword usage on your page for those search engines that use keyword frequency as a ranking item. (Of course, this should be in addition to the description of the image.)

Image Class The class attribute, new to the Property inspector in Dreamweaver MX 2004, is used to apply a style class to your image. You can use any styles defined for your page, or you can also choose to create a new style (New), edit an existing style (Edit), rename an existing style (Rename), or link to an external style sheet (Attach Style Sheet).

Vertical Space The vspace attribute is simply a number of pixels (default is "none") that act as a buffer zone above and below your image. This option and the Horizontal Space option are typically used if you are placing an image that is surrounded by text or other images and you do not want the other content right up against your image.

Horizontal Space Hspace is the same as vspace, but it's for the left and right side of your image rather than the top and bottom.

Link Target If you are using frames or if you want to control how the browser handles a link, this is the place to choose your options. Most of these pertain to frames. If you'd like to have a new browser window pop up over the window with your site displayed, choose "_blank."

Low Source This is an old-school style of placing images on a web page. You have the option of creating a very low quality version of your image and having it load first while the original, more detailed image is still loading. This was designed for the overwhelming number of site visitors who were using 28.8K (or slower!) modems—way before DSL, cable modems, and so on. We recommend that you use this feature only when you have a very large graphic—which you should avoid using anyway.

Border If you add a link to an image, Dreamweaver automatically places a 0 value in the Border setting. Otherwise, if you have a link associated with an image, the browser will automatically place a colored border (usually blue) around the entire image to indicate that it is a hotspot.

If you have an image that does not have a link, you can add a border (in pixels again) to give it some structure. Use a one- or two-pixel border around a photo for a nice touch.

Image Align Part II You'll notice three buttons on the far right of the Property inspector for aligning your image. These are for quickly centering your image or aligning left and right without having to go to the drop-down list.

Edit In Dreamweaver's preferences (Edit → Preferences → File Types/Editors), you can associate the Edit button with an image editor. By default, clicking it will open Fireworks, but you can set it to open whatever application you prefer.

In Dreamweaver MX 2004, additional image editing options are available in the Property inspector via the buttons to the right of the Edit button. The new image editing features use Fireworks technology, but are available in Dreamweaver even if you don't have Fireworks installed.

Dreamweaver's new image editing properties are easy to access, but they are meant for basic editing tasks and don't offer the range of options that a full-fledged graphics software program does.

Optimize You can also associate the Optimize button with an image editor. By default, Fireworks is selected. Clicking this button opens Fireworks and allows you to optimize (choose the appropriate image size and level of compression) your image. See the Sidebar, "Image Optimization," earlier in this section for more information on optimizing images.

Crop Clicking the Crop button adds a dotted crop border around your image. You can click and drag on this border to define the area to be cropped. You can also resize an image by selecting it and then dragging on the selection borders to resize it.

Resample After you resize an image in Dreamweaver, the Resample button becomes available (otherwise this button is grayed out). When a bitmap image is resampled, pixels are added or removed to make it larger or smaller.

Brightness and Contrast You can adjust the brightness and/or contrast of your image by adjusting the slider bars in the Brightness/Contrast dialog box that displays when you click this button.

Sharpen You can adjust the focus (sharpen) an image by adjusting the slider bar in the Sharpen dialog box that displays when you click this button.

All of Dreamweaver's image editing options change the original image stored in your site folder. Dreamweaver will display a message to this effect whenever you click one of the image-editing buttons. You should save a copy of the original image before you apply any of these options.

TEXT AS GRAPHICS

You can create a graphic for text display if, for example, you want to use a nonstandard font for displaying text information.

You can use either a GIF or a JPEG file for this, but GIFs are generally preferable. Text in images creates hard transitions that often appear blurred in JPEGs after compression; JPEG compression works best with images with gradual transitions.

Two issues to keep in mind when using text as graphics:

1. Using text as graphics increases the overall file size of your page. Make sure you don't overly increase the download time for the page with the additional graphics.

2. Text as graphics can create accessibility issues for viewers with visual disabilities. Be sure to include alternate text (via the <alt> tag) that contains the same text content as the graphic.

You can also easily create text as graphics directly in Dreamweaver itself by creating Flash text (Insert → Media → Flash Text). For more details on using Flash text, see Chapter 11, "Getting into Flash."

Designing with Image Placeholders (When the Art Isn't Ready Yet)

Sometimes you need to lay out your pages without having the final versions of the artwork ready. This is no problem. Use Dreamweaver's Insert Image Placeholder option from the Images pop-up menu on the Common Insert bar (or the Common tab, if you've selected tab view) to insert a dummy image tag. This brings up a dialog box where you can specify the name, alternate text, width, height, and background color of the placeholder.

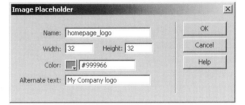

Choosing a color for the placeholder is optional, but it's a good idea to give it a name, just to remind you what's supposed to go there eventually. Dreamweaver will show a box to represent the image for now (see Figure 10.4).

When you have the art ready, double-click the placeholder to open the Select Image Source dialog box and choose the image to insert, or create the image directly in Fireworks (or whatever graphics program you specify in Preferences → File Types/Editors) by clicking the Create button in the Property inspector.

For in-depth information about web graphic file formats as well as how to slice and optimize images in Fireworks, Photoshop, Illustrator, and Dreamweaver, see the Chapter 10 supplement on the CD!

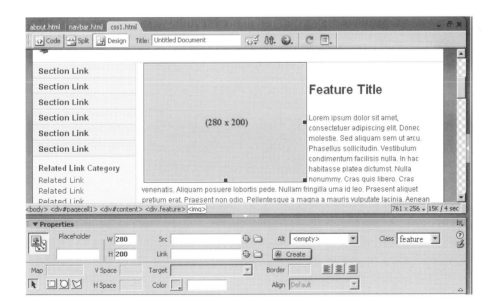

Figure 10.4

A placeholder has properties just like those of a real image.

Deciding to Include Multimedia

When you make a decision about including multimedia elements, you are performing an important part of the site planning and design process. But first, be sure that the multimedia element is necessary. Start with these questions:

- What is the overall purpose of the site? Is multimedia content necessary to meet these goals, or the objectives of a portion of the site?
- Does the multimedia element add content that can't be provided in any other way?
- Does the multimedia element enhance the rest of the page content?

Second, take a look at your audience definition, and pay particular attention to the following issues:

- Which browsers and browser versions are your audience most likely to be using to access your site?
- What kind of Internet connections are your audience likely to use?
- What percentage of your audience is likely to have broadband access?

Bandwidth is a very important issue to consider when you are using multimedia on the Web. Your site visitors will likely include users with both *broadband* connections and *narrowband* connections. Broadband connections are high-speed—200Kbps (kilobits per second) or higher—and include most DSL (Digital Subscriber Lines), ISDN (Integrated Services Digital Network), cable modem, T1, and T3 connections. Narrowband connections are less than 200Kbps, and include dial-up modems.

Third, be sure to consider how you're going to obtain multimedia files for the pages. Are you planning to create the multimedia files yourself or do you plan to contract with someone else to do this? If you're going to create them yourself, evaluate these issues:

- Do you have the necessary software and other materials (video camera, sound files, and so on) to do this?
- Do you already know how to use the software and materials, or do you need to plan on additional site development time to learn these skills?

If you've reviewed these issues for your website and have decided to go ahead with including multimedia elements on the pages, you're ready for the next steps: choosing multimedia file types, choosing a server, and deciding whether to use a multimedia player.

Visit the Macromedia site at www.macromedia.com for information on Macromedia's multimedia-authoring programs, including Director, Flash, and Authorware.

Understanding Web Audio and Video Formats

Many different types of files can be used for audio and video on the Web. The following two sections review the features of the most popular audio and video files.

Web Audio

There are six file types commonly used for web audio. Each type has advantages and disadvantages for use on the Web.

MIDI (Musical Instrument Digital Interface) MIDI files (with the `.midi` or `.mid` extensions) contain synthesized music. MIDI files are supported by most browsers, and don't require a *plug-in* (a program that is used to view effects that the browser doesn't support by itself). The sound quality is very good, and the files are relatively small, making MIDI a very good choice for web audio. Special hardware and software are required to synthesize MIDI files.

WAV (Waveform Extension) WAV files (with the `.wav` extension) contain high-quality sampled sound. WAV files are supported by most browsers and don't require a plug-in. You can record your own WAV files, but the large file size limits their use on the Web.

AIFF (Audio Interchange File Format) AIFF files (with the `.aif` or `.aiff` extensions) contain good-quality sampled sound. AIFF files are supported by most browsers and don't require a plug-in. You can record your own AIFF files but, like WAV files, large file size limits their use on the Web.

AU (basic Audio) AU files (with the `.au` extension) contain acceptable-quality sampled sound. AU files are supported by the widest range of browsers and don't require a plug-in.

MP3 (MPEG Audio Layer 3) MP3 files (with the `.mp3` extension) contain outstanding-quality sound. The MP3 format is a compressed format that greatly reduces the size of the files. MP3 files can still be very large, however. MP3 files can be *streamed*—the file plays as it downloads, rather than having to wait for the whole file to download before it starts to play. The disadvantage of the MP3 format is that it requires a browser plug-in or helper application.

RA, RAM (RealAudio) RealAudio files (with the `.ra`, `.ram`, or `.rpm` extensions) contain high-quality streaming sound in a compressed format. Real Audio files have a smaller file size than MP3 files. RealAudio files require the use of RealPlayer software, either a browser plug-in or a helper application.

Which audio format you choose will depend on what sound files you have available for your site. You can record your own sounds if you have a sound card and a microphone. You can also find thousands of sound samples on the Web—just be sure a sound file is in the public domain before you publish it on the Web.

FindSounds.com is a search engine for finding sound effects and sample sounds on the Web. Visit their site at www.findsounds.com.

Web Video

There are five file types commonly used for web video. Video files tend to be extremely large, however, so you must be sure a large video file is essential before you add it your site.

AVI (Audio Video Interleave) The AVI file format (with the `.avi` extension) was originally only supported on Windows platforms but is now also supported on the Mac platform. AVI files are often used for short video clips that aren't streamed. You can embed the AVI file in your page or create a link to it. In either case, the file must download entirely before playback can begin, so don't forget to keep it short!

MPEG (Moving Picture Experts Group) MPEG files (with the `.mpg` extension) are the most widely supported video file format on the Web. The MPEG file format is highly compressed so that the video file size can be made as small as possible. MPEG files, like AVI files, are often used for short video clips that aren't streamed.

QuickTime, RealMedia, Windows Media QuickTime, RealMedia, and Windows Media files are the most common web video file formats for streaming video. Each of these file formats requires a helper application unless the specific multimedia player is already installed on the user's computer.

Using Multimedia Players

Multimedia players are integrated packages of software that support almost all multimedia file types available on the Web. There are both free and commercial versions of all of the following multimedia players.

RealPlayer RealPlayer supports streaming audio and video including RealAudio and RealVideo as well as several other media types available as plug-ins. The RealOne Player is the current version of the RealPlayer software. RealOne Player combines features of RealPlayer and RealJukebox so that you can organize your media files or burn CDs. It also includes a built-in web browser for downloading media files. Although the preset defaults in the RealOne Player allow you to use it for every media file type, you can uncheck those selections during the installation process.

You can download the RealOne Player from `www.real.com/realoneplayer.html?src=R1Guide`.

QuickTime QuickTime supports over 200 types of digital media, including MP3, MIDI, AVI, streaming media, and digital video. The newest version of QuickTime is QuickTime 6.3. QuickTime 6.3 features 3GPP (3rd Generation Partnership Project), a new standard for multimedia on high-speed wireless networks. The 3GPP standard makes streaming multimedia available to multimedia-enabled cell phones and PDAs as well as computers.

The QuickTime 6.3 player supports playback of GSPP files, MPEG-4 video, streaming media, virtual reality (VR) media, and interactive content.

You can download the QuickTime player from `www.apple.com/quicktime/products/qt/`.

> You can import Flash 5 files in QuickTime 6.3.

Windows Media Player The Windows Media Player supports streaming media files, and includes a CD player and burner, a DVD player, an audio and video player, a media guide, a media library, and Internet radio.

The newest version is the Windows Media Player 9 for Windows XP, Windows 2000, Windows 98, and Windows Me. Versions are also available for many handheld devices, and for several other platforms including Mac OS 8.1–9.x and Mac OS X.

You can download the Windows Media Player from `www.microsoft.com/windows/windows-media/download/default.asp`.

> For more details on embedding a multimedia player in a web page, see "Embedding a Windows Media Player" by Adam Powell at `http://hotwired.lycos.com/webmonkey/01/49/index2a.html?tw=eg20020111`.

Adding Sound and Movies

Both sound and movie files are often very large files, so be sure to consider whether audio or video enhancement of your pages is worth the download time.

Adding Audio Files

Sounds on web pages include background sounds that play as soon as the page loads, sounds that play when the user clicks a link, or sounds that are part of other multimedia files such as Flash animations or video files.

> **CHOOSING A SERVER FOR MULTIMEDIA CONTENT**
>
> Another important issue to consider when you are adding streaming multimedia content to your website is the choice of a server for streaming multimedia files. Most web servers use HTTP, but streaming web servers that use RTSP and other protocols are becoming increasingly available. Streaming media files can be served from an HTTP server, but the media file download is not synchronized, so playback might not be synchronous either! Pauses in playback are also more likely to happen when you are using HTTP for downloading streaming media files.
>
> For more information on streaming media, visit `www.streamingmedia.com`.

Embedding Audio Files

Embedding an audio file in your page puts a sound player directly onto the page—the HTML that embeds the audio file also creates a visual display of a player that includes the controls that you specify. The user still needs the appropriate plug-in to play the file, but you have some control over the appearance of the player on the page.

To embed an audio file, follow these steps:

1. From the Common Insert bar, click the Media icon, and then click the plug-in icon (or choose Insert → Media → Plugin).

2. Browse to the audio file from the Select File display box (Figure 10.5), or enter the URL of the audio file.

3. Open the Property inspector (Window → Properties) and enter width and height values for the player display on the page.

Linking to Audio Files

When you have a link to an audio file, you give the user the most choice about whether to listen to the file or not, and by having such a link, you can get around the issue of browser support for embedding sound files.

To link to an audio file, follow these steps.

1. Select a block of text or a graphic from your page to use as the link to an audio file.

2. Open the Property inspector (Window → Properties).

3. Click the folder next to Link to browse to the audio file you want to link to, or enter the URL in the Link text box (Figure 10.6).

Figure 10.5

Inserting a plug-in

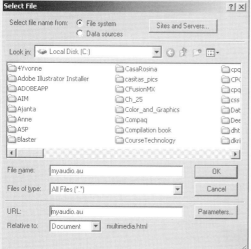

Adding Movies

Video files are becoming more and more common on web pages, particularly on entertainment and news websites. Video technology continues to develop rapidly, and smaller video file size is becoming much more common.

Newer versions of Internet Explorer support video streaming, MPEG video, and QuickTime movie playback in the basic installation. Netscape Navigator, however, has more limited support for video playback and video streaming, and even the latest version (Netscape Navigator 7.1) requires a plug-in to play QuickTime movies. Netscape 7.1 is, however, the first version of Netscape to support the Windows Media Player.

Figure 10.6

Linking to an audio file

To check which plug-ins are installed in your copy of Netscape, choose Help → About Plug-ins from the Navigator menu bar.

To add a video file to your page, follow these steps.

1. From the Common Insert bar click the Media icon and then select Flash or the Shockwave icon to add a Flash or Shockwave file to the page. Click the Plugin icon to add other video file types.

2. Browse to the video file from the Select File display window.

Adding Flash Movies

Dreamweaver includes both an `object` and an `embed` element when it inserts a Flash movie. This ensures that the movie can be viewed in both Internet Explorer and Netscape, as well as most other browsers. Dreamweaver automatically adds the appropriate code (Figure 10.7); you can modify it or add extra parameters for the Flash movie.

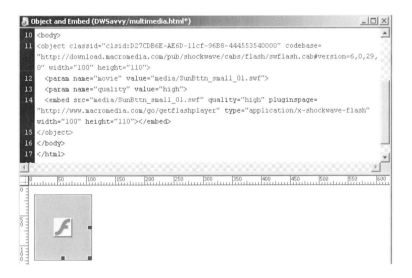

Figure 10.7

Inserting a Flash movie in Dreamweaver

To preview a Flash movie in the Dreamweaver Document window, select the Flash icon for the movie in Design view. Open the Property inspector (Window → Properties) and click the Play button.

Flash movie properties can be edited in the Property inspector in Dreamweaver. To edit a Flash movie, follow these steps.

1. Select the Flash movie icon in Design view.

2. Open the Property inspector (Window → Properties).

3. Add values for any attributes you want to change (see Chapter 11 for a table of common properties).

For more information on Flash and Flash integration with Dreamweaver, see Chapter 11, "Getting into Flash."

Adding Shockwave Movies

Macromedia Director MX is a multifaceted multimedia production program, and is generally used for creating multimedia content for CD, DVD, or kiosks. Director can generate Shockwave movies (`.dcr`) from Director source files (`.dir`). Shockwave movies are compressed versions of Director files designed for playback in a Web browser. Like Flash movies (`.swf`), Shockwave movies can't be edited directly—you must edit the source file (`.dir`) and then re-export the Shockwave file.

Figure 10.8 shows the Director MX workspace, with a timeline window at the top, and a cast window with storyboard at the bottom.

ACTIVE CONTENT AND CHANGES IN INTERNET EXPLORER

Microsoft is making changes to the next version of Internet Explorer due to a recent legal action. This change affects the browser display of any active content—content that uses Microsoft's ActiveX Controls for display (Macromedia Flash, Shockwave, and Authorware players, Apple QuickTime, RealAudio and RealVideo, Adobe Acrobat Reader, Microsoft Windows Media Player, and Java applets). For more details, see Chapter 11, "Getting into Flash", and check out these resources:

- `www.macromedia.com/devnet/activecontent/presentation/index.html`

- `http://msdn.microsoft.com/ieupdate/`

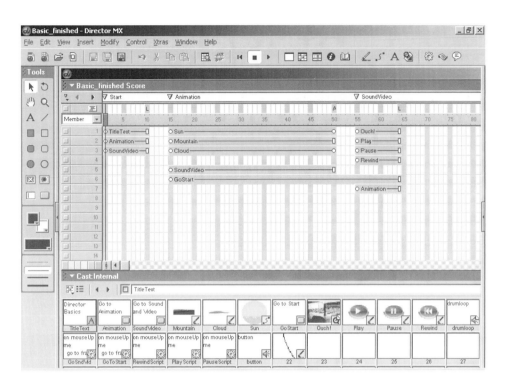

Figure 10.8

**Director MX
Workspace**

Director supports over 40 media types, including Real Media, Quicktime, and Flash. Director MX is integrated with both Flash and Fireworks. Director can import Flash files, and can Launch and Edit Flash. Director can also import Fireworks files, and can Launch and Edit Fireworks as well as Launch and Optimize in Fireworks.

Although you can use Macromedia Director to create Shockwave movies to add to your Dreamweaver pages, as well as export Shockwave movies in HTML files (Figure 10.9), you can't export directly from Director to Dreamweaver.

To add a Shockwave movie to your page, follow these steps.

1. From the Common Insert bar click the Media icon and then select the Shockwave icon to add a Shockwave movie to the page.

2. Browse to the Shockwave movie from the Select File display window.

Figure 10.9

**Exporting a
Shockwave movie
from Director to
an HTML file**

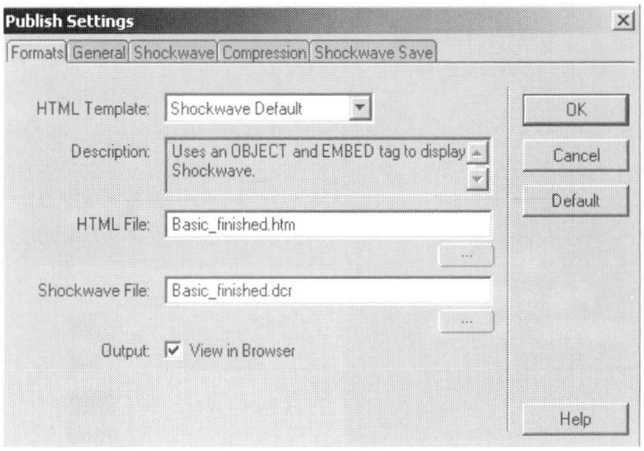

Adding Media Elements

Many other media elements can be added to your pages in Dreamweaver. These files can include Netscape plug-ins, ActiveX controls, Java applets, and animated GIFs.

Adding Netscape Plug-ins

Most multimedia files require plug-ins in order to be viewed in Netscape Navigator. Plug-ins act as though they are part of the browser and extend the capabilities of the browser. The most popular plug-ins are the Java plug-in (for viewing Java applets) and plug-ins for Adobe Acrobat Reader, Apple QuickTime player, Macromedia Flash player, and RealNetwork's RealPlayer.Developers can create new plug-ins for Netscape Navigator by using the Plugin API. For more details, see "Plug-in Basics" at `http://developer.netscape.com/docs/manuals/ communicator/plugin/basic.htm#1009627`.

> Internet Explorer for Windows beginning with versions 5.5 SP2 and 6.0 no longer supports Netscape-style plug-ins. This does not affect Mac users or Netscape users. Windows users can restore support for Netscape-style plug-ins by downloading an ActiveX control from Apple at `www.apple.com/quicktime/download/qtcheck/`.

To add a Netscape plug-in, use the Common Insert bar and click the Media icon, and then click the Plugin icon. Browse to the media file from the Select File display box (Figure 13.1), or enter the URL of the media file.

Netscape supports the `embed` element for inserting multimedia files. When you add a plug-in to your Dreamweaver page, an `embed` element with an `src` attribute (the location and filename of the multimedia file) and `width` and `height` attributes is automatically created.

To specify additional attributes for the `embed` element, follow these steps.

1. Select the Plugin icon in Design view.

2. Open the Property inspector (Window → Properties). The top part of the window displays the most commonly used properties for the Plugin object. To see all the properties, click the down arrow in the lower-right corner of the Property inspector (Figure 10.10).

3. Insert values for any attribute you want to include in the `embed` element.

Figure 10.10

Plug-in Property inspector—full view

Table 10.1 lists the most common properties of the Plugin object.

PROPERTY	DESCRIPTION
name	Identifies the plug-in, used in scripting
width	Identifies the width of the plug-in
height	Denotes the height of the plug-in
src	Describes the path (location and filename) to the plug-in file
Plg Url	Contains the URL of the pluginspace attribute[1]
align	Shows the alignment of the plug-in
vspace	Specifies the vertical space above and below the plug-in
hspace	Denotes the horizontal space to the left and right of the plug-in
border	Specifies the width of the border around the plug-in

Table 10.1

Common Plugin Properties

1 The browser uses this URL to download the plug-in if the viewer does not already have it installed.

The Property inspector also includes a Parameters button. Click this button, or right-click the Plugin icon on the Dreamweaver page to open the Parameters dialog box. The Parameters dialog box can be used to add attributes specific to the type of object being inserted and can be used with embed, object, and applet elements.

Click the plus (+) button and enter a name and a value to add a parameter. To remove a parameter, select it in the Parameters dialog box and click the minus (-) button. You can also change the order of parameters by selecting a parameter in the Parameter dialog box and then using the up and down arrow buttons.

To preview plug-in content in the Document window, select a media element you have inserted and choose View → Plugins → Play. To play all the media elements on the page, choose View → Plugins → Play All. You can also play a media element by selecting it, and then opening the Property inspector (Window → Properties) and clicking the Play button. Only media objects that use the embed element can be played in the Document window in this way. The appropriate plug-in to play the file must be installed on your computer.

The above table lists the common properties of the Plugin object.

Adding ActiveX Controls

ActiveX controls are small programs that add functionality to a web page. ActiveX controls use the ActiveX technologies developed by Microsoft.

> For further information on ActiveX, see "ActiveX Controls" at http://msdn.microsoft.com/library/default.asp?url=/workshop/components/activex/activex_node_entry.asp.

To add an ActiveX control, use the Common Insert bar and click the Media icon, then click the ActiveX icon. Browse to the media file from the Select File display box, or enter the URL of the media file.

Internet Explorer supports the object element for inserting ActiveX controls. When you add an ActiveX control to your Dreamweaver page, an object element with an src attribute (the location and filename of the multimedia file) and width and height attributes is automatically created.

To specify additional attributes for the object element, follow these steps.

1. Select the ActiveX icon in Design view.

2. Open the Property inspector (Window → Properties). The top part of the window displays the most commonly used properties for ActiveX objects. To see all the properties, click the down-arrow in the lower-right corner of the Property inspector.

3. Insert values for any attribute you want to include in the object element.

Table 10.2 lists the most common properties of the ActiveX object.

Additional ActiveX properties can be included by clicking the Parameters button in the Property inspector (as described in the preceding section on Netscape plug-ins), which results in the Parameters dialog box being displayed (Figure 10.11). To choose which additional parameters to include, check the documentation for the ActiveX control you're using.

> See the sidebar "Active Content and Changes to Internet Explorer" in the "Adding Movies" section earlier in this chapter for information on changes in ActiveX display in browsers.

	PROPERTY	DESCRIPTION
Table 10.2 **Common ActiveX Properties**	name	Identifies the ActiveX object, used in scripting
	width	Denotes the width of the ActiveX object
	height	Declares the height of the ActiveX object
	classid	Identifies the ActiveX control to the browser[1]
	embed	Adds an embed element within the object element[2]
	align	Shows the alignment of the ActiveX object
	src	Denotes the source of the data file to be used for a Netscape plug-in[3]
	vspace	Specifies the vertical space above and below the ActiveX object
	hspace	Specifies the horizontal space to the left and right of the ActiveX object
	base	Denotes the URL of the ActiveX control
	Alt img	Identifies the image file to be displayed if the browser doesn't support the object element
	id	Denotes an optional ActiveX id parameter
	data	Identifies the data file for the ActiveX control to load

1 The browser uses the class id to find the ActiveX control associated with the ActiveX object on the page. If the browser doesn't find the ActiveX control, it will download it from the URL value given for base.

2 If the ActiveX control has a Netscape plug-in equivalent, the embed element activates the plug-in.

3 This option only works if the embed element is included.

Adding Java Applets

Applets are small programs written in the Java programming language. You can use Java applets to add interactivity and animation to your pages. These applets can be embedded directly in your pages. Though applets are usually quite large, they don't require the additional download of a plug-in or helper application. Applets can be viewed in most browsers, including both Netscape and Internet Explorer.

Figure 10.11
Parameters dialog box

To add a Java applet, use the Common Insert bar and click the Media icon and then click the Applet icon. Browse to the applet file from the Select File dialog box, or enter the URL of the applet file.

Java applets use the `class` file extension. For simple applets, you only need to know the name of the applet to use it on your page. For more complex applets, you need to specify additional attributes, as follows:

1. Select the applet icon in Design view.

2. Open the Property inspector (Window → Properties). The top part of the window displays the most commonly used properties for applets. To see all the properties, click the arrow in the lower-right corner of the Property inspector (Figure 10.10).

3. Insert values for any attribute you want to include in the `applet` element.

   Table 10.3 lists the most common applet properties.

For complex applets, you may need to specify additional attributes. Additional applet properties can be included by clicking the Parameters button in the Property inspector (Figure 10.12) to open the Parameters dialog box (Figure 10.11). To decide which additional parameters to include, check the documentation for the applet you're using.

PROPERTY	DESCRIPTION
name	Identifies the applet, used in scripting
width	Denotes the width of the applet object
height	Denotes the height of the applet object
code	Specifies the location (URL) of the Java file on the server
base	Specifies the folder containing the applet[1]
align	Specifies the alignment of the applet object
alt	Denotes the alternative content that should be displayed if the browser doesn't support Java or if Java is disabled[2]
vspace	Denotes the vertical space above and below the applet object
hspace	Denotes the horizontal space to the left and right of the applet object

Table 10.3

Common Applet Properties

1 This attribute field is filled in automatically when you select an applet.

2 To make alternative content accessible in both Netscape and Internet Explorer with Java disabled (as well as text browsers), use both an image and an `alt` attribute to specify alternative content.

Figure 10.12

Applet Property Inspector

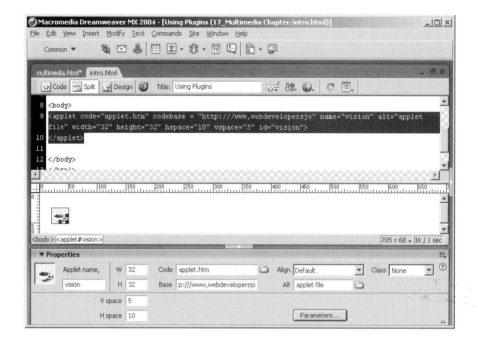

Adding Animated GIFs

Animated GIFs were one of the first multimedia elements to be added to web pages. They continue to be popular because their file sizes are usually small and because they are easy to create. You can create animated GIFs in graphics programs such as Fireworks, Photoshop, ImageReady, or Animation Shop. You can also use software specifically developed to create animated GIFs, such as Ulead GIF Animator (Windows) or GifBuilder (Mac). All of these programs include tools to combine individual GIF images into an animated GIF.

Ulead GIF Animator is available for free trial download from CNET's download.com site at `http://download.com.com/3120-20-0.html?qt=GIF&tg=dl-2001&search=+Go%21+`. GifBuilder is available for free download at `www.mac.org/graphics/gifbuilder/`.

You can add an animated GIF to a page in the same way you add any image. Use the Common Insert bar and click the Image icon. Select the animated GIF file in the Select Image Source dialog box.

Using Dreamweaver Behaviors to Control Media Elements

The following three Dreamweaver behaviors can be used with media elements:

Control Shockwave or Flash Stops, starts, rewinds, or goes to a specific frame in a Shockwave or Flash movie.

Play Sound Plays a sound when a specified event occurs.

Check Plugin Checks to see if site users have a specific Netscape-style plug-in installed, and sends them to different URLs based on whether or not the plug-in is installed.

> For more information on using Dreamweaver behaviors, including details on the preceding three behaviors, see Chapter 12, "Incorporating JavaScript Behaviors."

Hands On: Modifying a Graphic for Use on the Web

If you are working with web clients, you'll usually receive images in raw form and need to modify them for inclusion in a web page. The raw form may be a Photoshop PSD file, an Illustrator EPS file, or a photograph or illustration for you to scan and then modify. Even if the client provides a less raw form of the graphic, you'll often find that the image you were given to place in your web page won't look right. It might be a bit too large or you may need to crop it down to focus in on an object or a person.

In this Hands On tutorial, we'll use Photoshop 7 as our image editor, but you can use the graphics software of your choice.

In the Chapter 10 folder on this book's accompanying CD, copy the image named mod1.psd to your hard drive, then open it in the graphics program of your choice. If you want a preview of the completed image, open mod1_op.jpg, which is also in the Chapter 10 folder on the CD.

Figure 10.13

The Image Size dialog box in Photoshop 7.0

Resizing an Image

We are going to use this image (mod1.psd) as a logo and need to decrease its display size.

1. First, select Image → Image Size. This displays the Image Size dialog box (see Figure 10.13).

2. In the dialog box, the image's current dimensions are 624 pixels width and 608 pixels height. This is too large, particularly since we want to use this image as a logo. Make sure that the check box labeled Constrain Proportions is checked. Then, if you change the width, the height is adjusted automatically using the proportions of the original image.

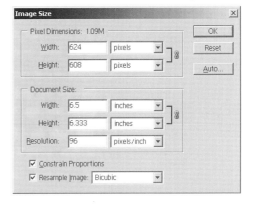

3. Highlight 624 in the width box, and change it to 200. Notice that the height is automatically changed to 195.

4. Save the image as mod1_a.psd (File → Save As). The original file remains unchanged, and is available as a backup in case we need to revert back to the original form of the image.

Optimizing an Image

Now we'll optimize this image for use on the Web. The image should still be open in your image editor (reopen it if it's not).

The following instructions apply to Photoshop 5.5 and above. If you're using a different image editor, check the Help menu for details on saving and optimizing (compressing) JPEGs.

1. Choose File → Save For Web. This opens the Save For Web dialog box.

2. At the top of the dialog box are four tabs: Original, Optimized, 2-Up, and 4-Up. Click on the 4-Up tab.

3. The original image is displayed in the upper-left corner. The other three images show previews of various levels of compression. JPEG compression ranges from 0 (lowest) to 100 (highest). The compression level is shown in the upper-right corner of the image caption.

4. Compare the quality of the three preview images to the saved PSD file. If the preview file display does not show the entire image, you can select the hand tool (on the left side of the page) to move the image so that you can view different areas. If you want to change the compression choices, select one of the optimized preview images. Click on the arrow to the right of the text box named Quality. Then adjust the slider bar that displays. This will automatically change the compression in the selected preview image.

5. Once you've found the optimal compression level (the greatest compression level with good image quality), click the Save button on the upper-right of the page, and save the image to the appropriate folder on your site. You can change the image name at this time, or simply save it with the same name but with a .jpg file extension.

6. If you're not sure whether a JPEG or a GIF is the best choice for your image, you can preview the image as a GIF by changing the selection in the drop-down menu directly under Settings. Notice the additional options for optimizing GIF images.

7. Although the GIF image is also acceptable, the file size is much larger than the JPEG version, so we'll stick with that.

Now our image is resized, optimized, and ready for use in a web page.

Can You Imagine?

What you've learned in this chapter should help you tremendously with putting together a clean, quickly loading site—a goal that many, many web designers miss completely. The decision to add graphic and multimedia elements to your pages is the essential question to answer during the site planning process. Once you've made the decision, it is easy to use Dreamweaver to add graphic and multimedia files.

For much more information on web graphics, and details on slicing and optimizing images with several graphics programs, see the Chapter 10 supplement on the CD.

There are many additional ways to add dynamic content to your Dreamweaver pages. See the next chapter for details on adding Flash to your site.

## CHAPTER 11

Getting into Flash

Flash was originally designed as a tool for creating vector-based animations for the Web. Vectors are the key to the small file sizes possible with Flash because they make it possible to scale a Flash movie without any change in the file size or any loss in image quality. Flash quickly became the standard for Web animation, but didn't stop there! In addition to improving its basic animation features, Flash evolved into a full-scale multimedia authoring tool that can create complex, interactive pages and navigation layouts, dynamic, data-driven pages, games, and cartoons.

With each new version of Dreamweaver and Flash, the integration between these two programs becomes tighter. From Dreamweaver itself, you can easily create Flash buttons and Flash text for your pages as well as launch-and-edit Flash files. Dreamweaver MX 2004 has added Flash elements, which are prebuilt Flash files that can be imported and customized in Dreamweaver.

This chapter explores the following topics:

- **Working with Flash files**
- **Exporting from Flash to Dreamweaver**
- **Adding Flash content**
- **Using Flash elements**
- **Creating Flash text**
- **Making Flash buttons**
- **Launch-and-edit**

Using Flash

Whether you are an experienced Flash developer and use it on a daily basis or you're totally new to Flash, you can add Flash content to your Dreamweaver pages. Dreamweaver MX 2004 provides prebuilt Flash elements that can be used whether or not you have Flash on your computer, and you can also create Flash text and Flash buttons in Dreamweaver. If you do have Flash installed, you can use Dreamweaver to launch and edit Flash files.

> Flash files present special accessibility challenges because the content may include graphics, audio, and video. You can, however, take steps to increase the accessibility of Flash, such as including text equivalents for the graphic content and adding keyboard navigation features. For more details, see Chapter 33, "Using Dreamweaver to Make Your Site Accessible."

Flash Files

When you create documents in Flash, they are in the Flash native file format (FLA format, with file extension .fla). These FLA files can only be opened and edited in Flash. They can be exported from Flash as Flash movie files (.swf). Flash SWF files are compressed versions of FLA files that are designed for viewing in browsers. These files can't be edited—to change them, you must change the FLA files and re-export them as new SWF files.

You can insert SWF files into your Dreamweaver pages (Insert → Media → Flash, or from the Media drop-down menu in the Common Insert bar). You create SWF files in Dreamweaver when you make Flash text or Flash buttons from Dreamweaver's built-in Flash template files (SWT format, with the .swt extension), and when you use Flash elements.

Flash *elements* (SWC format, with the .swc extension) are specialized prebuilt movie clips with predefined parameters. Flash elements are also called Flash *components*. Introduced in Flash MX, they can also be used in Dreamweaver MX 2004. Flash element parameters can be edited in the Tag inspector and the Property inspector in Dreamweaver. For more details, see the section, "Using Flash Elements," later in this chapter.

Exporting and Publishing Flash Files

You can export Flash FLA files (File → Export) as images or movies. A wide variety of export file formats are available, as shown in Table 11.1. The specific options available vary depending on the platform you're using (Windows or Mac) and on whether you are exporting as an image or as a movie.

FILE TYPE	FILE EXTENSION
Adobe Illustrator	ai
Bitmap	bmp
DXF Sequence and AutoCAD DXF Image	dxf
Enhanced Metafile (Windows)	emf
EPS 3.0 with Preview	eps
Flash movies	swf
Flash video (Flash Pro only)	flv
GIF and animated GIF	gif
JPEG	jpg
PICT (Macintosh)	pct
PNG	png
QuickTime	mov
WAV audio (Windows)	wav
Windows AVI	avi
Windows Metafile	wmf

Table 11.1

**Flash Export
File Formats**

Figure 11.1

**Choosing publishing
formats for Flash
files**

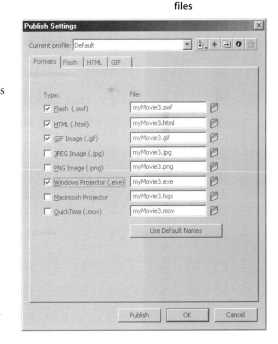

Most commonly, you'll want to publish Flash FLA files for playback in browsers. By default, Flash files are published as a SWF file and an HTML file. You can also include an option to display Flash files as image files (GIF, JPEG, PNG, and Quick-Time) if the Flash player is not available. In addition, Flash files can be published as projector files that are stand-alone movies that play in a freestanding Flash player window.

Figure 11.1 shows the Flash MX 2004 Publish Settings dialog box (File → Publish Settings). You can choose any or all of the available formats for publishing. Additional tabs display when you select the check box for that format. In this case, we've selected Flash, HTML, GIF, and a Windows projector format.

In the Flash tab of the Publish Setting dialog box, shown in Figure 11.2, you can specify several parameters for Flash playback including Flash player version, load order, ActionScript version, protection from import (to protect your FLA file content from editing), image quality setting, and audio settings.

The HTML tab (Figure 11.3) shows the options for templates to display the Flash movie on a Flash-generated HTML page. All of these display a SWF file in an HTML page unless otherwise noted:

Flash only The default choice

Flash for Pocket PC 2003 Page includes alignment for Pocket PC

Flash HTTPS Directs to an HTTPS server to obtain the Flash Player if it's not detected

Flash with AICC Tracking E-learning pages, with tracking connected to a server-side LMS (Learning Management System) that conforms to AICC (Aviation Industry CBT Committee) standards

Flash with FSCommand Includes support for Flash FSCommand as well as JavaScript

Flash with Named Anchors Includes anchors to allow bookmarking of Flash content

Flash with SCORM Tracking E-learning pages, with tracking connected to a server-side LMS (Learning Management System) that conforms to SCORM (Shareable Content Object Reference Model) standards

Image Map Image map in GIF, JPEG, or PNG format

QuickTime Inserts a QuickTime movie in an HTML page

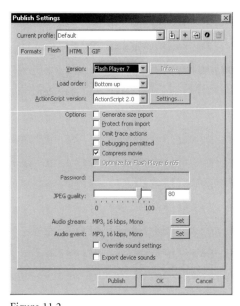

Figure 11.2

Flash playback parameters

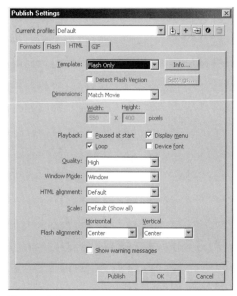

Figure 11.3

Displaying Flash in HTML files

Other options include Detect Flash Version (creates a detection file and alternate content page) and options for specifying dimensions, playback parameters, alignment, and scale.

You can choose the option to display Flash files as image files (GIF, JPEG, PNG, and QuickTime) by checking an image option in the Format tab of the Publish Settings dialog box (Figure 11.1). This displays the image file in the browser if the Flash player is not available. If you choose to include an image format, a separate tab for that image type displays in the Publish Settings dialog box with options for image display and playback.

> For detailed information on using Flash MX 2004, see *Flash MX 2004 Savvy* (by Ethan Watrall and Norbert Herber, Sybex 2003). Flash MX 2004 is available in two different versions, Flash MX 2004 (the basic version) and Flash MX 2004 Professional. For details on all the features in the new versions of Flash, visit the Flash section of the Macromedia website at www .macromedia.com/software/flash.

Adding Flash Content

You can easily add Flash movies to HTML pages in Dreamweaver. To insert a SWF file in a Dreamweaver page, choose Insert → Media → Flash, or select the Media drop-down menu in the Common Insert bar and choose Flash. The Select File dialog box displays. After you choose a SWF file, a Flash placeholder appears in the Document window.

> To preview a Flash movie in the Dreamweaver Document window, select the Flash placeholder for the movie in Design view. Open the Property inspector (Window → Properties) and click the Play button (Figure 11.4).

Using *object* and *embed* Elements

Dreamweaver automatically uses both an object and an embed element when inserting SWF files.

Figure 11.4

Previewing Flash movies in Dreamweaver

The object element is used by Internet Explorer (which is the browser included with Windows 9*x*/NT/2000/XP) and also by other browsers that support ActiveX controls. The object element includes four attributes (height, width, classid, and codebase) plus a variable number of param elements that contain additional parameters. The embed element is used by Internet Explorer for the Mac, Netscape, and also by other browsers that support Netscape-style plug-ins. The embed element includes all settings (such as height, width, quality, loop) as attributes.

The object and embed elements can both be used separately or together for inserting multimedia content on a page. If they are used together, the embed element is nested within the object element. Browsers that support the object element ignore the nested embed element, and those that don't support the object element ignore it and use the embed element instead.

The embed element is deprecated as of XHTML 1.0, but an equivalent element is not available in HTML or XHTML. (In other words, there is currently no option that uses the embed element and includes both cross-browser compatibility and web standards compliance.)

OBJECT, *EMBED*, AND CHANGES IN INTERNET EXPLORER

Due to a recent legal action, Microsoft is making changes to future versions of Internet Explorer. As of Internet Explorer 6 SP1b, IE 6 users will be shown a dialog box before ActiveX objects are loaded on a page. The dialog box says "Press OK to continue loading the content of this page," and displays every time IE encounters an object, embed, or applet tag unless

- The ActiveX controls are loaded from an external script

   or

- The ActiveX controls don't reference remote data

This change affects the browser display of any active content—content that uses Microsoft's ActiveX controls for display (Macromedia Flash, Shockwave, and Authorware players; Apple QuickTime; RealAudio and RealVideo; Adobe Acrobat Reader; Microsoft Windows Media Player; and Java applets).

Macromedia is actively working on developing tools to detect and repair HTML pages affected by this change. The Macromedia Active Content Developer Center offers a tutorial for manually repairing pages with an external JavaScript file. For more details, see

- www.macromedia.com/devnet/activecontent/articles/devletter.html

- www.macromedia.com/devnet/activecontent/articles/solution_summary.html

Solutions are also available on the Microsoft site for providing data inline and for using an external JavaScript file at http://msdn.microsoft.com/ieupdate/activexchanges.asp.

Saving Flash Files

When you create Flash movies, save the Flash source files and the Flash movie files in a Dreamweaver-defined site. This makes the source files easy to locate for you as well as anyone else working on the site files.

If you want to protect the source files from being updated, you can cloak the folder that contains the source files. For more details on cloaking, see Chapter 30, "Going Live or Delivering the Site."

Editing Flash Movie Properties

Flash movie properties can be edited in the Property inspector in Dreamweaver. To edit a Flash movie, follow these steps:

1. Select the Flash movie placeholder in Design view.

2. Open the Property inspector (Window → Properties) if it's not already open.

3. Add values for any attributes you want to change.

Table 11.2 lists the most-common properties of the Flash movies.

Additional Flash movie properties can be included by clicking the Parameters button in the Property inspector. To pass additional parameters to the Flash movie, it must be designed to accept these additional parameters.

PROPERTY	DESCRIPTION	
Name	Identifies the Flash movie, used in scripting (appears in the text box in the upper-left corner of the Property inspector, under the word Flash)	Table 11.2 **Common Flash Movie Properties**
W	Controls the width of the Flash movie	
H	Controls the height of the Flash movie	
File	Supplies the path to the Flash movie file (.swf)	
Src	Supplies the path to the Flash source file (.fla)	
Edit	Launches Flash for editing the Flash source file[1]	
Reset Size	Returns movie to original size	
Class	Applies a CSS style class	
Loop	Plays movie continuously (if checked), otherwise the movie plays once and stops	
Autoplay	Plays the movie when the page loads (if checked)	
V space	Controls the vertical space above and below the movie	
H space	Controls the horizontal space to the left and right of the movie	
Quality	Controls the degree of anti-aliasing during movie playback	
Scale	Controls how the movie fits into the specified width and height size	
Align	Controls alignment of the movie	
Bg	Controls the background color for the movie area	

[1]*This button is disabled if Flash MX is not installed on your computer.*

USING DESIGN NOTES

If you create a file in Flash or Fireworks and export it to Dreamweaver, a Design Notes file containing the name of the original source file is automatically created and exported along with the web-ready file. If you export slices from Fireworks to Dreamweaver, a Design Note will be automatically created and exported along with each slice.

Design Notes are notes associated with a file, but stored in a separate file. Design Notes are used to keep track of additional file information, such as the location of source documents. Design Notes can also be used to store information you don't want to display in the file itself, such as price and marketing data.

You can enable or disable Design Notes for a site by choosing Design Notes in the Advanced tab of the Site Definition window. To see if a file has an associated Design Note, click the Expand/Collapse icon in the Files panel to display the expanded Files panel view. A Design Notes icon appears in the Notes column if there is a Design Notes document for that file.

You can create a Design Notes file for any document, image, or media file in your site by right-clicking (Ctrl-clicking on Mac) on the file name in the Files panel, and then selecting Design Notes from the context menu. The Design Notes dialog box displays. Once you have filled in the information, the Design Notes file is saved in a folder called _notes in the same folder as the associated file. The Design Notes file name is the original file name plus an mno extension, such as `myFile.html.mno`.

Updating Links in Flash Files

If you have Flash installed, you can also edit links in a Flash movie file (SWF) in Dreamweaver, and then update the links in the Flash source file (FLA).

1. Create a Dreamweaver site and specify a home page, if you haven't already done so. If you have already designated a home page for the site, skip to step 7. (For more details on creating sites in Dreamweaver, see Chapter 3, "Setting Up Your Workspace and Your Site.")

2. Select Site → Manage Sites from the Dreamweaver application window.

3. Select the site in the Manage Sites dialog box, and click the Edit button.

4. Choose the Advanced tab in the Site Definition window.

5. Select Site Map Layout and enter a URL in the Home Page text box or browse to a file from the folders icon to the right of the text box.

6. Check the option labeled "Display Dependent Files."

7. Open the Files panel, and choose Map View from the drop-down menu on the right (Figure 11.5).

8. Click the Expand/Collapse icon (under the Menu bar) to expand the Files panel and display the Site Map in a larger window to the left of the Files panel.

9. Open the View menu and select Show Dependent Files (View → Show Dependent Files). The link appears below the Flash movie file.

10. Right-click the link and select Change Link from the drop-down menu (Figure 11.6).

11. Type the new URL in the URL text box or click the folder to the right of the text box to browse to the new file.

12. To change the link in the entire site, open the Site menu and select Change Link Sitewide.

13. Type the new URL in the Change All Links To text box, or click the folder to the right of the text box to browse to the new file.

Any links updated in the SWF file are updated in the FLA source file when a launch-and-edit is performed (see the section "Launch-and-Edit" later in this chapter).

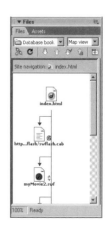

Figure 11.5

Using Map View in the Files panel

Figure 11.6

Changing a Flash link in the Site Map in the Expanded Files Panel

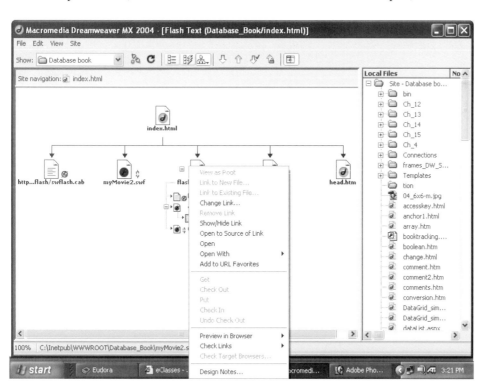

Working with Flash Elements

Flash elements are prebuilt Flash components that you can insert into your Dreamweaver MX 2004 documents. Flash elements are SWC files that help you create *Rich Internet Applications*.

Rich Internet Applications are a new type of Internet application that features more-interactive and more-responsive user interfaces for both computers and mobile devices. Rich Internet Applications run within a web page and host client-side applications that connect to application servers. For more information on Rich Internet Applications, see "Developing Rich Internet Applications with Macromedia MX 2004" at www.macromedia.com/devnet/mx/studio/whitepapers/rich_internet_apps.pdf. For an example of a Rich Internet Application, see the Broadmoor Hotel reservation system at http://reservations.ihotelier.com/onescreen.cfm?hotelID=2054.

A Flash element named Image Viewer is included with Dreamweaver MX 2004, and can be inserted into a page by selecting Insert → Media → Image Viewer. You can download additional Flash elements from the Macromedia Exchange website (www.macromedia.com/cfusion/exchange/index.cfm?view=sn120). You can also access the Macromedia Exchange by clicking the icon on the Dreamweaver MX 2004 Start page. You will need to use the Extension Manager to install additional Flash elements. For more details on using extensions in Dreamweaver MX 2004, see Chapter 32, "Customizing and Extending Dreamweaver."

Flash elements are also called Flash *components*, so be sure to also look for Flash components in the Macromedia Exchange.

Figure 11.7

Editing a Flash element in the Tag inspector

You can edit the attributes of a Flash element in the Tag inspector and the Property inspector. In the Tag Inspector, you can view and edit the parameters of a Flash element. Figure 11.7 shows the Tag inspector panel for the Image Viewer element.

You can also modify the display features of a Flash element in the Property inspector (see Figure 11.4). You can preview the Flash element in the Design view by clicking on the Play button in the Property inspector.

Creating Flash Objects

Dynamic Flash objects include Flash buttons and Flash text. These Flash objects are small Flash files that can be created in Dreamweaver. These can be simple additions that create interactivity on your page.

> The Control Shockwave or Flash behavior can be attached to Flash animations to control the playback, but these playback features do not apply to other interactive Flash objects, such as Flash text and Flash buttons. For more details on Dreamweaver behaviors, see Chapter 12, "Incorporating JavaScript Behaviors."

Flash Text

The Flash text object is an easy, efficient way to create text-as-graphics Flash movie files in Dreamweaver. Flash text is a Flash movie that contains only text and background colors. You can use the fonts of your choice and quickly make interactive text objects for your pages.

> For more information on using text-as-graphics, see Chapter 10, "Adding Graphics and Multimedia."

Figure 11.8

Setting parameters in the Insert Flash Text dialog box

To create a Flash text object:

1. Place the insertion point where you want the Flash text to be placed on the page.

2. Choose Insert → Media → Flash Text (or click the Media icon in the Common Insert bar and select Flash Text).

3. The Insert Flash Text dialog box (see Figure 11.8) displays.

You can specify any features you want included in your Flash text object:

Font Choose a font name from the Font drop-down menu, and enter a font point size in the Size field.

Font Style Click *B* for bold and/or *I* for italic to change the font style.

Choose left, center, or right alignment.

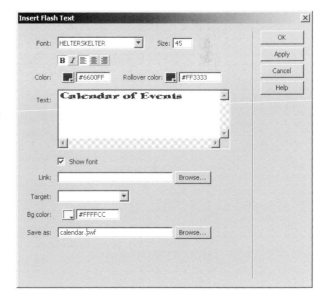

Color To choose the color of the text, click the Color field and choose a color from the color palette, or enter a color name or hexadecimal color value in the blank text field.

To choose the color that the text will appear during a rollover, click the Rollover Color field and choose a color from the color palette, or enter a color name or hexadecimal color value in the blank text field.

Text Enter the text in the Text box.

Select Show Font to see a preview of the text that displays in the selected font.

Link Enter an absolute URL or a document-relative URL in the Link field or click the Browse button to navigate to a file. Site-relative URLs can't be used for links because browsers don't recognize them in Flash movies.

Target Use the Target menu if you want to choose a target window or frame for the link.

Background color Click the Bg color field to choose a color from the color palette, or enter a color name or hexadecimal color value in the blank text field.

Save Enter a filename in the Save As field to name the Flash text file. Dreamweaver supplies a default name, such as `text1.swf`, if no other name is entered.

If you've included a rollover color, click the Play button in the Property inspector to preview the rollover effect in your Flash text in the Design view window. Presto! You've designed a Flash movie with your choice of font and a rollover effect and added it to your page—all within a minute or two.

Set Dreamweaver accessibility preferences (Edit → Preferences → Accessibility) to Show Attributes When Inserting Media. Then the Flash Accessibility Attributes dialog box (Figure 11.9) will display after you have set all the parameters and clicked the OK button. This allows you to enter a title for the Flash object that can be read by a screen reader. Otherwise, a visually disabled viewer will not be able to obtain any information about your Flash text object. You can also set an Access key and Tab order value.

Figure 11.9

The Flash Accessibility Attributes dialog box

Flash Buttons

You can create Flash buttons as easily as Flash text objects. Choose Insert → Media → Flash Button (or click the Media icon in the Common Insert bar and select Flash Button). The Insert Flash Button dialog box opens (Figure 11.10).

Choose a button style from the Style list, or click on the Get More Styles button on the right to go to the Dreamweaver Exchange and download additional button styles.

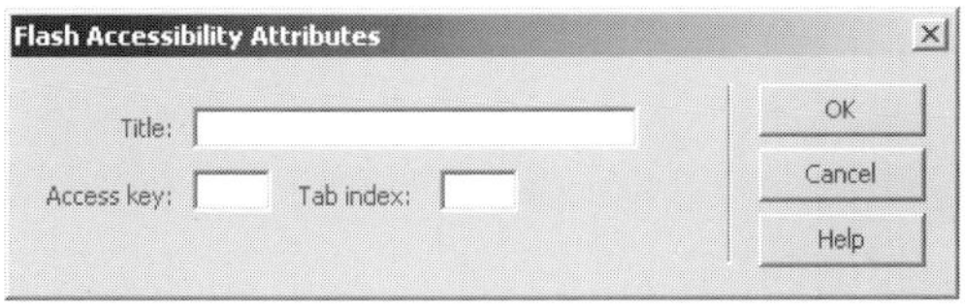

The additional options are the same as those in the Insert Flash Text dialog box, as detailed in the previous section.

There is no dynamic preview with the selected font, though, so you'll have to wait for a preview until the button is created. Then you can preview the button in Design view by selecting it and clicking the Play button in the Property inspector. You'll notice that the selected style displays when you mouseover the button.

> You can resize a Flash text object or a Flash button in Design view by selecting it and using the resizing handles. For Flash buttons, though, this may change the size of the background area of the movie in addition to the size of the button itself. Careful use of the resizing handles may enable you to get rid of the extra background area, depending on the overall button shape. You can also change the size of a Flash text object or Flash button by selecting it and then changing the values in the Property inspector's **W**idth and **H**eight boxes. You can return the button or text object to its original size by clicking the Reset Size button in the Property inspector.

You can modify Flash object properties in the Property inspector. Flash text objects and Flash buttons do not include a Loop or Autoplay option, but otherwise the Property inspector objects are the same as those shown in Table 11.2, earlier in this chapter. The other difference is the Edit button. For Flash text and Flash buttons, clicking the Edit button opens the Insert Flash Text or Insert Flash Button dialog box, where you can change any parameter of the object.

Figure 11.10
The Insert Flash Button dialog box

Launch-and-Edit

Dreamweaver MX 2004 includes launch-and-edit features for Flash. If you have both Flash MX 2004 (or Flash MX) and Dreamweaver MX 2004 (or Dreamweaver MX) installed on your computer, you can update the source files (.fla) for Flash movies that have been added to your Dreamweaver pages. To launch and edit Flash files from Dreamweaver, select the Flash placeholder in Design view, and then open the Property inspector (Window → Properties) and click the Edit button. Dreamweaver opens Flash and attempts to find the Flash source file for the selected Flash movie file. You can then work in Flash to make changes to the source file (.fla) and re-export it as a movie file (.swf).

Flash text and Flash buttons are created in Dreamweaver without requiring Flash to be installed on your computer. Flash text and buttons are also edited in Dreamweaver, not in Flash, and do not include a .fla source file. To edit Flash text or buttons, select them and then choose the Edit button in the Property inspector. This opens the Insert Flash Text or Insert Flash Button dialog box where you can change any of the parameters.

The Flash document window shows that you are editing from Dreamweaver. Flash closes after exporting the new movie file, and the focus returns to Dreamweaver. You can preview the new movie in Dreamweaver itself by clicking the Play button in the Property inspector.

The Flash source file is a different file type (.fla) than the Flash movie file (.swf). When you edit Flash files from Dreamweaver, you are editing the Flash source file and re-exporting it as a Flash movie file.

Hands On: Creating Flash Text

Creating Flash text is an easy way to make visually interesting text headers for your page display. If you haven't created Flash text before, follow the steps below to see how quickly you can do this! If you'd rather just test out a Flash text object, open the file flashtext2 .html in the Chapter 11 folder on this book's CD and preview it in a browser.

1. Open flashtext1.html in the Chapter 11 folder on the accompanying CD.

2. Put the insertion point at the top of the page.

3. Select Insert → Media → Flash Text (or click on the Media icon in the Common Insert bar and choose Flash Text). The Insert Flash Text dialog box opens.

4. First, choose a font from the Font drop-down menu.

5. Enter a number in the Size box. The default is 30.

6. Select Bold or Italic styling, if desired.

7. Choose a text alignment (left, center, or right). The default choice is left.

8. Choose a color, and a rollover color.

9. Enter your text in the Text box. Click the Show font box to preview the text in your selected font.

10. Enter a link in the Link box, or browse to the file you want the Flash text to link to.

11. Choose a Target, if desired.

12. Select a background color. Choose the page background color (#ffffcc, in this case) if you want the Flash text object to blend in with the rest of the page, or a different color if you want it to stand out.

13. Enter a name for the SWF file. The default is `text1.swf`.

14. Click OK to insert the object.

Now you can test your Flash text object. Select the Flash placeholder in Design view, then click the Play button in the Property inspector. You can also preview your Flash text by previewing the page in a browser (File → Preview in Browser).

To view our version of the new HTML page with the Flash text object, open `flashtext2.html` from the Chapter 11 folder on the accompanying CD. Figure 11.11 shows `flashtext2.html` in Internet Explorer 6.

Figure 11.11

Flash text object in Internet Explorer 6

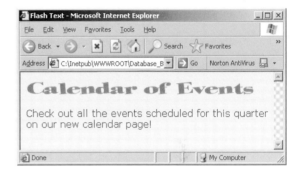

Put the *Multi* in Multimedia

Now you know how to export Flash files to Dreamweaver, and how to create and modify Flash objects within Dreamweaver itself. In the next chapter, we'll look at additional types of multimedia objects you can add to your pages to go beyond the basic text-and-pictures version of the Web.

## PART III

Adding Interactivity within Dreamweaver

The previous part *discussed building a web page, starting with layout and basic static page elements (text, graphics, frames, hyperlinks), and then moving on to dynamic page elements such as multimedia and Flash. The Web is a dynamic medium: it moves, and it interacts with the user. It doesn't just sit there. In this part, we continue with more dynamic features to add interactivity to your pages.*

In this part, we show you how to use Dreamweaver's catalog of behaviors to add interactivity to your site without having to master JavaScript; insert dynamic navigation elements, such as rollovers, navigation bars, and jump menus; create interactivity using forms; set up forms processing; and set up guest books, discussions, chats, and blogs for creating community.

## CHAPTER 12

Incorporating JavaScript Behaviors

Behaviors provide an easy way to use JavaScript to create interactive pages. Dreamweaver includes 22 built-in behaviors that are simple to use and do not require prior knowledge of JavaScript. Additional behaviors are available from Macromedia and third-party vendors. Experienced JavaScript users can also customize the built-in behaviors or create new ones.

This chapter covers the following topics related to Dreamweaver's behaviors:

- **Events and event handlers**
- **The Behaviors panel**
- **Events and browsers**
- **Introducing Dreamweaver's built-in behaviors**

Dreamweaver Behaviors

Behaviors are a combination of *events*—a browser's response to changes on a page, such as the page being loaded, or a user moving the cursor over an image—and *event handlers* (also called *actions*)—JavaScript code associated with a particular event and object.

Browsers generate events when changes occur on a page. For example, a browser generates an `onClick` event when a user clicks on an object, such as an image. The browser then checks to see if any action (event handler) is associated with an `onClick` event for that object (the image) and if there is one, it initiates the action (a block of JavaScript code) attached to the `onClick` event for that object.

Dreamweaver behaviors are designed to be cross-browser compatible, but the availability of specific actions and events depends on the browser and the browser version.

> For more information on browser compatibility issues, see Chapter 29, "Checking Browser Compatibility."

Using the Behaviors Panel

You can use the Behaviors panel (Figure 12.1) in Dreamweaver to attach behaviors to page elements. By default, the Behaviors panel is included in the Tag Inspector panel group. To access the Behaviors panel, open the Tag Inspector panel group and click on the Behaviors tab. If the Behaviors panel is not visible, choose Window → Behaviors, or Shift-F3.

Figure 12.1

The Behaviors panel

In the upper-left corner of the Behaviors panel (see Figure 12.1), there is a plus (+) button, which is used to add an action and an event, and a minus (–) button, which is used to delete a selected action and event. When you click on the plus (+) button, the Actions menu shows the actions that can be associated with the selected object. Unavailable choices for that object are grayed out.

To add a behavior to your Dreamweaver page, follow these steps:

1. Select an object (a page element, such as `h2` or `img`).

2. Open the Behaviors panel if it's not already open (Window → Behaviors, or Shift-F3).

3. Click the + button to display the available actions for the selected object.

4. The default event associated with the chosen action will automatically display once you choose an action. If you want to select a different event, click the down arrow in the Events column of the Behaviors panel to open the Events menu, and choose a different event.

You can download additional Dreamweaver behaviors from the Dreamweaver exchange at `www.macromedia.com/cfusion/exchange/index.cfm`. You can also access the Dreamweaver exchange by clicking on Dreamweaver Exchange on the Start page, or selecting Get More Behaviors… from the Actions menu.

If you are an experienced JavaScript user, you can write your own JavaScript code to create a custom action and add it to the Behaviors panel. For more details, choose Help → Extending Dreamweaver and also see Chapter 32, "Customizing and Extending Dreamweaver."

Behaviors in Fireworks are similar to Behaviors in Dreamweaver. They are used to attach behaviors to interactive image elements, such as rollovers and image maps. Fireworks also has a Behaviors panel that can be used to attach a behavior to a slice or hotspot in a Fireworks file. If a Fireworks rollover file is exported to Dreamweaver, the file can be edited in Dreamweaver's Behaviors panel.

Events and Browsers

Events are the key to creating interactivity with behaviors. If you know which events are accessible to scripting, you can make more choices about adding interactivity to your pages. The menu of events available for a particular action is determined by the choice of target browser. Newer browsers include more events. The target browser(s) is specified by choosing the Show Events For option in the Actions menu. The target browser determines which events display in the Events menu for the chosen action. The Show Events For submenu includes the following target browser choices:

3.0 and Later Browsers	IE 5.5
4.0 and Later Browsers	IE 6.0
IE 3.0	Netscape 3.0
IE 4.0	Netscape 4.0
IE 5.0	Netscape 6.0

Table 12.1 shows all the events available in the Events menu. The actual choices displayed in the Events menu vary, depending on the selected action and the target browser.

In addition to the events shown in the following table (Table 12.1), many more events are available. Internet Explorer 6 supports more events than any other browser at the present time. A list of events that can be used with Internet Explorer 6 can be viewed at `http://msdn.microsoft.com/library/default.asp?url=/workshop/author/dhtml/reference/events.asp#om40_event`.

EVENT	BROWSERS SUPPORTED	DESCRIPTION
onAbort	IE4+, NS4+	The user stops the browser from completely loading an image.
onActivate	IE5.5+	An object is selected as the active element.
onAfterPrint	IE5+	An associated document is previewed or printed.
onAfterUpdate	IE4+	A bound data element finishes updating the data source.
onBeforeActivate	IE6+	The focus is moved from the active element to another element.
onBeforeDeactivate	IE5.5+	The focus is moved from the active element to another element.
onBeforePrint	IE5+	An associated document is previewed or printed.
onBeforeUpdate	IE4+	A bound data element has been changed and the element has lost focus.
onBlur	IE4+, NS3+	A specified element loses focus.[1]
onBounce	IE4+	The contents of a marquee element reach the boundary of the marquee.
onChange	IE3+, NS3+	The user changes a value on the page.
onClick	IE3+, NS3+	The user clicks a page element.
onContextMenu	IE5+	The user right-clicks and opens a context menu.
onDblClick	IE4+, NS4+	The user double-clicks a page element.
onDeactivate	IE5.5+	The focus is moved from the active element to another element.
onDrag	IE5+	An object is dragged.
onDragEnd	IE5+	User releases the mouse at the end of dragging.
onDragEnter	IE5+	User drags an object to a drop target.
onDragLeave	IE5+	User drags an object out of a drop target.
onDragOver	IE5+	User drags an object over a drop target.
onDrop	IE5+	User releases mouse button during a drag.
onError	IE4+, NS3+	A browser error occurs when a page or page element is loading.
onFinish	IE4+	The contents of a marquee element complete a loop.
onFocus	IE3+, NS3+	A specified element gains focus.[2]
onFocusIn	IE6	Occurs just prior to an element gaining focus.
onFocusOut	IE6	Focus is moved to another element.
onHelp	IE4+	The user clicks the browser's Help button or Help menu.
onKeyDown	IE4+, NS4+	The user presses any key.
onKeyPress	IE4+, NS4+	The user presses and releases any key.[3]
onKeyUp	IE4+, NS4+	The user releases any key.
onLoad	IE3+, NS3+	A page or an image completes loading.
onLoseCapture	IE5+	The user clicks the mouse on an object while a previous object (for example, a menu) is still open. In this case, the menu has lost capture.
onMouseDown	IE4+, NS4+	The user presses the mouse button.
onMouseMove	IE3+, NS6	The user moves the mouse while over a specific element.

EVENT	BROWSERS SUPPORTED	DESCRIPTION
onMouseOut	IE4+, NS3+	The user moves the mouse pointer off a specific element.
onMouseOver	IE3+, NS3+	The user moves the mouse pointer onto a specific element.
onMouseUp	IE4+, NS4+	The user releases a pressed mouse button.
onMouseWheel	IE6	User rotates the mouse wheel button.
onMove	NS4+	A window or frame is moved.
onPropertyChange	IE5+	An object property changes.
onReadyStateChange	IE4+	The state of the specified element changes.[4]
onReset	IE3+, NS3+	A form is reset to default values.
onResize	IE4+, NS4+	The user resizes a window or frame.
onRowEnter	IE4+	The data source changes the current row.
onRowExit	IE4+	The data source is about to change the current row.
onScroll	IE4+	The user scrolls up or down.
onSelect	IE3+, NS3+	The user selects text in a text field.
onStart	IE4+	The contents of a marquee element begin a loop.
onStop	IE5+	User clicks the Stop button or leaves the page.
onSubmit	IE3+, NS3+	The user clicks the Submit button in a form.
onUnload	IE3+, NS3+	The user leaves the page.

1 For example, a user clicks in a text field in a form, and then clicks outside the text field.

2 For example, a user clicks in a text field in a form.

3 This event combines onKeyDown and onKeyUp.

4 This event is for objects that can have states, such as Loading, Initializing, or Complete.

The Built-In Behaviors

Behaviors are named for the 22 actions that are included in Dreamweaver. These built-in behaviors are detailed in the following pages.

> Once you have added a behavior, a default event displays in the Events column of the Behaviors panel. If you want to associate a different event with the action, click on the arrow to display the event options for that action.

Figure 12.2

Calling a JavaScript function using the Call JavaScript dialog box

Call JavaScript

The Call JavaScript behavior lets you attach custom JavaScript code to an event. This JavaScript can be original code or code from a JavaScript library.

In the Call JavaScript dialog box, enter the name of a JavaScript method or function, as shown in Figure 12.2, or enter one line of JavaScript code.

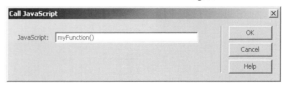

If you enter the name of a function, you need to include the function code in a script block (`<script>`...`</script>`) in the head or body section of the page.

Use your favorite search engine to find the many free online sources for JavaScript code. Two of our favorites are Dynamic Drive (`www.dynamicdrive.com`) and The JavaScript Source (`http://javascript.internet.com/toc.html`).

Change Property

The Change Property behavior dynamically changes the value of a property of 11 HTML elements including `div`, `form`, `img`, `layer`, `span`, `select`, `textarea`, and additional form elements such as check boxes, password fields, radio buttons, or text fields. Only certain properties of these 11 elements can be changed, depending on the specific element and the target browser.

Once you have selected a page element and added a Change Property action, the Change Property dialog box appears. From this dialog box, follow these steps to add a dynamic change to the value of a property.

1. Choose an object from the Type Of Object menu.

2. Choose the name of the object from the Named Object menu.

3. Choose the property you want to change from Property → Select, or click the Enter radio button and type the property's name. If you choose Select, you also need to choose a target browser and browser version. If you want to target more than one browser, you need to apply more than one Change Property action. The choice of target browser is important. Different browsers support different properties for some HTML elements.

Figure 12.3 shows the Change Property action for a `form` object. The `action` property is selected, and IE 4 is chosen as the target browser. The New Value for this property is `myscript.pl`.

Figure 12.3
Change Property dialog box

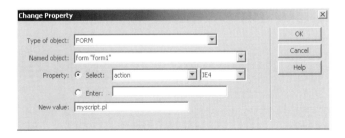

Knowledge of HTML and JavaScript is required to use the Call JavaScript and Change Property behaviors. You can obtain more information about HTML and JavaScript through Dreamweaver's Reference panel (Window → Reference, or Shift-F1).

Check Browser

The Check Browser behavior directs the user to a specific page depending on the user's browser and version. This behavior can be attached to a body element or can be used with a null link.

When the Check Browser action is added to an object, the Check Browser dialog box is displayed. In this dialog box, follow these steps.

1. Enter the version number of Netscape Navigator to check for. The default is 4.0.

2. Choose an action from the menu. This action tells the browser what to do if it is Netscape Navigator version 4.0 or later. The choices in this menu are the following:

    • Go To URL

    • Go To Alt URL

    • Stay On This Page

3. Choose an action from the second menu (otherwise). This tells the browser what to do if it is not Netscape Navigator 4.0 or later.

Figure 12.4

**Check Browser
dialog box**

4. Repeat steps 2 and 3 for Internet Explorer.

5. Choose an action from the menu labeled Other Browsers.

6. Enter values for URL and Alt URL, or click the Browse button to navigate to a file.
For a URL on a different site, you must enter an absolute path, such as `http://www`
`.macromedia.com/support/dreamweaver/`.

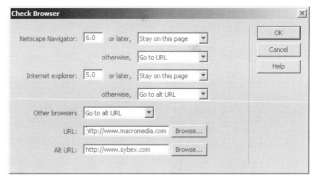

Figure 12.4 shows the Check Browser dialog box.

Dreamweaver MX 2004 includes a Check Browser Support icon on the Document toolbar. You can choose a list of Target Browsers, and Dreamweaver will automatically check for browser compatibility problems every time you save the document. You can add a Check Browser behavior to the page if there are browser compatibility problems with any of the features you've added, and send the user to the appropriate page. For more information on Check Browser Support, see Chapter 3, "Setting Up Your Workspace and Your Site."

Check Plugin

The Check Plugin behavior directs the user to a specific page depending on whether they have a specific plug-in installed.

When the Check Plugin action is added to an object, the Check Plugin dialog box is displayed. In this dialog box, follow these steps.

1. Choose a plug-in from Plugin → Select. The five choices follow:

   - Flash
   - Shockwave
   - Live Audio
   - Quick Time
   - Windows Media Player

   Plug-ins can't be detected by using JavaScript in Internet Explorer. If you select a Flash or Shockwave plug-in in the Check Plugin dialog box, VBScript code will be added to your page in order to detect those plug-ins in Internet Explorer in Windows. No plug-ins can be detected in Internet Explorer on a Mac.

2. Alternatively, enter the exact name of a plug-in in Plugin → Enter. On a PC, the exact plug-in names can be found in Netscape Navigator in the Help menu (Help → About Plugins). On a Mac, choose About Plugins from the Apple menu.

3. Enter a URL in the If Found, Go To URL text box. If you want users to stay on the page if they have the plug-in, leave this text box blank.

4. Enter a URL in the Otherwise, Go To URL text box.

If detection is not possible, the user is sent to the URL specified in Otherwise, Go To URL. Because the user might have the plug-in even though it is not detected, you might want the user to be directed to the address specified in If Found, Go To URL. In this case, check the box labeled "Always go to first URL if detection is not possible."

Figure 12.5 shows the Check Plugin dialog box.

Figure 12.5

Check Plugin dialog box

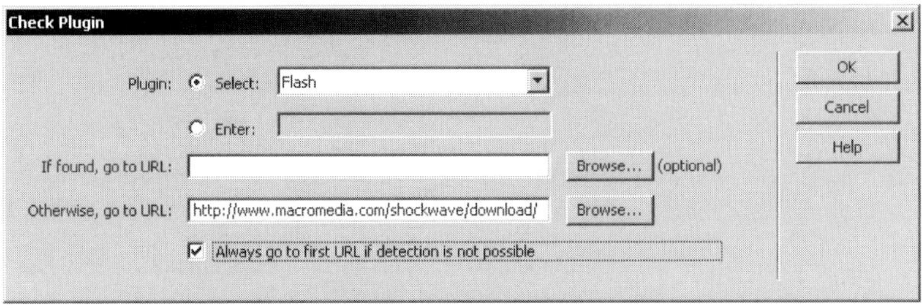

Control Shockwave Or Flash

The Control Shockwave Or Flash behavior directs a Shockwave or Flash animation to play, stop, rewind, or go to a specific frame in the animation.

To attach a behavior to a Shockwave or Flash movie, follow these steps.

1. Insert a Shockwave or Flash movie on the page (Insert → Media → Shockwave, or Insert → Media → Flash).

> To use this behavior, the media file extension must be `.dcr` or `.dir` for Shockwave files, or `.swf` or `.spl` for Flash files.

2. Open the Property inspector (Window → Properties).

3. Enter a name for the movie in the blank text field in the upper-left corner of the Property inspector. The movie must have a name in order to use the Control Shockwave Or Flash behavior.

4. Open the Behaviors panel and add Control Shockwave Or Flash. The Control Shockwave Or Flash dialog box is displayed.

5. Choose a movie from the Movie menu.

6. Choose one of the four available actions:

   • Play

   • Stop

   • Rewind

   • Go to Frame

Figure 12.6 shows the Control Shockwave Or Flash dialog box.

> If you choose the Go To Frame action, you must enter a frame number in the box next to that choice.

Drag Layer

The Drag Layer behavior allows the user to drag a layer. This behavior can be used to create movable elements on a page.

To attach a Drag Layer action to a layer, follow these steps:

1. Insert a layer (Insert → Layout Objects → Layer).

Figure 12.6

Control Shockwave Or Flash dialog box

2. Open the Property inspector (Window → Properties) and note the name for the layer in the text field in the upper-left corner. A default name is assigned by Dreamweaver, such as Layer1, but this name should be changed in the Property inspector.

3. Select the body element.

> The event that triggers the Drag Layer action must occur before the user can drag a layer, so it's generally easiest to attach this action to the body element (using an onLoad event).

4. Open the Behaviors panel and choose Drag Layer. The Drag Layer dialog box is displayed. By default, the Basic tab is shown in front.

5. Choose a layer from the Layer menu.

6. Choose Constrained or Unconstrained from the Movement menu.

7. For constrained movement, enter pixel values in the Up, Down, Left, and Right fields. The pixel values are relative to the starting position of the layer.

> For vertical movement only, enter 0 in the Left and Right fields. For horizontal movement only, enter 0 in the Up and Down fields.

8. Enter pixel values in the Drop Target Left and Top fields to specify the exact spot where the layer should be dragged. These values are relative to the top-left corner of the browser window. Specifying a drop target is optional.

9. Click Get Current Position to enter the layer's current Left and Top values. Use this option only if the current position is the target position for the layer.

10. Enter a pixel value in the Snap If Within field to specify how close the user must get to the target before the object snaps to the target.

    Figure 12.7 shows the Basic tab in the Drag Layer dialog box.

Figure 12.7

Drag Layer dialog box, Basic tab

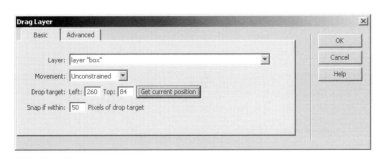

Take a look at the Advanced tab of the Drag Layer dialog box. Use the options on this tab to create a drag handle or specify the layer's position relative to other layers.

You can also use the Advanced tab to specify code that should be executed under different conditions. Enter JavaScript code in the Call JavaScript field to repeatedly execute the code while the layer is being dragged, or add JavaScript code in the When Dropped: Call JavaScript field to execute the code when the layer is dropped. You can also check the Only If Snapped box to specify that the code should be executed only if the layer has been dragged to the drop target.

Knowledge of JavaScript is required to use the advanced features of the Drag Layer behavior.

Figure 12.8 shows the Advanced tab in the Drag Layer dialog box.

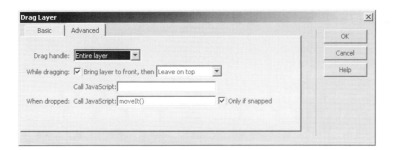

Figure 12.8

Drag Layer dialog box, Advanced tab

Go To URL

The Go To URL behavior opens a new page in the current window or in a specified frame.

When a Go To URL action is added, the Go To URL dialog box is displayed. In this dialog box, choose a frame or window from the Open In list, and then enter a URL in the URL field. Figure 12.9 shows the Go To URL dialog box. Click OK to close the dialog box.

Jump Menu

Jump menus are created from the Insert menu (Insert → Form → Jump Menu). It is not necessary to use the Behaviors panel to attach the Jump Menu behavior to an object. However, the Behaviors panel can be used to edit an existing Jump menu.

Figure 12.9

Go To URL dialog box

Select the Jump menu, open the Behaviors panel, and double-click Jump Menu in the Actions column. The Insert Jump Menu dialog box is displayed with the current settings for the menu (Figure 12.10). Edit these settings as desired, and click OK.

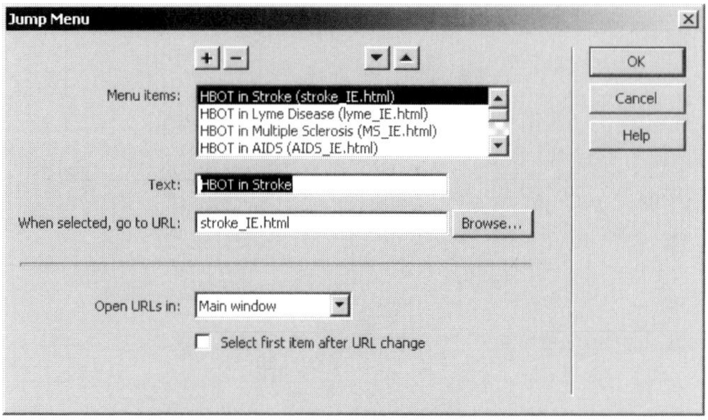

Figure 12.10

**Insert Jump Menu
dialog box**

For further information on jump menus, see Chapter 13, "Designing Navigation Objects."

Jump Menu Go

The Jump Menu Go behavior associates a Go button with an already existing Jump menu. A Go button is not always necessary but is useful when Jump menus are used in frames.

When a Jump menu is inserted (Insert → Form → Jump Menu), an Insert Jump Menu dialog box is displayed (see Figure 12.10). At the bottom of the dialog box, check the option Insert Go Button After Menu to insert a Go button next to the Jump menu.

Figure 12.11

**The Jump Menu Go
dialog box**

You can use a different image for the Go button instead of the default image. Select the object that you want to be the Go button. Open the Behaviors panel, and add Jump Menu Go. The Jump Menu Go dialog box displays (Figure 12.11). Choose a menu for the Go button to activate from the Choose Jump Menu drop-down list.

Open Browser Window

The Open Browser Window behavior opens a pop-up browser window. You can choose the properties of this window, including its size, toolbars, and name. If you don't specify any properties, the pop-up window will have the size and properties of the window it was launched from.

When an Open Browser Window action is added, the Open Browser Window dialog box is displayed. In this dialog box, follow these steps to add a pop-up window:

1. Enter a URL in the URL To Display text box, or click the Browse button to navigate to a file to display—for example, a new window that displays a larger graphic.

2. Enter pixel values for Window Width and Window Height. If you leave these fields blank, the new window will have the same size as the window it was launched from.

3. Specify the attributes of the new window. These include the following:

   • Navigation Toolbar (includes Back, Forward, Home, and Reload buttons)

   • Location Toolbar (shows the URL of the page being displayed)

   • Status Bar

   • Menu Bar (includes File, Edit, View, Go, and Help menus)

   • Scrollbars as Needed

   • Resize Handles (allow the user to resize the window)

4. Enter a name for the new window in the Window Name text field. This enables you to specify this window in JavaScript code, and allows you to use this window as a target in a link.

   Figure 12.12 shows the Open Browser Window dialog box.

Be sure it's really necessary to open another window. Many users, especially inexperienced users and users with visual disabilities, find it disorienting and confusing when a new window opens, and this can be compounded when they go to use the browser's Back button and discover that either it's not there or it's grayed out! Users who have installed pop-up-blocking software might not see the new window at all. Give users the option of opening a new window—for example, with a button to click—rather than having it open automatically.

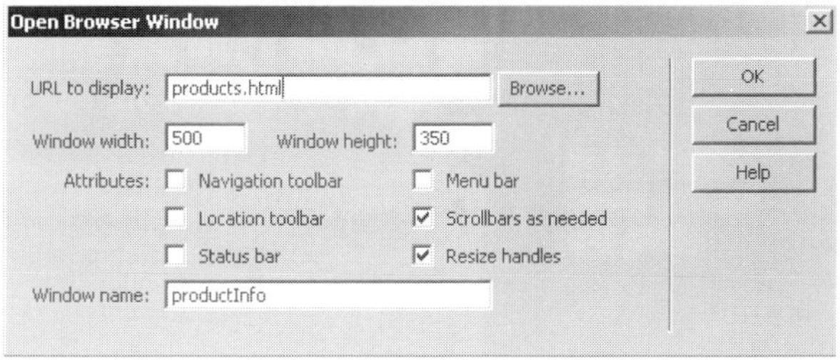

Play Sound

The Play Sound behavior plays a sound when a specified event occurs—for example, an audio clip that plays when the page is loaded. Automatically playing sounds without giving the visitor an option is not recommended, however. Combine a Play Sound behavior with a button or link that lets users decide if they want audio input from your page.

Figure 12.12

Open Browser Window dialog box

Figure 12.13

The Custom Print Gallery offers viewing and listening options for its visitors

The Custom Print Gallery (`www.santafehealingart.com/customprintgallery.html`) on the Santa Fe Healing Art site, shown in Figure 12.13, gives the viewer several options. Not only can visitors choose whether to listen to music while viewing the gallery, they can also select from three different types of music.

> Audio files may require audio plug-ins or specific types of media players. For more information on web audio and other multimedia files, see Chapter 10, "Adding Graphics and Multimedia."

When a Play Sound action is added, the Play Sound dialog box is displayed. In this dialog box, enter a path and filename or click the Browse button to navigate to a sound file.

Figure 12.14 shows the Play Sound dialog box.

Figure 12.14

The Play Sound dialog box

Popup Message

The Popup Message behavior creates a JavaScript alert box that displays the message you specify. Alert boxes are used to present information to the user. You can display a text message, or you can display other information by including JavaScript functions, variables, or expressions in the text. To use JavaScript code in the text, enclose it in curly braces {}. For example:

```
Today is {new Date()}
```

When a Popup Message action is added, the Popup Message dialog box is displayed (Figure 12.15). In the Message text area, enter a text message (and/or JavaScript code if you are experienced with JavaScript). Users have to click OK (Figure 12.16) to make the box go away before they can resume viewing and loading the page.

Figure 12.15

Popup Message dialog box

> Alert boxes should be used sparingly. They require a response from the user (clicking the OK button) and interrupt the user's viewing of the main page. All processing of the page pauses until the user responds to the alert box, so alert boxes can also increase page download time.

Preload Images

The Preload Images behavior is used to load images that might not automatically download when the page is first loaded; for example, when the user is using a Rollover link, a second image appears when the user moves the mouse over the first image. If the image is preloaded, it is displayed immediately because there is no delay waiting for the rollover image file to download.

> If you are using the Swap Image behavior, there is no need to add the Preload Images behavior—just check the Preload Images option in the Swap Image dialog box.

When a Preload Images action is added, the Preload Images dialog box is displayed. Follow these steps to preload images into the browser cache so there's no delay to download them after an action is triggered:

1. Enter the path and filename of the image you want to preload in the Image Source File text box at the bottom of the dialog box, or click the Browse button to navigate to an image file.

2. Click the plus (+) button at the top of the dialog box to add this image to the Preload Images list.

Figure 12.16

Alert boxes require a response from the user.

3. Repeat steps 1 and 2 to add additional image files.

4. Select an image from the Preload Images list and click the minus (–) button at the top of the dialog box to remove an image from the list.

> For more information on creating rollovers and preloading images, see Chapter 13, "Designing Navigation Objects."

Figure 12.17 shows the Preload Images dialog box.

Set Nav Bar Image

The Set Nav Bar Image behavior is used to edit the properties of navigation bar images; for example, you can change the display and/or actions associated with images in a navigation bar. You can set different images for each state of the navigation button (Up, Over, Down, Over While Down) as well as add more complex actions, such as changing the state of more than one image at a time when a user moves the mouse over an image (*multiple rollovers*).

A navigation bar can be created by using the Insert menu (Insert → Image Objects → Navigation Bar).

> For more details on image states and navigation bars, see Chapter 13.

To edit an existing navigation bar image, follow these steps:

1. Select an image in the navigation bar.

2. Open the Behaviors panel, and double-click the Set Nav Bar Image action in the Actions column. By default, the Basic tab of the Set Nav Bar Image dialog box displays.

3. In the Set Nav Bar Image dialog box, the Element Name text field displays the name of the selected image. This name is the same one that is displayed in the Property inspector under Image (size of file), or it can also be set by using a `name` attribute in the `img` element.

4. Edit the options in this dialog box. These include the following:

   • Up Image (*path and filename*): displays when the page loads

   • Over Image (*path and filename*): displays when the cursor moves over the image

- Down Image (*path and filename*): displays after the image is clicked
- Over While Down Image (*path and filename*): displays when the cursor moves over the image after its been clicked
- When Clicked Go To URL (*URL or frame name*): sets link for image

You don't have to select different images for every state. Often, you use two images: one for the Up state and one for all the other states.

5. Choose additional options by clicking the check boxes listed under Options:

- Preload Images
- Show "Down Image" Initially: lets the users know their location in the site by displaying the Down state rather than the default Up state

Figure 12.18 shows the Basic tab in the Set Nav Bar Image dialog box.

Ready to try it out? Create a navigation bar in the Hands On Tutorial in Chapter 13.

You can use the Advanced tab to create multiple rollovers—more than one image is changed by a single event. The event can be a click or a mouseover.

- When a user clicks on a navigation bar image, all the other images in the navigation bar automatically display in their Up state. If you don't want this to happen, you can select a different state for any of the images in the navigation bar.
- You can also add an action to change two images when a user mouses over one image.

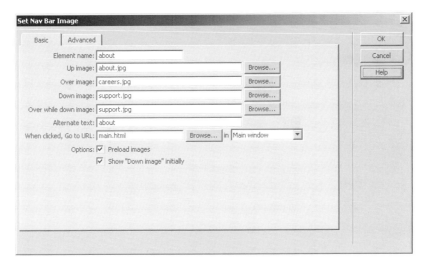

Figure 12.18

Set Nav Bar Image dialog box, Basic tab

Follow these steps:

1. In the When Element (*element name*) Is Displaying menu, choose an image state:

   - Over Image or Over While Down Image

     This option changes the display of a second image when the user moves the mouse over the first image.

   - Down Image

     This option changes the display of a second image when the first image is clicked.

2. Select a second image from the Also Set Image list.

3. Enter the path and filename of the image (or click the Browse button to navigate to an image file) to display when the event in step 1 occurs.

   Figure 12.19 shows the Advanced tab in the Set Nav Bar dialog box.

Set Text Of Frame

The Set Text Of Frame behavior changes the text display in a selected frame to new content and formatting that you specify. The content can include HTML code as well as JavaScript functions, properties, variables, or expressions. To include JavaScript, enclose it in curly braces {}; for example, here is how you would display the current year:

```
The year is {myYear()}
```

In this case, we've added our hand-coded (all four lines!) myYear function in a script block in the head section of the page so that it can be called from this statement. Here's the code:

```
function myYear(){
    var myYear = new Date();
    myYear = myYear.getFullYear();
}
```

Figure 12.19

Set Nav Bar Image dialog box, Advanced tab

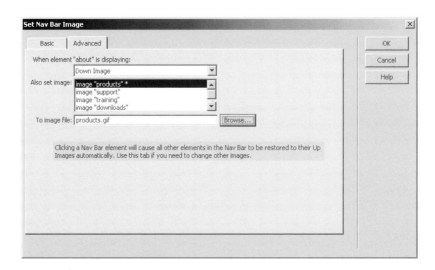

To add a Set Text Of Frame action, follow these steps:

1. Create a frameset (Insert → HTML → Frames → Frameset or click the frm icon in the HTML Insert bar).

> For more information about framesets and frames, see Chapter 7, "Interactivity with Framesets and Frames."

2. Select an object.

3. Open the Behaviors panel and click the plus (+) button to open the Actions menu.

4. Choose Set Text → Set Text Of Frame. The Set Text Of Frame dialog box appears.

5. Choose the target frame from the Frame menu.

6. Enter text, HTML source code, and/or JavaScript code in the New HTML text area field. You can also click the Get Current HTML button, which will copy the HTML contained in the body element of the current target frame into the New HTML field where it can be changed. However, this only updates the source code in the body element. Any other code in the targeted frame will be lost—for example, the code in the head element.

7. Check the Preserve Background Color box to maintain the background color of the frame when the new frame contents appear.

Figure 12.20 shows the Set Text Of Frame dialog box. When the user clicks the text in the original frame, the new text (You clicked me!) displays.

Set Text Of Layer

The Set Text Of Layer behavior replaces the content and formatting of an existing layer with new content and formatting that you specify. The current layer attributes are preserved. The new content can include text, HTML source code, and JavaScript functions, properties, variables, and expressions. To include JavaScript code in the new content, enclose it in curly braces {}.

To add a Set Text Of Layer action, follow these steps.

1. Create a layer (Insert → Layout Objects → Layer or use the Draw Layer icon in the Layout Insert bar and draw a layer by dragging the crosshairs in the Design window).

2. Select an object in the layer (for example, an image or a block of text) and open the Behaviors panel.

Figure 12.20

Set Text Of Frame dialog box

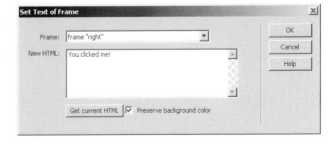

3. Click the plus (+) button and select Set Text → Set Text Of Layer from the Actions menu. The Set Text Of Layer dialog box displays.

4. Choose the target layer from the Layer menu.

5. Enter a text message, HTML source, and/or JavaScript code in the New HTML text area field.

6. Click OK to close the dialog box.

Figure 12.21 shows the Set Text Of Layer dialog box.

Set Text Of Status Bar

The Set Text Of Status Bar behavior displays a message in the status bar at the bottom of the browser window. With the Set Text Of Status Bar behavior, you can associate this message with an event, such as displaying a status bar message when the user moves the mouse over an image. The status bar message can be text, or you can include JavaScript functions, properties, variables, or expressions. To include JavaScript code, enclose it in curly braces {}; for example, here is how you would display the URL of the current page:

```
You are at {window.location}
```

When a Set Text Of Status Bar action is added, the Set Text Of Status Bar dialog box displays. In this dialog box, you can enter a text message and/or JavaScript code.

Figure 12.22 shows the Set Text Of Status Bar dialog box.

Set Text Of Text Field

The Set Text Of Text Field behavior replaces the content of a selected text field in a form with new content. The new content can be text, or you can include JavaScript functions, properties, variables, or expressions. To include JavaScript code, enclose it in curly braces {}.

Figure 12.21

Set Text Of Layer dialog box

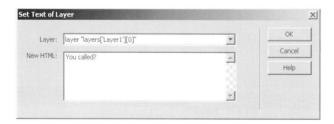

Figure 12.22

Set Text Of Status Bar dialog box

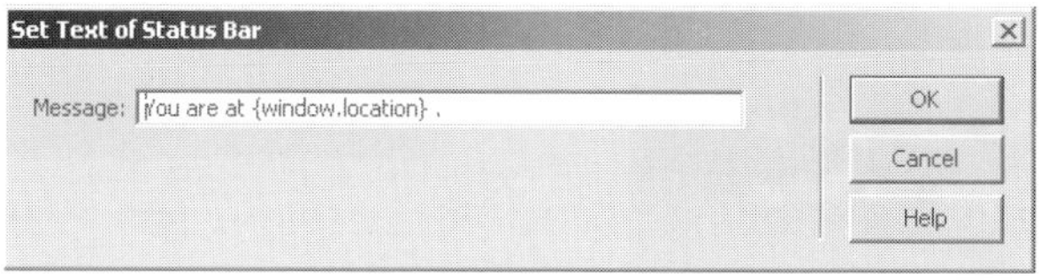

To add a Set Text Of Text Field action, follow these steps.

1. Insert a form (Insert → Form → Form or click the Form icon in the Forms Insert bar).

2. Create a text field (Insert → Form → Text Field or select Text Field after clicking the Form icon in the Forms Insert bar). The Tag Editor window displays.

3. Enter a name for the text field in the Input-General window of the Tag Editor (Figure 12.23). You can edit the name at any time in the Property inspector.

4. Open the Behaviors panel and click the plus (+) button to add an action.

5. Choose Set Text → Set Text Of Text Field from the Actions menu. The Set Text Of Text Field dialog box displays.

6. Select the target field from the Text Field menu.

7. Enter text and/or JavaScript code in the New Text text area.

Figure 12.24 shows the Set Text Of Text Field dialog box.

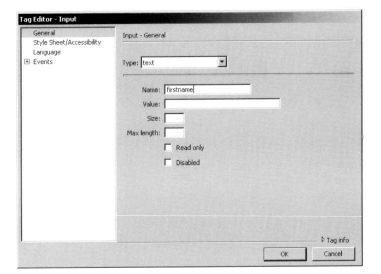

Figure 12.23

The Input-General window of the Tag Editor

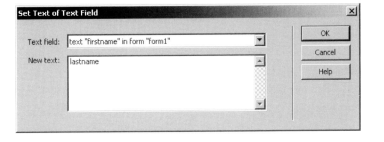

Figure 12.24

Set Text Of Text Field dialog box

Show-Hide Layers

The Show-Hide Layers behavior shows or hides one or more layers on a page. This behavior can be used to change the layer display as a user interacts with a page. For example, when a user moves the mouse over an image, another layer becomes visible, and this layer presents information about the image.

To add a Show-Hide Layers action, follow these steps:

1. Insert a layer (Insert → Layout Objects → Layer or use the Draw Layer icon in the Layout Insert bar and draw a layer by dragging the crosshairs in the Design window).

2. Open the Property inspector (Window → Properties) and note the name for the layer in the text field in the upper-left corner. A default name is assigned by Dreamweaver, such as Layer1, but this name can be changed in the Property inspector if you choose.

3. Deselect the layer by clicking the Document window, and open the Behaviors panel.

4. Click the plus (+) button and select Show-Hide Layers from the Actions menu. The Show-Hide Layers dialog box displays. If this choice is unavailable in the Actions menu, make sure you don't have a layer selected.

5. Select the target layer from the Named Layers list.

6. Click Show to make the layer visible, Hide to make the layer hidden, or Default to restore the default visibility of the layer.

7. Repeat steps 4 and 5 to change the layer visibility of additional layers.
    Figure 12.25 shows the Show-Hide Layers dialog box.

Swap Image and Swap Image Restore

The Swap Image behavior replaces one image with another. This behavior is used to create rollovers. The replacement image must have the same height and width as the original image, or the display of the replacement image may appear distorted.

For more information on creating rollovers, see Chapter 13.

Figure 12.25
**Show-Hide Layers
dialog box**

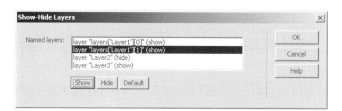

To add a Swap Image action, follow these steps.

1. Insert an image (Insert → Image or click the Image icon in the Common Insert bar and Select Image).

2. Open the Property inspector (Window → Properties) and enter a name for the image in the text field in the upper-left corner of the window. The Swap Image behavior can be used without naming the images; however, Dreamweaver automatically assigns default names to images (for example, Image 1, Image 2, and so on) if no image names have been assigned before the Swap Image action is added. It is much easier to identify an image if it has a name that means something to you.

3. Repeat steps 1 and 2 to add additional images.

4. Select an image and open the Behaviors panel.

5. Click the plus (+) button and select Swap Image from the Actions menu. The Swap Image dialog box displays.

6. Select the image you want to swap from the Images list.

7. Enter the path and filename of the new image in the Set Source To field, or click the Browse button to navigate to an image file.

8. Repeat steps 6 and 7 to change additional images.

9. Click in the Preload Images box to preload the additional images when the page is loaded.

Figure 12.26 shows the Swap Image dialog box.

To add the Swap Image Restore behavior, click the Restore Images onMouseOut check box in the Swap Image dialog box. This behavior restores the original image when the user moves the mouse off the image.

> Dreamweaver MX 2004 does not include timelines or timeline behaviors (Go to Timeline Frame, Play Timeline, and Stop Timeline).

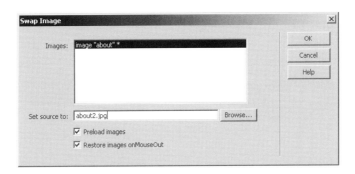

Figure 12.26

Swap Image dialog box

Validate Form

The Validate Form behavior checks the content of specified text fields in a form to make sure that the user has entered a value in required fields and that the user has entered the correct type of information for the field.

The Validate Form action can be used with an `onSubmit` event to check for entries in all required text fields when the user clicks the Submit button, or it can be used with an `onBlur` or `onChange` event to validate individual fields as the user fills out the form.

To add a Validate Form action, follow these steps.

1. Insert a form (Insert → Form or click the Form icon in the Forms Insert bar).

2. Insert a text field (Insert → Form → Text Field or click the Text Field icon in the Forms Insert bar). Repeat this step to add additional text fields to the form.

3. To validate individual fields, select the text field and open the Behaviors panel. To validate multiple fields when the user clicks the Submit button, select the `form` element and open the Behaviors panel.

4. Click the plus (+) button and choose Validate Form from the Actions menu.

5. If you are validating an individual field, select that field in the Named Fields list. If you are validating multiple fields, select any field in the Named Fields list.

6. Check the Value Required check box if the field must contain an entry.

7. Choose one of the following Accept options:

   Anything This option checks to make sure that a field contains an entry, but no particular type of entry is necessary.

   Email Address This option checks to see whether a field contains @.

   Number This option checks to see whether a field contains only numerals.

   Number From This option checks to see whether a field contains a number within a specified range.

8. If you are validating multiple fields at once, repeat steps 5, 6, and 7 for each field you wish to validate.

If you select the form element before adding a Validate Form action, the `onSubmit` event is automatically selected. If you select an individual text field before adding a Validate Form action, check that the event is `onBlur` or `onChange`. The `onBlur` event occurs whether or not a user has changed anything in the text field, but the `onChange` event occurs only if the user changes the contents of the text field.

Figure 12.27 shows the Validate Form dialog box.

Figure 12.27

Validate Form dialog box

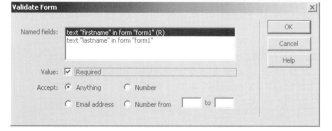

Show Pop-Up Menu

The Show Pop-Up Menu behavior allows you to add or edit a Dreamweaver MX pop-up menu or edit a Fireworks MX pop-up menu inserted in a Dreamweaver MX document.

> To edit the images in a Fireworks pop-up menu, use the Edit button in the Property inspector. You can edit the text in the menu in the Show Pop-Up Menu dialog box.

You can use the Show Pop-Up Menu dialog box to add a horizontal or vertical pop-up menu, and to edit the color, text, or position of the menu.

To add or edit a pop-up menu, follow these steps:

1. Select an object (an image or link) to attach the Show Pop-Up Menu behavior to, and open the Behaviors panel (Window → Behaviors, or Shift-F3).

2. Click the plus (+) button in the Behaviors panel and select Show Pop-Up Menu from the Actions pop-up menu. The Show Pop-Up Menu dialog box (Figure 12.28) displays.

3. From the Show Pop-Up Menu dialog box, set any of the following options. Each option is on a separate tab in the dialog box.

   Contents This option is used to specify the name, structure (outdent or indent), URL, and target for any individual menu item.

Figure 12.28

Show Pop-Up Menu dialog box

   Appearance This option is used to specify the appearance of the up and over states and to choose a font for the menu item text.

   Advanced This option is used to specify the properties of the menu cells, including cell width, cell height, cell padding, cell spacing, text indent, menu delay, and border properties.

   Position This option is used to specify the position of the pop-up menu relative to the triggering image or link.

Figure 12.28 shows the Show Pop-Up Menu dialog box.

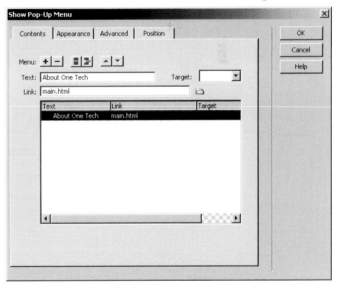

Hands On: Adding a Style Switcher to Your Page

JavaScript can be used to add a style switcher to a page that allows users to choose the style sheet they want to apply to your page. In this tutorial, almost all of the files you'll need are included on the CD: the JavaScript (`switch.js`) is provided as an external file, and you can use Dreamweaver's built-in CSS samples to create a variety of external CSS files.

Selecting Style Sheets

Begin by selecting the style sheets you want to use. You can use your own style sheets, or use the samples provided in Dreamweaver.

1. To view the Dreamweaver CSS Samples, choose File → New → CSS Style Sheets.

2. In the dialog box that displays, choose three or more CSS sample pages.

3. Open each of the selected sample pages, and save each one with a name of your choice, using a `.css` file extension.

The three sample CSS pages in the `Ch12` folder on the CD are named `bg.css`, `bgp.css`, and `red.css`.

Creating a New Document

Now you're ready to make a new document.

1. Create a new HTML document in Dreamweaver (File → New or choose Create New → HTML from the Start page).

2. Add any content you choose, but for the greatest effects, look at the CSS pages you're going to apply to see what elements have associated styles and include some of those elements.

We chose three CSS color pages as our samples, and our page content is displayed in headers (h1, h2, h3, h4) because each of these elements had associated styles.

Adding Links to the Style Sheets

In the head section of your page, add links to the style sheets. We are using three different kinds of style sheet links:

• Persistent: a persistent style sheet is always enabled.

• Preferred: a preferred style sheet is enabled when the page is loaded, but disabled if the user selects an alternate style sheet.

• Alternate: an alternate style sheet can be enabled by the user by selecting it in a link or menu.

For more details on the three different kinds of style sheet links, see "Alternative Style," by Paul Sowden, at www.alistapart.com/stories/alternate/.

In our sample file, gb.css is the persistent style sheet, bgp.css is the preferred style sheet, and red.css is the alternate style sheet. The links for the different types are slightly different, so let's review each one:

1. The persistent link:

```
<link rel="stylesheet" type="text/css" media="screen" href="gb.css">
```

This link element does not include a title attribute.

2. The preferred link:

```
<link rel="stylesheet" type="text/css" media="screen"
title="preferred" href="bgp.css">
```

This link element includes a title attribute. You'll need to use the value of the title attribute later in the page, so make a note of it.

3. The alternate link:

```
<link rel="alternate stylesheet" type="text/css"
media="screen" title="alternate" href="red.css">
```

This link element uses the value alternate stylesheet for the rel attribute, and also includes a title attribute.

Linking to an External JavaScript File

The JavaScript for the style switcher is all included in an external JavaScript file named switch.js. To link to this file, add a script element in the head section of the page:

```
<script type="text/javascript" language="JavaScript"
src="switch.js"></script>
```

At this point, the head section of your page should look something like this:

```
<head>
<title>Style Switcher</title>
<meta http-equiv="Content-Type" content="text/html; charset=iso-8859-1">
<link rel="stylesheet" type="text/css" media="screen" href="gb.css">
<link rel="stylesheet" type="text/css" media="screen" title="preferred"
href="bgp.css">
<link rel="alternate stylesheet" type="text/css" media="screen"
title="alternate" href="red.css">
<script type="text/javascript" language="JavaScript"
src="switch.js"></script>
</head>
```

You're almost there. Just one more thing to include!

Adding a Menu for Choosing the Style

In the body of the page, add a menu using the `select` element. In this menu, you will use the value of the `title` attributes in the style sheet links.

The `select` element includes an `onChange` event and a block of JavaScript code, written by Mike Golding at `www.mikezilla.com/exp0020/exp0020.html`. His article on style switching includes a detailed discussion of the code and some additional methods for creating a style switcher.

For our sample page, the code follows:

```
<select onchange="var v=this.options[this.selectedIndex].value;
if (v != '') selectStyle('style', v);">
<option value="">-- Select Style --</option>
<option value="preferred">Blue, Gray, Purple</option>
<option value="alternate">Red</option>
</select>
```

Note that the value in the `option` element is the same as the value of the `title` attribute in the associated `link` element. You can include as many `option` elements and style sheets as you want.

Preview Your File

Now it's time to take a peek at what you've done.

1. Save the HTML file and preview the file in a browser to see if your style switcher works properly. You'll notice that the default style displays when the page is loaded in Internet Explorer 6, but not when it's loaded in Netscape 6 and 7. The preferred and alternate styles, however, are displayed in both browsers.

2. If your file is not working properly, or if you would like to view the completed sample file, open the `switch.html` file from the Chapter 12 folder of the accompanying CD.

That's All, Folks!

We've covered the essentials of behaviors, but as you have seen, behaviors work closely with many other Dreamweaver features. To further advance your skills and knowledge in creating interactive and dynamic web pages using Dreamweaver, see the next chapter, where you'll learn how to create navigation objects such as buttons, navigation bars, rollovers, and jump menus.

## CHAPTER 13

Designing Navigation Objects

The most important part of a web page is the content, but the navigation, which lets users access the information they are looking for, is crucial to the user's experience. There are many types of visually interesting, interactive, and effective navigation aids that you can add to your pages to help the user move through your site.

In this chapter, you will learn to create a variety of navigation objects, including rollovers, buttons, navigation bars, pop-up menus, and jump menus. You'll also learn to use symbols, instances, and Library items.

These are the topics you'll delve into in this chapter:

- **Creating rollover effects**

- **Learning to use symbols, instances, and libraries**

- **Using buttons**

- **Making a navigation bar**

- **Creating pop-up menus**

- **Adding a jump menu**

Gathering Your Graphic Assets

Remember that Dreamweaver is not a graphics program and that you'll need to prepare your images first in the graphics software program of your choice (for detailed instructions, see the Bonus Chapter on the book's CD). As long as you have the images prepared (including whatever variations you want to display when a graphic link is hovered over, active, or clicked), you can assemble your rollovers and navigation bars directly in Dreamweaver.

If you use Fireworks or Flash to create your graphics, you can export them directly to Dreamweaver, including any HTML that's been created along with the graphics. If you have already created your entire interactive image in Fireworks (whether it be a simple rollover, a navigation bar, or something more complex), you can insert it into your document in Dreamweaver with Insert → Image Objects → Fireworks HTML. Then you just browse to the Fireworks file and click OK. If you use Photoshop or any other graphics software, just save your image files in the images folder in your site directory so that you can access them easily when working with Dreamweaver sites.

Creating Rollovers

Rollovers have a continuing appeal for both the novice and experienced Web user. What is it that makes a rollover effect so enticing? Maybe it's that we like movement on the Web. Not too much movement, of course. No, just a subtle color change or a new icon that pops up—enough of a change to show us that we are involved in the navigation of this particular site and that our actions on that web page have an effect.

So what exactly is a rollover? A rollover, also called a mouseover, is when a user moves the mouse pointer over an object, and that object changes. It can be something as simple as a picture changing to a different picture. It gets its name from an event (onMouseOver, technically speaking) that is associated with a behavior or action. For example, if the user moves the mouse over an image, a dynamic effect can be added that displays a different graphic in the same spot, somewhere else on the page, or both!

Image States

Understanding image states is essential to creating dynamic image effects. Before you start creating rollovers, buttons, and navigation bars, let's review the basics of image states.

Each image state represents a mouse event:

Up The default image that displays when the page first loads.

Over The image that displays when the user moves the mouse over the image.

Down The image that displays when the user clicks the image. The Down state image is often used to signify that the image represents the current web page when buttons are used as navigational objects.

Over While Down The image that displays when the user moves the mouse over the image after it's been clicked.

While this does not include every possible image state and mouse event, these four are the most common image states you will use for navigation objects. You don't have to include a different image for each of these four states. Very often, you'll only use an Up state and an Over state when creating simple rollover effects, for example.

Making a Rollover

A simple *rollover* is really just two different graphics with a little bit of scripting that tells the browser to swap one image for the other.

> The two graphics need to be exactly the same size in a simple rollover. Otherwise, the second image may appear distorted since the browser will display it as the same size as the original image.

You can also create multiple rollovers (change the state of more than one image at a time when the user mouses over an image) in both Dreamweaver and Fireworks. You can create *disjoint*, or remote, rollovers in Fireworks. A disjoint rollover occurs when you move the mouse over an image and a second image is displayed in a different location on the page.

Dreamweaver

To make a simple rollover, follow these steps:

1. Position the insertion point where you want the image to appear.

2. On the Common Insert bar (which defaults to whatever was last selected), click the Image icon and then click on the arrow and select Rollover Image (or select Insert → Image Objects → Rollover Image).

3. On the Insert Rollover Image dialog box that appears, type a name for the rollover (see Figure 13.1). The rollover action won't occur without a name to use in scripting.

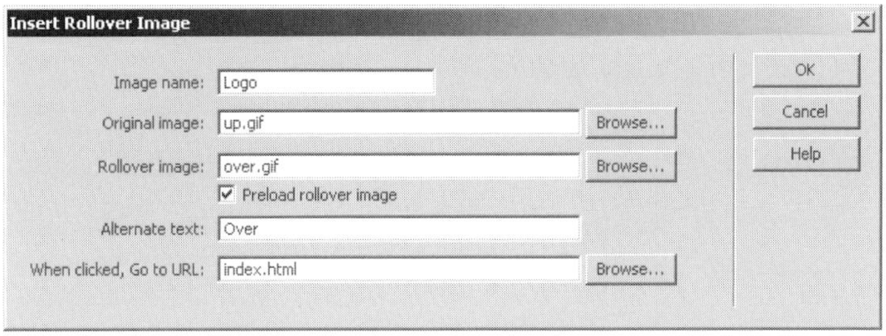

Figure 13.1

The Insert Rollover Image dialog box makes it simple to drop a rollover onto your page.

4. Browse to the original image (the one that should be displayed by default).

5. Then browse to the rollover image (the one that should be displayed when the action takes place—hovering, clicking, and so on).

6. Type alternate text for nongraphical browsers.

7. Browse to the destination for the rollover, assuming that you're using the interactive image as a link.

8. Click OK. Dreamweaver inserts the rollover.

> Dreamweaver won't display the rollover action for you. You'll need to preview your page in a browser (by pressing F12) to see the image in action.

By default, Dreamweaver makes rollovers that respond to the mouse when it is over the image. If you want to make a rollover that responds to another action, such as clicking, use the Behaviors feature to add an action called Swap Image (see Chapter 12, "Incorporating JavaScript Behaviors," for more on working with behaviors).

> The Chapter 13 folder on the accompanying CD includes a folder called Nav Practice. This is a group of four images (up, over, down, and over_down) for practicing dynamic effects.

To make multiple rollovers in Dreamweaver, you need to use the Set Nav Bar Image behavior, as detailed in Chapter 12. This means that the involved images need to be part of the same navigation bar.

Fireworks

Fireworks uses slices, hotspots, and buttons to create interactivity. Fireworks includes a "drag-and-drop" method to create simple interactivity and a Behaviors panel for more complex interactivity. If you export a Fireworks rollover to Dreamweaver, you can edit it in Dreamweaver's Behaviors panel.

> Buttons are covered later in this chapter. For more details on hotspots and image maps, see Chapter 8, "Making and Maintaining Hyperlinks." For additional information on using slices, see the Bonus Chapter on this book's CD.

To make a simple two-state (Up and Over) rollover, follow these steps:

1. Select, draw, or import the image you want as the trigger image or the Up state—the image that visitors see when they enter your site.

2. Place the image or button where you want it, right-click to access the contextual menu (Ctrl-click on a Mac), and choose Insert Slice.

3. In the Frames panel, add one more frame by clicking the New/Duplicate Frame icon. You don't need another slice for a new frame; you only need one slice for the target object, and it is in the Web layer for every frame automatically.

4. Select Frame 2, open or draw the second image (the same size as the first), and place it over the first image in your document.

> Here is an easy way to get an image to be the same size and in the correct location in Frame 2. First, return to the Layers panel, and select the object (not the slice). Then, choose Edit → Clone, then Edit → Copy, and Select Frame 2. Finally, choose Edit → Paste, and then make alterations to the clone.

5. On the canvas (or the Web layer in the Layers panel), select the slice you added.

6. Place the pointer over the behavior handle in the selected slice. The behavior handle is a round circle with crosshairs that appears in the center of a slice when it's selected. Hotspots and buttons also have behavior handles.

7. The pointer changes to a hand. Click the behavior handle and choose Simple Rollover from the menu that displays.

8. The Swap Image dialog box displays. From the Swap Image From menu, choose the frame you created in step 3.

Figure 13.2

The Simple Rollover behavior added to the Behaviors panel

In Figure 13.2 you can see that the onMouseOver Simple Rollover behavior has been added in the Behaviors panel. Figure 13.3 shows the selected slice with the behavior handle in the center and a line to the Frame beneath indicating a simple rollover.

> In Fireworks, you can preview the rollover behavior by clicking on the Preview tab in the Document window.

You can also create multiple and disjoint rollovers in Fireworks using Fireworks drag-and-drop technique.

To add a disjoint rollover:

1. Select, draw, or import the image you want as the trigger image or the Up state.

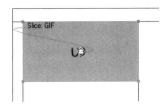

Figure 13.3

Selected slice with behavior handle and simple rollover

2. Place the image or button where you want it, right-click to access the contextual menu (Ctrl-click on a Mac), and choose Insert Slice.

3. In the Frames panel, add one more frame by clicking the New/Duplicate Frame icon.

4. Select Frame 2, open or draw the second image, and place it anywhere on the document other than over the first image.

5. Select the second image and choose Edit → Insert → Slice.

6. Select Frame 1 in the Frames panel.

7. Select the slice that contains the first image, and place the pointer over the behavior handle.

8. Drag the behavior handle to the slice you created in step 5.

9. The Swap Image dialog box displays. From the Swap Image From menu, choose the frame you created in step 3.

Figure 13.4

This slice includes both a simple and a disjoint rollover.

You can apply more than one rollover to a selected slice by dragging the behavior handle. Drag the handle to the upper-left of the selected slice to create a simple rollover, or drag the handle to a different slice to create a disjoint rollover. Figure 13.4 shows a slice with both a simple rollover and a disjoint rollover.

Creating Navigation Buttons

Dreamweaver allows you to make simple two-state (Up and Over) buttons by creating Flash buttons, as described in Chapter 11, "Getting into Flash." If you want to create buttons with more than two states, use Fireworks or Flash to create the buttons, and export them to Dreamweaver. Fireworks and Flash use symbols, instances, and libraries to design effective navigation buttons.

Symbols

Utilizing the same piece of artwork or the same object multiple times helps cut your production time and a page's download time. For example, web designers may use a small image for a background image on a page and let that image repeat, or *tile*, to fill the whole page. Fireworks and Flash use symbols to allow you to use the same object multiple times. The symbols that you generate are stored in libraries and instances are present in the document.

You can convert any object into a symbol. For example, if you have designed a custom button, you can make it a symbol, which can then be used over and over again. In addition to adding new symbols, you can convert any button or object that has already been produced to a symbol.

There are three types of symbols in Fireworks and Flash.

Graphic symbols These are any object or image that you'd like to use multiple times. Graphic symbols are static, meaning they have no behaviors, such as rollovers, attached to them.

Button symbols These usually contain multiple frames, which contain the different states of a button.

Animation symbols (Fireworks only) These contain all the frames and timing of your animation. A completed animation, including its links, is contained in the symbol.

Movie clip symbols (Flash only) These contain reuseable animations. Movie clip instances can be placed inside the Timeline of a button symbol to create an animated button.

Creating Symbols in Fireworks

To make any existing object or an animation into a symbol, follow these steps:

1. Draw any object you'd like, or open an existing object you've made.

2. Select the Pointer tool and select an object, choose Modify → Symbol → Convert To Symbol. The Symbol Properties dialog box will open as seen in Figure 13.5.

3. Name your new symbol and choose the type of symbol you want it to be (Graphic, Button, or Animation) by clicking the appropriate option.

4. Click OK when you are finished.

Symbols are also editable. As soon as you make a symbol, it is automatically stored in the Library panel (in the Assets panel group) and an instance is placed on the canvas.

When you double-click the instance, a dialog box will open. Which dialog box opens will depend on the type of symbol you are editing: a Graphic symbol will open the Symbol Properties dialog box, a Button symbol will open the Button editor, and an Animation symbol will open the Animate dialog box. When you edit the master symbol the changes will be made globally to all instances of that symbol.

Creating Symbols in Flash

To make any existing object into a symbol, follow these steps:

1. Select an element on the stage.

2. Select Modify → Convert To Symbol, drag the selection to the Library panel, or right-click (Ctrl-click on Mac) on the selection and choose Convert To Symbol from the context menu.

3. In the Convert To Symbol dialog box, type a name for the symbol, and choose the type of symbol (Graphic, Button, or Movie Clip).

4. Click OK when you are finished.

Figure 13.5

The Symbol Properties dialog box in Fireworks

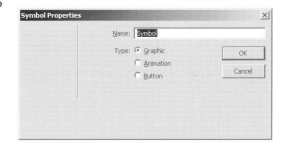

Flash automatically adds the symbol to the Library panel, and an instance is placed on the stage. You can edit the symbol by double-clicking an instance on the stage or by double-clicking the symbol's icon in the Library panel.

Using Instances and Libraries

Symbols are stored in the library. Once you have a symbol, you can drag additional instances from the library onto your canvas (Fireworks) or stage (Flash)—but when you do, you should be aware that it's not the actual symbol you see, it's an *instance* of the symbol, a copy.

An instance maintains a link to the parent symbol. If you edit the parent symbol, all of the instances are also changed. You can, however, edit certain properties of instances without affecting any other instances or the symbol itself. In Fireworks, you can use the transform tools and alter the opacity on individual instances, and you can add effects to an instance, which can be edited instance by instance. In Flash, you can modify the color, scale, rotation, alpha transparency, brightness, tint, height, width, and location of an individual instance without affecting any others.

You can export and import symbols from one document to another, and in Flash you can share symbols between documents as shared library assets.

Making Buttons

In both Fireworks and Flash, buttons are the most common type of symbol used for navigation. Because buttons can have multiple states, you can use them to create dynamic navigation effects and offer additional clues to the user about where they are in your site.

Figure 13.6

The Button editor dialog box

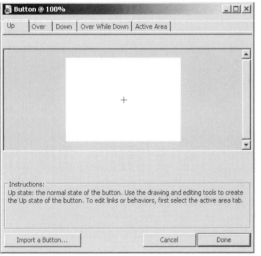

Fireworks

In Fireworks, you can make a button directly in the Button editor or you can convert an existing button into a Button symbol and edit it in the Button editor. A Button symbol encapsulates up to four different button states (Up, Over, Down, Over While Down). Instead of spending a lot of time reproducing similar buttons, you simply have to place an instance of a symbol onto your canvas and edit the text and link.

You can use this editor to help streamline your workflow because you can apply up to four different states for the same button as well as add links and a slice. All the JavaScript code for the different rollovers gets exported with the button. Figure 13.6 shows the Button editor.

To use the Button editor, follow these steps:

1. Choose Edit → Insert → New Symbol. When the Symbol Properties dialog box opens, enter the name **Green Button** and choose Button for the Type. Click OK.

2. The Button editor will open with the Up state tab active. Select the Rectangle tool and draw a rectangle with the following properties (which you should set in the Property inspector):

    Size: **130 × 25**

    Fill: **Gradient → Linear, # 66FF00 (green)** is the color we used for the left side of the gradient, and **# 003366 (blue)** was used on the right.

    Fill Texture: **Parchment, 50%**

    Stroke: **Pencil 2, dark gray**

    Effects: **Inner Bevel, Frame 2, Width 4**

3. Center the button by using the Align panel (Window → Align). Select the To Canvas icon (should be orange) and the center icon in each group of three in the Align section (center horizontally, center vertically).

    Figure 13.7 shows the button in the Up state.

4. Select the Text tool and type the text you want on the button (for this exercise, type **Home**). Remember that the text is fully editable and can easily be changed later. Use any font and size that looks good on your button.

5. To center this text, use the Align panel. Select the To Canvas icon (should be orange) and the center icon in each group of three in the Align section (center horizontally, center vertically).

6. Click the Over tab and click the Copy Up Graphic button to put a copy of the Up state in the Over state's editing box.

7. Select the button and change the stroke color to yellow and the text color to gold.

8. Click the Down tab and then click the Copy Over Graphic button. Leave the Include Nav Bar Down state option checked so that the Down state will be active when the corresponding page loads.

9. Change the stroke color to gray and click the + sign in the Property inspector to access the Effects list.

10. Then choose Bevel and Emboss → Inset Emboss and accept the default settings.

Figure 13.7

Up tab of the Button editor

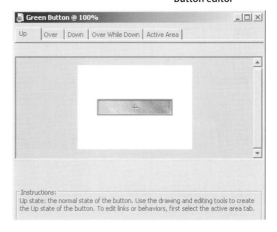

11. Click the Active Area tab; you will see a slice added to your document automatically. The Active Area is set to Automatic by default and generates a slice large enough to cover all the button states. There is one slice for all four button states; you can change the size of the slice by unchecking the Automatic option and dragging the slice points.

12. Open the Property inspector to view the slice properties. You can add links and Alt text to your buttons in the Slice Property inspector. When you add it to the Up state, all the states are updated automatically.

13. Click the Done button when you are finished with all the states of the button. An instance of the button is automatically placed in your document (Figure 13.8), indicated by the little arrow in the corner, and the button is automatically added as a symbol to the Library panel.

14. To add more buttons to your document, drag them from the Library panel (in the Asset panel group) by clicking and dragging either the Button symbol or the name of the symbol onto your document.

15. To preview the button, click the Preview tab in your document window, pass your mouse over the button, and click the button to see the different states.

Use the Property inspector to edit the buttons you have made. The following is a list of the different portions of your buttons and the steps for editing each portion:

Text Select the button. If you want to change the text characters, use the Text box in the Button Property inspector. If you want to edit text properties such as font, color, or size, double-click the button to open the Button editor. Select the text, then make changes in the Text Property inspector. You should add Alt text and can also add a Link.

Button characteristics Double-click to open the Button editor, click the tab for the state or states you'd like to alter, and make your changes. Click the Done button when you're finished.

Imported symbols Editing an instance of an imported button doesn't affect any documents containing the original symbol. But if you choose to Update (Library Options pop-up menu), the symbol will return to its original state. If you truly want to break the link between the original imported symbol and your new document, make a duplicate through the Library Options pop-up menu. Then drag an instance of this button onto your document (the copy won't say Import).

Active area If you want to change the active area of the button slice, you can now do it right in your document. Click and drag the red slice lines to adjust the active area.

Figure 13.8

A button instance is automatically placed in your document.

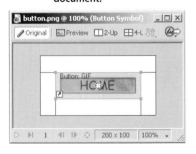

Flash

Buttons in Flash are four-frame movie clips. When you create a symbol and choose button as the symbol type, Flash creates a Timeline with four frames. The first frame is the Up state, the second frame is the Over state, the third frame is the Down state, and the fourth frame is the Hit state that defines the active area of the button.

To create a button in Flash, follow these steps:

1. Select Insert → New Symbol.

2. In the Create New Symbol dialog box, give the button a name, and select the Button radio button from the Behavior group.

3. Flash switches to symbol editing mode and a Timeline with four frames displays (Figure 13.9)

4. Create an Up state for the button by importing a graphic and dragging it onto the stage, dragging an instance of another graphic or movie clip onto the stage, or by using the drawing tools in Flash to create a graphic. You can also use the button graphics in the Common Library (Window → Other Panels → Common Libraries → Buttons).

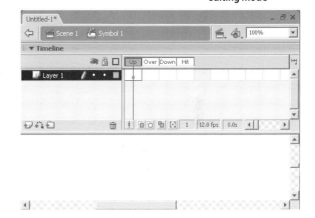

Figure 13.9

Timeline with four frames in button symbol editing mode

You can use a graphic or movie clip symbol in a button, but you can't use another button in a button. Use a movie clip symbol if you want the button to be animated.

5. Click the second frame in the Timeline and choose Insert → Timeline → Keyframe. Flash automatically copies the previous frame (Up) into the new frame (Over).

6. Modify the graphic, or repeat the steps in step 4 to obtain a new graphic.

7. Repeat steps 5 and 6 for the Down state and the Hit state.

8. The Hit state shows the area on the button where the button is active and responds to clicks. Make sure the hit area is large enough to click easily. The Hit state is not visible, so you can make it as large as you choose.

9. Select Edit → Edit Document to leave symbol editing mode.

10. Drag your button from the Library to the stage to create a new instance in your document (Figure 13.10).

Figure 13.10

Button instance on the stage

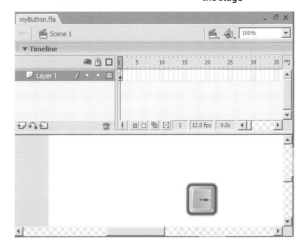

To preview your button:

1. To preview buttons in authoring mode, select Control → Enable Simple Buttons.

2. To preview animated buttons, or buttons with attached actions, choose Control → Test Movie.

You can edit your button in Symbol editing mode in four ways:

1. Open the Edit Symbols menu on the right side of the information bar above the Timeline for the movie and select the name of the button you want to edit.

2. Right-click (Ctrl-click Mac) the button instance on the stage and choose Edit from the context menu.

3. Select the button instance on the stage and choose Edit → Edit Symbols from the application menu bar.

4. Open the Library panel and double-click the symbol's icon or select the symbol and choose Edit from the Library options menu.

Flash offers additional options for creating complex buttons, including multilayered buttons with additional dynamic effects, animated buttons, and buttons with sound. See the Flash Help panel for more information.

Adding a Navigation Bar

A navigation bar is a group of images that link to different areas of a site. The navigation bar usually stays the same from page to page and provides a consistent navigational scheme for the user.

Before you can insert a navigation bar into the pages of your site, you first have to prepare the images that will appear as the links, menu choices, or buttons. For each button, you'll need up to four images, one for each of the four possible states (Up, Over, Down, Over While Down).

Once you have the graphic images ready, you can use either Dreamweaver or Fireworks to assemble a navigation bar.

Dreamweaver

Dreamweaver makes the assembly of even complicated nav bars easy.

To make a navigation bar, follow these steps:

1. Position the insertion point where you want the navigation bar to appear on the page.

2. On the Common Insert bar, click the Navigation Bar icon or select Insert → Interactive Images → Navigation Bar.

3. On the Insert Navigation Bar dialog box that appears, type a name for the first button (see Figure 13.11).

4. Browse to the location of the Up image or type in the path and filename.

5. Then (optionally) type in the path and filename of (or browse to the location of) the Over, Down, and Over While Down images.

6. Type alternate text for nongraphical browsers.

7. Type a URL or browse to the location of the linked file for the Down state.

8. If the current button represents the current page (as, for example, a Home button would do on the home page of a site), click the Show Down Image Initially option.

9. To add the next button, click the Add Item button (the plus (+) sign at the top of the dialog box) and then repeat steps 3 through 8. Do this as many times as needed.

10. Indicate if the nav bar is to be inserted vertically or horizontally.

11. Check the Use Tables box if you want to insert the nav bar as a table.

12. Click OK. Dreamweaver inserts the navigation bar.

You can edit the nav bar by choosing Modify → Navigation Bar, which opens the Modify Navigation Bar dialog box (Figure 13.12).

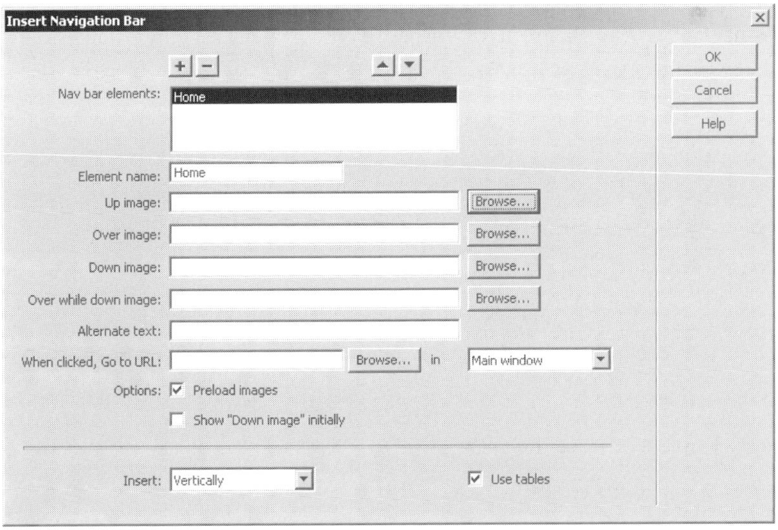

Figure 13.11

The Insert Navigation Bar dialog box streamlines the process of assembling a nav bar.

Figure 13.12

**The Modify Naviga-
tion Bar dialog box**

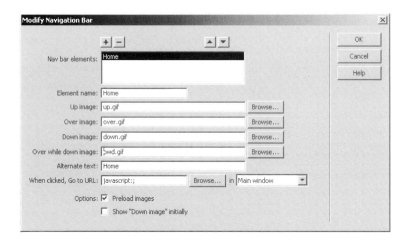

You can also use the Set Nav Bar Image behavior to edit the properties of navigation bar images; for example, to change the display and/or actions associated with images in a navigation bar. For more information, see Chapter 12, "Incorporating JavaScript Behaviors."

To make a single navigation bar available to numerous pages in your site, insert the bar into a template and then attach the template to your pages (or build your pages based on the template). See Chapter 4, "Saving Labor with Templates and Libraries," for more on templates.

You can also do this in Fireworks by dragging the button symbol into a new Fireworks document and then cloning the instance on the page to create as many copies as you want. You can use the Property inspector to edit the important attributes for each instance. The Dreamweaver way is easier, though!

Pop-Up Menus

Pop-up menus are very popular on the Web. You can make them in Dreamweaver or build them in Fireworks.

In Dreamweaver, you can use the Show Pop-Up Menu behavior to create a Dreamweaver pop-up menu or to edit a Fireworks pop-up menu that's inserted in a Dreamweaver document.

In Dreamweaver, you start with an object and attach the Show Pop-Up Menu behavior to the object. For more details, see "The Built-In Behaviors" section in Chapter 12.

You can also build pop-up menus in Fireworks, but if you've already created the graphics, the Dreamweaver method is quicker and easier. If you need to create the graphics, then Fireworks offers many more options, including submenus.

Adding a Jump Menu

You can create jump menus in Dreamweaver. A jump menu is a drop-down menu in a document that is visible to your site visitors; it contains links that allow them to go to other documents or files. You can create links to documents in your website, documents on other websites, e-mail links, links to graphics, or links to any file type that can be opened in a browser.

Jump menus allow for more link options in a smaller amount of space on a page. There are three basic components of a jump menu:

- A menu selection prompt, such as a category description for the menu items, or instructions such as "Choose one." This is an optional element.

- A list of linked menu items from which a user chooses an option, which causes a linked document or file to open. This is a required element.

- A Go button. This is an optional element.

Figure 13.13 displays a jump menu that shows your search categories. This jump menu also uses the optional Go button, so this is a combination of two elements, although Dreamweaver lets you create them together.

> The Jump Menu Go option can be confusing and difficult to use in Dreamweaver. For an easy, workable option, see the section "Using a Go button" later in this chapter.

Inserting a Jump Menu

Because the jump menu must be part of a form object, Dreamweaver automatically creates one if you don't already have one defined. Therefore, to insert a jump menu into your document, you use the Jump Menu form object.

1. Select Insert → Form → Jump Menu. This opens the Insert Jump Menu dialog box shown in Figure 13.14.

Figure 13.13

Search Category jump menu

2. To create an optional selection prompt, type the prompt text in the Text field of the dialog box.

3. If you use a selection prompt, select the "Select First Item After URL Change" check box at the bottom of the dialog box.

4. Click the plus (+) button to add a menu item.

5. In the Text field of the Insert Jump Menu dialog box, type the text you want to appear in the menu list.

6. In the When Selected, Go To URL field, select the file to open by browsing for the file, or entering the file's path.

Figure 13.14

**Insert Jump Menu
dialog box**

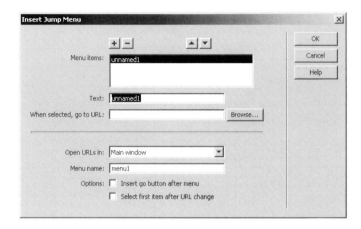

7. In the Open URLs In drop-down menu, select a location in which the file will open, either the main window, or a frame.

> If your target frame doesn't appear on the Open URLs In pop-up menu, close the Insert Jump Menu dialog box and name the frame.

8. If you want to add a Go button instead of a menu selection prompt, under Options, select the Insert Go Button After Menu option. (To make your Go button functional, see the section "Using a Go Button" later in this chapter.

9. To add additional menu items, click the plus (+) button and repeat steps 3 through 6 of this procedure (see Figure 13.15).

10. Click OK.

Figure 13.15

**Completed Insert
Jump Menu
dialog box**

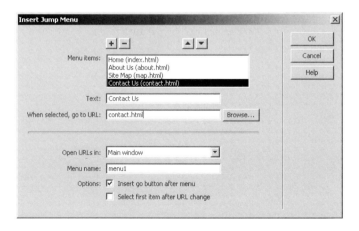

Figure 13.16 shows both the jump menu and the Go button the user sees from the information entered for Figure 13.15.

Editing Jump Menus

In order to make jump menu changes, use the Property inspector or the Behaviors panel. You can change the list order or the file an item links to, or you can add, delete, or rename an item. However, if you are changing the location in which a linked file opens, or even adding or changing a menu selection prompt, you must use the Behaviors panel.

Figure 13.16

Jump Menu and Go Button

In order to edit a jump menu item using the Property inspector, follow these steps:

1. Open the Property inspector (Window → Properties).

2. In the Document window's Design view, select the jump menu object.

3. The List/Menu icon should appear in the Property inspector.

4. In the Property inspector, click the List Values button. Figure 13.17 shows the List Values dialog box that displays as a result.

Figure 13.17

List Values dialog box

5. Make changes to the menu items, then click OK.

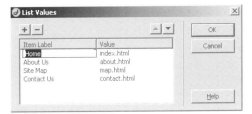

As with any software application, there are always different ways of doing something. If you're using frames as a destination for your jump to take the user to a new page, then the user can't navigate backwards. The next section shows how to create a workaround for this accessibility problem.

Jump Menu Workarounds

As just mentioned, once users choose a jump menu item, they will not be able to reselect that menu item if they navigate back to that page, or if the Open URL In field specifies a frame. You have to work around this problem, and there are two ways to do it.

First, you can use a menu selection prompt, such as a category, or a user instruction, such as "Choose one." This menu selection prompt is reselected automatically after each menu selection.

Second, you can use a Go button, which allows a user to revisit the currently chosen link.

Select only one of these options per jump menu because they cannot be used at the same time on the same jump menu.

Using a Go button

Macromedia support (www.macromedia.com/support/dreamweaver/ts/documents/gobutton.htm) states that the Go button is designed only for the case where the user wants to go to the page that's already selected in the menu, and therefore needs an additional trigger to make that possible. (Otherwise, the jump menu itself should trigger the action of going to the selected page).

However, this is confusing for both users and developers! There is an easy and free option that makes the Go button active for any selection in the menu, and it works in both Internet Explorer and Netscape.

Visit the Drop-Down Menu Generator page on the JavaScript Builders site at www.ricocheting.com/js/drop.html. The automatic Drop-Down Menu Generator will create *all* the code you need to insert a functional drop-down menu with a Go button in your page.

If you don't need a Go button, then Dreamweaver's jump menus work fine, but for those occasions when you want to add a Go button feature, the Drop-Down Menu Generator is a better option than working to configure Dreamweaver's Go button.

Here's sample code for a simple drop-down menu (two items) that includes a fully functional Go button that opens new pages in the original window.

```html
<html>
<head>
<title>Jump</title>
<meta http-equiv="Content-Type" content="text/html;
charset=iso-8859-1">
</head>

<body>
<form name="form1">
<select name="menu">
<option value="http://www.example.com/index.html">Home</option>
<option value="http://www.example.com/about.html">About Us</option>
</select>
<input type="button" onClick="location=this.form.menu.options
[this.form.menu.selectedIndex].value;" value="GO">
</form>

</body>
</html>
```

Hands On: Making a Nav Bar

In this tutorial, you will create a navigation bar for the Info Tech sample site that uses an Up image and an Over image for each navigation element.

1. Open the Chapter 13 folder on the accompanying CD. This folder contains 12 images for the navigation bar—6 for the Up state and 6 for the Over state. Copy all the Chapter 13 tutorial files to your computer so that you can browse to their location.

2. Open a new HTML file in Dreamweaver.

3. Position the insertion point where you want the navigation bar to be located on the page. In this case, you want the navigation bar to be as close to the top and left of the page as possible, so add `marginwidth` and `marginheight` to the body tag, as follows:

    ```
    <body marginwidth="0" marginheight="0">
    ```

4. Choose Insert → Image Objects → Navigation Bar (or click the Images icon in the Common Insert bar and choose Navigation Bar). The Insert Navigation Bar dialog box opens.

5. Browse to the image file for the first element in the nav bar (About). The first Up image is `about.jpg`. The first Over image is `about.gif`.

6. Enter **about.html** in the Go To URL box, or browse to the file.

7. Check the option to preload images.

8. Choose horizontally from the Insert menu at the bottom of the dialog box, and check the option to Use Tables.

9. Click on the + at the top of the dialog box to add another element. Repeat steps 5–8 for the remaining five elements as shown in Table 13.1.

10. Click OK when you have entered all the elements, images, and links.

11. Save the file as `nav.html`, and preview it in a browser. Test the navigation elements and make sure the mouseovers and links work.

12. To view the completed nav bar as part of the Info Tech frameset, open `frames.html` in the Chapter 7 `frames_complete` folder in the Chapter 7 folder on the CD.

ELEMENT NAME	UP IMAGE	OVER IMAGE	LINK
about	about.jpg	about.gif	about.html
product	product.jpg	product.gif	product.html
support	support.jpg	support.gif	support.html
training	training.jpg	training.gif	training.html
downloads	downloads.jpg	downloads.gif	downloads.html
careers	careers.jpg	careers.gif	careers.html

Table 13.1

Navigation Bar Items

Keeping It Simple

So now you know how to create rollovers, buttons, navigation bars, pop-up menus, and jump menus using Dreamweaver, Fireworks, and/or Flash. Use your newfound knowledge well and make sure you create navigation schemes that are user-friendly and accessible. Remember that rollovers—from a design point of view—should be used to enhance an already clean website design. Your site should already have great—not just good—navigation that is easy to use and even easier to understand, and colors and graphics should not detract from the content and purpose of the site.

Keep it simple and clean—subtly integrate your rollovers into your existing design and you'll do just fine. In other words, make sure that you don't make your fancy-schmancy rollovers the focus of the site.

To further advance your skills and knowledge in creating interactive and dynamic web pages, see Chapter 14, where you'll learn how to use forms to create interactivity on your pages.

CHAPTER 14

Collecting Information with Forms

Any time you submit information online, you fill out a form. Forms can range from complex collections of fields such as you might find in a survey, to a single field that lets you select a file to download. The front-end experience of filling out a form is easy to grasp and familiar to most software users. The back-end automation of a form, which controls how the information is processed, is a black box to most users. But if you want your forms to *do* anything, then you or your team will have to be comfortable with both creating the display of the form as well as processing the form results with scripts.

Forms are used in a variety of situations. No matter how you use your form, it remains a tool for collecting information or enabling interaction with your site, and it operates through a collection of scripts and HTML form elements.

This chapter explains how to create forms using the tools provided within Dreamweaver with the following topics:

- Using the elements of HTML forms

- Creating hidden form fields

- Using form-processing scripts with Dreamweaver forms

- Editing scripts in a text editor

- Creating target pages for form responses

- Using FormMail to process form results

Exploring Form Elements

HTML forms, as created by Dreamweaver or any other HTML editor, use a combination of HTML elements and attributes to define, collect, and process the information requested by the website owner or administrator.

Dreamweaver allows you to create HTML-based forms using its built-in form field controls located on the Forms Insert bar. These elements are used to create the form struc-

Figure 14.1

**A basic
webpage form**

ture, text fields, buttons, radio buttons, check boxes, images, file fields, list/menu selections, hidden tags, labels, fieldsets, and legends that are discussed in the following sections. Once all of these form objects are combined, you will find that your form can be an efficient collection of fields that can collect the information you require. Figure 14.1 shows a form for requesting further information.

The formatting of this form is controlled by using a series of table cells that allow you to align each label, as well as each text field, while still keeping the information easy to read and readily accessible to the individual filling out the form. If you don't have a form that fits on a single screen, you can break the form into sections so that the form doesn't become an overwhelming, monotonous task for your site visitors.

Application servers (such as ASP or ColdFusion) can use session variables to retain user information so it's not lost, for example, as the user moves from one page to the next in a multi-page form. The information in session variables can be reused for as long as the session (visit) lasts. Session variables function only if the user's browser is configured to accept cookies.

Specifying Your Form Structure

Dreamweaver uses the HTML `<form>` tag to create a form on your web page. You can use the Property inspector to access several form attributes (Figure 14.2), including `name`, `method` (`get` or `post`), `action`, `enctype` (content type for form data submitted using the post method), `target`, and style attributes. The form element can also include event handlers, such as `onclick`, and a `title` attribute. We'll look at all these properties shortly.

Figure 14.2

Form properties

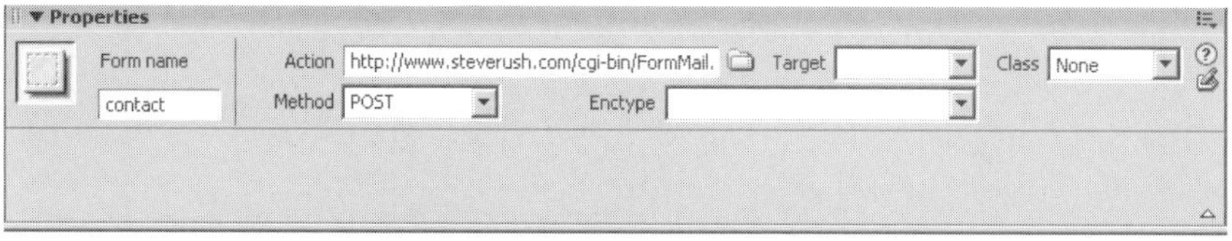

To insert a form into your Dreamweaver document, select Insert → Form → Form, or use the icons shown on the Forms Insert bar. This inserts `<form name="form1" method="post"` `action="">  </form>` tags into your document. The form itself, when seen in Design view (View → Design) appears as a red dashed outline on your screen. To add form objects, text, and formatting, you must place your cursor in this red box prior to the addition of your information. Figure 14.3 shows a form with a text box and two check boxes in Design view.

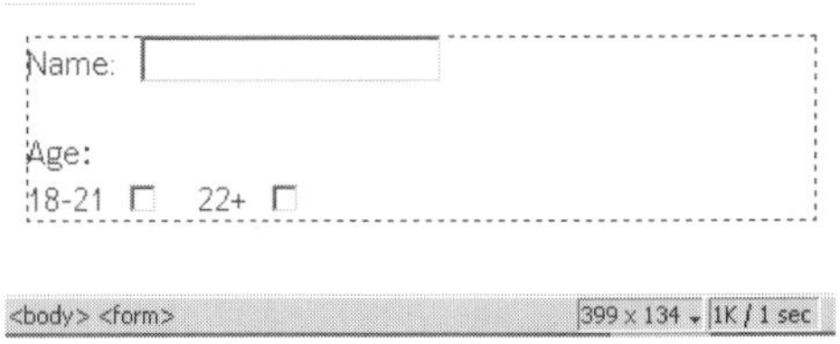

Figure 14.3

Form in Design view

The Property inspector for each form in your document contains these fields, which correspond to the `<form>` tag's attributes of the same name:

Name This stores the name used to reference the form in scripts. You can place any unique alphanumeric string, such as `form1` or `contact_form`, in this field. This field corresponds to the `name` attribute of the `<form>` tag. Dreamweaver automatically supplies a default name, such as `form1`, but site maintenance is easier if you use a more descriptive name.

Action The Action field in the Property inspector specifies the file/script name and location that will receive the contents of the form when the Submit button on the form is pressed. This field corresponds to the `action` attribute of the `<form>` tag.

Most of the time, the contents of the action field will specify the name and location of a CGI script (`.cgi`), a Perl script (`.pl`), a Java applet or Java Server Page (`.jsp`), a ColdFusion document (`.cfm`), an Active Server Page (`.asp`), a Hypertext Preprocessor file (`.php`), or one of any number of other formats for coding HTTP behaviors. You'll learn more about form processing scripts in the section, "Working With CGI Scripts," later in this chapter. Here are some examples of strings that can be used to specify an action:

```
http://www.myserver.com/cgi-bin/formmail.pl
http://www.myserver.com/mydocument.cfm
/cgi-bin/links.pl
/myprocessingdocument.asp
scripts/login.php
```

Target This drop-down menu is used to specify a target window to display the results of the form processing. This can be a named window or frame, or any of the standard target choices (`_blank`, `_parent`, `_self`, `_top`). For more information on using targets, see Chapter 7, "Interactivity with Framesets and Frames."

Class This drop-down menu is used to apply a style class to a form or form element. Any formatting you apply to a form or part of a form will be automatically saved as a style. This property corresponds to the `class` attribute of the `<input>` tag.

Method This drop-down menu has three options: default, GET, or POST. This field corresponds to the `method` attribute of the `<form>` tag. The default option uses the browser's default method (usually GET) to send the form data.

The GET HTTP method will append the contents of the form fields to the URL specified in the action attribute, for example:

```
http://www.example.com/cf/add.cfm?fname=rose&lname=smith
```

This URL submits form entries for first and last name. There are two main disadvantages to the GET method:

- URLs are limited to 8192 characters, so you can only submit a limited amount of data
- Confidential form information (such as passwords) is visible if included in a URL

The POST HTTP method sends the form data directly to the script specified in the action attribute. There are no restrictions on the amount of information that can be submitted using the POST method. POST can also be used to send binary information, such as files and images.

Enctype This drop-down menu allows you to specify a MIME encoding type for the form content. These are the two built-in options:

- application/x-www-form-urlencoded, the default type used with the POST method
- multipart/form-data, for a file upload

You can also type in other encoding types in this field. This field corresponds to the enctype attribute of the <form> tag.

Once you have set each form attribute, your <form> tag will look something like the following in Code view (View → Code):

```
<form action="/cgi-bin/formmail.pl" method="post" enctype="application/
x-www-form-urlencoded" name="form1">
```

Using Form Text Fields

There are three types of text fields used in HTML forms: single-line text fields, multiline text fields, and password text fields. Although the functions of these three fields are much the same, their appearance and abilities widely differ. *Single-line text fields* contain, understandably, a single line of text and are typically used to collect information such as names and addresses or other short-phrase answers. *Multiline text fields* can contain and display multiple lines of text including comments, full paragraph queries, and in-depth descriptions of problems and solutions that you wish to share with, say, an online discussion board. *Password text fields* substitute asterisks for the entered text to keep sensitive information private.

To insert a text box into your Dreamweaver document, select Insert → Form → Text Field. As you can see from the TextField Property inspector (shown in Figure 14.4), the difference between these three types of text field is controlled by setting the values in the PI's property fields. Each of these properties corresponds to an attribute of the same name, or a similar name, for the <input type="text"> tag.

Figure 14.4
Text Field properties

Name The TextField Name field in the Property inspector stores the name used by scripts to reference the text field. You can place any unique alphanumeric string in this field, such as `text1` or `contact_name`. This value is the name of the variable that stores the data entered in this field, and is sent to the server for processing along with the data entered by the user. This property corresponds to the `name` attribute of the `<input type="text">` tag.

The combination of the variable name and the entered data is known as a *name-value pair*.

Char Width The Character Width attribute sets the total number of characters that are visible in the field. This property corresponds to the `size` attribute of the `<input type="text">` tag.

Max Chars The Maximum Characters attribute sets the total number of characters that can be stored in the field. This property corresponds to the `maxwidth` attribute of the `<input type="text">` tag.

Wrap The Wrap attribute allows the contents of a multiline text field to wrap to a second line in the text box, rather than run continuously on a single line. This property corresponds to the `wrap` attribute of the `<input type="text">` tag.

Type The Type property specifies that the box should be drawn as a single line, a multiline, or a password field. This property corresponds to the `type` attribute of the `<input>` tag.

Class This attribute is used to apply a style class to a form or form element. Any formatting you apply to a form or part of a form will be automatically saved as a style. This property corresponds to the `class` attribute of the `<input>` tag.

Init Val The Initial Value attribute sets up the value that will originally be displayed in the field when the HTML document is displayed. This property corresponds to the `value` attribute of the `<input type="text">` tag.

The following sections show each of the three types of text fields in action.

Single-Line Text Fields

Single-line text fields are best used to collect answers to single-phrase requests (such as "What is your name?" or "What is your Address?" or even "What Product do you wish to order?"). Anything that requires a more complex answer ("How do you feel about widgets?") should be answered in a multiline text field, as shown in the next section.

When you select Insert → Form → Text Field, a single-line text field is created automatically. You can ensure that you are creating a single-line text field, and not a password field, by selecting Single Line from the Type property in the Property inspector.

Multiline Text Fields

Multiline text fields are best used to collect answers to complex questions, such as "How do you use widgets at home compared with how you use them at work?" or "What is your favorite vacation?" If you have a request that will require more than a single line of text to answer, you should give the visitor the space to answer it fully.

As we saw, when you selected Insert → Form → Text Field, a single-line text field was created automatically. To change this into a multiline text field, select Multi Line from the Type property in the Property inspector. Notice how the `max chars` property is replaced by a `num lines` property. Dreamweaver allows you to specify the character width and number of lines for a multiline text field, but not a maximum number of characters. As odd as this restriction may sound, it exists because a multiline text field isn't created using an `<input type="text">` tag, but is created using a `<textarea>` tag, which doesn't support an attribute specifying a maximum number of characters.

When you use a multiline text field, you can also specify a value for the `wrap` attribute that specifies how to display the user's text entry if it exceeds the width of the textarea box:

Default or Off Prevents wrapping and continues the text entry in a single horizontal line, adding a horizontal scrollbar. The user must use a return to move to the next line in the textarea box.

Virtual Displays the text as if it is wrapping, but actually submits the entry as a single line.

Physical Applies wrapping to the display as well as the submitted data.

In Figure 14.5, you can see a sample of a six-line text box. You can make your boxes display as many lines as you wish, but keep in mind that it is more comfortable to fill out a form in which the space allotted is neither too small nor so large that it seems as if you are requesting a small novel.

Password Text Fields

Password text fields look just like single-line text fields in Dreamweaver, but users' entered text displays as asterisks or bullets (see Figure 14.6). If you are asking the visitor for a password or wish to hide a credit card number you are collecting, the use of a password text field is handy and makes visitors feel that your site is more secure.

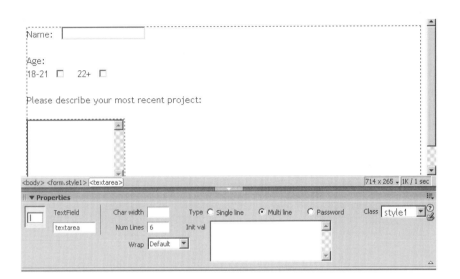

Figure 14.5

A multiline text field

Password text fields hide the information displayed on screen, but they do not encrypt the data as it is sent through your server. Do not use password text fields to collect private data unless you are also encrypting the form contents before you deliver it through e-mail or store it in a database. For more information on passwords, see Chapter 26, "Controlling Access to the Site."

To change a single-line text field into a password text field, select Password from the Type field in the Property inspector.

Inserting Check Boxes and Radio Buttons

Check boxes and radio buttons serve a similar purpose in forms. Both allow you to select from a list of options, or objects, and make one or multiple selections. Radio buttons force a single selection, while check boxes allow you to make multiple selections.

To insert a check box into your form, select Insert → Form → Check Box. In Figure 14.7, you can see the Property inspector for the first check box on the form in Figure 14.5.

The properties for check boxes include the following:

Name The Check Box Name property stores the name used to reference the check box in scripts. You can place any unique alphanumeric string in this field, such as `color1` or `career_farmer`. This property corresponds to the `name` attribute of the `<input type="checkbox">` or the `<input type="radio">` tag.

Figure 14.6

A password text field entry displayed as bullets in Internet Explorer 6

Figure 14.7

**The Check Box Prop-
erty inspector**

Checked Value   This property stores the value that will be sent to the form's processing application when the form is submitted and the box is checked. This property corresponds to the `value` attribute of the `<input type="checkbox>` or the `<input type="radio">` tag.

Initial State   This property can be set to either Checked or Unchecked to control how the check box or radio button first appears. This property corresponds to the `checked` attribute of the `<input type="checkbox>` or the `<input type="radio">` tag.

Class   This attribute is used to apply a style class to a form or form element. Any formatting you apply to a form or part of a form will be automatically saved as a style. This property corresponds to the `class` attribute of the `<input>` tag.

   Both check boxes and radio buttons have the same available properties in the Property inspector, but radio buttons must be grouped in order to force the user to make a single selection. To group radio buttons together, you must give all of the radio buttons in that group the same name (shown as "Age" in Figure 14.8). This will force the form to allow only one of the buttons to be checked at a time, and send only one value to the form's processing script when the form is submitted. Because radio buttons work as part of a group, you can only set the Initial Value of one radio button to be checked. All others will automatically be reset to Unchecked. (You can also leave them all unchecked.) Check boxes allow you to set multiple boxes to be checked.

   You can also create a series of radio buttons using the Radio Group option. To create a series of radio buttons, which are automatically part of the same group, follow these steps:

1.   Select Insert → Form= → Radio Group.

2.   Type a name for the group in the Name field. This will be the name applied to all the radio buttons used in this group.

3.   Click the plus (+) button to add additional radio buttons, or use the minus (−) button to remove buttons that have already been added.

4.   Use the up-arrow and down-arrow buttons to control the order in which the radio buttons are displayed on your page.

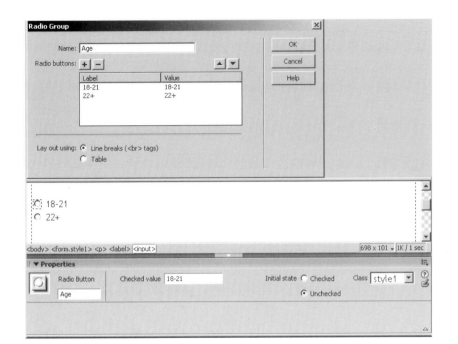

Figure 14.8

A selection of radio buttons, the Radio Button Property inspector, and the new Radio Group dialog box, which automatically groups radio buttons for you

5. Enter a label and a value for each button. The label is the text that displays next to the button on the page. If the radio button is checked, the value is the data that's sent to the form script for processing when the form is submitted. The label and value can be the same or have different values.

6. Select either Line Breaks (
 tags) or Table in the Lay Out Using option to control the layout of your radio buttons.

Once you have completed your selections, the Radio button group will be created. Figure 14.8 shows a Radio button group inserted in a form. Dreamweaver also allows you to insert form components without requiring an enclosing form tag. Sometimes you want to use a form component without submitting information to a script—for example, using a scripting language such as JavaScript to dynamically write messages into text fields.

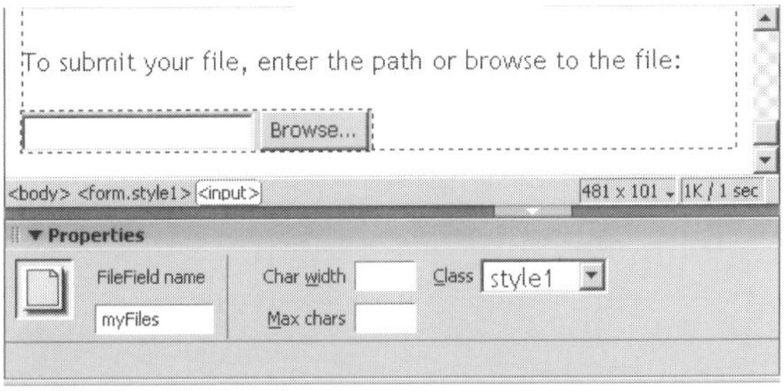

Figure 14.9

Selecting a File field allows you to share files using web forms.

Using Form File Fields

One of the great things about the Internet is the ability to share files and other documents. For instance, you can add a File field to your HTML forms and allow people to send you files from their computers.

To add a File Selection field to your form, select Insert → Form → File Field. File fields, as shown in Figure 14.9, allow users to use the Browse button to search their own hard drives. Once a file is selected, the filename and location appear in the text field next to the button. You must use the POST method to submit the file information as form data. The data is sent to the location you specify in the Action text box in the Form Property inspector. A Submit button then uses this information to send the file to your server.

As you can see from the File Field Property inspector, file fields have the following properties that need setting:

Name The FileField Name field stores the name used to reference the File field in scripts. You can place any unique alphanumeric string in this field, such as `file1` or `upload_file`. This property corresponds to the `name` attribute of the `<input type="file">` tag.

Char Width This property sets the total number of characters that can be visible in the text portion of the File field. This property corresponds to the `size` attribute of the `<input type="file">` tag.

Max Chars This property sets the total number of characters that can be stored in the text portion of the file field. This property corresponds to the `maxlength` attribute of the `<input type="file">` tag.

Class This attribute is used to apply a style class to a form or form element. Any formatting you apply to a form or part of a form will be automatically saved as a style. This property corresponds to the `class` attribute of the `<input>` tag.

You can insert a label (Insert → Form → Label) before or after the file field to display additional information about the field.

Creating List/Menu Form Selections

List/Menu fields, as shown in Figure 14.10, allow you to create a group of options that can be selected either from a list of constantly visible items or from a drop-down menu system. Lists are great for providing immediate access to just a few settings, while menus work better when you are working with a long list of options.

Figure 14.10

Form showing the same options in both a list format (right) and a menu format (left)

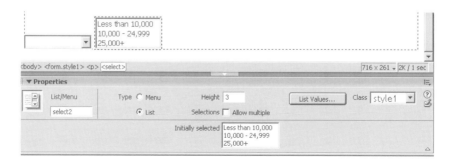

CONCERNS WITH UPLOADED FILES

Don't have files that have been uploaded to your site automatically sent to your e-mail or some other system that may automatically try to execute the file. This is a great way to get and spread viruses. Keep in mind that many mail clients now have a preview pane that automatically shows and activates the contents of the message as soon as it is selected in your mailbox. Instead, you should have all files sent to a secure location where they can be inspected for viruses and other bugs well in advance of them interacting with your personal computer.

To add a List/Menu selection to your form, select Insert → Form → List/Menu.

As you can see from the List/Menu Property inspector, these fields have the following properties:

Name The List/Menu property stores the name used to reference the field in scripts. You can place any unique alphanumeric string in this field such as `list1`, `menu1`, or `site_urls`. This property corresponds to the `name` attribute of the `<select>` tag.

Type This property specifies that the field should be drawn as a list or drop-down menu. The type is `list` if there is a `size` attribute in the `<select>` tag. Otherwise, the type is `menu`.

Height This property sets the total number of lines that are visible simultaneously in a List field. This option isn't available when the Type property is set to Menu. This property corresponds to the `size` attribute of the `<select>` tag.

Selections: Allow Multiple This property allows you to select a series of options from a list. This option isn't available when the Type property is set to Menu. This property corresponds to the `multiple` attribute of the `<select>` tag.

You can include a `multiple` attribute and still have the options display as a drop-down menu. Just leave the Height text field blank. Although Dreamweaver changes the Type to list, it will display and function as a drop-down menu.

Figure 14.11
**List Values
dialog box**

List Values This button opens the List Values dialog box, shown in Figure 14.11, which allows you to add (+), remove (–), and move the options on your list or menu. Each option you add is stored within a series of `<option></option>` tags in your HTML document.

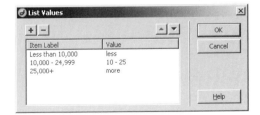

Initially Selected This property selects the item in your list or menu that will be highlighted by default when the form first loads. This property corresponds to the `selected` attribute of the `<option>` tag.

Class This attribute is used to apply a style class to a form or form element. Any formatting you apply to a form or part of a form will be automatically saved as a style. This property corresponds to the `class` attribute of the `<select>` tag.

Using Form Images

Admittedly, forms can be somewhat boring to view at times. By using images in place of Submit buttons or even Reset buttons, you can spruce up the appearance of your pages. Image fields on forms look much like any other image on your web pages (see Figure 14.12), but they have the added function of working like buttons when you wish them to.

To insert an Image field into your form, select Insert → Form → Image Field. As you can see from the Image Property inspector, these fields have the following attributes:

Name The Image field Name property stores the name used to reference the field in scripts. You can place any unique alphanumeric string in this field, such as `image1` or `image_option`. If you set the name of the image to "Submit" and then click it, the image will function the same as if you clicked a Submit button. This property corresponds to the `name` attribute of the `<input type="image">` tag.

W The Width property sets the width, in pixels, of the image being displayed. This property corresponds to the `width` attribute of the `<input type="image">` tag.

H The Height property sets the height, in pixels, of the image being displayed. This property corresponds to the `height` attribute of the `<input type="image">` tag.

Figure 14.12

Form images

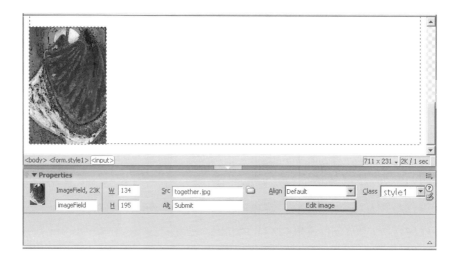

Alt The Alternate Text property specifies the text that will appear if the image can't be loaded for any reason. This property corresponds to the `alt` attribute of the `<input type="image">` tag.

Src The Src property identifies the location of the image file on the server. This property corresponds to the `src` attribute of the `<input type="image">` tag.

Align The Align property controls the alignment of the image in your document. This property corresponds to the `align` attribute of the `<input type="image">` tag.

Class This attribute is used to apply a style class to a form or form element. Any formatting you apply to a form or part of a form will be automatically saved as a style. This property corresponds to the `class` attribute of the `<input>` tag.

Inserting Form Buttons

Buttons are used to submit form information to the processing application. They don't all have to be labeled Submit or Reset. When you are working with a search form, the button is often labeled Go or Search. At other times, you will have a button labeled Browse to help you find a file, or even Open to load a new website from a menu list. The sample buttons, shown in Figure 14.13, give you just a few examples of the types of labels that can be shown on your Form buttons.

To insert a button into your form, select Insert → Form → Button. As you can see from the Button Property inspector, these fields have the following attributes that need setting:

Name The Button Name field stores the name used to reference the field in scripts. You can place any unique alphanumeric string in this field. This property corresponds to the `name` attribute of the `<input type="submit">`, the `<input type="reset">`, or the `<input type="button">` tag.

Label The Label property sets the text that appears on the face of the button, such as Submit, Reset, or Go. This property corresponds to the `value` attribute of the `<input type="submit">`, the `<input type="reset">`, or the `<input type="button">` tag.

Figure 14.13
Form buttons

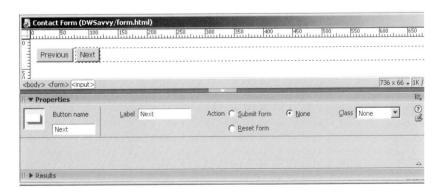

Action The Action property controls the function of the button. The actions that you can choose from are Submit Form, Reset Form, and None. When set to Submit Form, the button's action will send the form data to the processing application, and the `type` attribute of the `<input>` element will be set equal to "submit." When set to Reset Form, the button's action will reset all of the values in the form to either a blank state or to the value specified in the form object's Initial Value field, and the `type` attribute of the `<input>` element will be set equal to "reset." When set to None, the button will require a script to manipulate the processing of the information from the form and the `type` attribute of the `<input>` element will be set equal to "button."

Class This attribute is used to apply a style class to a form or form element. Any formatting you apply to a form or part of a form will be automatically saved as a style. This property corresponds to the `class` attribute of the `<input>` tag.

Using Hidden Fields

Hidden fields are invisible to visitors and are commonly used to collect information on forms and pass it to the forms' processing applications without the site visitors' knowledge. Although some people don't like not knowing what information their computer is sending out, this isn't necessarily a bad use of form controls. Sometimes hidden fields are used to provide detailed instructions about which target page to load after the processing application is complete. (See the section "Creating Target Pages" later in this chapter for more details.) At other times, they can be used to specify which e-mail address should receive the content of the form.

Hidden fields can also be used to collect such information as what browser a visitor is using or what their IP address is. You can accomplish this by adding JavaScript code to the values of your hidden form field.

The following sample statements send the last modified date of the document to the form processor as part of the hidden information in the file.

```
<input type="hidden" name="hiddenField" value="{document.lastmodified}">
```

To learn more about JavaScript, check out *Mastering JavaScript Premium Edition* by James Jaworski (Sybex, 2001).

To add a hidden field to your HTML form, select Insert → Form → Hidden Field. As you can see from the HiddenField Property inspector, these fields have the following attributes that need to be set:

Name The HiddenField Name field stores the name used to reference the field in your processing script. You can place any unique alphanumeric string in this field such as `Target` or `Recipient`. This property corresponds to the `name` attribute of the `<input type="hidden">` tag.

Value The Value property sets up the value that will be sent to the processing application when the script is submitted. Values can be anything from e-mail addresses to JavaScript code. This property corresponds to the value attribute of the `<input type="hidden">` tag.

> Although the HiddenField Property inspector shows a Class property, this field does not display on the page. Applied styles won't be visible.

Adding Form Labels

Forms work best with labels for each of the forms' fields. Labels let the user know exactly what information is expected in each field.

For those of you who have actually read the HTML 4.01 or the XHTML specification, you may remember that there is actually a `<label>` element that provides labels for your form elements.

To add a label using Dreamweaver, select Insert → Form → Label. This opens Code view, in addition to Design view, allowing you to directly modify the name of your label, as shown in Figure 14.14. Type in the text you wish to appear as a label between the `<label></label>` tags.

Once you have typed in the appropriate label text, press F5, or click the Refresh button in the Property inspector. This will update all of the information you have updated in Design view as well as in Code view.

Using Fieldsets and Legends for Form Organization

Dreamweaver supports the `<fieldset>` and `<legend>` tags. The sole purpose of the `<fieldset>` tag is to group sets of form elements, while the `<legend>` tag provides a label for those groups. By dividing your form fields into groups, you can make their relationships easier to comprehend (for your site visitors) and still improve the function of tab-based navigation methods. When you use the `<legend>` tag with your `<fieldset>` tag, you can provide a description for the group of controls.

For instance, assume you are taking a survey and wish to know an individual's age range. By creating a `<fieldset>` tag that holds all of the radio buttons representing the age range values, and by adding a legend to that `<fieldset>` tag, you end up with a meaningful combination of elements that can then be interpreted by your processing application in a more succinct manner.

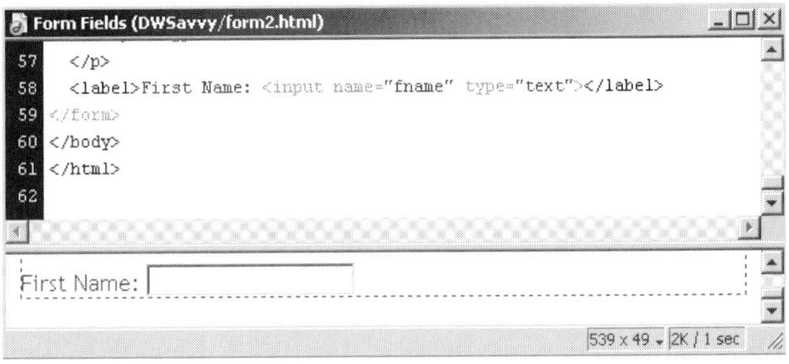

Figure 14.14

You must edit the HTML code to add a label using Dreamweaver's installed feature.

```
57   </p>
58   <label>First Name: <input name="fname" type="text"></label>
59   </form>
60   </body>
61   </html>
62
```

First Name:

539 x 49   2K / 1 sec

Figure 14.15

Fieldset dialog box

If you wish to add your own `<fieldset>` and `<legend>` elements, you can add them manually in Code view (View → Code) or use the Insert → Form → Fieldset. The Fieldset dialog box displays (Figure 14.15). Enter the label text in the Label field and click OK to insert a legend tag with the label text.

Your code, once complete, would look something like this:

```
<form action="..." method="post">
 <p>
 <fieldset>
  <legend>Contact Information</legend>
  Last Name:
  <input name=" lastname" type="text" tabindex="1">
  <br>
  First Name:
  <input name=" firstname" type="text" tabindex="2">
  <br>
  Address:
  <input name=" address" type="text" tabindex="3">
  <br>
  ...more contact information...
 </fieldset>
 <fieldset>
    ...more form controls...
 </fieldset>
 </p>
 </form>
```

Working with CGI Scripts

All forms must be processed or they just sit there and don't do anything. Here are the basic steps:

1. The user enters information in a form on a web page.

2. After the user clicks a button to submit the information, the data is sent as name/value pairs (e.g., `name="last"`, `value="Jones"`) to a script on a web server.

3. The script processes the information, and then directs the web server to return ("serve") a page to the user's browser. This page usually says something like "Thanks for filling out our form." It is important to let the user know that their forms information has been received—otherwise you may receive multiple copies of the same information as the user repeatedly resubmits the information. See the section "Creating Target Pages" later in this chapter for more details.

FORM TIPS

Below are some tips on forms:

- Use text fields for questions with short answers, such as "Favorite color?".

- Use multiline text fields for questions with long answers, such as "How would you like to change the world?".

- Use radio buttons when you want the user to choose one and only one item from a group.

- Use check boxes when you want to allow the user to choose zero, one, or more items from a group of selections.

- Label all the fields so the user knows what information you want to collect from any form field.

- Make sure to use a target page—users will submit form information multiple times unless they receive a confirmation message that the information was sent. See the section, "Creating Target Pages," later in this chapter.

- Unless you can add session variables to retain the information entered by the user, limit the form to one page.

For more tips on creating and designing forms, see "Good Forms" at `http://hotwired` `.lycos.com/webmonkey/99/30/index4a.html`.

You have a lot of options for processing forms, but Common Gateway Interface (CGI) scripts are probably the most common. CGI is a protocol, not a language in itself. CGI scripts can be used to e-mail the contents of your form to you or to another designated individual, to write the information collected in the form to a database, or to post the information to another web page. They can also be used as the input to search a database.

For more information on CGI, see the overview of the CGI interface at the NCSA site at `http://hoohoo.ncsa.uiuc.edu/cgi/overview.html`.

Perl, a scripting language, is commonly used for the "server-side" of form processing, although any server-side language can be used. Your ISP or web hosting service may offer a "pre-made" script for you to use for form processing, or it may be necessary for you to contract with a web developer/web programmer to write a custom script for your form.

Many free scripts are available on the Web. Check the listings at www.cgi-resources.com or www.freescripts.com, and see additional suggestions in the "Forms Resources" section later in this chapter.

CGI Script Requirements

Depending on the type of web server you are using, most CGI scripts will be created in either Perl or C. Perl is typically the language used to develop CGI scripts for use on a Unix/Linux platform; C is most commonly used on Windows platforms.

Most free scripts for form processing are written in Perl, so it's important to be familiar with the requirements for using these scripts.

If you are using Perl-based CGI scripts, your server must have all of the following:

- A compatible version of Perl installed
- A properly configured cgi directory
- The proper CHMOD settings for each directory and file in your cgi-bin directory

Compatible Version of Perl

Although most Unix/Linux-based servers do have Perl installed, they may have an older version than the one for which your script is designed. You can find out the requirements for your script by reading its documentation; then you can find out what version of Perl is running on your server by checking with your server administrator, ISP, or web hosting service.

Properly Configured *cgi* Directory

There are typically two options for using CGI scripts on your Unix/Linux-based web server. The first, and most common, is to run all of your programs out of a cgi-bin directory, which has been configured in your server files to store and run Perl and CGI files. The second commonly used option is to use a CGI-wrapper that will allow scripts to run on a server but also allows the server administrator more security over the types of scripts that can be run, who can run them, and how they are run.

Proper CHMOD Settings

CHMOD is a Unix command, an abbreviation of "change mode"—it is used, among other things, to assign read/write privileges for directories.

You must have proper file access settings for each file used by your CGI script in order for this script to work properly. There are varieties of permission settings that can be used for these files, but you should always set those permissions to be just what you need to run the script without giving away any extra access.

CHMOD permissions on Unix and Linux machines are broken down into Users, Groups, and Others identification classifications. You set permissions for an individual user, a group of users, or all others. Each user is identified by a user ID.

> For additional information on Unix permissions and CHMOD settings, visit www.perlfect.com/articles/chmod.shtml.

Each of these groups is allotted permissions individually. These permissions are controlled by the assignment of a numerical value to that specific set of users. Permission values are Read=4, Write=2, and Execute=1. In order to apply a Read and Execute permission, you would add the assigned numerical values and come up with 5.

For instance, if you want to set the script file permissions so that you (user) can modify the script file, but your group and all others can read and run the script but not change it, you would set a permission of 755:

User	Read + Write + Execute	=	7
Group	Read + Execute	=	5
Other	Read + Execute	=	5

If you were to type in the command CHMOD myfile 755, you would be stating that it is OK for anyone to read or execute the file, but only you can modify it (write).

Once all of your file permissions are correct, your cgi directory is properly set up and installed, and you have a valid version of Perl running on your computer, you are ready to start writing and testing the CGI scripts you wish to use.

Using the Perl Declaration

One of the primary pieces of any Perl script is the Perl declaration that identifies the location of the Perl interpreter on your machine. This statement is typically located at the top of every .pl or .cgi file running on a Unix or Linux server. If this statement doesn't properly identify the location of Perl, then none of your scripts will work, even if everything else on the server is properly configured. Common Perl declaration statements include these:

```
#!/usr/bin/perl
#!/usr/local/bin/perl -wT
```

A Perl declaration must be the first line of the Perl script. These declarations tell the Unix/Linux shell where to find Perl, and then they pass the rest of the script to that program where it can be executed. You can also specify additional options to be used when the script is run, as shown above in the second declaration.

Of course, the path specified in this statement will change, depending upon where Perl is installed. For instance, if you have multiple versions of Perl on your system, you may have a `perl5` directory, rather than just a `perl` directory.

```
#!/usr/bin/perl5
#!/usr/local/bin/perl5 -w
```

The `-w` switch shown in the second statement generates warning messages when the Perl program is run. Without this switch, you won't receive any error messages other than those generated by the software that you are using to view the results of your Perl program. Whenever you are testing out a script, be sure to turn warnings on. This will help you keep a log of errors and find erroneous code lines deep in your program.

For more information on Perl, see `www.perl.com` or `http://perl.oreilly.com/`.

Editing a CGI Script

CGI scripts written in Perl are simple text files. When you need to edit a Perl CGI script, you will often need to modify variable values, define new variables, add fields to databases, or even modify the HTML created by your script.

Because Perl-based CGI scripts are simple text files, you can easily view and modify their source code in a program such as Windows Notepad or in PICO on your Linux server.

When you go to modify your documents, simply open them in your text editor and scroll down through the mix of comments and code to find the section you wish to modify. Read the comments (preceded by #) carefully as you go. They will tell you what portion of the script you are in, what it does, and what the variables are referring to, as seen in the following code snippet:

```
# Variable Definitions
#
# $sitetitle
#     Identifies the title to use for all instances
#     of the <title> elements in the resulting HTML documents.
$sitetitle = 'Happy's Wholesale Haven'

# $siteadmin
#     Identifies the login name of the individual
#     that has administrative control over pages.
$siteadmin = 'beaudiddley'
```

In order to modify this code, you simply need to follow the existing format and add or update the information it contains. For instance, in the `$sitetitle` variable, if your site's name isn't Happy's Wholesale Haven, then you need to modify this path to represent the actual title of your site. It could be something like `'WebGuru's Script Haven'`.

After you are done making changes to your CGI scripts, you will need to re-upload them to your web server. When you do, make sure that you set the script back to its original file permission settings, discussed previously.

Using Languages Other Than Perl

CGI scripts can be developed in many languages. Perl has been known to use the best constructs of C, awk, and sed, so using a strict version of C isn't much different from using Perl. It just depends on what you know best, and which language your server supports. A CGI program can be written in any language that allows it to be executed on the system; some possibilities include the following:

- Any Unix shell script
- AppleScript
- C/C++
- Fortran
- Perl
- PHP
- Visual Basic
- ASP
- ASP.NET
- ColdFusion

The configuration of your server may force you to use a language other than Perl or C. Most Unix/Linux servers come with a Perl interpreter. Most Windows servers come with either a Visual Basic or C/C++ compiler. And most Apple servers come with a version of the AppleScript compiler. One of these four languages is used by most people, and therefore, it is rare to see a Fortran CGI script nowadays.

An additional consideration for choosing a language for writing CGI scripts is your task. For instance, C++ is a full-fledged programming language that allows you to create just about anything that you can think of. Perl doesn't have the full features of C++, and therefore it may limit you in the tasks that you can accomplish with it. C code is faster than Perl so speed might also be a factor in your decision.

Dreamweaver MX 2004 supports five server technologies: ASP, ASP.NET, ColdFusion, JSP, and PHP. For more information on choosing a server technology, see Chapter 16, "Building Web Applications." For details on specific server technologies, see Chapters 20 through 25.

If you have already chosen a server technology but would like more information on form processing for a specific application server, see one of the following sites:

- ASP: `http://hwang.cisdept.csupomona.edu/asptutorial/form_processing-post.asp`

- ASP.NET: `www.sitepoint.com/article.php/815`

- ColdFusion: `http://livedocs.macromedia.com/coldfusion/6/Getting_Started_Building_ColdFusion_MX_Applications/cfml_basics6.htm`

- JSP: `www.jsptut.com/Forms.jsp`

- PHP: `www.apptools.com/phptools/forms/forms1.php`

Creating Target Pages

After the user completes a form and submits the data (usually by clicking a Submit button), the script runs, and the user has to be given a new page to land on. This resulting page is called a *target page*. Target pages are used by form processing applications as a destination for the script after the information in the form has been processed. In the case of a simple form e-mail processing script, the page might just be something as simple as a "Thank You" with links to the primary areas of your website.

If you are processing your form information with ColdFusion, JavaServer Pages (JSP), or Active Server Pages (ASP), then your target page might be a lot more complicated. For instance, assume that you have a survey that runs off a ColdFusion server. The target page might be the compiled answers for your survey and a list of suggested reading based upon the answers that you made.

In general, when you are creating a target page for your form processing script, you need to ensure that it has the following features:

- Links to every primary page on your website

- Contact information (phone, e-mail, and so on) for your company

- Verification that their information was properly received

- Assurance that they will be getting a response in an appropriate time frame

- A description of how they should expect to receive a response to any questions they might have posed

Target pages, with all of this information, may look like the simple page shown in Figure 14.16.

Creating your target page is no different than creating any other page in your website. Simply use the tools you learned in Part II of this book to create a page, preferably one with a format similar to what is found in the remainder of your website, that can be used to reassure your visitors that they have submitted information to your company and your company only.

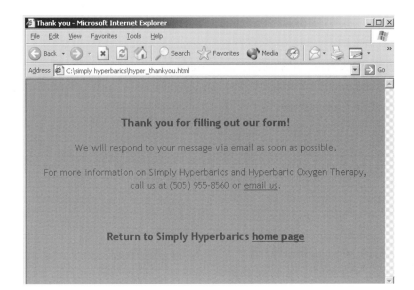

Figure 14.16

A simple target page for an e-mail processing application

Forms Resources

You can create your own form processing applications in any server-side language, but you can also use a form processing host or use a free form processing script.

A forms host processes form information for you, so you don't have to create or find your own script. There are both free and commercial forms hosts. The free hosts aren't really "free," of course—like other "free" things on the Web, the price is often advertising on your site for the provider of the service. To see a list of available free forms hosts, go to: `www.webfreebees.net/webpages-forms.html`, or use your favorite search engine and search for free forms hosting.

There are also many free scripts for form processing. If you want to send form results via e-mail, the easiest script to use is form mail by Matt Wright. The nms project at Source-Forge has created an updated, more secure version of this script that's available as a free download from Matt's Script Archive site at `www.scriptarchive.com/nms.html`.

You need to check with your ISP or web hosting service to see if they support form mail (most do). Then follow the instructions for form mail *exactly* and put your form mail script in the `cgi-bin` folder or whatever location your ISP or host uses for scripts. Form mail is designed to send form information via e-mail only—it does not create a data file, or send information to a database. If you need these capabilities, you need a more complex script.

You can find free CGI scripts online that will do everything from create a search engine to a guest book to a shopping cart to a calendar. Visit any of these sites:

- eXtropia: `www.extropia.com`
- Matt's Script Archive: `www.scriptarchive.com`
- BigNosedBird.com: `http://bignosebird.com`
- Perl Archive: `www.perlarchive.com`
- CGI Resource Index: `www.cgi-resources.com`
- MegaCGI cgi scripts: `www.megacgi.com`

As you might have guessed, there are many other script archives available on the Internet. If you wish to find them, simply type "cgi scripts" into your favorite search engine and wait for the thousands of links to come back to you.

Hands On: Using FormMail

In this hands-on tutorial, you'll create a simple form and configure the FormMail Perl script to e-mail the form results. FormMail is a very simple solution for form processing.

To use FormMail, complete the following steps:

1. Download the nms version of the FormMail script from `www.scriptarchive.com/nms.html` and install it into your `cgi-bin` directory on your web server. Be sure to read all of its documentation so that you don't have to repeat steps multiple times. CGI scripts, especially on Unix/Linux machines, require that file permissions are set correctly for every file on the machine—be especially careful when setting these permissions.

2. Open the compressed file in your favorite expander program, then open `FormMail.pl` in a text editor.

3. The first line in the FormMail script is:

   ```
   #!/usr/bin/perl -wT
   ```

   Ask your server administrator, ISP, or web host for the location of Perl on the server. Change this line as necessary to specify the location of the Perl interpreter.

4. Find the User Configuration section of the script and locate this line:

   ```
   $mailprog = '/usr/lib/sendmail -oi -t';
   ```

   This line specifies the location of the sendmail program on the server. Ask your server administrator, ISP, or web host for the location of sendmail on the server, and change this line as necessary.

5. Also locate this line in the User Configuration section of the script:

   ```
   @referers    = qw(dave.org.uk 209.207.222.64 localhost);
   ```

This line specifies the domains where you want to allow forms to reside and use this installation of FormMail. Add any domains that always receive e-mail results from the script—in other words, if the results are e-mailed to info@example.com, then add www.example.com to this list:

```
@referers = qw(www.example.com dave.org.uk 209.207.222.64 localhost);
```

6. Save the FormMail.pl file and upload it to the cgi-bin on your server. On some servers, you will have to change the file name to FormMail.cgi.

7. Set file permissions for the script.

8. In Dreamweaver, open the HTML page where you want to insert the form (or create a new HTML page).

9. Choose Insert → Form → Form to insert a new form on the page. The following code is inserted on your page:

```
<form name="form1" method="post" action="">
</form>
```

10. In the action attribute, put the URL for the FormMail.pl file, for example:

```
<form name="contact" method="post" action="http://www.example.com/
cgi-bin/FormMail.pl">
```

11. Add any form objects you want in the form. For this tutorial, add two text fields. The first is named *fullname* and the second is named *email*.

```
<input name="fullname" type="text" size="50" maxlength="50">
<input name="email" type="text" size="50" maxlength="50">
```

12. Add five hidden fields to provide additional information to FormMail.pl when it processes the form. The first hidden field is:

```
<input type="hidden" name="recipient"
value="info@simplyhyperbarics.com">
```

The recipient field specifies where the e-mail with the form results should be sent. You can add additional recipients by separating the values with commas; for example:

```
<input type="hidden" name="recipient"
value="info@simplyhyperbarics.com, ken@simplyhyperbarics.com">
```

The recipient field is required in order for FormMail to e-mail the form results.

13. Include a hidden field to specify a subject for the form results e-mail.

```
<input type="hidden" name="subject" value="hyperbaric form">
```

This is optional, but it helps you identify that an e-mail contains form results.

14. Add a redirect hidden field to direct the user to a specific page on your site after they click the Submit button on the form.

```
<input type="hidden" name="redirect"
value="http://example.com/thankyou.html">
```

15. Add a hidden field to specify which form fields are required. In this case, both the `fullname` and `email` fields are required fields.

    ```
    <input type="hidden" name="required" value="fullname,email">
    ```

16. Add another redirect hidden field to direct the user to a specific page on your site if they don't fill out the required fields. This page informs them that these are required fields and asks them to use the browser back button to return to the form.

    ```
    <input type="hidden" name="missing_fields_redirect"
    value="http://www.example.com/error.html">
    ```

17. Add any other forms fields you choose, then save the page and upload it to your server.

18. Create a target page for the user to be redirected to after submitting the form, as in step 14.

19. Create an error page for the user to be redirected to if all required form fields are not filled out when the form is submitted.

20. Upload the target page and the error page to your server.

21. Test out your form and make sure it's functional.

22. If your form does not work, check for any errors in your HTML code or in the modifications you made to `FormMail.pl`. Check with your server administrator, ISP, or hosting service to make sure of the following:

    - They support FormMail
    - The path to the Perl interpreter on the server is correct
    - File permissions are correct

    Also, check the FormMail documentation (README file).

From Forms to Discussions

Forms are the fundamental means of interactivity on the Web—the primary way that a website's user can respond or give information. Other interactive features you can build into your site include discussion boards where users can post messages in threaded discussion topics and guest books where users can post comments and questions. See Chapter 15, "Community Building with Interactive Site Features," for more details on setting up additional interactive features using Dreamweaver.

Community Building with Interactive Site Features

Interactive site features can involve your visitors and help to create a virtual online community. In previous chapters in this section, the focus has been on interacting with your site visitors via behaviors and navigation objects, and obtaining input from visitors from HTML forms and form-processing scripts. You can also allow your visitors to send input that's published on the site using features such as guestbooks or discussion boards. This lets visitors interact with each other and view each other's input, and helps to build a sense of community. You can also interact with your users by creating a blog where they can read your postings regarding news related to the site or other topics of interest.

Although Dreamweaver doesn't directly support these kinds of community-building features, you can certainly add these features to your Dreamweaver sites and use Dreamweaver to customize the look and feel of the pages you create. In this chapter, you'll find resources for adding user input to your pages via guestbooks, discussion boards, chats, and blogs.

- **Creating community**
- **Adding a guestbook**
- **Using discussion boards**
- **Hosting a chat**
- **Creating a blog**

Creating Community on the Web

The first step in building an online community is that familiar but often overlooked first step of designing and creating a website: know your audience.

What is the purpose of your site? Who's likely to visit your site, and why? Are they likely to return for additional information and interaction? Do users have the opportunity to interact with you and send you comments and questions? Are your users likely to benefit from having an opportunity to share information with each other online?

There are many ways to create community on your site, from simple to complex. An easy first step is to create links with related sites, and ask for links back to your site. This helps create a larger community of visitors interested in a particular topic or product, and increases the traffic to all the linked sites. Link popularity, or the number of links to and from your site, is also used as a ranking criteria by search engines such as Google. (For more information on search engines, see Chapter 26, "Controlling Access to the Site.")

Adding a Guestbook

A guestbook provides a way for site visitors to leave messages, and to read messages from previous visitors. Visitors can't directly respond to each other's messages in a guestbook, though—that requires a discussion board, as discussed in the following section, "Using a Discussion Board." Many ISPs and Web Hosting services offer free guestbook scripts, or you can use your favorite search engine and do a search for free guestbooks.

The following sites offer a multitude of free scripts of all types, including guestbook scripts:

- Matt's Script Archive (`www.scriptarchive.com/`)
- BigNoseBird.com (`http://bignosebird.com`)
- CGI Resource Index (`www.cgi-resources.com`)

Guestbook scripts are generally CGI scripts written in Perl.

If you are an experienced Perl programmer, you can probably write your own guestbook script. If not, though, you can adapt a prewritten script for your site.

> Although Dreamweaver does not include support for Perl, you can open and edit Perl scripts in Dreamweaver.

The first step is to find out the requirements for your script by reading its documentation, then check with your server administrator, ISP, or Web Hosting service to see if it supports those requirements. Since most CGI scripts are written in Perl, your server needs to have a compatible version of Perl installed. You'll need to know the path to the Perl inter-preter (generally it's `/usr/bin/perl` or something similar) and the location of the cgi-bin.

For more information on using and editing CGI scripts, see Chapter 14.

A very easy script to adapt is available at `http://bignosebird.com/carchive/bnbbook.shtml`. This script is freeware, and can be freely used and adapted as long as you include the notice at the top of the script that identifies the source of the script.

You can view a working example at `http://bignosebird.com/guestbook.html`. You can modify the appearance of this page as well as the function of the script. The Chapter 15 folder on the book CD includes a modified guestbook page that uses this script (`guestbook.html`), shown in Figure 15.1. Let's take a closer look at how to adapt the script:

1. Download the script from `http://bignosebird.com/carchive/bnbbook.shtml`.

2. Unzip the file. There are three files included: `bnbbook.cgi`, `README.txt`, and `gbook.html`.

3. `README.txt` contains the full directions for adapting the script, but we will review the major steps here.

4. Open `bnbbook.cgi` in Dreamweaver.

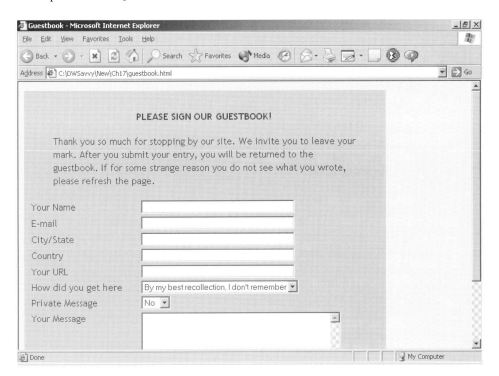

Figure 15.1

Our modification of `guestbook.html`

5. Go to line 46 :

   ```
   $HTML="YES";
   ```

   If you want to block users from using HTML tags in their input, change this from YES to NO.

6. Change line 51:

   ```
   $GUESTBOOK="/home/www/gbook.html";
   ```

   Specify the full path to the guestbook file (gbook.html) on your server. This path is specific to the server, so you may need to contact your ISP or hosting service to find out details of the path.

7. Go to line 56 and enter the absolute URL to the guestbook file. This redirects the user back to the guestbook page after they submit their entry.

   ```
   $GUESTBOOK_URL="http://df132domain.com/gbook.html";
   ```

8. Change line 73:

   ```
   $MY_EMAIL="me\@dfdfdomain.com";
   ```

   Enter your e-mail address here. Be sure to include a \ before the @.

9. Go to line 106:

   ```
   $VALID_DOMAIN="dfdfdomain.com";
   ```

   Enter your domain name.

   Okay, you've now changed all the significant script parameters (for more options, see the README.txt file). Now, let's change the response page and the guestbook format.

10. Go to Line 113 and adapt the thank you message for the response page. This is the message that displays after the user clicks the Submit button. You can change anything between these two lines:

    ```
    $THANK_YOU=<<__END_OF_THANK_YOU__;
    ```

    and

    ```
    END_OF_THANK_YOU
    ```

    but be sure not to delete either of these two lines.

11. Go to line 142. You can change the display of the user's post by modifying your code in between these two lines:

    ```
    $PAGE_ENTRY=<<__END_OF_PAGE_ENTRY__;
    ```

    and

    ```
    __END_OF_PAGE_ENTRY__
    ```

12. Save the changes you made to bnbbook.cgi .

13. Open `gbook.html` and modify the page display as desired. You can also add a link to a style sheet (see `guestbook.css` in the Chapter 15 folder on the CD).

14. Upload `bnbbook.cgi` and `gbook.html` to your server. The `bnbbook.cgi` file should be uploaded to the cgi-bin. Set file permissions of 755 for `bnbbook.cgi` and 644 for `gbook.html`. (For more details on setting file permissions, see Chapter 14.)

You should now have a functional guestbook on your site. Test it out by opening the guest page online and making an entry. If it does not work as expected, see the troubleshooting tips in the `README.txt` file or contact your server administrator, ISP, or Web Hosting service.

> This script instantly posts a user's message to your page. Although this script lets you include filters for words you don't want to allow in posts, you may want to use a guestbook script that lets you review visitors' entries before they're posted on your page.

Using Discussion Boards

You have even more options if you want to include a discussion board (also known as discussion lists or bulletin boards). A discussion board usually includes threaded postings, so that users can respond to each other's entries. All responses to one topic are grouped together as discussion threads. Generally, you can view all the responses in chronological order, and archives are often available of previous threads. A discussion board can be open to all visitors, or you can limit participation to registered members. Many discussion boards include a moderator, or administrator, who reviews entries before they are posted to the board.

Free discussion board scripts are available from the sources mentioned in the previous section, or may be available from your ISP or Web Hosting service. You can set up a discussion board on your own site or on another site—for example, Yahoo Groups. To see an example, see Figure 15.2 or visit the Yahoo discussion group for this book at `http://groups.yahoo.com/group/dreamweaversavvy/`. You'll need to create a free Yahoo user ID and password to join a discussion group or to create a discussion group of your own. To create a Yahoo discussion group, go to `http://groups.yahoo.com/start` and follow the instructions.

If you use ColdFusion, there are several free discussion board extensions available for download on the Macromedia Exchange site at `www.macromedia.com/cfusion/exchange/index.cfm`, or just click the Dreamweaver Exchange link on the Dreamweaver start page. Go to the ColdFusion section of the Macromedia Exchange, and search for discussion boards. For additional information on using ColdFusion, see Chapter 20, "Working with ColdFusion," and for more details on using extensions, see Chapter 32, "Customizing and Extending Dreamweaver."

Figure 15.2

The Dreamweaver Savvy discussion at Yahoo Groups

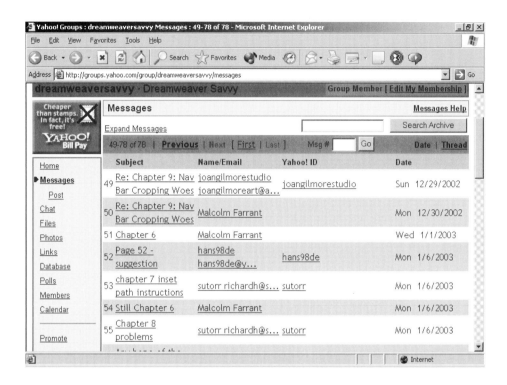

Hosting a Chat

If you want to give your visitors the opportunity to interact with each other in real time or if you want to be available to answer questions—for example, to provide real-time customer service—you can include a chat room on your site. A chat is an instant messaging service, or instantaneous e-mail interaction, so it's more like having an actual conversation than a threaded discussion. The conversation in a chat is not limited to two participants; several people (up to the limit for your chat room) can interact at the same time.

A chat display can be just a scrolling display of text, or it can include a more graphic display with graphic characters, props, and text balloons, such as the chat rooms available at `www.thepalace.com`. Newer chat rooms offer voice and video services as well as text display. Apple's iChat AV (`www.apple.com/ichat/`) offers video conferencing over any broadband connection.

Many Hosting Services offer free chat room services for their clients, or you can find many free chat services as well as chat scripts online. See the collection of free Perl scripts named Ralf's Chat at `www.2createawebsite.com/enhance/create-chat-room.html` or the free Java applet chat at `www.freejavachat.com/`. Commercial chat software, such as DigiChat (www.digichat.com) is also available, and offers increased security, privacy features, and other enhanced chat features.

You can offer a public chat room, or you can create a private chat, with participants limited to members and/or invited guests. If you choose to host a chat room on your own site, consider the load on your web server and how many participants you can support at one time. You will probably want to use a chat hosting service if you are planning on an active chat room with a large number of participants.

> A list of free and commercial chat services is available at http://cgi.resourceindex.com/ Remotely_Hosted/Chat/.

Creating a Blog

Blogs, or *web logs,* first came on the Web scene around 1998. Originally, blogs consisted of web pages with dated entries containing a combination of links, news, commentary, and personal observations. These blogs served to highlight and filter web content that might otherwise go unnoticed by the majority of Web users, and offered brief descriptions and commentary in addition to links to the actual content. This original type of blog is still widely used; for an example, see Macromedia's John Dowdell's blog, "News for MX Developers," at www.markme.com/jd/, Eric Meyer's "Thoughts from Eric" at www.meyerweb.com/, and Jeffrey Zeldman's "Daily Report" at www.zeldman.com/.

Blog content can be syndicated through RSS (Rich Site Summary), an XML language for sharing news information. RSS files include static information about your site plus dynamic news entries that include a title, a URL, and a brief description of the linked content. Your RSS files can be registered with an RSS aggregator and made available as RSS feeds. You can also download RSS feeds from other sites to display news items on your site. The news content is dynamically updated as new RSS feeds become available, so it's always up to date.

In August 1999, Blogger (http://new.blogger.com/) introduced a free, web-based tool for quickly creating blogs. Blogger's tool requires no skills in coding or web development, and was one of the tools that enabled rapid expansion and proliferation of blogs. Basically, Blogger and similar software enable you to type in a block of text, which is added to a template to create a new file, which is then uploaded to a server. Although Blogger was not the only version of web log tool available, it quickly became the most popular blog tool. In part because it is so easy to use, a new form of blog became popular—the short journal form of blog, such as Jason Sutter's blog at http://jason.similarselection.org/index.php. Blogger provides a web-based application that is hosted on Blogger's server, and frees the user from maintenance and configuration issues.

You can also choose a more customizable blog tool such as Greymatter (`http://noah-grey.com/greysoft/`) or Moveable Type (`http://www.movabletype.org/`). These tools both offer a set of customizable CGI scripts that you upload to your server, and give you more control over the display and features of your blog.

Radio Userland 8.0.1 (`http://radio.userland.com/`) is an easy-to-use, full-featured tool for creating blogs, syndicating, aggregating, and displaying news content. Radio Userland software is installed on your own computer, rather than being a web-based application, and allows you to work locally until you're ready to upload your blog files. Radio Userland includes a newsreader that lets you subscribe to any RSS feeds you choose, checks for updates every hour, and displays your news updates in a single page for quick scanning.

For additional information on blog, see the following websites:

- "The Weblog Tool Roundup" `http://hotwired.lycos.com/webmonkey/02/18/index3a.html`

- "weblogs: a history and perspective" `http://www.rebeccablood.net/essays/weblog_history.html`

- "Introduction to RSS" `http://www.webreference.com/authoring/languages/xml/rss/intro/index.html`

Hands On: Create Your Own Blog with Blogger

Blogger is free, easy to use, and a great tool for creating your first blog. If you're an experienced blogger, skip this tutorial and move on to building web applications in Chapter 16, "Building Web Applications."

Your blog can be a filtered combination of links and commentary, a personal journal, or anything you want it to be! Blogs make web publishing available to anyone who has a connection to the Internet.

1. Start by opening `http://new.blogger.com/` in the browser of your choice. Click the button labeled "Start Now" in the section at the top of the page titled "Create Your Own Blog!".

2. The "Create a Blogger Account" page displays. Fill out the form with your username, first name, last name, e-mail address, and a password to register as a Blogger user. Review the Terms of Service agreement, and click the check box if you agree. Then click the "Sign Up" button at the bottom of the page to complete your Blogger registration.

3. Click on the button labeled "Create a New Blog" on the right side of the Blogger home page. The first page of the Create a New Blog form displays.

4. Step 1: Provide a title and description for your blog, and choose public or private (public means it may appear in the Blogger directory).

5. Step 2: Select free hosting (with ad) at Blogspot.com or choose to FTP your blog file to your server.

6. Step 3: If you chose free hosting, enter a name for your page on this third page. If you chose FTP, enter your FTP parameters on this page.

7. Step 4: Choose a template for the presentation of your blog page. You can change this choice at any time, and can also use your own style template.

8. The Create New Post window of the Publishing tab opens. Enter your blog text in the box, and then click the button at the bottom of the window to Preview your blog. Edit the text as needed in this window.

9. Click on the Publish Status window in the Publishing tab. Click the button at the bottom of the window to publish your blog.

10. Click on the Settings tab to change any of the settings from steps 1 through 3. Click on the Template tab to display the code in the selected template from step 4, or to choose a different template style.

That's it—your blog is now published online, and you have officially joined the ranks of bloggers worldwide!

From Community to Web Application Development

In this section, you have learned how to create a guestbook and a blog to add community-building interactivity to your site. In the next chapter, you can start to explore the back end of site construction—building web applications using Dreamweaver's web development features and support for server technologies such as ASP, ASP.NET, ColdFusion, JSP, and PHP.

## PART IV

Developing Web Applications

Dreamweaver *is more than a designer's tool for constructing file-based websites: It is now a full-featured development environment for database-backed web applications. In this Part, we show you how to set up web applications in Dreamweaver; how to customize, streamline, and automate your coding workspace; how to tie your pages to database tables; how to work with ColdFusion sites; how to incorporate the XML and XHTML standards into your site; and how to work with cutting-edge technologies such as .NET.*

## CHAPTER 16

Building Web Applications

In Part I, before you started making pages, you learned how to set up a website in Dreamweaver. If you're building a dynamic site (a web application), there are a few more steps you will need to take.

First, you need to choose a local or remote web server, and then you can make a choice of server technology and application server. Dreamweaver supports a number of different popular server technologies (ASP, ASP.NET, Cold Fusion, JSP, and PHP), and the process for each is analogous, though the specific steps vary somewhat.

This chapter will show you how to get set up so that you can start building web applications in Dreamweaver.

- Building and testing web applications

- Working with a local or remote web server

- Choosing a server technology

- Working with an application server

- Setting up the site in Dreamweaver

Designing and Testing Web Applications

The difference between developing web applications and developing static sites in Dreamweaver starts with the setup. There are three basic steps to setting up a site for building web applications in Dreamweaver: specifying local information, specifying remote information, and specifying testing server information. These steps can be accessed from the Advanced tab in the Site Definition dialog box: Site → Manage Sites → New to set up a new Dreamweaver site or Site → Manage Sites → Edit to edit an existing Dreamweaver site. From the Advanced tab, click each of the following categories to set this information.

Local Info

You set up the local site information the same way for Web applications as you do for non-dynamic websites (see Chapter 3, "Setting Up Your Workspace and Your Site," for more information on setting up a site in Dreamweaver).

Remote Info

The remote site can be set up to point to a web server running on your local computer or network, or it can be set up on a remote server.

> The term *server* can be used for both software and hardware products. In web application development, web servers and application servers are software.

Testing Server

You specify a server model and a testing server (a.k.a. application server) in order to preview dynamic pages (and connect to databases) from Dreamweaver. An application server is software that works with a web server and processes dynamic pages.

First, choose a server model from the drop-down menu in the Testing Server window. Note that there are seven choices, depending on which scripting/programming language you use with ASP (Active Server Pages) or ASP.NET (Figure 16.1). See the sections "Choosing a Server Technology" and "Defining a Testing Server" later in this chapter for more details on these choices.

This testing server can be local or remote, depending on where your web server is located.

Figure 16.1

Choosing a server model from the Testing Server options

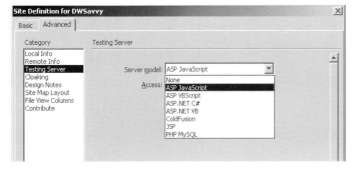

If your web server is local, then you specify a folder (usually the root folder) on the web server as the testing server folder. Figure 16.2 shows the testing folder setup for ASP running locally on IIS (Internet Information Services).

If your web server is remote, then you specify the details for that connection. This connection can be the same as the one set up in the Remote Info window, but it can also be different if the application server runs on a different system than the web server.

Databases are a major source for dynamic content on a web page, but not the only source. You can also use HTML form values, server object values (for example, date and time), Java Bean properties, and other sources of dynamic content. For more information on using databases and setting up a database connection in Dreamweaver, see Chapter 19, "Database Connectivity."

Working with a Web Server

In order to run an application server to test your site, you first need a web server. If you use Windows, you may have a web server (IIS) already installed or even running on your machine. If you use Mac OS X (10.1 or later), then you already have the Apache server installed. See Table 16.1 for operating system and web server. You can also install several web servers on the same computer and choose which one to run for a given application.

OS	INSTALLED WEB SERVER
Win 2000	IIS 5
Win XP Home	none available
Win XP Pro	IIS 5
Win Server 2003	IIS 6
Mac OS X 10.1+	Apache

Table 16.1

Operating System and Installed Web Server

If IIS in installed on your computer, an `Inetpub` folder will be in place on your hard drive. If IIS isn't already installed and you're using Windows 2000 or Windows XP Professional, open the Control Panel → Add/Remove Programs → Add/Remove Windows Components.

You might prefer to work with a web server installed at a remote location. For example, you could set up a free hosting account at `www.brinkster.com` to test your ASP pages remotely instead of using a local web server.

We prefer the convenience of using a local web server for testing. Even the quickest file upload to a remote server is not as fast as previewing pages locally. For more details on setting up a web server, see Chapter 30, "Going Live or Delivering the Site."

Figure 16.2

Setting a testing server folder on a local web server

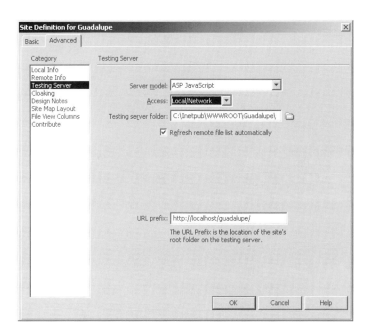

> Though ASP sites can be developed on any version of IIS, ASP.NET sites require IIS 5 running on Windows 2000 or XP Pro systems, or IIS 6 running on Windows 2003. You can still develop ASP.NET sites anywhere, but you need the aforementioned setup plus the .NET framework to test them as you go.

Choosing a Server Technology

To build a web application, you have to decide what type of server technology you want to use, and then choose the application server it will run on. Dreamweaver MX and MX 2004 support a broad range of server models, from Microsoft's web services framework (.NET), through Macromedia's own ColdFusion server, to open source frameworks based on Java or Apache/PHP.

> The following section, "Setting Up Your Application Server," provides links to further information and downloads for application server software.

The ASP and ASP.NET models ASP stands for Active Server Pages and is a Microsoft standard that is being replaced by a newer Microsoft standard, .NET (for web services). See

Chapter 25, "Emerging Technologies," for a further discussion of .NET site development and web services. ASP can use IIS as an application server, as well as Sun ONE Active Server Pages software (formerly known as Chili!Soft ASP). ASP.NET uses IIS with the .NET framework.

The ColdFusion model ColdFusion sites run on the ColdFusion MX application server using the ColdFusion scripting language. Studio MX 2004 includes the developer edition of ColdFusion MX 6.1 Server (for Windows only).

The JSP Model JSP stands for Java Server Pages. In order to use Java Server pages, you need an application server that supports JSP. You have many choices, including Macromedia JRun, Sun ONE Application Server, IBM WebSphere, Apache Tomcat, and BEA Web Logic.

The PHP model PHP is an open source scripting language and application server. Although PHP can work with many different databases, MySQL is commonly the only database supported for PHP by many web hosts, and it is the only database supported for PHP in Dreamweaver. The term PHP, by the way, is just another recursive acronym (good examples include GNU, which stands for Gnu's Not Unix, and PINE, which stands for Pine is not Elm). Officially it stands for "PHP: Hypertext Preprocessor."

Which One to Choose?

Any of the five server technologies supported by Dreamweaver can do similar tasks, such as connecting to a database, making a query, displaying recordsets, adding or deleting recordsets, creating dynamic tables, and user authentication. The chapters in Part IV will introduce you to each of the five server technologies and show you how to use Dreamweaver for any of these tasks.

In general, the choice of a server technology is not based on what any particular technology can do. Rather, it's a choice based on what programming languages, if any, you are already familiar with and what operating system you are working with.

Our personal choice? If you are using Dreamweaver MX 2004 for web application development, we recommend ColdFusion for a server technology. CFML (Cold Fusion Markup Language) is tag-based and easy to use, and a free developer edition of the Cold-Fusion MX 6.1 Server is included with Studio MX (or can be downloaded for free at www.macromedia.com/cfusion/tdrc/index.cfm?product=coldfusion—the free trial version becomes the developer edition after 30 days). Macromedia's extensive online support network includes many articles and tutorials on ColdFusion web application development. See Chapter 20, "Working with ColdFusion," for additional details and examples.

Setting Up Your Application Server

You'll use the application server to test your site while it's in development. Most application servers can be downloaded and installed on a local or network machine. You might also be working with a host or client who has the application server you need installed on a remote site.

Table 16.2 shows some web locations where popular application servers can be obtained.

> When setting up an application server, be sure to define a root folder for the application you're building. The root folder is on the local or remote computer running the web server. For more details, see the section "Defining the Testing Server" later in this chapter.

Table 16.2

Application Servers and Download Sites

APPLICATION SERVER	SERVER TECHNOLOGY	DOWNLOAD	DOWNLOAD SITES
IIS	ASP	Free	IIS comes with Win 2000 and Win XP Pro
Sun ONE Active Server Pages	ASP	Trial	`wwws.sun.com/software/chilisoft/index.html`
IIS 5+ and .NET framework	ASP.NET 1.0	Free	`http://msdn.microsoft.com/netframework/downloads/v1.0/default.aspx`
IIS 6 and .NET framework	ASP.NET 1.1	Free	`http://msdn.microsoft.com/library/default.asp?url=/downloads/list/netdevframework.asp` (IIS 6 comes with Windows Server 2003)
ColdFusion MX	ColdFusion MX	Free Developer version	`www.macromedia.com/cfusion/tdrc/index.cfm?product=coldfusion`
JRun	JSP	Free Developer version	`www.macromedia.com/cfusion/tdrc/index.cfm?product=jrun`
Sun One Application Server	JSP	Free Developer version	`wwws.sun.com/software/products/appsrvr_pe/home_appsrvr_pe.html`
IBM WebSphere	JSP	Trial	`www7b.software.ibm.com/wsdd/downloads/WASsupport.html#download`
Apache Tomcat	JSP	Free	`http://jakarta.apache.org/tomcat/`
BEA WebLogic	JSP	Free Developer version	`www.bea.com/framework.jsp?CNT=index.htm&FP=/content/products/server/`
PHP	PHP	Free	`www.php.net/downloads.php` (and, for Mac OS X users who want to run PHP on their built-in Apache server, `www.entropy.ch/software/macosx/php/`)

Setting Up Your Web Application as a Dreamweaver Site

Once you've got the infrastructure in place, setting up your dynamic site or web application in Dreamweaver is no more complicated than it is for setting up an ordinary static site full of HTML pages.

Defining the Local Folder

Defining the site starts with setting up your local folder for staging copies of your files, which is really not any different from how you would do it for a static site (see Chapter 3 for more information on this).

Select Site → Manage Sites → New. This brings up the Site Definition dialog box. If the wizard is showing, click the Advanced tab. You should automatically start in the Local Info category.

Give your site a name, browse to the local root folder, and indicate the eventual URL of the site for link-checking purposes.

Defining the Remote Folder

Next, set up access to your web server. Choose the Remote Info category, and start by choosing an Access type (see Figure 16.3).

Here's how to choose the right Access type:

FTP Choose FTP if the web server is at a remote host without any special source-code security database running.

Local/Network Choose this if the web server is on your local computer or network.

RDS (Remote Development Services) Choose this option if the web server is a ColdFusion MX server.

SourceSafe Database Choose this if you are collaborating on a project where the code is stored in a SourceSafe database.

WebDAV (Web-based Distributed Authoring and Versioning) Choose WebDAV if your code is secured using the WebDAV extensions to HTTP.

Depending on your access choice, indicate the path to the local/network server, the FTP login information, or the RDS, SourceSafe, or WebDAV settings (path, username, and password).

If you're collaborating on this site, consider the Check In/Check Out option. (RDS, SourceSafe, and WebDAV will all require

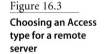

Figure 16.3

Choosing an Access type for a remote server

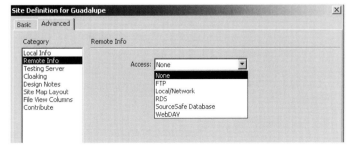

Check In/Out automatically.) See Chapter 3 for more discussion of these remote setup options.

Defining the Testing Server

Finally, set up your application server as the testing server for your site so that Dreamweaver can process your dynamic components. To do so, choose the Testing Server category in the Edit Sites or Site Definition dialog box (refer back to Figure 16.1).

For your server model, choose one of the following options:

ASP JavaScript For ASP sites using JavaScript as the scripting language.

ASP VBScript For ASP sites using VBScript as the scripting language.

ASP.NET C# For ASP.NET sites using C# ("C-sharp") as the scripting language.

ASP.NET VB For ASP.NET sites using Visual Basic as the scripting language.

ColdFusion For ColdFusion sites.

JSP For JSP sites.

PHP MySQL For PHP sites (MySQL is the only database type supported for Dreamweaver PHP sites).

After choosing a server model, you need to tell Dreamweaver how to get access to the testing server and where to find the site's root folder on the testing server:

Access Choose FTP if the application server is remote or Local/Network if the application server is on your local computer or network.

- If you choose FTP, Dreamweaver will suggest the FTP server and path to your remote server. Use that if the testing server is the same server as the remote server. Otherwise, replace it with the correct FTP server and path information for your testing server.

- If you choose Local/Network, Dreamweaver will suggest the local site's root folder for the Testing Server Folder. Use that or browse to the correct local folder.

Root Folder The web server you choose must be able to serve any file in your root folder in response to an HTTP request from a browser. To test it, place a test HTML page in the root folder and then attempt to access it by entering the URL in a browser. If the web server is local (installed on your computer), then you can use localhost in place of a domain name, for example, if your test file is `myTest.html`:

- IIS - `http://localhost/myTest.html`
- Apache (Windows) - `http://localhost:80/myTest.html`
- Apache (Mac) - `http://localhost/~your Mac user name/myTest.html`
- ColdFusion MX - `http://localhost:8500/myTest.html`

For other web servers, consult the documentation for the location of the root folder.

> The file path is not the same as the URL. For example, the file path to the test page in your IIS folder may be `C:\Inetpub\WWWRoot\myTest.html`, but the URL is `http://localhost/myTest.html`. If you open the page in a browser by using the file path, you won't be able to test dynamic features.

URL Prefix The URL Prefix indicates the web address of the application server, including the root folder specified when you set up the testing server. If the application server is on your own computer, the URL will start with `http://localhost/`.

Then click OK. You're now ready to start building a dynamic site.

From Applications to Transactions

If you're building a web application that involves transactions, you have e-commerce—online behavior that generates payments. Chapter 17 takes you through the process of developing an e-commerce site. If you'd rather plow ahead and start hooking up to databases, skip ahead to Chapter 19.

Building an E-Commerce Site

Dreamweaver makes starting up an e-commerce website practically as easy as swiping a credit card, whether you're a business tycoon or a web design expert.

Because e-commerce websites have different goals, they require different strategies than informational or community-building websites. To reach your ultimate goal—getting potential customers to purchase your goods or services—you need to make products easy to find and select, provide good customer service, and process transactions.

In addition to setting up your site in the most appealing way, you will need to perform other strategies that fall into the category of traditional business activities; it's up to you to accomplish many basic tasks the old-fashioned way. Dreamweaver can't do much to help you write a good sales pitch, solve a shipping problem, or satisfy a customer who calls you with a question about your products. But the software *can* help you design your store's look-and-feel. Dreamweaver can also provide a starting point for important back-end activities like shopping carts.

This chapter explores the following topics:

- **Establishing a graphic identity**
- **Marketing your website**
- **Setting up a sales catalog**
- **Creating a shopping cart**
- **Processing online transactions**

Creating an Identity for an Online Store

All of the activities that go into creating a website—creating a look-and-feel, gathering compelling content, organizing the pages, going live, and performing ongoing maintenance—become more critical when your website represents some or all of your income. This section presents a quick rundown of what creating a graphic identity means when your goal is e-commerce.

> *E-commerce* refers to the process of generating revenue through transactions that take place on the Internet. Business-to-consumer (B2C) e-commerce occurs between a website that has something to sell and an individual who wants to buy it. Business-to-business (B2B) e-commerce involves the exchange of supplies between companies.

Why care about developing a look-and-feel for your site? Here are a few reasons:

Trust and confidence A consistent graphic identity builds trust and confidence in your business for those customers who might be reluctant to shop and make purchases online due to security concerns.

Communication Your visual image strikes a chord with customers you have already identified as the people you want to reach—the people who are likely to need and buy what you have to offer.

Like any website, an e-commerce site conveys its look-and-feel through color, type, and graphics. Your company's name—not just your "brick-and-mortar" name, but your domain name—makes your store easy to find and revisit. Be sure to pick a short, understandable domain name that reflects what you do and is easy for your customers to remember and type into their browsers' Address box.

Including a Logo

A *logo*—a small graphic image that includes the name of your company and, often, a drawing that visually represents the product or service that you provide—plays one of the most important roles in creating an online store's identity. (The logo, together with the site's look-and-feel, contributes to the online aspect of what's called the *branding* of your store.) A good logo gets your company's name across in a single glance while also establishing color and type choices that will be used consistently throughout the site.

If you create your own logo, you can easily add it to your Dreamweaver website. But suppose your organization already has a logo for its printed material, which you (or your designer) have created using a popular program like Adobe Photoshop and saved in a print file format such as a TIF file. Such an image can't be put online as a Photoshop file because it's too complex; it needs to be compressed using one of the standard image formats used on the Web—GIF, or JPEG, or PNG (see the bonus chapter on the book's CD for more information about these graphics formats).

See the logo for our example e-commerce site (Obscura Camera Supplies) in Figure 17.1.

Figure 17.1
Logo for Obscura Camera Supplies

Using Color and Type

Every website needs good color and type selections. Other chapters have covered the basics of using color and type to get your message across. But you may be wondering what issues are specific to choosing color and type for an e-commerce site. It's all a matter of matching what your customers want to what you and your company have to offer.

Matching Customer Tastes

The best colors for an online store are ones to which your customers will respond positively, and ones that will not interfere with the presentation of your sales items. If you're looking to reach customers with conservative tastes, or if your products reflect traditional values, use simple color schemes. The home page for our e-commerce site, shown in Figure 17.2, is designed to appeal to photographers. It uses a black and grey color theme for the headers and menu items, with a plain white background behind the color images of the products. Other sites use vivid colors, bright backgrounds, and Flash animation to reach an audience looking for excitement—check out the Wired News Animation Express (`www.wired.com/animation/`) for an example of eye-catching type and color.

Figure 17.2
Successful e-commerce sites match color and type selections to the tastes of their target audience. The color and type choices should reflect the products being sold and the emotion they produce in the customer.

Matching Corporate Colors

If you are creating an e-commerce site that functions as an outgrowth of an existing brick-and-mortar business, your website can be a great place to build your brand recognition. To match colors your organization uses on its existing printed material, use the eyedropper tool. Click on the color box in any Dreamweaver dialog box or in the Property inspector to open the color picker, and then use the eyedropper to select a color. The Dreamweaver eyedropper lets you choose a color that you have scanned from one of your corporate publications. Click anywhere on your screen—even outside your Dreamweaver windows—to select the color with the eyedropper.

A *pure play* is a company that operates only online. A *brick-and-mortar* business has a physical location where customers can shop. Many brick-and-mortar businesses are developing websites so that they can do *cross-channel e-commerce*—selling both online and through their physical store (for example, Barnes & Noble).

Let's say you've scanned a piece of stationery and the colors you see on screen are the ones you want to duplicate on your website. Start up Dreamweaver and follow these steps to do the copying.

1. Open the file that has the color you want to duplicate. This file can be in a program other than Dreamweaver.

2. Click the color box in Dreamweaver's Property inspector. The color picker appears, and the mouse arrow turns into the eyedropper.

3. Hold down the mouse button when you move from the Dreamweaver window to the window that contains the color you want. (You need to have both windows visible on your screen to do this.) This keeps the eyedropper on screen even when you move outside of Dreamweaver. When you pass the eyedropper over the desired color, that color appears in the color sample box in the upper-left corner of the color picker.

4. Release the mouse button. The selected color appears in the color box in the Property inspector. You can now assign the color to text or images on your web page.

Style sheets give you another way to develop an online identity for your store by applying colors consistently from page to page. Cascading Style Sheets (CSS) also let you specify type size and leading (the space between lines) precisely, if you want to emulate the look of printed publications. (See Chapter 9, "Cascading Style Sheets," for more about style sheets.)

The key word is *emulate*. You won't be able to exactly duplicate printed type specs on your Dreamweaver web page. Nor should you; most of the typefaces used in print won't display on the Web unless viewers have those same fonts installed on their own computer systems, and there's no way you can guarantee that. Stick to common type fonts, such as Arial, Verdana, or Times Roman, that your users are likely to have installed on their system.

Marketing Your Site

An e-commerce site owner needs to do targeted, smart marketing to build traffic. Traffic can make or break an e-commerce site. Attract enough visitors, and you can earn revenue by charging other businesses to place advertisements on your site. Attract shoppers who are already looking for what you have to offer, and you make sales. This section runs through the basics of marketing your online store.

Listing with Search Services

How do potential customers find their way through the scores of web stores to the one you've just set up with Dreamweaver? Chances are they search for you or your products by entering a word or phrase in the search box of a search engine such as Google (`www.google.com`). When they submit the information, a search program scours a database of web pages and their contents and returns pages that contain the desired word or phrase.

BE A PROFILER: IDENTIFY YOUR IDEAL CUSTOMERS

One of the most important aspects of online marketing is something you need do on your own before you even start up Dreamweaver. Know exactly whom you want to reach. Only when you identify those people can you market your goods and services to them.

How do you get to know them? Here are some suggestions:

- Find them online. Single out websites where your likely customers hang out. Check out newsgroups to get a feel for their concerns.

- Create customer profiles. Try to describe three of your customers in as much detail as possible. Tell yourself where they live, how they dress, what they do for a living. Print out the profiles, paste them on your bulletin board near your computer, and keep them in mind when you create content for your site.

- Talk to people who already buy what you have to offer at your competitors' stores.

- Look at other sites that offer similar goods and services.

Most people who shop online are looking to save time and money. They are too busy to drive, park, and trudge through shopping malls. They want efficiency and good service as well as good value. Check out the demographics information at CyberAtlas (`www.cyberatlas.com`). You'll find some useful information there about online shoppers and their characteristics. Once you know who these people are, you can then market to them.

Search services use special programs that scour the Web's contents and build a database that anyone can search. If you tap your toes long enough, your site will probably be added to the search service's database automatically. To enhance the effectiveness of this type of search, add many descriptive words about your site into the keywords on your site. This way, you'll get pulled up more often by web searches (find more about this in the "Adding Keywords" section that follows).

But instead of just waiting for a search engine to list you, you can register your site and add yourself to the database. To register, you fill out a form that provides the service with your store's name and URL, as well as a description of what you do. As you may have guessed, filling out each service's form can be time consuming. You can streamline the process by using a service that submits your site's information to multiple search sites at once. Some will submit your information to a handful of sites for free and to a larger number of sites for a fee. Check out SiteOwner.com's Submit It! Free service (`www.siteowner.com/sifree.cfm`).

Think twice about paying a fee to a commercial service to submit your information to a large number of search engines. It's generally more efficient and productive to do submissions to the most popular search engines and to any specialized search engines for your product or service rather than a large number of obscure search engines that your customers are unlikely to use. A review of major search engines and directories is at `www.searchenginewatch.com/links/article.php/2156221`.

If you can get your site listed on Yahoo! (`www.yahoo.com`), you'll get visitors because this indispensable index to the Internet is so popular. It's worth taking the time to register there, though it can take weeks to get your site registered with them. You can bypass the wait by using Yahoo! Express. This currently costs $299 annually, but guarantees that your site will be reviewed within seven business days. Some categories of commercial sites are required to use Yahoo! Express for Yahoo listings.

META TAGS

A meta tag is an HTML tag that provides information about an HTML document (such as the author or copyright) but doesn't provide any information that's displayed on the page. There are several different kinds of meta tags, but the most commonly used ones are the keyword and description tag types. Some search engines rely heavily on meta tags, while others don't use them at all.

Adding Keywords

The way you present your online store is an essential component of your marketing success. For that reason, be sure you go behind the scenes to add keywords to the home page of your site.

Keywords are terms you create that describe your business or the goods or services you sell. For a site that sells hardware, you might add keywords like `hardware`, `tools`, `repair`, `building`, `electrical`, `paint`, and so on. Adding keywords may increase the frequency with which your site appears in a search service's list of results (depending on the search engine). If the user's search term matches one of your keywords, your site is presented in the list. The more specific your keywords are, the more likely that your site will come up in a search. For example, if your site sells Southwest shamanic art prints, be sure to include `Southwest art`, `shamanic art`, and `Southwest shamanic art` in your keywords rather than more general terms like `art` and `prints`.

Like all HTML tags, you can insert `meta` tags manually or have Dreamweaver do it for you. You add keywords by clicking the Head icon on the HTML Insert bar and selecting Keywords. Type the keywords in the Keywords box of the Insert Keywords dialog box (see Figure 17.3), and then click OK.

> For more information about how search engines work and how to optimize your site for search engines, see Chapter 30, "Going Live or Delivering the Site."

Advertising with Banners

Advertising on the web is a big business. The most common online ads take the form of rectangular graphics (usually one inch by four or five inches in size) called *banners*. They appear on a web page and publicize someone else's website. When viewers click the graphics, their browsers go to the sites being advertised. The site that displays the ad usually charges a fee for displaying these banners. The fee is either based on the popularity of the site doing the displaying, the number of times the page bearing the ad is viewed, or the number of times visitors click through to the advertiser's site (these are called *clickthroughs*). Banners can be expensive to place on sites that receive a lot of traffic—for instance, Yahoo! charges thousands of dollars for the privilege of placing ads on some of its more popular index pages.

> Users might be irritated by banner ads, and many have now installed software that blocks the display of banner ads. The clickthrough rate for banner ads is extremely low.

Figure 17.3

Adding keywords to your site's home page increases your chances of being found by a potential customer using a search service.

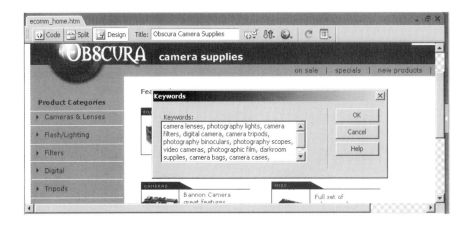

You can save money and still market your business by exchanging banners with other websites. First, you need to create a banner for your own site, either in a graphics program or by using an online service such as Animation Online (`www.animationonline.com/freebanners.html`). Once you have your banner, you can trade it with other websites using a service such as Microsoft bCentral's free Banner Network (`www.bcentral.com/products/bn/default.asp`).

> A Dreamweaver extension called Universal Bookmarks lets you take a proactive approach to making your website easier to find. Once you install the extension, you can automatically add a link that the user can click on to add your site to the user's Favorites (IE) or Bookmarks (Netscape or Opera) menu. The Universal_Bookmarks extension is in the Extensions folder on the CD included with this book.

Processing Transactions

Many activities go into making an e-commerce operation successful. But there's only one that really counts as far as your bottom line is concerned: getting your customers to close the deal. Online shoppers like to be able to complete purchases within a few mouse clicks. The closer you can get to making the transaction process easy, the more likely you are to generate sales.

This section discusses how to use Dreamweaver as a starting point to create the essentials of completing purchases online—a sales catalog, a shopping cart, and a credit card processing system.

Creating an Online Catalog

Many e-commerce websites force shoppers to do an excessive amount of searching just to figure out how to purchase something. The first thing you can do to avoid such confusion is to create a well-organized sales catalog. An effective online catalog meets these criteria:

- Consists of a set of web pages that presents sales items with clear descriptions and (usually) photos

- Contains buttons or links that enable the shopper to store the items in a shopping cart for later purchase

- Includes links to other parts of the company's catalog, as well as to all other parts of the website, so that the shopper can jump from one sales category within the catalog (such as men's formalwear) to another (such as children's outerwear)

Figure 17.4 shows a page from the online catalog of the Obscura Camera Supplies site. Each item includes a button that links to a detail page and a button to add the item to the shopping cart. A product detail page is shown in Figure 17.5.

Dreamweaver's predesigned web page components include several catalog layouts. They contain the features that are essential to virtually all online catalogs, and you should browse through them before you start to create catalog pages on your own. Open the site you want to contain the catalog, and then follow these steps:

1. Choose File → New to open the New Document dialog box.

2. Click Page Designs in the Category column.

Figure 17.4

Online catalog page from the Obscura Camera Supplies site. The View Details and Add To Cart buttons help make online shopping easy and efficient.

Figure 17.5

**Product detail page
from the Obscura
Camera Supplies
site.**

3. Click one of the Catalog options at the top of the Page Designs column to view a preview and description on the right side of the dialog box.

4. Click the catalog layout you want, and click Create. The catalog page is created.

For example, if you click Commerce: Product Catalog A, the layout shown in Figure 17.6 appears. You can add your images and type your descriptions, replacing the placeholder text.

When you think about catalogs, you probably think about selling discrete consumer goods. However, you can describe your services if you are in a service field and don't sell individual commodities. The most important thing is to anticipate what customers want from your catalog. Ideally, your website should provide customers with the look-and-feel of walking into a store and approaching a sales clerk who will handle the entire transaction in real time—with no delays in processing, with strong customer service, and with complete answers to questions.

Some web hosting services that specialize in e-commerce, like Microsoft bCentral (www.bcentral.com) for small business solutions, include utilities that streamline the process of creating a catalog. If you don't want to create your catalog from scratch, consider signing up with such a service.

Keep It Fresh

If you update your catalog on a regular basis, you give your customers an incentive to return to your site. Be sure to include links to new items, seasonal sales, and inventory clearances in a prominent place on your home page.

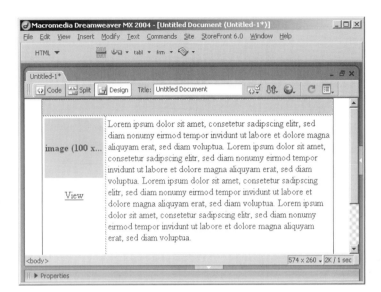

Figure 17.6

Dreamweaver MX 2004 provides pre-designed layouts you can use to create a sales catalog.

Don't be reluctant to sprinkle words like New! or Sale! liberally around your home page or other parts of your site. Also consider inviting your visitors to sign up for your special sales and promotions list so that you can send them announcements of upcoming sales and online events to remind them of your site and to encourage them to revisit it—Amazon.com does this on a weekly basis, sending out ideas about what you might like that is new, and what items in their warehouse of inventory are on sale.

Keep It Organized

Divide your sales items into categories and subcategories, if that's possible. This not only makes your total selection seem less intimidating, but it makes it easier for the shopper to immediately hone in on the specific item that they want. You can set up jump menus (see Chapter 13) to lead people from one category to another instantly.

Make It Complete

Shoppers on the Web have an insatiable desire for information. Don't hold back when it comes to images and descriptions of your products. At the same time, you don't have to present everything all at once. In the catalog page shown in Figure 17.4, you see a thumbnail of the product, a brief description, and the price. Shoppers can click the View Details button to view a larger version with further product details.

It doesn't matter whether each catalog page contains a single item or a group of items—only that it's easy to navigate the site and do the shopping. It's generally better to present only the bare essentials about an item on a catalog page, while giving shoppers the option of clicking elsewhere to find out more. Inviting prospective customers to explore your site further keeps them involved; the longer they stay on your e-commerce site, the more likely they'll make a purchase.

Creating a Shopping Cart

A *shopping cart* is software that performs the same function as the metal device you push around a brick-and-mortar store. Dreamweaver doesn't come with a built-in shopping cart. You have several options for adding one to your e-commerce website:

- Write your own shopping cart program and install it on the server that hosts your site.

- Buy a commercial shopping cart program and install it on the server that hosts your site.

- Use a Dreamweaver extension to add a shopping cart that uses PayPal for processing transactions (PayPal eCommerce Toolkit, free download from the WebAssist Products site at `www.webassist.com/Products/ProductResults.asp`).

- Create your own shopping cart for no charge at Mal's e-commerce site (`www.mals-e.com/`)—see the tutorial at the end of this chapter for more details.

- Host your site with a company that provides you with a cart as part of its services.

When combined with an online catalog, the shopping cart performs another set of essential e-commerce functions. First, it enables shoppers to make selections. By clicking Add To Cart, or a similarly named button, items are stored in the cart (see Figure 17.7). Once shoppers have added an item to the cart, they have the option of either continuing to shop for more selections or proceeding to the checkout area.

Figure 17.7

A shopping cart gives e-commerce website owners an Add To Cart button that they can add to each page of their sales catalog. Shoppers click the button to store the selected item in the cart until checkout.

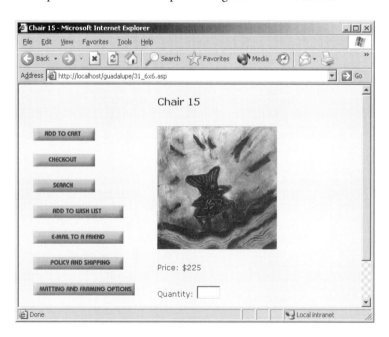

The cart stores the catalog items that customers select in a safe location—a secure server that uses encryption to protect customer information. When the customer decides to check out, the cart totals up the selected items and gives the shopper the option of rejecting unwanted items. Finally, the cart contains a button labeled Proceed To Checkout that sends the shopper's browser to an area where payment and shipping information is requested so that the transaction can be completed. Figure 17.8 shows LaGarde's Store-Front shopping cart, which can be installed as a Dreamweaver extension. It's used as the shopping cart for Santa Fe Healing Art (`www.santafehealingart.com`), an online art and healing products store.

StoreFront offers a variety of e-commerce products, from simple solutions for small businesses to sophisticated, full-featured e-commerce products for larger businesses that include wish lists, sales features, mailing lists, inventory management, back ordering, merchant account and gateway integration, and real-time rates from major shippers at checkout. For more information and an online demo, visit the StoreFront site at `www.storefront.net`.

The New Document dialog box includes a shopping cart layout you can add in a flash. Just open the web page that you want to contain the shopping cart layout, position the cursor where you want the cart to appear, and follow these steps:

1. Choose File → New to open the New Document dialog box.

2. Click Page Designs in the Category column.

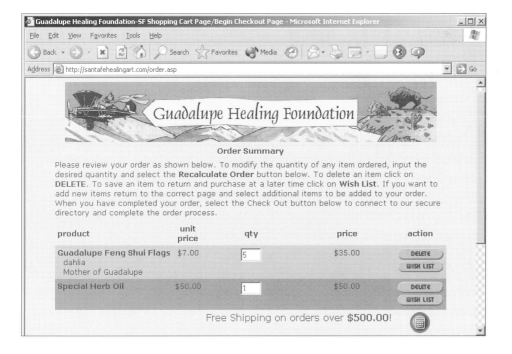

Figure 17.8

This store's shopping cart comes as an extension for Dreamweaver. It stores selections, calculates totals, and gives shoppers the ability to continue shopping, delete selected items, or proceed to the checkout area.

3. Click Commerce: Shopping Cart in the Page Designs column.

4. Click Create.

A shopping cart layout appears in the current page (see Figure 17.9).

Processing Credit Card Payments

Some shoppers, squeamish about online security, prefer to pay for their web-based purchases by phoning or faxing their credit card billing information and shipping address. For that reason, you should include your phone and fax numbers on your web pages. But you should also make it possible for shoppers to follow their impulses and complete transactions in just a minute or two by submitting their credit card data to you online. There are two options for obtaining what you need: You can do it yourself, or you can sign up with other online businesses that will do some or all of the work for you.

Doing It Yourself

If you're the do-it-yourself type and you want to process your customers' sensitive financial information, you need to set yourself up with the following:

- A merchant account with a financial institution that can charge the customer's credit card and credit your account. Expect to wait anywhere from several days to several weeks for your application to be approved; you'll also have to pay application fees of $300 to $800 as well as "discount fees" of 1 to 4 percent per transaction.

- A secure server that protects your customers' credit card numbers and other personal information with Secure Sockets Layer (SSL) encryption.

- Point-of-sale (POS) hardware or software that transmits your customers' credit card numbers to your bank. The hardware device is a terminal of the sort that most retail stores use. The software is a program like Keystroke (`www.keystrokepos.com`). Both communicate with the bank through your modem.

It's not difficult to find online businesses that are eager to set you up with merchant accounts. (Perhaps you've received unsolicited e-mail messages from some of these organizations already.) You can check out a well-established online financial institution like Wells Fargo Bank (`www.wellsfargo.com`) or scan the lengthy list of merchant account providers on Yahoo!'s site:

```
http://dir.yahoo.com/Business_and_Economy/Business_to_Business/
Financial_Services/Transaction_Clearing/Credit_Card_Merchant_Services/
```

If you have an existing store and already process credit cards, you should probably stick with that bank for your online transactions. The advantage of using your current financial institution is that it saves you the trouble of having to shop around for a credit card vendor and, as an existing customer, you're more likely to have your merchant account application approved.

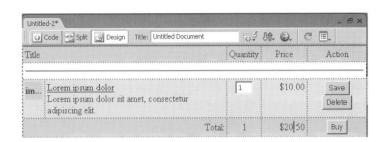

Figure 17.9

Dreamweaver MX 2004 includes a predesigned shopping cart you can add with a single mouse click, and then customize to suit your needs.

But if you're starting up a new web-based business, consider the many shortcuts to the merchant account application process that are provided by e-commerce hosting companies. You don't have to shop around for a financial institution; you don't have to convince them that your online business is a "real" one; and since the merchant already has an affiliation with your hosting service, you're likely to be approved. But be sure to read the fine print—credit card merchants affiliated with e-commerce hosts are likely to carry the same hidden charges such as application fees and "discount fees" as traditional banks. (The term *discount fee* is commonly used to describe the charges the financial institution makes you pay it for each transaction it processes.)

Letting Your Host Do the Processing

You can save yourself some time and trouble by renting web space on the system of another company that already has credit card processing systems in place. In this situation, you pay a fee to a website that sets you up with a merchant account, provides you with the forms you need, gives you space on a secure server, verifies the customer information, and processes the data.

At Yahoo! Store, for instance, you pay a $39.95 per month for a hosting fee plus a 1.5 percent fee for each transaction for the Starter plan. Despite all these charges, being a Yahoo! merchant has its advantages. For instance, as a Yahoo! Store merchant, you can use an affiliated credit card payment service called Paymentech, and the process of applying for a merchant account will be streamlined. Paymentech processes applications in three days or less, so you will be up and running in no time. However, there are charges here too. Paymentech charges a monthly service fee of $22.95 for processing credit card purchases. In addition, it offers you a discount fee of 2.52 percent plus a 20-cent transaction fee to MasterCard International Inc. or Visa International as well.

Similarly, if you pay $24.95 per month to become a Microsoft bCentral merchant, you can apply to Cardservice International to become a credit card merchant. If you are a bCentral customer, Cardservice will process credit card transactions for 2.35 percent of each transaction for Mastercard and Visa (3.5 percent for American Express) plus a fee of $19.95 per month.

Obtaining a merchant account through your web host doesn't mean you're not involved with completing transactions. On the contrary, you need to answer questions, handle returns, make sure items are shipped, and be able to track shipments if they're lost or delayed.

Having read about all the fees you have to pay to be a credit card merchant, you might wonder why you should go through all the trouble in the first place. The main reason is that online shoppers love to purchase with credit cards. Filling out forms and clicking a few buttons is what they're used to. If you force shoppers to send in checks or phone in credit card information, you won't get nearly as many sales.

Some online merchants prefer to process credit card payments themselves rather than leaving the work to a processing service. When they do this, they assume responsibility for making sure that the credit card number is valid, that the customer's name is correct, and that the credit card limit has not been reached. That way, they can be on the watch for obvious signs of fraud, such as a billing address in one country and a shipping address in another country.

Some credit cards, like American Express and Discover, might not be covered by the merchant account you obtain through your web host. If you want to accept these cards, you might need to apply to the credit card companies separately.

Hands On: Create a Shopping Cart

As stated in the section "Creating a Shopping Cart," the New Document dialog box includes a predesigned shopping cart design that you can add to a web page in a flash. But that's only the front end of the cart, the part that the user sees. To get the cart to actually function, you need to manually capture session variables yourself using ColdFusion, ASP, ASP.NET, or PHP (see Chapter 20, "Working with Cold Fusion," Chapter 21, "Working with ASP," Chapter 22, "Using PHP in Dreamweaver," and Chapter 25, "Emerging Technologies").

Alternatively, you can add full shopping cart functionality to your e-commerce website using Mal's e-commerce—and it's free! Mal's is a great way to set up a shopping cart for any size store, but is particularly useful for a small business that wants to "test the e-commerce waters" by offering a few products online for their customers and seeing what the response is. You can store credit card numbers securely on Mal's site for retrieval and manual processing by you or, with Mal's premium account ($18 per three months), you can link directly to payment processors.

Follow these steps to add a shopping cart to the Obscura Camera Supplies site.

1. Go to www.mals-e.com/services/create.htm and fill out the form to sign up for a free account with Mal's e-commerce. If you'd like to check it out first, go to www.mals-e.com/services/index.htm and click on the link for the Demo Store.

2. Open the product detail page for the Obscura Camera Supplies site (`Obscura_ product.htm`) in the Chapter 17 folder on the CD.

> To see the completed product detail page with e-commerce links, open the `Obscura_ product_final.htm` file in the Chapter 17 folder on the CD.

3. Select the Add To Cart button under the item price on the Obscura product detail page. Open the Property inspector if it's not already open.

4. In the Link text box in the Property inspector, or directly in the Code window, type the following link for the Add To Cart graphic:

    ```
    <a href="http://www6.aitsafe.com/cf/add.cfm?
    userid=89136789&product=Cameratek+Flatbed+Scanner&price=2450.99">
    ```

    If you created an account, replace this user id with your own. Also, make sure to use the correct server address, as assigned to you when you created the account—in this case, `www6.aitsafe.com`.

5. Add a return attribute to the link you just created so that users return to the page of your choice when they click the Continue Shopping button at checkout. In this case, users will return to the same page where they placed the order (`Obscura_product.htm`):

    ```
    <a href="http://www6.aitsafe.com/cf/add.cfm?
    userid=89136789&product=Cameratek+Flatbed+Scanner
    &price=2450.99&return=www.obscura.com/Obscura_product.htm">
    ```

> You might recognize this as a link that uses the GET method. You can also use HTML forms and the POST method if you prefer. See the web page, "The Basics to Get You Running," for details (`www.mals-e.com/support/helpscr.htm?pg=help1a`).

6. Now add a link to the View Cart/Checkout button in the upper-right corner. (Note that we no longer have an ongoing total displayed, since Mal's cart does not support this kind of feature.) This allows the customer to view the contents of the shopping cart at any time.

    ```
    <a href="http://www6.aitsafe.com/cf/review.cfm?userid=89136789">
    ```

7. Add a return attribute to this link so the user can return directly to this page from the cart:

    ```
    <a href="http://www6.aitsafe.com/cf/review.cfm?
    userid=89136789&return=www.obscura.com/Obscura_product.htm">
    ```

8. Now that the basic functions are in place, let's configure the look of the cart. Click on the link at the top of the page labeled "Admin Area." You'll need your user ID and password to log in to the Admin Area.

9. The Administration window displays. Click on Admin home on the left side of the window. A box labeled My Admin displays on the right of the page. Check Show Cart and click the Update button.

10. Click Yes in the next window that asks whether you'd like to create a shopping cart, then click on the "Cart set-up" link that appears on the left side of the window.

11. The Shopping Cart Set-Up window opens. You can set the look of the cart to match your site, add shipping information, e-mail messages to confirm the order, and any other parameters you choose to complete your shopping cart. Instructions are provided for each setting when you click the links on this page.

12. You can test your cart by clicking the Buy Now link for testing at the bottom of the page.

13. When you're finished with customizing and testing the shopping cart, click the Log Out link on the left of the page.

That's it—you just created a functional shopping cart for your site! Upload your catalog pages to your web server (see Chapter 16 for details), and your shopping cart is open for business. If you want to create carts for additional sites, just open another free account.

Now all you have to do is administer your website and make those sales!

Putting the *e-* in Everything

Sure, a basic e-commerce storefront is just the tip of the iceberg when it comes to e-business, but that's what some of your customers will be looking for. For more sophisticated business-to-business, business-to-employee, or business-to-supplier sites (often called corporate or enterprise portals), you'll want to pull together most of what there is to learn in this book, from designing pages, to working with forms, databases, and XML, and finally to administration.

The more you get into working with the code, as opposed to layout and other design issues, the more you might want to work in Code view. The next chapter shows you how to set up a coding environment to your liking in Dreamweaver.

Dreamweaver MX 2004 Savvy in Color

The Web is a color medium—like television and magazines and the front page of *The New York Times*. In this section, we'll demonstrate some of the more colorful features of Dreamweaver MX 2004, including

- **Choosing colors in Dreamweaver**
- **The nested template feature in Dreamweaver MX 2004**
- **CSS design examples from the CSS Zen Garden**
- **Frames-based pages**
- **Graphic techniques for optimizing an image**
- **Design-oriented e-commerce**
- **Page display in an assortment of browsers**

Setting Page, Text, and Link Colors

One of the ways that you maintain a consistent look-and-feel across an entire website is by standardizing the use of color on each page. Page elements that can be given default colors include the page's background, ordinary text, and link text. (See Chapter 6 for further discussion of text formatting.) Link text can have a different color depending on whether it has never been clicked, is currently being clicked, or has already been clicked. Any of these colors can be added to the Assets panel or hardwired into a template (as discussed in Chapter 4).

To indicate your color preferences for a page, select Modify → Page Properties (Ctrl-J/Cmd-J). On the Page Properties dialog box that appears, choose the Appearance category to select colors for page background and text. Select the Links category to specify colors for links, visited links, and active links. Click OK to save your changes.

Each time you open the color menu, you can choose a color from the palette shown, choose one from elsewhere on your screen, or use your system's built-in color picker. Dreamweaver's color palette can display colors using several different formats, which are shown here.

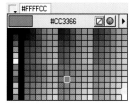

Color cubes (showing related colors together)

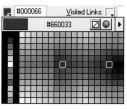

Continuous tone (showing colors in a spectrum)

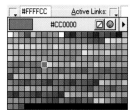

Windows OS (showing the colors of the Windows palette)

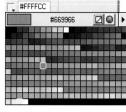

Mac OS (showing the colors of the Mac palette)

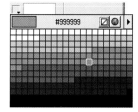

Grayscale (showing shades of gray)

For all these cases, you have the choice of having the color palette snap to the web-safe colors or to display a wider range of colors (some of which will not be rendered accurately on all browsers).

If you prefer to choose colors using the color chooser built into your operating system, then choose the System Color Picker option on any color palette.

The first image is what you get in Windows XP, and the second is what Mac OS X users see.

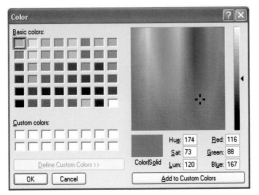 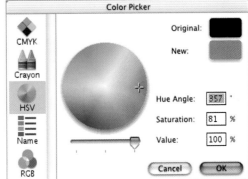

Working with Nested Templates

One of the features in Dreamweaver MX 2004 is nested templates—templates that are based on existing templates. (For more information on using Dreamweaver templates, refer to Chapter 4.) When would you want to use this feature? Well, let's say that every page at your site is going to have the same banner across the top of the page, but some of the pages will also have a navigation bar down the left side of the page, some will have several columns of copy, and others will have a single text area below the banner.

To efficiently maintain consistency, you can create a base template that designates the banner at the top of the page. Then you could create three or more nested templates from the base template. Here's how you would do it.

To create a new template from scratch, click the Templates icon on the Common Insert bar and select Make Template from the drop-down menu. Give your base template a file-name and save it. Now create the content that you will want to appear on every page, and designate the rest of the template as an editable region (bordered in aquamarine). Be sure to save your changes.

To base a nested template on the template you've already created, first make an ordinary page from the existing template (also called an "instance" of the template) by choosing File → New, selecting the Templates tab and your current site, and then double-clicking the name of the template you just created.

Then click the Templates icon on the Common Insert bar, and select Make Nested Template from the pop-up menu. Save the new nested template. Now you can define further editable areas in addition to the content that will pass through (regions bordered in orange are passed through from the parent template).

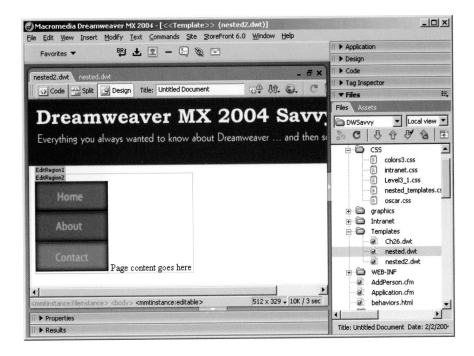

Develop pages for this section of the site using the nested template you just designed. For sections of the site that require other variants of the master design, create new nested templates from the base template.

CSS-Based Design

The CSS Zen Garden is an ongoing demonstration of the power of using CSS-based design. An HTML file and a sample CSS file are available for download from the site at www.csszengarden.com. Graphic designers are invited to create a new page look by creating a new style sheet to attach to this HTML file. Submissions are posted on the site and change frequently.

Keep in mind that all of these pages are based on exactly the same HTML file—only the CSS has changed. The four designs you see here were all contributed by the site's founder, Dave Shea.

See Chapter 9 for more information on using CSS in Dreamweaver.

tranquille by Dave Shea

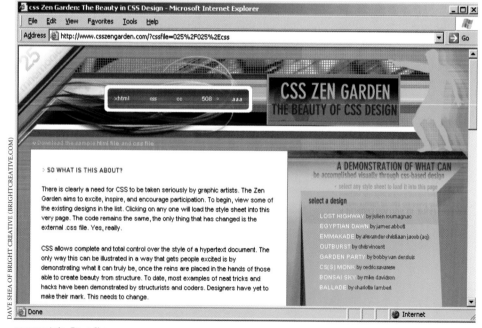

mnemonic by Dave Shea

Night Drive by Dave Shea

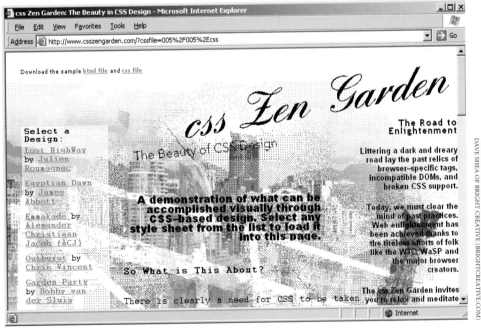

Blood Lust by Dave Shea

Frames-Based Design

The most common reason to use frames is to keep one sort of content static and always on screen while the content of other frames changes. The static content is usually a logo, ad, or navigation bar.

These figures show the frames-based layout used for the Simply Hyperbarics website (www.simplyhyperbarics.com). The site owner likes a "framed" look for the site, including the logo and navigation bar at the left, a static graphic for the page header, and a scrollable window on the right for variable page content. Clicking the HBOT FAQ'S link in the static navigation bar in the left frame makes the FAQs page display in the scrollable frame on the right.

It's very common to inherit some sites done in frames, and you'll need a basic idea of how frames work to update these sites. For more information on the pros and cons of using frames and suggestions for alternatives to frames-based design, see Chapter 7.

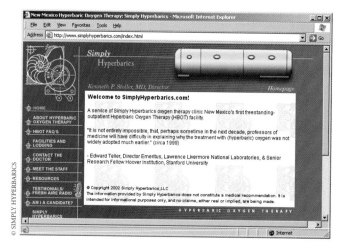

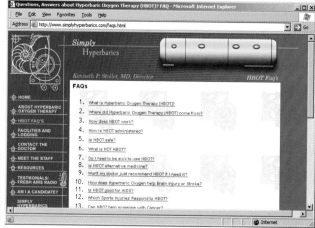

Optimizing Images

Optimizing an image is a balance between file size and image quality. This page shows optimization in Fireworks MX 2004, but you can also optimize images for the Web in Photoshop, Illustrator, Paint Shop Pro, and other graphics software programs. See the bonus graphics chapter on the CD for detailed information on slicing and optimizing images.

Before exporting a Fireworks MX 2004 image for use in Dreamweaver MX 2004, take the time to optimize it. High quality is important, but so is making sure that your pages will download rapidly for all users. The Preview feature in Fireworks enables you to compare up to four different versions of your image side-by-side.

To rapidly compare optimization choices, click the 4-Up Preview and select Window → Optimize (F6). Then, for each of the preview areas, you can choose different optimization options.

- The original image (upper-left) is a JPG and is very large (1145K).

- Turning the image into a GIF (upper-right) with a 30% dither maintains quality but only gets the file size down to 345K.

- Choosing the JPEG option that tries to maintain maximum quality (lower-left) only manages to get the file down to about 656K.

- The JPEG option that trades off more quality gets it down to under 33K with adequate image quality.

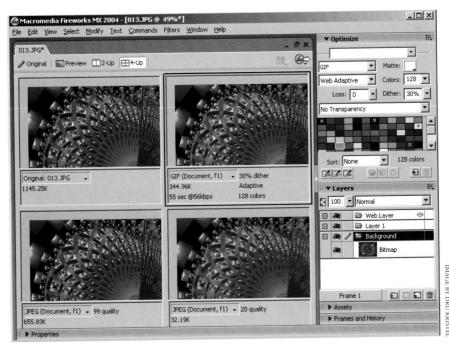

Speaking of dithering, this 4-Up Preview shows how three different dither settings affect a GIF image (all four views are zoomed in 300%).

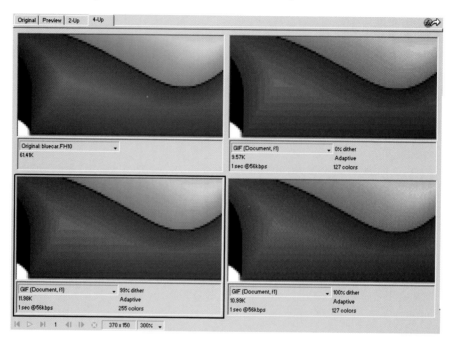

- The original image has a nearly continuous tone.
- The GIF in the upper-right has 0% dither and the continuous tone is clearly rendered in a series of discrete color areas.
- The GIF in the lower-left has 99% dither, which roughens the edges of the color areas but still leaves them looking blocky.
- The GIF in the lower-right has 100% dither, which manages to blur the jumps in color tone more effectively.

Design-Oriented E-Commerce

Designed and produced by a group of highly creative individuals, the Santa Fe Healing Art site (www.santafehealingart.com) is a graphic-intensive site created mainly in Flash. When they added e-commerce capabilities to their site using StoreFront's e-commerce add-on for Dreamweaver, they maintained the design integrity of the site while providing e-commerce features.

The shops page, done in Flash, features links to the shopping areas of the site as well as the search page.

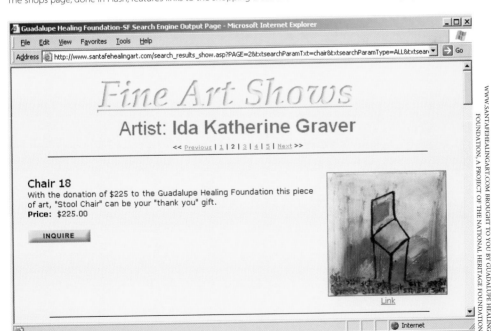

A search of the Fine Art Shows returns this print by Ida Katherine Graver.

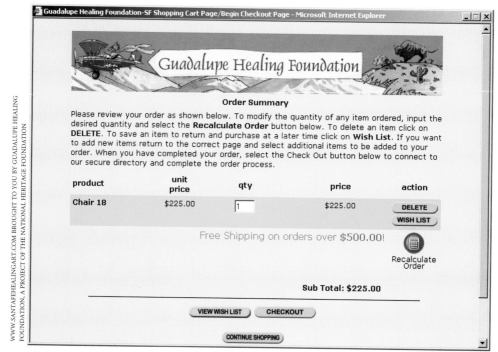

http://www.santafehealingart.com/detail_pop1.asp?prodID=208 - Microsoft Internet Explorer

Chair 18
Ida Katherine Graver
6" x 6"
Mixed Media

With the donation of $225 to the Guadalupe Healing Foundation this piece of art, "Stool Chair" can be your "thank you" gift.

Original Art	$225	Purchase
Tax Deductible Amount	$225	

Please contact us with any questions.
Phone: 505-955-1850
Email: contact@santafehealingart.com

zoom

CLOSE | CHECKOUT

Clicking the link on the search results page takes us to a detail page where we can order the print.

Guadalupe Healing Foundation-SF Shopping Cart Page/Begin Checkout Page - Microsoft Internet Explorer

Guadalupe Healing Foundation

Order Summary

Please review your order as shown below. To modify the quantity of any item ordered, input the desired quantity and select the **Recalculate Order** button below. To delete an item click on **DELETE**. To save an item to return and purchase at a later time click on **Wish List**. If you want to add new items return to the correct page and select additional items to be added to your order. When you have completed your order, select the Check Out button below to connect to our secure directory and complete the order process.

product	unit price	qty	price	action
Chair 18	$225.00	1	$225.00	DELETE / WISH LIST

Free Shipping on orders over $500.00!

Recalculate Order

Sub Total: $225.00

VIEW WISH LIST | CHECKOUT

CONTINUE SHOPPING

After clicking the Purchase button on the detail page, we can view the order details.

Checking Browser Compatibility

Unless you're designing for an intranet where everyone is using the same platform and the same version of the same browser, you need to check your site pages on both Windows and Mac OS and in a variety of browsers. Luckily, the days of major browser incompatibility are past, and the newer browsers (level 6+) are very compatible for most features.

We've used the example sites from the chapter tutorials for our browser compatibility tests. The first site we tested is the One Tech site used in the Chapter 7 tutorial.

Safari 1.0, Mac OS X

AOL 7.0, Windows 2000

The next site we tested is the Obscura Camera Supplies site used in the Chapter 19 tutorial.

IE 5.2, Mac OS X

Netscape 4.78, Windows 2000

The preceding four images are screenshots from www.browsercam.com. Browsercam offers screenshots from a wide variety of browsers and platforms. You supply a URL and specify which browser/platform combinations you would like for screenshots. You can then save the screenshots you want. Browsercam offers a free eight-hour trial of their service.

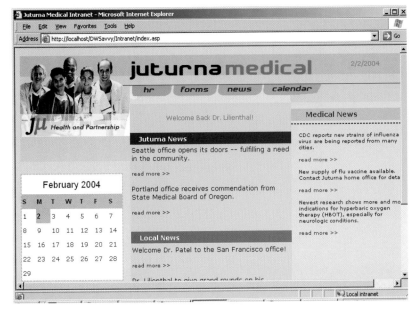

IE 6, Windows XP

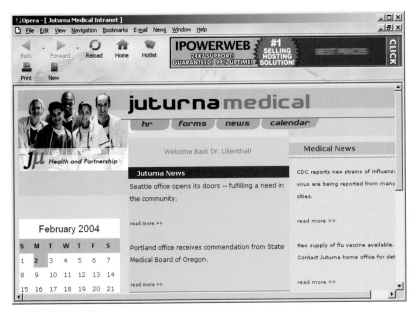

Opera 6, Windows XP

The final site we tested is the Juturna Medical Intranet site from Chapter 28. Although we would expect intranet users to be using the same platform and browser, for this example, we tested the site in two different browsers.

As you can see, our sites appear to be compatible in all the browsers and platforms we tested. However, never assume compatibility—always preview your pages in the browsers your audience is likely to use to view your site.

## CHAPTER 18

Handcrafting Your Code

Dreamweaver is designed to generate code as automatically and efficiently as possible. You can, if you choose, work in Design view only and never look at raw code. If you prefer a more "hands-on" approach to coding, Dreamweaver also offers a powerful, timesaving, and customizable coding environment.

Here are some of the issues we'll be discussing in this chapter:

- ▪ **Setting up your coding environment**

- ▪ **Writing code longhand or with a plethora of shortcuts**

- ▪ **Working with an external or integrated editor**

- ▪ **Working with tag libraries and custom tags**

- ▪ **Debugging your code**

The Ergonomics of Coding

Working with code involves an entirely different approach to the project. You see it as lines of code, whether script files, HTML pages, or database queries. The minute-to-minute habits that define the actual real-world user experience for humans using a piece of software will be different when you are working with code than when you work from a design-centered perspective. So, if you prefer to work directly with code and want to use Dreamweaver as your *coding environment*, set aside a little time (less than half an hour) to decide how you'll view, enter, and edit code.

Viewing the Code

If you plan to do most of your work directly at the code level, then you'll probably work in Code view (or possibly Code and Design view but with the design portion kept pretty short), using Design view only for previewing a page, if that. To choose a view, do one of the following:

- To view just code, select View → Code.

- To view both code and design, select View → Code And Design.

- Click a view icon (Code, Split, Design) from the Document toolbar.

If you're more comfortable viewing design in one window and code in another, use Design view and then choose Window → Code Inspector to display the code in a separate window.

Figure 18.1

Designating code-only file formats

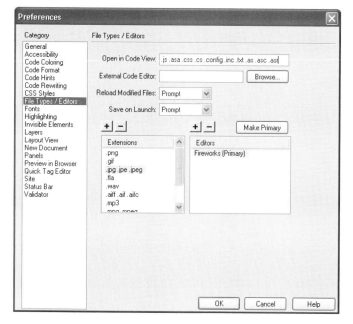

Some documents, such as script files, make sense only in Code view. They don't present visual information and therefore don't have a Design view. You can tell Dreamweaver that files with specific extensions should always be opened in a code-only view (the Code and Design and Design options are disabled). To do so, go to your Preferences dialog box (Ctrl-U/Cmd-U), and in the File Types/Editors category, add the file extension (preceded by a dot, as in .txt) to the list in the Open in Code View box, and then click OK (see Figure 18.1).

PC code jockeys may want to choose the Coder style variation of the integrated MX 2004 workspace (as discussed in Chapter 3).

Code Display Options

If you are new to coding, you can probably skim or skip this section because Dreamweaver's default settings for code display are a good place to start. If you have some longstanding preferences for the look and structure of your code, possibly developed while you were working in some other coding environment or application, then this section will tell you how to overrule the default preferences for such options. First, though, there are a few simple Code view options you can toggle easily from the View → Code View Options submenu shown here.

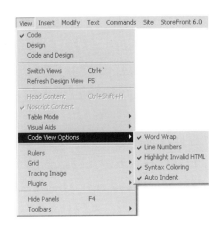

Word Wrap   This option makes sure that lines are visible even if the code window is narrow (see the next section for setting limits for hard word-wrapping when entering code).

Line Numbers   This option shows or hides the numbers. (We like to see them—it makes it easier to troubleshoot the code.)

Highlight Invalid HTML   This is what it sounds like. The only reason you might want to turn this off is if you are deliberately inserting fragmented HTML, as you would do when you are expecting embedded scripts to complete the pages dynamically when they are loading.

Syntax Coloring   This turns the colors on and off. We like syntax coloring. For us, it makes the code easier to read.

Auto Indent   It is a good idea to use this option to automatically structure your code. It keeps things easy to read.

For advanced code-format, structure, and display options, start by going to the Preferences dialog box (Ctrl-U/Cmd-U). The four categories related to Code preferences are clustered together (see Figure 18.2).

The Code Format Category

The Code Format options are generally straightforward, but the context of each may not be clear. Remember, features accumulate in mature software to meet recognized needs for both large and small numbers of users. You

Figure 18.2

Code Format is the primary code-related category in the Preferences dialog box, but there are three others.

These four categories all deal with code.

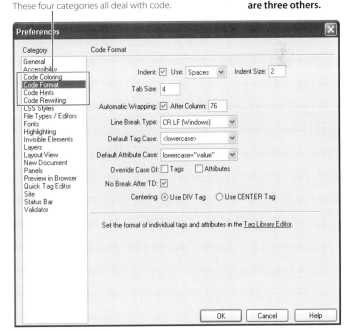

may not care about some of the options, which is fine. Most of them are very easy to understand, but here are a few tips you may find helpful:

Automatic Wrapping After Column   In this context, a column means the width of a single character. The default column number (line length in characters) before word-wrapping is set to 76, which is considered a number safely shy of the old 80-character maximum for certain terminals. Pick a lower number if you like, but we don't recommend going up to or over 80.

Line Break Type   This determines which ASCII character is used to indicate a new line in your code files. Don't necessarily choose the option that corresponds to your own platform! Choose the one that corresponds to the platform of the eventual production (live) server. If you are developing on a PC but going live on a Unix (or Linux) box, for example, choose LF (Unix), not CR LF (Windows).

Default Tag Case and Default Attribute Case   The default tag and attribute case (that is, lower- or uppercase) can be an aesthetic choice, but if you are concerned with forward-compatibility, you should bear in mind that XML and XHTML require lowercase for tags and attributes. Lowercase code is also much easier to read and troubleshoot.

Centering   Centering with the center tag is a backward-compatible approach that should be avoided if possible (this will depend on what browsers your audience uses), but some—those who prefer CSS and standards-compliant code, would consider the div tag not that much more forward-looking, although it is supported by XHTML as of this writing. (CSS mavens would recommend creating a .center style that could be attached to any tag.)

The Code Coloring Category

The next most useful code-related category is Code Coloring. It stores all the color-syntax choices for an incredible number of file types (see Figure 18.3).

To change any one scheme to your own preferences, select it in the Document Type box and click the Edit Coloring Scheme button. In the resulting dialog box, choose any element, change its color (or background color, or make it bold and/or italic), and repeat as often as you like before clicking the OK button to seal the changes.

Figure 18.3

The scrolling Document Type box shows only a partial list of the types of files that Dreamweaver can parse for syntax coloring.

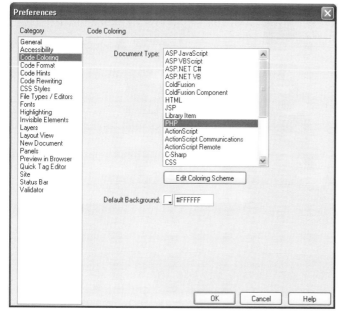

The Code Rewriting Category

Use the Code Rewriting category to control whether and how Dreamweaver will change the code for imported documents (see Chapter 6 for a discussion of this in the context of importing Word or Excel files). By default, Dreamweaver now maintains a "hands off" posture, but you can check Rewrite Code and then specify any of several specific situations in which Dreamweaver is authorized to make changes.

For instance, if you were using an earlier version of Dreamweaver (2.0 or 3.0) to try to help the team speed up some .asp development, you could offer to enter your copy changes directly into the files, using Dreamweaver for the editing and the FTP. At the time when these versions of Dreamweaver were current, the software would clean up imported files by default, and consequently strip all the scripts from your first attempt. We have since learned how to overrule that option, but it is no longer really a concern because now Dreamweaver will not rewrite your code unless you explicitly enable rewriting, and even then, it defaults to excluding a long list of known scripting formats that should not be exposed to this kind of scrutiny (see Figure 18.4).

The Code Hints Category

The Code Hints category mainly enables you to turn off hints (in case you find them annoying) or change the speed with which they pop up as you are entering code (more on this later).

Advanced Setup

If you are going to be working with additional custom tags or libraries of tags that Dreamweaver doesn't inherently recognize, you can extend Dreamweaver by importing tag libraries and custom tags, and you can create and edit custom tags with the tag editors. But, first, a few definitions are in order:

Tag library A collection of tags associated with a programming language or some other custom set of tags, defined with XML or some other convention. The tag library defines how each tag is to be displayed.

Custom tag A tag that is defined by an XML Document Type Definition (DTD) file or schema, or by an external tag library (Dreamweaver supports ASP.NET, JSP, and JRun custom tags).

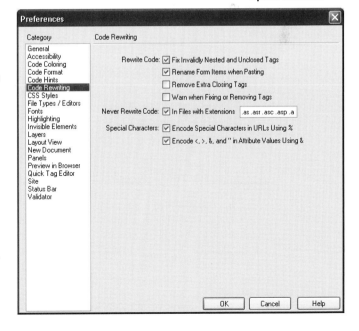

Figure 18.4

You won't accidentally overwrite ASP, JSP, or PHP files (among others) if you leave the Never Rewrite Code option checked.

Tag Library Editor An editor that enables you to make, change, and delete tag libraries and to import custom tags.

> A *tag editor* is something else entirely—it is one of Dreamweaver's many helpful shortcuts for inserting tags, which will be discussed in the next major section of this chapter. The *Quick Tag Editor* is a tool for inserting tags, primarily from Design view.

To work with libraries and custom tags, choose Edit → Tag Libraries. The Tag Library Editor dialog box comes up with the HTML tag library expanded, but you can collapse it to see the base set of libraries that are installed with Dreamweaver (see Figure 18.5).

Making, Editing, and Deleting Tag Libraries

You can make a new library easily. Just click the plus (+) sign at the top of the Tags list box in the Tag Library Editor dialog box and select New Tag Library on the pop-up menu (see Figure 18.6). Then type the library name and click OK. It's immediately added to the list of libraries and made available to HTML files. You can then check off any other file formats that might need access to your new library.

Adding tags to a library is a two-step process—first you add the tags and then you specify the attributes for the tags you've added.

To add tags to your empty new library, click the plus (+) sign and choose New Tags, and then (making sure that the correct library is selected), type a list of tags separated by commas and no spaces, and click OK. Dreamweaver will specify the end tags unless you don't want it to.

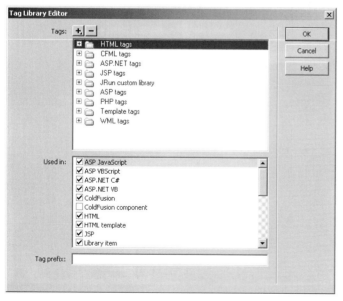

Figure 18.5

The Tag Library Editor dialog box represents Dreamweaver's collected wisdom about how to display many sets of tags with legibility-enhancing structured formatting.

To customize the display of a new tag, decide whether and where line breaks should appear within the tag, and whether the tag should get formatting and indentation, just one or the other, or neither. You can also choose a case for the tag, bearing in mind that XML and XHTML will expect lowercase. If you choose mixed case, you'll have to show Dreamweaver exactly which characters are uppercase and which are lowercase (see Figure 18.7).

To add attributes to a tag, click the plus (+) sign and choose New Attributes, and then (making sure that the correct library and tag are selected), type a list of attributes separated by commas and no spaces, and click OK.

To customize the display and allowable values for an attribute, choose a case (same comments as for tags) and an attribute type. If you choose Enumerated, list the allowable choices in the Values box (see Figure 18.8), and you know the drill (comma, no space between entries).

To delete an attribute, tag, or library, click the minus (–) sign.

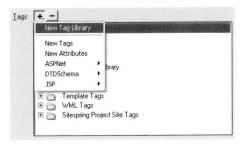

Figure 18.6

Making a new tag library

> Be careful with that minus (–) sign! Dreamweaver gives you a chance to think twice before deleting an entire library, but it deletes tags and attributes without quarreling, and those deletions are irreversible.

Importing Custom Tags

To import a library of custom tags from an external source, click the plus (+) sign and choose one of the ASPNet, DTDSchema, or JSP submenus. Each represents a different custom tag source that Dreamweaver can understand. Choosing Import XML DTD or Schema, for example, brings up a dialog box where you can browse to a source file or enter a URL for an external source. Several modes for importing JSP tag libraries are supported (file, folder, and server), and the ASP.NET option includes the choice of importing only selected tags.

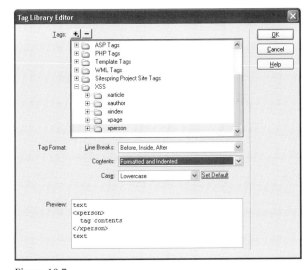

Figure 18.7

Describing the tag format for a new tag

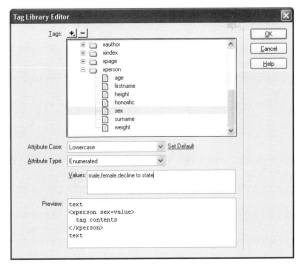

Figure 18.8

Select the case and type of the attribute, and sometimes the allowable values.

When you're finished customizing your tag libraries, click OK.

Writing Code

Despite the color and indentation, code is basically meant to be typed and read as raw, unformatted text. There's a reason that coders have often preferred to do all their word-processing in bare bones text-editing environments. On that level, it's silly for us to be telling you how to write code. You type it in the window. End of story, right? Well, not really. It's true that you will type in code, either most of the time or just some of the time, but you may also cut it from another source and paste it in place, and that's really just the beginning.

> Changes made in Design view always update Code view automatically, but changes made in Code view do not reciprocate. To see code changes reflected in Design view, you must either save the file (generally a good idea anyway—use Ctrl-S/Cmd-S) or refresh the view without saving by clicking the Refresh button in the Property inspector, pressing F5, or selecting View → Refresh Design View. Just choose whatever's easiest for you to remember.

Structuring Your Code

If you aren't using Auto Indent (see the previous major section) or if you want to override the automatic indenting while you're entering code, use Edit → Indent Code to indent the selection or Edit → Outdent Code to push it back.

> In addition to syntax coloring and structured code, be sure to use comments in anything complicated so that others can tell what your intentions are even if you're not around to narrate the code personally.

Using Code Shortcuts

Dreamweaver offers a plethora of shortcut tools to help you insert code. At times, the quantity of these seems almost ridiculous, and to some extent, this wealth of tools represents the software's legacy as products like HomeSite and ColdFusion Studio have been brought into the Macromedia fold and features have been duplicated for compatibility's sake. But there's no harm in it. Chances are you will use three of these approaches from time to time and mostly ignore the rest.

Code Hints While-U-Type

As soon as you type the < symbol, the Code Hints menu pops up.

You can press the Esc key to make this pop-up go away, or you can just start typing and the pop-up Code Hints menu will jump to the tag you appear to be typing. Hit Enter to accept the suggestion at any time. A matching closing tag appears immediately after your insertion point as soon as you close the tag so that you can start typing anything that you need to put between the opening and closing tags. Or, instead of closing the tag, you can type a space and then the Code Hints pop-up menu will show you available attributes. (Code Hints can also show available functions and methods.)

Reference Materials

If you're not sure about what a particular tag is for or what it's supposed to do, Dreamweaver MX 2004 has reference materials for you to read as you code. These materials come from a variety of sources, and after you type in a tag name (such as meta) and press F1, you can read the description of the tag, and how it is to be used, in the Reference panel of the Code panel group (see Figure 18.9). Note that you can also open the Reference panel by right-clicking on the tag and then selecting Reference from the context menu. If you are using the Code Inspector window for entering your code, you can open the Reference panel by clicking on the icon in the Code Inspector toolbar.

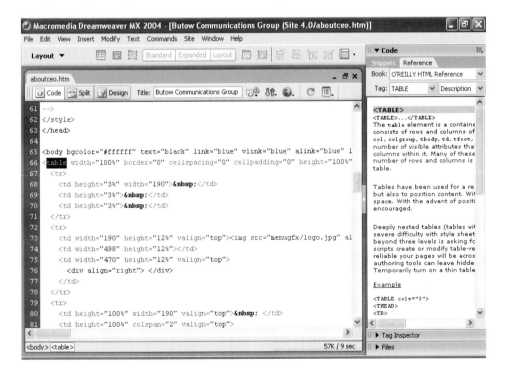

Figure 18.9

The Reference tab in the Code panel group displays information about the tag and its use.

Inserting Tags with the Tag Chooser

To choose and insert a tag directly from a library, press Ctrl-E/Cmd-E or choose Insert →
Tag (or click the Tag Chooser icon in the Common Insert bar) to bring up the Tag
Chooser (see Figure 18.10).

Choose a library and then a tag, and click the Insert button. The flexible Tag Editor dialog box will appear and prompt you for attributes if any are required. If there are only a
few settable attributes for a tag, the Tag Editor dialog box may be compact, as shown here
for the base tag:

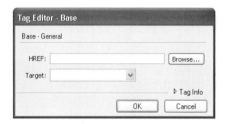

For other tags, multiple categories of options can be applied, including tag-specific
options, style sheets, language, event handlers, "browser version" categories, and so on,
based on the features of each tag.

Click the Close button when you are done inserting tags.

Inserting and Storing Snippets

Just because you want to work with raw code and not in Design view, that's no reason to
turn your nose up at useful shortcuts (such as keyboard shortcuts, as discussed in Chapter 34). Hardcore coders find it useful to maintain a library of boilerplate code samples
that can be pasted in place with very little tweaking. The tool for managing such useful
pieces of code (or *snippets*, as Dreamweaver calls them) is the Snippets panel (the Snippets tab of the Code panel group), which you can bring up with Window → Snippets if
you don't already have it showing.

The panel is seeded with some existing snippets—mostly drawn from the design templates that ship with Dreamweaver.

To insert a snippet, follow these steps:

1. Position the insertion point or select the code you want to surround with the snippet.

2. Browse to the snippet you want to insert, preview it, and then double-click.

To store a new snippet, follow these steps.

1. If you have an example (even if it's just close but not exact) of the entire snippet (including any surrounding material if necessary to get the opening and closing part of the snippet), select it.

2. Then click the New Snippet icon in the bottom-right of the Snippets panel.

3. In the Snippet dialog box that appears (see Figure 18.11), type a name for the new snippet (it has to work as a legitimate filename, so avoid funky characters).

4. Press Tab and type (optionally) a description.

5. Click Wrap Selection if this snippet is supposed to surround the selection or Insert Block if not.

6. Depending on your choice in step 5,

   • Type or edit the opening code in the Insert Before box, and type or paste the closing code in the Insert After box, for wrapping snippets.

   • Type or edit the code in the Insert Code box for block snippets.

7. Decide if the snippet should be previewed in the panel as code or design.

8. Click OK.

Use short bits of dummy copy to indicate replaceable text in snippets. Snippets are not interactive dialog boxes like tag editors. They just insert or surround the selection with whatever you tell them to.

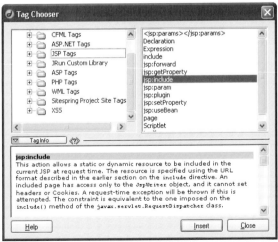

Figure 18.10

The Tag Chooser is overkill for run-of-the-mill tags, but for scripts and complicated attributes you may find it helpful.

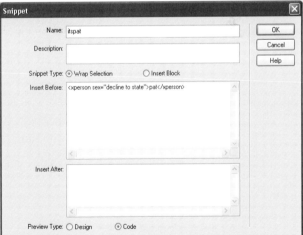

Figure 18.11

If you made a selection first, it will appear in the Insert After or Insert Before box.

DESIGN-ORIENTED SHORTCUTS

Note that you can also insert tags using several shortcuts that are more suited to Design-view editing, all of which are discussed in Chapter 5. These shortcuts include the following:

- The Quick tag editor, for inserting and editing individual tags quickly. This is accessed through a context menu that appears when you right-click on the tag in the tag selector and choose Edit Tag. You can also open the Quick Tag editor in Design view with Ctrl-T/Cmd-T.

- The Text Insert bar, including the Font tag editor and several text formatting icons.

- The Property inspector, which shows status but also enables you to apply formatting and some other attributes quickly.

Tag Selector

If you would rather edit your tags without having to switch to Code View, Dreamweaver makes it easy with the Tag Selector. The Tag Selector is actually a list of tags at the bottom of the Document window. When you select an object on your page, the corresponding tag appears as one of a series of tags, with the selected tag as the rightmost tag in the series and all its parent tags appearing to the left (see Figure 18.12).

Figure 18.12

The Tag Selector appears as a series of tags at the bottom of the Document window.

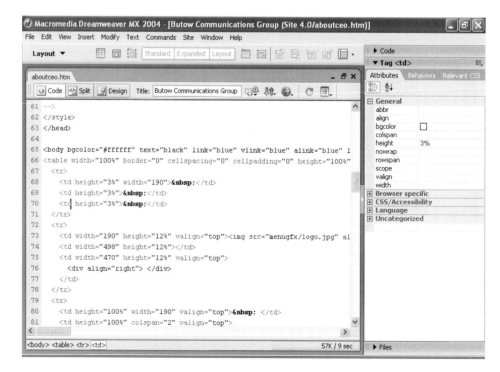

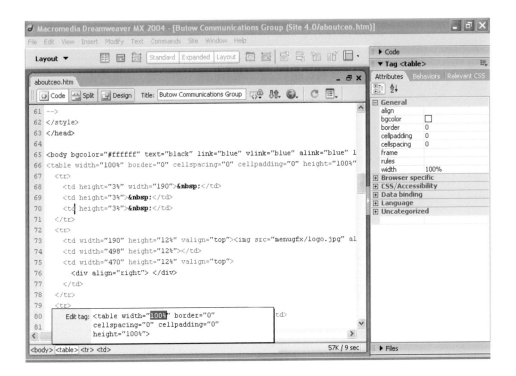

Figure 18.13

The Quick Tag Editor appears above the selected tag in the Tag Selector.

Each tag appearing to the left of the previous one denotes a tag that is higher up in the hierarchy until you reach the highest tag. In most cases, this is the <body> tag since it is one of the top-level tags. If you click on a top-level tag, all you will see in the Tag Selector is that top-level tag. The Tag Selector does not show any tags on a lower level than the current tag.

You can edit a tag in the Tag Selector by right-clicking on it, and then choosing Edit Tag from the context menu. The Quick Tag Editor appears (Figure 18.13) so you can edit the code associated with the tag.

Using the Quick Tag Editor

The Quick Tag Editor appears just above the tag you have selected in the Tag Selector. Here you can edit the tag and its associated code without having to wade through all of the surrounding code. With this unencumbered view of your tag and its associated code, you can make your code changes quickly. When you press Enter after typing your code, the new code appears in the Document window as if you typed it directly in the Code view window.

When you're in Design view, the Quick Tag Editor gives you several more options to choose from. You can click on a location, text, or graphic on your page and then press

Ctrl-T (or Command-T on the Macintosh) to select from one of three editing modes. The mode in which it opens depends on the current selection in Design view, but you can cycle through these three modes by clicking Ctrl-T or Command-T in succession.

The first mode, Insert HTML, lets you add a new HTML tag to a location when you click on an insertion point in your document. The Quick Tag Editor displays with an empty tag. If you move your mouse pointer over the empty tag, a drop-down list appears so you can select the tag you want to add (see Figure 18.14).

Press Ctrl-T (or Command-T) a second time to switch to Edit Tag mode. The Quick Tag Editor displays the code for the selected tag or for the object immediately preceding the insertion point. You can then edit the code (or add new code) directly in the Quick Tag Editor. After you finish editing your code, the Document window reflects your handiwork.

When you press Ctrl-T (or Command-T) a third time, the Quick Tag Editor switches to Wrap Tag mode. This mode "wraps" a selected unformatted paragraph or object, or the paragraph or object directly before the insertion point, in a particular tag. For example, you can click within a regular text paragraph and apply the bold (<b>) tag in the Quick Tag Editor: Your entire paragraph will switch from regular text to bold text just like that.

You can switch back to Insert HTML mode by pressing Ctrl-T/Cmd-T again. Exit the Quick Tag Editor by pressing Esc or by clicking elsewhere in the Document window.

Figure 18.14

The Insert HTML mode of the Quick Tag Editor lets you add HTML code at the insertion point.

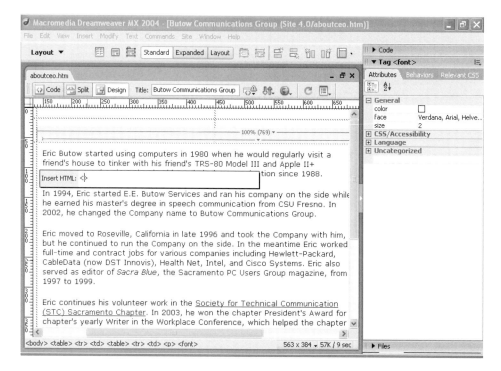

Editing Code

Unless you always type (or insert) your code flawlessly and never need to make any changes, you'll want to know how to edit your code as well. As with code entry, you can edit code by hand, of course, deleting and inserting characters at will, but to avoid further typos and mistakes, consider using these shortcuts.

> To make sure you have the right tags selected before editing them, you can use Edit → Select Parent Tag and Edit → Select Child.

Using the Tag Editor

To edit an existing tag, right-click or Control-click it in the Code view window (or right-/Control-click an object in the Design view window) to access the context menu select Edit Tag. This brings up the Tag Editor window for the selected tag (Figure 18.15). (As discussed earlier in this chapter, access the context menu from a tag in the Tag Selector at the bottom of a document window to gain access to the Quick Tag editor for that tag.)

By default, Dreamweaver colors and indents text so you can see the different levels tags have. For example, a table row (with the tag <tr>) has the <td> tag for each table cell one level below the <tr> tag. Thus, Dreamweaver indents the <td> tags one tab to the right to signify that the <td> tag is one level below, or a child of, the parent <tr> tag.

With this in mind, Dreamweaver figures that you don't want to edit every single child tag (or child of a child tag, and so on) within every single parent tag. So the Tag Editor selects all the code within the parent tag. For example, if you select a table row, Dreamweaver selects all the child tags within the <tr> and </tr> tags. Then Dreamweaver knows what setting options to make available to you in the Tag Editor so you can make changes.

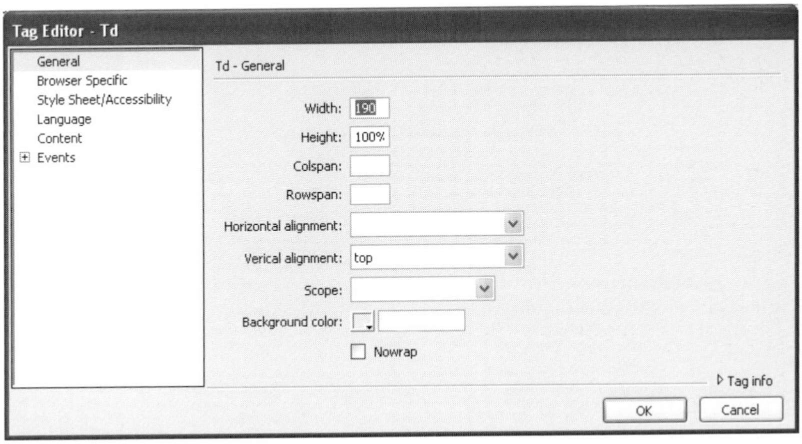

Figure 18.15

The Tag Editor window for editing a table

For example, in Figure 18.15 we see the options available for a table. You can edit the alignment and color; select browser settings; apply style sheets; set the language for the text that will appear in the table; and even add code that performs an action when an event, such as a mouse-click on the table, takes place. In other words, Dreamweaver lets you select from settings related directly to editing the table. Different settings appear for different tags.

When you change the information in the Tag Editor, Dreamweaver adds and modifies the child tags within the parent tags per your settings. So if you're a bit intimidated by editing a lot of code, the Tag Editor breaks down your tasks into manageable chunks in an easy-to-navigate window.

Get Hints

What if you could have each HTML tag available to you as you type your code so you could ensure that you're entering the right code and avoiding mistakes? It's not a dream anymore—the Code Hints feature in Dreamweaver MX 2004 lets you ensure that any tag, attribute, CSS property name, and more are correct as you type your code.

Code Hints are actually pop-up lists that appear as you start typing a tag, attribute, or CSS name. Dreamweaver is smart enough to pick up on what you're writing in your code and to suggest different options for completing your code before you finish typing it. The suggestions appear as a pop-up list as you start to write your code. For example, if you start writing a tag, the list appears when you type the left angle bracket (see Figure 18.16).

Figure 18.16

The Tag Editor list as you edit a table

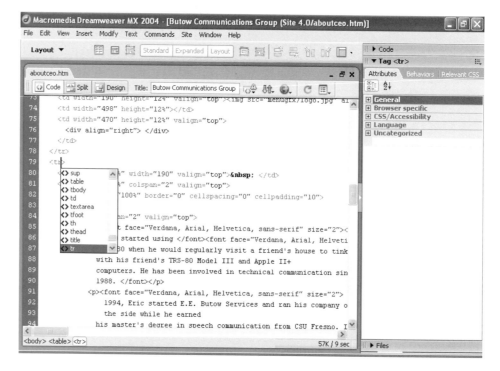

If you enter another character, such as *t,* then the Code Hints list will move to the first entry in the list that starts with <t. Then you can scroll down the list to see if there are any code tags that start with <t that match what you're looking for. Or, if you prefer, you can scroll up and down the Code Hints list to find the tag you want. When you click on a tag from the list (or use your keyboard's arrow keys to select the tag you want, then press Enter), Dreamweaver adds the tag to your code automatically.

Not everyone finds the Code Hints list to be useful. You can turn off Code Hints easily from the Preferences window. When you select Code Hints in the Category list, a number of options are at your disposal (see Figure 18.17). You can determine the timing of the list's appearance (or disable the list entirely), choose what sorts of tags you want to appear in the list, and even add or remove specific tags and attributes from the list by clicking the Tag Library Editor link.

The Tag Library Editor

Click the Tag Library Editor link in the Code Hints window of Preferences or select Edit → Tag Libraries to open the Tag Library Editor. The Tag Library Editor contains the Tags list of all available HTML tags, and this list appears as a folder tree (Figure 18.18). When you click on the arrow to the left of the tag name, all the potential attributes for that tag appear in a list below the tag name.

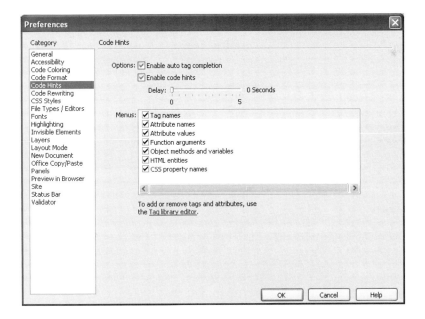

Figure 18.17

The Preferences window Code Hints page lets you change how Code Hints display, or if they display at all.

You can change either the format of the tag itself or the attributes that appear within the tag. When you select a tag or an attribute from the list, the available options display below the Tags list. For example, in Figure 18.18, when you click the tr tag several options become available to change the tag format. If you select an attribute, such as align, the formatting options change. Some tags and attributes have more formatting options than others. No matter what tag or attribute you select, the Preview area at the bottom of the Tag Library Editor window shows you what your new tag will look like.

Figure 18.18

The Tag Library Editor lets you control the format of tags and their attributes.

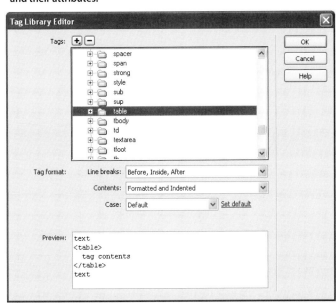

If none of the tags or attributes are what you're looking for, you can take advantage of Dreamweaver's powerful tag customization features and add your own tag or attribute, import another tag library, or import ASP, XML DTD, XML schema, or JSP tags. You can add a tag, attribute, or new tag library by clicking on the plus (+) button just above the Tags list.

Don't like a tag or attribute in the Tags list? Just select the tag or attribute and click the minus (–) button above the Tags list and the tag or attribute goes away. Be careful, though: When you delete a tag, all its attributes are also deleted.

Using the Tag Inspector

To view and edit code in the Tag Inspector, first click on a tag's name or content in Code view, select an object in Design view, or select a tag in the Tag Selector. Then open the Tag Inspector panel group (or select Window → Tag Inspector) and choose the Attributes tab. Click on an icon above the Attributes list to view the attributes in categories or as an alphabetical list. (See Figure 18.19.)

Figure 18.19

View and edit all the current and possible attributes of a tag in the Tag Inspector.

To edit or add an attribute, click in the attribute values column and type a new value, or use the available shortcuts for that attribute, such as a drop-down list of possible values, the Color Picker, browsing to a URL, or selecting a dynamic data source.

BEHAVIORS

When you click the Behaviors tab in the Tag Inspector panel group, you can view a list of behaviors associated with a selected element or block of code (see Figure 18.20). Behaviors are Dreamweaver's built-in JavaScript code blocks. For more details on using behaviors in JavaScript, see Chapter 12, "Incorporating JavaScript Behaviors."

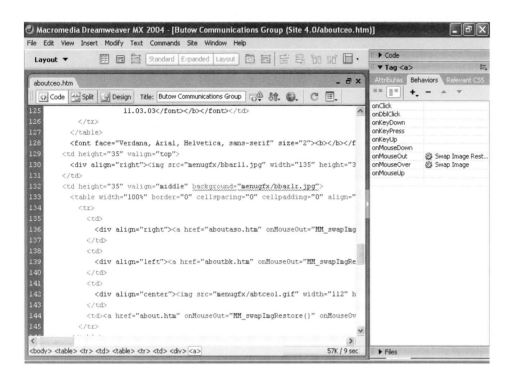

Figure 18.20

The Behaviors panel

The Show Set Events and Show All Events icons are at the top-left of the Behaviors panel. You can choose Show Set Events to view behaviors for the selected tag, or Show All Events to list all available events for the selected tag.

When you want to add a behavior to the selected event, click on the empty cell to the right of the event in the list, and then click the plus (+) button, which is just above the list. A pop-up menu will show you the list of available behaviors you can attach to that event. When you select a behavior, the appropriate dialog box appears that lets you specify the settings for the behavior.

You can change a behavior that's currently in the list by double-clicking on the behavior name next to the event. An editing window appears so you can change the behavior settings. You can also choose a different event by selecting the current event and then selecting a new event from the pop-up menu of possible events for the attached behavior. If you right-click/Ctrl-click on the event name, a context menu appears that includes options for Editing, deleting, and adding a new behavior.

RELEVANT CSS

When you click the Relevant CSS tab, the list of CSS styles in your document displays with a list of properties for each style underneath the CSS styles list. See Chapter 9 for more information about how to use this panel and for more details on Dreamweaver's new CSS features.

Cut, Copy, Paste

While in Code view, you can use the ordinary Cut (Ctrl-X/Cmd-X), Copy (Ctrl-C/Cmd-C), and Paste (Ctrl-V/Cmd-V) shortcuts available in most applications on the planet.

Adding and Converting Code

Dreamweaver MX 2004 makes it easier than ever for you to apply changes to your code on the fly so your code is readable and easy to manage. (If you want to be a professional web developer, having properly formatted code can help you stand out from the crowd.) You can do this in Code view by right-clicking on the block of code or at the insertion point, then choosing Selection in the menu. The Selection submenu appears with several options for tweaking your code.

CONVERT SPACES AND TABS

You can convert spaces to tabs and tabs to spaces by clicking Convert Tabs To Spaces and Convert Spaces To Tabs, respectively, in the Selection submenu. When you convert spaces to a tab, Dreamweaver counts the number of spaces you have in the selected text and converts these spaces to one or more tabs based on the tab size value. When you convert a tab to spaces, Dreamweaver counts the number of tabs and converts them to the appropriate number of spaces based on the tab size value.

> So how do you know what the tab size value is? Open the Preferences window and click Code Format in the Category list to view and change your tab size value settings.

COMMENT AND UNCOMMENT LINES

If you want to change a block of code to a comment, such as a piece of code that is no longer used but which you want to keep as a reference, you can select the code and then select Comment Out Lines from the Selection submenu. When you decide that you want a commented piece of code to lose its comment marks and be an active part of your code again, select Uncomment Lines from the submenu.

INDENT AND OUTDENT

Selecting Indent in the submenu indents the selected code by shifting it to the right. Selecting Outdent shifts the selected code to the left. You can set the size of the indent or outdent in the Preferences window Code Format category.

REMOVE ALL TAGS

You can remove all tags in the selected text by clicking Remove All Tags in the Selection submenu. For example, you can highlight a block of text that is enclosed in one or more formatting tags and remove those tags in preparation for applying a CSS style.

CONVERT LINES TO TABLES

When you have a block of text that you think would look better in a table, you can automatically wrap the text into a table by selecting the text and clicking Convert Lines To Table in the Selection submenu. Dreamweaver places table tags on either side of the selected text without any attributes so you can continue to build your table.

ADD LINE BREAKS

If you want to add line breaks (the <br> tag) to the end of each line in the selected piece of code, all you have to do is click Add Line Breaks from the Selection submenu. Placing line breaks in your code can have unintended consequences for your code's appearance, so you may have to click Undo from the Edit menu more than once to figure out the best way to apply line breaks.

CONVERT THE CASE OF TEXT OR TAGS

All coders like their code to appear a certain way—theirs. Some like all their tags with uppercase text, and others like it in all lowercase text. You may also have some text that needs its case changed, such as a sentence written in all uppercase text you want converted to lower. The Selection submenu gives you the option of converting selected text—both text and tags—to uppercase or lowercase. You can also just convert all tags and the attributes contained within those tags to uppercase or lowercase text and leave the rest of the selected text alone.

Search and Replace

When you need to make global changes to your code, you can use Edit → Find And Replace. See Chapter 6, "Inserting and Formatting Text Content," for more details.

Create CSS Style

If you create an element that has its own attributes, such as a piece of text you use as a heading, you can easily create a CSS style by right-clicking on the object in Design View or the code block in Code view, then selecting CSS Styles in the context menu. In the New CSS Style window that appears, you can choose a selector type, and decide whether you want the style to be available only in the current document or saved as a style sheet that's available to other documents.

Refer to Chapter 9 for more information about how to apply CSS styles to pages and how to manage CSS style sheets.

Code Navigation

If you are working on a script file with functions, you can instantly jump to any function with the Code Navigation button in the Document toolbar of the Code Inspector window (Window → Code Inspector).

Hold down Ctrl (Windows) or Option (Mac) to see all functions in alphabetical order.

REGULAR EXPRESSION SUPPORTED

Regular expressions are a Unix standard for specifying searches with remarkable precision. Like all Unix-type syntax, regular expressions involve a list of teeny (single-character mostly) commands and switches. The Find And Replace box supports regular expression–based searches. Just check the Use Regular Expressions option. For a good online resource about regular expressions beyond the brief introduction in the Dreamweaver documentation, see the website `http://sitescooper.org/tao_regexps.html` (A Tao of Regular Expressions).

Dreamweaver MX and MX 2004 include a Print Code command on the File menu (Ctrl-P/Cmd-P).

Using an External or Integrated Editor

If you have an HTML or plain text editor that you prefer for your coding, Dreamweaver isn't jealous. It will "play nicely" with that external editor. In fact, the Windows version of Dreamweaver MX 2004 comes bundled with HomeSite+, a popular HTML editor now part of the Macromedia family. On the Mac side, Dreamweaver has always closely integrated with BBEdit. Beyond that, you can choose any external editor you want.

Setting Up an Editor

To set up an external editor, go to the Preferences dialog box and choose the File Types/Editors category (see Figure 18.21).

Mac users only must uncheck the Enable BBEdit Integration option to integrate with a different editor.

After you have made the appropriate choice depending on your operating system, browse to the application you want to use.

Figure 18.21

Browse to your preferred external editor.

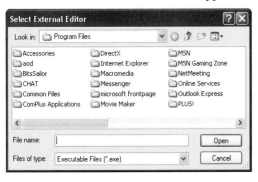

For the Reload Modified Files option, choose Always, Never, or Prompt to determine whether Dreamweaver will automatically reload file changes in the external editor, not do so, or ask you each time.

Similarly, the Save On Launch option determines whether Dreamweaver automatically saves the current file before opening it in an external editor, or never does so, or asks you each time.

Launching an External Editor

To open a file in an external editor (whether "integrated" or not), select Edit → Edit With *external editor name*. When you are finished editing, save the document in the external editor and switch back to Dreamweaver. To change the settings that govern whether Dreamweaver saves the document before you go to the external editor or reloads it when you come back, see the previous section.

Roundtrip HTML

Dreamweaver calls its approach to HTML and code from other sources "Roundtrip HTML." Because it's too easy for software applications to break code inserted externally (especially in the interest of cleaning up the code), Dreamweaver is completely configurable, enabling you to disable code rewriting entirely or for certain file types (as discussed in Chapter 5, "Page Layout," and earlier in this chapter).

Debugging Your Code

If you've got Dreamweaver highlighting any invalid HTML (as discussed at the beginning of this chapter) and cleaning up any imported code, and if you're using tag libraries and choosers and editors and an inspector to insert everything, then your code should all be valid and functional, right? Well, no. You can always insert stuff where it doesn't belong or delete something that breaks a working set of nested tags. For that matter, if you're writing script for applications, there are all kinds of errors you can include in your code undetected.

There are a few things you can do, though, to comb through your code and keep it as clean and bug-free as possible. For example, you can

- Make sure that opening and closing tags are balanced.
- Clean up your HTML or XHTML code.
- Validate your HTML or XHTML code.
- Debug your ColdFusion code.

If you're unfamiliar with debugging concepts, such as setting break points, or stepping through code, then this section of this chapter will not be enough to get you completely up to speed, but if you are familiar with such basic debugging concepts, you can learn how to apply them in Dreamweaver.

Balancing Your Tags and Braces

One quick way to check for egregious errors is to make sure that all of your opening and closing tags are balanced or, in the case of script code, that all of your braces are balanced.

- To balance your tags in an HTML document, select a tag and choose Edit → Select Parent Tag (Ctrl-[/Cmd-[). Repeat this until you arrive at the <html> and </html> tags.

- To balance your braces in a script file, put the insertion point inside a function and select Edit → Balance Braces. The entire expression between the braces will be selected. Repeat this to work your way through surrounding braces.

Formatting Your Code

As you read earlier in this chapter, Dreamweaver makes it easy to change how your code looks via the Preferences window. Unfortunately, there is one drawback: If you have one or more documents already open when you make those changes, those changes won't automatically apply to your open document(s). The changes only apply starting with new files. Never fear, though, for Dreamweaver has you covered.

All you have to do to apply the changes to the document you're currently working on is to select Commands → Apply Source Formatting. This reformats your entire document. If you want to apply the new formatting to only a block of code but leave everything else alone, select the code and then select Commands → Apply Source Formatting To Selection. Only the code you selected will reflect your new format.

Cleaning Up HTML (or XHTML)

You can have Dreamweaver review and clean up all of the HTML in your document at once by selecting Commands → Clean Up HTML. This brings up the Clean Up HTML/XHTML dialog box, as shown here. Dreamweaver can also clean up XHTML, as discussed in Chapter 26, "Controlling Access to the Site."

These options are fairly self-evident but here are a few comments:

- Don't use the (Remove) Non-Dreamweaver HTML Comments option if you tend to insert comments manually, because Dreamweaver will only recognize the types of comments the software itself inserts, such as to mark off areas in templates.

- For the (Remove) Specific Tag(s) option, you can list multiple tags, separated by commas. You only need to list the opening tag of any pair.

- We recommend that you use the Show Log On Completion option so that you can see what Dreamweaver did!

Click OK when you're ready.

If you use Dreamweaver to open an HTML file created in Microsoft Word, use the Clean Up Word HTML command rather than the Clean Up HTML command. For more details, see Chapter 6, "Inserting and Formatting Text Content."

Validating Your HTML Code

Another way to check your code for errors is to validate it.

Validating your code is easy, but it's a crucial step to take before handing anything over. You can also use it as a quick-and-dirty debugging tool to detect errors quickly.

From the Validator category in the Preferences window, choose a document type for your file to be validated against if no DOCTYPE is included—for example, HTML 4.0 or XHTML 1.0 Transitional. If you do include a DOCTYPE (and, for web standards compliance, we recommend that you do), Dreamweaver will validate your page against that DOCTYPE.

Dreamweaver automatically inserts a DOCTYPE in any HTML/XHTML pages it creates.

To validate your HTML code, select File → Check Page → Validate Markup. Dreamweaver will display any errors it finds on the Validation tab of the Results panel (see Figure 18.22).

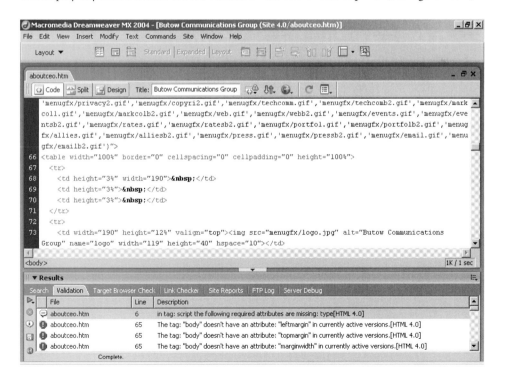

Figure 18.22

Validate your code before you're through.

You can also validate XML files by selecting File → Check Page → Validate As XML. For more information on XML and XHTML, see Chapter 24, "Working with XML and XHTML."

Debugging ColdFusion Code

If you are a ColdFusion developer running Dreamweaver on a PC, then you can use ColdFusion MX 6.1 Developer Edition (included with Dreamweaver MX 2004) as your Dreamweaver testing server (see Chapter 22 for more on working with ColdFusion applications).

To enable debugging in ColdFusion MX 6.1:

- In the ColdFusion MX Administrator, select Debugging and Logging → Debugging Settings to display the Debugging Settings page.

- Check the Enable Debugging check box to enable any selected debugging options.

Debugging information is appended to the bottom of the page when it's previewed in a browser.

As of Dreamweaver MX 2004, the JavaScript Debugger is no longer included in Dreamweaver.

Hands On: Creating Your Own Code

Now it's time to put what you've learned in this chapter into practice. Through adding code in this tutorial you will learn how to apply many of Dreamweaver's coding features, starting with setting your preferences and creating a tag library. Then you get into writing your code and editing, debugging, and validating it so your code is neat and tidy. When you're all done, your final code will appear as shown in Figure 18.23.

Setting Preferences

The first step is to set your preferences to ensure your code looks the way you want it to in the Document window. Follow these steps:

1. Open a new HTML document.

2. Choose Edit → Preferences.

3. Select Code Format from the Category list.

4. Set your indent size to 5 spaces.

5. Set your tab size to 10.

6. Select Code Coloring from the Category list.

7. Click the Edit Coloring Scheme button.

Figure 18.23

Completed tutorial file

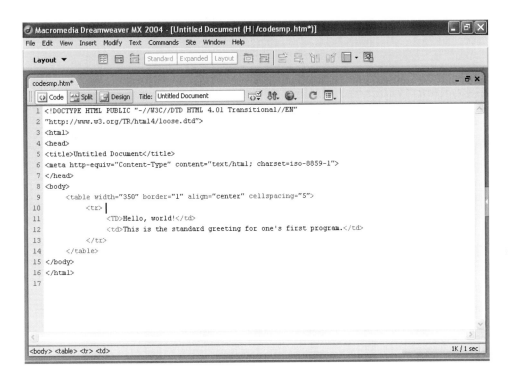

8. Select HTML Table Tags from the Styles For list.

9. Change the text color to green (or a shade of your choosing).

10. Keep the background color as is.

11. Click OK.

12. Click Code Hints from the Category list.

13. Set the Code Hints delay from 0 to 5 seconds.

14. Click OK.

15. Save the HTML file as codesmp.htm.

Editing Tags

Next, you're going to edit the Tag Library to make a couple of tags stand out a bit more in your code.

1. Choose Edit → Tag Libraries, and then choose the HTML tags library.

2. Select the body tag.

3. Set the Contents to Formatted and Indented.

4. Select the `tr` tag.

5. Set line breaks to Before, Inside, After.

6. Click OK.

7. Save the HTML file.

Writing Code

Now it's time to work on your code by creating a small table with two columns. Type the following code between the `<body>` and `</body>` tag, then save your HTML file:

```
<table width=66%" border="1">
<tr><td>Hello, world!</td><td>
This is the standard greeting for one's first program.
</td></tr></table>
```

Editing Your Code

Okay, you've added your code, and now it's time for you to edit it using the Tag Selector and the Tag Inspector. Follow these steps:

1. Place your insertion point in the `<table>` tag.

2. Right-click on the `<table>` tag in the Tag Selector.

3. Click Edit Tag in the menu.

4. In the Quick Tag Editor, set the width of your table to 350 pixels and add cell spacing of 5 pixels.

5. Click OK.

6. Choose Window → Tag Inspector (if the Tag Inspector isn't already open).

7. Click the Refresh button.

8. Place the insertion point inside your `<table>` tag.

9. Expand the General category in the Tag Inspector list.

10. Set the table alignment to Center.

11. Set the background color for the table to Light Blue.

12. Set the width to 80 percent.

13. Save the HTML file.

Browser Check and Validation

Finally, you need to validate your code so you can rest assured that it's ready to publish.

1. Open the Results panel (Window → Results).

2. If you haven't previously configured the Target Browser Check, click the Target Browser Check tab.

3. Click the arrow under the Search tab to display the pop-up menu, and choose Settings.

4. The Target Browser's window opens. Choose the minimum browser versions you want to check.

5. Open the pop-up menu again and select Target Browser Check.

> You can also click the Browser Check icon in the Document toolbar and select Check Browser Support from the pop-up menu. The results display in the Target Browser Check panel in the Results panel group. In addition, you can choose Auto-Check On Open from the pop-up menu to automatically check browser support whenever a document is opened in Dreamweaver.

6. View the results in the Target Browser Check panel.

7. Choose File → Check Page → Validate Markup.

8. View the Validation panel in the Results panel group to verify that no errors or warnings have been found.

9. Save the HTML file.

10. Preview the file in a browser (File → Preview In Browser).

Coding an Application

So you've set up Dreamweaver to build a web application and you've got your coding environment working the way you want it to. Now the time has come to plunge into the heart of any application: the data tables. In Chapter 19, you'll learn how to work with databases, add logic with scripting languages, and insert dynamic content into your web pages.

Database Connectivity

So far you've learned to create static pages, and now we're going to tackle a whole new beast—working with live databases. The amazing thing about Dreamweaver MX 2004 is that this version allows you to do back-end management of your web pages, thereby creating dynamic content powered by a database. No other application integrates databases so well.

This chapter will help you determine whether a data-driven page is right for you, and then it will help you with the nuts and bolts of creating that database-backed page to impress your relatives, friends, and business partners. Topics addressed in this chapter include the following:

- **Using databases in Dreamweaver MX 2004**

- **Working with databases**

- **Mastering web database concepts**

- **Troubleshooting database problems**

Using Databases in Dreamweaver MX 2004

Dreamweaver MX 2004 allows you to pick a development model, make a database connection, and create pages with dynamic content tags in them. Essentially, Dreamweaver MX 2004 creates a framework for building database-driven pages. Database-driven pages allow you to create websites like www.amazon.com, where information is remembered about you and your purchase history, as well as your billing and shipping information. There are two major components of creating an interactive web page: the web server and the database. The interaction with the database will be discussed fully throughout the course of this chapter.

Creating Dynamic Pages

All dynamic pages begin as blank or static pages. First you build a static page, and then you transform it into a dynamic one. Your page might start out simply with some logos, text, links to the rest of your site, and a table. In order to make this information dynamic, you could modify the table to display information gathered from a database. In order to create dynamic data-driven pages, you follow a four-step process:

1. Lay out the page.

2. Define a Dreamweaver MX 2004 data source.

3. Add dynamic content.

4. Add server behaviors.

Server behaviors are functions that you can assign to a web page after you establish a database connection and a query. These could be actions like moving to the next record, deleting a record, or inserting a record.

To build data-driven web applications in Dreamweaver MX 2004, you need the following:

- A web server

- An application server that runs on your web server, or a web server that doubles as an application server, such as Internet Information Server (IIS)

- A development model

- A database

- A database driver that supports your database

System requirements for Studio MX 2004 for Windows are Windows 98 SE, Windows 2000, or Windows XP. PWS (Personal Web Server) is included with Windows 98, and IIS (Internet Information Services) is included with Windows 2000 and Windows XP Pro. There is no support for web servers on Windows XP Home Edition.

Implementing a Web Server

A web server allows you to preview your dynamic web pages "live" from a browser. The web server is important when you have dynamic content because it performs the process of dynamically building your pages. If you aren't creating dynamic pages, then you can simply access the files locally without using a web server. Technically, this process is conducted through an application server, which dynamically generates web pages from code on the server.

> For details on setting up and using a web server, see Chapter 16, "Building Web Applications," and Chapter 30, "Going Live or Delivering the Site."

Now let's look at development models (the programming languages and application servers that let you craft dynamic pages), the differences between them, and what might be the best environment for you to use.

Selecting a Developmental Model

Dreamweaver MX 2004 produces your dynamically updated web pages by placing snippets of code to perform data-related functions. Dreamweaver does its best to hide the details of the code from you so that you don't have to be a programmer to use it. It does, however, support several types of code, so you must pick which type you will use. Your choice of development model will also affect how you connect to the database, which we'll talk more about later in this chapter. ASP, ASP.NET, JSP, PHP, and ColdFusion are development models. Each uses a different programming language and application server:

Active Server Pages.NET (ASP.NET) ASP.NET is a new development model from Microsoft. It works much the same as the ASP model but it supports the Microsoft .NET framework. In order to use ASP.NET you must download and install the ASP.NET framework, which is currently available in two versions from the Microsoft website: version 1.0 (`www.asp.net/download.aspx`) and version 1.1 (`http://msdn.microsoft.com/library/default.asp?url=/downloads/list/netdevframework.asp`). ASP.NET includes support for Visual Basic and C#. C# is a full-featured object-oriented programming language from Microsoft.

Active Server Pages (ASP) Active Server Pages (ASP) was developed by Microsoft. ASP functions can be called from either JavaScript or VBScript, which are two languages used to call code. ASP code is actually executed by the application server, which in the case of ASP is usually IIS. ASP is being phased out in favor of the newer technology, ASP.NET.

Java Server Pages (JSP) Java Server Pages (JSP) are generated by running Java scriplets (which are written in Java, which was developed by Sun). If you choose to have Dreamweaver MX 2004 insert JSP snippets of code, you'll need to have an application server that is able to execute this code. You may still use IIS, but you'll also need a separate application server. Two popular choices are WebSphere (by IBM) and Jserv, an Apache add-on. In addition, you'll need the Java Development Kit (JDK) from Sun. It is a free download, available from `http://java.sun.com/products/`.

PHP Dreamweaver MX 2004 supports the PHP dynamic page development model. You must have a PHP application server installed before you can process PHP pages. The PHP application server can be downloaded from the PHP site (`www.php.net/`). There is a separate file to download depending on whether you use IIS or Apache. Although PHP can actually work with many different databases, Dreamweaver only supports a MySQL database connection for PHP.

ColdFusion ColdFusion is a development system by Macromedia. The language used by ColdFusion is called ColdFusion Markup Language (CFML). As you do for ASP, for Cold-Fusion you need a web server—IIS, for example. You'll also need Macromedia's ColdFusion Application Server.

Once you've selected the development model, you need to specify it, because Dream-weaver inserts code based on the development model type. For example, if you're using JSP, Dreamweaver inserts Java code. The development model is defined as part of the site definition. To select a model, select Site → Manage Sites from the main application window and then click the New button. You can modify the name and location that Dreamweaver MX 2004 uses to store your site. On the Testing Server tab the Server Model drop-down list has seven development model choices: ASP JavaScript, ASP VB Script, ASP.NET C#, ASP.NET VB, ColdFusion, JSP, and PHP MySQL.

Once you've picked a development model, you can also specify the remote folder where Dreamweaver MX 2004 uploads your code. Your code has to reside in the same directory that the web server/application server publishes from in order for it to be viewed. This is generally not the same directory that your project resides in. For example, if you are using IIS, the remote folder could be `c:\Inetpub\wwwroot\test`.

Databases

Databases provide a way to store information that changes between visits to a web page. There are several major vendors of databases, including Microsoft and Oracle.

Microsoft offers two database choices: Access and SQL Server 7 or 2000. Access is good for setting up a small, simple database when you're first learning about how a database works and are not concerned with performance. SQL Server 7 and 2000 are more complicated to set up and run, but they offer more database procedures than Access and they have the power to handle many simultaneous web users.

PICKING THE RIGHT DATABASE

If you are going to create a large site, don't bother even booting up Microsoft Access; go full-steam ahead to a database like SQL Server, or Oracle. If these choices seem too enterprise-wide and too big for your needs, you could use Access with a SQL database engine called MSDE. The MSDE database engine processes SQL commands.

However, enterprise databases like SQL Server give you programming and business logic within the database (often referred to as stored procedures). Picking the right database is important because you don't want a lot of rework if you make significant changes to your pages.

In addition, Oracle offers their 9*i* and 10*g* databases, which support many users as well as complex logic that can be built into the database. SQL Server and Oracle9*i* fight for major website dominance, but currently Oracle is the industry leader for busy websites.

MySQL is another database option that you should consider. MySQL is available for free from `www.mysql.com/downloads/index.html`. It's available for free because it's open source, and it is supported on the Mac OS X, Windows, and Linux. MySQL supports ODBC connectivity. ODBC is useful because Dreamweaver MX 2004 also supports ODBC.

Oracle is a more robust system, but also more complicated and pricey compared to free MySQL. In addition Oracle requires more resources, including CPU and memory. If you're just starting out, you probably want to use Access or MySQL.

Drivers

Dreamweaver MX 2004 builds pages that access the database through one of the three standard protocols described here. The drivers tell Dreamweaver MX 2004 how to "talk" to each type of database. You can think of them as translators.

ODBC The most common and flexible way to build pages is by using Open Database Connectivity (ODBC). ODBC connections are managed under the Windows ODBC Connection Administration screen. Database vendors provide ODBC drivers with their database to allow easy access by applications. Dreamweaver MX 2004 supports any database that provides an ODBC driver.

OLE DB ASP and ASP.NET applications can talk to databases through a standard called Object Linking and Embedding database (OLE DB) or through ODBC. OLE DB connections are generally faster than ODBC and are available for most databases. OLE DB can be used with Windows NT, 2000, and XP.

JDBC JSP applications talk to databases natively through Java Database Connectivity (JDBC). If your database supports JDBC directly, this is the fastest way to go. Oracle and

IBM's DB2 provide JDBC drivers. For compatibility, Sun also provides a bridge driver that translates JDBC into ODBC, thereby allowing you to use any ODBC-supported database. See `http://industry.java.sun.com/products/jdbc/drivers` for more information on JDBC drivers available from Sun.

> ColdFusion accesses the database using the same methods as JSP. PHP uses a MySQL-specific database interface, and a MySQL driver.

Using a Macintosh

If you're using a Macintosh, you will use a Java Database Connectivity (JDBC) driver to connect to an Access database, or any Open Database Connectivity (ODBC) data source, located on a Windows server. If you don't have access to a database with a JDBC driver, you can search a list of JDBC drivers and vendors on the Sun Microsystems website at `http://industry.java.sun.com/products/jdbc/drivers`. The more-popular JDBC database drivers are those from Oracle and Microsoft.

The Application Panel Group

The Application Panel Group includes the Databases, Bindings, Server Behaviors, and Components panels. In this section, we'll review the first three panels in this group— the Components panel is covered in Chapter 20, "Working with ColdFusion," and in the Web Services sections of Chapter 25, "Emerging Technologies."

The Databases Panel

When you begin building a data-driven page, you need to define at least one data source. The *data source* is the description of the database that you will use to query and store information. The data source definition includes all of the information that Dreamweaver needs to access the database and a name for the connection. Required information includes the type of connection, such as ODBC, OLE DB, or JDBC; the database name; and the login.

Any data source that you define is added to your list of data sources in the Databases panel, and is available to you from the Bindings panel and the Server Behaviors panel. To define a data source, follow these steps:

1. Open the Databases panel; if it isn't already open on your screen, select Databases from the Window menu.

2. From the plus (+) sign menu, select Data Source Name (*DSN*). This opens a window in which you can select a DSN.

3. Click the radio button to use a local DSN, which is defined on your local computer instead of on a remote server.

> If you're using a Mac, the radio button should be clicked for using DSN on testing server.

4. Select a DSN to use from the DSN drop-down list. Dreamweaver uses the standard naming convention where connection names start with "con" or "conn." For example, conTrio could be a name of a DSN.

5. DSN points to ODBC database connections. If you want to create your own DSN, click the Define button on the Data Source Name window. This button is a shortcut to the Windows Control Panel's ODBC Data Sources applet, which defines DSNs. However, you don't have to define one since Macromedia provides a sample Microsoft Access database called Trio, as designated in the Data Source Name field of the ODBC Microsoft Access Setup window (see Figure 19.1).

6. After you define your data source, it is a good idea to test your database connection definition by pressing the Test button.

> For details on creating your own DSN, see Chapter 26, "Controlling Access to the Site."

If you've chosen to develop in JSP, you'll have more choices when you create a new database. These choices will include Oracle, MySQL, IBM DB2, SQL Server, and Sun's JDBC-to-ODBC driver. Each of these drivers requires you to enter some information in the URL field. The required information needs to be enclosed in brackets. For example, the Sun ODBC driver requires that the ODBC DSN be entered in the URL field where it says "odbc dsn"—for the Trio DSN, you would type `jdbc:odbc:[Trio]` for the actual entry.

Figure 19.1
ODBC Microsoft Access Setup window

The Bindings and Server Behavior Panels

In order for you to manage the dynamic objects on your web pages, you'll need to use the Bindings and Server Behaviors panels.

The Bindings and Server Behaviors panels are used to define data driven objects for your web page. The current server model is displayed in these panels. For example, "ASP-VBScript" represents an ASP server model using VBScript to call the ASP functions. The plus (+) and minus (–) buttons of each tab are used to add and remove data objects and bindings.

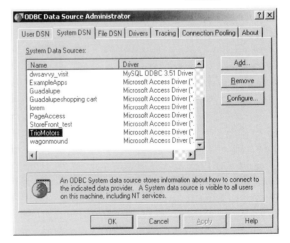

Data binding allows you to define the sources of data for your dynamic content; server behaviors allow you to move through and manipulate that data. The Binding and Server Behavior panels are the reference for the dynamic data that is being used on the current page. You'll need to set up a query on the Bindings panel before you can add server behaviors to your page. Figure 19.2 displays a Recordset in the Bindings panel.

Figure 19.2

The Bindings panel

The Server Behaviors panel lists existing server behaviors that are present on the current page that you are editing. To remove an existing server behavior from a page, select the server behavior and press the minus (–) button. You'll be using the Server Behaviors panel to insert dynamic content later in this chapter.

Defining a Recordset

Before you can work with the data from a table that is made available through a Data Source, you must define a recordset. Databases group collections of information in tables. A recordset is a set of data resulting from a query of one or more database tables, and it specifies which table and columns will be selected when you retrieve data.

To define a recordset, select RecordSet (Query) from the plus (+) sign menu on the Bindings panel. Your choices for columns include All or selecting which ones you want to include.

The final parameter on the RecordSet definition screen is the Sort parameter. This parameter allows you to select the order in which records are returned. The Result columns and Ascending or Descending can be selected.

Defining a Database Filter

Once you have selected the table, you can further limit the records that are returned by defining a database filter. Database filters allow you to specify which records of a recordset you are interested in—otherwise you get everything in the table. The filter is the same as the WHERE clause used in the Structured Query Language (SQL). By using this filter/clause, you limit the rows returned from a database query.

Dreamweaver gives you the choice of using their GUI to select the WHERE clause or specifying the SQL WHERE clause yourself. We'll talk more about using SQL to do an advanced query in "Exploring SQL," later on in this chapter.

The GUI allows you to select not only which column to filter by, but also the type of comparison, and where the comparison value comes from. Possible sources include a URL parameter, a form variable, or an entered variable.

Live Data View

You can preview and edit your dynamic pages by using Live Data view. To open Live Data view, click the Live Data view icon on the Document toolbar or choose View → Live Data. You'll see a preview of dynamic content in the Design View window.

If the application server has any problems returning a page, a warning box will display with suggested sources of errors and possible solutions. Should you encounter problems using the Live Data feature, a good site to check for troubleshooting information is www .macromedia.com/support/ultradev/ts/documents/common_server_errors.htm. Even though this article was written for Dreamweaver UltraDev, it's still applicable to Dreamweaver MX 2004 and application server problems. These tips also apply to problems that you might encounter while you are viewing the pages directly from your web server.

For additional information on using Live Data, see Chapter 21, "Working with ASP."

Next, we'll introduce the concept of adding dynamic content to your page, including radio buttons, images, lists, and text.

Adding Dynamic Content to Your Page

Once you've defined a database connection or another source of dynamic data such as a session variable, you may want to include some dynamic content on your page. If you are in Live Data view, you will see the dynamic text as soon as you enter it. Otherwise, you'll see a placeholder that describes the data source of the text.

In this section we discuss the various types of dynamic content that can be added to your page. These include dynamic text, lists or menus, radio buttons, and images. All of these items can be customized by database information.

Inserting Dynamic Text

The simplest dynamic object to work with is dynamic text. To insert dynamic text into a page, do the following:

1. Select the Bindings tab from the Application panel group. You can also get to this window by selecting Bindings from the Window menu.

2. Select the data source from the list of available sources. In the case of a recordset, select the column of the recordset to include.

3. Select the text to replace or the point to insert your dynamic text from the Design view of your page.

4. Click the Insert button or simply drag the data source from the Bindings panel to the insertion point.

Inserting Dynamic List/Menus

What if you want to dynamically change the contents of a list or menu in your page? No problem; just follow these steps.

1. Insert a list/menu item into your page.

2. From the Server Behaviors panel, click the plus (+) sign.

3. Select Dynamic Form Elements → Dynamic List/Menu.

4. A dialog appears in which you must select the recordset as well as the fields that will populate both labels and values (see Figure 19.3).

5. Make your selections and click OK.

Inserting Dynamic Radio Buttons

What if you want to dynamically set whether a check box is checked based on a data source? An example of this is if you need to have a radio button on your page indicate which department an employee is part of. The radio button's value defaults to the value that matches the database column. By using the default database value, the user won't have to change the selection. To do so, you'll need to specify the data source and the value you want to see in it for the check box to be checked. Do the following to set the initial value:

1. Insert a radio button item into your page.

2. From the Server Behaviors panel, click the plus (+) sign.

3. Select Dynamic Form Elements → Dynamic Radio Buttons. A dialog box appears from which you can select the recordset as well as the fields that will populate both labels and values (as shown in Figure 19.4).

4. Make your selections and click OK.

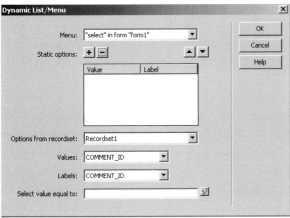

Figure 19.3

Select a recordset from the drop-down list.

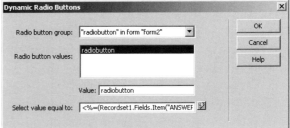

Figure 19.4

Dynamic Radio Buttons dialog box

Inserting Dynamic Images

Oracle allows you to store binary images to display on your web page, but Dreamweaver doesn't allow for this functionality, which means that you must keep the images on the web server and use your database to figure out which image to use. Once you have your images on the web server, you can set up Dreamweaver to dynamically generate the image source path for the image you want. First you'll need to store the filenames of the images in a table before they are viewable by the end user. You can then add the image tag to your site by doing the following:

1. Add the image by selecting Image from the Insert menu.

2. Click the Data Source check box.

3. Select the column that contains the image location information (as shown in Figure 19.5).

An example of what might be in your Image Source database column is Sales.jpg if the department is Sales and Marketing.jpg if the department is currently Marketing. Both Sales.jpg and Marketing.jpg must be in the same directory, and that directory must be specified in the static part of the image path. You can also simply store the path to the image in the Image Source column rather than just the filename.

Now that we've added dynamic content, you're probably wondering how to get rid of it if you decide to revamp your site. You can either delete content, or change it.

Figure 19.5

Select Image Source dialog box with data sources option

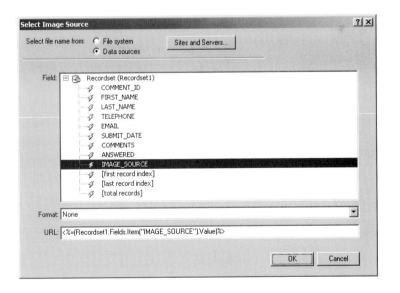

Changing or Deleting Dynamic Content on Your Page

Often, we'll insert content on our web page that needs to change, or be deleted completely. The easiest way to change the dynamic content on your page is to select it from the Server Behaviors panel (as seen in Figure 19.6). When you double-click an entry, you are allowed to edit its properties. And by selecting an entry and clicking the minus (–) sign, you can delete a Server Behavior.

Defining a Search and Result Page Set

After you've added your dynamic content, you need to consider how your users will be accessing your website data. Users may want to specify parameters for their search, and then they'll want to see a page with results. For example, say you're searching through the employee records and you want to see all the records that match a last name. You would create this type of interaction for the user by defining a search and results page set.

A typical web page interaction for retrieving database records is to have your user specify search parameters on a search page using a form. This page, which we'll call the search page (it's actually just taking the search parameters), then calls the results page with the user's search criteria sent as URL parameters. The results page does the actual database query.

The results page takes the parameters from the search page and plugs them into the filter section (WHERE clause) of a recordset. Depending on how you set up your results page, you can display one record or a whole set of records at one time. The results page can also be a stepping-stone to viewing details of a record or record deletion page.

Setting Up the Search Page

To set up your search page, start with a new page, preferable with "search" in its name. This page will need a form object to contain one or more parameters with which the user will search. You should change the names of the variables for each form object to reflect what the fields will hold. This makes it easier to match up the parameters when you define your recordset filter.

Figure 19.6
Server Behaviors panel

If you have only one search parameter, you can use Dreamweaver MX 2004's simple Recordset query on the results page. Otherwise, you'll need to use the advanced SQL WHERE clause.

You'll also need to include a search button on your form for users to press when they have finished entering their parameters. The form needs to have the destination page set in its parameters and a submission type of GET.

Setting Up the Results Page

To set up your results page, start with a new page. It helps if you include "results" some-where in its name. Add the recordset to the results page by selecting Recordset (Query) from the Add (+) menu of the Bindings panel. Select all of the columns that you want to be part of your recordset. If you have only one search parameter, you can specify it using the simple version of the recordset definition window. If you have multiple search param-eters, you'll need to use the advanced WHERE clause to add all of them. Be sure to specify URL parameter as the source of your filter parameters.

You can now add the Recordset field to a table row as described earlier in the "Inserting Dynamic Text" section. If you'd like to use a Repeat Region, you can also set that up to dis-play more than one record at a time. A Live Preview, accessed by the Live Data command in the View menu of the results page, displays the first record or records of a recordset. Up until this point, you may have been using a sample database, such as the Trio database that comes bundled with Dreamweaver MX 2004. You will now learn how to set up your own database.

Designing Your Database Schema

A *database schema* is a set of user-defined tables and columns that holds all the dynamic information that your website uses. Because this is referred to so often, it is vital that you lay out the database tables correctly. In this section, you will see how to lay out your data-base tables. If you don't design your database properly, you will experience problems not only while you are developing your site, but also with the end user performance.

Grouping Data Together into Tables

You should group the data that you are collecting logically. For example, if you are collect-ing human resources information, you will want to group data like the following:

Employee	Dependents	Department
Employee ID	Employee ID (links to the Employee table)	DeptID (links to the Employee table)
First Name	DeptID (links to the Department table)	Department Name
Last Name	First Name	Head of Department
Gender	Last Name	Location
Start Date	Gender	
DeptID(links to Department table)	Relationship to Employee	
Extension	Birth Date	
Birth Date		
Home Phone		
Supervisor ID (links to another entry in Employee table)		

In our example, we broke up the information to allow employees to have multiple dependents without duplicating all of the employee information for each dependent entry. Likewise, department-specific information is stored only once for each department, and only the name of the department needs to be stored with the employee record. In your database, try to find redundant data and put it in a separate table, as we did in this example. Setting up your database in this way eliminates performance problems, as well as page errors.

However, there's more to defining tables than just the column names—we also need to define how the tables are accessed and the type of data they store.

Primary Keys

Each table should have a field that is used by default to look up the rest of the entries in the table. This field is called the Primary Key field and it usually has a unique value for each record in the table. For the employee table, the primary key is the Employee ID because each employee has a unique employee ID. This unique ID streamlines the lookup process. For example, the employee ID can also be used to look up an employee's information in another table such as the Dependents table.

Data Types

Each column in a database table has a data type associated with it. The most common types are character strings, numbers, dates, and Booleans. When you create a table, either through a GUI interface or using SQL, you will need to specify the types for tables.

Boolean logic is a form of algebra in which all values are reduced to either TRUE or FALSE. For example, the expression 3 < 7 (3 is less than 7) is considered Boolean because the result is TRUE. Any expressions that contain relational operators, which the less-than sign (<) is, are Boolean. The following operators are Boolean operators: AND, OR, XOR, NOR, and NOT.

Let's use an employee table as an example. You can see in Table 19.1 that the Employee ID has a data type of Number.

Table 19.1 **Employee Table**	COLUMN	TYPE OF DATA	SQL SERVER TYPE
	Employee ID	Number	NUMBER
	First Name	Character String	VARCHAR(30)
	Last Name	Character String	VARCHAR(30)
	Gender	Character ('M' or 'F')	CHAR
	Start Date	Date	DATE
	Dept ID	Character String	NUMBER
	Extension	Number	NUMBER
	Birth Date	Date	DATE
	Home Phone	Number	NUMBER
	Supervisor ID	Character String	VARCHAR(30)

> The number specified after VARCHAR is the maximum length of the string that the database
> will store.

Dreamweaver MX 2004 attempts to isolate you from the language used to query the
database, which is fine, but you should have some basis in understanding the language
used, so we will now briefly discuss SQL.

Exploring SQL

SQL describes both Database Manipulation Language (DML) and Database Definition Language (DDL) operations in a standard way. DML operations are instructions to add, update,
or delete data rows. DDL operations instruct the database to create or delete database
objects, such as the tables and indexes that are used to speed up access to rows in a table.

In this section you'll learn how to create and drop database objects such as tables and
indexes. You'll also learn how to add and remove data from the database tables.

Creating and Dropping Tables with SQL

Dreamweaver considers SQL to be an advanced option, but don't worry—with a little
practice, it's really quite simple. Let's start with an example of a DDL statement that is
being used to create the employee table in SQL.

```
CREATE TABLE employees
(employee_id      NUMBER,
 first_name       VARCHAR(30),
 last_name        VARCHAR(30),
 gender           CHAR,
 start_date       DATE,
 dept_id          VARCHAR(30),
 extension        NUMBER,
 birth_date       DATE,
 home_phone       NUMBER,
 supervisor_id    VARCHAR(30)
)
```

The column names have their spaces replaced by underscores because spaces are not
allowed in user-defined database names in some database management systems.

> You will need to verify which data types and naming formats can be used in the specific data-
> base management system you're using.

The case of the text in the statement is driven more by convention. Commands and
keywords are typed in caps while user-defined names, such as the table name and column

names, are typed in lowercase. Typically, databases consider table and column names to always be uppercase unless they are enclosed in double quotes when defined, but it's best not to use the mixed-case names.

> If you learn SQL, your website can have more elaborate interactions. Learning how to write SQL or Stored Procedures may be difficult at first, but in the long run it will pay off because you will have snazzy, complicated web pages!

To remove the Employees table with a SQL command, execute the following:

```
DROP TABLE employees;
```

Remember to use this command with caution because once you drop a table it is permanently removed. You might need to remove a table if you've decided to split up the information in one table into two tables. You may find that as you add information to a table that it becomes clear that several tables should represent that information.

Creating and Dropping Indexes with SQL

A *database index* is a special database object that speeds up access to rows in database tables if it is given queries on the indexed field. The nuts and bolts of an index are built using a b-tree (binary tree index). We will not go into too much detail here about how this works because you are not required to know how to use it. What is important about indexes is that they speed up access to rows. The downside of using indexes is that they use more database space and take up additional processing time when you are adding records. To create an index that accelerates querying up rows from the employee table based on first name and last name, you would use the following query:

```
CREATE INDEX employee_name
            ON employees (first_name,
                                    last_name);
```

If you've created an index that you aren't really using, delete it to release its resources and to speed up inserts into the database. To delete the employee_name index we just created, execute the following command:

```
DROP INDEX employee_name;
```

In general, the syntax to drop an index is

```
DROP INDEX [index name];
```

If you drop a table, all indexes associated with it are automatically dropped.

Selecting Rows from a Table

Now that we've gone over the basics of how to create database objects with SQL, we'll move on to selecting data from an existing table. The command that is used to select data is naturally called SELECT. The following is the basic syntax for the SELECT command:

```
SELECT [COLUMNS]/[*]
FROM table
[WHERE] column=value;
```

To select the employee name and phone extension from the Employees table, use the following:

```
SELECT first_name,
            last_name,
            extension
    FROM employees;
```

Figure 19.7

Recordset dialog box

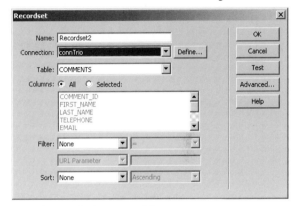

Dreamweaver lets you build SELECT queries by using the filter portion of the Recordset definition screen, an example of which is shown in Figure 19.7. You can use the more advanced and flexible WHERE clause of the SELECT statement by clicking the Advanced button of this screen.

The Advanced Recordset dialog box, shown in Figure 19.8, shows the actual SQL query that Dreamweaver is using for the current filter. You can modify the text in the SQL window directly, or you can use the Database Items tree view at the bottom of the Advanced Recordset dialog box to select items to be included (the Select button), limited by (the Where button), or the order in which records are returned (the Order By button). The Database Items tree and these action buttons are present to help you write the SQL query.

Figure 19.8

Viewing a SQL query in the Advanced Recordset dialog box

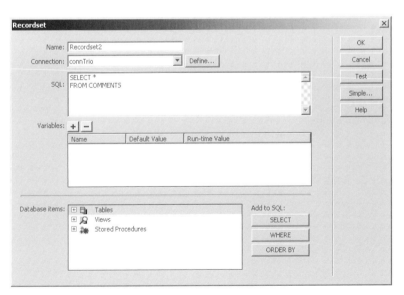

> In order to streamline your process, you should write your database code in your database. Ask any Oracle or SQL Server guru and they will tell you that it's handier to write the code in the database instead of in Dreamweaver because, by doing so, you keep your code in the application instead of on a web page. If you end up making a platform change down the road, all of your code won't have to be rewritten.

Inserting Rows into a Table

To insert rows into a database table, use the SQL command INSERT. INSERT uses the following syntax:

```
INSERT INTO table_name (column1, column2,...)
                VALUES (value1, value2,....)
```

For example, to add an employee to our Employees table you could use the following statement:

```
INSERT INTO employees (employee_id,
                       first_name, last_name, gender,
                       start_date, dept_id, extension,
                       birth_date, home_phone, supervisor_id)
         VALUES (1,
                 'Bob','Smith','M',
                 '13-NOV-2001','Engineering',3923,
                 '11-JAN-1950','(612)823-2312',2);
```

This statement creates an employee whose name is Bob Smith and who works in the Engineering department. The list of columns can be omitted if you specify the values in the same order as they are listed in the table definition and you provide all of the values.

Deleting Rows from a Table

Now that you have added rows to your database table, you may wish to delete some. This can be done with the SQL DML command DELETE. DELETE uses the following syntax:

```
DELETE FROM table_name WHERE column_name = value;
```

The DELETE command syntax is very similar to the syntax of the SELECT command except matched rows are deleted instead of displayed. To delete the row we just added, execute the following:

```
DELETE FROM employees WHERE employee_id = 1;
```

Though we could have also specified the WHERE clause as first_name = 'Bob', it is safer to use the primary key, which we know is unique. Otherwise, we could end up unintentionally deleting all employees with the first name of Bob.

Now that you've worked with database objects, which make up a database schema, we'll talk about how to manipulate data from the web page.

Manipulating Database Records

Records are generally displayed as collections of dynamic database text on your web page. By default, only the first record of a recordset displays on your page. Server behaviors are used to display and manipulate database records. As you add server behaviors to your page, they appear in the list of in-use server behaviors in the Server Behaviors panel.

We will now discuss inserting and removing database records; the database would be useless if you didn't have the ability to add and remove data from it.

Inserting Database Records

You might want to give your users the ability to add records to the database. For example, in the employee database scenario that we were discussing earlier, a manager might want to add a new employee.

To insert database records, you would need to perform the following steps:

1. Set up a page with a form that has fields for all of the columns you want entered.

2. Add the Insert Records Server Behavior from the Server Behaviors panel. In the Insert Records window, you will be able to define which table you will be adding to, the page you want to go to after you perform the insertion (which should inform the user that the insert was successful), and the appropriate HTML form's field to database table column that is mapped during insertion. This mapping defines which field in the form contains the data for each database column when inserting the data.

3. For each field in the form, select the data type from the Dreamweaver MX 2004 drop-down list.

4. Click OK to add the Server Behavior to your page.

Dreamweaver also provides an Application Object called Record Insertion Form Wizard that further automates the process of building pages to insert records. The Record Insertion Form Wizard asks for the same information as the Insert Records server behavior, but it also creates the form for you.

Removing Database Records

You might also want to give your users the ability to delete a record. Using our employee database example, this scenario might arise—an employee leaves the company and you want to delete that record from the Employees table. Typically, such a deletion is done in a multistep process:

1. Create a new page by selecting File → New. This will be your Search page. The simplest search page simply displays all records from a recordset as deletion candidates.

2. From the Server Behaviors plus (+) sign pop-up menu, select Go To Detail Page. The page must have a Go To Detail Page Set server behavior to launch the delete page.

3. In the Go To Detail Page window, leave Link: as Create New Link. This tells Dreamweaver MX to create the link for you that indicates the deletion.

4. Set Detail Page to `delete.asp` by entering **delete.asp**.

5. Select Recordset1 from the Recordset drop-down list. Then select Code from the Column drop-down list. This tells Dreamweaver where to get all of the details for the record you are about to delete.

6. From the Site window, double-click `delete.asp` to open the delete page. Dreamweaver will have already added the code to display the record.

7. To add a Delete button, you must add a form to hold it and choose a location for it. To do so, click to the right of the table of information for the displayed record and select Insert → Form → Form. A new form appears below the record.

8. To Add the Delete button, select Button from the Form submenu of the Insert menu.

9. In the Properties inspector window for the button, change Label from Submit to Delete.

10. You'll now add the Delete Record server behavior by selecting Delete Record from the Server Behaviors plus (+) sign menu. The Delete Record Server Behavior window is shown in Figure 19.9.

11. In the Delete Record server behavior window, select your database connection from the Connection drop-down list.

12. Then select which table to delete from by selecting it from the Delete From Table drop-down list.

13. Select the recordset from the Select Record From drop-down list that you used in the search page.

14. Select the unique key column from the Unique Key Column drop-down list. This corresponds to the key value that your delete page used to display the record. The Delete By Submitting drop-down list should specify the form name to which you added your delete button.

Figure 19.9

Delete Record dialog box

15. Specify the page to which you want to go to in the After Deleting, Go To field. If the deletion was accomplished successfully (without a database error), you will be sent to the page you specify here. The detection of database problems is handled for you by the server behavior.

16. Click OK to add the server behavior. Your delete page is now complete.

Dreamweaver also provides you with the ability to change database records through stored procedures.

Stored Procedures

Dreamweaver MX 2004 includes support for database stored procedures. *Stored procedures* are pieces of code that reside within the database. A stored procedure can take parameters, and when executed, it modifies data in the database. Stored procedures also have the advantage of being able to execute programming logic, such as conditional statements, whereas plain SQL cannot. Not all databases support stored procedures, however. Specifically, Oracle and SQL Server do; Access and MySQL do not, although the next major release of MySQL will support them.

> How you create stored procedures varies by database and is beyond the scope of this chapter. To learn how, consult a database administrator or your database's documentation.

Dreamweaver displays available stored procedures in the database on the Database tab of the Application panel group. The stored procedures appear under the tree branch called Stored Procedures.

The way that you add a stored procedure to your page varies slightly depending on the development model you are using. In general, you should follow these steps:

1. Go to the page that you want to add the stored procedure call to and select Command (Stored Procedure) from the pop-up menu that appears when you click the plus (+) sign of the Bindings panel.

2. From the Command dialog box's Connection drop-down list, select the database where the stored procedure you want to add resides.

3. Choose Stored Procedure from the Type drop-down list. This tells the Command dialog box that you want to execute a stored procedure.

4. Select the stored procedure to call from the Stored Procedures tree branch in the Database Items box. This tells Dreamweaver which procedure to call.

5. If your procedure requires parameters, associate them in the Variables table to variables from your page. For each variable, click the plus (+) sign and enter the name and Run-Time Value (which variable your form puts the value into). You may want to create a page that collects the information to send to the procedure before it is called.

6. Click OK on the Command dialog box to accept your stored procedure execution options. Dreamweaver will now add the code to your page.

Dreamweaver MX 2004 also provides server behaviors that allow you to move through recordsets; this is discussed in the next section. It's important to be able to view more results from a recordset.

Navigating Recordsets

Naturally, the web page user wants to be able to step through records when there is more than a single record. One of the ways to make this happen is to assign images or text to the server behaviors that are responsible for moving to the next or previous record in a recordset. To assign the server behaviors for navigation, follow these steps:

1. First add images or text to your page that indicate the action.

2. Then select the image or text that indicates you are interested in moving to the next or previous records.

3. From the Server Behaviors panel, select Recordset Paging → Move To Next Record from the plus (+) sign's pop-up menu. There are other options on the same menu for going to the first, previous, last, or specific record.

4. The Move To Next Record dialog box has options for selecting the Recordset. Select the Recordset and then select OK.

5. Repeat steps 2–4 for each direction you want on your page.

6. Then upload your pages to a server because Live Data does not support these server behaviors.

7. After your page is uploaded, view it using your web browser. You will be able to use the icons you created to move through a recordset.

If all the records displayed do not fit on the page, you'll use a Repeated Region to specify how many are displayed at a time.

Repeated Region

A repeated region is a server behavior that allows you to display dynamic content—for example, database records. This means that the formatting assigned to the first record is assigned to all subsequent records. When you define a repeated region you select the recordset and how many records to display at a given time. Use the Repeated Region dialog box to define the recordset and the number or records to display. If a repeated region is used and all of the records cannot be displayed at once, the server behavior displays the next set of records.

To apply a repeated region, follow these steps:

1. Select the table row of one of the fields of the recordset that you are already displaying on your page.

2. Click the <tr> tag in the footer of the window to select the entire row.

3. Next, select Repeated Region from the Add Server Behaviors menu.

4. The Repeated Region is automatically added to the page.

Sometimes you'll want to add a group of server behaviors all at once to accomplish a goal. Adding a group of server behaviors simultaneously is similar to running a macro. For example, in Word you can create a macro using VBScript that will install an entire set of styles for the user to access while creating a document. In the database world, this is called using Application Objects.

Application Objects

Dreamweaver MX 2004 provides the ability to add Application Objects to your site. Application Objects are really just collections of server behaviors that are packaged together to do a task. An example of an Application Object is a Recordset Navigation Bar. You can build this yourself as we discussed in "Navigating Recordsets" or you can use the Application Object to do it all at once. The following Application Object allows you to get more detail about a record.

Master/Detail Pages

A master/detail page is a Live Object that Dreamweaver allows you to zoom in on. On the master page, generally, fewer columns are displayed about each record. When a user clicks the master record, a detail page displays with all of the recordset information. You create only one detail page that is used no matter which master record the user selects to zoom on.

The master/detail pages can be created using a Live Object (Insert → Application Objects → Master Detail Page Set) to do everything at once or piecemeal by using Server Behaviors (+ Menu → Go To Detail Page). To apply a detail page, insert text or an image indicating details into the row of the resultset and apply the detail record to it. Figure 19.10 shows an example of the Go To Detail Page parameters window

The detail page options specify which page to jump to for details as well as the URL parameter to send to the detail page. This parameter is generally going to be the primary key of the resultset.

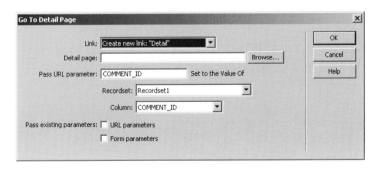

Figure 19.10

Go To Detail Page dialog box

Troubleshooting

Dreamweaver MX 2004 is certainly very powerful and flexible when it comes to building the code to make your dynamic web pages run. Unfortunately, you might encounter problems when you try to execute the pages that Dreamweaver has built. We'll discuss some of the strategies for minimizing the pain this may cause you and also how to avoid some of these problems.

The first time that you'll notice problems is when you attempt to use the Live Data view feature. The Live Data view feature displays the Live View of your page by actually running the code on the page though the application server. You will likely see the same type of errors here as you would when you execute the code by using your browser to access it though the web server; this is because the code is executed through the application server in either case.

You might want to display the Code view of the page that is giving an error and check the code that Dreamweaver has built for you. Because you might need to do this, you should understand the code that your development model uses.

Application Server Problems

Macromedia recommends running the latest version of Windows 2000 Professional or XP Pro if you're on a PC. This should minimize errors with IIS, especially the processing of the ASP code on your pages. Make sure that you have installed the latest Microsoft Service Pack. You should be running at least Service Pack 4 for Windows 2000 and 1a for XP. The service packs are available from the following addresses:

```
www.microsoft.com/windows2000/downloads/servicepacks/default.asp
www.microsoft.com/windowsxp/pro/downloads/default.as
```

Most of the errors you will encounter happen during the application server's processing of the page. Both Macromedia and the vendor who makes your application server should have pages with problem FAQs and/or searchable databases of problems.

The error type appears in the page that your application server returns. Here is an example of such an error:

```
Error Type:
        Provider (0x80004005)
        Unspecified error
        /MyTutorialSite/Results.asp, line 10
```

Macromedia's help page for Application Server errors is `www.macromedia.com/support/ultradev/ts/documents/common_server_errors.htm`. This web page also provides links to the help sections of all of the major application server vendors.

Database Problems

If you are experiencing a database access problem, it will appear when you try to process your page. ODBC/Access database errors can be permission related. For instance, you might see this error:

```
80004005 - Couldn't use '(unknown)'; file already in use.
```

This indicates that you probably have a Windows 2000 file permissions error or too low a timeout. The files in question are either the project files in IIS's wwwroot directory or the file and directory that hold the MDB file. This location can be found by checking the ODBC data sources applet definition for the database. Assign these files to access groups that the IIS server belongs to.

Under Windows 2000 and XP, the application servers access files as the user IUSR_ [machine name]. You can go to Control Panel → Administrative Tools and select the Computer Management applet to give more permission to that user or to change each of the files that need access to be updateable by that user or "Everyone."

To increase the ASP timeout for the test database, do the following: Open the ODBC Datasource Administrator from the Control Panel's Administrative Tools folder. Select the System DSN tab. Next, select the database you're using—for example, TriMotors. Click the Options button. Change the Page Timeout value to 5000.

If you are having a problem getting the results you expect from a database query, try executing the query outside of Dreamweaver. Each database provides its own interface for executing SQL queries. For example, Oracle's tool is called SQL*Plus. The SQL query executed on its own with the parameters that you wish Dreamweaver to search by will tell you if your query is correct.

Backups

It's a good strategy to periodically back up your project files (specified in the local directory section of your site definition). This way, should you encounter a problem with your site after adding functions, you can go back to the last working version without having to start all over. At the very least, you should back up the file that you're currently working on.

Hands On: Rapid Development of a Master Detail Page Set

In this tutorial, we will take you through the steps of defining a Master Detail page set that zooms in on Location records from the trio.mdb database that Macromedia provides with Dreamweaver MX 2004. We will use the ASP JavaScript development model, but the steps in the tutorial are the same for any development model.

To Develop a Master Detail Page Set, perform the following steps:

1. Set up your site to use your locally defined application server to process the ASP pages (or another application server if you have chosen to use a different development model).

2. Select Data Source Name from the plus (+) sign drop-down list of the Databases tab of the Application Panel group.

3. Type **connTrio1** in the Data Source Name dialog window's Connection Name text box.

4. Select TrioMotors from the Data Source Name drop-down list of the Data Source Name dialog box and click OK.

5. Now create two new pages for your site by selecting File → New. Call them `testMaster` `.asp` and `testDetail.asp`. Use File → New File from the Site tab to add these files.

6. On the testMaster page created in the last step type **Master Page Test** (this is cosmetic only, but it will help you identify the Master page).

7. Create a recordset to retrieve locations from the Trio database by selecting Recordset (Query) from the plus (+) sign's drop-down menu on the Bindings tab.

8. In the resulting Recordset window, type **Recordset1** in the Name field.

9. Set the connection to connTrio1 from the Connection drop-down list. Then select Locations from the Table drop-down list. Leave Columns set to All.

Figure 19.11

**Insert Master-
Detail Page Set**

10. Click OK to add the Master Detail Page Set.

11. Click after the Master Page Test text. Press the Enter key to add a new line on the Master Page.

12. Insert the Master/Detail object at the line you just added. From the main document window, choose Insert → Application Object →Master Detail Page Set.

13. From the Insert Master-Detail Page Set window that appears (see Figure 19.11), select Recordset1 from the Recordset drop-down list.

14. Then use the minus (−) sign to remove all but LOCATION_NAME, CITY, and STATE_ COUNTRY from the Master Page Fields list. This defines which fields to include on the master page.

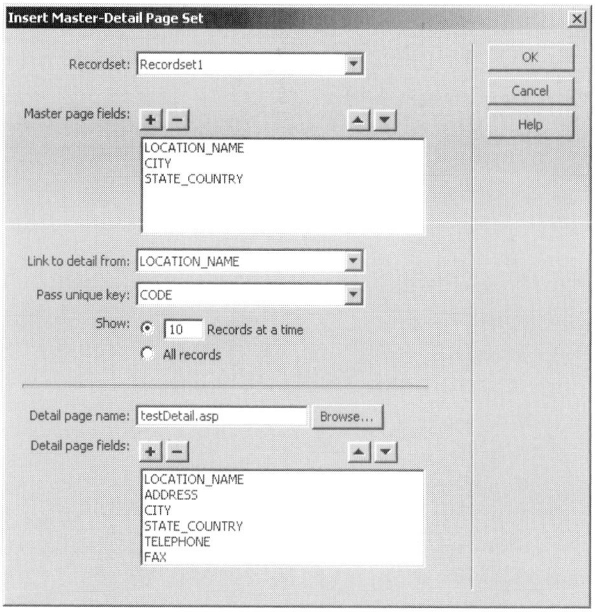

15. Then select LOCATION_NAME from the Link To Detail From drop-down list, and select CODE from the Leave Pass Unique Key drop-down list.

16. Next, use the Browse button to select `testDetail.asp` using the file selection dialog that appears.

17. Use the minus (–) button to remove CODE and REGION_ID from Detail Page Fields list. This list defines which fields to include on the detail page, so by removing these items, you have eliminated them from the detail page.

18. Click OK to save your changes and close the Insert Master-Detail Page Set window.

19. Save the `testMaster` and `testDetail` files, and then upload the files to the application server (by highlighting each file and pressing the up-arrow icon on the Site tab).

20. Finally, test the testMaster page by entering a URL (`http://127.0.0.1/mytutorialsite/testMaster.asp`, for example) into your web browser for the project directory appended with the filename, which is `testMaster.asp`. Figure 19.12 shows how the Master Detail Page Set window will appear through your web browser.

You can now zoom in on a database record using pages that were created by the Master Detail Page Set Live Object.

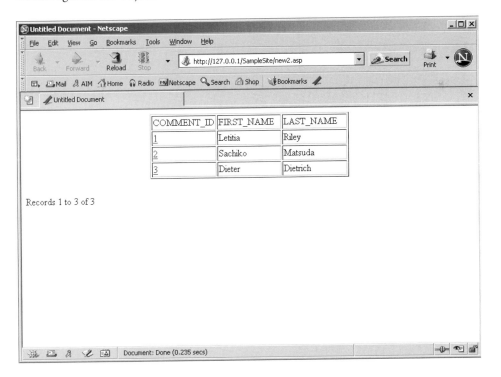

Figure 19.12

Testing Master-Detail Page Set

Dynamic Sites with ColdFusion

Dreamweaver MX 2004 makes creating data-driven dynamic pages easy. A variety of databases and development models are supported for ease of use and personal preference. Now that Macromedia also owns the ColdFusion MX server product, Dreamweaver includes support specifically designed for that server model. The next chapter helps you work with ColdFusion-based sites. As your expertise with the development model and database grows, Dreamweaver MX 2004 allows you to manipulate the code directly, if you so desire. You can also use Dreamweaver to customize your own application objects and extensions. Good luck creating your web interactions with a database that you are comfortable with, and may your dynamic content rock!

Working with ColdFusion

ColdFusion, one of Macromedia's server products, is a popular application server whose core rests in the execution of template files. These template files have .cfm extensions and use ColdFusion Markup Language (CFML), a tag-based language, to direct logic and invoke functionality through the server. More than any other web scripting language, CFML has the benefit (with a few exceptions) of working in a fashion that Dreamweaver understands—using tags.

ColdFusion MX 6.1 brings further performance and third-party integration enhancements. This chapter includes ColdFusion basics as well as highlights of the features meant to entice ColdFusion developers into using Dreamweaver.

The following topics will be discussed in this chapter:

- Introducing ColdFusion
- Exploring the features of ColdFusion
- Setting up a Dreamweaver site for ColdFusion
- Connecting to ColdFusion data sources
- Setting up bindings
- Using server behaviors

Introducing ColdFusion

ColdFusion is an application server that works with a web server to generate dynamic Web applications. Other application servers include Macromedia's JRun, IBM's WebSphere, and Sun's iPlanet.

> For more information on application servers, see Chapter 16, "Building Web Applications," and Chapter 19, "Database Connectivity." JRun 4 is included with ColdFusion MX 6.1. For more details on using JRun and JSP, see Chapter 23, "Working with JSP."

ColdFusion MX includes two major components: CFML (ColdFusion Markup Language) and the ColdFusion MX application server software. Dreamweaver MX 2004 provides a development tool to produce ColdFusion code, and includes:

- Built-in query tools and server behaviors
- Visual design environment
- Live Data preview
- Direct access to ColdFusion code

ColdFusion can be used as a stand-alone server or as an application running on top of another Java application server such as JRun or WebSphere. ColdFusion also includes the ColdFusion Administrator, a set of browser-based administration tools.

> The Windows version of Studio MX 2004 includes the developer edition of ColdFusion MX 6.1. It can be used locally and/or with one remote hosting provider.

Important Features for ColdFusion Developers

Because working with ColdFusion templates is not unlike working with other tag-based files, Dreamweaver excels in its tool applicability. The sheer number of built-in parsing tools, commands, and behaviors makes working with ColdFusion templates incredibly easy. Here are some of the best examples.

Code Editor

For a ColdFusion developer, the core of the Dreamweaver tool is the editor, or Code view as it is called in Dreamweaver. The Code view portion of the UI (user interface) is extremely flexible about its presentation of files. Dreamweaver allows you to have multiple files open at once, and they can be stacked in workbook fashion (like Excel and ColdFusion Studio) or in a more traditional Multi-Document Interface (MDI) style. The MDI style allows you to see two or more files simultaneously, which can be very useful when migrating code.

Two of the more powerful features found in ColdFusion Studio, Tag editors and Code Hints, have been incorporated into the editing environment of Dreamweaver MX 2004.

Tag Editors One of the truly powerful features of ColdFusion is the Tag editor. Merely by right-clicking a tag the user can launch a dialog box that will assist with the completion of the tag's attributes, similar to the Tag Editor in Dreamweaver.

Code Hints Another feature that ColdFusion users will find familiar in Dreamweaver is Code Hints. This mechanism provides automatic assistance for the developer by displaying a pop-up menu of tags and attributes. The developer can select a desired tag or attribute from the display and it will be inserted. This display automatically updates as the developer continues to type—trying to match names to the letters being typed. How quickly the pop-up menu displays is a setting that can be adjusted in the Code Hints section of the Preferences dialog box.

New Features in ColdFusion MX 6.1

ColdFusion MX 6.1 has been improved in a couple of major ways that developers will certainly notice. First, skipping the intermediate step of producing Java source code has substantially reduced compilation time. Java Byte Code is now directly compiled. Functionally, ColdFusion MX 6.1 supports multiple instances running with JRun 4 (included with the application) or exporting to a number of J2EE-compatible third-party application servers. Operating system support has also been added for Solaris 9 and Red Hat Linux systems.

Application Panel Group

Nothing will really prepare the ColdFusion MX 6.1 user for the power that Dreamweaver MX users have known for some time through the Application panel group. This panel group includes four panels that contain tools for creating application logic with the click of a few buttons. Though there will be some familiar points of functionality, the overall toolset is a major leap ahead for ColdFusion developers.

Databases Panel

This panel is analogous to the Database tab in ColdFusion Studio. It provides a view of the data sources configured with the ColdFusion Administrator on the targeted server.

What appears to be missing from this panel, from a ColdFusion Studio user's perspective, is the Visual Query Builder. Not to fear, though—Dreamweaver MX 2004 has a powerful solution on the Bindings panel.

Bindings Panel

This panel allows the developer to manage all the queries and variables for a template from a single interface. What's more, Dreamweaver MX 2004 allows the cacheing of queries for testing during development time.

Though features of this panel aren't much different from ColdFusion Studio's Visual Query Builder tool, the panel is considerably more powerful. What this panel can do that Studio's Visual Query Builder cannot do is look at data sources that have been abstracted with variable names. The common practice of defining a variable in the `Application.cfm` for use as the `CFQUERY` tag's `DATASOURCE` attribute can be handled from this interface and will remain persistent not only while working in a template but for the whole configured site.

Server Behaviors Panel

The closest things that ColdFusion Studio has to server behaviors offered by Dreamweaver are snippets and wizards. However, these do not compare to the scriptable versatility in even the basic kit that comes with Dreamweaver MX 2004.

There are some similarities between the Server Behaviors panel and the Bindings panel when it comes to managing recordsets, but that is where the similarities end. A server behavior (SB) provides tools not only for creating recordsets but also for manipulating them by inserting, updating, and deleting records within them. There are SBs for conditional logic that will insert CFIF statements, authentication tools, and HTML Form tools for creating elements bound to CFML variables.

The single most powerful feature of this panel, though, is its ability to be extended. Custom behaviors can be added, and in fact, they can be created using existing behaviors as templates.

Components Panel

Another new feature of ColdFusion MX 6.1 is ColdFusion Components or CFCs. CFCs are a powerful new language extension for building reusable components in CFML. The Components panel is Dreamweaver's tool for creating and manipulating CFCs. ColdFusion components are a kind of super CFML container to facilitate modular re-use of code.

Setting Up a Dreamweaver Site for ColdFusion

Configuring a site specifically for handling ColdFusion is not that much different than configuring one for other application servers. See Chapter 16, "Building Web Applications," for more on setting up web applications in general.

A ColdFusion-configured site is required before any of Dreamweaver MX 2004's Cold-Fusion features can really be explored. The following process will help you set up the site needed for the other exercises in this chapter.

1. Launch Manage Sites window (Site → Manage Sites…).
2. Click the New button on the Site window.
3. Select Site from the drop-down list.
4. Select the Advanced tab on the Site Definition wizard.

5. Select Local Info in the Category list on the left and set the values as they are shown in Figure 20.1. We have named our site EmployeeInformation, as shown in the figure.

6. Select Remote Info in the Category list on the left and set the values as they are shown in Figure 20.2.

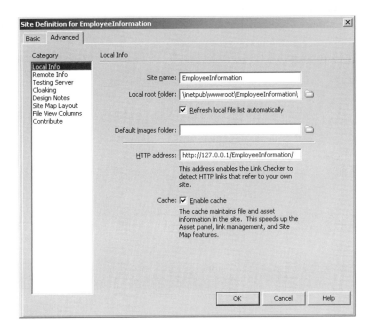

Figure 20.1

EmployeeInformation Site's Local Info settings

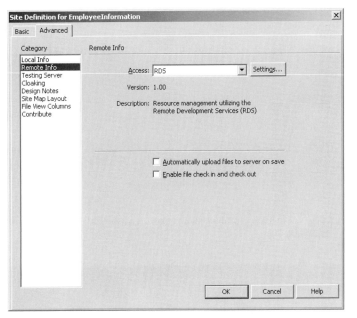

Figure 20.2

EmployeeInformation Site's Remote Info settings

7. Select Testing Server in the Category list on the left and set the values as they are shown in Figure 20.3.

Connecting to ColdFusion Data Sources

Opening your ColdFusion site allows the various ColdFusion-specific features of the Application panel group to be enabled. The Databases panel will display a four- or five-step prompter if there is no prior information available for connecting to your Cold-Fusion site.

The prompter steps are as follows:

1. Create a site for this file.

2. Choose a document type.

3. Set up the site's testing server.

4. Specify the RDS login information.

RDS stands for Remote Development Services. RDS is a proprietary component in ColdFusion Studio that allows remote access to files and databases.

5. Create a ColdFusion data source.

Figure 20.3

EmployeeInforma-tion Site's Testing Server settings

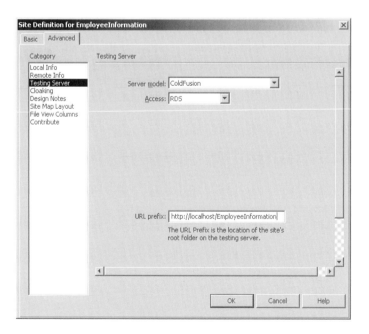

If everything in your site configuration is set up, you have only to click the login link for step 4. This will display the RDS Login dialog box and allow you to get authenticated, provided that a ColdFusion Studio/RDS client password has been configured in the Cold-Fusion Administrator.

Once this is done, all of the data sources configured with that ColdFusion Server will be displayed. You can access the ColdFusion Administrator from Program Files → Macromedia ColdFusion MX → Administrator, or by entering `http://localhost/CFIDE/administrator/index.cfm` in a browser.

Three databases are included with ColdFusion MX 6.1: `cfexamples.mdb`, `cfsnippets.mdb`, and `company.mdb`. They are in the `db` folder within the directory where you installed Cold-Fusion. You set data sources in ColdFusion in the ColdFusion Administrator, as shown in Figure 20.4. CompanyInfo is the DSN we created for `company.mdb`. We'll be using this DSN for the examples in the rest of this chapter.

These settings are for using ColdFusion locally with IIS and remotely with RDS. If you config-ure ColdFusion locally with Apache, you can set up your ColdFusion site with the local Apache web server for the Local Info, Remote Info, and the Testing Server.

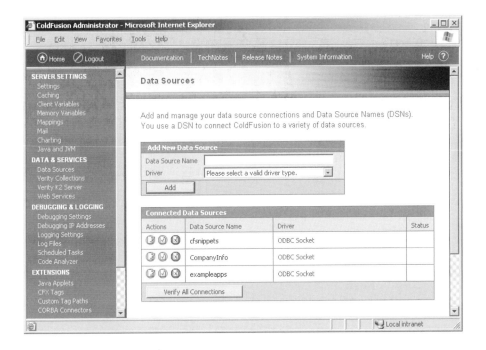

Figure 20.4

Configuring Data Sources in the ColdFusion Administrator

Follow these steps to connect to the CompanyInfo database:

1. Select the EmployeeInformation site on the Manage Sites window (Site → Manage Sites).

2. Open a new ColdFusion template. Select File → New, and from the resulting dialog box, click the General tab. From the General tab, click the Dynamic Page entry in the Category list. Then from the Dynamic Page list select ColdFusion. It is necessary to have a dynamic page open (specifically a ColdFusion page in this case); otherwise the panels in the Application panel group will be grayed out and inaccessible.

3. Click the RDS login information prompter and log in if a list of databases is not displayed in the Databases panel of the Application panel group.

Use the ColdFusion Administrator to set an RDS password.

4. Inspect the CompanyInfo database.

Setting Up Bindings

There are many powerful capabilities on the Bindings panel—each individually worthy of discussion. If you have not read about the Bindings panel in Chapter 19, you should pause and do so now.

A common practice in developing database-backed applications is to abstract the data source name to a variable. This makes pointing the application at different test and production databases a little easier. Typically, third-party development environments don't handle this abstraction very well, but this is not the case with Dreamweaver. Using the Data Source Name Variable binding tool, a developer can identify to Dreamweaver, within the context of a ColdFusion site, the variable used to abstract the name of the data source. Once this is done, the variable is available to server behaviors and recordsets. Using this variable, the results of the query used in the recordset can even be viewed during development by Dreamweaver.

The following steps will walk you through setting up this binding.

1. Remove all of the HTML and save the blank ColdFusion template created in step 2 of the process described in the previous section as `Application.cfm`.

2. Insert a variable into this template from the Bindings panel (by clicking the Add button and selecting the CFParam menu item from the resulting pop-up menu), and set the following values in the resulting dialog box:

> Name: **Datasource**
>
> Default: **CompanyInfo**
>
> Type: leave empty

3. Click OK

4. Bind the variable created in step 2 as the Data Source Name Variable (by clicking the Add button and selecting the Data Source Name Variable menu item from the resulting pop-up menu), and set the following values in the dialog box:

> Variable Name: **Datasource**
>
> Data Source: **CompanyInfo**

5. Save the template.

Using Server Behaviors

The basic toolkit of server behaviors that comes with Dreamweaver seems paltry when contrasted with the nearly 100 tags (and roughly double that in functions) of CFML. While this is true on the surface, most of the Dreamweaver SBs center on the two most common operations facing a developer when building a ColdFusion application: gathering data in forms and manipulating database content.

Using the exercises in the following two sections as examples, you will explore the point-and-click power that Dreamweaver SBs provide you as a ColdFusion developer. While the exercises seem rather involved, with 17 steps and 5 steps, respectively, they really aren't at all difficult.

Creating the Main Page

Here you will walk through the steps to create the main page of the EmployeeInformation application that we worked with earlier in the chapter. What will be produced is a simple page that displays groups of records from the database and allows the user to scroll through them using Back and Next Image buttons on the page (not to be confused with the Back and Next buttons of the browser). There is a hyperlink for creating new records that we will tend to in the next section.

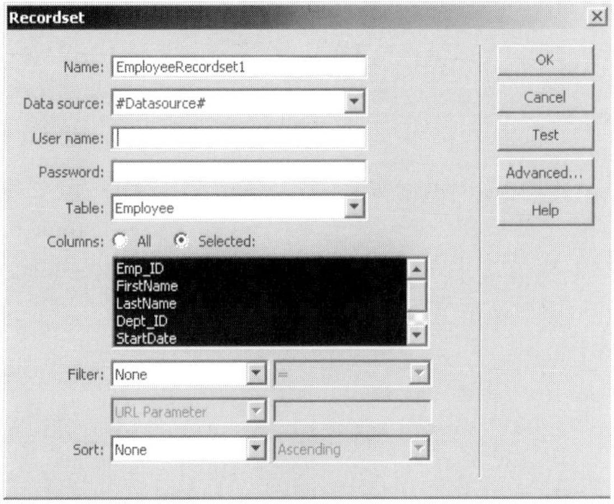

Figure 20.5

Simple Recordset dialog box

1. Create a new ColdFusion template. Select File → New, and from the resulting dialog box, click the General tab. From the General tab, click the Dynamic Page entry in the Category list. Then from the Dynamic Page list select ColdFusion. Once this is done, immediately save it as index.cfm.

2. From the Server Behaviors panel, add a Recordset object to the template by clicking the Add button and selecting the Recordset menu item from the pop-up menu. Enter EmployeeRecordset1 in the Name text box, then select #Datasource# from the Data source drop-down menu.

3. Choose Employee from the Table drop-down menu. Click the Selected radio button next to Columns, and select these fields: Emp_ID, FirstName, LastName, Dept_ID, and StartDate (use Ctrl to select multiple fields). Figure 20.5 shows the Simple view of the Recordset dialog box. Click the Advanced button to view the Advanced Recordset dialog box, as shown in Figure 20.6.

4. Insert a table within the body tag and set the following values in the Table window:

> Rows: **3**
>
> Columns: **4**
>
> Table width: **75%**
>
> Border thickness: **0**
>
> Cell padding: **2**
>
> Cell spacing: **0**

5. Choose Top from the Header row, then click OK.

6. Enter these values in the first table row's three table cells: First Name, Last Name, and Start Date. Select each value, then choose Left from the Horz drop-down menu in the Property inspector.

Figure 20.6

Advanced Recordset dialog box

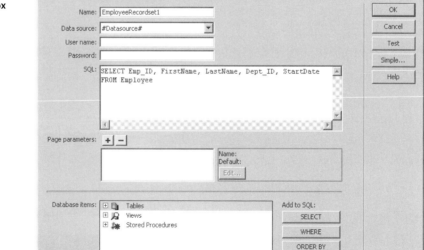

7. Click in the second table row's first table cell, then click the Add (+) button in the Server Behaviors panel and select Dynamic Text from the pop-up menu. From the resulting Dynamic Text dialog box, expand the Recordset named EmployeeRecordset1, select the FirstName field and click the OK button. This will insert the following CFOUTPUT block in the cell:

```
<td><cfoutput>#EmployeeRecordset1.FirstName#</cfoutput></td>
```

8. Repeat step 6 for the second table row's second table cell. Select the LastName field from the Dynamic Text dialog box, then click OK.

9. Repeat step 6 for the second table row's third table cell. Select StartDate from the Dynamic Text dialog box, then click OK.

10. Insert two images in the fourth cell in the second row, edit.gif and delete.gif (images are in the Chapter 20 folder on the CD).

11. Select the entire <tr> blocks that are the second and third row of the table, insert a Repeat Region SB (click the Add button and select the Repeat Region menu item from the pop-up menu), and set the following values in the resulting dialog box:

> Recordset: **EmployeeRecordset1**
>
> Show: **10 Records at a Time**

12. Click OK.

13. Insert two images (back.gif and next.gif) in the first table cell of the third table row.

14. Insert empty hyperlinks around each of the two img tags from step 12:

```
<td><a href=""><img src="back.gif" width="25" height="25" border="1">
</a><a href=""><img src="next.gif" width="25" height="25" border="1">
</a></td>
```

15. With the cursor is in the first empty hyperlink from step 13, add the Move To Previous Page SB (click the Add button and select the Move To Previous Page menu item from the Recordset Paging pop-up menu) and set the following values:

> Link: Select the empty hyperlink around back.gif.
>
> Recordset: **EmployeeRecordset1**
>
> Pass Existing URL Parameters: Make sure this is checked.

16. While the cursor is in the second empty hyperlink from step 13, add the Move To Next Page SB (click the Add button and select the Move To Next Page menu item from the Recordset Paging pop-up menu) and set the following values:

> Link: Select the empty hyperlink around next.gif.
>
> Recordset: **EmployeeRecordset1**
>
> Pass Existing URL Parameters: Make sure this is checked.

17. Insert a hyperlink in the third table row's fourth table cell and set the following values:

Text: New Person

Link: AddPerson.cfm

Target: leave empty

Title: Add a New Person

Access Key: leave empty

Tab Index: leave empty

     The resulting ColdFusion template (see Listing 20.1, which can also be found in the Chapter 20 folder on the accompanying CD), while not truly complex, does contain a considerable amount of code. The beauty of this is that nearly all of it was produced via point-and-click.

Listing 20.1

Main page (*index.cfm*)

```
<cfset CurrentPage=GetFileFromPath(GetTemplatePath())>
<cfparam name="PageNum_EmployeeRecordset1" default="1">
<cfquery name="EmployeeRecordset1" datasource="CompanyInfo">
SELECT Emp_ID, FirstName, LastName, Dept_ID, StartDate
FROM Employee
</cfquery>
<cfset MaxRows_EmployeeRecordset1=10>
<cfset
  StartRow_EmployeeRecordset1=Min((PageNum_EmployeeRecordset1-1)
  * MaxRows_EmployeeRecordset1+1,
  Max(EmployeeRecordset1.RecordCount,1))>
<cfset EndRow_EmployeeRecordset1=Min
(StartRow_EmployeeRecordset1+MaxRows_EmployeeRecordset1-1,
EmployeeRecordset1.RecordCount)>
<cfset TotalPages_EmployeeRecordset1=Ceiling
  (EmployeeRecordset1.RecordCount/MaxRows_EmployeeRecordset1)>
<cfset QueryString_EmployeeRecordset1=Iif(CGI.QUERY_STRING
  NEQ "",DE("&"&XMLFormat(CGI.QUERY_STRING)),DE(""))>
<cfset tempPos=ListContainsNoCase
  (QueryString_EmployeeRecordset1,
  "PageNum_EmployeeRecordset1=","&")>
<cfif tempPos NEQ 0>
  <cfset QueryString_EmployeeRecordset1=ListDeleteAt
    (QueryString_EmployeeRecordset1,tempPos,"&")>
</cfif>
<!DOCTYPE HTML PUBLIC "-//W3C//DTD HTML 4.01 Transitional//EN"
  "http://www.w3.org/TR/html4/loose.dtd">
```

```
<html>
<head>
<title>Employee Information </title>
<meta http-equiv="Content-Type" content="text/html;
  charset=iso-8859-1">
</head>

<body>
<table width="75%"  border="0" cellspacing="0" cellpadding="2">
  <tr>
    <th align="left" scope="col">First Name </th>
    <th align="left" scope="col">Last Name </th>
    <th align="left" scope="col">Start Date </th>
    <th scope="col"> </th>
  </tr>
  <cfoutput query="EmployeeRecordset1"
    startRow="#StartRow_EmployeeRecordset1#"
    maxRows="#MaxRows_EmployeeRecordset1#">
  <tr>
    <td>#EmployeeRecordset1.FirstName#</td>
    <td>#EmployeeRecordset1.LastName#</td>
    <td>#EmployeeRecordset1.StartDate#</td>
    <td><img src="edit.gif" width="25" height="25" border="1">
      <img src="delete.gif" width="25" height="25" border="1"></td>
  </tr>
  <tr>
    <td><a href="#CurrentPage#?PageNum_EmployeeRecordset1=
      #Max(DecrementValue(PageNum_EmployeeRecordset1),1)
      ##QueryString_EmployeeRecordset1#">
      <img src="back.gif" width="25" height="25" border="1">
    </a>  <a href="#CurrentPage#?PageNum_
      EmployeeRecordset1=#Min(IncrementValue(PageNum_
      EmployeeRecordset1),TotalPages_EmployeeRecordset1)
      ##QueryString_EmployeeRecordset1#">
      <img src="next.gif" width="25" height="25" border="1">
    </a></td>
    <td> </td>
    <td> </td>
    <td><a href="AddPerson.cfm" title="Add a new person">
      New Person</a></td>
  </tr>
  </cfoutput>
</table>
</body>
</html>
```

New Records

The following steps will walk you through creating a form for adding new records to the database's Employee table.

1. Create a new ColdFusion template. Select File → New, and from the resulting dialog box, click the General tab. From the General tab, click the Dynamic Page entry in the Category list. Then, from the Dynamic Page list, select ColdFusion. Save it as AddPerson.cfm (the link that you created in step 16 of the previous exercise).

2. Insert a <form> tag within the <body> tag of this document (click the Form icon on the Forms Insert bar or select Insert → Form → Form) and from the Property inspector, make the following changes:

   Form Name: **NewPerson**

   Action: leave empty

   Method: **POST**

3. Select Insert → Form → Text Field. Add seven <input> tags within the <form> tag for each of the seven fields in the Employee table. (You can view the field names in the Employee table in the Databases panel.) Set name attributes to correlate to field names in the table, and the type attributes for each of them should be "text."

4. Add a Submit button to the <form> tag.

Figure 20.7

The Insert Record dialog box

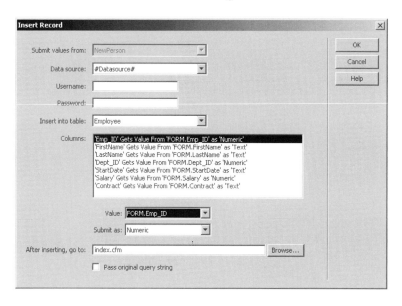

5. Place the cursor at the top of the page in the Code view window. Add an Insert Record SB (click the Add button and select the Insert Record menu item from the pop-up menu). Choose #Datasource# from the Data source drop-down menu, and Employee from the Insert Into Table drop-down menu. Dreamweaver will automatically set the values for the Columns. Enter `index.cfm` in the After Inserting, Go To text box, as shown in Figure 20.7.

The resulting ColdFusion template (see Listing 20.2, which can also be found in the Chapter 20 folder on the accompanying CD) contains a considerable amount of Cold-Fusion code inserted by the Insert Record SB.

Listing 20.2

New Person Page (*AddPerson.cfm*)

```
<cfset CurrentPage=GetFileFromPath(GetTemplatePath())>
<cfif IsDefined("FORM.MM_InsertRecord")
  AND FORM.MM_InsertRecord EQ "NewPerson">
  <cfquery datasource="#Datasource#">
  INSERT INTO Employee
(Emp_ID, FirstName, LastName, Dept_ID, StartDate, Salary,
  Contract) VALUES (
  <cfif IsDefined("FORM.Emp_ID") AND #FORM.Emp_ID# NEQ "">
    #FORM.Emp_ID#
      <cfelse>
      NULL
  </cfif>
  ,
  <cfif IsDefined("FORM.FirstName") AND #FORM.FirstName# NEQ "">
    '#FORM.FirstName#'
      <cfelse>
      NULL
  </cfif>
  ,
  <cfif IsDefined("FORM.LastName") AND #FORM.LastName# NEQ "">
    '#FORM.LastName#'
      <cfelse>
      NULL
  </cfif>
  ,
  <cfif IsDefined("FORM.Dept_ID") AND #FORM.Dept_ID# NEQ "">
    #FORM.Dept_ID#
      <cfelse>
      NULL
  </cfif>
```

```
      ,
      <cfif IsDefined("FORM.StartDate") AND
        #FORM.StartDate# NEQ "">
        '#FORM.StartDate#'
          <cfelse>
          NULL
      </cfif>
      ,
      <cfif IsDefined("FORM.Salary") AND #FORM.Salary# NEQ "">
        #FORM.Salary#
          <cfelse>
          NULL
      </cfif>
      ,
      <cfif IsDefined("FORM.Contract") AND #FORM.Contract# NEQ "">
        '#FORM.Contract#'
          <cfelse>
          NULL
      </cfif>
      )
      </cfquery>
      <cflocation url="index.cfm">
</cfif>
<!DOCTYPE HTML PUBLIC "-//W3C//DTD HTML 4.01 Transitional//EN"
  "http://www.w3.org/TR/html4/loose.dtd">
<html>
<head>
<title>Add Employee</title>
<meta http-equiv="Content-Type" content="text/html;
  charset=iso-8859-1">
</head>
<body>
<h3>Add Employee Form</h3>
<table>
<form action="<cfoutput>#CurrentPage#</cfoutput>" method="POST"
  name="NewPerson">
<tr><td>Employee ID</td><td><input name="Emp_ID" type="text"></td>
</tr><br>
<tr><td>First Name</td><td><input name="FirstName" type="text"></td>
</tr><br>
<tr><td>Last Name</td><td><input name="LastName" type="text"></td>
</tr><br>
<tr><td>Department ID</td><td><input name="Dept_ID" type="text"></td>
</tr><br>
```

```
<tr><td>Start Date<td><input name="StartDate" type="text"></td>
</tr><br>
<tr><td>Salary</td><td><input name="Salary" type="text"></td>
</tr><br>
<tr><td>Contract</td><td><input name="Contract" type="text"></td>
</tr><br>
<tr><td><input name="" type="submit" value="Submit"></td><td> </td>
</tr>
<tr><td><input type="hidden" name="MM_InsertRecord" value="NewPerson">
  </td><td> </td></tr>
</form>
</table>
</body>
</html>
```

Continuing Work

The EmployeeInformation application is very simple. It could easily be expanded in a number of different directions. The main page (`index.cfm`) alone has numerous opportunities for continuing exercises and exploration. Here are some exploration options:

Delete Form You can use the Delete Record SB to create a form to delete existing Employee records from the database. Link it to the obvious image on the main page's Delete icons displayed for each record in the fourth column of the table.

Edit Form You can use the Update Record SB to create a form to edit existing Employee records in the database. Link it to the obvious image on the main page's Edit icon that is displayed for each record in the fourth column of the table.

To the Bleeding Edge

The sheer power of the features in Dreamweaver MX 2004 truly makes rapid application development in ColdFusion MX possible. Just leveraging the server behaviors could improve a developer's productivity massively. Further still, the extensibility of Dreamweaver means that as new features become available in the future versions of ColdFusion, Dreamweaver will be able to adapt without a serious need for an upgrade.

In the next chapter, you'll learn about using Dreamweaver to work with ASP (Active Server Pages), a Microsoft server technology that works with either JavaScript or VB Script to create dynamic web applications.

## CHAPTER 21

Working with ASP

Active Server Pages (ASP) is a Microsoft server technology for creating dynamic web pages. ASP is not a scripting language, but is used with a scripting language that supports ActiveX, such as VBScript or JavaScript. When an ASP page is processed on a web server, it dynamically generates HTML at the time of the request and sends it to the browser. Although an ASP page must be processed on a computer that supports ASP, ASP pages can be viewed on any computer with almost any browser.

If you are familiar with HTML and a scripting language, ASP is easy to learn and to use. Dreamweaver MX 2004 provides several tools for using ASP to develop dynamic web applications, and includes a set of ASP sample files as well as a tutorial for developing a sample web application using ASP.

The following topics will be discussed in this chapter:

- Getting started with ASP

- Setting up a Dreamweaver site for ASP

- Connecting to a database with ASP

- Creating a dynamic page with ASP

- Viewing Live Data

- Using ASP in Dreamweaver

Getting Started with ASP

To develop dynamic pages with ASP, you need a web server that supports ASP, either a local web server on your computer or a remote web server. Unlike HTML, ASP is a server-side technology, and requires a server to translate the ASP into HTML before passing it on to a browser.

If you are using Windows 98, 2000, or XP Pro, web server software (either PWS or IIS) that includes an ASP engine is included with the operating system software. The advantage of using a local web server is that you can test pages quickly without uploading them to a remote server. If you don't have access to a computer with a web server that supports ASP, you can also use a remote computer to test your ASP pages.

You can set up a free ASP hosting account at `www.brinkster.com` to test your ASP pages.

PWS or IIS may already be installed on your computer. Both PWS and IIS create a folder named `Inetpub` during installation, so you can check for this folder on your hard drive. If you're using Windows 98, a PWS installation file is included on the Windows 98 CD. Otherwise, you can install IIS via the Add/Remove Program feature in the Control Panel. Choose Add/Remove Windows Components, then select IIS and follow the instructions. For more information on installing a web server, see Chapter 30, "Going Live or Delivering the Site."

You can't install IIS or run ASP locally if you're using Windows XP Home edition.

An alternative to using a Microsoft web server is to use Sun ONE Active Server Pages. This enables Sun ONE and Apache web servers to run ASP on Sun Solaris, Linux, HP-UX, and IBM AIX operating systems. For more information, go to `www.chilisoft.com`.

The Root Folder

In order to use a local web server, you need to save your files in the root folder of the web server. If you are using PWS or IIS, the default root folder is named `wwwroot` and is located in the `Inetpub` folder. You can also create separate root folders within the `wwwroot` folder to test separate ASP applications.

Unlike an HTML page, which you can open directly in a browser by double-clicking the file or by entering the file path, you need to open your ASP pages via the root folder of the web server. You can test your web server by entering the following URL in a browser:

```
http://localhost
```

If the web server is working correctly, the web server default page (for example, `local-start.asp`) will open in the browser.

Setting Permissions

If you create a separate root folder, you need to make sure that Read and Script permissions are enabled for the folder:

- For PWS, open the Personal Web Manager. Choose Advanced options, and then select Home and choose Edit Properties. Select the Read and Scripts options.

- For IIS, open the Control Panel, and then choose Administrative Tools. (In XP Pro, choose Performance And Maintenance → Administrative Tools.) Double-click the Internet Information Services icon to open the Microsoft Management Console. Find the folder you created under local computer → Web Sites → Default Web Site → *your folder*. Right-click the folder and select Properties from the context menu. On the Directory tab, make sure that Scripts Only is selected in the Execute Permissions drop-down menu.

For more information on setting IIS web server permissions, see this Macromedia TechNote: www.macromedia.com/support/dreamweaver/ts/documents/web_server_permissions.htm.

Setting Up an ASP Site in Dreamweaver

Setting up a dynamic ASP site in Dreamweaver is not much more complicated than setting up a static site. For more information on setting up Dreamweaver sites in general, see Chapter 3, "Setting Up Your Workspace and Your Site." For additional details on setting up a dynamic site in Dreamweaver, see Chapter 16, "Building Web Applications."

Figure 21.1

Defining the Local Info

Creating a Root Folder

Create a separate root folder named MyASP within the wwwroot folder of the Inetpub folder on your hard drive. Enable permissions for this folder as described in the section "Setting Permissions" earlier in this chapter.

Defining the Local Info

Select Site → Manage Sites → New. This brings up the Site Definition dialog box. If the wizard is showing, click the Advanced tab. You should automatically start in the Local Info category.

As shown in Figure 21.1, name your site Trio, browse to the local root folder, and indicate the HTTP address of the site. Leave the Site Definition dialog box open.

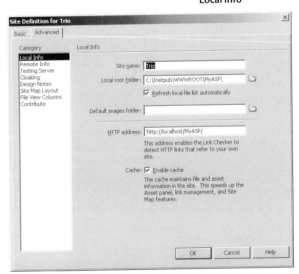

Defining the Remote Info

Select the Remote Info category in the Site Definition dialog box. Choose Local/Network from the Access drop-down menu (unless you are using a remote host). Browse to the MyASP folder and select it as the Remote Folder, as shown in Figure 21.2. Leave the dialog box open.

Defining the Testing Server

Next, select the Testing Server category in the Site Definition dialog box. Choose ASP VBScript as the Server model, then select Local/Network from the Access drop-down menu (unless you are using remote hosting). Dreamweaver should automatically copy your settings from the Remote Info window into the Testing Server folder text box and the URL prefix text box, but double-check to make sure these are correct (see Figure 21.3). Click OK to close the Site Definition dialog box.

Connecting to a Database with ASP

During installation, Dreamweaver automatically copies a sample Microsoft Access database to your hard drive. This database, named trio.mdb, can be found in the Database folder within the Samples folder in the folder where Dreamweaver MX 2004 is installed.

To use ASP to make a database connection in Dreamweaver, you need to have an ASP page open in Dreamweaver. You'll be creating an ASP page in a moment, but for now open the time2.asp page in the Chapter 21 folder on the CD, copy it to the MyASP folder, and then open it in Dreamweaver.

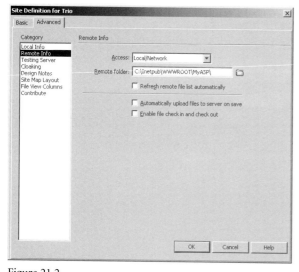

Figure 21.2

Defining the Remote Info

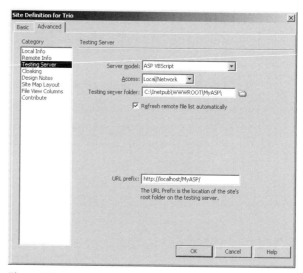

Figure 21.3

Defining the Testing Server

To create an ASP database connection (Figure 21.4):

1. Open the Applications panel group and click on the Databases tab. ASP JavaScript should be displayed next to the – (minus) sign at the top of the tab.

2. Click on the + (plus) sign and select Data Source Name (DSN).

3. In the Data Source Name (DSN) dialog box, enter **conTrio** in the Connection name textbox.

4. Choose TrioMotors from the Data Source Name (DSN) drop-down menu.

5. Select Using Local DSN (for a local web server) or Using DSN On Testing Server (for a remote web server).

6. Click Test. An alert box displays to let you know if the connection was successful.

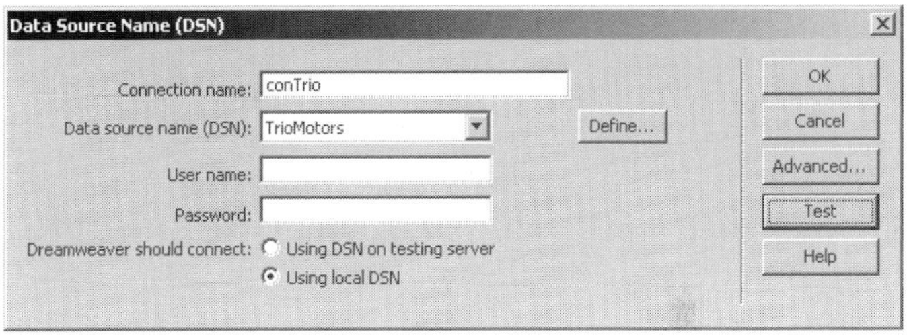

Figure 21.4

Creating an ASP database connection

For more information on using databases in Dreamweaver, see Chapter 19, "Database Connectivity."

Creating a Dynamic ASP Page

Now let's create a simple ASP page to show the current date and time, and test it in our web server. This page accesses the current date and time on the server that processes the ASP page. If you're using a local web server, it will display the local values for time and date. If you're using a remote web server, it will display the time and date for the server location.

1. Open a new ASP file in Dreamweaver (File → New → Dynamic Page → ASP VBScript).

2. Save the file as time.asp.

3. Open the Design panel group and click the Options menu in the upper-right corner. Select "Attach Style Sheet." From the Attach External Style Sheet window, click on the Sample Style Sheets link at the bottom. Choose the Full Design: Arial, Blue/Green/Gray style sheet.

4. Add the following HTML text to highlight the time:

```
<h2>Welcome!</h2>
<h3>And now for the time:</h3>
The current time ... at this very moment ... is
```

5. Add the following code to request the current time from the server and write it to the page:

```
<%
Response.Write Time
%>
```

Note the <% and %> tags, which indicate that this is an ASP script block.

6. Add HTML to highlight the date:

```
<h3>And maybe you'd like to know the date,too?</h3>
```

7. Add another ASP script block. This block declares (Dim) four variables and then uses ASP date functions to extract the current date information from the server.

```
<%
Dim TDate, TDate_Month, TDate_Day, TDate_Year
TDate = Date
TDate_Month = DatePart ("m", TDate)
TDate_Month = MonthName (TDate_Month)
TDate_Day = DatePart ("d", TDate)
TDate_Year = DatePart ("yyyy", TDate)
Response.Write TDate_Month
Response.Write " "
Response.Write TDate_Day
Response.Write ", "
Response.Write TDate_Year
%>
```

8. Add one more block of HTML to send a goodbye message to the viewer:

```
<h3>Thanks for stopping by ... <br>
come back and see us again ... <br>
if you have the time!</h3>
```

9. Save the page.

The complete code is shown in Listing 21.1, and is also included in the Chapter 21 folder on the CD.

Listing 21.1

time.asp

```
<%@LANGUAGE="VBSCRIPT" CODEPAGE="1252"%>
<!DOCTYPE HTML PUBLIC "-//W3C//DTD HTML 4.01 Transitional//EN"
"http://www.w3.org/TR/html4/loose.dtd"><html>
<head>
<title>As Time Goes By</title>
<link href="CSS/Level3_1.css" rel="stylesheet" type="text/css">
```

```
<meta http-equiv="Content-Type" content="text/html; charset=iso-8859-1">
</head>
<body bgcolor="#ccffcc">
<h2>Welcome!</h2>
<h3>And now for the time:</h3>
The current time ... at this very moment ... is
<%
Response.Write Time
%>
<h3>And maybe you'd like to know the date,too?</h3>
<%
Dim TDate, TDate_Month, TDate_Day, TDate_Year
TDate = Date
TDate_Month = DatePart ("m", TDate)
TDate_Month = MonthName (TDate_Month)
TDate_Day = DatePart ("d", TDate)
TDate_Year = DatePart ("yyyy", TDate)
Response.Write TDate_Month
Response.Write " "
Response.Write TDate_Day
Response.Write ", "
Response.Write TDate_Year
%>
<h3>Thanks for stopping by ... <br>
come back and see us again ... <br>
if you have the time!</h3>
</body>
</html>
```

Using Live Data View

You can preview and edit your dynamic pages by using the Live Data window. To open the Live Data window, click the Live Data view icon on the Document toolbar or choose View → Live Data. Dreamweaver automatically sends a temporary copy of the dynamic page to the application server for processing. The resulting page is displayed in the Live Data window and the temporary copy on the server is deleted. That's it! If the application server has any problems returning a page, a warning box will display with suggested sources of errors and possible solutions.

If the page expects URL parameters from an HTML form using the GET method, you can enter that data in the text box on the toolbar of the Live Data window. Click the Refresh icon (circle-arrow) after entering the data.

You can also enter the data in the Live Data Settings dialog box (see Figure 21.5). To do so, open the Live Data Settings dialog box (View → Live Data Settings), and enter data in the Name and Value columns. For example, if the

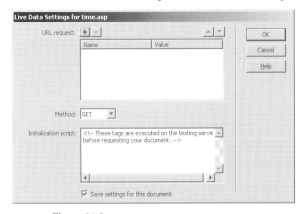

parameter name is city and the value is Chicago, you would enter `city=` in the Name column, and `Chicago;` in the Value column.

Open `time.asp` in Design view. Click the Live Data view icon on the Document toolbar to preview the page.

You can also test your dynamic pages by previewing them in a browser (F12). Complete the Testing Server category in the Site Definition dialog box before you preview the page.

Figure 21.5

Live Data Settings dialog box

Using ASP in Dreamweaver

Dreamweaver includes a set of ASP sample files that can be used with the tutorial, "Developing a Web Application." These files are in the `Samples` folder (`Samples/GettingStarted/4-Develop/asp`) that was installed at the time of the Dreamweaver MX 2004 installation. This tutorial can be used with any of the five server technologies that Dreamweaver supports (ASP, ASP.NET, ColdFusion, JSP, and PHP). It can be accessed by choosing Help → Getting Started And Tutorials. In this tutorial, you learn to use a database and an application server to define a recordset, display database records, add dynamic fields to a table, set a repeated region, and create a record insert form. These procedures are basically the same in Dreamweaver regardless of the server technology you choose to use.

> If you created the sample files in Chapter 20, "Working with ColdFusion," you have already gone through all the steps in this tutorial.

Dreamweaver MX 2004 provides built-in tools to use databases with ASP, but this requires knowledge of ASP as well as JavaScript or VBScript.

Although ASP is easy to learn, it's beyond the scope of this chapter to cover the details of learning and using ASP. If you are new to ASP and would like to learn more about creating your own ASP pages, check out the online ASP tutorials at these sites:

- www.4guysfromrolla.com

- www.w3schools.com/asp/

- www.learnasp.com/learnasp/

- www.aspin.com/

From Proprietary to Open Source

Dreamweaver MX 2004 offers tools for rapidly creating ASP web applications and database connections. Although Dreamweaver supports ASP development, you need some basic knowledge of ASP and either VBScript or JavaScript in order to use ASP in Dreamweaver. To learn about the latest version of ASP technology supported by Dreamweaver, see the information on ASP.NET in Chapter 25. In Chapter 28, we'll explore using ASP for dynamic content management.

In the next chapter, you'll learn about PHP, an open-source server technology supported in Dreamweaver MX 2004.

## CHAPTER 22

Using PHP with Dreamweaver

PHP is an open-source server technology for creating dynamic web pages. Dreamweaver MX 2004 includes native support for PHP via its own PHP MySQL server model that developed from a Dreamweaver UltraDev extension to a full server technology. (For more information on Dreamweaver's extensibility features, see Chapter 32, "Customizing and Extending Dreamweaver.")

When a server receives a request for a PHP page from a user's browser, the PHP page is *preprocessed* by the PHP interpreter, and these results are sent to the web server where HTML code is created and sent on to the user's browser. The viewer sees only the resulting HTML page, not the original PHP source code.

You can use Dreamweaver MX 2004's rich visual interface for rapid PHP application development without delving into all the details of writing PHP code. In this chapter, you'll learn how to set up PHP and MySQL on your computer, set up a database connection to MySQL using PHP, and create a PHP application to retrieve and display information from a database on dynamically generated web pages.

The following topics will be discussed in this chapter:

- Getting started with PHP

- Introducing MySQL

- Setting up a Dreamweaver site for PHP

- Connecting to a MySQL database with PHP

- Using PHP in Dreamweaver

Getting Started with PHP

To develop dynamic pages with PHP, you need the PHP application server software. PHP is open-source, and can be downloaded online. Versions of PHP are available for Windows, Linux, Unix, HP-UX, Solaris, and Mac OS X systems. You can use the PHP application server with any of a number of web servers, including Apache, Microsoft IIS or PWS, Sun ONE servers, and most web servers that support the Common Gateway Interface (CGI). You can develop PHP pages locally using a web server on your computer or on a remote web server that supports PHP. Unlike HTML, PHP is a server-side technology, and requires a server to translate the PHP into HTML before passing it on to a browser. (PHP is a recursive acronym that stands for "PHP: Hypertext Preprocessor.")

> If you want to develop with an open-source web server as well as an open-source application server (PHP), download the Apache web server from the Apache Software Foundation at www.apache.org/ and run PHP under Apache. Alternatively, you can download a package installation that includes PHP, MySQL, and Apache at www.firepages.com.au/.

All versions of PHP can be downloaded from the PHP website at www.php.net/downloads.php. There are several options, including complete source code and Windows binaries. The complete source code is in the C language, and needs to be compiled to work on your system. If you are working on a Linux system, you can compile the source code with the tools available in Linux. If you're working on a Windows system, the Windows binaries are a better choice. If you're using IIS or PWS, then download the Windows binaries installer version, or if you're using another web server in Windows, download the Windows binaries zip package. The Windows binaries installer version automatically configures IIS for you, but doesn't include all the external extensions of the Windows binaries zip version—if you'll only be using PHP with IIS, the Windows binaries installer version is easier to install. You'll notice that Beta versions of the newest PHP version are also available, but for starting out we recommend that you choose the most current stable version—PHP 4.3.4 at the time of this writing.

> If you are running Mac OS X 10.1 or later, you can install the PHP module for Apache available at http://www.entropy.ch/software/macosx/php.

For this chapter, we'll install PHP 4.3.4 under Internet Information Services (IIS). If you are using Windows 98, 2000, or XP Pro, web server software (either PWS or IIS) is included with the operating system software. The advantage of using a local web server is that you can test pages quickly without uploading them to a remote server. If you don't have access to a computer with a web server, you can also use a remote computer to test your PHP pages.

> For links to free PHP web hosting services, see `http://www.0php.com/free_PHP_hosting.php`.

PWS or IIS may already be installed on your computer. Both PWS and IIS create a folder named `Inetpub` during installation, so you can check for this folder on your hard drive. If you're using Windows 98, a PWS installation file is included on the Windows 98 CD. Otherwise, you can install IIS via the Add/Remove Program feature in the Control Panel. Choose Add/Remove Windows Components, then select IIS and follow the instructions. For more information on installing a web server, see Chapter 30, "Going Live or Delivering the Site."

> You can't install IIS or run PHP locally if you're using Windows XP Home edition.

Installing PHP

To install the Windows binaries for IIS, download the Windows binaries installer or the Windows binaries zip version. Unzip the file if necessary once the download is complete, and double-click the resulting `.exe` file to start the Windows installer. This process is mostly automatic. You'll be asked where to install PHP (usually `C:\PHP`), and also which server you want to configure to run PHP, as shown in Figure 22.1.

Next, if you downloaded the Windows binaries zip version, you need to let IIS know that PHP is installed (this is automatically done if you use the Windows installer version, so you can skip the next nine steps):

1. Start the Internet Services Manager. In Windows XP Pro, the path is Start → Control Panel → Performance And Maintenance → Administrative Tools.

2. Double-click the Internet Information Services icon to open the Internet Information Services window.

3. Click the arrow next to your computer's name in the displayed list, then click the arrow next to Web Sites. Right-click on Default Web Site (see Figure 22.2), and choose Properties from the contextual menu.

Figure 22.1

Choosing a web server for the PHP application server installation

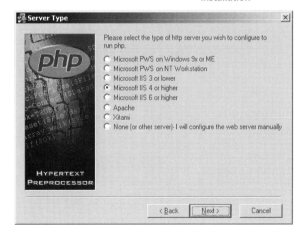

Figure 22.2

Default Web Site in the Internet Services Manager window

4. Choose the Home Directory tab, and click on the Configuration button.

5. Select the Mappings tab, and click the Add button.

6. In the new window that opens, browse to the location of the PHP executable file (usually `C:\PHP`) and select the PHP executable file (`php.exe`).

7. For extension, type **.php**. Make sure that the Script engine and Check That File Exists check boxes are checked.

8. Click OK.

9. Shut down and restart IIS so the changes can take effect. Open a command prompt (Start → All Programs → Accessories → Command Prompt) and type:

```
net stop iisadmin
```

to shut down IIS, then type:

```
net start w3svc
```

to restart it with the new configuration.

Finally, for either installation of PHP, test your PHP installation.

1. Open Dreamweaver and create a new PHP page (File → New → Dynamic page → PHP or click PHP from the Create New list on the Start page).

2. Using Code view, choose Edit → Select All to select all the existing code. Replace this code with:

```
<?php phpinfo() ?>
```

3. Save this file as `testing.php` in the root folder of your web server—for IIS, that's the `WWWROOT` folder within the `Inetpub` directory.

4. Open the page in a browser using this address: `http://localhost/testing.php`. If your installation is successful, the PHP info page should display, as shown in Figure 22.3.

5. If the PHP info page does not display, check the PHP documentation available at `www.php.net/docs.php`.

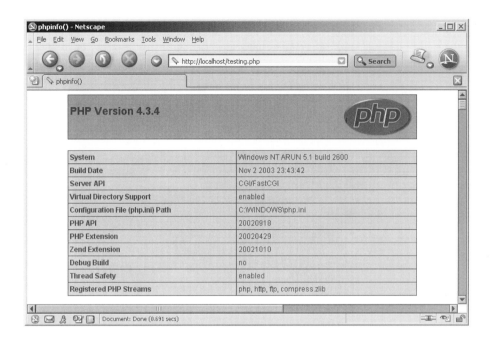

Figure 22.3
This PHP Info page displays after a successful installation of PHP.

For additional information about PHP and online tutorials, see:

- The PHP Info Center on the Zend site: www.zend.com/zend/docs.php
- The PHP Resource Index: http://php.resourceindex.com/Documentation/
  Examples_and_Tutorials/
- PHP Links: www.php.net/links.php

Using MySQL with PHP

To use PHP with a database in Dreamweaver MX 2004, you need to install MySQL on your computer or set up an account with a host that supports MySQL. MySQL is an open-source database server. Although PHP can work with many different database management systems (DBMS), MySQL is the only database supported for PHP in Dreamweaver, and is often the only database supported for PHP by many web hosts.

For free MySQL hosting, see the Free PHP and MySQL hosting directory at http://
free-php.cjb.net/.

MySQL lacks some of the advanced features of commercial database systems, but will likely meet your database needs. There is extensive documentation on the MySQL site (`www.mysql.com`), several resource sites for tutorials and news (see the next section for details), and a large community of MySQL users.

To download MySQL, go to `www.mysql.com/downloads/mysql.html`. At the time of this writing, MySQL 4.0 is the current version of the production release of MySQL. Follow the link to MySQL 4.0, and then select the Windows (or other operating system) downloads. You can choose a version with or without an installer. For more information, see the documentation on the MySQL site (`www.mysql.com/documentation/index.html`).

> You can also install MySQL on a Mac. Download a current version for Mac OS X at `www.entropy.ch/`.

Configuring MySQL

Once you've installed MySQL, you have created all the files you need to run the server. Next, you need to activate MySQL as a service, and configure it.

First, open the WinMySQL administrator by double-clicking on the `winMySQLadmin.exe` file that is located in the `bin` directory of your `mySQL` folder. You need to run this program at least once after you install MySQL. This program does several things:

- Creates the `my.ini` configuration file
- Lets you set a username and password to connect to the MySQL server
- Creates, registers, and starts the MySQL service

You can turn the service on and off by using the services console (Start → Control Panel → Performance And Maintenance → Administrative Tools → Services) or by using a command prompt and typing `net start mysql` to start the service, or `net stop mysql` to stop the service.

Next, open the MySQL console. It's located in the `bin` directory of the folder where you installed MySQL. To use the console:

1. Open a command prompt (Start → All Programs → Accessories → Command Prompt).

2. Type in the following code to navigate to the `bin` directory (adjust as necessary for the version of MySQL you installed and the location of the `bin` directory):

```
cd c:\
C:\> cd c:\mysql-4.0.16\bin
```

3. Then, type the following code to activate the MySQL monitor:

```
mysql.exe
```

You should see a welcome message from the MySQL monitor. This is where you will type commands to the MySQL server so that you can do things like sending queries or creating database tables.

When you're ready to shut down the command prompt, just type `exit`.

While it's beyond the scope of this chapter to give all the details about using MySQL, the following list shows additional online resources for further information and tutorials:

- MySQL Language Reference

    `www.mysql.com/documentation/mysql/bychapter/index.html`

- MySQL tutorials

    `www.devshed.com/Server_Side/MySQL/`

- Webmonkey's PHP/MySQL tutorial

    `http://hotwired.lycos.com/webmonkey/programming/php/tutorials/`
    `tutorial4.html`

Okay, now that you have PHP and MySQL installed (or hosting set up), let's get back to Dreamweaver MX 2004 and set up a PHP site.

Setting Up a Dreamweaver PHP Site

We won't review all the details of setting up a Dreamweaver site in this chapter, but the following list shows the necessary steps, and refers you to other chapters in this book for more details:

1. Set up a root folder (Chapter 21, "Working with ASP").

2. Set permissions for the root folder (Chapter 21, "Working with ASP").

3. Set up a Dreamweaver site. Provide details for Local Info, Remote Info, and Testing Server categories in the Site Definition Dialog box (Chapter 3, "Setting Up Your Workspace and Your Site," and Chapter 16, "Building Web Applications").

Connecting to a Database with PHP MySQL

If you're connecting locally, you'll also need to download an ODBC (Open Database Connectivity) driver for MySQL and create a DSN (data source name). At the time of this writing, the current version can be downloaded at `www.mysql.com/downloads/api-myodbc-3.51.html`. Download the appropriate version for your operating system, and follow the instructions on the download page.

See Chapter 26, "Controlling Access to the Site," for more details on creating a DSN (data source name), and Chapter 19, "Database Connectivity," for more information on using databases in Dreamweaver.

Creating the Database

You can use the MySQL console to set access privileges for users and create a database and table. Follow the instructions in the "Configuring MySQL" section earlier in this chapter to activate the MySQL console. See the file dwsavvy2.txt in the Chapter 22 folder on the CD for the commands to use to create the dwsavvy2 database and set privileges so that visitors can access table1. You can copy the commands from dwsavvy2.txt and paste them in the MySQL console. Paste one block at a time at the mysql> prompt.

A great resource for writing commands for MySQL is available in the Quick Reference Section of "A Gentle Introduction to SQL" at http://sqlzoo.net/.

Connecting to the Database

To use PHP to make a database connection to MySQL in Dreamweaver, you need to have a PHP page open in Dreamweaver. You'll be creating a PHP page in a moment, but for now, open the testing.php page you created earlier in the chapter to test your PHP installation.

To create a PHP database connection (Figure 22.4):

1. Open the Applications panel group and click on the Databases tab. Document Type : PHP should be displayed next to the – (minus) sign at the top of the tab.

2. Click on the + (plus) sign and select MySQL Connection.

3. In the MySQL Connection dialog box, enter a name of your choice in the Connection name textbox.

4. In the MySQL server textbox, enter **localhost** if you are running PHP and MySQL locally.

5. Enter **visitor** in the User name textbox and **11xx3** in the Password textbox.

6. Click the Select button next to the Database text box to browse to a list of available MySQL databases. Choose dwsavvy2.

7. Click the Test button to the right. An alert box displays to let you know if the connection was successful.

Using PHP in Dreamweaver

Figure 22.4

Creating a PHP database connection

Now that the database is created and a database connection is established, you're ready to use PHP and Dreamweaver MX 2004 to access the database and display database records by creating a dynamic master page and detail pages.

Dreamweaver gives you two options for creating master and detail pages. You can create these pages block by block using the Server Behaviors panel, or you can create them all at once by using the Master/Detail Page Set application object. We'll review both techniques in this section.

Using PHP Server Behaviors

First, create the master page:

1. Create a new PHP page in Dreamweaver (File → New → Dynamic page → PHP).

2. Open the Bindings panel (Figure 22.5) in the Application panel group.

3. Click the + (Plus) button at the top of the Bindings panel and choose Recordset (Query). The Recordset dialog box (Figure 22.6) opens.

4. From the Connection drop-down menu, choose the DNS you set up in the last section of this chapter (our DNS is named `dwsavvy_visit`).

5. In the Table drop-down menu, select `table1`.

6. In the Columns radio buttons, choose Selected and then select the `name` row.

7. Click the Test button to display a preview of the selected records.

8. Click OK.

9. Insert a dynamic table (Insert → Application Objects → Dynamic Data → Dynamic Table) to display the selected records on the master page. The Dynamic Table dialog box displays (Figure 22.7).

10. Choose Show All Records, and then click OK.

Next, create the links to the detail page:

1. Select the dynamic content placeholder (in this case, `Recordset1.name`).

2. Open the Property inspector and enter **detail.php** in the Link textbox.

3. Create a URL parameter so that the links in the master page can pass the ID of the selected record to the detail page. The detail page uses the ID to find the selected record in the database.

4. Select the first link in the dynamic table. In the Property inspector, add the following string to the end of the link URL:

```
?name=<?php echo $row_Recordset1['name']; ?>
```

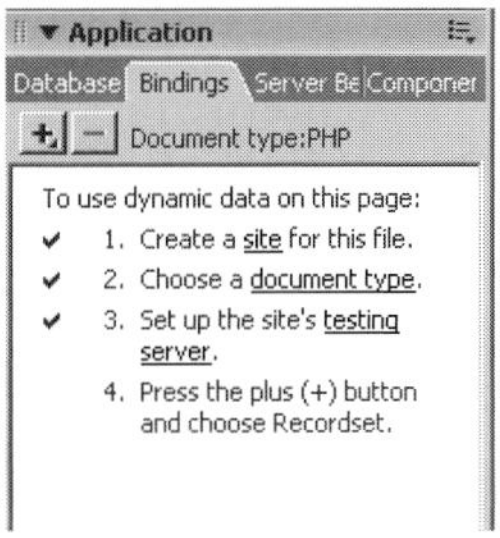

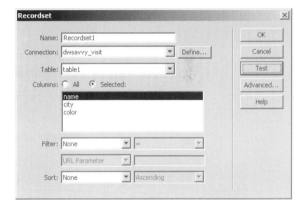

Figure 22.5

The Bindings panel in the Application panel group

Figure 22.6

Using the Recordset dialog box to select records to display on the master page

Figure 22.7

The Dynamic Table dialog box

5. Save the page as `master.php`.

The last step is to create the detail page:

1. Create a new PHP page (File → New → Dynamic page → PHP).

2. Open the Bindings panel (Figure 22.5).

3. Click the + (Plus) button at the top of the Bindings panel and choose Recordset (Query). The Recordset dialog box (Figure 22.8) opens.

4. Select a connection and a database table as in the master Page settings.

5. Choose all columns.

6. Choose `name` from the Filter drop-down menu, and = from the drop-down menu to the right.

7. In the next row, select `URL Parameter`, and then `name` from the drop-down menus.

8. In the Sort row, select `name` and `ascending` from the menus.

9. Click the Test button to preview the data.

10. Click OK.

11. Save the page as `detail.php`.

Make any additions you'd like to the design of the pages. We chose to attach one of Dreamweaver's sample CSS style sheets to both pages, and made a table on the detail page to display the results.

Now you're ready to test your dynamic pages. Open `master.php` in Dreamweaver, and then select File → Preview in Browser. Your page should look like the one shown in Figure 22.9.

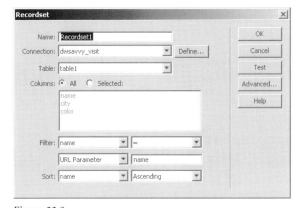

Figure 22.8

Recordset dialog box settings for the detail page

Figure 22.9

The Master page previewed in Internet Explorer

Using Application Objects

This time, you'll use a Master/Detail Page Set application object to create a master and detail page at the same time.

1. Create a new PHP page in Dreamweaver (File → New → Dynamic page → PHP).

2. Open the Bindings panel (Figure 22.5).

3. Click the + (Plus) button at the top of the Bindings panel and choose Recordset (Query). The Recordset dialog box (Figure 22.6) opens.

4. Select a connection and a database table as in the previous master page settings.

5. Choose all columns.

6. Click the Test button to preview the data.

7. Click OK.

8. Save the page as `master2.php`.

9. Open the page in Design view.

10. Insert the application object (Insert → Application Objects → Master Detail Page Set). The Insert Master-Detail Page Set dialog box opens.

11. Specify settings as shown in Figure 22.10. Basically, you select the fields you want to display on the master page first, specify link field, and the primary key field. Then specify a name for the detail page—Dreamweaver will create one if it doesn't already exist—and choose the fields to display on the detail page.

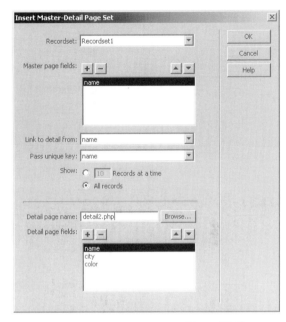

Figure 22.10

Using the Insert Master-Detail Page Set dialog box

That's it! Dreamweaver automatically creates a table on both pages to display the results, and adds a record count to the bottom of the master page.

The four PHP pages are included in the Chapter 22 folder on the CD.

Dreamweaver includes a set of PHP sample files that can be used with the tutorial, "Developing a Web Application." These files are in the Samples folder (`Samples/GettingStarted/4-Develop/php`) that was installed at the time of the Dreamweaver MX 2004 installation. A MySQL database file (`insert.sql`) is included in the Database folder (`Samples/Database`). This tutorial can be used with any of the five server technologies that Dreamweaver supports (ASP, ASP.NET, ColdFusion, JSP, and PHP). It can be accessed by choosing Help → Getting Started and Tutorials. In this tutorial, you learn to use a database and an application server to define a recordset, display database records, add dynamic fields to a table, set a repeated region, and create a record insert form. These procedures are basically the same in Dreamweaver regardless of the server technology you choose to use.

JavaBeans and JRun

PHP and MySQL are a powerful combination for creating dynamic data-driven web pages. Dreamweaver makes it easy to use these open-source server technologies to create dynamic web applications.

In addition to ColdFusion, ASP, and PHP, Dreamweaver MX 2004 supports two additional server technologies, Java Server Pages (JSP) and ASP.NET. We'll explore JSP, Java-Beans, and the JRun application server in the next chapter, and ASP.NET in Chapter 25, "Emerging Technologies."

## CHAPTER 23

Working with JSP

Java Server Pages (JSP) is a technology for creating dynamic web applications. Java Server Pages contain a combination of JSP scripts and HTML. The JSP server compiles the JSP scripts into Java *servlets* (small Java programs that run on a web server in response to browser requests). These servlets generate dynamic content that is sent back to the client browser as HTML. The servlet stays active in the server memory until the server is shut down, responding to client requests, and making JSP a very fast server technology. For more complex Java code, you can use *JavaBeans*—compiled Java code that is accessed through a JSP script.

Dreamweaver MX 2004 provides several tools for using JSP and JavaBeans to develop dynamic web pages, and includes a set of JSP sample files as well as a tutorial for developing a sample web application using JSP.

The following topics will be discussed in this chapter:

- **Getting started with JSP**

- **Setting up a Dreamweaver site for JSP**

- **Connecting to a database with JSP**

- **Creating a dynamic page with JSP**

- **Using JSP in Dreamweaver**

Getting Started with JSP

To develop dynamic pages with JSP, you need a web server that supports JSP and servlets, either a local web server on your computer or a remote web server. If your web server of choice doesn't support JSP, you may be able to use an add-on JSP engine to enable the web server to process JSP and servlets. Several combinations of web server, application server, and add-on engines are possible. For more details, see the list at `java.sun.com/products/jsp/industry.html`.

JSP works with several application servers, including the following:

Macromedia JRun Available for Windows, Mac OS X, Linux, Unix, and Solaris. JRun is available as a server or as an add-on engine. JRun Developer Edition is available for free download at `www.macromedia.com/downloads/`.

Apache Tomcat An open-source application server for JSP, available for Windows, Mac OS X, and Unix. Apache Tomcat is available as a server or as an add-on engine. It can be downloaded free at `http://jakarta.apache.org/tomcat/`.

IBM WebSphere Available for Windows and Linux. A trial version can be downloaded at `www7b.software.ibm.com/wsdd/downloads/WASsupport.html#download`.

> You can sign up for free JSP hosting at `www.mycgiserver.com`.

In this chapter, we'll be using Macromedia JRun 4.0 connected to IIS via JRun's easy-to-use Web Server Configuration Tool. (Jrun also supports Apache HTTP Server, Netscape Enterprise Server, Netscape iPlanet, and Zeus Web Server.)

The Root Folder

In order to use a local web server, you need to save your files in the root folder of the web server. If you are using PWS or IIS, the default root folder is named `wwwroot` and is located in the `Inetpub` folder. You can also create separate root folders within the `wwwroot` folder to test separate JSP applications. (We created a folder named JSP within the IIS `wwwroot` folder.)

Unlike an HTML page, which you can open directly in a browser by double-clicking the file or by entering the file path, you need to open your JSP pages via the root folder of the web server. If you have added a JSP engine to IIS, and created a folder named JSP within the IIS `wwwroot` folder, you can test your web server by entering the following URL in a browser:

```
http://localhost/JSP/filename
```

Setting Permissions

If you create a separate root folder, you need to make sure that Read and Script permissions are enabled for the folder:

- For PWS, open the Personal Web Manager. Choose Advanced options and then select Home and choose Edit Properties. Select the Read and Scripts options.

- For IIS, open the Control Panel and then choose Administrative Tools. (In XP Pro, choose Performance and Maintenance → Administrative Tools → Internet Information Services). Find the folder you created under local computer → Web Sites → Default Web Site → *your folder*. Right-click the folder and select Properties from the context menu. On the Directory tab, make sure that Scripts Only is selected in the Execute Permissions drop-down menu.

Setting Up a JSP Site in Dreamweaver

Setting up a dynamic JSP site in Dreamweaver is not much more complicated than setting up a static site. For more information on setting up Dreamweaver sites in general, see Chapter 3, "Setting Up Your Workspace and Your Site." For additional details on setting up a dynamic site in Dreamweaver, see Chapter 16, "Building Web Applications."

Creating a Root Folder

Create a separate root folder named JSP within the wwwroot folder of the Inetpub folder on your hard drive. Enable permissions for this folder as described in the section "Setting Permissions" earlier in this chapter.

Defining the Local Info

Select Site → Manage Sites → New. This brings up the Site Definition dialog box. If the wizard is showing, click the Advanced tab. You should automatically start in the Local Info category.

As shown in Figure 23.1, name your site JSP, browse to the local root folder, and indicate the HTTP address of the site. Leave the Site Definition dialog box open.

Figure 23.1

Defining the Local Info

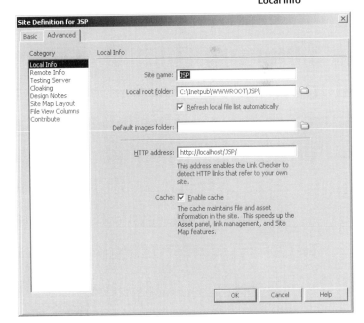

Defining the Remote Info

Select the Remote Info category. Choose Local/Network from the Access drop-down menu (unless you are using a remote host). Browse to the JSP folder and select it as the Remote Folder, as shown in Figure 23.2. Leave the Site Definition dialog box open.

Defining the Testing Server

Select the Testing Server category. Choose JSP as the Server Model, then select Local/Network from the Access drop-down menu (unless you are using remote hosting). Dreamweaver should automatically copy your settings from the Remote Info window into the Testing Server Folder text box and the URL Prefix text box, but double-check to make sure these are correct (see Figure 23.3). Click OK to close the Site Definition dialog box.

Connecting to a Database with JSP

The first step in connecting to a database with JSP in Dreamweaver MX 2004 is to make sure you have the appropriate driver installed. Dreamweaver supports the following drivers for JSP connections, as well as custom JDBC connections:

- IBM DB2 App Driver
- IBM DB2 Net Driver
- MySQL Driver

- Oracle Thin Driver
- Inet Driver
- Sun JDBC-ODBC Driver

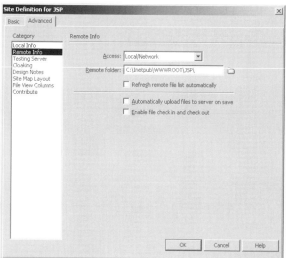

Figure 23.2

Defining the Remote Info

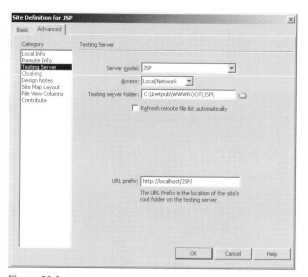

Figure 23.3

Defining the Testing Server

A list of JDBC drivers and vendors is available at:

`http://servlet.java.sun.com/products/jdbc/drivers`

If you are using Windows, you can use an ODBC driver, create a DSN (as described in Chapter 26, "Controlling Access to the Site"), and then use the Sun JDBC-ODBC driver to make a connection to the database. This driver comes with the Sun Java 2 SDK, version 1.2 or higher, Standard Edition for Windows—check your hard drive for a folder named `jdk1.2`, `jdk1.3`, or `j2sdk 1.4`. You can download the Java 2 SDK 1.4 .2 at `http://java.sun.com/j2se/1.4.2/`.

For the examples in this chapter, we use the TrioMotors database that installs with Dreamweaver MX 2004. The TrioMotors database is an Access database and uses an ODBC driver.

> See Chapter 19, "Database Connectivity," for more information on using databases in Dreamweaver.

Creating the Database Connection

Once you have the right drivers (and a DSN, if you're using PWS or IIS), you're ready to make a JSP database connection in Dreamweaver.

Open a JSP page in Dreamweaver. You'll be creating a JSP page in a moment, but for now open the `today.jsp` page in the Chapter 23 folder on the CD, copy it to the JSP folder, and then open it in Dreamweaver.

To create a JSP database connection (Figure 23.4), follow these steps:

1. Open the Applications panel group and click on the Databases tab. JSP should be displayed next to the – (minus) sign at the top of the tab.

2. Click on the + (plus) sign and select Sun JDBC-ODBC Driver.

3. In the Sun JDBC-ODBC Driver dialog box, enter **TrioMotors** in the Connection name textbox.

4. In the URL textbox, enter **jdbc:odbc:TrioMotors**.

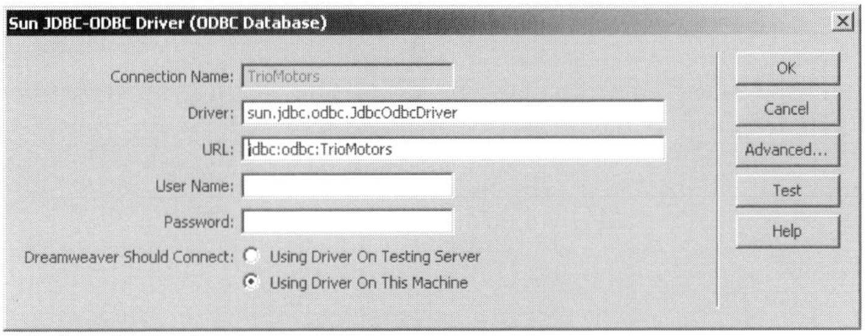

Figure 23.4

Creating a JDBC database connection

5. Specify the location of the JDBC-ODBC driver. Select "Using Driver On This Machine" (for a local web server) or "Using Driver On Testing Server" (for a remote web server).

6. Enter a user name and password if necessary to access the database.

7. Click Test. An alert box displays to let you know if the connection was successful.

> For more information on using databases in Dreamweaver, see Chapter 19, "Database Connectivity."

Creating a Dynamic JSP Page

Now let's create a simple JSP page to show the current date and time, and test it in our web server. This page accesses the current date and time on the server that processes the JSP page. If you're using a local web server, it will display the local values for time and date. If you're using a remote web server, it will display the time and date for the server location.

1. Open a new JSP file in Dreamweaver (File → New → Dynamic Page → JSP).

2. Save the file as `today2.jsp`.

3. Open the Design panel group and click on the Options menu in the upper-right corner. Select "Attach Style Sheet." From the Attach External Style Sheet window, click on the Sample Style Sheets link at the bottom. Choose the Colors: Yellow/Brown style sheet (it's included in the Chapter 23 folder on the CD as `colors4.css`).

4. Add the following HTML text to highlight the time:

   ```
   Today is
   ```

Figure 23.5

Using the JSP Server to display the current date and time.

5. Leave a space, then add the following code to request the current time from the server and write it to the page:

   ```
   <%= new java.util.Date() %>
   ```

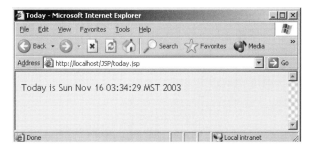

Note the `<%` and `%>` tags, which indicate that this is a JSP script block.

6. Save the page.

7. Preview the page in a browser (File → Preview In Browser). It should resemble Figure 23.5.

Using JSP in Dreamweaver

Now that a database connection is established, you're ready to use JSP and Dreamweaver MX 2004 to access the TrioMotors database and build a search and result page.

You'll build a search page using an HTML form. You'll use a single parameter from the TrioMotors database (region) to search for all TrioMotors locations in that region, and then display those results to the user via a results page.

First, create the search page:

1. Open a new JSP page in Dreamweaver (File → New → Dynamic Page → JSP).

2. Open the Design panel group, click the Options menu at the upper-right, and select Attach Style Sheet. Browse to the location of the `colors4.css` file.

2. Insert an HTML form (Insert → Form → Form).

3. Enter `results.jsp` for the action, and GET for the method.

4. Add a List (Insert → Form → List/Menu). In the Tag Editor dialog box, enter `region` for the Name and 1 for the size.

5. Click on the opening `select` tag and open the Property inspector.

6. Click on the List Values button, and then enter the following values in the Labels column of the List Values dialog box:

   - North America
   - South/Central America
   - Europe
   - Africa
   - Asia
   - Australia

7. Enter values in the Values column of the dialog box, starting with **1** for North America and ending with **6** for Australia, as shown in Figure 23.6.

8. Add a Submit button (Insert → Form → Button). Choose submit from the drop-down menu, and enter `Submit` in the Name and in the Value field.

9. Save the page as `search.jsp`.

Figure 23.6

List Values dialog box for JSP Search Page

Next, create the results page:

1. Create a new JSP page (File → New → Dynamic Page → JSP).

2. Save the page as results.jsp.

3. Open the Design panel group, click the Options menu at the upper-right, and select Attach Style Sheet. Browse to the location of the colors4.css file.

4. Open the Bindings panel in the Application panel group.

5. Click the + (Plus) button at the upper-left of the panel and choose Recordset.

6. The Recordset dialog box displays in Simple view. Choose TrioMotors from the Connection drop-down menu, select the LOCATIONS table, and all columns, as shown in Figure 23.7.

7. From the first row of drop-down menus in the Filter area, choose REGION_ID and =; in the second row, choose URL parameter (because you're using the GET method) and the name of the form object on the search.jsp page that accepts the search parameter (region).

8. From the Sort drop-down menus choose REGION_ID and Ascending so that the locations for that region will display in alphabetical order. Your settings should now look like those in Figure 23.8.

9. Click the Test button to preview the data display. Keep the page open.

Finally, add a dynamic table to display the results:

1. Insert a dynamic table after the opening body tag (Insert → Application Objects → Dynamic Data → Dynamic Table).

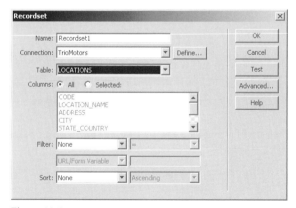

Figure 23.7

Choosing the results display from the Recordset dialog

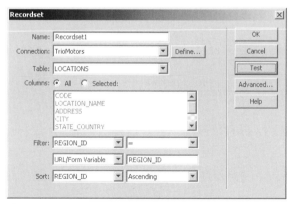

Figure 23.8

Finalizing the settings in the Recordset dialog

2. In the Dynamic Table dialog box, select Show 10 Records At A Time, and then click OK to insert the table.

3. Save the page.

4. Open the `search.jsp` page, and preview it in a browser (File → Preview in Browser). Choose a region from the drop-down menu and click the Submit button. The results for that region should display on the `results.jsp` page. Figure 23.9 and 23.10 show the display in Internet Explorer.

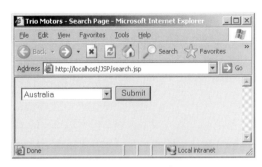

Figure 23.9
`search.jsp` in **Internet Explorer**

Advanced JSP in Dreamweaver

If you are an experienced JSP developer, you can also use Dreamweaver to create JavaBeans or use JSP stored procedures or prepared statements to modify a database.

For more information, see the Dreamweaver Help menu and the JRun section of the Macromedia site (`www.macromedia.com/software/jrun/`). If you have installed JRun, see the `Getting_Started_with_JRun` section in the `html` folder in the `docs` folder in the directory where JRun is installed (usually `C:\JRun4`).

Other Technologies

In addition to the four server technologies that you've learned about in the last four chapters (ColdFusion, ASP, PHP, and JSP), Dreamweaver also supports a fifth server technology: ASP.NET, which along with emerging technologies is covered in Chapter 25.

Dreamweaver also includes support for Extensible Markup Language (XML). The next chapter explores the use of XML and XHTML in Dreamweaver MX 2004.

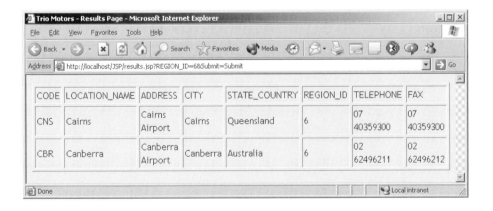

Figure 23.10
`results.jsp` in **Internet Explorer**

## CHAPTER 24

Working with XML and XHTML

HTML is fine for most person-to-machine interactions, but machines have a hard time reading HTML. This is because HTML is mostly formatting information (which machines don't care about) and links (which they do), and machines don't read the content the way humans do. Basically, machines read data and need metadata or some sort of context to help them understand the meaning or applicability of that data. For day-to-day websites, this may not be very important. But for B2B (business-to-business) websites, it can make or break the project.

One way that both humans and machines can understand is to encode the meaning or metadata surrounding data with XML (Extensible Markup Language), which is used to create custom markup languages (XML applications). You can design your own language by creating a set of tags that describe the content they contain. You can use this set of custom tags to specify a structure for the content of your XML document.

This chapter covers the following topics:

- **The basics of XML**
- **Using XML in Dreamweaver**
- **XHTML in Dreamweaver**
- **Validating XML and XHTML documents**
- **Using XML news feeds**

XML Concepts

Why should you care about XML? XML and its associated technologies are one of the most rapidly growing areas in web development today. Even if you never deal with "data" on the websites you design, XML can be used to efficiently update and maintain the text content of web pages. Check out the resources listed at the end of this section to continue your introduction to XML. Flash 2004 and ColdFusion both include extensive support for XML application development, and future versions of Dreamweaver are likely to include much more support for XML and XHTML.

One of the most important and basic features of XML is extensibility. *Extensibility* means that, in contrast to HTML, there is no core set of tags that make up the language. You can create whatever tags you need to structure your XML document so that the content is in a form that meets your needs. If you give your tags meaningful names that describe the content, it is easy for you and others to understand what information is contained in the document.

> Dreamweaver itself is written partly in XML as well as HTML and JavaScript. For example, the configuration of your menus is stored in an XML file. Dreamweaver also supports the use of XML, through the use of Dreamweaver templates to import and export XML.

Creating XML documents requires planning. If you are sharing XML documents with a larger group or industry, it's important to make sure that the documents are structured in a consistent way so that the information can be accessed and exchanged easily and efficiently.

For example, to create an XML document (`inventory.xml`) that can be used for parts inventory information, follow these steps:

1. Start the XML document with an XML declaration like this one:

   ```
   <?xml version="1.0"?>
   ```

   This XML declaration tells the processor that this is an XML file, and it also specifies which version of XML is used in the document. Version 1.0 is currently the only version of XML available, so it's the only one we can specify in our XML declaration!

2. Add a root element to the document. In this case, the root element is `inventory`. Everything that follows the XML declaration is contained within this root element.

   ```
   <inventory>
   ```

3. Add a `part` element. This element is the first child of the `inventory` element.

   ```
   <part>1971</part>
   ```

4. Add additional child elements of the `inventory` element. These child elements contain information about a specific part in our inventory.

   ```
   <name>Maxwell Silver Hammer</name>
   ```

```
<description>12" hammer with silver coating on head</description>
<warranty>lifetime</warranty>
<costRetail>25.00</costRetail>
<costWholesale>12.50</costWholesale>
<discount>yes</discount>
<shipping>7.95</shipping>
<stock>5</stock>
```

5. Close the `inventory` tag to complete the document.

```
</inventory>
```

The complete markup for `inventory.xml` is shown in Listing 24.1 and is also included in the Chapter 24 folder on the accompanying CD.

Listing 24.1

XML File for Inventory Data (*inventory.xml*)

```
<?xml version="1.0"?>
<inventory>
    <part>1971</part>
    <name>Maxwell Silver Hammer</name>
    <description>12" hammer with silver coating on head</description>
    <warranty>lifetime</warranty>
    <costRetail>25.00</costRetail>
    <costWholesale>12.50</costWholesale>
    <discount>yes</discount>
    <shipping>7.95</shipping>
    <stock>5</stock>
</inventory>
```

The markup in XML documents is often indented, as shown in Listing 24.1, to highlight the underlying structure of the document and to make it easier to read the code.

This XML document (`inventory.xml`) illustrates the following basic rules of XML syntax:

An XML document must contain a root element that contains all the other elements in the document. The XML declaration, links to other documents, and comments are the only components that can be outside of the root element container. The root element in this example is `inventory`.

Every element must have a closing tag. Most commonly, XML elements contain content, either text or data, and need both an opening and a closing tag. However, XML can also include empty elements (elements that contain no content). Empty elements can use a combined opening and closing tag

```
<warehouse/>
```

or can use separate opening and closing tags

```
<warehouse></warehouse>
```

Empty elements often include attributes, but the attributes are contained within the tag itself: `<warehouse branch="east"/>`.

Elements must be properly nested. If you open one element and then open a second element before you close the first one, you must close the second element before you close the first one. For example, this is correct XML syntax:

```
<apples>
<oranges>
</oranges>
</apples>
```

This is incorrect:

```
<apples>
<oranges>
</apples>
</oranges>
```

Unlike HTML, XML syntax has strict rules that must be followed. XML documents will not function correctly if the syntax is not correct.

XML is case sensitive. Case matters in XML. The elements APPLES, Apples, and apples are three different elements in XML. It doesn't make a difference which case you use, but you must be consistent.

All attribute values must be quoted. An attribute's value must be enclosed in either single or double quotation marks; for example:

```
<part number="1971">
```

Figure 24.1

`inventory.xml` **in Internet Explorer 6**

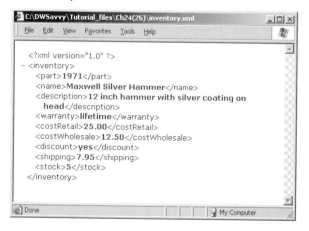

An XML document that follows the rules of XML syntax is a *well-formed* XML document. An XML document that is well-formed will display in a browser; however, the display itself varies with the browser. Internet Explorer 6 displays the source code of the XML document. Figure 24.1 shows `inventory.xml` as displayed in Internet Explorer 6.

Unlike Internet Explorer 6, Netscape 6+ displays the content of all the tags. Because XML does not include any information about the presentation of the content,

the content is displayed in a straight line without any formatting. Figure 24.2 shows
`inventory.xml` as displayed in Netscape 7.

Style information can be added to an XML document by using
a Cascading Style Sheet (CSS) or Extensible Style Language Trans-
formations (XSLT) style sheet. Since the content is separated from
the style, XML information exchange is not limited to the Web,
but can also be used on other devices such as wireless appliances.

In addition to being well-formed, XML documents should be
valid. To determine if an XML document is valid, test it against
another document that specifies the rules for the structure of the
XML document. Either a *document type definition (DTD)* or a *schema* can be used for validating XML documents. A DTD is a set of rules for the elements and attributes in a document. The syntax of a DTD is based on *Standardized General Markup Language (SGML)*,
the parent language of many other markup languages, including XML and HTML. A
schema is also a set of rules for a document's structure. Schemas are written in XML itself.

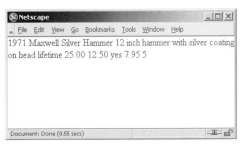

Figure 24.2
`inventory.xml`
in Netscape 7

For additional information about XML, check out the following online resources:

- The W3C XML 1.0 (Second Edition) specification at `www.w3.org/TR/REC-xml`

- XML tutorial at `www.w3schools.com/xml/default.asp`

- IBM Developer Works at `www-106.ibm.com/developerworks/views/xml/tutorials.jsp`,
  which offers several XML tutorials including "Intro to XML" and "Validating XML"

- "What the Hell Is XML?" an article by Troy Janisch at `www.alistapart.com/stories/`
  `hellxml/`

- "How Should My XML Look? Using Style Sheets with XML," an article by Jennifer
  Kyrnin at `http://html.about.com/library/weekly/aa110600a.htm`

XML in Dreamweaver MX 2004

XML's main role in Dreamweaver at the current time is for the underlying configuration
of the Dreamweaver program itself. If you look at the files in the Configuration folder
included in the Dreamweaver installation (the default path to the folder on a PC is usually
`C:\Program Files\Macromedia\Dreamweaver MX 2004\Configuration\`), you'll see that most
of Dreamweaver's configuration files are either XML, JavaScript, or HTML files.

Open the Configuration folder and then open the folders named `CodeColoring`, `CodeHints`,
`Menus`, or `Toolbars`, for example, and you'll find XML files. The following code snippet is
taken from Dreamweaver's `toolbars.xml` file (in the Toolbars folder) that specifies the
appearance of toolbars in Dreamweaver.

```
<menubutton id="DW_ValidatorErrors"
  image="Toolbars/images/MM/validatornoerrors.png"
```

```
arguments="'valmenu'"
tooltip="Browser target check"
file="Toolbars/MM/ValidatorErrors.htm"
update="onViewChange,onValidationChange"/>
```

This part of the code specifies the appearance of the Check Browser support section of the Document toolbar.

One of the most valuable features of Dreamweaver is the availability to the user of the program's configuration. Dreamweaver is unusual in that it allows you access to the program files themselves so that you can customize and extend the program to meet your needs. For example, you can change the display of the Dreamweaver toolbars and menus, as discussed in the preceding paragraph. You can also create custom tags to use in Dreamweaver by using XML to create the specific features of the tags. These aspects of Dreamweaver are covered in detail in Chapter 32, "Customizing and Extending Dreamweaver."

How else can you use XML in Dreamweaver?

- You can open an XML file for editing directly in Dreamweaver. Dreamweaver will open the file in code view and you can enter changes and save the file in Dreamweaver. If you spend much time working on XML files, though, you will probably want to use a full-fledged XML editor and development tool such as Altova's XML Spy (www.xmlspy.com).

- You can import and export XML to and from Dreamweaver with XML templates. However, Dreamweaver requires the XML to be in a Dreamweaver-specific, nonstandard form. If you work with XML files regularly, it's not likely you'll want to take the extra time to convert your XML files to Dreamweaver format. If you work with XML only in Dreamweaver, and want to display XML content in your HTML pages, Dreamweaver's XML templates can be an effective way to do this. The details of the XML import and export process are covered in the following section of this chapter.

- You can import XML tags from XML DTD (Document Type Definition) and XML Schema files. These tags are then available for use in Dreamweaver documents. Details are provided in the section "Importing Tags from XML Files," later in this chapter.

Importing and Exporting XML with XML Templates

XML can be imported and exported from Dreamweaver by using templates. The templates can be used to import XML content into the editable regions of a template and then display that information as part of an HTML page. Content can also be exported from the editable regions of a template to create an XML file.

For more information on using templates, see Chapter 4, "Saving Labor with Templates and Libraries."

CDATA SECTIONS AND XML VALIDATION

CDATA sections are used in XML documents to enclose any content that you would like to display, but not parse. Because these sections are not available to the XML parser, your content will not be available for validation. The *structure* of your document can still be validated, just not the content that is enclosed in CDATA sections. If your content is mainly text, validating the content may not be a big issue. If your content is mainly data, however, validating the content is a major advantage of using XML. The easiest way to get your XML document into a format that's compatible with Dreamweaver is to create a Dreamweaver template, use the template to create an HTML page, and then export the editable regions from this HTML page to create an XML file. This XML file can then be used to create other XML files in a format that can be imported into Dreamweaver.

XML must be formatted in a very specific way in order to be imported into a Dreamweaver template, and any XML exported from Dreamweaver will also be formatted in this way. Dreamweaver uses CDATA (character data) sections to enclose any content contained in your XML tags, as shown in the following example:

```
<item name="warranty"><![CDATA[lifetime]]></item>
```

This example shows the sixth line of markup from the `inventory.xml` file you created earlier in this chapter after it has been converted to Dreamweaver XML format.

In the following example, you will import the `inventory.xml` file you created earlier in this chapter into Dreamweaver and use it to create other XML files in a format that can be imported into Dreamweaver and displayed in HTML pages. To do this, follow these steps:

1. Open the `inventory.dwt` file from the Chapter 24 folder of this book's accompanying CD. This is a template file based on `inventory.xml`. The template file was created in Dreamweaver in order to display the inventory information on a HTML page. Figure 24.3 shows `inventory.dwt` in Dreamweaver's Design view (View → Design).

   As you look at this view, you will see that the names of the XML elements from `inventory.xml` are the same as the names of the editable regions in the Dreamweaver template. This is so that Dreamweaver knows where to insert the XML content.

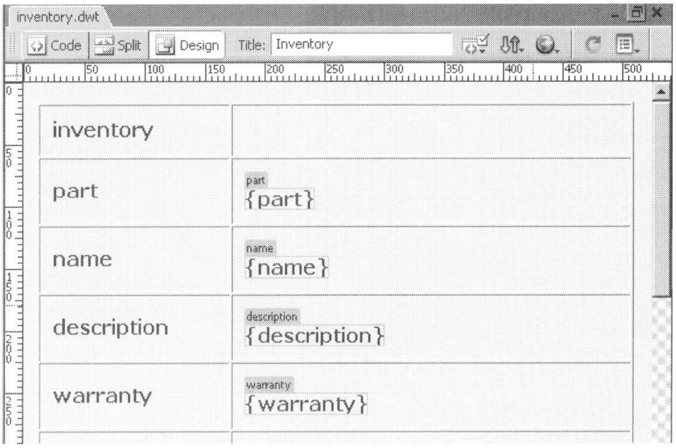

Figure 24.3

`inventory.dwt` in **Design view**

2. From the `inventory.dwt` file, choose File → Import → XML Into Template. An Import XML dialog box displays, as shown in Figure 24.4. Choose `inventory2.xml`. This file is in the Chapter 24 tutorial folder. The difference between this file and your original file is the addition of CDATA sections to enclose any content in the tags and Dreamweaver's `templateItems` and `items` tags.

> If your XML document is not in Dreamweaver XML format (it does not have all the content enclosed in CDATA sections), the new HTML page that is created by Dreamweaver may show no XML content, or may display content incorrectly. Generally, in this case, the HTML file looks the same as the template file; in other words, no content has been inserted.

3. If the XML file you choose to import is already in Dreamweaver XML format, such as `inventory2.xml`, the HTML file that's created will display the data correctly. In this case, you don't need to go through the rest of the steps that follow—just save your file from Step 2 as `inventory.html` and you're done! Preview the file in a browser to see a display of the data contained in `inventory2.xml`.

4. If the XML file you choose to import is not in Dreamweaver format, such as `inventorya .xml`, you will need to add XML content to the appropriate areas in the HTML file that's created, as shown in Figure 24.5. Save this file as `inventory2.html`.

> The `inventorya.xml` file contains a `template` attribute that specifies the template to use for import. Otherwise, Dreamweaver will not allow you to import the XML data from the file.

Figure 24.4

Import XML dialog box

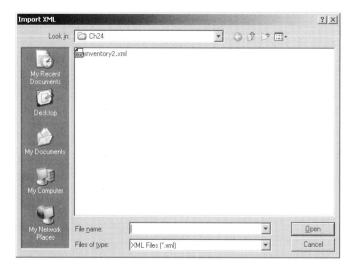

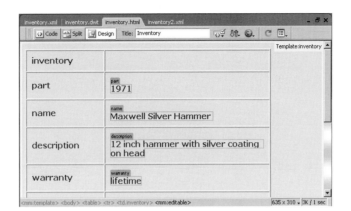

Figure 24.5

An HTML file (`inventory.html`) created by importing an XML file

5. From the `inventory.html` file, choose File → Export → Template Data As XML. The Export Template Data as XML dialog box displays, as shown in Figure 24.6.

6. Click a radio button to choose the type of notation for the XML file. You can choose either Use Standard Dreamweaver XML Tags or Use Editable Region Names As XML Tags. The standard Dreamweaver XML tags use an `item` element. The name of the item element is the same as the name of the editable region. Listing 24.2 shows markup for `inventory2.xml` (also included on the accompanying CD). This file uses Dreamweaver XML tags. The content is exactly the same as our original file, `inventory.xml`, but the tag structure is different. This file has a root element named `templateItems` that includes a `template` attribute that specifies the path and filename of the template file (`inventory.dwt`).

Figure 24.6

Export Template Data as XML dialog box

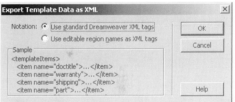

7. If you choose to use editable region names as XML tags, your XML file will use the names themselves as tags, and no Dreamweaver `item` elements will be included. The markup in that case will be similar to `inventoryb.xml`, shown in Listing 24.3. The root element is still `inventory`, but it now includes a `template` attribute to specify the path and filename of the template file.

Listing 24.2

Using Standard Dreamweaver XML Tags (*inventory2.xml*)

```
<?xml version="1.0"?>
<templateItems template="inventory.dwt" codeOutsideHTMLIsLocked="false">
    <item name="part"><![CDATA[1971]]></item>
    <item name="name"><![CDATA[Maxwell Silver
        Hammer ]]></item>
    <item name="description"><![CDATA[12
```

```
        inch hammer with silver coating on head]]></item>
    <item name="warranty"><![CDATA[lifetime]]></item>
    <item name="costRetail"><![CDATA[25.00]]></item>
    <item name="costWholesale"><![CDATA[12.50]]></item>
    <item name="discount"><![CDATA[yes]]></item>
    <item name="shipping"><![CDATA[7.95]]></item>
    <item name="stock"><![CDATA[5]]></item>
</templateItems>
```

Listing 24.3

Using Editable Region Names as Tag Names (*inventoryb.xml*)

```
<?xml version="1.0"?>
<inventory template="inventory.dwt" codeOutsideHTMLIsLocked="false">
    <doctitle><![CDATA[<title>Inventory</title>]]></doctitle>
    <warranty><![CDATA[lifetime]]></warranty>
    <shipping><![CDATA[7.95]]></shipping>
    <part><![CDATA[1971]]></part>
    <description><![CDATA[12
        inch hammer with silver coating on head]]></description>
    <costRetail><![CDATA[25.00]]></costRetail>
    <name><![CDATA[Maxwell Silver
        Hammer ]]></name>
    <costWholesale><![CDATA[12.50]]></costWholesale>
    <discount><![CDATA[yes]]></discount>
    <stock><![CDATA[5]]></stock>
</inventory>
```

The exported XML file can be used to create other XML files with the same structure but different content. Because these XML files are in Dreamweaver XML format (either using item elements or using editable region names as tag names), they can be directly imported into Dreamweaver templates to create HTML files.

Importing Tags from XML Files

Dreamweaver MX 2004 allows you to import tags from an XML DTD (Document Type Definition) or XML Schema document. These imported tags are added to the Tag Library and then are available for use in Dreamweaver.

To add XML tags from an XML document, follow these steps:

1. Open the Tag Library editor (Edit → Tag Libraries).

2. Click the plus (+) sign and choose DTDSchema from the drop-down menu, and then select Import XML DTD or Schema File.

3. Enter the filename or URL of the DTD or schema document in the File or remote URL box, or click the Browse button to the right of the box to navigate to the DTD or schema file.

4. If you want to identify a tag as a part of a specific tag library, enter a prefix for the tags in the Tag Prefix box.

5. Click the OK button.

These tags are now available for you to use when you are creating Dreamweaver documents.

Supporting XHTML in Dreamweaver

XHTML (Extensible Hypertext Markup Language) is HTML written in XML syntax. XHTML is a transition between HTML and XML, and it provides an easy and useful way to write code that is compliant with W3C standards.

Dreamweaver MX 2004 includes support for XHTML documents in its basic configuration, and it allows you to create XHTML documents as well as convert HTML documents to XHTML documents.

XHTML is a reformulation of HTML using XML syntax. It is very similar to HTML but uses the stricter XML syntax rules. The basic rules of XHTML syntax are the same as the rules for XML syntax in the "XML Concepts" section earlier in this chapter. Dreamweaver automatically applies the following rules of XHTML syntax to the XHTML files it creates:

- The root element of the document must be the `html` element. XHTML files are saved with an `.html` file extension.

- If the character encoding of an XHTML document is anything other than UTF-8, an XML declaration that includes the character encoding is included in the document, as shown in the following:

      `<xml version="1.0" encoding="iso-8859-1"?>`

- A `DOCTYPE` declaration must precede the root element, such as the transitional XHTML 1.0 doctype shown in the following example:

      `<!DOCTYPE html PUBLIC ""-//W3C/DTD XHTML 1.0 Transitional//EN""`
      `    "http://www.w3.org/TR/xhtml1/DTD/xhtml1-transitional.dtd">`

There are three types of XHTML doctypes: strict, transitional, and frameset. A doctype is required for a valid XHTML document. Dreamweaver MX 2004 automatically uses the transitional XHTML doctype for any XHTML document that is not in frames, in which case it uses the frameset XHTML doctype. The strict XHTML doctype is not available in Dreamweaver MX 2004, although you can always manually change the doctype to XHTML strict.

Other rules for valid XHTML include the following:

- The XHTML namespace must be associated with `html` root element, as in the following example:

  ```
  <html xmlns="http://www.w3.org/1999/xhtml">
  ```

- Use an `id` attribute in addition to a `name` attribute (with the same value) to identify elements.

- Attributes that do not include a value, such as `checked` in a check box form element, must include a value in XHTML. This is specified by using the attribute name for the value—for example `checked="checked"`.

- All `script` and `style` elements must include a `type` attribute. Any `script` elements must also include a `language` attribute.

- All `img` and `area` elements must include an `alt` attribute.

The complete markup for a simple XHTML file named `xhtml_example.html` is shown in Listing 24.4 and is also included in the Chapter 24 folder on the accompanying CD. Note that all attribute values are quoted, even color name attributes such as `white`.

Listing 24.4

An XHTML Document Created in Dreamweaver (*xhtml_example.html*)

```
<!DOCTYPE html PUBLIC ".//W3C/DTD XHTML 1.0 Transitional//EN"
   "http://www.w3.org/TR/xhtml1/DTD/xhtml1-transitional.dtd">
<html xmlns="http://www.w3.org/1999/xhtml">
<head>
<title>XHTML sample</title>
<meta http-equiv="Content-Type" content="text/html; charset=iso-8859-1" />
<style type="text/css">
<!--
body {
   background-color: #99CC99;
   font-family: "Trebuchet MS"
}
body,td,th {
   color: #663300;
}
-->
</style></head>
<body>
<hr />
<p>This is an XHTML file. It is saved as an HTML file so that
   browsers can display it.</p>
<br />
</body>
</html>
```

XHTML is easy to learn, and helps ensure that the documents you create are W3C standards compliant.

The W3C provides a free online validator for XHTML documents at `http://validator.w3.org/file-upload.html`. For information about validating XHTML documents in Dreamweaver MX 2004, see the next section, "Validating XML and XHTML Documents."

It's easy to create XHTML documents in Dreamweaver. There are three options for creating XHTML documents.

To create a new XHTML document, follow these steps:

1. Open a new file (File → New).
2. In the Category column, select Basic Page.
3. In the Basic Page column, select HTML.
4. Check the box labeled Make Document XHTML Compliant.
5. Click the Create button.

To convert an HTML document to an XHTML document, follow these steps:

1. Open an existing HTML file (File → New).
2. Convert it to XHTML (File → Convert → XHTML).

If the HTML document is part of a frameset, each frame and the frameset document must be selected and converted separately. See Chapter 7, "Interactivity with Framesets and Frames," for more information on saving documents in frames and framesets.

Then follow these steps to create XHTML documents by default:

1. Open the Preferences dialog box (Edit → Preferences).
2. Select the New Document category.
3. Select a document type and check the Make Document XHTML Compliant box.

Whether you use the Start page and choose Create New → HTML, or use File → New → HTML, Dreamweaver MX 2004 will now create an XHTML file by default.

You can clean up XHTML code by opening a document in Dreamweaver and then choosing Commands → Clean Up XHTML.

For more information on XHTML, check out the following:

- "XHTML: The Clean Code Solution," an article by Peter Wiggin at `http://www.oreillynet.com/pub/a/network/2000/04/28/feature/xhtml_rev.html`

- "What is XHTML?" an article by Jennifer Kyrnin at `http://html.about.com/library/weekly/aa013100a.htm?once=true&`

- The XHTML Resource page at `http://xhtml.startkabel.nl/`, which includes links to XHTML articles and tutorials

- XHTML tutorial at `http://www.w3schools.com/xhtml/`

- The XHTML section of the W3C HTML home page at `http://www.w3.org/MarkUp/`, which includes links to all of the W3C XHTML specifications

Validating XML and XHTML Documents

Dreamweaver MX 2004 supports validation of XML and XHTML documents (as well as several other types of documents) through the built-in Validator. Using the Validator helps you find tag and syntax errors in your code and helps ensure that your XML and XHTML documents work properly.

You can set preferences for the Validator, including the tag-based languages it should check against, the problems it should check for, and the types of errors it should report. To set these preferences, follow the following steps:

1. Open the Validator Preferences dialog box (Edit → Preferences → Validator).

2. Check the boxes for the tag libraries you want to validate against.

3. Click the Options button. The Validator Options dialog box displays.

4. Check the boxes in the Display option list for the types of errors you want to be included in the Validator report.

5. Check the boxes in the Check For option list for the problems the Validator should check for.

6. Click OK to close the Validator Options dialog box, and then click OK again to close the Validator Preferences dialog box.

Once you have set the Validator preferences, you can run the Validator for a document by following these steps.

1. Open an XML or XHTML file.

2. Select Check Page from the File menu, and then select Validate as XML from the drop-down menu (File → Check Page → Validate as XML).

3. If there are no errors in your document, the message No Errors Or Warnings is displayed in the Results panel below the document.

4. If the Validator found errors, the error messages are displayed in the Results panel. Double-click an error message to highlight the relevant code in the document.

5. Right-click (Control-click on a Mac) in the Results panel to save the report as an XML file or to open the report in a browser.

> XML Schema, the newest XML validation tool, offers sophisticated datatyping that allows you to create very specific rules for the format of valid content.

Using XML News Feeds

XML news feeds are commonly used to syndicate content and make it available as news links to anyone who chooses to subscribe to a particular news feed. These news feeds are usually written in an XML language called RSS (Rich Site Summary).

Dreamweaver doesn't yet support direct use of XML/RSS news feeds, but you can use XML/RSS news feeds in both Flash and ColdFusion:

1. The Flash Player can parse an XML document such as a news feed document and extract the information you choose. For more details, see `www.macromedia.com/ devnet/mx/flash/articles/learning_xml.html`.

2. ColdFusion includes support for XML. You can use an XML news feed as a data source in ColdFusion to produce dynamic content for an HTML page. For more information, see Volume 3 of the DevNet Resource Kit at `www.macromedia.com/ software/drk/productinfo/product_overview/volume3/sample_apps.html`.

Macromedia publishes an XML/RSS news feed of DevNet content at `www.macromedia.com/ go/devnet_rss`. You can use a news reader, also known as a news aggregator, to read and organize data from XML news feeds.

> For more details on RSS and blogs, see Chapter 15, "Community Building with Interactive Site Features."

Figure 24.7 shows a DW MX 2004 Savvy blog using the Radio Userland 8.0.8 news aggregator to retrieve and display selected news feeds. For this blog, we use news feeds from Macromedia DevNet, Macromedia's John Dowdell (JD on MX), Jeffrey Zeldman (Daily Report), Eric Meyer (meyerweb.com), and Wired News. You can see the current page at `http://radio.weblogs.com/0132492/`, or you can download a 30-day trial of Radio Userland at `http://radio.userland.com/` and create your own!

Figure 24.7

**DW MX 2004 Savvy
Radio Weblog**

Using XML and XHTML

Although Dreamweaver has strong support for creating and using XHTML, XML's role in Dreamweaver is still mainly behind the scenes in configuration files. Although you can edit XML files in Dreamweaver, for serious XML development work, we recommend an XML editor such as XMLSPY rather than Dreamweaver.

In the next chapter, you'll learn about using emerging web technologies with Dreamweaver MX 2004, including how to use special types of XML files (WSDL and SOAP files) to add web services to your pages, and you will also find out how to use the .NET framework with Dreamweaver MX 2004.

## CHAPTER 25

Emerging Technologies

Dreamweaver MX 2004 features extensive support for web development, including five server-side languages (ASP, ASP.NET, ColdFusion, JSP, and PHP) and emerging web technologies such as web services.

The preceding chapters in this section present information on web application development, connecting to databases, using server technologies, and using XML and XHTML. This chapter focuses on using Dreamweaver to access web services and .NET.

Both web services and the .NET framework can be used with Dreamweaver MX 2004 to create dynamic web applications. *Web services* are remote applications (accessed via a web page) that carry out specific tasks or functions. Through the use of web services technology, the Web can be accessed not only to share information but also to share services. Using Dreamweaver MX 2004, you can create pages to connect to web services applications using ASP.NET, ColdFusion, or JSP. Microsoft .NET is the Microsoft platform for XML web services, and it can be used in Dreamweaver with ASP.NET to create web applications.

This chapter includes the following topics:

- **Understanding web services**

- **Accessing web services**

- **Adding a web service to a page**

- **Understanding .NET**

- **Introducing Rich Internet Applications (RIA)**

Understanding Web Services

Web services allow digital services, such as currency conversion, language translation, and user authentication, to be shared by multiple web sites. The web services platform includes WSDL (Web Services Description Language), SOAP (Simple Object Access Protocol), and UDDI (Universal Description, Discovery, and Integration Service). Any language can be used to develop a web service application and web service applications can be run on any platform.

> Dreamweaver MX 2004 allows you to select a web service online and then create a web service proxy that lets your web page communicate with the remote web service application. A web client can connect to a web service application via this page, and can use the application as needed. You can use Dreamweaver to add web service proxies to ASP.NET, ColdFusion, and JSP pages. For more details, see the Hands On tutorial later in this chapter. Dreamweaver is not a tool for creating the web service applications themselves, but if you're familiar with ColdFusion, you can use that to create your own web service applications.

Web services allow application developers to combine software components from different web service providers to create distributed applications. Web service applications are made available by web service providers that can be located through online registries. The registries use UDDI to describe the services available from various web service providers.

Many registries are available, including the following.

XMethods (`www.xmethods.com`) Lists publicly available web service applications.

SalCentral (`www.salcentral.com/salnet/webserviceswsdl.asp`) Provides a search engine that looks for commercial web service applications that meet your criteria.

Microsoft UDDI Registry (`http://uddi.microsoft.com/default.aspx`) Offers a free copy of the UDDI registry, but you must register to use it.

In order to create a web page that accesses a web service application, you need to know the server implementation and the protocol used. This information is available as part of the online registry listing, or directly from the service provider.

Accessing Web Services

A web service is accessed through a web page. A typical scenario involves a web browser that sends a request to a web server for a particular page. The page is a portal to dynamic content—news stories, for example. The page on the web server makes a call to other servers that supply updated news content. After the latest news information is obtained from the web service providers, the information is inserted into the web page and returned to the web browser.

The three major components of the web services platform (WSDL, SOAP, and UDDI) provide the technology that supports this dynamic information transfer.

WSDL

To access a web service application, your web page needs a way to communicate with the application to determine the programmatic interface (available methods and parameters). WSDL is the proposed standard for this communication. WSDL is an XML format that describes the basic form of web service requests with different network protocols. It can be extended to any network protocol or message format.

Each web service includes a WSDL file that describes the bindings, methods, and data inputs and outputs. WSDL defines a *service* as a collection of ports. A *port* is specified by associating a network address with a binding. A *binding* is a protocol and data format specification for a specific port type.

> For more information on WSDL, see "Web Services Description Language (WSDL) Explained" at `http://msdn.microsoft.com/library/default.asp?url=/library/en-us/dnwebsrv/html/wsdlexplained.asp`.

WSDL 2.0 is a W3C Working Draft as of November 2003 (`www.w3.org/TR/wsdl20/`, `www.w3.org/TR/wsdl20-patterns/`, and `www.w3.org/TR/wsdl12-bindings/`). The W3C Working Drafts describe bindings with SOAP 1.2, HTTP 1.1 GET/POST, and MIME (*Multipurpose Internet Mail Extensions*), but it is not limited to these bindings. More information about current W3C work in the web services area is available on the W3C Web Services Activity page at `www.w3.org/2002/ws/`.

SOAP

The web page requesting the service and the web service application usually communicate using SOAP, although other bindings can also be used. SOAP is a protocol that is independent of platform and language. A SOAP message is an XML document that is sent via a transport protocol—usually HTTP, but SOAP can also work with other transport protocols.

SOAP 1.2 is a W3C Recommendation and consists of four basic parts:

- An envelope that describes what's in a message and how to process it
- A set of encoding rules for application-defined data types
- A convention for remote procedure calls (RPCs) and responses
- A binding convention for exchanging messages using an underlying protocol

The SOAP 1.2 Recommendation was released in June 2003 and includes four parts:

- Part 0: Primer: `www.w3.org/TR/soap12-part0/`
- Part 1: Messaging Framework: `www.w3.org/TR/soap12-part1/`
- Part 2: Adjuncts: `www.w3.org/TR/soap12-part2/`
- Specification Assertions and Test Collection: `www.w3.org/TR/soap12-testcollection/`

SOAP allows applications to invoke object methods on remote servers. Because SOAP is platform and language independent, the application and the server can use different languages as long as they both use the SOAP protocol.

> For more details on using SOAP, see "Getting Your Feet Wet with SOAP" at `http://hotwired.lycos.com/webmonkey/02/08/index0a.html`.

UDDI

UDDI is a method for finding web services. UDDI is built upon SOAP, and is independent of platform and implementation. A UDDI interface is used to connect to services provided by external partners. A UDDI registry provides a place for businesses to publish services, as well as a place for clients to obtain services. Three types of information are provided in a UDDI registry:

White pages Contact and general business information (services, categories, URLs).

Yellow pages Information about web services a business provides and how an application finds a particular service.

Green pages Technical details and binding information.

> For more information on UDDI, see "About UDDI" at `www.uddi.org/about.html`.

Understanding .NET

Microsoft .NET is the Microsoft XML Web Services platform. The .NET platform includes four main areas:

Smart clients and devices "Smart" client software that allows PCs and smart devices to access XML Web Services.

XML Web Services A core set of web services.

.NET servers Servers that integrate XML and XML Web Services in a distributed computing model. These include .NET Enterprise, Windows 2000, and Windows 2003 servers.

Developer tools Visual Studio .NET, Visual Studio .NET 2003, and the .NET Framework.

The .NET Framework

The .NET Framework is Microsoft's programming model for developing and using XML Web Services. It consists of three major components:

Common language runtime Takes responsibility for executing the application and making sure that all application dependencies are met.

Unified core classes Ensure that any type of application uses the same core classes; these classes also support code reuse.

Presentation classes Include ASP.NET, ADO.NET (for loosely coupled data access), XML Web Services, and Windows forms (for smart client applications).

The .NET Framework supports the integration of applications using different programming languages and allows application developers to use any programming language to develop applications.

The .NET Framework is a free download. If you're using Windows 2000 or XP Pro and running IIS 5 or later, you can install the .NET framework directly on your computer. If you're using Win 98 or a Mac, you will need to use a hosting service that supports ASP.NET.

If you're running IIS 5, go to `http://msdn.microsoft.com/netframework/downloads/v1.0/default.aspx` and download and install version 1.0 of the .NET Framework SDK. If you are running IIS 6, go to `http://asp.net/download-1.1.aspx?tabindex=0&tabid=1` and download version 1.1 of the .NET Framework redistributable. Once it's installed, download and install version 1.1 of the .NET Framework SDK. Be sure to use the correct version of .NET for your operating system—otherwise your ASP.NET pages won't function on your local web server.

> Microsoft also recommends installing Microsoft Data Access Components (MDAC) 2.7 after installing the .NET Framework. It's available for free download at `www.microsoft.com/data/downloads.htm`.

For more information on .NET and the .NET Framework, check out the following articles:

- "What is the Microsoft.NET framework?" at:

  `http://www.microsoft.com/net/basics/framework.asp`

- "Using the .NET Framework" at:

  `http://msdn.microsoft.com/netframework/using/`

In the Hands On tutorial at the end of this chapter, you will add a web service to a Dreamweaver MX 2004 page using ASP.NET.

Introducing Rich Internet Applications

Studio MX 2004 introduces Rich Internet Application (RIA) development with Flash MX 2004. RIAs are a new form of web application that let you do the following:

- Present a single screen interface for an application with multiple steps rather than requiring a new page load for each step
- Redraw sections of the screen without refreshing the page
- Process on the client side and decrease the number of requests to the server
- Progressively download content and data
- Use two-way interactive audio and video

An RIA can be a stand-alone application, or can be used in a hybrid form as a Flash module embedded in an HTML page. For more information on RIAs, see:

- The Rich Internet Application resource center:

  `www.macromedia.com/resources/business/rich_internet_apps/`

- The Rich Internet Application Starter Kit:

  `www.macromedia.com/go/ria_starterkit/`

To view a functioning RIA online, see Footjoy golf shoes at `www.myjoys.com`. This site is a Flash application connected via Flash Remoting and .NET services to a content management system.

> Flash Remoting is available for Flash MX Pro 2004. It can be used to connect a Flash interface with a database using ColdFusion, .NET, J2EE, XML, and web services. For more details on using Flash Remoting with .NET, see "Introduction to Flash Remoting with .NET" at www `.macromedia.com/devnet/mx/flashremoting/articles/intro_flremoting_net.html`.

Macromedia Flex

Macromedia Flex (previously called Royale) is a server designed for RIAs. Flex uses XML-based graphical user interfaces to extend Flash and also provides back-end features such as remote service invocations using SOAP. Flex runs on top of a J2EE application server such as Macromedia JRun or Apache Tomcat (and will also work with .NET in the future). For more information, see the Flex white paper:

`www.macromedia.com/software/flex/whitepapers/pdf/flex_tech_wp.pdf`

MXML is an XML markup language introduced with Flex. MXML is used to specify user interfaces that are rendered by the Flash Player. Flash ActionScript is used for the programming language. For more details on MXML, see "An Overview of MXML" at

`www.macromedia.com/devnet/flex/articles/paradigm.html`

DREAMWEAVER AND RIAS

Currently, Flash is the Macromedia application used to create RIAs. Macromedia is working to extend Dreamweaver MX 2004 to handle Flex code and visual layout with project Brady. For more information, see the Flex white paper.

Hands On: Creating a Web Service Using ASP.NET

In this tutorial, you'll create an ASP.NET page and create a functioning web service for the page. If .NET is not already installed on your computer, you will need to download .NET (as detailed earlier in this chapter) or use an ASP.NET hosting service to complete this tutorial.

If you have already installed .NET, you can skip ahead to the "Creating a Virtual Directory" section of this tutorial.

Installing ASP.NET

If you are developing and testing dynamic web pages, you need both a web server and an application server. (The application server is also called a testing server in Dreamweaver.) The application server for ASP.NET is IIS with the .NET Framework.

To use ASP.NET in Dreamweaver MX 2004, you need the following:

- Windows 2000 or Windows XP Professional

- Web server software—IIS 5 or higher on your computer or a networked Windows computer

IIS may already be installed on your computer. You can check by searching for a folder named Inetpub that IIS creates during installation.

- Application server software—NET Framework:

        http://msdn.microsoft.com/netframework/downloads/v1.0/default.aspx

Creating a Virtual Directory

Create a sub-web in IIS so that your web service and your web application act as if they are on physically separate computers. To create a virtual directory in IIS, follow these steps:

1. Make a new folder on your hard drive named myTemp_web.

2. Open the Internet Services Manager (Control Panel → Performance and Maintenance → Administrative Tools → IIS).

3. In the left side of the IIS window, expand the view until you see the Default Web Site node.

4. Right-click on the node and choose New → Virtual Directory (Figure 25.1).

Figure 25.1

**Creating a Virtual
Directory in the
IIS Manager**

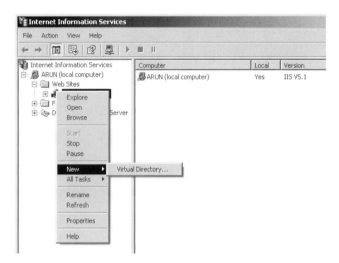

5. The Virtual Directory Creation Wizard displays.

6. Type `myTemp_web` for the Virtual Directory Alias.

7. In the next screen, click on the Browse button and navigate to the location of the folder from Step 1.

8. In the screen that follows, leave the default choices selected, and click Next.

You will now be able to access your web service by typing this URL in IE—`http://localhost/myTemp_web`.

Creating a Dreamweaver ASP.NET Site

Create an ASP.NET Dreamweaver site for your web service and web application. Use the Site Definition dialog box (Site → Manage Sites → New) to create the site. If your folder is located at `C:\myTemp_web`, then follow these steps:

1. In the Local Info category, enter the location of the root folder as `C:\myTemp_web\`, and the HTTP address as `http://localhost/myTemp_web`.

2. In the Remote Info category, choose Local/Network from the Access drop-down menu, and enter `C:\myTemp_web\` for the remote folder location.

3. In the Testing Server category, choose ASP.NET VB for the server model, and Local/Network access. Enter `C:\myTemp_web\` for the Testing server folder, and `http://localhost/myTemp_web/` for the URL prefix.

4. Click OK when you are finished, and then click Done to close the Manage Sites dialog box.

> For more details on creating a Dreamweaver site, see Chapter 3, "Setting Up Your Workspace and Your Site."

Creating a Web Service

You can create your own web service and add it to a Dreamweaver page, or you can use Dreamweaver MX 2004 to add a prebuilt web service to a Dreamweaver page (ASP.NET, ColdFusion, or JSP).

In this tutorial, you'll create your own simple web service and then add it to a Dreamweaver ASP.NET VB page.

If you prefer to use a prebuilt web service, see the next tutorial. You will need to know some scripting language basics in order to adapt web service methods for your Dreamweaver page, even with a prebuilt web service.

> To use a prebuilt web service, see the following Hands On section. You will need to know some scripting language basics in order to adapt web service methods for your Dreamweaver page, even with a prebuilt web service.

In this tutorial, you will create a web service to convert Fahrenheit temperature to Celsius. Copy the `celsius.asmx` file from the Chapter 25 folder on the CD into the `myTemp_web` folder on your hard drive, then open `http://localhost/myTemp_web/celsius.asmx` in Internet Explorer. A help page displays automatically—it should resemble the one shown in Figure 25.2.

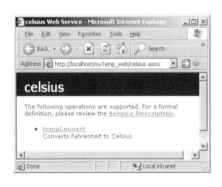

Figure 25.2

Web Service Help window

> If you'd like to view the source code for the convertTemp web service, open `celsius.asmx` in Dreamweaver or a text editor. Basically, it's a VB.NET class with a single method.

Now create a WSDL file for your web service by entering this URL in Internet Explorer: `http://localhost/myTemp_web/celsius.asmx?WSDL`, as shown in Figure 25.3. Make a note of this URL—you'll use it to generate a proxy in Dreamweaver.

Generating a Proxy

Your ASP.NET page doesn't interact directly with the web service. It uses a file called a proxy for the interaction. Dreamweaver MX 2004 can automatically create the proxy file as well as the `.dll` file you'll need.

To generate a proxy for our web service:

1. Open a new ASP.NET VB page in Dreamweaver.

2. Save this page in your ASP.NET site root folder as `celsius.aspx`. Leave the page open in Code view in the Dreamweaver workspace.

Now you can create a web service proxy class. This proxy is software that is used by the web page to communicate with the web service application. The proxy is created from the WSDL file that describes the web service, and then this proxy class is used to create a `.dll` component. Dreamweaver MX 2004 includes several proxy generators, and you can also add others.

To add a web service proxy to the page from Step 1 above, follow these steps.

1. Choose Window → Components to display the Components panel.

Figure 25.3

Automatically creating a WSDL file

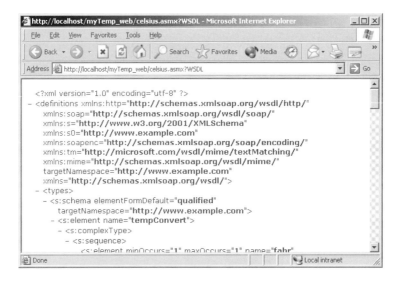

2. Make sure that there is a check mark in front of each of the four steps shown in the Components panel (Figure 25.4); otherwise, complete any unchecked steps now.

3. In the Components panel, choose Web Services from the drop-down menu at the upper-left.

4. Click the plus (+) button to the right of the drop-down menu and choose Add Using WSDL. The Add Using WSDL dialog box (also called the Web Service Chooser dialog box; Figure 25.5) is displayed.

5. The Proxy Generator box should be set to *.NET VB.*

6. Enter the URL of the WSDL file (`http://localhost/myTemp_web/celsius.asmx?WSDL`) and then click OK.

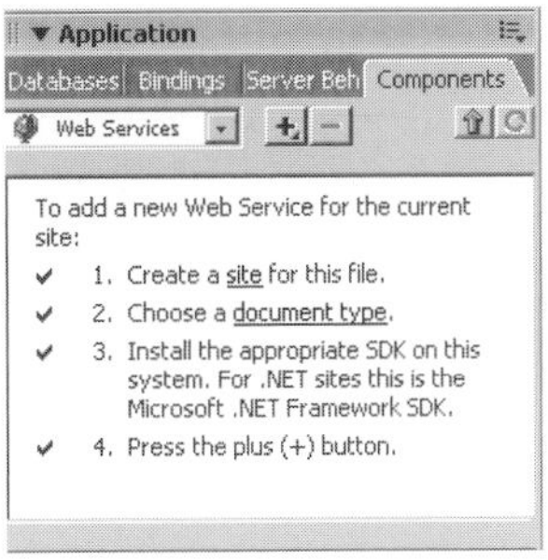

Figure 25.4

The Components panel

Two files will be automatically generated: `celsius.vb` and `celsius.dll`. Create a directory within the site folder (`C:\myTemp_web`) named `bin`, and move the `celsius.dll` file into this directory.

The web service now displays in the Components panel, as shown in Figure 25.6 for the web service named Fortune.

Now, one more step. You need to add the web service to your Dreamweaver ASP.NET VB page (`celsius.aspx`). Adding a web service to a page is also called "consuming" a web service in your web application. Add the Celsius web service to your page by following these steps:

1. Switch to Code view (View → Code).

2. Open the Components panel (Window → Components).

3. In the Components panel, click a method of the web service and drag it into the Code view window. Dreamweaver then adds the method and dummy parameters to the page.

4. Edit the inserted code with the data types, parameter values, and service instance names as required by the web service application.

Figure 25.5

Add a WSDL service here.

Figure 25.6

Web service icon in the Components panel

We have adapted the Celsius web service methods to create an interactive interface using a form with a button and two text fields. Listing 25.1 shows the complete code listing for celsius.aspx, and it is also included in the Chapter 25 folder on the CD. In the listing, the code between the bold script tags is what we adapted and inserted in the head section of the page; the dynamic form code we inserted in the body of the page is between the bold form tags.

Listing 25.1

celsius.aspx

```
<%@ Page Language="VB" ContentType="text/html"
   ResponseEncoding="iso-8859-1" %>
<!DOCTYPE HTML PUBLIC "-//W3C//DTD HTML 4.01 Transitional//EN"
   "http://www.w3.org/TR/html4/loose.dtd">
<html>
<head>
<title>Fahrenheit to Celsius</title>
<meta http-equiv="Content-Type" content="text/html; charset=iso-8859-1">
<script language="vb" runat="server">
sub btnConvert_Click(Sender as Object, E as EventArgs)
...dim myTemp as new celsius
...dim fahr as integer
......
......fahr = txttempConvert.text
......lblResult.text = myTemp.tempConvert(fahr).toString
...end sub
</script>
</head>
<body bgcolor="#99CC99" text="#663333">
<form runat="server">
   <p><strong>Fahrenheit to Celsius Conversion</strong></p>
   <p>Enter Temperature in Fahrenheit:
      <asp:TextBox id="txttempConvert" size="5" runat="server" /><br><br>
      <asp:Button id="btnConvert" text="Convert Now!" runat="server"
         onclick="btnConvert_Click" />
   </p>
   <p>Celsius Temperature: <asp:Label id="lblResult" runat="server" /></p>
</form>
</body>
</html>
```

Open celsius.aspx in your web server and test out the convertTemp web service. Your page should resemble Figure 25.7.

Hands On: Adding a Prebuilt Web Service to a Page

In this tutorial, you'll use Dreamweaver to add a "prebuilt" web service to an ASP.NET page. Dreamweaver MX 2004 includes several features for creating pages that connect to web service applications, including the following:

- Browsing the web from within Dreamweaver to find available web service applications

- Binding a web page to a web service application by creating a proxy object

- Viewing the methods and properties of web service applications

To add a web service to a Dreamweaver ASP.NET page:

1. Open Dreamweaver and create a new ASP.NET page with C# or VB (File → New → ASP.NET C# or ASP.NET VB).

2. Save this page (with a `.aspx` file extension) in your ASP.NET site root folder. (In this case you don't need to use a virtual directory because the web service is located on a different computer.) Leave the page open in Code view in the Dreamweaver workspace.

Now you can add a web service proxy; to add a proxy to this page, follow these steps:

1. Choose Window → Components to display the Components panel.

2. Make sure that there is a check mark in front of each of the four steps shown in the Components panel (refer back to Figure 25.4); otherwise, complete any unchecked steps now.

3. In the Components panel, choose Web Services from the drop-down menu at the upper-left.

4. Click the plus (+) button to the right of the drop-down menu and choose Add Using WSDL. The Add Using WSDL dialog box (also called the Web Service Chooser dialog box; Figure 25.5) is displayed.

5. The Proxy Generator box should be set to either .NET C# or .NET VB, depending on the document type you initially created.

6. Leave the Adding Using WSDL dialog box open.

Figure 25.7

Consuming a web service

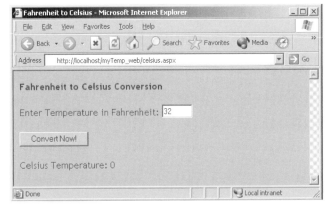

You can also use a proxy generator that is not supplied with Dreamweaver. To do so, you must obtain the proxy generator and any necessary software and software libraries from the vendor. After installing and configuring the proxy generator, you also need to configure it to work with Dreamweaver.

Next, you need to locate a web service that provides the functionality you desire, and download its WSDL file. To locate a web service application, follow these steps:

1. In the Add Using WSDL display box, specify the URL of the web service you want to use.

2. If you don't know the URL, click the globe to the right of the URL text box and select one of the web service registries. The three selections are IBM UDDI, Microsoft UDDI, and XMethods. Dreamweaver will launch your specified primary browser and open the selected registry. You can also select Edit UDDI Site List to add additional registries or web service providers to the list, or you can select Edit Browser List to change the primary and secondary browsers. Select a web service from this registry, and enter the URL in the URL of the WSDL File text box.

Implementation information is provided as part of the registry listing so that you can determine if the web service is available for your chosen web service server model. Be sure that the selected proxy generator is installed and configured on your system.

Figure 25.8

The Default Proxy Generator

3. The web service now appears in the Components panel (Window → Components) and can be inserted in a web page (Figure 25.6).

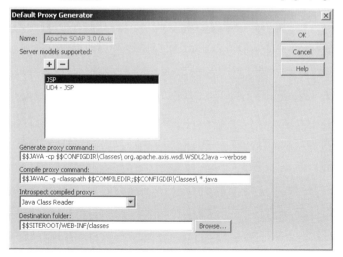

The proxy generator creates a proxy for the web service and *introspects* it. Through introspection, the proxy generator queries the internal structure of a web service proxy and makes its methods, properties, and interface available through Dreamweaver. An introspector can be chosen in the Default Proxy Generator dialog box (Figure 25.8) from the drop-down menu labeled Introspect Compiled Proxy.

Once you have selected a web service and generated a proxy, you can insert the web service on your web page, as shown at the end of the preceding Hands On section.

For more details on using the Web Services Chooser dialog box to generate a proxy, see "Setting the Web Services Chooser dialog box options" and "Configuring proxy generators for use with Dreamweaver" in Dreamweaver Help (Help → Using Dreamweaver).

When you use Dreamweaver to upload your site files to a web server, Dreamweaver automatically copies the pages, the proxy, and any necessary library files to the web server. These items must be available to the web server or your pages will not be able to communicate with the web service application. If you do not use Dreamweaver to upload your site files, make sure you include the proxy and any necessary library files.

What's Ahead

Web services applications, the .NET platform, and Rich Internet Applications are rapidly evolving. With public web service applications such as those listed in the XMethods registry (www.xmethods.com) and the free download of the .NET Framework, you can test out these new technologies in Dreamweaver MX 2004.

The final part of this book deals with site administration. You'll learn how to prepare a site (or web application) for turnover to a client, how to test the site and then go live with it, and how to maintain it throughout the rest of its life cycle.

## PART V

Site Administration from Start to Finish

Too many designers, architects, and consultants build websites that look great when they launch and then slowly begin to gather dust when it becomes apparent that nobody put thought into how to maintain them. There should be a convenient and well-designed interface for administering the site if you expect anyone to bother updating it.

In this part, we'll show you how to set up user registration and login, how to implement static and dynamic content management, how to make sure your site is compatible with the browsers your audience will be using, how to handle the turnover of a site ("going live"), how to maintain a website after the launch, how to customize and extend Dreamweaver, and how to use Dreamweaver's accessibility features.

## CHAPTER 26

Controlling Access to the Site

Dreamweaver MX 2004 makes it easy to control access to individual pages as well as entire sites. By using a database and Dreamweaver, you can set up user registration, passwords, and login procedures.

There are many reasons to control site access. For example, your visitors may include both members and non-members, with a members-only section of the site, or you may want to welcome return visitors and let them skip the introduction page. In order to do this, you will need to establish roles for various users and follow a protocol of user and content administration.

This chapter addresses all of these access control features and topics including the following:

- Developing user administration
- Creating a database
- Making a registration page
- Using server behaviors
- Setting up user login pages
- Restricting access
- Adding personalization features

Developing User Administration

Dreamweaver MX 2004 gives you the tools that help you restrict user access to your website. Here are examples of access control:

- Users register when they arrive at the site for the first time.

- Users log in every time they visit the site.

- Only certain authorized users can view specific pages.

In addition to setting up a dynamic site, in order to control site access, you'll need the following:

A database table that stores your users' pertinent information, and a form that allows entry of personal data, including a user ID and a password. The database table you create holds this form's information so that it can be recalled every time a user logs in to your system.

Server behaviors including Insert Record, which updates the database user information, and Check New Username, which ensures that the username each user enters is unique.

Creating a Database Table for User Authorization

When you create your database table to store the user information, think about what type of data you want to collect from the users—their username, password, name, address, and phone number, for instance—and set up the table columns accordingly. Remember to create as many columns as you need to store each type of data that you want to collect in its own column. For example, if you want to collect a username and password only, then your database table would have two columns.

> If you are collecting personal information other than a username and password, you need to take additional steps to secure this data. Database security is beyond the scope of this book, but a good place to start is the article "Securing Your Web Database" at www.notestips.com/ 80256B3A007F2692/1/TAIO-5TGFJK.

If you want to assign different privileges to different users, make sure you create a privileges column in your database table. To do this, you would first create a database column that specifies each user's access privileges, and then you would assign each user one of the following privilege types: Administrator, User, or Guest.

You can also assign a default level of access to this Privileges column so that each user has a standard level of access—let's say User. Then you would go back and give more or less access to individual users based on what permissions you want to give those specific users.

The following steps show how to create a user's table using Microsoft Access. However, each database works differently, so the process for Access is different than that for Oracle, SQL Server, or MySQL. If you don't have Access installed on your computer, you can use the database file (user_admin.mdb) provided in the Ch 26 tutorial file on the CD.

1. Select File → New and then choose New → Blank Database from the list of new file types on the right. Save the database as users.mdb.

2. Choose Create Table In Design View from the Database window that displays.

3. Name the first field UserName and choose Text as the Datatype.

4. Make it a required field by entering Yes next to Required in the table that displays at the bottom left. Don't change any other settings.

5. Create a second field named Password and repeat steps 3 and 4.

6. Create a third field named Access Level. Repeat steps 3 and 4, but also add a default value of "User" in the table at the bottom left.

7. Make the ID field the Primary Key by putting the cursor in the ID field, and then selecting Edit → Primary Key. Save the table as PageAccess (File → Save As → PageAccess) and choose As Table from the drop-down menu.

8. Save the database file *outside* of the root folder on your testing server.

Site Preparation

In order to create a dynamic site with a database connection for user administration in Dreamweaver MX 2004, you need to complete these tasks:

- Create a DSN (DataSourceName). See the following section for more details.

- Create a site in Dreamweaver (see Chapter 3, "Setting Up Your Workspace and Your Site," for more information).

- Choose a document type from the eight dynamic page types available in Dreamweaver (ASP JavaScript, ASP VBScript, ASP.NET C#, ASP.NET VB, ColdFusion, ColdFusion Component, JSP, PHP). In this chapter, we'll be using ASP JavaScript as our document type. See Chapter 16, "Building Web Applications," and Chapter 19, "Database Connectivity," for more details on server technologies.

- Set up the site's testing server (see Chapter 16 for more details).

- Create a database connection (see Chapter 19 for more information).

Creating a DSN (DataSourceName)

The first step in setting up a database connection in Dreamweaver MX 2004 is to create a DSN. To create a DSN in Windows XP Pro for an Access database, follow these steps:

> If you're using Windows 98, see the instructions at `http://support.microsoft.com/default.aspx?scid=kb;en-us;300595`. If you're using Windows 2000, check out `http://support.microsoft.com/default.aspx?scid=kb;en-us;300596`.

1. Start → Control Panel → Performance And Maintenance → Administrative Tools.
2. Double-click the DataSources (ODBC) icon.
3. Click the System DSN tab, and then click Add.
4. Choose a database driver. In this case, choose Microsoft Access Driver (`*.mdb`), and then click Finish.
5. Type a name for the DSN. You'll use this name later when you set up the database connection in Dreamweaver.
6. Click on the Select button under Database to browse to the database file. This file should be outside the root folder of your testing server.
7. Click OK. Your DSN should now display in the list on the System DSN tab.

Creating a Registration Form

A registration page is a form that your front end uses to collect information from the user. In this form you specify that the user should create a username, a password, and any other information you want to collect.

To create such a form in Dreamweaver MX 2004, follow these steps:

1. Create a new page (File → New). In the New Document window, select Dynamic page from the category column. From the Dynamic page list select the page type that matches your configuration.

> User authentication methods in Dreamweaver are the same for ASP, ColdFusion, JSP, and PHP; however, Dreamweaver does not provide user authentication server behaviors, discussed in the following section, for ASP.NET.

2. Select Insert → Form → Form. This creates an empty form on your Dreamweaver page where you can add in username and password text fields.
3. To establish text fields on this form, for example User and Password fields, select Insert → Form → Text Field. This creates a text field in which users can add their information.

4. Add text labels to your fields by choosing Insert → Form → Label.

5. After your fields are designated, add a form Submit button by using Insert → Form → Button. Choose Submit for the Type from the drop-down menu in the Tag Editor window that displays.

6. Save the page as form.asp (or appropriate page type for the configuration you're using).

You now have everything you need on your form to capture login information.

In order for your form to store the information it collects in the database, you'll need to add an Insert Record server behavior. In the next section, you'll learn how to add the Insert Record server behavior to save the user's registration information.

Adding Server Behaviors

Whenever you need to add a server behavior, use the Server Behaviors panel (see Figure 26.1). This window lists the active server behaviors on your page; in addition, it lists the new behaviors that can be added. During the process of making a registration page for your users, you will use this window to add two server behaviors: Insert Record and Check New Username, which will be discussed in more detail in the following sections.

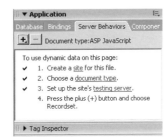

Figure 26.1

The Server Behaviors panel

Updating the Database with the Insert Record Server Behavior

Whenever you add, change, or delete information, your database needs to reflect these changes. Once the user has submitted the registration form with the information you requested (username, password, and any additional information you requested), you need to save these registration changes to the database so that the user can use these values to log in.

In order to update the database table of users, follow these steps to use the Insert Record server behavior (see Figure 26.2):

1. In the Server Behaviors panel, click the plus (+) button and select Insert Record. The Insert Record server behavior window displays.

2. To specify the table of users in the database, select the connection to use from the Connection drop-down list. Also select the database table to insert into from the Insert Into Table pop-up menu.

Figure 26.2

Insert Record dialog box

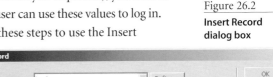
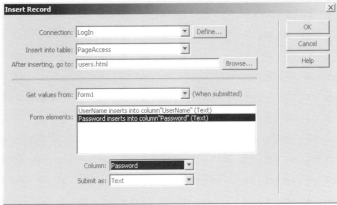

3. In the After Inserting, Go To box, enter the page that should be opened after the login information is inserted into the table.

4. In the Get Values From pop-up menu, select the form that was used to obtain the user's username and password.

5. Map each value in the login form to the database column it will be stored in. For each field in the form, first highlight the field from the Form Elements list and then select the database column it uses from the Column drop-down list as well as the data type from the Submit As menu. For example, the UserName form field should map to the UserName database column as a text data type.

> The *data type* is the kind of data the column in your database table is expecting (text or numerals). Password or username columns usually expect text, but sometimes numbers might be used.

6. Click OK.

Figure 26.2 shows the Insert Record dialog box after these steps have been used to fill in its values with sample data.

Making Sure Usernames Are Unique

No matter what the size of your site, you will find that getting users to use unique user names is a challenge. You need to set up your database to check its tables to see if a specific username is unique.

To have your database check for existing usernames, use the Check New Username server behavior (see Figure 26.3).

This dialog box specifies the field to check and the page to go to if the username already exists. By using this behavior, when a new user clicks Submit, or Enter (whatever button name you've selected to indicate that the user has completed filling out the data), this server behavior compares the username they just entered with all the registered usernames stored in the database.

Figure 26.3
**Check New User-
name dialog box**

When the Check New Username performs its search and there isn't a matching username, Insert Record creates a new record for that user and lists the username that they chose.

If there is an existing record, Check New User-
name cancels the Insert Record function and delivers an error to the user. This is the process that you should follow to find out if the username is unique.

1. Click the plus (+) button from the Server Behaviors panel and choose Check New Username from the User Authentication sub-menu.

2. From the Username Field drop-down list of the Check New Username window, specify the form field name that contains the user's username.

3. Use the Browse button to select a page to go to if the username already exists. This page should tell the user to pick a different username.

4. Click OK to save your changes.

The registration process is now complete. Once they are registered, your users will have a login name and a password that they will use every time they enter your site, or the portions of it that they visit if they are restricted to specific groups.

Login Pages and Processes

Now that you can register users, you'll need a login page to authenticate them each time they visit your site. When a user completes a successful login, Dreamweaver MX 2004 places their login information in a session variable. After logging in, the user will be able to access the pages that match their access level as long as their current session is open.

To add a login page, follow these steps.

1. Create a new page (File → New). In the New Document window, select Dynamic page from the category column. From the Dynamic page list select the page type that matches your configuration.

2. Add a form object, by selecting Insert → Form → Form, to create an empty form in which you can add username and password fields.

3. Use Insert → Form → Text Field to add field definitions. Insert labels (Insert → Form → Label) so that your users understand what data to enter in each separate field.

4. After your fields are designated, add a form Submit button by using Insert → Form → Button and then choosing submit from the Type field in the Tag Editor window.

5. You may now add the Log In User server behavior to your page. Click the plus (+) button from the Server Behaviors panel and choose the Log In User from the User Authentication sub-menu. See Figure 26.4 for an example of how the Log In User dialog box can be filled out.

6. The Log In User dialog box prompts you for the name of the form you just created. In this case, the form name was login.

7. Then use the Browse button to select the pages that the user will be sent to after successful and failed logins.

8. You can then select the connection that includes the database table that holds the access information from the Validate Using Connection drop-down list.

9. Select the table that is used for validation from the Table drop-down list.

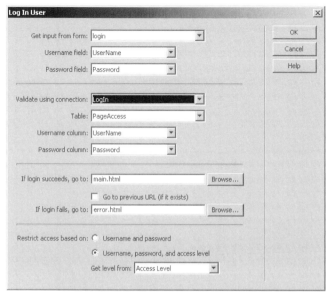

Figure 26.4

**Log In User
dialog box**

10. Select the UserName column from the Username Column drop-down list.

11. Select the Password column from the Password Column drop-down list.

12. Click OK to save your changes.

This produces a functional login page. You'll still need to develop the static content, attach a template or style sheet, and otherwise finish the design of the page (as discussed in Parts II and III of this book). You could also design your page so that the login form occupies just the upper-right corner, for example, and other content is displayed on the rest of the page.

If you want to make your login process Amazon-slick, you can use a cookie to identify your users, as we will discuss next. *Cookies* store information on the user's computer for later reference by your site.

For security's sake, users should be able to log out of your site. If you don't make your users log in every single time they access your site, or if the information is incredibly sensitive, you can provide a logout button for your users to end their session. For example, a bank site requests usernames and passwords when users log in order for the database to show the user their customized information. Because it's a banking site, they also have a logout button in order to close out the display of sensitive information.

Logging Users Out

Security conscious users will want the ability to log out of a website (so that someone else using the same computer cannot access their information). Dreamweaver MX 2004 provides the Log Out User server behavior to accomplish this (see Figure 26.5).

This server behavior offers two ways to tie the login behavior to the site. You can create a logout link (you may want to include it in your navigation bar or template header) that invokes the behavior or you can choose to have the logout server behavior launch automatically when the page that contains it loads. The login page should usually be the page that you specify to go to after logout.

Figure 26.5

**Log Out User
dialog box**

USING COOKIES TO STORE PERSISTENT USER DATA

Cookies are data structures used by a website to deliver data to a user, store user information, and return that stored information to a website when the user returns. This enables websites to "remember" user information in order to deliver the user's custom preferences. For example, a cookie could be used to automatically default to the user's username on the login page (or even skip the login page altogether and automatically log in the user, which is obviously less secure).

Dreamweaver supports the use of session variables in ASP, ColdFusion, JSP, and PHP to gather cookies from a user. You can access these variables by clicking the + in the Bindings panel:

- ASP and JSP
- Bindings → Request Variable
- ColdFusion and PHP
- Bindings → Cookie Variable

Cookies can also be accessed by the JavaScript functions readCookie and writeCookie.

For more information on creating and using cookies, check the documentation for the server technology you're using. Additional resources include:

- "How to Create and Retrieve Cookies Using ASP":
  www.powerasp.com/content/code-snippets/cookies.asp
- "Using Session Variables to Maintain State":
  http://coveryourasp.com/Session.asp

Restricting Page Access

When you want to restrict access to a page, you use the Restrict Access server behavior. When a user attempts to access a restricted page, the user is redirected to another page that alerts them of their access *faux pas.*

The options that you can control from this dialog box include restricting access to include which access levels are valid for the page and which page to go to if the user isn't logged in. Usually, the login page is specified as the Access Denied Go To page.

Restricted pages should always contain a link to log out.

When you are assigning levels of access, remember that a single user cannot have multiple levels of access. Because of this rule, if you want to set up multiple privileges for a certain page of content, you will need to set those privileges at the page level instead of at the user level. Here's how you do it:

1. Open the page you want to restrict, then click the Server Behaviors panel.

2. Click the plus (+) button, and from the resulting pop-up menu, select User Authentication ► Restrict Access To Page. The Restrict Access To Page dialog box displays (Figure 26.6).

3. Click the Username, Password, and Access Level radio button to assign individual access levels to different users.

4. Click the Define button next to the Select Levels box and add three levels (User, Administrator, and Guest).

5. Enter a URL in the "If Access Denied, Go To" text box to set the page you want to display if the visitor is denied access to the page.

6. Click OK.

> Dreamweaver MX 2004's server behavior, Restrict Access To Page, redirects the user to another page if the user attempts to access the protected page. (This page will typically say something to the effect of "You are not permitted to access this page," with a link to return to the accessible areas of the site.)

Now that user access has been established, we can customize the content to a specific user based on their role or group; this is also called *personalization*.

Using User Information to Add Personalization Features

Once you know who is logged in to your site, you may want to do more than just whimsically restrict or grant access to pages and sections of your site. Whether you've grouped your users by role or you simply want to exploit an attribute of their database profile, you've got plenty of choices of ways that you can personalize their web experience. Generally, users are happiest when they are presented with information that is relevant to them.

Figure 26.6

Restrict Access To Page dialog box

Let's use an e-commerce site that sells clothing as an example. A user with a registration profile that specifies that their home state is Minnesota could be offered an initial page with heavy winter coats featured, whereas a user from Arizona might be offered windbreakers.

As this example illustrates, by using the demographic and personal information you have about a user, you can customize every small detail of the web page that user will see. This unique treatment enhances the user's experience and also increases the probability that they will continue using your site. For example, if you are a frequent purchaser on Amazon.com, your cookies identify you, and then Amazon.com offers suggestions for new purchases in music, books, and toys (wherever your interest was in prior purchases).

Here are some other things to consider in personalizing a site:

Changing the presentation of a page Though you may just send different groups of users to different pages, you can also make more subtle changes such as including a different CSS definition for different roles. Either the path of the CSS definition or the name of the definition can be generated dynamically. This changes the way the page appears and feels but not the content. For example, users in the U.S. might see a page with red, white, and blue, while users from Germany would see yellow, red, and black (the colors of the German flag).

Modifying the content of a page You can also change the content of your pages by using the Show Region server behaviors as well as all of the other dynamic objects, such as dynamically changing images.

Your end users aren't the only ones who benefit from dynamically built pages based on their login. You can create profiles and groups for administrators to help you or them get the job done faster.

Testing, 1, 2 ...

As you can see, with a little thought, creativity, and knowledge, setting up the crucial back end aspects of a website can be an exciting adventure. You can enhance your website in myriad ways, and all of these can help ensure that your users (or community members) come back again, and again, and again. You can use what you've learned here to create a customized site. Next, you will learn about using Contribute for site content management.

## CHAPTER 27

Static Content Management with Contribute

Web developers and web designers often create websites that, when complete, are managed by the site owner. It's economical and convenient for the client to maintain and update the site using Macromedia Contribute 2. Handing off routine maintenance lets you, the web developer/designer, concentrate on creating new sections of the site, making CSS pages for the site, working on the back end with scripting and databases, and constructing Dreamweaver templates for the client to use for content changes to the site pages.

A Contribute site needs an administrator. Generally it's most efficient if you, the web designer/developer, serve as the Contribute administrator, performing site administrative tasks such as setting permissions and managing version control for the site pages. In this way, the integrity of the site code and design can be maintained while at the same time the client can make content updates at any time. The administrator specifies what parts of the site and its pages can be changed, and then the client or the client's staff are free to make content changes at any time and upload the changed pages directly to the web server.

Contribute 2 also allows you to transform documents into the new FlashPaper format and insert them as SWF files (file extension .swf) in the Contribute site pages.

The following topics will be discussed in this chapter:

- **Getting started with Contribute 2**
- **Administering Contribute sites from Dreamweaver**
- **Making new Contribute pages from Dreamweaver templates**
- **Adding FlashPaper to Contribute documents**

Introducing Contribute 2

Although it's a tool for distributing the work of maintaining a website, Macromedia's Contribute 2 is basically a browser and a page editor. The browser is part of Contribute itself, and allows you to view site pages before and after published changes. Contribute 2 is incredibly easy to use, and you can learn its basics by using the tutorial and sample website that install with it. The tutorial takes about 10 to 15 minutes to complete—no kidding, it's that quick and easy to get started with Contribute 2.

In this chapter you will learn to administer the Contribute 2 sample website from within Dreamweaver MX 2004. A 30-day trial version of Contribute 2 is included on the CD, so go ahead and install it now if you'd like to get hands-on practice. Once you've used it, you'll see how easy it is for clients to use this software. You don't have to use Dreamweaver to use Contribute—Contribute can also be used with Microsoft Front Page, Adobe GoLive, or hand-coded HTML pages.

Preparing a Dreamweaver Site for Contribute

You can configure a Dreamweaver site for Contribute compatibility when you initially create the site, or edit the site settings later to enable Contribute compatibility.

> For more details on creating a Dreamweaver site, see Chapter 3, "Setting Up Your Workspace and Your Site."

To enable Contribute compatibility, follow these steps:

1. Select Site → Manage Sites to open the Manage Sites dialog box.

2. Choose a site, and then click Edit.

3. Click the Advanced tab in the Site Definition dialog box.

4. Choose Contribute from the Category list (see Figure 27.1).

Figure 27.1

The Contribute category in the Advanced Site Definition dialog box

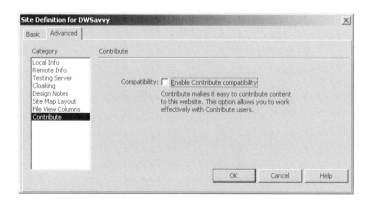

Figure 27.2

Enabling Design Notes and file Check In/Out is required for Contribute compatibility

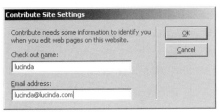

Figure 27.3

The Contribute Site Settings dialog box

5. Check the box labeled Enable Contribute compatibility. As shown in Figure 27.2, a confirmation box displays. Click OK to enable Design Notes and file Check In/Out, as required for Contribute compatibility.

For more information on Design Notes and Check In/Out, see Chapter 31, "Maintaining a Site."

6. The Contribute Site Settings dialog box displays. Enter a user name and e-mail for file Check In/Out (see Figure 27.3).

7. Click OK, and then click Done.

Administering Contribute from Dreamweaver

If you have Contribute installed on the same computer as Dreamweaver, you can use Dreamweaver to perform site administration tasks in Contribute.

Figure 27.4

Open the Site Definition's Contribute category.

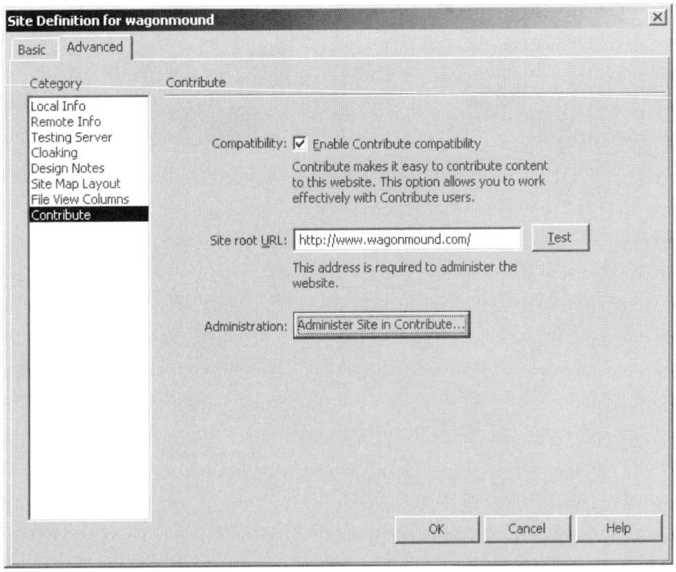

To administer Contribute from Dreamweaver, follow these steps:

1. Select Site → Manage Sites.

2. Choose a site that you've enabled for Contribute compatibility (as shown in the previous section), and click the Edit button.

3. Click the Advanced tab in the Site Definition dialog box, and then choose the Contribute category (Figure 27.4).

4. If you've enabled Contribute compatibility, a button labelled Administer Site In Contribute is displayed. Click this button to open Contribute. The Administrator password dialog box displays. Enter the

password and click OK. If no administrator has been specified, a box displays asking if you want to be the administrator. Click Yes, and then enter a password. The Administer Website dialog box displays (see Figure 27.5).

From this dialog box, you can choose to change Sitewide Settings, set permission groups, and send a connection key.

Sitewide Settings

Click the Sitewide Settings button to display the Sitewide Settings dialog box (Figure 27.6). From this dialog box you can set an administrator email address, change the administrator password, enable rollbacks (saved previous versions of site pages), set the number of rollbacks, and access Index and URL Mapping if needed.

Creating and Editing Permission Groups

From the Administer Website dialog box (Figure 27.5), you can also edit or create permission groups. Contribute automatically creates an Administrator and a Users group, but you can also create new groups. Select a permission group and click the Edit button to edit default permissions. The Permission Group dialog box opens. There are seven available categories, including General, File/Folder Access, Editing, Styles and Fonts, New Pages, and New Images. You can set permissions in any or all of these categories. Figure 27.7 shows the default selections for the Editing category.

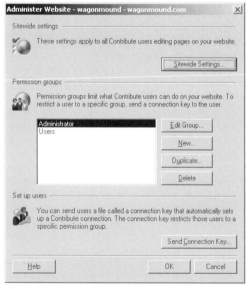

Figure 27.5

Administer Website dialog box in Contribute 2

Figure 27.6

Sitewide Settings dialog box

Sending Connection Keys

You can manually set up a connection to a site in Contribute, but you can also send a content provider a connection key that automatically creates a connection for them and also automatically restricts them to a certain permission group.

To create a connection key for a Contribute user, click the button named Send Connection Key at the bottom of the Administer Website dialog box to open a wizard (see Figure 27.8). Follow the steps to create an encrypted connection key for a user. You will be prompted to enter a password to encrypt the key. The user will need this password to use the connection key, as shown in Figure 27.9.

Using Dreamweaver Templates in Contribute

Users need access to the Templates folder in a Contribute site in order to use templates. You can set file and folder permissions in the Folder/File Access category of the Administer Website dialog box in Contribute, but you will also need to create read access for the Users group on the server itself. For more details on setting permissions on the server, see the section, "CGI Script Requirements," in Chapter 14, "Collecting Information with Forms."

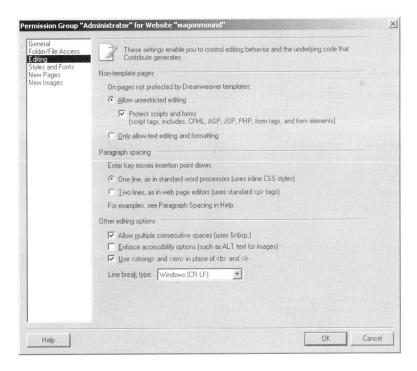

Figure 27.7

Editing category of the Permissions Group dialog box

In general, you will want to give users read access to these folders:

- the /_mm folder (a subfolder of the root folder), where the shared settings are stored in a file named contribute.xml

- the /Templates folder, where templates are stored

- any folders that contain assets you want the users to be able to access

To create a new Contribute page from a template, click the New Page button at the top of a page in the Contribute browser. The New Page dialog box opens (see Figure 27.10). Select the template you want to use to create the new page, enter a file name in the Page title box, and click OK.

The template opens in the Contribute document window. Dreamweaver templates include editable and locked regions. The editable regions have a tab at the upper-left showing the name of the editable region and dashed borders around the regions, as shown in Figure 27.11. If you pass the cursor over a locked region, a circle with a slash through it displays to indicate that the region is not editable.

For more information on using and creating Dreamweaver templates, see Chapter 4, "Saving Labor with Templates and Libraries."

Make changes to the editable regions, and then click the Publish button at the top of the page to save the page and upload it to the web server.

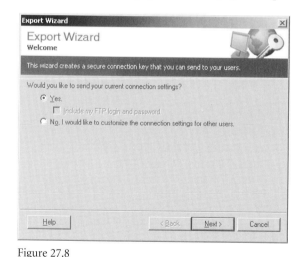

Figure 27.8

The Connection Wizard in Contribute

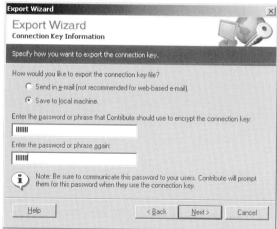

Figure 27.9

Encrypting a connection key

You can also use Contribute sample pages as templates to create new pages. To access the sample pages, click the New Page button at the top of a Contribute page, then select a sample page template in the New Page dialog box.

Using FlashPaper in Contribute 2

Contribute 2 enables Windows users to convert any printable document into a Flash SWF file, insert it in a web page, and view it in a browser. It allows the viewer to see files that were not designed for Web viewing, such as Microsoft Excel files, and it also allows the viewer to see files even if they don't have the software that created the file, such as Microsoft Excel or Word.

In your draft Contribute document, place the insertion point where you want to insert a FlashPaper file, then choose Insert → Document As FlashPaper. Browse to the location of the file in the Open File dialog box. Make sure to choose All Files from the Files Of Type drop-down menu unless the file is already in SWF format. The FlashPaper dialog box (see Figure 12.12) opens. Choose portrait or landscape display, and then choose a page size for the FlashPaper file.

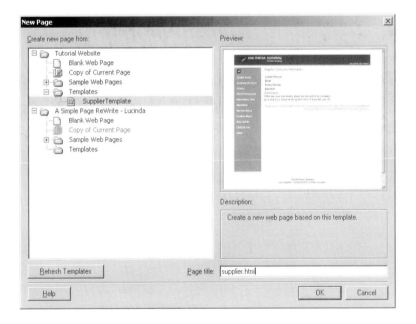

Figure 27.10

Choosing a template in the New Page dialog box

The FlashPaper file is inserted into your page, along with several controls, including Print, Zoom, Fit, and Navigate.

FlashPaper is a printer driver, so you can also create FlashPaper files from any application that includes printing. To insert the file into your page in this case, choose Insert → Flash Movie → From My Computer.

For more details on using FlashPaper in Contribute, see Joseph Lowery's article in the "Macromedia Edge" newsletter at `www.macromedia.com/newsletters/edge/july2003/section3.html`.

Dynamic Pages in Contribute Sites

By default, Contribute users can't select or delete dynamic content or invisible elements pages in Contribute sites. You can change permissions to allow them to select and or delete dynamic content by following these steps:

1. Click the Administer Site In Contribute from the Contribute category in the Site Definition dialog box.

2. Enter the administrator password in the Administrator Password dialog box.

3. The Administer Website dialog box opens. Select a permission group, and click the Edit button.

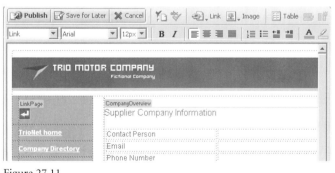

Figure 27.11

Using a Dreamweaver template in Contribute

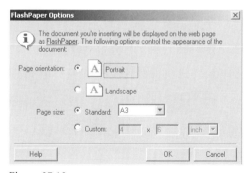

Figure 27.12

FlashPaper Options dialog box

4. Select the Editing category (see Figure 27.7). Uncheck the Protect Scripts And Forms check box and click OK to close the Permissions Group dialog box. Click OK again to close the Administer Website dialog box.

> Contribute users can't change CSS style sheets in Contribute. To change these files, use Dreamweaver.

Content Management: From Static to Dynamic

Contribute 2 can be an extremely useful tool for site content management for both web developers and their clients. Contribute is mainly designed for changing content on static pages. In the next chapter, you'll learn about managing content dynamically using Dreamweaver, ASP, and a database.

## CHAPTER 28

Dynamic Content Management

Dreamweaver MX 2004 offers several ways to use dynamic content in web pages, including HTML forms, server objects, JavaBeans, and databases. You can add dynamic content to a static page, such as adding time and date to a static page, or you can generate dynamic pages from database content.

Using a database to store content is another way to separate design and content. You can design a page or template and then connect to a database for updated content every time the page is requested. You only have to change the content in one location—the database—and the new content is retrieved and displayed dynamically in response to user requests.

Previous chapters focused on database connections and using databases with the five server technologies supported in Dreamweaver MX 2004. In this chapter, you'll learn more about using a database to dynamically manage page content.

The following topics will be discussed in this chapter:

- **Dynamic content in Dreamweaver MX 2004**
- **Using the client side for dynamic content**
- **Connecting to a database for dynamic content**
- **Creating master detail page sets with ASP**
- **Dynamic updates of an ASP page using an Access database**

Using Dreamweaver with Dynamic Content

Dreamweaver MX 2004 includes several automated and easy to use techniques for using dynamic content in your pages, including:

Recordsets To include dynamic data on a Dreamweaver page, you must first create a recordset to store the retrieved data. A recordset is created by a SQL query, and retrieves an entire database table or specific columns and rows. Dreamweaver automatically creates simple SQL queries, or you can use SQL code in Dreamweaver to generate more complex queries.

> You need to set up a database connection before you can create a recordset. See the section "Connecting to a Database for Dynamic Content," later in this chapter for more information.

URL and Form Parameters URL and form parameters are used to store input from users. An HTML form can use either URL parameters (GET method) or form parameters (POST method) to transmit data from users. You can also use a hyperlink with the HTTP GET method to transmit data in the form of name/value pairs at the end of a URL; for example:

```
http://www.example.com/cf/add.cfm?fname=rose&lname=smith
```

> See Chapter 14, "Collecting Information with Forms," for more details on the HTTP GET and POST methods.

Session Variables Session variables allow you to store information for the duration of a user's visit (*session*) to your site. You can create session variables in your source code and then define them for easy access in the Bindings panel of the Application panels group.

> See the section "Login Pages and Processes" in Chapter 26, "Controlling Access to the Site," for more details on creating and using session variables.

Application Variables (ASP and ColdFusion) Application variables store information that persists from user to user and is maintained for the life of the application. You can create application variables in ASP or ColdFusion in the Bindings panel of the Application panels group.

Server Variables Server variables are server objects that can store information and can be used as dynamic content sources. The available server variables differ depending on the particular server technology you are employing—the most extensive collections are available for ASP and ColdFusion, but server variables are also available in JSP and PHP.

In ASP, use the Request Variable dialog box in the Bindings panel (click + and then select Request Variable). This lets you access ASP request collections including `Request.Cookie`, `Request.QueryString`, `Request.Form`, `Request.ServerVariables`, and `Request.Client-Certificates`. In ColdFusion, click + in the Bindings panel and choose from any of these server variables (Client Variable, Cookie Variable, CGI Variable, Server Variable, or Local Variable). For JSP and PHP, click + in the Bindings panel and select Request Variable (JSP) or select the variable (PHP).

JavaBeans and JSP JavaBeans are JSP components and can be used as dynamic content sources in Dreamweaver JSP pages. JavaBeans appear in the Bindings panel where you can double-click a JavaBean to display its properties, and then drag individual properties from the Bindings panel to a JSP page.

> Chapter 19, "Database Connectivity," presents details on using databases with Dreamweaver MX 2004, and includes information on using Dreamweaver to create dynamic text, dynamic list/menus, dynamic radio buttons, and dynamic images.

Working on the Client Side

Although most dynamic content sources are on the server side, you can also use client-side scripting in JavaScript or VBScript to use dynamic data without a trip to the server. You won't be able to use a database from the client (browser) without accessing the server, but you can use the client browser to access dynamic data such as time and date. You can also use a combination of client-side and server-side scripting on the same page—for example, using JavaScript or VBScript in an ASP page.

To include the current date using VBScript in an ASP page, simply add this script block to your ASP page:

```
<script language="vbscript" type="text/vbscript">
  Document.Write Date
</script>
```

This code displays the date in `mm/dd/yr` format. See the Hands On tutorial at the end of this chapter for an example of using VBScript and ASP for dynamic content updates.

> To see a server-side method for inserting the current date on a page, see Chapter 21, "Working with ASP."

Using a Database for Dynamic Content

For dynamic content updates, you need to connect to a database. Database creation and design is a huge topic and beyond the scope of this book. If you are not already familiar with using databases, Microsoft Access is a great place to start learning about them. An Access database (`lorem.mdb`) for use with the examples in this chapter is included in the Chapter 28 folder on the CD.

> If you are new to databases, see the "Beginner's Guide to Databases" in Dreamweaver MX 2004 Help. For more details on using databases in Dreamweaver, see *Mastering Dreamweaver MX Databases* by Susan Harkins, Bryan Chamberlain, and Darren McGee (Sybex, 2003).

Microsoft Access

In this chapter, you'll be using an Access `.mdb` file. Microsoft Access is easy to learn and to use, and is included as part of the Microsoft Office suite, so it is available to many PC users. For large database-driven sites with heavy traffic, Access is not a good choice (Access is limited to 255 concurrent connections), but it can work well for smaller sites and databases.

> For more information on using Access 2002 for database-driven sites, see `http://msdn` `.microsoft.com/library/en-us/dnacc2k2/html/odc_adap.asp`.

Figure 28.1 shows the Tables view of `lorem.mdb`, with the DailyNews table selected (you'll use this table in the Hands On tutorial at the end of this chapter). Figure 28.2 shows this table in Design view. Notice that the table has an ID field, which serves as the

Figure 28.1

The `lorem.mdb` file in Access

primary key for the table. This field is auto-numbered, so it increments automatically as you make entries in the table. You'll use this field in the tutorial to filter the database results when the page is updated. The other fields use Access's Memo data type. A Memo data type can hold up to 65,535 characters, so it works well when you have more than a sentence or two of text data. Use the Access Text data type (can hold a maximum 255 characters) for small text blocks.

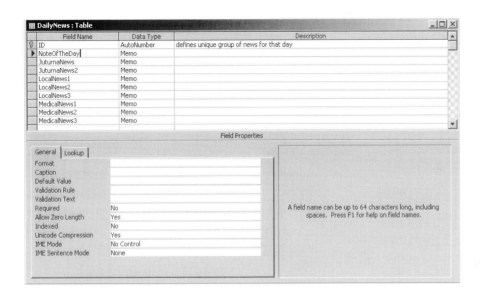

Figure 28.2

`DailyNews` **table in Design view in Access**

Making a DSN

The first step in creating a database connection is to make a DSN.

Briefly, to create a DSN for the `lorem.mdb` database included in the chapter CD, follow these steps in Windows XP (for more details on creating a DSN, see Chapter 26, "Controlling Access to the Site"):

1. Open Control Panel → Performance And Maintenance → Administrative Tools → Data Sources (ODBC).

2. In the ODBC Data Source Administrator dialog box (Figure 28.3), click the System DSN tab, and then click Add.

3. Choose Microsoft Access Driver (*.mdb) in the Create New Data Source window.

4. Enter a name in the ODBC Microsoft Access Setup window, and then click the Select button in that window and browse to the location of the `lorem.mdb` file on your computer. You will need the name to create a database connection in Dreamweaver.

Figure 28.3

ODBC Data Source Administrator dialog box

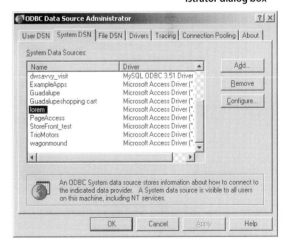

Creating a Connection

To create a connection using this DSN, follow these steps:

1. Open an ASP site in Dreamweaver MX 2004, or create a new ASP site with a local or remote host.

2. Open a new or existing ASP page in the site, and then open the Databases panel in the Applications panel group. Click the + and select Data Source Name (DSN). The Data Source Name (DSN) dialog box displays (see Figure 28.4).

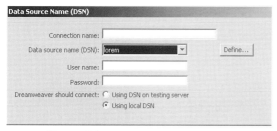

3. Choose the DSN you created in the previous section from the drop-down menu and give the connection a name. Click the Test button to verify that the connection is functional, then click OK. This connection is now listed in the Databases panel.

4. Leave the ASP page open (you'll use it in the following section).

Figure 28.4
Data Source Name (DSN) dialog box

This connection includes more than one table—you'll use one table (`Oscar`) for creating a Master Detail set in the following section, and one (`DailyNews`) for the Hands-on tutorial at the end of this chapter.

Creating Master Detail Page Sets with ASP

Using Master Detail page sets is one way to display dynamic content from a database, and is available for all the server technologies supported by Dreamweaver MX 2004. Basically, records from a database recordset are displayed on the master page, with links to dynamically created detail pages for any record listed on the master page.

In previous chapters, you created Master Detail page sets with ASP JavaScript (Chapter 19) and PHP (Chapter 22). The procedure is basically the same for any server technology, so feel free to skip to the Hands On tutorial at the end of this chapter if you're already comfortable with creating Master Detail page sets in Dreamweaver. In this section, you'll use ASP JavaScript and the `Oscar` table from the `lorem` database connection to create dynamic pages.

> If you'd just like to view the completed pages, copy `oscar.asp` and `detail.asp` from the Oscar folder in the Chapter 28 folder on the CD into the site folder on your computer that contains the `lorem` database connection information, and preview the pages. You'll need to update the connection information in these files for them to access the database from your computer.

To create a Master Detail page set to display Oscar Wilde quotations, you'll need an open ASP page and the DSN and database connection that you created in the previous section. Then, follow these steps:

1   Open the Bindings panel in the Application panel group. Click the + and choose Recordset (Query).

2. In the Recordset dialog box (Figure 28.5), enter a name for the Recordset in the Name textbox, and select a connection name from the Connection drop-down menu.

3. Select Oscar from the Table drop-down menu.

4. Leave the All radio button checked to include all the columns.

5. Click the Test button to preview the recordset, and then click OK to close the dialog box.

6. Save your page.

7. Choose Insert → Application Objects → Master Detail Page Set from the main Dreamweaver application menu.

8. In the Insert Master-Detail Page Set dialog box (Figure 28.6), select the Quotation field and then click the minus (−) button to remove this field. Only the Topic field will display on the Master page.

9. Choose All Records from the Show radio button group.

10. Enter a filename for the Detail page, and then click OK. The Detail page is automatically created.

11. Save both files, and then preview the Master page in a browser (File → Preview In Browser).

Figure 28.7 and 28.8 show the Master and Detail pages in Internet Explorer. Both pages are linked to a style sheet named Oscar.css that's included in the CSS folder in the Chapter 28 folder on the CD.

Figure 28.5

Creating a Recordset

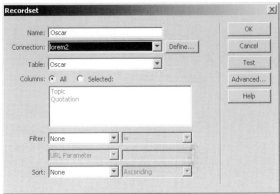

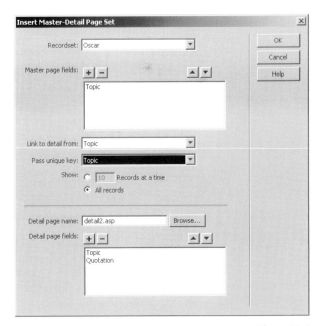

Figure 28.6

Creating a Master and Detail page

Figure 28.7

Previewing the Master Page in Internet Explorer

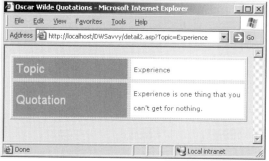

Figure 28.8

The dynamically created Detail Page previewed in a browser

Hands On: Adding Dynamic Content with ASP and Access

In this tutorial, you'll use the DailyNews table from the lorem database to add dynamic text content to update the Juturna Medical intranet site. The Juturna Medical home page has been generated from slices created in Fireworks MX 2004 from the working design file, and linked to one of Dreamweaver's sample CSS pages that we modified and renamed intranet.css.

The completed home page (index.asp) is included in the Intranet folder in the Chapter 28 folder on the CD. A starter page (index_start.asp) to use with this tutorial is also included in the folder.

Creating the Components

First, create a DSN and a database connection:

1. Open or create an ASP site and open a new or existing ASP VBScript page.

2. Create a DSN and a connection to the lorem database as described earlier in this chapter. Name the connection Intranet.

    Then make a new recordset:

1. Open the Bindings panel in the Application panel group. Click the + and choose Recordset (Query).

2. In the Recordset dialog box (see Figure 28.9), enter Intranet1 for the Recordset in the Name text box, and select the Intranet connection from the Connection drop-down menu.

3. Select the `DailyNews` table in the Table drop-down menu.

4. In the Filter section, choose `ID` from the first drop-down menu and = from the second drop-down menu. Select `Entered Value` from the third drop-down menu, and enter the value **1** in the textbox to the right.

5. Click OK to close the dialog box.

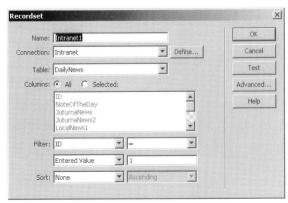

Figure 28.9

Using the Recordset dialog box

The `ID` is the primary key for the `DailyNews` table. The value entered in the text box is the value used to filter the Recordset data—in other words, if you enter **1**, the data from the row with an `ID` of `1` (the first row of the table) is used.

Adding a Dynamic Date

To add a dynamic date to your page:

1. In the upper-right corner of the `index_starter` page, select the last cell on the right side of the first row of the table. The code for this cell:

```
<td bgcolor="#bcc4cf" class="date"> </td>
```

2. Replace ` ` with the following VBScript code that inserts the client date automatically whenever the page is opened.

```
<script language="vbscript" type="text/vbscript">
   Document.Write Date
</script>
```

3. Save the page as `index.asp`, and preview it in a browser (File → Preview In Browser). The current date should be displayed on the page.

Inserting Dynamic Text

To adjust the text content of your page on the fly, follow these steps:

1. Find the cell above the Juturna News graphic. Select ` ` in the code for this cell.

2. Select Insert → Application Objects → Dynamic Data → Dynamic Text.

3. In the Dynamic Text dialog box (see Figure 28.10), select NoteOfTheDay and click OK. A placeholder for dynamic text will appear in the cell in Design view.

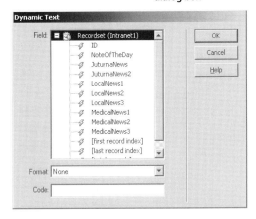

Figure 28.10

Dynamic Text dialog box

4. Repeat steps 1 through 3 for Juturna News, Local News, and Medical News. Select the fields with these names one at a time from the `Intranet1` recordset. Insert Dynamic Text between the opening `td` tag and the first `br` tag, marked *HERE* in the following code sample for the first Juturna news item:

```
<td rowspan="3" class="sidebar">HERE<br><br>
```

5. Insert two Dynamic Text placeholders for Juturna News, three for Local News, and three for Medical News. Once all the Dynamic Text is inserted, save the page and preview in a browser (File → Preview In Browser).

6. See the completed page (`index.asp`) in the `Intranet` folder for an example of the final code.

A few additional notes on the Juturna Medical home page:

- The URLs for the links on this page are all in the form a `href="#"`, so the links don't load a new page. You can add a URL field to the `lorem` database and use Dynamic Text to insert the URLs and create links dynamically.

- The graphic at the top of the page can be made into an image map, and links added for HR, Forms, News, and Calendar. See Chapter 8, "Making and Maintaining Hyperlinks," for more information on image maps.

- The dynamic calendar on the left side of the page is created using ASP. The current day is automatically highlighted when the page loads.

- The Medical News on the right side of the page could be updated using an RSS feed from a medical news site online. See Chapter 15, "Community Building with Interactive Site Features," for more information on blogs and RSS feeds.

Figure 28.11 shows the completed Juturna Medical home page, with dynamic content updates from Row 1 of the `DailyNews` table. Of course, for only one page, it would be just as fast and easy to do content updates using a template or Contribute, but for larger sites with multiple pages to update, using a database to store dynamic content for updates can be very easy and efficient.

A Walk on the Browser Side

In this chapter you learned about using dynamic content on the client side or server side to update Dreamweaver pages. All five server technologies supported in Dreamweaver can be used with a database to create dynamic content updates.

In the next chapter, the focus is on the browsers and using Dreamweaver MX 2004 to preview pages and test for browser errors before you upload your pages to a web server.

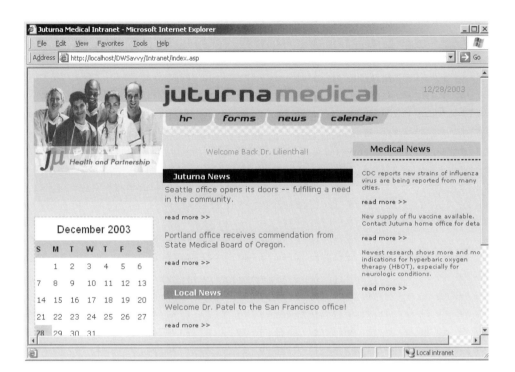

Figure 28.11

Juturna Medical home page after dynamic content updates

## CHAPTER 29

Checking Browser Compatibility

Browser compatibility continues to be an issue for web designers. Unless you are designing pages for a very specific audience—an office intranet where everyone is using computers with the same operating system and the same browser, for example—it's necessary to design pages with browser compatibility in mind. You should also test your pages in multiple browsers before uploading them to a web server.

This chapter covers the following topics:

- **Defining the target audience**

- **Evaluating browsers for JavaScript, CSS, and XML support**

- **Testing browser compatibility in Dreamweaver**

- **Avoiding common problems**

- **The future of browsers**

Defining the Target Audience

The vast majority of web surfers are using computers with the Windows operating system. In 2003, according to statistics from Statmarket (`www.statmarket.com`), 35 percent of the web audience used Windows XP, and 25 percent used Windows 98. Other versions of Windows accounted for another 30 percent of web users, Mac users made up 3 to 5 percent, and the remaining 4 to 5 percent included users of all other platforms combined.

Internet Explorer 6 is currently the most popular browser for web surfers. Overall, statistics at the Browser News site (`www.upsdell.com/BrowserNews/stat.htm`) from four diverse sources show that 50 to 70 percent of the web audience uses Internet Explorer 6, 12 to 26 percent use Internet Explorer 5, and 3 to 20 percent use Gecko-based browsers (Netscape Navigator 6+ and Mozilla 1+). Also of interest are the stats for level 4 browsers. Currently, one percent or less of the web audience uses IE 4, and only 1–2 percent use Netscape 4.*x*.

Keeping these statistics in mind, look at your target audience again. Which browsers are they likely to use? Do your pages include JavaScript or CSS? Do your pages include special features that require the latest browsers, such as XML or CSS absolute positioning support? Are your pages viewable by users with disabilities? You should review all of these important issues at the beginning of the site design process, and again during the testing phase.

See Chapter 1, "Planning and Preparing for a Dreamweaver Project," for more information on audience definition and site planning, and Chapter 33, "Using Dreamweaver to Make Your Site Accessible," for details on using Dreamweaver's accessibility features.

Evaluating Browsers

All browsers support basic HTML, but browser support varies widely for JavaScript, CSS, and XML. If you are using these additional features in your pages, it is very important to evaluate and test the browser support for the specific features you want to include.

Table 29.1 provides general information about browser support for JavaScript, CSS, and XML. In addition to the most popular browsers (Internet Explorer and Netscape Navigator), Opera has been included. Although Opera does not have a large number of users in the United States, it is much more popular in Europe. If your site targets an international audience, it may be important to include Opera in your browser evaluation and testing.

BROWSER	JAVASCRIPT VERSION	CSS VERSION	XML	
Apple Safari 1	1.5 ECMA[1]	CSS1, partial CSS2	Yes	Table 29.1
Explorer 6	1.5 ECMA	CSS1, partial CSS2	Yes	**Browser Support for JavaScript, CSS, and XML**
Explorer 5.5	1.5 ECMA	CSS1, partial CSS2	Partial	
Explorer 5	1.3 ECMA	CSS1, partial CSS2	Partial	
Explorer 4	1.2 ECMA	CSS1	No	
Mozilla Firebird 0.7	1.5 ECMA	CSS1, partial CSS2	Partial[2]	
Netscape 6, 7	1.5 ECMA	CSS1, partial CSS2	Partial[2]	
Netscape 4.7	1.3 ECMA	CSS1	No	
Opera 6, 7	1.4 ECMA	CSS1, CSS2	Yes	
Opera 5	1.3 ECMA	CSS1, CSS2	Yes	

[1] *ECMA is an open standard for JavaScript*

[2] *XML support is very different in IE and Gecko-based browsers. See a comparison at* `http://wp.netscape.com/ browsers/future/standards.html`.

Table 29.1 provides general guidelines for browser support, but for information about support of specific features, check out the following sources:

- QuirksMode Compatibility Tables at `www.quirksmode.org/dom/`
- Safari Developer FAQ at `http://developer.apple.com/internet/safari_faq.html`
- WebReview's Browser Compatibility Chart at `www.afactor.net/toolbox/notes/HTML/ info/browsersCompatability.html`
- WebReview's CSS master grid (now posted on the Dr. Dobbs site—you'll need to register (free) to access the article) at `www.ddj.com/webreview/style/`

Information regarding browser support of specific CSS, HTML, and JavaScript features is also available in Dreamweaver itself. Choose the Window menu and select Reference. A Reference window displays. From this window, choose O'REILLY CSS Reference, O'REILLY HTML Reference, or O'REILLY JavaScript Reference, and then choose the specific feature you are interested in from the drop-down list. Browser information is shown to the far right of the feature name.

Dreamweaver includes built-in JavaScript in Dreamweaver behaviors. (For more information on Dreamweaver behaviors, see Chapter 12, "Incorporating JavaScript Behaviors.") To specify one or more target browsers, choose the Show Events For item in the Action or Events menu of the Behaviors panel. The target browser determines which events are shown in the Events menu for the chosen action. The Show Events For submenu includes the following target browser choices:

- 3.0 and Later Browsers
- 4.0 and Later Browsers
- IE 3
- IE 4
- IE 5
- IE 5.5
- IE 6
- Netscape 3
- Netscape 4
- Netscape 6

Testing Browser Compatibility in Dreamweaver

Dreamweaver includes two features for testing pages in browsers and determining browser compatibility: Preview in Browser and Check Target Browsers. The Target Browser Check has been expanded in Dreamweaver MX 2004 to include the Check Browser Support feature in the Document toolbar.

You can also modify browser profiles or create new ones to customize your browser compatibility testing.

Preview in Browser

The Preview In Browser feature allows you to view your pages in the browser(s) of your choice.

Pages don't have to be saved in order to use this feature, so you can test them at any time. All browser-related functions work in Preview mode, so you can test JavaScript and CSS functions as well as links, plug-ins, and ActiveX controls. Although absolute and relative URLs function in preview mode, root-relative links can be viewed only if the file is on a server.

To use the Preview In Browser feature, select Preview In Browser from the File menu in the page you want to preview, and then choose one of the browsers from the list. You can also add or remove browsers from the list by choosing File → Preview In Browser → Edit Browser List and then clicking the plus (+) button to add a browser to the list, or the minus (−) button to delete a selected browser from the list.

You can also specify a primary browser and secondary browser. This enables you to use function keys to activate Preview In Browser. F12 opens the current page in the primary browser, and Control-F12 (Cmd-F12 for the Mac) opens the current page in the secondary browser.

You can include up to 20 browsers in the Browser List. You must, however, have all these browsers installed on your computer.

You can also choose to preview using a temporary file by checking this option in the Preview In Browser category of the Preferences menu (Edit → Preferences).

> The Debug In Browser feature for testing JavaScript is no longer included in Dreamweaver as of Dreamweaver MX 2004.

Check Target Browsers

The Check Target Browsers feature allows you to check for any elements or attributes that are not supported by the target browser. Dreamweaver uses preset browser profiles for Netscape Navigator versions 3, 4, 6, and 7; for Internet Explorer versions 3, 4, 5, 5.5, and 6; for Opera versions 2.1, 3, 3.5, 4, 5, 6, and 7; for Mozilla 1; and for Safari 1.

> These profiles can be modified, and new browser profiles can be created. See the "Using Browser Profiles" section later in this chapter for more information.

Check Target Browsers can be used to check a document, a directory, or an entire site. Dreamweaver generates a browser compatibility report that opens in the Target Browser Check panel in the Results panel group. This report includes the following:

- The name and location of the files with potential problems
- The specific line where the problem occurs
- A description of the problem

If you double-click the error message, the affected code is highlighted in the Code view window.

The report includes three types of problems:

error May cause serious display problems in some browsers.

warning Won't display correctly in some browsers, but no serious problems.

informational message Feature not supported, but has no effect on page display.

Errors are marked with a wavy red underline in the Code view window. If you put the cursor over the red underline, a tooltip displays showing which browsers don't support this item.

Here are some ways to use the Check Target Browsers feature:

- To check a file, save the file first. The check is done on the last saved version of the file. With the file open in Dreamweaver, choose File → Check Page → Check Target Browsers. The results of the check will then display in the Check Target Browser panel in the Results panel group.

You can now do this easier with the Check Browser Support feature in the Document toolbar. For more details, see the following section, "Check Browser Support."

- To check a folder or a site, open the site files in Local view in the Files panel. Select a group of files or the site folder. Open the Results panel and click on the Check Target Browser tab. Choose Site Report from the Show drop-down menu. Right-click the Site Report choice and select Check Target Browser For Selected Files/Folders in Site.

Check Target Browsers checks only HTML and CSS, not scripts.

Check Browser Support

The Check Browser Support feature in the new Document toolbar (see Figure 29.1) enables you to specify browsers and browser versions and test your page for errors based on level of browser support for the features included in your page.

By default, Dreamweaver automatically runs Check Browser Support when a document is opened. You can uncheck this option if you want, but it's an extremely useful reminder to check browser compatibility.

Dreamweaver automatically tests to make sure you are not using tags or CSS features that the target browsers do not support. You specify target browsers by selecting Settings from the pop-up menu and checking options in the Target Browser dialog box (see Figure 29.2).

Using Browser Profiles

Browser profiles are text files that include detailed information about the elements and attributes supported by specific browser versions. The browser profile files are contained in the `Configuration/BrowserProfiles` folder in the Dreamweaver application folder. Dreamweaver uses browser profiles for the Check Browser Support and Check Target Browsers features. You can edit these profiles to change how Dreamweaver validates your files in your chosen target browsers. For example, you might want to include errors or warnings when you use tags such as font or align (rather than CSS).

Figure 29.1

The Check Browser Support feature in the Document toolbar

The following code shows an excerpt from the browser profile for Netscape Navigator 7.

```
<!ELEMENT BLOCKQUOTE >
<!ATTLIST BLOCKQUOTE
    cite
    id
    class
    lang
    dir
    title
    style
    onclick
    ondblclick
    onmousedown
    onmouseup
    onmouseover
    onmousemove
    onmouseout
    onkeypress
    onkeydown
    onkeyup
```

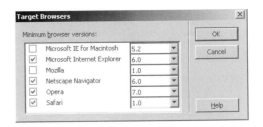

Figure 29.2

Select minimum browser versions in the Target Browser dialog box.

The browser profiles are very similar to Document Type Definitions (DTDs) and are mainly written using DTD syntax. These files specify exactly which elements and attributes a particular browser supports. HTML pages can be tested (validated) against the browser profiles. In the preceding code example, the BLOCKQUOTE element is specified as a valid element in this browser. The additional lines of code specify that the BLOCKQUOTE element can contain any of the listed attributes.

Browser profiles can also include warnings, error messages, and suggested substitutions for the unsupported element or attribute.

Browser profiles must have a very specific structure to function correctly. The rules for this structure include the following:

• You must use a unique profile name. This name appears in the Check Target Browsers list, and it must appear as the first line of the document, as shown in the first line of code in the Netscape Navigator 7 profile:

```
Netscape Navigator 7.0
```

• You must use the following form for the second line, which identifies this document to Dreamweaver as a browser profile:

```
PROFILE_TYPE=BROWSER_PROFILE
```

- You can use only the following elements in a browser profile:

`!ELEMENT`	HTML elements
`!ATTLIST`	Made up of HTML attributes for a specified element
`!Error`	Adds an error notice in the Check Target Browsers report
`!msg`	Messages in plain text that are added to error notices
`!htmlmsg`	Messages in HTML that are added to error notices

- You cannot use HTML comments `<!-- -->` in a browser profile. You can include comments by using `--` at the beginning of a line.

- You can include `!Error` within `!ELEMENT` or `!ATTLIST`.

- You must include a space in the following locations: before the closing angle bracket (`>`) in an `!ELEMENT` declaration, after the opening parenthesis in a list of attribute values, before the closing parenthesis in a list of attribute values, and before and after each pipe (`|`) in a list of attribute values.

For example, the format for the `BR` element is shown in the following excerpt from the Netscape Navigator 7 profile:

```
<!ELEMENT BR >
<!ATTLIST BR
    id
    class
    title
    style
    clear
```

The first line is an element declaration for the HTML element `BR`. A `Name` attribute is optional, but if it is included, this name (`Line break`) can be used in error messages. Otherwise, `BR` will be used in error messages.

The second line is an attribute list declaration. The `BR` following `!ATTLIST` specifies that this is a list of valid attributes for the `BR` element. These attributes include `id`, `class`, `title`, `style`, and `clear`.

To edit a browser profile, open an existing profile in Dreamweaver or in a text editor (Notepad, SimpleText, or another text editor of your choice).

If you don't want to see an error message for a particular unsupported element or attribute, change its format. For example, to stop seeing error messages for the `style` element in Netscape 3, change its format from this:

```
<!ELEMENT Style !Error >
```

to this:

```
<!ELEMENT Style >
```

If you edit a browser profile, save the original profile with a new file name. This preserves the original profile in case you want to use it again. Save the new profile with the original file name so Dreamweaver uses the new profile.

To add a custom error message, add either `!msg` or `!htmlmsg` after `!Error`. For example, you can modify the error messages for the attributes of any element that includes attributes. Take a look at this code from the Netscape Navigator 3 browser profile for the UL element and its attributes:

```
<!ELEMENT UL name="Unordered List" >
<!ATTLIST UL
        Type ( disc | circle | square )
        Class !Error
        ID    !Error
        Style !Error
>
```

This can be modified to include messages regarding errors, as shown in the following:

```
<!ELEMENT UL name="Unordered List" >
<!ATTLIST UL
        Type ( disc | circle | square )
        Class !Error !msg "Netscape Navigator 3 does not support the Class
attribute."
        ID    !Error !htmlmsg "<b>Netscape Navigator 3 does not support the
ID attribute.</b>"
        Style !Error
>
```

To create a new browser profile, follow these steps:

1. Open an existing profile in Dreamweaver or in a text editor (Notepad, SimpleText, or other text editor of your choice).

2. Replace the profile name in the first line of the browser profile file.

3. Add any new elements or attributes using the format shown above for the BR element and its attributes.

4. Delete any elements or attributes not supported by the browser. If you are creating a profile for a new browser, it is unlikely you will need to delete any elements or attributes.

Dreamweaver MX 2004 adds CSS validation to browser profiles. Each browser that supports CSS has a CSS profile (XML file) in addition to a browser profile (text file). The CSS profile includes all the CSS properties and supported name and value attributes, as shown in the following code excerpt for the margin style property from the Internet Explorer 6 CSS profile:

```
<property name="margin">
    <value type="units" names="%,em,ex,px,in,cm,mm,pt,pc"/>
    <value type="named" name="auto"/>
    <value type="named" name="inherit" supportLevel="warning" message=""/>
</property>
```

These XML files can be edited or you can create new CSS profiles.

Avoiding Common Problems

Browser compatibility issues are best addressed by preventing them from taking place. Take a close look at your target audience, including which browsers and platforms they are most likely to be using to view your pages. The more features you add to your pages—including complex layouts, JavaScript, CSS, animation, interactivity, and multimedia content—the more likely you will have problems with browser compatibility.

Feature Detection

In the past, designers and developers often decided that it was easiest to include different versions of pages for different browsers rather than try to design one page that displays the way you want it to in several browsers. JavaScript can be used to include browser detection and to direct users to different pages depending on the browser version they're using to view your page.

This method, however, can become ridiculously complex when you include every possible browser and version and platform. Web developers also realized that what really matters is features detection. You can look at the features your pages include and then use the Check Browser Support option in the Document toolbar to see if those features are supported in your target browsers. If you find that some features aren't supported in a target browser, you can use Dreamweaver's built-in JavaScript code snippets for simple browser detection and redirect.

If you prefer hand-coding JavaScript, see "Browser Detection and Cross Browser Support" for more information on using JavaScript for browser features detection (`http://devedge .netscape.com/viewsource/2002/browser-detection/`).

Designing for Browser Compatibility

To design the most browser-compatible page, consider the following when you design the pages for your site:

- Don't save browser-compatibility testing until the last moment. It's much easier to make changes early in the design process. Test your pages in multiple browsers (and on both the PC and the Mac platform, if possible). Web designers tend to use the latest, greatest browsers, but that is often not the case with your audience.

- Allow some flexibility in your design layout. Don't expect your pages to look the same in all browsers and on all platforms—they won't! A pixel-precise design might work well in some browsers, but it is unlikely to work the way you had in mind in all browsers.

- Use multimedia elements wisely and offer viewers the choice of listening to audio files and viewing long segments of animation.

- Specify margin width, margin height, and left and top margin attributes in the body element to ensure that browsers display your page margins in a similar way.

- Use layers wisely. If possible, use CSS instead of tables or layers to lay out your pages.

- Use the Reference panel and the Check Browser Support feature to check support for tags and CSS properties in your target browsers.

- Think twice about including several complex features in a single page. Be sure these features are really necessary to convey the intent of your page.

Web Standards

Browser compatibility can be very complex, and a major headache for web designers and web developers. Newer browsers—including Netscape 6+, Internet Explorer 6, Mozilla, Mozilla Firebird, Opera 6+, and Safari—are designed to be much more compliant with the web standards developed by the Worldwide Web Consortium (W3C) and make it much easier to design a single version of a page that will display approximately the same in each of these browsers. Although browsers are certainly nowhere near being totally compliant with web standards, these newer browsers are a huge step in the right direction.

For more information on web standards, visit the Web Standards Project site at www.webstandards.org and A List Apart at www.alistapart.com.

In addition to the usual choices, Dreamweaver MX 2004 includes Apple Safari 1 and Mozilla 1 in the Check Browser Support feature.

Apple Safari 1 (see Figure 29.3), the default Mac OSX web browser, is standards-compliant and includes tabbed browsing and a built-in Google search menu. Safari is—at least so far—only available for the Mac platform.

Mozilla, an open-source choice, has introduced an additional browser, Mozilla Firebird (see Figure 29.4). Firebird is a fast and efficient browser, because it's only a browser. It doesn't include e-mail or newsgroups or all the features of Mozilla.

As long as your audience includes viewers using 4.*x* browsers or earlier, you will have to consider browser compatibility issues carefully.

Figure 29.3

Apple Safari 1 homepage

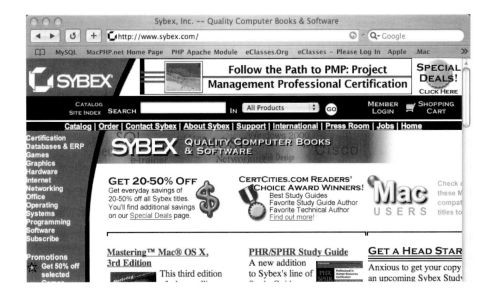

Figure 29.4

Mozilla Firebird 0.7 homepage

Resources for Exploring Browser Compatibility Issues

A good start to exploring browser compatibility issues is to learn the features of the browsers well. For more information about specific browsers, see the following:

- "Netscape Navigator 7 Review"

    www.web-user.co.uk/products/prod_rev.php?rid=621&cid=221

- "IE 6 Overview"

    http://hotwired.lycos.com/webmonkey/01/30/index3a.html?tw=eg20010824

- "Opera 7 Released"

    www.evolt.org/article/Opera_7_Released/1/54851/

- "Safari Developer FAQ"

    http://developer.apple.com/internet/safari_faq.html

- "Why You Should Switch to the Mozilla Firebird Browser"

    www.mozilla.org/products/firebird/why/

For more-complex browser compatibility issues, particularly if you are using DHTML (JavaScript and CSS) in your pages, see the following:

- "Common Browser Implementation Issues"

    www.ddj.com/webreview/browsers/browser_implementation.shtml

- "Browsers! Browsers! Browsers! A Strategic Guide to Browser Interoperability"

    www.ddj.com/documents/s=2728/nam1012432163/

- "Scripting for the 6.0 Browsers"

    www.scottandrew.com/weblog/articles/dom_1

> See the "Color Tutorials" section for screenshots from www.browsercam.com of the same page viewed in different browsers and platforms.

The Future of Browsers

Just like most everything else on the Web, the browser scene is in constant flux. In June 2003, Microsoft announced that they would not be making new stand-alone versions of Internet Explorer. All future versions of IE will be integrated with the Windows OS, and there will be no further versions of IE for the Mac.

Soon after this news, in July 2003, Netscape announced that there will be no new versions of Netscape. Sadly, this meant the end of the Netscape DevEdge team, which produced such great work for the web development community.

There are other browser choices, of course, such as Opera, Safari, and Firebird. Most end-users, though, use the browser that came with their computer, and it continues to be difficult to convince them to download a newer or different browser.

Getting Ready to Launch

Before you make a new site or project public, it's natural to want to get everything just exactly perfect. Of course, this is an ideal result that is almost impossible to achieve (particularly if perfection is defined subjectively, usually by the person paying the bills). However, you now know how to plan around the likely browsers your audience will be using, and you can validate your site code one last time using the methods described in Chapter 18, "Handcrafting Your Code." In the next chapter you'll finally get to that most important milestone, the site launch, also known as "going live."

## CHAPTER 30

Going Live or Delivering the Site

Once you've finalized the code and the design of your site, checked the navigation, and tested the pages in different browsers and platforms, it's time to complete the final phases of testing the site for useability and accessibility. Once that's done, you're ready to "go live" with the site—in other words, upload the files to the production server so that they can be viewed online. This chapter discusses synchronizing your local and remote files, uploading files to a server, and turning the site over to the client.

The following topics will be discussed in this chapter:

- Final testing and QA
- Section 508 accessibility standards
- Optimizing the site for search engines
- Finding or preparing a host server
- Going live (from staging to production)
- Working live with Dreamweaver
- Transferring just the right files
- Documenting your work

Quality Assurance and Final Testing

I know we just got done with a lot of testing in Chapter 29, but that was validation—making sure that your code won't break in any of your user's browsers. When a project is concluding, a few other types of testing might be needed:

Useability testing The final stage. Though useability testing can start during storyboard/thumbnails, it continues when HTML templates have been made, and it can be done even here at the end of a project to avoid costly post-launch retrofixes.

QA Quality assurance testing. This must be completed before turnover.

User-acceptance testing This can be carried out on the production server as a beta test before the site or application officially goes live. Though it's a bit late in the game to make changes, if users aren't going to adopt your new application or site, then it is worth making changes so that they will.

Useability Testing

Though you can test a site's interface reasonably well from mockups and prototypes, there's no real substitute for watching first-time users attempt to navigate and use your final site. To facilitate this process, design a series of procedures you want to see tested, and then ask your subjects to attempt to accomplish them. Don't give them any help or feedback; just observe what the users do when presented with the interface. Some large-scale projects can benefit from highly quantitative testing done in lab conditions, but even on a shoestring budget you can find some way to bring people into your office (or home) and watch them interact with your site.

QA Testing

Like useability testing, QA testing could warrant an entire book to itself, but we'll address it here briefly. The classic way to do quality assurance testing is to design a "coverage matrix" of features and functionality based on the user requirements you gathered at the beginning of the project. The same people who did the analysis and requirements gathering can also design the QA tests, or you can bring in a specialist for the end game. In addition to testing the features and functionality, the QA expert will identify what platforms and web browsers the intended audience will be using and then test each procedure in every possible environment.

Often, you grab every warm body you can, and set them up in front of Internet Explorer for Windows NT, Opera for OS X, Mozilla for Windows XP, and so on. In each environment, each tester needs to work their way through the coverage matrix and log any bugs they find. Bugs are prioritized in a three- or five-point scale (examples of priority types might include "serious," "minor," and "suggested enhancements"), and then the top-priority bugs are fixed in the time permitted—ideally you would get to everything except for perhaps some nice-to-have enhancements that don't break the site for anybody if they don't get added.

User-Acceptance Testing

User-acceptance testing is often confused with useability testing, but it is different. It is less scientific and usually involves bringing some of the intended end users in to test the site after it has been handed over (as discussed in the next few sections) but before it has officially gone live. Similar to what you would do for useability testing, you can develop a set of tasks for the user-testers to perform, but it's not as important to avoid helping them or commenting on the interface. If problems arise that aren't egregious, they can possibly be addressed through help material, documentation, and training. The primary goal of user-acceptance testing is to verify that the site operates as intended and can be comprehended and used effectively by those who are going to be stuck with it once you're on to your next project.

Meeting Section 508 Accessibility Standards

The U.S. Federal Government has mandated a set of accessibility standards (in the 1998 Rehabilitation Act), usually referred to as "Section 508" standards collectively for sites developed for the government or using government funding. These have become *de facto* standards for other organizations and it is becoming more common for Section 508 compliance to show up as a requirement in RFPs (requests for proposals).

> See Chapter 3, "Setting Up Your Workspace and Your Site," for a discussion of how to turn on prompting for accessibility attributes when you are designing your sites. See Chapter 33, "Using Dreamweaver to Make Your Site Accessible," for more details on Dreamweaver's accessibility features.

Figure 30.1

Getting ready to check the accessibility of an entire site.

As a result, it is important that your site meets these standards. To run an accessibility report to make sure your site complies, follow these steps.

1. Select your site from the drop-down menu in the Files tab of the Files panel group.

2. From the main Dreamweaver application window, choose Site → Reports. This brings up the Reports dialog box.

3. Select Entire Current Local Site in the Report On drop-down menu.

4. Under HTML Reports, click the Accessibility check box (see Figure 30.1).

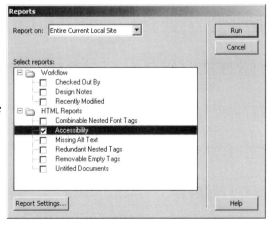

5. Click the Run button. Dreamweaver analyses your site and produces a report keyed to the Section 508 regulations (see Figure 30.2).

6. Double-click any line in the report to jump to the problem code and fix it, if need be.

Even if your client or employer does not require total compliance with Section 508 standards, you can still benefit from reviewing the accessibility of your site from this perspective. For more information about the guidelines, see the government's site at www.section508.gov/. Note that this site is itself compliant with the standards (of course).

Optimizing Your Site for Search Engines

Now that you've checked accessibility features on your site, make sure that you've optimized the site for search engine listings. Usually, you will want to involve the client early in the site development process to help prepare a list of keywords for you to include in the site pages. You can also help the client check the keywords of similar sites so that they can get a better idea of what to include in a keywords list. Generally, the more specific the keyword is, the better it will work for searches.

Figure 30.2

It looks like we've got a lot of code to clean up to make sure our site is as compliant as possible.

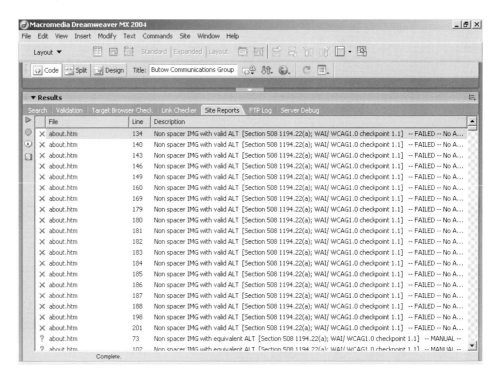

Keyword Searching

Keyword searches are the most common form of text searching done on the Web. Most search engines do their text query and retrieval using keywords. Keywords are added using HTML `meta` tags. Some search engines rely heavily on them, but others don't use them at all. It might be wise to optimize your `meta` tags for the search engines you believe are sending the most traffic to your site.

If no keywords are specified, then the search engine needs to determine them. This means that search engines pull out and index words that are believed to be significant. Words that are mentioned toward the top of a document and words that are repeated several times throughout the document are more likely to be deemed important.

> It's important to understand how search engines operate in order to understand the best ways to optimize your pages for search engine rankings. For a guide to understanding how search engines operate, submitting to search engines, and optimizing your site for inclusion in search results, see Danny Sullivan's "Search Engine Submission Tips" at www.searchenginewatch .com/webmasters/index.php.

Here are some additional suggestions for using keywords:

- In the keyword tag, list a few synonyms for, or foreign translations of, keywords. Make sure the keywords refer to, or are directly related to, the subject or material on the page. Don't use false or misleading keywords in an attempt to gain a higher ranking for your pages.
- Use keywords that are appropriate to your subject, and make sure they appear in the top paragraphs of actual text on your webpage. Many search engine algorithms score the words that appear toward the top of your document more highly than the words that appear toward the bottom.
- Words that appear in HTML header tags (`h1`, `h2`, `h3`, etc) are also given more weight by some search engines.
- Use keywords in your image `alt` tags too.
- Use relevant keywords in your title, and vary the titles on different pages that make up your website in order to target as many keywords as possible.

Concept-Based Searching

"Concept-based" searching tries to determine what you mean, not just what you enter in their fields. A concept-based search returns hits on documents that are about the subject/ theme you're exploring, even if the words in the document don't match the words entered into the query. Excite is currently the best-known general-purpose search engine site that relies on concept-based searching. This is also called clustering, which means that words are examined in relation to the other words found near the words in your search.

> This is a key concept in web optimization. If you have a website like the Pillsbury Bake Off site sponsored by General Mills, you could hypothetically link all 150 web pages to one another, thereby creating each document with links to the other 149 documents. Even if it seems "cheating" because all the pages reside on the General Mills server, and are linking to all other Pillsbury Bake Off pages, the reality is that these are considered links and will therefore boost the relevancy rating in Google and other search engines.

Other Techniques

Another key is to maintain the same domain name for a long time. Longevity on the web usually helps your ranking, as does an original, unique, and thought-provoking domain name. With attention to these criteria, you could be one of the first hits on a search engine's pages.

Often, the amount of time you spend optimizing a site for inclusion in search engines depends on the site budget and how important the client considers search engine rankings for the success of the site. Search engine optimization should be included in the overall plan and budget for a site.

Now that you've tested the site, checked for compliance with accessibility guidelines, and optimized the site for search engine rankings, you're almost ready to move to a live environment.

From Staging to Production

The big step you take at turnover or when your site goes live is moving the site from the staging environment (whether that's a testing server, a local version of the site, or what have you) to a production environment—a live environment that makes the site or application available to the public (or to its intended audience—it might be on a secure intranet, after all).

If you are building your own site and do not have access to an Internet host, then you'll need to contract with a hosting service and set up an FTP account for publishing the site live. You should be able to do this inexpensively, assuming your site is not too large and the expected traffic not high enough to require premium pricing. (If you are developing a high-traffic site, then you need to factor the costs of hosting the site into your business model!) There are many sources of opinion available online about hosting providers. The market changes rapidly and we wouldn't feel comfortable recommending a specific hosting service.

In any case, the staging server and the production server should be set up exactly the same way. If there are services enabled, they should be configured the same way, and the directory structure of one should mirror the other.

Implementing a Web Server

Before your site goes live, you may want to use a local web server as a staging server to test your pages. The advantage of using a local web server is that you can test pages quickly without uploading them to a remote server. The web server is even more important when you have dynamic content because it performs the process of dynamically building your pages. If you aren't creating dynamic pages, then you can simply access the files locally without using a web server. Technically, the process of testing dynamic pages is conducted through an application server, which dynamically generates web pages from code on the server. (For more information on application servers, see Chapter 16, "Building Web Applications," and Chapter 19, "Database Connectivity.")

The easiest way to go is to use the Microsoft web server that is available with your operating system. Depending on what version of Windows you're running, this web server will either be Internet Information Services (IIS) or Personal Web Server (PWS). We'll talk about IIS first because it is available with the most advanced versions of Windows, such as XP Pro and 2000.

Installing Internet Information Server (IIS)

In Chapter 21, "Working with ASP," and Chapter 25, "Emerging Technologies," you learned about using Microsoft's Internet Information Services (IIS) to process Active Server Pages (ASP) and ASP.NET pages. IIS is Microsoft's enterprise-class web server, which is available in Windows 2000 and the Professional version of Windows XP.

If you develop ASP pages, you must use IIS to publish your ASP pages, because without it you won't be able to install all ASP components when you upload your site to a remote web server. However, it takes two to tango, and you need to ensure that the version of IIS on the remote web server is the same or later than the one you're using locally.

Windows 2000 uses IIS 5.0, and Windows XP Professional uses IIS 5.1. Windows 2000 Server supports IIS 5.0 and 5.1, and Windows Server 2003 supports IIS 6.0. If you're using Windows NT 4.0, which uses IIS 4.0 for either your client or server, consider moving up to Windows 2000 or XP Pro for your client and to Windows Server 2003 for your server so you can take advantage of the latest features, including security features, available with IIS.

If you're using IIS, be sure you have the latest IIS information and patches; otherwise your computer may become infected with various unpleasant viruses. Information regarding IIS can be found at http://www.microsoft.com/WindowsServer2003/iis/default.mspx.

To install IIS, select Control Panel → Add/Remove Programs → Windows Components, which is shown in Figure 30.3. (Note that in Windows XP Home you won't see IIS listed in the Windows Components window.)

IIS will create a directory structure including `inetpub` and `wwwroot` as follows: `C:\Inetpub\wwwroot`. This directory is the default location from which IIS will publish documents, as shown in Figure 30.4.

Figure 30.3

The Windows Components wizard for IIS installation

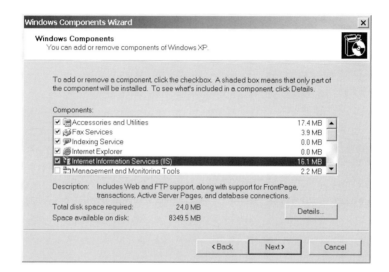

Figure 30.4

The `wwwroot` **directory**

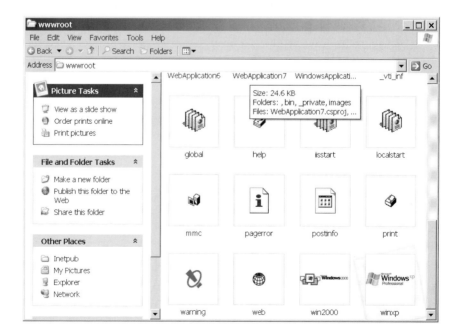

Using Personal Web Server (PWS)

Personal Web Server (PWS) is the predecessor to IIS, and is supported by Windows NT 4.0 Workstation as well as Windows 98. Like IIS, PWS also has a built-in application server for ASP pages, and it also serves pages out of the C:\Inetput\wwwroot directory. The latest (and last) version of PWS is version 4.0.

PWS is designed more as a test environment for your ASP pages than for use in production. Once you test your ASP pages locally, you can upload them to your site.

To install PWS, use your Windows 98 CD; browse to Add-Ons → PWS and select setup.exe. The Microsoft Personal Web Server Setup dialog box displays, as shown in Figure 30.5.

Using a Macintosh

If you're using a Macintosh, you will use a Java Database Connectivity (JDBC) driver to connect to an Access database, or any Open Database Connectivity (ODBC) data source, located on a Windows server. If you don't have access to a database with a JDBC driver, you can search a list of JDBC drivers and vendors on the Sun Microsystems website at http://industry.java.sun.com/products/jdbc/drivers. The more popular JDBC database drivers are those from Oracle and Microsoft.

Hosting Options

Once you determine whether you want to create your own site in Dreamweaver or just edit files using Dreamweaver (for more details, see Chapter 3, "Setting Up Your Workspace and Your Site"), you should determine what sort of web host you want to use.

You might not need to choose a host because you may be designing a website for your company either to be posted on the company's web server or on an intranet. Or you may already have an existing host. If you don't, you have plenty of options available.

Paid hosting services abound, and the sheer number of them can make it difficult to choose one. A good place to start is with your own Internet service provider (ISP). Many ISPs offer their own hosting services at reasonable rates. Of course, reasonable doesn't always mean the least expensive, and being less expensive doesn't mean you receive the best service.

So where do you start to find a hosting company? You can search through your local area

Figure 30.5

Microsoft's Personal Web Server Setup wizard

chamber of commerce to see what ISPs are listed there. You can even go through low-tech services such as computer user groups, the Yellow Pages, and computer publications. Friends, colleagues, and even owners and/or webmasters at companies you frequent can also offer recommendations. And, of course, you can always do an online search for web hosting companies.

There are also a number of hosting companies that offer free services, such as Brinkster for ASP hosting. However, with free services you have to agree to one or more compromises. For example, with Brinkster's free accounts, you have limited ASP support and no e-mail boxes, which come standard with most paid ISP plans. Free hosts generally require you to run their banner ads on your website, and only after you pay a monthly fee will you be able to host your site without the mandated ads appearing on your site.

FTP Using Dreamweaver

File Transfer Protocol (FTP) is the standard transmission protocol for transferring files between your computer and a remote web server. In Chapter 16, you learned how to set up web applications using Dreamweaver tools as opposed to just creating static pages. If you only need to upload static pages and don't have anything more sophisticated than CSS documents and scripts to go along with it, then Dreamweaver's FTP features will probably be all you need.

To FTP files from a Dreamweaver site, use the Remote Info category in the advanced tab of the Site Definition window (Site → Manage Sites). If you want to use Dreamweaver for FTP without defining a Dreamweaver site, Dreamweaver MX 2004 offers the option of connecting to an FTP or RDS server to upload and download files without formally setting up a Dreamweaver site.

> For additional details on FTP in Dreamweaver, see Chapter 3, "Setting Up Your Workspace and Your Site."

Working Directly with a Remote Server

If you've defined a site and included information about the remote server (in the Remote Info category of the Site Definition window), Dreamweaver gives you the option of staying connected to your remote web server while you work on site files.

You connect to your remote folder via the Files panel. The top of the panel displays your current site by default in the sites drop-down list. The view drop-down list tells you that you're looking at files in the local folder (called the local view), and this view opens by default.

We recommend that you save a backup copy of any site files you edit—at least until you know your new version works correctly.

The Files panel also contains a toolbar just above the folder tree that contains a series of seven buttons (see Figure 30.6). The Connect button on the far left (the one with the plug and the socket) connects you automatically to the remote host you have defined in the site. Once you connect, you can get files from the remote folder and put files into the remote folder, check files in and out if your site is set up to do so, and refresh your files list—all while you work on one or more open files in the Dreamweaver MX 2004 workspace.

Figure 30.6

The Files panel drop-down lists and toolbar

Though working in the Files panel is an easy way to manage your files and edit files at the same time, you can't see what's going on in your remote folder. But you can change this in one of two ways. First, you can select Remote View (instead of Local View) from the drop-down view list just above the toolbar, or you can click the Expand/Collapse button at the right side of the toolbar.

You have to be connected to the remote server to view the remote files, and if you are not connected when you select Remote View from the view list, Dreamweaver will remind you to click the connection button in the toolbar. You can maintain your connection to the remote server at the same time that you're working on your site pages. When you make changes to pages in your local folder, be sure to remember to upload those files to your remote server so you will see your changes when you access your website.

If you check Automatically Upload Files To Server On Save" in the Remote Info category of the Site definition window, files will be automatically uploaded to the remote server when you save them.

If you want to see your local and remote folders side by side, click the Expand/Collapse button. The Files panel expands so you can view both the remote folder in the left pane and the local folder in the right pane (see Figure 30.7). In this view you can drag and drop files between your local and remote folders.

When you open the expanded Files panel, the toolbar at the top of the window also expands and adds several new buttons. One of those buttons, View Site FTP Log, lets you view a text log of the FTP transfer sessions. To the right of the View Site FTP Log button is a series of three buttons. The button on the left, Site Files, is selected by default. The middle button, Testing Server, lets you view files in the testing folder. The right button, Site Map, lets you view your site as a hierarchical tree so you can see how pages in your site relate to one another.

Figure 30.7

You can drag and drop files between your local and remote folders in the expanded Files panel.

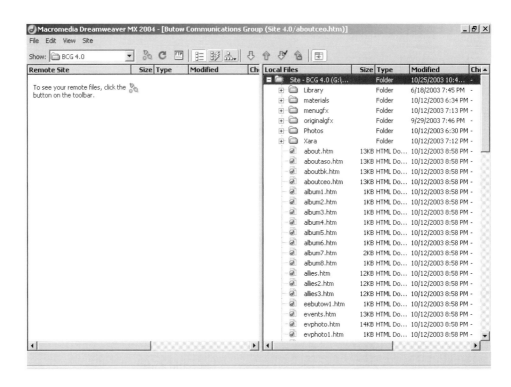

When you want to return to the Document window, click the Expand/Collapse button. The Files panel returns to its original size and location.

So what happens if you want to disconnect from the remote site? Just click the Connect button again in the Files panel (in either Expanded or Collapsed mode). Even if you disconnect from the remote server, the Files panel displays the list of remote folder files. Remember that you have to reconnect to the remote server to get an updated list of what's in your remote folder and to transfer files between your local and remote folders. Also remember that if you select a different site to edit and then go back to your original site, you will not be able to see your remote folder files—you have to reconnect.

Turnover (At Last!)

There are two different ways to upload a finished site to a production server from your testing/staging environment:

- Export the entire site as a single XML file
- Synchronize the local site with a remote site

The first approach makes sense when you won't have regular access to the production server but need to deliver or send the site to the new server for installation. This approach makes sense only if Dreamweaver will be used on both ends, so that the site can be both exported and imported as a Dreamweaver XML .ste file.

The second approach works best when you can set up the production server as your remote site (as opposed to using the staging server as a remote site and keeping a local site too).

Exporting a Site As XML

It's easier than it sounds to export a site as XML. Just follow these steps.

1. Choose Site → Manage Sites.

2. Click the Export button. The Export Sites dialog box appears.

3. Browse to the location where you want to save the site. When you click Save, the site is saved as an XML file with a .STE extension.

   To import the XML version of an entire site, the process is similar.

1. Choose Site → Manage Sites.

2. Click the Import button. The Import Sites dialog box appears.

3. Browse to and select the STE file.

4. Click the Open button. Dreamweaver unpacks the site and adds it your list of sites.

5. Click Done.

   So, one way to make a clean handoff of site code if the client is using Dreamweaver is to simply deliver the XML (STE) file exported from the completed site.

Synchronicity

Another, more common way of delivering the final site is to put it all from your local server to a remote server. If you've been using a staging or testing environment as your remote server, you should first synchronize that entire version of the site with your local copy, and then set up the production ("live") server as your remote server and synchronize again.

Cloaking Folders and Files

If there are any folders or files on the local server that don't belong in the official release of the site, you can *cloak* them before synchronizing so that they will be ignored during the mass PUT (upload) of folder and files to the remote server.

> Besides hiding files and folders from the synchronize command, cloaking also hides them from the PUT and GET methods, Check In and Check Out, reports, "select newer," all sitewide operations, Asset panel content, and template and Library updating.

To cloak a specific folder or file, first make sure that cloaking has been enabled. To enable cloaking, right-click on the file you want to cloak in the Files panel, click Cloaking, and then click Enable Cloaking. Right-click on the file again, and choose Cloaking → Cloak. The file or folder now appears in the Files panel with a red line across it (Figure 30.8). To turn off cloaking, right-click on the cloaked file or folder, then select Cloaking → Uncloak.

To have all files of a specific type cloaked automatically, right-click on a file in the Files panel, choose Cloaking, and then choose Settings. The Site Definition dialog box opens. In the Advanced tab, click the Cloak Files Ending With check box and enter the file extensions of any file types you want to cloak (see Figure 30.9).

You can also uncloak all cloaked files at your site in one fell swoop by right-clicking on a file in the Files panel, then selecting Cloaking, and then choosing Uncloak All.

Be aware that the step of uncloaking all files at the site is irreversible. Dreamweaver will "forget" which files and folders were cloaked and, if you change your mind, you will have to recloak each file or folder individually.

Synchronizing to the Remote Server

When the time comes to duplicate the site on the production server, the easiest way to do this is with the site Synchronization feature. This is simply an automatic way of handling the PUT operation for the entire site.

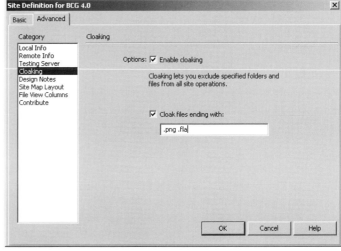

Figure 30.8

A cloaked folder in the Files panel

Figure 30.9

Dreamweaver can automatically cloak all the files of a specific type for you.

See Chapter 3 for an explanation of getting, putting, Check In, and Check Out.

To upload your site this way, follow these steps:

1. In the Files panel, open the site you want to synchronize from the drop-down list.

2. Right-click a site file in the Files panel and choose Synchronize. The Synchronize Files dialog box will appear (Figure 30.10).

3. Select the Select Entire Site option in the first drop-down list.

4. Select Put Newer Files To Remote in the second drop-down list.

5. Click the Delete Remote Files Not On Local Drive check box if you're sure there's nothing at the remote site (aside from the files you're uploading) that should be preserved.

6. Click the Preview button. Dreamweaver will list the files to be put to the remote server. Uncheck any files you don't want put there (see Figure 30.11).

7. Click OK. Dreamweaver will report Synchronization Complete when done.

8. To save a record of the upload, click the Save Log button.

9. Click Close.

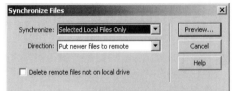

Figure 30.10
The Synchronize Files dialog box

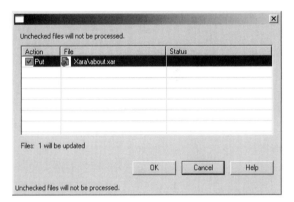

Figure 30.11
Dreamweaver lists the files to be updated.

Teach Them to Fish: Knowledge Transfer

Once you've handed over the code for a site, your project might involve supporting whoever will have to work with and maintain the site (if this is not you). Dreamweaver can help with some aspects of what's called *knowledge transfer* (which is just consultant jargon for training your client to help them understand how their new system works). Here's a list of some of the key aspects of knowledge transfer, with notes on whether Dreamweaver can be of any help in executing each process:

- Consider using Macromedia Contribute so that the site owner can make changes to the site with Contribute templates without knowing all the ins and outs of coding (and without making changes to areas that should not be changed). This will require you to be a Contribute administrator, to enable the site in Dreamweaver for using Contribute, and to supply the client with Contribute templates. See Chapter 27, "Static Content Management with Contribute," for more details.

- By supplying the client with Dreamweaver site templates, you will make it easier for them to maintain and update the site in the future. If you did not use templates in the building of the site, you still may want to create templates from the key pages for this purpose. Although Contribute is more efficient, and created specifically for this purpose, you and the client can still use Dreamweaver templates. See Chapter 4 for an explanation of templates.

- You must use clean, readable code if you may have to maintain a site or application developed by someone else. Dreamweaver can structure and highlight your code (as discussed in Chapter 18). You can also insert comments into your code to help explain it using the Comment button on the Common Insert bar (it brings up a dialog box; and you type your comment and click OK).

- You can add design notes to any file that might benefit from explanation, by choosing File → Design Notes. (Enter your notes in the primary text box and then click OK.)

- You should provide the client with documentation (a manual for maintaining the site) or—at minimum—a clean copy of the requirements used to develop the site. Dreamweaver can't help with this!

- You should also provide the client with training. Again, Dreamweaver won't help you with this.

- And then there's always good old-fashioned handholding.

Hands On: Working Live

Now it's time to put Dreamweaver to work checking your website and sending your work onto the Web. You're going to start by opening a web page you created in an earlier chapter (`frames.html` from Chapter 7) and checking its accessibility. Then you're going to keep that page open as you build a new site around it, connect to the site, and upload your files to the remote server. Finally, you will edit the page in your site and synchronize your edited local file with the file in your remote folder.

Since you have the option of selecting the website of your choice and using the web hosting service of your choice, what you see happen in Dreamweaver will vary depending on your own situation. In each of the three tasks listed in this section, references to the relevant figures in this chapter are included so you can see an example of what your results might look like.

Check Accessibility of Your Page

To check the accessibility of your page,

1. Open `frames.html` or any existing web page from your computer.

2. Select Site → Reports.

3. Click Accessibility.

4. Click Run.

Refer back to Figure 30.2 to see an example of an accessibility report in the Site Reports tab of the Results panel group. If you have no accessibility problems, there will be no listings in the Site Reports panel.

Create and Connect to a New Site

Follow these steps to create and connect to a new site:

1. Select Site → Manage Sites.

2. Click New.

3. Click Site.

4. Enter the new site name.

5. Enter the local root folder.

6. Click Remote Info in the category list.

7. Select FTP from the Access drop-down list. (Look back at Figure 30.9 to see an example of the Remote Info screen for an FTP connection.)

8. Enter the FTP host, host directory, login, and password information for your web server. (You might need to get information from your hosting provider.)

9. Click OK.

10. Click Done in the Manage Sites window.

11. Click the Expand/Collapse button in the File Inspector. (See Figure 30.13 on the CD to see an example of the expanded File Inspector.)

12. Click the Connect button in the toolbar.

13. Put your website on the remote server. The Remote Site pane will display the same files that are in your Local Files pane.

Synchronize to the Remote Server

To synchronize to the remote server,

1. Edit the web page on your site.

2. Right-click the web page name in the Files panel.

3. Click Synchronize.

4. Click Preview.

5. From the Synchronize Files dialog box (see Figure 30.16 on the CD), you can choose to synchronize the entire site or selected files only. You can also choose to Get (download), Put (upload), or both Get and Put files on the remote server. Click OK.

6. Verify the file was put onto your remote server.

7. Disconnect from the server.

8. Click the Expand/Collapse button to collapse the Files panel.

9. Save your web page.

The Long Haul

So, now you know what to do at the end of a web development project. You go live with your new site, or you deliver a working site or application to your client, and that's the end of the story, right? Well, no. The Web is not a printing press and a website is not a book. Most websites and some web applications require constant maintenance and oversight, which brings us to Chapter 31.

Maintaining a Site

In Chapter 3, "Setting Up Your Workspace and Your Site," you learned how to use some of the Dreamweaver tools that enable you to set up and organize a website. After you have published your site, the same tools allow you to perform the ongoing maintenance that keeps your content fresh and your pages useable. Ongoing website administration may not be glamorous, but it's essential—it's what keeps visitors coming back consistently.

Luckily for anyone tasked with having to keep a website running smoothly, Dreamweaver offers an unmatched range of tools for keeping track of files, cleaning up HTML, and collaborating with members of a team. This chapter examines the typical website administration functions you'll need to perform once your site is online. They include the following:

- **Managing content with the Site Map and Files List views**
- **Synchronizing your local site with online files**
- **Collaborating with your team using Check In/Check Out and Design Notes**
- **Making your workflow run smoothly**
- **Keeping records of changes and backups**

Managing Content

Your website might start out at a manageable size—say, three to six pages—but it can soon begin to grow exponentially and at a rapid rate. If your site presents an online catalog of goods for sale, for example (a fairly static one, where you're not using a dynamic database), you will need to delete items as they go out of stock and change descriptions as prices change. If you are managing a corporation's informational website, you will also need to perform regular updates of personnel, financial information, press releases, and more.

When your website contains hundreds or even thousands of files, even a single change, such as renaming a file or repairing a broken link, can have big consequences. Happily for both inexperienced and expert webmasters, Dreamweaver presents you with a toolbox full of utilities for keeping track of your site's content.

Using the Site Map and File List Views

The first challenge faced by many website administrators is simply being able to get an overview of all of the files the website contains. Some like to get a visual picture of how their site is organized. Others prefer to view the folders, subfolders, and files in the form of a hierarchical list. Dreamweaver gives you access to both ways of viewing your site's content through the Files panel. Figure 31.1 shows two views of the Files panel. The left side shows the remote version of the site in File List view. The right side displays the site's contents in Site Map view.

Figure 31.1

File List view (left) shows folders and files in a hierarchical list. Site Map view (right) gives you a picture of how your files and folders are linked.

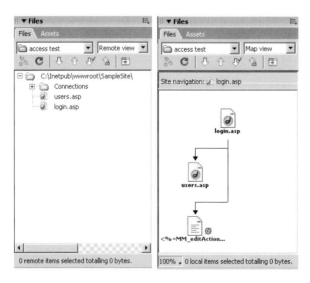

The Files panel, which contains the Site Map and Files List views, lets you do much more than just see your site; it gives you a way to perform routine administrative functions. Not only that, but when you use the Files panel to create or rename files or move documents from one location to another, you can instantly see the result and how the change fits into the overall structure of your site.

In order to work both on the local version of your site and on the one you've already published, you need to define your site as described in Chapter 3, "Setting Up Your Workspace and Your Site," and connect to it with FTP or another protocol (see Chapter 30, "Going Live or Delivering the Site"). Continue by opening the Files panel and choosing the site's name from the drop-down list on the left and Local view from the drop-down list on the right to open your local Files List view. Click the icon at the far left of the Files toolbar at the top of the panel to connect to your remote site. You can click the Expand/Collapse icon at the far right of the Files toolbar to expand the Files panel window and display remote files on the left and local files on the right. When you have both the remote and local sites open in the two panes of the Files panel, you can start moving files between the two.

FTP isn't the only option you have for gaining access to your website and transferring files. If the server that hosts your website supports it, you can also connect to your remote website using the WebDAV (Web-based Distributed Authoring and Versioning) and Visual SourceSafe protocols. These let you do source-control and version-control integration. You can also use RDS (Remote Development Services) to connect to a remote site on a server that supports ColdFusion.

Moving Files

Dreamweaver, like some FTP programs, uses the terms Get and Put to move the files between your website and your filesystem. Click the options menu to the right of the Files panel, and then choose Site → Get to move a selected file from the remote server to your computer; choose Site → Put to move a file from your local site to the remote server.

Selecting a single file in either the remote or local pane of the Files panel moves that file when you select Get or Put. But you can also select multiple files and then move them all at once. Shift-click to select contiguous folders or files; Ctrl-click (Cmd-click on a Macintosh) to select discontiguous folders or files.

You can configure Dreamweaver to automatically save files before you put them on the remote site. Choose Edit → Preferences to open the Preferences window. Click Site in the Category List in the Preferences window, check the box next to Save Files Before Putting, and then click OK.

Creating and Deleting Files

The Files panel makes it easy for you to revise the content of both your remote and your local website. You can remove or create both individual files and folders. To create a new folder, either in the remote site or on your local directory, follow these steps:

1. Select the folder that you want to contain the new folder.

2. Do one of the following:

   • Click the Option menu icon at the upper-right corner of the Files panel group. Choose File → New Folder from the menu.

   • Press Ctrl-Alt-Shift-N (Cmd-Shift-Option-N on a Mac).

The new folder is created. The default name New Folder is highlighted so that you can type a new name and then press Enter to rename it.

To add a new file to the site, the steps are similar:

1. Select either the folder that you want to contain the new file or an existing file in the folder that you want to contain the file.

2. Do one of the following:

   • Choose File → New File from the main menu or from the context menu.

   • Press Ctrl-Shift-N (Cmd-Shift-N on a Mac).

The new file is created. The file's name is highlighted so that you can type a new name and then press Enter to rename it.

Double-click the file's icon in the Files panel to open the file in a new Dreamweaver window so that you can edit it.

If you connect to your site with FTP, Dreamweaver will disconnect you if you're inactive for more than 30 minutes. You can change this limit: Choose Edit → Preferences, click Site, and replace the number 30 in the Disconnect After 30 Minutes Idle box.

Renaming Files and Folders

You can rename an existing file or folder on either the remote or local site by following these steps:

1. Highlight the file's name in one of two ways:

   • Right-click the file or folder (Windows) or Control-click the file or folder (Mac) and choose Edit → Rename from the pop-up menu.

   • Click the file name and then click F2 (Windows) or click the filename, pause, and then click the file name again (Mac).

2. Type the new name and press Enter.

If your site presents content generated by a small- to medium-sized company, you might suddenly find yourself awash in content. Consider adding on a program designed to automate content creation. See Chapter 28, "Dynamic Content Management," for more details.

Synchronizing Local and Remote Sites

If you want to verify whether an individual file or folder in one location exists in the other location, Dreamweaver can save you some time looking. Right-click (Control-click—Mac) the folder you want to locate and choose either Locate In Remote Site or Locate In Local Site from the pop-up menu. When Dreamweaver finds the file, it is highlighted in the opposite pane of the Files panel. The Locate In Remote/Local Site command is especially helpful if the file you're looking for is buried within folders and subfolders and would take some searching to find otherwise.

After you've created, deleted, or renamed files in one pane of the Files panel, you need to make sure your changes are carried over to the other pane of the window. Rather than making you search and replace files and folders one by one, Dreamweaver saves you time and effort by enabling you to automatically synchronize both sites.

For more details on synchronizing local and remote sites, see the "Synchronicity" section in Chapter 30, "Going Live or Delivering the Site."

Cleaning Up Your HTML

It's up to the editors and writers who create content for your site to make sure the words that make up your web pages are free of grammatical errors and typos. (Of course, if you're doing everything yourself, you need to proofread the content as well as design the web pages.) But no matter what, it's up to you to make sure your site's behind-the-scenes content—its HTML code—has the correct syntax.

If you create all of your content from scratch using Dreamweaver, you can be certain that your HTML is correct. But few webmasters type all the text themselves in the Dreamweaver window. More often, they import text from word processing programs such as Microsoft Word, which adds unnecessary HTML commands to your web page code. You can tell Dreamweaver to clean up the code, whether it comes from Word or from another source. You get other options of automatically cleaning up the HTML when the application opens a file, or when you manually tell it to perform a cleanup.

> For more information on cleaning up the code in imported files, see Chapter 6, "Inserting and Formatting Text Content," and Chapter 18, "Handcrafting Your Code."

Cleaning up your HTML isn't just a matter of good housekeeping. It ensures that your website content will appear the way you want, with no "extra" tags showing in your pages, and no extra spaces due to unnecessary commands.

> Don't forget to take advantage of the Assets panel when you are called upon to perform ongoing website maintenance. The Assets panel enables you to select groups of items quickly, or move individual assets to or from a website. See Chapter 4, "Saving Labor with Templates and Libraries," for more about the Assets panel.

Workflow

Workflow is all about getting the tasks associated with creating a website done efficiently and on deadline, and getting everyone on your production team to work in a cooperative way. It means collaborating efficiently with the members of your production team and communicating effectively with your clients.

Part of maintaining smooth workflow is up to you: you need to set a schedule and make sure everyone in your workgroup knows what they're supposed to do. But you can take advantage of some special Dreamweaver utilities to improve your communication and make sure your website progresses smoothly—Design Notes and Check In/Check Out.

Communicating with Design Notes

Sticky notes are great, but you can't attach them to a web page that exists not on paper but on a computer screen. With that limitation in mind, Dreamweaver provides a counterpart called Design Notes—computer files that can contain messages and that can be electronically attached to web pages.

Design Notes enable you to attach important information to your files. When coworkers open the files, they can view the information. The notes stay with their files when the files are copied, moved, or renamed. You might record the file's author or the program in which the file's contents were originally created. You can also communicate less technical information, such as the individuals who need to approve the document, or policy decisions that went into its creation.

Enabling Design Notes

Before you can begin using Design Notes, you have to set up this feature for the website on which you're working. Follow these steps:

1. Choose Site → Manage Sites… to open the Manage Sites dialog box.

2. Select a site and click Edit to open the Site Definition dialog box.

3. In the Category list, click Design Notes.

4. Check the box next to Maintain Design Notes, if it's not already checked, to enable Design Notes for this site.

5. If you need to share your Design Notes with your coworkers, make sure Upload Design Notes For Sharing is selected.

6. Click OK to close the Site Definition dialog box and Done to close the Manage Sites dialog box.

If you are working alone on your site, deselecting the Upload Design Notes For Sharing option can save some time when you transfer files from one location to another. However, when this option is deselected, your Design Notes won't be transferred when you upload your files to your remote server.

Creating Design Notes

Once you have enabled Design Notes, you can start attaching them to files within your site. Open the file to which you want to attach a note, and choose File → Design Notes to display the Design Notes dialog box (see Figure 31.2).

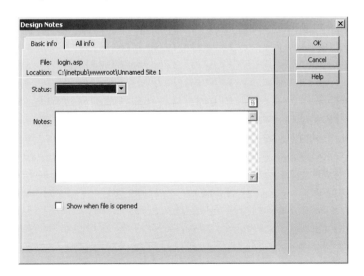

Figure 31.2

Use this dialog box to designate a status for a file, such as Draft, Beta, or Needs Attention, and to type Design Notes that you can share with your coworkers.

You can also right-click a file's name in the Files panel and choose Design Notes… from the context menu to open the Design Notes dialog box.

In the Basic Info tab, you can choose a status to assign to the file to remind you or your coworkers exactly where the file stands in the production process. You enter notes about the file in the Notes text box. Check the Show When File Is Opened box if you want the Design Notes file to appear whenever the file is opened.

In the All Info tab, you can add information about the file in the form of name-value pairs. You might enter type of information (such as **Author** or **Date**) in the Name field and then the specific data (such as **Becky** or **11/7/03**) in the Value field. If you need to enter another name-value pair, click the plus (+) sign; to remove a name-value pair, click the minus (–) sign.

When you're done, click OK. The notes are saved in a subfolder of your website named _notes. Each Design Notes file is assigned the filename extension .mno.

Figure 31.3

You or your team members can identify a file that has Design Notes in the Site Reports panel after running the Design Notes report.

You can run a report that generates a list of all the files in a site that have Design Notes attached to them. To do so, open the site, choose Site → Reports, check Design Notes in the Workflow section of the Reports dialog box, and click Run. A sample of the report results is shown in Figure 31.3.

In order to view notes for an individual file, you or your coworkers can do one of two things:

- Right-click the file's icon in the Files panel and choose Design Notes from the context menu.

- Select the file in the Files panel, click the Option menu icon at the upper-right of the panel, and choose File → Design Notes from the menu.

If the author of the notes checked Show When File Is Opened, the Design Notes will appear when the file is opened.

Web pages are only the most obvious kinds of files that can have Design Notes attached to them. You can also attach Design Notes to images, Flash animations, Java applets, and other website contents. You can attach Design Notes to web page templates, but be aware that documents created with the template don't inherit its Design Notes.

Using Check In/Check Out

After a website has been created and is online, you might be called upon to perform regular updates. You might receive new files from writers, and editors and designers might need to work on pages to change colors or images. When you're part of a larger workgroup of individuals with different responsibilities, you need to keep track of who has worked on a file, and when the work was completed, so as not to duplicate effort or miss important stages. The need to track workflow becomes more important if more than one team member needs to work on a web page, and if workers are scattered in different locations.

The Check In/Check Out system of file management that you learned about in Chapter 3 can be just as useful for ongoing website administration as it is for site creation. You can use Check In/Check Out even if you're the only one doing the work on the site. For instance, you can enter different check-out names depending on which computer you're working on (such as `GregH-Production Mac`, `GregH-Home PC`, and so on) so that you know where the most recent changes are located should you forget to check a file back in.

> Don't forget that if other team members aren't using Dreamweaver for uploading files, they can still access and overwrite files on the remote server regardless of Dreamweaver's Check In/Check Out system.

In terms of ongoing maintenance, it's particularly useful to keep in mind that you can activate Check In/Check Out on some sites and make it inactive on others. Use Check In/Check Out when you're revising files on your local site. When the revisions are done and you want to move new files to the remote server and/or delete outdated files, you can disable Check In/Check Out to save time. This also makes sense if you're the only one authorized to publish files on the remote server and there's no chance of confusing your work with anyone else's.

MANAGING CONTENT WITH DREAMWEAVER TEMPLATES

All the Design Notes in the world won't prevent coworkers from changing parts of your site that they aren't supposed to tamper with. Even a Design Note that says "Don't Change This!" doesn't guarantee that they won't click a heading and delete it accidentally, or change the look of boilerplate text that isn't supposed to be altered.

Unless, that is, you mark such content as non-editable through the use of Dreamweaver's Templates. You can use templates to create your own content management system, by only allowing certain contents to be changed. As you learned in Chapter 4, templates can contain regions that you specify as either editable or non-editable. By using templates to design your site, you can restrict what others can change. This enables contributors to input content without compromising site design.

Dreamweaver MX 2004 also gives you the ability to designate regions of a template as "optional." You can set parameters that let either the template author (that's you) control which regions show and hide without letting a user edit the content, or, alternately, let your colleagues edit content and specify whether the region shows or hides. See Chapter 4 for more information about creating editable regions in templates.

You can also do site management using Contribute and Contribute templates. See Chapter 27, "Static Content Management with Contribute," for more details.

Journaling and Rollback

Guarding against lost data is an essential part of ongoing website administration. Once your site is online, you need to protect yourself and your clients or employers against viruses, security breaches, or disasters that can not only take a site offline, but can also force you to spend considerable time rebuilding a site.

Dreamweaver can help you guard against such disasters by enabling you to perform such functions as journaling and rollback. By using reports to keep track of the most recent versions of your files, you gain the ability to return to the last correct version of your website when something goes wrong.

A journal is a record of transactions you've conducted or events you've encountered over a period of time. In the world of computer software, *journaling* is the process of keeping a record of system writes so that you can know what files have been copied to a filesystem recently. *Rollback* is a term usually used in connection with databases. If data is lost or the current database becomes corrupted in some way, a system administrator needs to roll back to the most recent correct version.

Generating Reports

Most web hosting services provide you with log file reports that analyze how your site has been used. You can also generate reports that tell you when files were created or modified or when they were moved to the server.

Dreamweaver has a built-in reports utility of its own, but it's primarily used to track Design Notes and Check In/Check Out records as well as specific HTML problems such as bad external links or unnecessary tags.

You can, however, create your own website journal of recent changes, and thus have a higher degree of control over the information you need, by installing some Dreamweaver extensions.

Site Import and Export

The Site Import and Export functions enable you to save site information for a website. You can export the data to a file that you can either share with your coworkers or open up in case your files are damaged. The extension produces an electronic snapshot of a site that can help others work on it or even recreate it if necessary.

This functionality used to be provided as an extension to Dreamweaver but is now built into the application. The following steps show you how to start using it:

1. From the Site menu, choose Manage Sites. The Manage Sites dialog box opens.

2. Select the site you wish to export from the listed sites. Only one site can be exported at a time.

3. Click Export. The Exported Site dialog appears.

4. Navigate to the folder in your filesystem that you want to contain the exported site data, or click the New Folder button to create a new folder.

5. Click Save to export the website data.

The exported website information appears with the generic name `DWSite.ste` in your selected location. The file contains the XML representation of the site. To view the file, you can either open it in the Dreamweaver window or import the file by clicking the Import button from Site → Manage Sites, locating the site file, and clicking OK. The site is added to the list of sites in the Manage Sites dialog box.

The Site Summary Reports Extension

An extension provided by Macromedia, Site Summary Reports, is intended for users who are migrating to Dreamweaver from another popular website design tool—Microsoft FrontPage. But the extension works just as well with Dreamweaver-created sites. It enables you to create reports listing different types of information about the files in your site. You can use the extension to report on all files created or modified after a certain date, which can prove helpful if you need to roll back to a previous version. After you download and install the extension, from

```
www.macromedia.com/cfusion/exchange/index.cfm#view=sn100&viewName=
Macromedia%20Exchange&
```

quit and restart Dreamweaver if necessary. Then follow these steps:

1. Open the site that you want to report on.

2. Choose Site → Reports.

3. The Site Summary Reports extension adds a new category to the Reports dialog box: FrontPage Migration Kit (see Figure 31.4). Check one or more of the options in this category. If you want a list of files created in a certain period of time, click either File Creation Date Range or File Modification Date Range.

4. Choose an option from the Report On drop-down list, such as Entire Current Local Site.

5. Click Report Settings.

6. In the File Creation Date Range dialog box (which appears if you have selected File Creation Date Range or File Modification Date Range), specify the start and end dates you want to report on.

7. Click OK to return to the Reports dialog box.

8. Click Run.

Figure 31.4

Clicking one of the new report options under the FrontPage Migration Kit category can help you take a snapshot of your site so that you can restore it if need be.

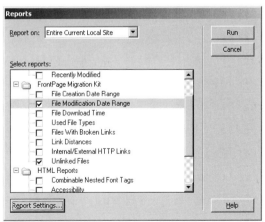

Figure 31.5

The Site Summary
Reports extension
provides you with
lists of files created
or modified after a
certain date.

Report results appear in the Results panel (see Figure 31.5). To save your results, click Save Results (the Floppy Disk icon). Choose the location on your computer or network where you want to save the file, and click Save. You can then open the file either with Dreamweaver or with a text editor.

Another extension, Web Kitchen, lets you sort only files modified after a certain date. It also includes utilities for such website maintenance functions as finding and replacing text, repairing instances of "smart" quotes, performing word counts, and converting accent marks. You can download a 30-day trial version from the Macromedia Exchange and then purchase the product for $49.95 from Matterform Media. Find out more at `http://matterform.com/webkitchen/help/frames.php?page=general/list.htm`.

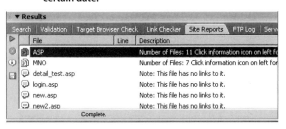

Rolling Back Your Site

Of course, it's important to save information about your site and compile a list of recently created or modified files. But in order to move back to a previous version of the site, you've got to *save* a backup version in a place where you can retrieve it easily.

It's up to you to come up with a schedule for making regular backups and then observe that schedule. If you use a backup program, such as one of the popular Retrospect packages by Dantz Development Corporation (`www.retrospect.com`), you can schedule your backups to take place automatically. Here are some other ideas:

- Duplicate your site by choosing Site → Manage Sites… and then clicking Duplicate in the Manage Sites dialog box. A copy of the site is created and stored in `C:\Program Files\Macromedia\Dreamweaver 5\Configuration`. Move the duplicate to a safe location so that you can retrieve it if your server or your local computer is damaged.

- Like many webmasters, you may want to mirror your site on a completely different server so that people can get access to it if the original server goes down.

Hands On: Updating an Existing Website

Now try out some of the common website administration tasks in a project. You'll update a website template, change some basic content, adjust the site navigation, and use Dreamweaver's link checking feature.

From the Chapter 31 folder on the accompanying CD, copy the folder `sample_website` to your computer. Start Dreamweaver, and define the site by choosing Site → Manage Sites… → New, then locate and name the site in the Site Definition dialog box. Open the site by displaying the Files panel and then choosing the site from the drop-down list.

Correcting the Website Template

The Stylus Media website contains seven separate web page files, each created from a template called `StylusTemplate.dwt`. Your first administrative task is to change the template, which is something that frequently occurs as organizations change their products or services.

1. Open the `StylusTemplate.dwt` template file, which is located in *[directory you used when copying the files from the CD]*/sample_website/Templates folder.

2. At the bottom of the template page, change 2001 to 2004.

3. Add a new editable region after the editable region labeled Heading. Position the cursor just after the word *Heading*.

4. Press Shift-Return to move to a new blank line.

5. Choose Insert → Template Objects → Editable Region.

6. In the New Editable Region dialog box, enter **Subhead**.

7. Click OK.

8. Replace the placeholder word *Subhead* with `Stylus Media`.

9. Select the words Stylus Media. In the Property inspector, choose the Arial typeface group, font size 1, and press Return. The new subheading is shown in Figure 31.6.

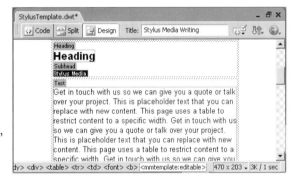

Figure 31.6

Edited website template

Change Website Content

Next, you'll fulfill one of the most common website administrative tasks—changing the basic content on your web pages. Suppose your client has directed you to change the words "editorial services" at the top of every web page to "content management." The quickest way to make the change across the entire site is to use Find And Replace.

1. From the Document window menu bar, choose Edit → Find And Replace.

2. In the Find And Replace dialog box (see Figure 31.7), choose Entire Current Local Site from the Find In drop-down list.

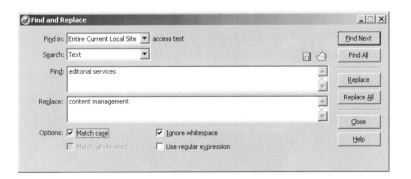

Figure 31.7

Making textual changes across an entire website

3. Enter **editorial services** in the box next to the Search For drop-down list.

4. Enter **content management** in the Replace With box.

5. Check the Match Case box.

6. Click Find All.

7. When a dialog box appears telling you the changes have been made, click OK.

Adjusting Website Navigation

Figure 31.8

Changing the navigational structure of a website

Next, you'll perform another common administrative task—you'll change the navigation for your site. Go to the Files panel and view the site map for the sample website. You'll notice that, although there are seven files in the site, only four are included in the map. You need to make sure the home page index.htm links to all of the six second-level pages.

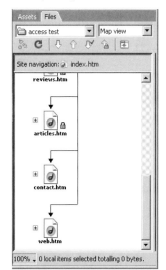

1. In the Files list of the Files panel, click the file index.htm to select it.

2. Drag the Point-to-File icon 🌐 to one of the pages not included in the site map, contact.htm, in the Files panel (see Figure 31.8). Release the mouse button when contact.htm is selected. The file is added to the map.

3. Repeat step 2 for the file web.htm to add it to the site map.

Checking Links

Checking the links in a website and repairing those that are broken is another common administrative task that you'll perform. Here's how.

1. Click the Option menu icon at the upper-right corner of the Files panel. Choose Site → Check Links Sitewide from the menu.

2. Click Close to close the Link Checker window after it reviews the links in your site.

Changing a Link

Next, you'll change an e-mail link that occurs on each of your site's web pages.

1. Select the file index.htm in the Local Folder pane of the Files panel.

2. Click the Option menu icon at the upper-right corner of the Files Panel. Choose Site → Change Link Sitewide from the menu.

3. In the Change Link Sitewide box (see Figure 31.9), enter `mailto:jdoe@mywebsite.com` in the Change All Links To box, and enter `mailto:webmaster@stylusmedia.com` in the Into Links To box.

4. Click OK.

5. In the Update Files dialog box, click Update.

6. Double-click any one of the files in the website to view it and check the link.

Extend Your Reach

Granted, website maintenance isn't the most thrilling part of going online. But like seeing your doctor for checkups or getting your oil changed, it's a necessary part of keeping a site healthy as it grows. After all, sites that undergo regular tune-ups maintain regular visitors and stay useful for their owners—and that's the ultimate goal of using Dreamweaver.

Next, you'll learn how to do some *really* exciting things with Dreamweaver. First, you'll discover how to extend your reach and make the program work just the way you want by customizing it. Then, you'll learn how to extend Dreamweaver's own reach by installing extensions that enable Dreamweaver to do even more amazing things.

Figure 31.9

Changing a link sitewide

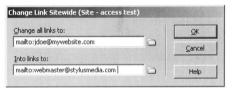

## CHAPTER 32

Customizing and Extending Dreamweaver

You might not find all of the features you want straight out of the box with Dreamweaver, but its extensibility allows you to create or download extensions for the features you need. You can add, or download, any of the premade third-party extensions available from the Macromedia Exchange for Dreamweaver website. You can also modify your menus and shortcut keys, record macros to create shortcuts for multiple steps that you repeat often, add objects to your Insert bar, and even change the way that Dreamweaver's dialog boxes and default document templates appear.

In this chapter, you will find descriptions of how to completely customize and modify your Dreamweaver interface and functionality:

- **Using the Extension Manager**

- **Setting up custom shortcut keys**

- **Changing the default template**

- **Making custom commands (macros)**

- **Making custom menus**

- **Making custom tags**

- **Modifying the Insert bar**

- **Changing dialog boxes**

Using the Extension Manager

Though Dreamweaver is incredibly malleable (in how many other programs can you edit the menus and dialog boxes yourself?), you might quite naturally find it a little intimidating to start mucking around in the software's innards without some practice or a few examples to follow. Fortunately, the community of Dreamweaver users has already collectively developed and tested quite a few extensions that you might find handy. You can download these examples from the Macromedia Exchange for Dreamweaver site at www.macromedia.com/exchange/dreamweaver/.

Dreamweaver end users or the Macromedia developers have provided these extensions. Other software companies that work closely with Macromedia also create some of the extensions. To learn how to create your own extensions and share them with others, refer to the "Creating Extensions" section later in this chapter.

Not all of the extensions are available for both Windows and Macintosh operating systems. The pages that describe each extension will list the operating systems for which the selected extension is available.

Using Macromedia Exchange for a Dreamweaver Site

The purpose of the Macromedia Exchange for Dreamweaver website is to provide a forum where developed additions for Dreamweaver can be shared. The extensions provided on this website come with no warranty of functionality, so you should be careful when you add any extension into your installation of Dreamweaver.

You can open the Macromedia Exchange for Dreamweaver site, using any of the following options:

- Click the Dreamweaver Exchange link on the Dreamweaver MX 2004 start page.

- Visit the website directly at www.macromedia.com/exchange/dreamweaver/.

- Select Help → Extensions → Extending Dreamweaver.

- Select Commands → Get More Commands.

- Select File → Go to Macromedia Exchange from the Extension Manager menu bar, or click the Go to Macromedia Exchange tool on the toolbar.

- Select Get More Styles… inside the Insert Flash Button (Insert → Media → Flash Button) dialog box.

- Select Get More Server Behaviors… from the plus (+) menu in the Server Behaviors dialog box.

Extension Categories

As you browse the Macromedia Exchange for Dreamweaver website, you will see that the many different extensions for Dreamweaver are divided into different categories. Each category provides a collection of extensions that can assist you when you go to develop your own websites. The categories available within the Exchange are listed here:

Accessibility Provides features that make using your website easier for people using portable devices, MSN TV, speech synthesizers, and other related hardware. The extensions here also include controls for creating and setting cookies, adjusting image attributes, validating your HTML code, and for assessing the accessibility of your pages.

App Servers Provides extensions for querying, viewing, and formatting data that is fed to your web page dynamically using server-side languages such as Active Server Pages (ASP and ASP.NET), ColdFusion, Java Server Pages (JSP), and PHP. This category even includes the addition of search functions and a Java-based web mail system.

Browsers Provides controls for checking on browser versions, redirecting pages, adding pages to your Favorites/Bookmark lists, controlling the appearance of your document titles, and controlling the toolbars on your browser window.

Commerce Provides links to shopping carts, counters, banner advertising systems, and site searches that can be easily installed on your pages without the problems associated with trying to run customizable Common Gateway Interface (CGI) scripts, or other more complex systems.

Content Provides frameworks for management of media resources, such as online photo albums.

DHTML/Layers Provides extensions and updates that support the dynamic web components on your pages. The extensions in this category provide capabilities such as aligning layers, creating scrollable and draggable layers, and adjusting the stacking order of layers dynamically.

Extension Development Provides links to a variety of extensions that assist you in developing your own extensions.

Fireworks Provides all the extensions that can be used to help Dreamweaver use Fireworks functions to complete tasks faster than would be possible without an automatic system.

Flash Media Provides sets of new Flash button images, text, and other Flash objects.

Learning Provide sets of extensions that allow you to easily create learning/testing-oriented web pages. The ever-popular CourseBuilder extension is included in this category.

Navigation Provides commands that allow you to create more dynamic effects, such as button rollovers, in your navigation bars. Some of these extensions provide lists of site structure, while others create collapsible menus, format Cascading Style Sheet (CSS) styles on your menu text, and check all of the links on your pages.

Productivity Provides additional features that will help you get more done faster on your existing sites. You can use one of these extensions to add additional Meta tags to your document templates, while others create calendar pages, automatically title documents, and update document dates and times.

Rich Media Provides extensions that add multimedia to your web page. Some of these extensions work with audio files, while others allow you to insert movies, CAD drawings, and news services.

Scripting Provides sets of commands that can be used to rotate banner images, test colors, adjust CSS code, and create dynamic form fields. All of the extensions in this category work by adding JavaScript to your document.

Security Provides extensions that keep your pages from being set up inside a frame on another site; they also help restrict the language used in form submittals.

Style/Format Provides a list of customized CSS effects that can be added to your documents.

Tables Provides access to extensions that work directly with Open Database Connectivity (ODBC) databases to populate your tables, as well as controls that change the formatting axis of the table and its appearance.

Text Provides advanced text formatting options, such as changing character case, inserting math symbols, and displaying your text in graduations of color.

Web Analysis Provides information on site users and what pages they're visiting.

Downloading Extensions

When you find an extension, either using the category listing or the Search function, you are taken to a page devoted to the extension you selected. On this page, you can read about the extension, discuss it in a chat group, rate it, and find a link to download it.

To download an extension, you will need to be a member of the Macromedia site. This registration is free, and after you complete the registration information, a cookie is placed on your computer so that you will be recognized whenever you visit the Macromedia website. Keep in mind that not all the extensions you see on the Macromedia Exchange for Dreamweaver website are free. Some of them are for sale, with or without a free 30-day trial. Read the extension explanation page carefully for information about the extension with which you are working.

Once you have found an appealing extension, you'll want to download it. Notice that on the right side of the extension's page are links to both Windows and Macintosh versions of the extension, if both are available. Extensions are written in combinations of HTML documents and JavaScript files, which are just standard text files. This makes it relatively easy for a developer to provide the same functionality for both operating systems. Extensions are stored in MXP files, which are used by the Extension Manager to install the appropriate files for the extension. MXP files are specific to the Macromedia Extension Manager, so you likely won't see this type of file anywhere else on your computer. The Extension Manager reads an MXP file in much the same way WinZip reads a ZIP file, collecting the information it needs out of the MXP file and placing that information where it needs to be stored.

To start the download process, all you have to do is click the link for your operating system, which will automatically trigger the download to start, and then wait for the download to complete. After the download is finished, you can start the Extension Manager and install the extension.

> If you don't have a copy of the Extension Manager, or you wish to download the latest copy, go to the main Macromedia Exchange Help page at `www.macromedia.com/exchange/help/about_exchange.html#manager`.

Installing Extensions

After you have downloaded your extensions, you need to start the Extension Manager to install them. The Extension Manager, shown in Figure 32.1, can be opened in a variety of ways:

- Select Commands → Manage Extensions… from within Dreamweaver.
- Select Help → Extensions → Extending Dreamweaver from within Dreamweaver.
- Select Start → Programs → Macromedia → Macromedia Extension Manager from your Windows desktop.
- Double-click the Extension Manager application in your Finder window on your Macintosh.

The Extension Manager is installed automatically with Dreamweaver MX 2004, but not all of the extensions available for previous versions of Dreamweaver will work in Dreamweaver MX 2004. You will need to check the extensions documentation to determine compatibility.

Figure 32.1

Dreamweaver Extension Manager window. Information about the selected extension is displayed in the bottom section of the window.

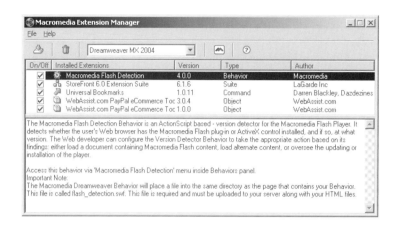

To complete the installation of your extension, follow these steps:

1. Select either the Install New Extension button on the Extension Manager toolbar, or select File → Install Extension… (Ctrl-I in Windows or Cmd-O on a Macintosh).

2. When the Select Extension To Install dialog box opens, select the MXP file you wish to add to your installation.

3. Answer any questions, including those in the licensing statement, required during the installation of the extension.

4. Restart Dreamweaver if you are prompted.

5. Ensure that the new extension is checked in the Extension Manager.

To find out how to run the extension, select the extension in the list of installed extensions and read the information about the extension in the lower window of the Extension Manager, where you will find the instructions for starting, using, and configuring the options in this extension.

Figure 32.2

An additional Insert bar (Link Builder), made with Dreamweaver extensions

Using Extensions

Once you have downloaded and installed your extensions, you will be able to use them as you would any other feature of Dreamweaver. In Figure 32.2 you can see a Dreamweaver

Insert bar showing a variety of additional objects that you can use to add functionality to your web pages. Other extensions will be found on your Commands menu, as shown in Figure 32.3.

To use the new extension(s), simply select it from your objects or commands, and answer any of the prompts that control the configuration of the extension. For assistance with any of the extensions you download off the site, you will need to return to the extension's page and ask your questions in the chat group, if chat is available.

Creating Extensions

You can create your own Dreamweaver extensions if you know HTML and some JavaScript, but the detailed description that would be required to teach you how to create a fully functional extension is outside of the scope of this book. Hopefully the information and resources provided here will point you in the right direction.

Figure 32.3

Additional options on the Commands menu

Resources for Creating Extensions

There are many books and websites devoted to the development of Macromedia Dreamweaver extensions. If you have questions about developing your own extensions, check out these Macromedia resources first.

- Select Help → Extensions → Extending Dreamweaver in the main Dreamweaver application window. This takes you to the Extending Dreamweaver manual. This manual takes you through the nitty-gritty details of how Dreamweaver works, and how the files used in the creation of an extension must be formatted.

- Select Help → Extensions → API Reference. This takes you to the API Reference manual. This manual details two Dreamweaver Application Programming Interfaces (APIs): the Utility API and the JavaScript API. These APIs let you perform supporting tasks when developing Dreamweaver extensions and adding code to your Dreamweaver pages.

> If you look on your Dreamweaver installation CD, you will find copies of both the `Extending_DW.pdf` and the `DW_API.pdf` files that document how to extend the program.

- Select Help → Extensions → Creating And Submitting Extensions. This option takes you to a document that provides an overview of the process used to create and submit extensions to the Macromedia Exchange for Dreamweaver website. Before you submit an extension to Macromedia to be added to the Exchange, be sure to read this file thoroughly.

- Visit the Extending Dreamweaver section of the Macromedia Support Center (`www.macromedia.com/support/dreamweaver/extend.html`) to read more about extensions themselves and how to customize Dreamweaver in general.

- View the files that were installed by other extensions, and see how they accomplished their appointed task.

Extension Creation Overview

In general, extensions are no more difficult to create than your own customizations to Dreamweaver. The following steps should help outline the extension creation process for you.

1. Create the primary HTML file that serves as the base file for the extension. This file references the JavaScript program created in step 2.

2. Create the JavaScript files that will actually provide the functionality for the extension. In some cases, the JavaScript will be a part of the HTML file; other times it will be an external JavaScript (`.js`) file that must be called and loaded when the extension is used.

3. Create the icons, or menu items, that will be used to start the extension after it is installed within Dreamweaver.

4. Ensure that your dialog boxes and other effects comply with the Macromedia UI Guidelines available from `www.macromedia.com/exchange/help/ui_guidelines.html`. This document tells you how things must function and appear in order for them to be accepted into the Exchange program.

5. Complete a thorough testing procedure of your extension on multiple operating systems, multiple system configurations, and with multiple browsers. Macromedia also provides some instructions for testing extensions at www.macromedia.com/exchange/help/test_standards.html.

6. Create a staging area on your computer, and move the relevant extension files to that location. This must be done before the files can be packaged.

7. Create an MXI file (Macromedia Extension Installation) that specifies the locations and controls used when installing the extension. You can view the `Blank.mxi` file located in the `Extension Manager/Samples/Dreamweaver` folder in your Extension Manager installation. Within this MXI file, you will need to define shortcut keys, menu options, object buttons, and so on. You can find additional information on formatting this file and other extensions related customizations at the Macromedia Exchange for Dreamweaver website `www.macromedia.com/exchange/dreamweaver/`.

8. Open the Extension Manager, and select File → Package Extension…. This will start the packager that creates an MXP file out of the individual pieces of your extension. This file contains compressed versions of all of the pieces you created in the previous steps. Because of the nature of the files, you can typically use the same MXP file on both a Windows or Macintosh platform.

9. Test out the MXP file you just created on your own machine, preferably with a fresh install of Dreamweaver so that none of your old pieces and parts from previous tests or the creation of the extension are still hanging about. At this point, you need to retest all of the features of the extension so you can be sure they all work as expected.

10. You can now submit the extension to the Macromedia Exchange for Dreamweaver site using the File → Submit Extension option located in the Extension Manager window. You can also submit an extension by visiting `www.macromedia.com/exchange/help/upload_help.html`. From this location you can start the submission process for your extension.

For more information on using extensions, see the section, "Hands On 1: Using the Advanced Random Images Extension" later in this chapter.

Creating Custom Shortcut Keys

There are two ways to modify your keyboard shortcut keys. The easiest, and the method discussed here, is to use the Keyboard Shortcuts editor. The alternative is to modify the `menus.xml` file, which will be discussed later in the section entitled "Creating Custom Menus."

To modify your keyboard shortcuts using the Keyboard Shortcuts editor, select Edit → Keyboard Shortcuts. This opens the Keyboard Shortcuts dialog box shown in Figure 32.4, which lets you edit your keyboard shortcuts for Dreamweaver or select an alternative set of shortcuts.

This editor allows you to customize sets of keyboard shortcuts. You can't directly edit the existing sets, but you can use the Duplicate Set button to create a copy of the set closest to your needs and then make your modifications to the copy. To duplicate a set, select the set from the Current Set list and then click the Duplicate Set button to the right of the field. By default, the Macromedia Standard set is used for Dreamweaver MX 2004.

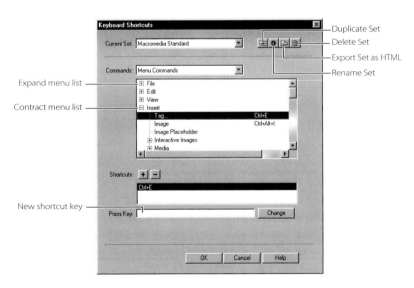

Figure 32.4

Keyboard Shortcuts dialog box

Once you have duplicated a set of keyboard shortcuts, you are ready to start making your changes using these steps:

1. Select the set of keyboard shortcuts that you wish to modify.

2. If you wish to modify a menu item's shortcut key, select Menu Commands from the Commands drop-down menu. Options on this menu include the following:

   Code Editing Commands that function only in the Code view of the document window.

   Document Editing Commands that function in the Design view of the document window.

   Menu Commands Commands found on the main menu bar in Dreamweaver.

   Site Panel (Windows only) Commands found on the option menu in the Files panel group.

   Site Window (Windows only) Commands that are available when a document is open in the Dreamweaver workspace.

   Snippets (Windows only) Commands that are available when the Snippets panel is open.

3. From the Menu list, select the menu item you wish to modify. Use the plus (+) button and minus (–) button (Windows) or the triangle icons (Macintosh) to expand the contents of the menus.

4. The list of current shortcuts for that command are shown in the Shortcuts field. To add an additional shortcut, press the plus (+) button. To remove one of the shortcuts, press the minus (–) button.

5. When you are adding a shortcut, place your cursor in the Press Key field and press the key combination that you wish to use for this shortcut. If the shortcut is already assigned to a different command, you will be given the opportunity to change it.

> Download a reference card showing all the default keyboard shortcuts in Dreamweaver at
> www.macromedia.com/support/dreamweaver/documentation/dwmx_shortcuts/.

6. Click the Change button to add it to the list of shortcut keys.

7. Repeat steps 2 through 6 for every command or menu option you wish to modify.

8. Once you are done modifying your keyboard shortcuts, click the OK button. After you have altered your keyboard shortcuts, you will need to restart Dreamweaver before the shortcuts become active.

When you are modifying your keyboard shortcuts, it's a good idea to use the Export Set As HTML button to create a printable list of your shortcuts. This way you always have a reference of your shortcuts in case of a computer crash or if you take a long hiatus from your Dreamweaver development tasks.

You can also modify your keyboard shortcuts in the `menu.xml` file located in your Dreamweaver Configuration/Menus folder. This document contains a series of tags that create sets of shortcuts. These shortcuts are modified in much the same way as the menu options, also contained in this file.

Changing the Default Document Template

Every time you open a new Dreamweaver document, you get the same page. This page is created from a default template located in the `Configuration/Templates/Default.html` file. The contents of this file are used on every file that you create in Dreamweaver. So if you set this document to have a pink background, every new file that you create using Dreamweaver will have a pink background. The default document template is different from the site templates discussed in Chapter 4 that provide you with a customized layout for each site. If you work on multiple sites with Dreamweaver, you might prefer to do only minor modifications to the default document template and otherwise rely on customized site templates.

The default document template does not have locked (non-editable) regions, as does a site template. A page based on the default document template can be modified at will. There are many ways you can adjust your default document template to save you time. Anything that appears on every page should be added, such as background and text color, copyright statements, comments, banner logos, footers, and so on.

No matter what you plan on doing with the default document template, you need to save a copy of the original template before you start making changes to it. To do this, open the `Configuration/Templates/Default.html` document and save it as `original_Default.html`.

Here is the code for the default document template.

```
<!DOCTYPE HTML PUBLIC "-//W3C//DTD HTML 4.01 Transitional//EN">
<HTML>
<HEAD>
<TITLE> </TITLE>
<meta http-equiv="Content-Type" content="text/html; charset=">
</HEAD>

<BODY>

</BODY>
</HTML>
```

As you can see from this code, the default document template is quite empty. This code creates that blank white page that you see whenever you open a new document. To change that information, simply modify this page just as you would any other document. You can add tables, text, images, background colors, layers, behaviors, or any thing else that strikes your fancy.

If you are working on multiple sites, you might want to limit your modifications to simple changes, such as copyright notices, default page backgrounds, and text colors. But if you develop for only one site, you can make your default template as complex as you want, as shown in Figure 32.5.

Figure 32.5

Default document template with modifications

After you have made your changes, be sure to save the file using File → Save As, rather than File → Save As Template. Remember, using the Save As Template option creates a site template, rather than modifying your document template. Now whenever you open a new document it will have the changes that you made.

Creating Dreamweaver Commands

If you ever find yourself repeating the same sequence of commands over and over, such as inserting navigation buttons at the bottom of each page, you might consider automating the task. Hey, doing stuff over and over is computer work, not people work!

There are actually a few ways to automate your tasks:

- Repeat single steps listed in the History panel.

- Record steps from the History panel (Window → History).

- Record a command as you perform the steps.

The History panel (see Figure 32.6) tracks all of the menus that you have opened, characters you have typed, and items that you have moved to the current document. It doesn't keep track of mouse movements per se; so if you wish to record a selection of complex menu selections, use your keyboard to open the menus. Remember, you can use the Tab and arrow keys to navigate through options in dialog boxes.

Figure 32.6

The History panel

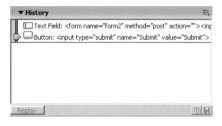

Replaying Steps from the History Panel

To repeat a series of steps, or a single step that you have already made in your document, you just need to select it from the History panel. To replay steps, select the step you wish to repeat from the History list and choose the Replay button located at the bottom of the panel.

When you are replaying steps from the History panel, you don't have the option of changing their order, but you can selectively choose which steps to replay. By pressing Ctrl while you click steps in the History panel, you can select just the steps you want to repeat. For example, you could select the first five steps that you took, and then skip to step 10 and continue making your selections. Once you hit the Replay button, only the steps that you have selected will be played.

> If you see a step in your History panel with a red "X" in the lower-right corner of the icon, or one that is marked by a thin black line between steps, you won't be able to repeat that step. It will be skipped when the steps are replayed, and therefore it may cause your results to be skewed.

Creating Commands from the History Panel

You can save yourself a lot of work by recording the steps that you have already taken and saving them as a Dreamweaver command on the Commands menu.

To create a command from your History panel of precompleted steps, follow these instructions.

1. Select the steps you wish to save from the History panel. You can use the Ctrl key to select multiple discontinuous steps.

2. Click Save Selected Steps as a command button in the lower-right corner of the History panel.

3. In the Command Name dialog box, type in a name for the new Dreamweaver command. When you are done, click the OK button.

4. Open the Command menu and you will be able to see your new command, shown highlighted in Figure 32.7, at the bottom of this menu.

Figure 32.7

New option on the Command menu

Recording Commands

In addition to converting precompleted steps into a Dreamweaver command, you can also record the steps for these commands as you perform them. To start the command recorder, select Commands → Start Recording or press Ctrl-Shift-X (Cmd-Shift-X on the Macintosh).

With the recorder going, you will be able to see that your mouse pointer has a cassette tape attached to it, and you can perform all of the steps required for your command. When you are done recording your steps, press Ctrl-Shift-X (Cmd-Shift-X) again to stop the recorder. You won't be able to find the commands recorded in this fashion on your Commands menu because they are stored for immediate playback and can be accessed by selecting Commands → Play Recorded Command or by pressing Ctrl-P (Cmd-P on the Macintosh).

If you wish to save your recorded command so that it can be used outside of this current document, you need to save the command from the History panel as addressed in the previous section.

Creating Custom Menus

It might seem drastic to be changing around the menus for Dreamweaver, but once you've worked with the program for a while, you'll realize that there are some features you (and your team) rely on heavily and some that just aren't part of your normal routine. You can create a custom configuration of the Dreamweaver menus to maximize your efficiency and put the most useful commands all together.

Dreamweaver menus are stored in Dreamweaver's `Configuration/Menus/menus.xml` file. The `menus.xml` file defines all of the menus, menu bars, menu options, and even the primary shortcut keys included in Dreamweaver. Despite the `.xml` extension, this file isn't true XML, and therefore can't be modified using an XML-compliant editor. However, it can be modified in any text editor, such as Windows WordPad (the file is too large for Notepad) or the Mac's BBEdit. But don't try to edit the menu files from within Dreamweaver! If Dreamweaver is running, then those files are in use.

Before you make any of these changes to your Dreamweaver installation, be sure you have made a backup copy of any of the Dreamweaver configuration files you plan to change. This way, if your changes don't work, then you still have a sure-fire way to restore your Dreamweaver installation. If you create a file with invalid menu options, a variety of results could occur. You might simply have a few menu options that won't work, or you could end up with Dreamweaver not even being capable of loading correctly. Most of the time you will end up with an entire menu that won't work, or even open, rather than just a menu option that won't work.

Here is a segment of the `menus.xml` file. This file is used to specify the name, shortcut key, platform, command, and so on, that is used by Dreamweaver when the menu option

is selected. The part of the file shown defines the menu item name and key for the File →
New, Open, and Open Recent commands.

```
<menubar name="Main Window" id="DWMainWindow">
  <menu name="_File" id="DWMenu_File">
    <menuitem name="_New..." key="Cmd+N" domRequired="false"
      enabled="true" command="dw.newDocument()" id="DWMenu_File_New" />
    <menuitem name="_Open..." key="Cmd+O" domRequired="false"
      enabled="dw.getDocumentDOM() == null || (dw.getDocumentDOM() !=
      null && !dw.getDocumentDOM().getEditNoFramesContent())"
      command="dw.openDocument()" id="DWMenu_File_Open" />
  </menu>
  <menu name="Open Recent" id="DWMenu_File_RecentFiles">
    <menuitem dynamic name="(No Recent Files)"
      file="Menus/MM/File_RecentFiles.htm"
      id="DWMenu_File_RecentFiles_None" />
  </menu>
</menubar>
```

If you are familiar with JavaScript, a quick read of this code shows you that many of the
commands invoked to perform the menu options are based on JavaScript. As a result,
once you learn JavaScript, you can easily modify your menus to add functionality. Simply
create a JavaScript (.js) file containing all the code for creating your function's interface,
such as an HTML form, and then write the JavaScript code that will generate the appropriate HTML and/or JavaScript into your document.

If this sounds complicated, simply read through some of the existing Dreamweaver
command files and study how they accomplish their given tasks. These files are all stored
in the /Configuration/Commands directory or the /Configuration/Shared/ directory.

Adding Menus and Menu Bars

Menus and menu bars can be added quite easily. Menu items, on the other hand, can be a
bit more difficult because they have additional attributes and command requirements.

To add a menu bar to Dreamweaver, you simply need to type in the
code. As you can see from the previous code sample, the <menubar> code must precede,
with </menubar> at the end, each set of menus you wish to appear on a single bar in your
document.

The <menubar> element has the following attributes that can be set:

id This required attribute defines the unique ID of the menu bar or menu.

Do not change the id attributes of existing menus because doing so prevents them from displaying properly in Dreamweaver.

name This required attribute defines the name of the menu bar or menu that appears. If you are creating a shortcut menu, this would be left empty (`""`), but the attribute must be present.

platform This attribute defines whether the menu is available on the Macintosh (`mac`), Windows (`win`), or both (attribute omitted).

Menu bars must contain at least one `<menu>` tag, which in turn must contain at least one `<menuitem>` or `<separator>` element. Individual menus are created by adding the tags `<menu>` `</menu>` between your `<menubar>` tags. So, imagine you want to create a menu bar called "Popup Menu" to let you quickly access a set of folders; your code might look like this:

```
<menubar name="Popup Menu"  id="DWSiteSpecific" platform="win">
    <menu name="_Folders"   id="DWFolders" platform="win">
    </menu>
</menubar>
```

As you can see from the previous example, both the `<menu>` and the `<menubar>` elements have the same attributes, so once you become familiar with one, you can implement the other. You can add submenus to your menus by inserting `<menu>` tags within other `<menu>` tags, as shown here:

```
<menu name="_Open Image" id="DWOpenImage" platform="win">
    <menu name="_Clipart" id="DWClipart" platform="win">
    </menu>
</menu>
```

To create a menu name with a shortcut key, such as Ctrl-F (Command-F for the Mac), place the underscore character in front of the letter that should serve as the hot key. In the previous example, the Open Image menu could be opened by pressing Ctrl-O (Command-O on the Mac).

Adding Menu Items

Once you have created your menu bar and menus, you are ready to create individual menu items. Menu items can be created using the `<menuitem>` tag in conjunction with these attributes:

id This required attribute defines the unique ID of the menu item.

name This required attribute defines the name of the menu item as it should appear in the menu. Place an underscore in front of the character that you wish to serve as the hot key to activate that menu in Windows.

arguments This attribute allows you to specify a comma-separated list of arguments that should be passed to the file, specified by the `file` attribute. Each argument should be enclosed within single quotations (') inside the attribute value's double quotations ("). For example, to pass the information that a table cell should get a background color and that the color should be yellow, you might use the following: `arguments="'true','yellow'"`.

checked This specifies a JavaScript function that will return a value of `true` if the menu item should have a check mark appearing next to it in your Dreamweaver menus when it's active.

command This specifies the JavaScript function that is executed whenever this menu item is selected.

isdomrequired This attribute controls whether both the Design and Code views should be synchronized before the code specified by the menu item is executed. If set to `true`, then the document must be synchronized prior to running the code specified by this menu. When set to `false`, the document does not need to be synchronized.

dynamic This identifies a menu item that is configured dynamically by an HTML file. If you include this attribute, you must also include the `file` attribute.

enabled This specifies a JavaScript function that will return a value of `true` if this menu item should be currently enabled. For instance, this attribute can be used to cause a script to run to ensure that a table is selected before the Insert Row function is available in the Table menu.

file This specifies the file used to dynamically configure a menu item as specified by the `dynamic` attribute. The documents specified here are HTML documents that use JavaScript code to manipulate the Dreamweaver interface, such as opening a dialog box.

showIf This specifies if a menu item should appear if a particular Dreamweaver enabler (for example, _SERVERMODEL_ASP) has a value of *true*.

platform This defines whether the menu is available on the `mac` (Macintosh), `win` (Windows), or both (attribute omitted).

key This defines the shortcut key that can be used to activate this menu option. When you are specifying a key combination, use the plus (+) sign to separate each key (for instance, Ctrl+Alt+F). Options for your keys include the following:

Alt or Opt Indicates the Alt key in Windows or the Option key on a Macintosh.

Cmd Indicates either the Ctrl key in Windows or the Cmd key on a Macintosh.

Ctrl Indicates the Ctrl key for either Windows or Macintosh.

Shift Indicates the Shift key for either Windows or Macintosh.

Special Keys Such as F1 through F12, Home, End, Ins, Del, Tab, Esc, Backspace, Space, PgUp, and PgDn.

It is easier to use the Keyboard Shortcuts editor to modify these values than it is to modify them yourself in the menus.xml file. The Keyboard Shortcuts editor dialog box was discussed earlier in the chapter in the section entitled "Creating Custom Shortcut Keys."

If you add a new menu and menu items to your Dreamweaver interface, you could end up with a screen similar to Figure 32.8.

The following code is used to create the sample menu shown in Figure 32.8. The sample menu shown in Figure 32.8 is created by inserting this code into menus.xml (inserted in between the Text menu code and the Commands menu code).

```
<menu name="_Addition" id="DWMenu_Text_NewAddition">
  <menuitem name="Addition1" enabled="true"
    command="dw.add1('site files')" id="Addition1" />
  <menuitem name="Addition2" enabled="true"
    command="dw.add2('site map')" id="Addition2" />
  <menuitem name="Addition3" enabled="true"
    command="dw.add3('assets')"  id="Addition3" />
  <separator />
  <menuitem name="Addition4" enabled="true"
    command="dw.add4(true)" platform="Win" id="Addition4" />
  <menuitem name="Addition5" enabled="true"
    command="dw.add5(false)" platform="Win" id="Addition5" />
</menu>
```

The <separator> tag is used to create a gray line in the middle of your menu to separate the menu contents into sections of more-closely related options. This tag has no attributes.

Third-Party Tags: Creating Custom Tags Using XML

Dreamweaver can be extended to support the use of custom tags through its Tag Library Editor and through its third-party tag feature. The Dreamweaver MX 2004 tag libraries include HTML, CFML, ASP.NET, JSP, JRun, ASP, PHP, and WML (Wireless Markup Language) tags that you can edit and manage using the Tag Library Editor (Edit → Tag Libraries). For more details, see Chapter 18, "Handcrafting Your Code."

Figure 32.8

Customized Dreamweaver menu and menu items

The third-party tag feature is not limited to custom tags to be used in XML documents, but it can include custom tags for other applications such as ASP.NET, JSP, or JRun.

When you define a custom tag in Dreamweaver, a tag database file is created that defines how Dreamweaver reads and interprets the tag. The tag database file is saved as an XML file in the `Third Party Tags` subfolder of the `Configuration` folder.

You can create two kinds of custom tags: HTML-style tags that include an opening and a closing tag, or string-delimited tags that are empty tags without a separate opening and closing tag. The `<br>` tag in HTML is an empty tag because it contains no content and has no opening and closing tag. ASP tags are string-delimited tags that start with `<%` and end with `%>`, as shown in the following example that specifies that the scripting language used in this ASP file is VBScript:

```
<%@ Language = VBScript %>
```

> An empty tag in XML and XHTML includes a forward slash before the closing angle bracket to close the tag. For example, an HTML `<br>` tag would be formatted in XML and XHTML as `<br/>` or `<br />`. The extra space before the closing angle bracket allows empty tags to display properly in browsers.

A custom tag consists of one XML element, `tagspec`, with up to seven attributes:

`tag_name` The `tag_name` attribute specifies the name of the custom tag.

`tag_type` The `tag_type` attribute specifies whether a tag is empty or nonempty. This attribute is ignored for string-delimited tags because they are always empty.

`render_contents` The `render_contents` attribute specifies whether the contents of the tag rather than an icon should appear in the Design view of a document. It is a required attribute for nonempty tags but is ignored for empty tags. Values are Boolean (`true` or `false`).

`content_model` The `content_model` attribute specifies what kind of content is allowed in the tag and where the tag can appear in the document. There are four choices for the value of this attribute:

`block_model` Block-level elements that can appear only in the body of the document or within other block-level elements such as `div`.

`head_model` Elements that contain text content and that can only appear in the head section of the document.

`marker_model` Elements that can contain any valid HTML code and that can appear anywhere in the document, usually used for inline tags.

`script_model` Elements that can appear anywhere in the document and usually used for markup that Dreamweaver should not parse, such as ASP markup.

start_string The start_string attribute is used to mark the beginning of a string-delimited tag. A string-delimited tag can appear anywhere in the document where a comment can appear. If this attribute is used, an end_string attribute is also required.

end_string The end_string attribute is used to mark the end of a string-delimited tag. If this attribute is used, a start_string attribute is also required.

detect_in_attribute The detect_in_attribute attribute specifies whether to ignore everything between a start_string value and an end_string value even if this information appears within an attribute. This attribute is usually set to false for string-delimited tags. The default value is true.

parse_attribute The parse_attribute attribute specifies whether to parse the attributes of the tag.

icon The icon attribute specifies the path and filename of the icon associated with the tag. It is required for empty tags and for nonempty tags whose contents are not displayed in Design view.

icon_width The icon_width attribute specifies the width of the icon image in pixels.

icon_height The icon_height attribute specifies the height of the icon image in pixels.

To create a custom tag for the description element in inventory.xml, the following markup could be used:

```
<tagspec tag_name="description" tag_type="nonempty"
    render_contents="true" content-model="marker-model">
```

The markup is then saved in an XML file and placed in the ThirdParty Tags subfolder in the Dreamweaver Configuration folder. You can save more than one custom tag in the same XML file.

You can now access this tag for any Dreamweaver document. Figure 32.9 shows the Code and Design view for the description.html file. The content of the description tag is displayed in the Design view window.

Modifying the Insert Bar

The Insert bars provide shortcuts for inserting all of the objects (images, horizontal rules, layers, and tables) that we used in earlier chapters to create our web pages. This might sound similar to what a Library object does, but the effect is much different. A Library item can insert only HTML code into your document, while an object on an Insert bar can insert both HTML code and JavaScript.

The configuration file for Dreamweaver's Insert bar is insertbar.xml (Configuration\Objects\insertbar.xml). Similar to the menus.xml file for menus, insertbar.xml contains XML code for all the Insert bars. This file consists of categories and objects within those categories; for example, as shown in the following code from `insertbar.xml`, the Common Insert bar is a category, and Hyperlink is an object within that category.

```
<category id="DW_Insertbar_Common"
    MMString:name="insertbar/category/common" folder="Common">
    <button id="DW_Hyperlink" image="Common\Hyperlink.png"
        MMString:name="insertbar/hyperlink" file="Common\Hyperlink.htm" />
```

Dreamweaver lets you modify any category or object in an Insert bar. You can move an object from one Insert bar to another, remove an object from an Insert bar, change the order of objects in an Insert bar, or create a new object and/or an additional Insert bar.

If you look at the above code for a Hyperlink object, you can see that this object includes an image file (`Hyperlink.png`) and an HTML file (`Hyperlink.htm`), and both of these files are contained in the Common folder within the Objects folder. The HTML file is linked to several JavaScript files and also contains the HTML code for the display of the Hyperlink dialog box.

To create a new object, you need to create an image file for display in the Insert bar, an HTML file, and a JavaScript file. You also need to modify the `insertbar.xml` file to include your new object.

Figure 32.9

description .html—**Code and Design view**

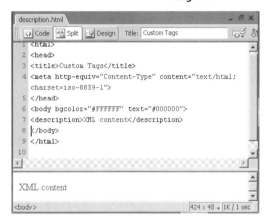

> When creating your own object, you should always place all of the files related to a single object in the same folder.

Dreamweaver MX 2004 includes a new Insert bar category—Favorites—that is easy to customize and use:

1. Display any Insert bar.
2. Right-click on any icon in the Insert bar and select "Customize Favorites."
3. The Customize Favorite Objects dialog box opens (Figure 32.10).
4. Choose any object from any Insert bar on the left side of the window. Click the >> button to transfer that object to your Favorites Insert bar.

> For more information on customizing Insert bars, see Hands On 2, "Add Custom Characters to an Insert Bar," later in this chapter. For additional details on creating new objects for Insert bars, see Extending Dreamweaver (Help → Extensions → Extending Dreamweaver).

Figure 32.10

Customizing the Favorites Insert bar in the Customize Favorite Objects dialog box.

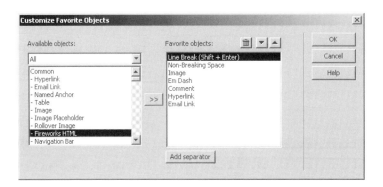

Figure 32.10

Customizing the Favorites Insert bar in the Customize Favorite Objects dialog box.

Updating Dreamweaver Dialog Boxes

Did you know that all of the dialog boxes you see when you open up a function in Dreamweaver are created from HTML forms? Because they are all HTML documents, you can make changes to a form and then have those changes made active for all uses of Dreamweaver, not just the one site with which you are currently working.

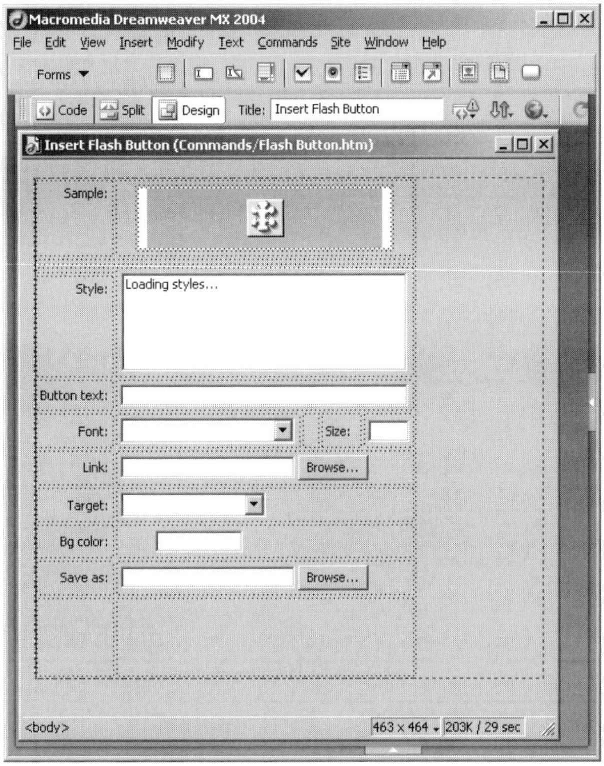

Figure 32.11

The *Flash Button.htm* file opened for editing in Dreamweaver.

There are many reasons to modify Dreamweaver's dialog boxes. You might simply want to add an additional comment to a dialog box so that you don't forget to do something that you have a tendency to forget. Or you might want to add a field to a dialog box in order to set the values for an option or attribute that wasn't previously available through Dreamweaver but is available in your browser base.

The hardest part of modifying your dialog boxes' content is finding the code for the dialog boxes in the first place. Most of the documents that make up the Dreamweaver dialog boxes can be found in Dreamweaver's `Configuration/Commands` folder. A few dialog boxes are stored in the `Configuration/Shared` folder.

To modify the appearance of the dialog box, edit the HTML file. To modify the function of the dialog box's options, edit the JavaScript document(s) that is called from within the HTML document.

Take, for instance, the Flash Button dialog box. Figure 32.11 shows you what the dialog box looks like when it is opened in Dreamweaver. This dialog box, stored as `Configuration/ Commands/Flash Button.htm`, appears almost identical to the actual dialog box shown in Figure 32.12. A few things to note about these dialog boxes include the following:

- The title of the HTML document is the title used for the dialog box.

- The buttons on the form might not show up the same as they do on the actual dialog box, or they might not be there at all. JavaScript generates most of those buttons.

To modify the Insert Flash Button dialog box, open the `Flash Button.htm` file in Dreamweaver and modify it as you would any other document. Be sure not to remove any of the scripting code at the top of the document or you will lose part of your dialog box's functionality. In Figure 32.13, you can see the modified version of the dialog box made by adding the following code to the `Flash Button.html` document.

```
Be sure to save your Flash Button in a folder that will be uploaded
    and accessible through your templates.<br>
```

> If you want to share these types of customizations with other users, simply copy the files you have modified and manually install them in each user's `Configuration/Commands` folder.

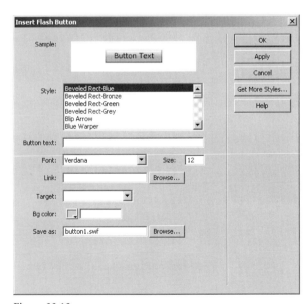

Figure 32.12

The Insert Flash Button dialog box as it is normally seen in Dreamweaver

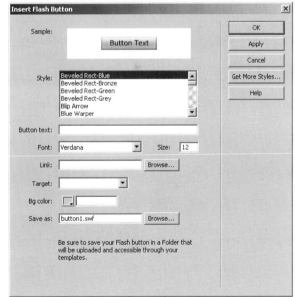

Figure 32.13

The modified Insert Flash Button dialog box.

Hands On 1: Using the Advanced Random Images Extension

There are a wide variety of extensions available, but one of the most useful is the Advanced Random Images extension. Not only is this extension one of the most useable, but it is also one of the most popular. This extension allows you to display a random image, a daily image, or even a set of sequential images on your website. This is a great tool if you wish to create a series of rotating banners for advertising, or even if you want to easily change the appearance of your website for daily visitors.

The Advanced Random Images extension is available on the companion CD. To install and use this extension, follow these steps.

1. Open the Chapter 32 folder on the CD and double-click the Advanced Random Image extension file (`advRandImage3.mxp`).

2. The Extension Manager dialog box should display automatically. If it doesn't, you can also use one of these:

   - Select Start → Programs → Macromedia → Macromedia Extension Manager from your Windows desktop.

   - Double-click the Extension Manager application in your Finder window on your Macintosh.

3. In the Extension Manager window, select File → Install Extension. This will open the Select Extension To Install dialog box shown in Figure 32.14. This dialog box will automatically open to the location where extensions were last installed. Click Install to start the installation procedure.

4. Click Accept to agree to the terms of the licensing agreement for the extension. The rest of the installation should complete, and you should be returned to the Extension Manager with the Advanced Random Image extension selected and checked.

5. Open Dreamweaver and the document to which you wish to add the random images.

This document must be saved into your current site for the extension to work properly.

6. Select Commands → Kaosweaver.com → Advanced Random Images to open the Random Images dialog box shown in Figure 32.15.

7. In the Random Images dialog box, select the type of display you wish to create from the Actions drop-down menu. Your options include the following:

   Random Image Images in the list are displayed randomly.

   Daily Image One image is displayed to all visitors each day.

   Random Slideshow Images are displayed randomly in a slideshow format.

   Sequential Slideshow Images are displayed in their listed order in a slideshow format.

8. Use the + (Plus) button and Folder icon to add images to your Image List. If you wish to delete some, select them and click the - (Minus) button.

9. In the Subdomain field enter the trailing part of the URL if your site is not at the root for your web server.

10. Set the following properties for each image in your list.

    Auto Automatically set width and height of the images.

    Width Controls the width, in pixels, of the image.

    Height Controls the height, in pixels, of the image.

    Align Sets the image alignment.

    Title & Alt Sets the alternate text for the image.

    Border Controls the width of the images border.

    Link Specifies the document to open when that image is clicked.

    Target Specifies the target of the link.

11. The properties affect only the currently selected image in the image list.

12. Click OK when you are done.

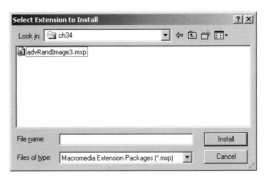

Figure 32.14

The Select Extension To Install dialog box with the Advanced Random Images extension selected

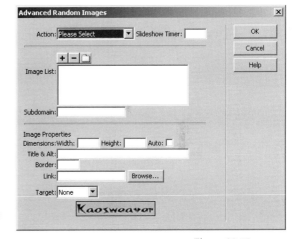

Figure 32.15

The Random Images dialog box, which allows you to configure the Advanced Random Images extension

The code created by this extension is visible only when you have View Invisible Elements turned on, so don't worry if you don't see any results on your Design view screen. You can see them in Code view.

When you view this page in your browser, you will see that the images appear in the order, and sizes that you configured in the dialog box.

Hands On 2: Add Custom Characters to an Insert Bar

The steps outlined in this tutorial allow you to create your own custom characters and add them to the Character menu of the Text Insert bar.

1. Open one of the HTML files in your /Macromedia/Dreamweaver MX 2004/Configuration/ Objects/Characters directory in Dreamweaver. For instance, you can use the Trademark .htm file shown in this example.

2. Change to Code view, by selecting View → Code. This opens the Trademark.html file shown below.

```
<!-- MENU-LOCATION=NONE -->
<HTML>
<HEAD>
<!-- Copyright 2000, 2001, 2002, 2003 Macromedia, Inc.
     All rights reserved. -->

<title><MMString:LoadString id="insertbar/trademark" /></TITLE>
<SCRIPT SRC="characters.js"></SCRIPT>
<SCRIPT LANGUAGE="javascript">

function isDOMRequired() {
  // Return false, indicating that this object is available in code
view.
  return false;
}

function objectTag() {
  checkEncoding();
  // Return the html tag that should be inserted
  // <!ENTITY trade    CDATA "&#8482;" -- trade mark sign, U+2122
ISOnum -->
  return "&#8482;";   // Supported starting in 4.0 browsers, valid HTML
  //return "&trade;"; // Supported starting in 5.0 browsers, valid HTML
  //return "&#153;";  // Generally supported, but not valid HTML
(refers to windows specific character)
}
</SCRIPT>
</HEAD>
<BODY BGCOLOR="#FFFFFF">

</BODY>
</HTML>
```

In this file, there are two JavaScript functions that insert a named entity—such as ¡, which inserts an inverted exclamation point—into your document. This entity is also referred to numerically by ¡.

3. Modify the Trademark.htm file so that it inserts your entity item, ¡. This is done by replacing the existing entity string on line 19 (you can view the line numbers in your document by selecting View → Code View Options → Line Numbers) with either the ¡ or the ¡ numerical entity.

The named entity ¡ is only supported by 4.0 and newer browsers such as Internet Explorer 4+, Netscape Navigator 4+, and Opera 4+. For users of your site using other browsers or devices, you might want to consider using the numerical entity ¡ because it has more global support.

When you have finished, and as long as you are using the ¡ character, your document will appear as follows:

```
<!-- MENU-LOCATION=NONE -->
<HTML>
<HEAD>
<!-- Copyright 2000, 2001, 2002, 2003 Macromedia, Inc. All rights
reserved. -->

<title><MMString:LoadString id="insertbar/trademark" /></TITLE>
<SCRIPT SRC="characters.js"></SCRIPT>
<SCRIPT LANGUAGE="javascript">

function isDOMRequired() {
  // Return false, indicating that this object is available in code
view.
  return false;
}

function objectTag() {
  checkEncoding();
  // Return the html tag that should be inserted
  return "&#161;";   // Supported starting in 4.0 browsers, valid HTML
}
</SCRIPT>
</HEAD>
<BODY BGCOLOR="#FFFFFF">

</BODY>
</HTML>
```

4. Select File → Save As and save your new character description in the `/Macromedia/Dreamweaver MX 2004/Configuration/Objects/Characters` directory. Name the file `iexcl.html`.

5. Using your favorite graphics program, create an 18- × 18-pixel GIF image that contains the image you wish to serve as the button that will represent your new character in the Character category on the Text Insert bar. This graphic file also needs to be saved in your `/Macromedia/Dreamweaver MX 2004/Configuration/Objects/Characters` directory.

6. Restart Dreamweaver. When you restart Dreamweaver, your new icon will appear as the last icon in the Character category view of the Text Insert bar. You can add as many characters to your panel in this fashion as you want.

Be careful to use only valid named entities within your modified configuration files. If these entities are invalid, you will insert non-supported information into your document, which might be displayed incorrectly or not at all by web browsers.

Hands On 3: Using an Extension to Create a Bookmark to Your Web Page

In this tutorial we'll walk through installing an extension to create a Universal Bookmarks link on your web page. This extension adds a script to your page that provides a browser-specific link so that a user can add your URL to Netscape Bookmarks, Internet Explorer Favorites, or Opera's Hotlist.

1. Open the Chapter 32 folder on the CD and double-click the Universal Bookmarks extension file (`Universal_Bookmarks.mxp`).

2. The Extension Manager dialog box should display automatically. If not, you can also:

   - Select Start → Programs → Macromedia → Macromedia Extension Manager from your Windows desktop.

   - Double-click the Extension Manager application in your Finder window on your Macintosh.

3. In the Extension Manager window, select File → Install Extension. This will open the Select Extension To Install dialog box. This dialog box will automatically open to the location where extensions were last installed. Click Install to start the installation procedure.

4. Click Accept to agree to the terms of the licensing agreement for the extension. The rest of the installation should complete, and you should be returned to the Extension Manager with the Universal Bookmark extension selected and checked.

5. Create a new HTML file by selecting File → New.

6. From the General Tab select Basic under Category and HTML from the Basic page type list.

7. From the File menu, select Save As and type a name of your choice.

8. Choose either Design view or Split view (with the cursor in the Design view window).

9. Choose Commands → Dazdezines → Universal Bookmarks.

10. The Universal Bookmarks Dialog box displays. In the Basic tab (see Figure 32.16), type the URL that you want the user to bookmark. This is the only field you need to fill out for the extension to work. Don't include `http://`; that will be automatically added by the script.

11. The Advanced tab, shown in Figure 34.17, displays the link text for different browsers. You can customize this text, but Dazdezines recommends reading the Help page before you do this. To display the Help page, click the Help button on the right side of the dialog box. You can also customize the display of the link by adding a style sheet.

> For additional information on this extension, see the Universal Bookmarks page at
> `www.dazdezines.com/mme/extensions/unversal_bookmarks.htm`.

12. Click the Add button.

13. Be sure your page has a title; otherwise the bookmark will be saved as Untitled Document. Save the file.

14. You can view the script in the Code view window, but you won't see any changes in Design view. Preview the file in different browsers to view the link.

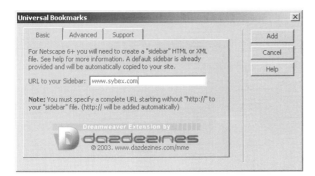

Figure 32.16

The Basic tab of the Universal Bookmarks dialog box.

Figure 32.17

You can change the link text in the Advanced tab of the Universal Bookmarks dialog box.

Ready, Set, Go!

Dreamweaver's customization and extension features are among the outstanding features of Dreamweaver and make it possible to totally customize your use of Dreamweaver. But before you head out into the fast-paced world of web application development, you'll need one more item for your web development tool kit: a good understanding of Dreamweaver's accessibility features. In the next chapter, you'll learn how Dreamweaver can help you quickly and easily implement accessibility on all your pages and sites.

Using Dreamweaver to Make Your Site Accessible

Accessible design enables users with disabilities—whether visual, auditory, or other forms of disability—to access, navigate, and use the Web. Accessibility is a part of web standards, is required for U.S. government sites (under the law known as "Section 508"), and should certainly be a consideration for today's designers and developers. Many other government, educational, and corporate organizations around the world now require compliance with accessibility guidelines.

Dreamweaver MX 2004 makes it easier than ever to create pages and sites that are accessible to Web users with disabilities. You can configure your Dreamweaver workspace so that the program prompts you to use accessibility features when you insert page elements, and you can also run an accessibility report to test a page or site's compliance with accessibility guidelines.

Dreamweaver includes several features for Dreamweaver users with disabilities, including support for using screen readers and keyboard navigation.

The following topics will be discussed in this chapter:

- ■ **Setting Accessibility Preferences in Dreamweaver**

- ■ **Detailing the Section 508 guidelines**

- ■ **Using Dreamweaver's Sample Accessible Pages**

- ■ **Generating an Accessibility Report**

- ■ **Support for Dreamweaver users with disabilities**

Using Dreamweaver's Accessibility Preferences

Dreamweaver includes a multitude of accessibility features but, as always, leaves it up to you to choose which features you want to include in your workspace. You can set these preferences in the Accessibility category of the Preferences dialog box (Edit → Preferences → Accessibility), as shown in Figure 33.1.

Four categories of page elements are included: form objects, frames, media, and images. If you check the box in front of a category, dialog boxes with accessibility tags and attributes will automatically display when you insert these page elements. In the next section, we'll review Section 508 guidelines and show how Dreamweaver's accessibility dialog boxes help you stay in compliance with the Section 508 law.

The Accessibility preferences settings also include an Offscreen Rendering check box for screen reader users. This is checked by default, but you can uncheck it if you are having any problems with your screen reader.

Section 508 Guidelines

Section 508 includes 16 guidelines for Internet information; reviewing these guidelines is a good introduction to web accessibility issues in general.

> You can download a zip file with Section 508 Web Development Guidelines from Macro-media at www.macromedia.com/macromedia/accessibility/508_guidelines.html.

Figure 33.1

**Accessibility
Preferences**

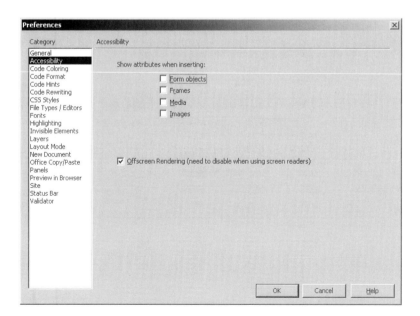

These 16 guidelines are taken directly from the Section 508 Law, technical standard 1194.22 (web-based intranet and internet information and applications). To see the complete text of technical standard 1194.22, visit `www.access-board.gov/sec508/guide/1194.22.htm`.

A text equivalent for every non-text element shall be provided. The `alt` attribute of the `img` tag is used to provide alternate text for viewers with visual disabilities who use screen readers and viewers who turn off image display in browsers. You can use up to 256 characters in an `alt` attribute.

You can also add a `longdesc` attribute to provide a longer text description. A `longdesc` attribute is a link to another page that contains only the text description. Screen readers open and read the `longdesc` page, but standard browsers ignore it.

If you check Images in the Accessibility preferences, then when you insert an image in a Dreamweaver page, the Image Tag Accessibility Attributes dialog box (see Figure 33.2) automatically displays.

Equivalent alternatives for any multimedia presentation shall be synchronized with the presentation. You can add captions for screen readers or alternative auditory content for multimedia presentations, and synchronize these with the visual presentation.

> See the "Introduction to Screen Readers" movie at `www.doit.wisc.edu/accessibility/video/intro.asp` for more details on captioning.

Web pages shall be designed so that all information conveyed with color is also available without color, for example from context or markup. Make sure that your page design does not rely on color alone to convey information.

Documents shall be organized so they are readable without requiring an associated style sheet. Your page should still be readable without an associated style sheet. For best results, if you use styles, use an external CSS stylesheet with your page, and make sure there is no presentational markup in your page code (for example, `<b>` tags or `align` attributes).

Redundant text links shall be provided for each active region of a server-side image map. Dreamweaver creates client-side image maps, not server-side, but the same principle can be used for client-side image maps—include text links for each image map link.

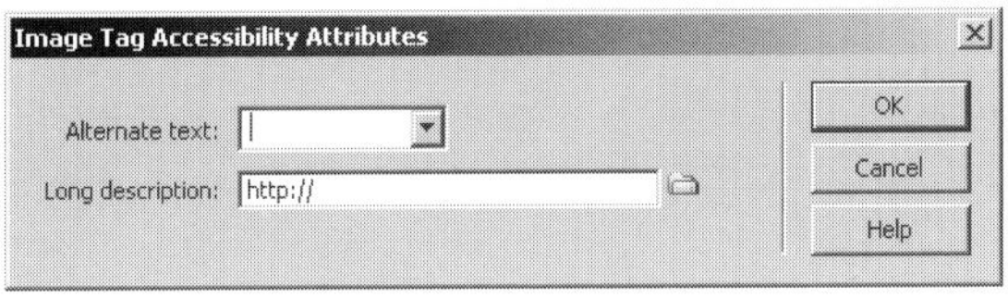

Figure 33.2

Image Tag Accessibility Attributes dialog box

Client-side image maps shall be provided instead of server-side image maps except where the regions cannot be defined with an available geometric shape. The available shapes are rectangle, polygon, and oval. Server-side image maps are rarely used.

Row and column headers shall be identified for data tables. Tables were created for displaying tabular data. Dreamweaver automatically displays accessibility options in the Table dialog box (see Figure 33.3) that displays when you insert a table. Choose a header style (none, top row, left column, or both) from the graphic icons. You can also specify a caption, caption alignment, and a table summary, although these features aren't required under Section 508.

Markup shall be used to associate data cells and header cells for data tables that have two or more logical levels of row or column headers. Screen readers have difficulty with complex tables unless additional attributes are added to relate the header cells with the correct data cells: an `id` and a category attribute (`axis`) for the header (`th`) cells, and a `headers` attribute for the `td` cells. You'll need to add these attributes by hand to your Dreamweaver code. (See the Macromedia article for an example and more details.)

Frames shall be titled with text that facilitates frame identification and navigation. Use meaningful titles for frames. If you checked Frames in the Accessibility Preferences, the Frame Tag Accessibility Attributes dialog box (see Figure 33.4) displays when you insert a frameset. Choose the frame name from the Frame drop-down menu and enter a title in the Title text box.

Pages shall be designed to avoid causing the screen to flicker with a frequency greater than 2 Hz and lower than 55 Hz. You can use scripts to control the refresh rate of the user's monitor. We recommend not using flickering graphics, but if you must, avoid the frequencies listed above (which can trigger seizures in individuals with photosensitive epilepsy) or provide a warning that links to alternative content.

Figure 33.3
Accessibility features in the Table dialog box

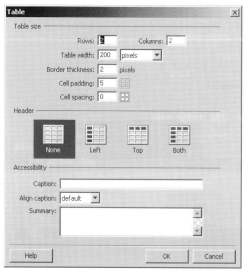

A text-only page, with equivalent information or functionality, shall be provided to make a website comply with the provisions of this part, when compliance cannot be accomplished in any other way. The content of the text-only page shall be updated whenever the primary page changes. If you can't comply with accessibility guidelines, it's also acceptable to provide a link to the page content as a text-only page. Update the text page whenever the original page changes.

When pages utilize scripting languages to display content or to create interface elements, the information provided by the script shall be identified with functional text that can be read by assistive technology. If you use JavaScript for important content, make sure you provide non-JavaScript alternatives. Also consider using server-side scripting, because the final output is HTML content that can be read by a screen reader.

When a web page requires that an applet, plug-in, or other application be present on the client system to interpret page content, the page must provide a link to a plug-in or applet that complies with 1194.22(a) through (l) [the previous 12 guidelines]. Provide a link to necessary players, plug-ins, and helper applications.

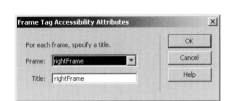

Figure 33.4

Frame Tag Accessibility Attributes dialog box

When electronic forms are designed to be completed on-line, the form shall allow people using assistive technology to access the information, field elements, and functionality required for completion and submission of the form, including all directions and cues. If you checked form objects in Accessibility Preferences, the Input Tag Accessibility Attributes dialog box (see Figure 33.5) displays when you insert form input elements such as a text field. You can add any of three additional accessibility elements through this dialog box:

Label	The label element associates a text label with a form element.
Access key	Keystroke that is used with the Alt key to put focus on a specific form element.
Tab order	Specifies a sequence that form elements are tabbed through.

> For more information on using access keys, see "Accesskeys: Unlocking Hidden Navigation" at www.alistapart.com/articles/accesskeys/. For additional details on forms, see "Accessible Forms" at www.htmldog.com/guides/htmladvanced/forms.php.

A method shall be provided that permits users to skip repetitive navigation links. Add a graphic link and a text link to an anchor where the actual page content begins. This enables screen reader users to skip going through the navigation links on every page.

Figure 33.5

Input Tag Accessibility Attributes dialog box

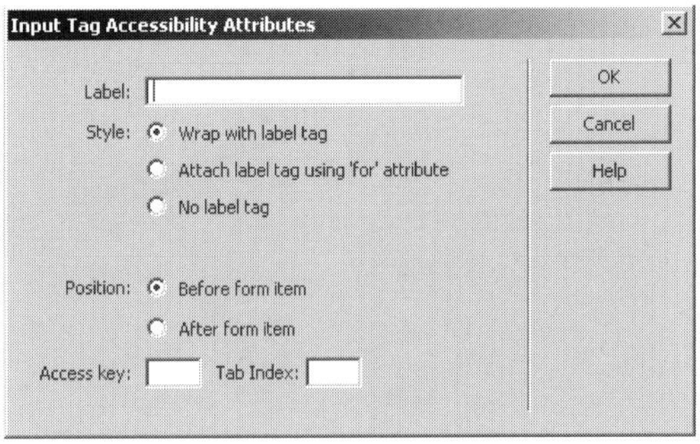

When a timed response is required, the user shall be alerted and given sufficient time to indicate more time is required. This requirement addresses sites where the content "expires" if a response is not received, such as online testing pages or secured sites. Screen readers might process a page more slowly than other users, so time limits must be clearly stated on the testing web page, and users should have a way to reset the timer if additional time is needed.

Using Dreamweaver's Accessible Page Samples

To use one of Dreamweaver's Sample Accessible Page Designs, choose Page Designs (Accessible) from the Start page Create From Samples list, or from the main menu choose File → New → Page Designs (Accessible). The New Document window (see Figure 33.6) displays. Select a sample page from the Page Designs list, and then click the Create button to close the window. Your new page opens in the Document window.

Generating an Accessibility Report

You can test a page or a site to check compliance with accessibility guidelines. To create a report:

1. Select Site → Reports to open the Reports dialog box. Check the Accessibility option (see Figure 33.7).

2. Click the Report Settings buttons at the bottom left to open the Accessibility dialog box (see Figure 33.8).

3. All of the guidelines are enabled by default. To select specific Accessibility guidelines to test against, select All and click the Disable button to disable all the options. Select the guidelines you want to test against and click the Enable button. Click OK to close the window and return to the Reports dialog box.

4. Click the Run button. The results display in the Site Reports panel in the Results panel group.

Figure 33.6

Selecting an Accessible Page Design sample page

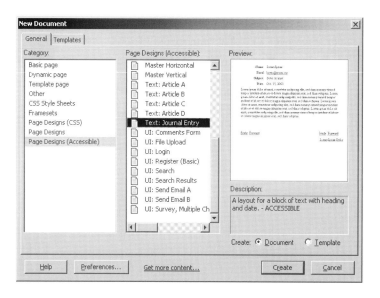

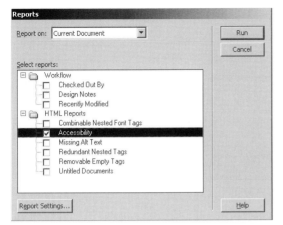

Figure 33.7

Reports dialog box with Accessibility option selected

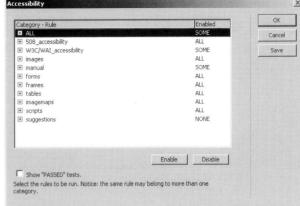

Figure 33.8

Accessibility dialog box

Support for Dreamweaver Users with Disabilities

Dreamweaver also provides features for Dreamweaver users with disabilities, including screen reader support, support for Windows high contrast mode, and keyboard navigation.

Screen Reader Support Screen readers read screen text content, as well as non-screen text content such as links, alternative text in images, and accessibility attributes. You can use a screen reader when creating pages in Dreamweaver MX 2004, which supports the JAWS for Windows (www.freedomscientific.com) and Window Eyes (www.gwmicro.com) screen readers.

> For more details on screen readers and CSS, see "Screenreader Visibility" at http://css-discuss.incutio.com/?page=ScreenreaderVisibility.

Windows High Contrast Mode Dreamweaver supports the Windows high contrast mode. You access this via the Windows Control Panel. Dialog boxes and panels use system color settings, and will be in high contrast mode. Code view syntax coloring is turned off in this mode.

Keyboard Navigation You can use keyboard navigation in Dreamweaver to navigate panels, the Property inspector, dialog boxes, frames, and tables. However, using tabbing and arrow keys is supported for Windows only.

For additional information on accessibility and creating accessible pages, see these online resources:

- "Building Accessible Websites," Joe Clark's free online version of his accessibility book at `http://joeclark.org/book/sashay/serialization/`.
- Web Accessibility Initiative at `www.w3.org/WAI/`
- "HTML Techniques for Web Content Accessibility Guidelines 1.0" at `www.w3.org/TR/WCAG10-HTML-TECHS/`.

Ready, Set, Go!

You're now ready to enter the fast-paced world of rapid website and web application development with Dreamweaver MX 2004.

See the appendices that follow for information on online resources (Appendix A), keyboard shortcuts (Appendix B), and an overview of new features in Dreamweaver MX 2004 (Appendix C).

## PART VI

Appendices

Dreamweaver *inspires loyalty and enthusiasm among its users, and you can see evidence of this in the many websites and discussion groups devoted to the software. The enjoyment that designers and developers get from using the program encourages them to share what they've learned, discovered, or created. Going online is the best way to get the latest information about Dreamweaver and other Macromedia products, and to contact other web designers/developers if you have questions or problems you can't solve.*

The first appendix collects some websites, mailing lists, and other online resources that will help you continue to learn about Dreamweaver after you finish this book. The second appendix will help you get around in Dreamweaver. We hope that you will find this extensive list of keyboard shortcuts helpful and informative. The third appendix is a summary of all the new features in Dreamweaver MX 2004.

APPENDIX A ■ Online Resources

APPENDIX B ■ Keyboard Shortcuts

APPENDIX C ■ New Features in Dreamweaver MX 2004

Online Resources

There are so many websites related to Dreamweaver that it can be helpful to begin with sites that collect links to other resources as well as providing their own software or instructional materials. The following websites are good starting points for finding out about Dreamweaver online.

These sites are Macromedia resources:

Dreamweaver Developer Center (www.macromedia.com/devnet/mx/dreamweaver/) The Dreamweaver Developer Center features links to articles, tutorials, and sample files for Dreamweaver MX 2004 as well as Dreamweaver MX. It also includes information on Contribute and on server technologies supported in Dreamweaver. For links to additional articles on Dreamweaver MX 2004, see www.macromedia.com/devnet/mx/dreamweaver/dw_mx2004.html.

Macromedia On Demand Seminars (www.macromedia.com/macromedia/events/online/ondemand/index.html) On Demand seminars are free multimedia presentations and demonstrations of Macromedia products that can be viewed at any time over a broadband connection. Several presentations are already available for Dreamweaver MX 2004.

Dreamweaver Support Center (www.macromedia.com/support/dreamweaver) Any problems with Dreamweaver are reported here. You'll also find patches, how-tos, and tips.

Dreamweaver Documentation (www.macromedia.com/support/documentation/en/dreamweaver/) Download Dreamweaver product manuals and release notes.

Dreamweaver Templates (www.macromedia.com/devnet/mx/dreamweaver/templates.html) The Dreamweaver Developer Center Template section includes links to several articles on various aspects of using templates. You can also download sample design templates at www.macromedia.com/software/dreamweaver/download/templates.

Dreamweaver Online Forums (http://webforums.macromedia.com/dreamweaver) Macromedia's own web-based discussion groups for Dreamweaver include General Discussion, Application Development, and Exchange Extensions.

Here are a few more starting points for more information, from non-Macromedia sources:

Dreamweaver FAQ (`www.dwfaq.com/default.asp`) Dreamweaver FAQ offers an assortment of tutorials, articles, and Dreamweaver news, and also features an exchange for code snippets.

edgeofmyseat (`www.edgeofmyseat.com/resources.do`) This site features Dreamweaver articles, tutorials, and extensions created by Rachel Andrews.

Essential Dreamweaver Resources (`www.thepattysite.com/essential_resources.cfm`) Patty Ayers' links to Dreamweaver resources, tutorials, FAQs, and extensions.

Charon Internet (`www.charon.co.uk/default.aspx`) Julian Robert's Charon Internet offers Dreamweaver articles, tutorials, and extensions, including both a free and a commercial version of a shopping cart extension. This site is a great source for information on using ASP.NET with Dreamweaver.

Robgt.com (`http://robgt.com/index.asp`) Rob Turnbull's site includes a variety of Dreamweaver tutorials, especially for ASP/VB Script.

Dreamweaver Software

Dreamweaver can do a lot, but some enterprising designers who have used the program in real-world situations have found ways to make it do more. They've come up with their own extensions, templates, commands, and other goodies that can be added to the program. Some are available for free, but don't expect the software to be updated or supported. Other extensions have to be purchased from their developers.

Third-Party Extensions

Macromedia Exchange for Dreamweaver (`www.macromedia.com/exchange/dreamweaver`) Macromedia makes a number of extensions available that add additional capabilities to Dreamweaver. Be sure to read the comments posted by individuals who have actually used (or tried to use) the extensions.

Dreamweaver Dabbling (`www.pawluk.com/public`) Self-proclaimed dabbler Hal Pawluk makes some nifty extensions available for download, including JavaScript code snippets and a tell-a-friend-about-this-site form.

Dreamweaver Fever (`http://dreamweaverfever.com/grow/`) Drew McLellan provides some unusual extensions, including one that automatically adds two paragraphs of mock Latin text, which designers can use as filler text to mock up pages.

Yaromat (www.yaromat.com/dw) Web designer Jaro von Flocken gives back to the Dreamweaver community by providing extensions, objects, behaviors, and other goodies on this site for free.

Project Seven Development (www.projectseven.com) This is consistently one of the best commercial sources for Dreamweaver design packs and extensions, including a variety of dynamic menu styles.

Website Templates

Templates2go.com (www.templates2go.com) Designer Linda Locke presents four packages of 25 predesigned websites for business, publishing, personal, and e-commerce use. Cost is $50 per package.

Dreamweaversites.com (http://store.dreamweaverwebmaster.com/dwtemplates.asp) Restrained, tasteful designs intended for business and e-commerce sites. You can buy one template at a time, typically for $15 to $30.

Heeha.com (www.heeha.com) A wide range of personal and business templates, many of which use a clean white page background. Some templates are available for free; others typically cost about $16.

Newsgroups and Mailing Lists

There's nothing like finding personal support when you run into a problem you can't solve or a question you can't answer immediately. Newsgroups and mailing lists not only give you a great place to get help, but you can also answer questions yourself and be part of the Dreamweaver community.

Macromedia_Dreamwvr (http://groups.yahoo.com/group/Macromedia_Dreamwvr) One of the Yahoo! discussion groups, it's for beginners as well as advanced users. You need a Yahoo! ID to subscribe, but you can obtain one for free from Yahoo!.

Dreamweaver Talk (www.blueworld.com/blueworld/lists/dreamweaver.html) An e-mail discussion group run by software developer Blue World Communications, Inc.

Blogs

These blogs are an excellent source for news and tips about Dreamweaver MX 2004 and other Macromedia software.

JD on MX (www.markme.com/jd/) Macromedia's John Dowdell's blog features news updates for web developers who use Macromedia products. Also see JD's Forum at www.macromedia.com/devnet/jd_forum/.

Dan's Shorts (`http://blog.web-shorts.com/`) Dan Short is a Team Macromedia member, author, and web designer. His blog focuses on web development with Macromedia software.

Macromedia XML News Aggregator, Dreamweaver section (`www.markme.com/mxna/index.cfm?category=Dreamweaver`) This blog includes a selection of Dreamweaver news and tips from 208 news feeds.

fullasagoog (`www.fullasagoog.com/index.cfm?blogcat=DreamweaverMX`) This section of the fullasagoog blog includes updates from Dreamweaver news feeds.

Keyboard Shortcuts

This appendix lays out some essential keyboard shortcuts that will help you get around in Dreamweaver MX 2004. If you keep this reference handy when you are working with the application, you will be able to save yourself a lot of mouse-clicks.

You can also customize Dreamweaver's keyboard shortcuts. Choose Edit → Keyboard Shortcuts, then add, delete, or change shortcuts.

CATEGORY/COMMAND	WINDOWS SHORTCUT	MACINTOSH SHORTCUT
Managing Files		
New document	Ctrl-N	Command-N
Open an HTML file	Ctrl-O	Command-O
Open in frame	Ctrl-Shift-O	Command-Shift-O
Close	Ctrl-W	Command-W
Close all	Ctrl-Shift-W	Command-Shift-W
Save	Ctrl-S	Command-S
Save as	Ctrl-Shift-S	Command-Shift-S
Exit/quit	Alt-F4 or Ctrl-Q	Command-Q
General Editing		
Undo	Ctrl-Z or Alt-Backspace	Command-Z
Redo	Ctrl-Y or Ctrl-Shift-Z	Command-Y or Command-Shift-Z
Cut	Ctrl-X or Shift-Delete	Command-X or Shift-Delete
Copy	Ctrl-C or Ctrl-Insert	Command-C
Paste	Ctrl-V or Shift-Insert	Command-V or Shift-Insert
Clear	Delete	Delete
Bold	Ctrl-B	Command-B
Italic	Ctrl-I	Command-I
Select all	Ctrl-A	Command-A
Move to page up	Page Up	Page Up
Move to page down	Page Down	Page Down
Select to page up	Shift-Page Up	Shift-Page Up

continued

CATEGORY/COMMAND	WINDOWS SHORTCUT	MACINTOSH SHORTCUT
Select to page down	Shift-Page Down	Shift-Page Down
Select line up/down	Shift-Up/Down	Shift-Up/Down
Move to start of line	Home	Home
Move to end of line	End	End
Select to start of line	Shift-Home	Shift-Home
Select to end of line	Shift-End	Shift-End
Go to previous/next paragraph	Ctrl-Up/Down	Command-Up/Down
Go to next/previous word	Ctrl-Right/Left	Command-Right/Left
Select until next word/paragraph	Ctrl-Shift-Right/Down	Command-Shift-Right/Down
Select from previous word/paragraph	Ctrl-Shift-Left/Up	Command-Shift-Left/Up
Delete word left	Ctrl-Backspace	Command-Backspace
Delete word right	Ctrl-Delete	Command-Delete
Select character left/right	Shift-Left/Right	Shift-Left/Right
Find and replace	Ctrl-F	Command-F
Find next/find again	F3	Command-G
Replace	Ctrl-H	Command-H
Copy HTML (in Design view)	Ctrl-Shift-C	Command-Shift-C
Paste HTML (in Design view)	Ctrl-Shift-V	Command-Shift-V
Preferences	Ctrl-U	Command-U
Page Views		
Table Layout view	Ctrl-F6	Command-F6
Expanded Tables view	F6	F6
Live Data view	Ctrl-Shift-R	Command-Shift-R
Refresh Live Data	Ctrl-R	Command-R
Switch to next document	Ctrl-Tab	Command-Tab
Switch to previous document	Ctrl-Shift-Tab	Command-Shift-Tab
Switch between Design and Code views	Ctrl-~	Command-' (backquote)
Server debug	Ctrl-Shift-G	Command-Shift-G
Refresh Design view	F5	F5
Viewing Page Elements		
Show/hide visual aids	Ctrl-Shift-I	Command-Shift-I
Show/hide rulers	Ctrl-Alt-R	Command-Option-R
Show/hide grid	Ctrl-Alt-G	Command-Option-G
Snap to grid	Ctrl-Alt-Shift-G	Command-Option-Shift-G
Show/hide head content	Ctrl-Shift-H	Command-Shift-H
View page properties	Ctrl-J	Command-J

continued

CATEGORY/COMMAND	WINDOWS SHORTCUT	MACINTOSH SHORTCUT
Code Editing		
Switch to Design view	Ctrl-~	Command-' (backquote)
Print code	Ctrl-P	Command-P
Validate markup	Shift-F6	Shift-F6
Open Quick Tag Editor (Design view)		Ctrl-T Command-T
Open snippets panel	Shift-F9	Shift-F9
Show code hints	Ctrl-Spacebar	Command-Spacebar
Indent code	Ctrl-Shift->	Command-Shift->
Outdent code	Ctrl-Shift-<	Command-Shift-<
Insert tag	Ctrl-E	Command-E
Edit tag (Design view)	Ctrl-F5	Command-F5
Select parent tag	Ctrl-[	Command-[
Select child (Design view)	Ctrl-]	Command-]
Balance braces	Ctrl-'	Command-'
Move to top of code	Ctrl-Home	Command-Home
Move to end of code	Ctrl-End	Command-End
Select to top of code	Ctrl-Shift-Home	Command-Shift-Home
Select to end of code	Ctrl-Shift-End	Command-Shift-End
Text Editing		
Create a new paragraph	Enter	Return
Insert a line break 	Shift-Enter	Shift-Return
Insert a nonbreaking space	Ctrl-Shift-Spacebar	Command-Shift-Spacebar
Move text or object	Drag item	Drag item
Copy text or object	Ctrl-drag item	Control-drag item
Select a word	Double-click	Double-click
Open/close the Property inspector	Ctrl-F3	Command-F3
Switch between Dreamweaver and other open programs	Alt-Tab	Option-Tab
Check spelling	Shift-F7	Shift-F7
Formatting Text		
Indent (inserts blockquote tags; using CSS for indenting is preferred)	Ctrl-Alt-]	Command-Option-]
Outdent	Ctrl-Alt-[	Command-Option-[
Format as paragraph	Ctrl-Shift-P	Command-Shift-P
Apply headings 1–6	Ctrl-1–6	Command-1–6
Align left/center/right/justify	Ctrl-Alt-Shift-L/C/R/J	Command-Alt-Shift-L/C/R/J
Working in Tables		
Select cell (with cursor inside the cell)	Ctrl-A	Command-A

continued

CATEGORY/COMMAND	WINDOWS SHORTCUT	MACINTOSH SHORTCUT
Insert a row (before current)	Ctrl-M	Command-M
Add a row at end of table	Tab (in the last cell)	Tab (in the last cell)
Delete current row	Ctrl-Shift-M	Command-Shift-M
Insert a column (to left of current column)	Ctrl-Shift-A	Command-Shift-A
Delete a column	Ctrl-Shift-- (hyphen)	Command-Shift-- (hyphen)
Merge selected table cells	Ctrl-Alt-M	Command-Option-M
Split table cell	Ctrl-Alt-S	Command-Option-S
Increase column span	Ctrl-Shift-]	Command-Shift-]
Decrease column span	Ctrl-Shift-[	Command-Shift-[
Working in Frames		
Select a frame	Alt-click (in frame) or Alt-Up	Shift-Option -click (in frame)
Select next frame or frameset	Alt-Right	Command-Right
Select previous frame or frameset	Alt-Left	Command-Left
Select parent frameset	Alt-Up	Command-Up
Select first child frame or frameset	Alt-Down	Command-Down
Add a new frame to frameset	Select frame, then Alt-drag frame border	Select frame, then Option-drag frame border
Working with Layers		
Select a layer	Ctrl-Shift-click	Command-Shift-click
Select and move layer	Shift-Ctrl-drag	Command-Shift-drag
Add or remove layer from selection	Shift-click layer	Shift-click layer
Move selected layer by pixels	Arrow keys	Arrow keys
Move selected layer by snapping increment	Shift-Arrow keys	Shift-Arrow keys
Resize selected layer by pixels	Ctrl-Arrow keys	Option-Arrow keys
Resize selected layer by snapping increment	Ctrl-Shift-Arrow keys	Option-Shift-Arrow keys
Toggle the display of the grid	Ctrl-Alt-G	Command-Option-G
Snap to grid	Ctrl-Shift-Alt-G	Command-Shift-Option-G
Align layers left	Ctrl-Shift-1	Command-Shift-1
Align layers right	Ctrl-Shift-3	Command-Shift-3
Align layers top	Ctrl-Shift-4	Command-Shift-4
Align layers bottom	Ctrl-Shift-6	Command-Shift-6
Make same width	Ctrl-Shift-7	Command-Shift-7
Make same height	Ctrl-Shift-9	Command-Shift-9
Getting Help		
Using Dreamweaver Help topics	F1	F1
Using ColdFusion Help topics	Ctrl-F1	Command-F1
Reference	Shift-F1	Shift-F1

continued

CATEGORY/COMMAND	WINDOWS SHORTCUT	MACINTOSH SHORTCUT
Inserting Objects		
Any object (image, Shockwave movie, and so on)	Drag file into the Document window	Drag file into the Document window
Image	Ctrl-Alt-I	Command-Option-I
Table	Ctrl-Alt-T	Command-Option-T
Named anchor	Ctrl-Alt-A	Command-Option-A
Managing Hyperlinks		
Check links sitewide	Ctrl-F8	Command-F8
Create hyperlink (select text, image, or object)	Ctrl-L	Command-L
Remove hyperlink	Ctrl-Shift-L	Command-Shift-L
Drag and drop to create a hyperlink from a document	Select the text, image, or object, then Shift-drag the selection to a file in the Files panel	Select the text, image, or object, then Shift-drag the selection to a file in the Files panel
Drag and drop to create a hyperlink using the Property Inspector	Select the text, image, or object, then drag the Point-to-File icon in Property inspector to a file in the Files panel	Select the text, image, or object, then drag the Point-to-File icon in Property Inspector to a file in the Files panel
Open the linked-to document in Dreamweaver	Ctrl-double-click link	Command-double-click link
Previewing and Debugging in Browsers		
Preview in primary browser	F12	F12
Preview in secondary browser	Shift-F12	Shift-F12
Managing a Site		
Refresh view	F5	F5
Create new file	Ctrl-N	Command-F5
Open file	Ctrl-O	Command-O
Copy file	Ctrl-C	Command-C
Paste file	Ctrl-V	Command-V
Duplicate file	Ctrl-D	Command-D
Rename file	F2	F2
Get (selected files or folders from remote site)	Ctrl-Shift-D	Command-Shift-D
Put (selected files or folders to remote site)	Ctrl-Shift-U	Command-Shift-U
Check out	Ctrl-Alt-Shift-D	Command-Option-Shift-D
Check in	Ctrl-Alt-Shift-U	Command-Option-Shift-U
View site map	Alt-F8	Option-F8
Using a Site Map		
View site files	F8	F8
Link to existing file	Ctrl-Shift-K	Command-Shift-K
Change link	Ctrl-L	Command-L
Remove link	Ctrl-Shift-L	Command-Shift-L

continued

CATEGORY/COMMAND	WINDOWS SHORTCUT	MACINTOSH SHORTCUT
Show page titles	Ctrl-Shift-T	Command-Shift-T
Zoom in site map	Ctrl-+ (plus sign)	Command-+ (plus sign)
Zoom out site map	Ctrl- - (hyphen)	Command- - (hyphen)
Opening and Closing Panels		
Insert bars	Ctrl-F2	Command-F2
Properties	Ctrl-F3	Command-F3
CSS styles	Shift-F11	Shift-F11
Behaviors	Shift-F3	Shift-F3
Tag inspector	F9	F9
Snippets	Shift-F9	Shift-F9
Reference	Shift-F1	Shift-F1
Databases	Ctrl-Shift-F10	Command-Shift-F10
Bindings	Ctrl-F10	Command-F10
Server behaviors	Ctrl-F9	Command-F9
Components	Ctrl-F7	Command-F7
Files	F8	F8
Assets	F11	F11
Results	F7	F7
Code inspector	F10	F10
Frames	Shift-F2	Shift-F2
History	Shift-F10	Shift-F10
Layers	F2	F2
Show/hide panels	F4	F4

New Features in Dreamweaver MX 2004

Dreamweaver MX 2004 features a diversity of new and improved features in several areas. The key improvements are a streamlined and more efficient user interface and a major upgrade in CSS features and support, but other new features and changes have been added to make Dreamweaver an even more effective and easy to use web production and development tool.

If you have used previous versions of the program, you'll notice the change as soon as you open it, but even if you're a new Dreamweaver user you'll appreciate all the new features. And wherever this book discusses a new feature, you'll see the MX 2004 icon.

Useability

Dreamweaver MX 2004 offers a trimmed-down and less-cluttered workspace that allows you to access even more features of the program more easily than before. New features and changes include these:

Document toolbar The new Document toolbar makes it easy to use features that were previously in separate locations in the Dreamweaver workspace. The Document toolbar provides quick and easy access to just about every feature of the program and most of Dreamweaver's essential tools—tools that let you switch between viewing modes (Code, Split, Design), change the document title, manage files, check browser support, preview your site in a browser of your choice, refresh Design view after changes to the code, and change view options for both Code and Design view.

Dreamweaver MX 2004 automatically checks your files for cross-browser compatibility whenever you open a file. You choose target browsers, and Dreamweaver creates a report listing errors, warnings, or other information about cross-browser issues.

Start page When you open Dreamweaver (or anytime that no documents are open in the workspace), the new Start page appears in the workspace. The Start page includes options to open recent documents, create a new document, or create a new document from sample files (CSS style sheets, Framesets, Table Based Layouts, and Accessible Page Designs). The Start page also gives you access to Help and to the Dreamweaver Exchange on the Macromedia site.

Tabbed document interface (Windows workspace only) When documents are maximized, they display a tab at the top, and the contents of a single document fill the Dreamweaver workspace. You can shift back and forth easily between multiple open documents by clicking the tabs, and you can see at a glance the file names of all open documents. If you want to compare the content of multiple documents at the same time, just reduce the document size and arrange them however you wish in your workspace.

Multiple Insert bars Dreamweaver MX 2004 includes a drop-down menu with a set of insert bars for various tasks rather than a single insert bar. Not only are the medium-sized icons easier to read than the small icons of Dreamweaver MX, but the new insert bar is smaller and takes up less space. The insert bar selections include Common, Layout, Forms, Text, and HTML as well as two new choices: a Favorites insert bar where you can add icons for the features you most often use and a Flash elements insert bar. Flash elements, also new in Dreamweaver MX 2004, are prebuilt Flash components that can be inserted in your Dreamweaver pages to create RIAs (Rich Internet Applications). See Chapter 11, "Getting into Flash," for more information on Flash and RIA.

Improved table editing Dreamweaver MX 2004 includes three modes for creating and editing tables: Standard mode, Layout mode, and the new Expanded Tables mode. Expanded Tables mode makes it easy to select areas within and around table cells. Improvements in Layout mode provide better visualization of table and cell size and boundaries, and instantly show changes to the code when cells are resized.

Siteless connections From Dreamweaver MX 2004, you can connect to a server, download files, make changes, and upload files—all without having to create a Dreamweaver site. If you want to use Dreamweaver's comprehensive site management tools, though, you'll need to create a Dreamweaver site.

> For additional details on all the changes to the Dreamweaver workspace and document window, see Chapter 3, "Setting Up Your Workspace and Your Site."

CSS (Cascading Style Sheets)

One of the biggest changes in Dreamweaver MX 2004 is the addition of many more CSS features. CSS in Dreamweaver is now web standards–compliant; when Dreamweaver checks your pages for browser compatibility, it checks CSS as well as HTML/XHTML. Whether you use an external CSS editor, such as Top Style Pro, or create all your CSS in Dreamweaver itself, you'll find a host of features to help you use CSS in your pages, including:

CSS Styles in the text Property inspector By default, Dreamweaver MX 2004 automatically creates text styles when you format text, and lets you apply these styles to other selections of text. A style drop-down menu is now included in the text Property inspector, listing all Dreamweaver-created styles as well as any additional styles available in attached style sheets. The style drop-down menu displays sample text in the available styles, so you can easily preview any style choice before you apply it.

> CSS styles can be also be accessed and applied from the new Class drop-down menu available in Dreamweaver's other Property inspectors.

CSS Page Properties The page properties dialog box is expanded in Dreamweaver MX 2004, and now includes options for CSS-based page properties (such as background color and font characteristics), link display features, and heading styles.

Relevant CSS panel The new Relevant CSS panel in the Tag Inspector panel group displays any CSS rules that have been applied to the current selection. The top part of the panel displays the applied rules and any affected tags, and the bottom part displays the details of the applied style rules. You can modify the rules in the bottom section, and changes will be immediately applied to your document.

CSS Rule inspector The CSS Rule inspector displays details of any style rule selected in the CSS panel, an associated style sheet, or the head section of an HTML page. The CSS Rule inspector opens the CSS properties panel in the Tag Inspector panel group where you can view and edit the CSS properties directly.

> You can also edit Dreamweaver's CSS rules by right-clicking the rule in the CSS Styles panel (Control-clicking on a Mac) and selecting Edit, which opens the CSS Style Definition dialog box.

CSS Code Hints CSS Code Hints are now available in Code view when hand-coding CSS rules.

Using Dreamweaver's CSS sample pages When you attach an external style sheet to a Dreamweaver page, you can choose sample style sheets directly from the Attach External Style Sheet dialog box. This automatically applies the selected style sheet sample to the current page, and makes it easier than ever to use CSS in your pages.

Additional New Features

Dreamweaver MX 2004 has even more new features, including:

Increased integration with Microsoft Word and Excel You can now copy and paste Word and Excel documents directly into Dreamweaver pages and preserve the Word or Excel formatting while displaying the content as HTML.

Integrated image editing The new image editing features in the image Property inspector enable you to edit JPEG and GIF images directly in Dreamweaver. You can crop, resize, resample, sharpen, or modify brightness and contrast.

Secure FTP Dreamweaver now allows you to connect to SFTP servers and enables you to do encrypted file transfers from Dreamweaver.

XML namespaces Dreamweaver now supports the use of XML namespaces in Dreamweaver XML documents.

Index

Note to the Reader: Throughout this index **boldfaced** page numbers indicate primary discussions of a topic. *Italicized* page numbers indicate illustrations.

Soluti👁ns™ FROM SYBEX®

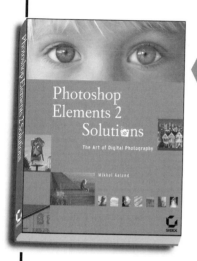

Photoshop® Elements 2 Solutions™
by Mikkel Aaland
ISBN: 0-7821-4140-4
US $40.00 💿 full color throughout

iMovie™ 3 Solutions™: Tips, Tricks, and Special Effects
by Erica Sadun
ISBN: 0-7821-4247-8
US $40.00 💿 full color throughout

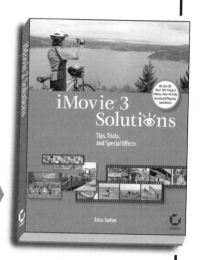

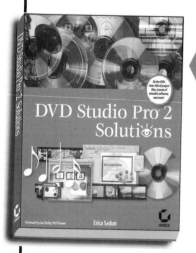

DVD Studio Pro® 2 Solutions
by Erica Sadun
ISBN 0-7821-4234-6
US $39.99 💿 📀

Acrobat® 6 and PDF Solutions
by Taz Tally
ISBN 0-7821-4273-7
US $34.99 💿

SYBEX®

www.sybex.com

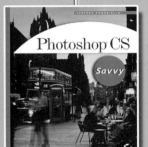
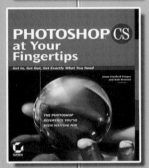

ABOUT SYBEX

Based in the Bay Area since 1976, Sybex is the oldest independent computer book publisher. We were founded at the very start of the personal computer revolution and we've been an innovator in the field for more than twenty-five years.

While lecturing in the mid-1970s, Sybex's founder, Dr. Rodnay Zaks, realized there wasn't much documentation available to help people grapple with the rapidly changing technology of the day. Starting with books based on his own classes, he launched Sybex simultaneously in his adopted home of Berkeley, California, and in his original home of Paris, France.

Over the years, Sybex has continued to forge an independent path, offering unique, innovative books on everything from the first word processors in the early 1980s to digital photography, 3D graphics, and Mac OS X at the start of the 21st Century. Now in our third decade, we publish dozens of books each year on topics related to graphics, web design, digital photography, and digital video. With each book, our goal remains the same: to provide exceptional books on exciting topics, written by some of the best authors in the field—experts who know their topics as well as they know you, their readers.